Text and Interpretation

Imam Jaʿfar al-Ṣādiq and His Legacy in Islamic Law

Hossein Modarressi

Library of Congress Control Number:
2022930797

Printed in the United States of America
978-0-674-27189-0

Contents

Introduction

This book attempts to define the nature and main characteristics of the legal thought of Imam Jaʿfar al-Ṣādiq, a preeminent religious scholar and jurist of Medina in the first half of the second century of the Muslim calendar (mid-eighth century CE).

During the reign of the Umayyad caliphate, which ruled the Muslim world from 41 to 132 AH (662–750 CE), various trends in legal interpretation and reasoning emerged, mainly in the Ḥijāz and Iraq. A generation of jurists with circles of devoted students and the subsequent debates and disputes between supporters of rival positions gradually turned these trends into brands and, over a few further decades, into local schools of legal interpretation. Some of these local schools managed to attract followers beyond their lands of origin and spread to other parts of the Muslim world. Each of these schools is usually identified by the name of the prominent jurist in early Islam who started or led the trend that the school represents. The schools made invaluable contributions to the legal thinking of the young Muslim community. A few survived the test of time, formed vast communities of followers, and continued to inform the Muslim legal mind down to our time.

The school that is the focus of the present study emerged in the late Umayyad period. Its eponym was Imam Abū ʿAbd Allāh Jaʿfar b. Muḥammad al-Ṣādiq, a highly respected jurist of Medina who was also a revered member of the House of the Prophet (*ahl al-bayt*), as was known to his contemporaries. Ever since his lifetime, the school has been known as the Jaʿfarī school, and its adherents are known as the Jaʿfarīs.[1] Like all other schools of Islamic law, it developed over time into a well-established school with a specific legal theory and distinctive methods of analysis. The school embodies a living tradition that endured for thirteen centuries and presently has more than two hundred million followers worldwide, and its legacy is

1 For some of the earliest references to the name from the time of Jaʿfar al-Ṣādiq to later in the second century, see the reports in Kulaynī, *Kāfī*, 2:77, 636 (also 2:233, 5:467); Kashshī, *Rijāl*, 162, 255, 306; Qāḍī Nuʿmān, *Daʿāʾim al-Islām*, 1:73 (also 1:71, 82 [in which the word *Jaʿfariyya* is obscured as *fulāniyya*]; Qāḍī Nuʿmān, *Sharḥ al-akhbār*, 3:504); Ibn Bābawayh, *Faqīh*, 1:251. See also Ḥimyarī, *Qurb al-isnād*, 357. For some early non-Shīʿī references, see, for instance, Abū Tammām, *Dīwān*, 3:242; Ibn Qutayba, *Maʿārif*, 215; Ibn ʿAbd al-Barr, *Tamhīd*, 2:66.

preserved in thousands of books conveying the ideas of a long list of original legal thinkers. In the two areas of legal interpretation and contracts, in particular, this tradition has expanded to a degree unmatched by any of its counterparts in the Muslim legal tradition.

Numerous works in different languages, including a 1984 English monograph by the present author,[2] have appeared in the past half century to introduce this school of Islamic law, its history, legal theory, and contents. All of this literature, however, has focused on later stages of the school in its developed and expanded form. The goal of the present study as an essay in intellectual history is to show how the school began and to sketch the background and past that it represented.

There are other aspects of the character of Imam Jaʿfar al-Ṣādiq that this study will not touch upon. The most important is his leadership of the Shīʿa Muslim community of his time and its recognition of him, to the present day, as the sixth Imam from the House of the Prophet. This matter is too well known to require deep explanation. The following paragraph provides a brief summary for readers who may require it:

For the first twenty years after the death of the Prophet in the year 11, the community remained united under rulers commonly known as caliphs. A protest by some members of Muslim society against certain administrative policies of the third caliph, ʿUthmān b. ʿAffān (r. 24–35), got out of hand and ended with his killing, but the hostility between his supporters and opponents continued and culminated in a civil war during the caliphate of ʿAlī b. Abī Ṭālib (r. 35–40), which broke the unity of the Muslim community. The civil war subsided after ʿAlī's assassination and the accession to the caliphate of his rival and opponent, Muʿāwiya (r. 41–60), who assumed rule over the entire Muslim community and established the Umayyad dynasty, which subsequently governed the lands of Islam for close to a century. However, support for ʿAlī and his descendants and hopes that they would one day come to lead the community again did not die away. The supporters of the ʿAlids' cause[3] were involved in a number of unsuccessful uprisings against the Umayyads. The latter, for their part, chased and prosecuted the supporters of the ʿAlids in a ruthless manner, as is well known to students of the history of Islam.[4]

2 Modarressi, *Introduction to Shīʿī Law*.

3 "Those who have affection for us" (*ahl mawaddatinā*), as they were called by Jaʿfar al-Ṣādiq in a report in ʿAlī b. Ibrāhīm, *Tafsīr*, 1:67.

4 The first civil war as an historical event thus ended with the establishment of the Umayyad dynasty. However, the pro-ʿUthmān versus pro-ʿAlī conflict had an enduring effect on Muslim society. In a statement quoted from Jaʿfar al-Ṣādiq in Kulaynī, *Kāfī*, 8:159, he advised his

As the most learned and esteemed member of the House of the Prophet in his time,[5] Jaʿfar al-Ṣādiq was the focus of both public reverence and governmental jealousy and suspicion for most of his life. His supporters were not limited to proponents of the ʿAlids' cause, who were by then known as

followers not to mention the name of ʿAlī in public in order to protect themselves from harm, given the general pro-ʿUthmān sentiment of the time:

إيّاكم وذكر علي وفاطمة فإنّ الناس ليس شيءٌ أبغض إليهم من ذكر علي وفاطمة.

Beware of mentioning ʿAlī and Fāṭima, for people detest nothing more than mention of ʿAlī and Fāṭima.

See further Ibn Abī al-Ḥadīd, *Sharḥ Nahj al-balāgha*, 11:44–45 (quoting the historian Abū al-Ḥasan ʿAlī b. Muḥammad al-Madāʾinī [d. 225] in his *Kitāb al-Aḥdāth*).

5 See, for instance, the letter that his contemporary caliph, Manṣūr, allegedly wrote to another member of the House with a claim to the caliphate, Muḥammad b. ʿAbd Allāh al-Nafs al-Zakiyya:

وما وُلد منكم بعد وفاة رسول الله أفضل من علي بن الحسين. وما كان فيكم بعده مثل ابنه محمّد بن علي. ولا مثل ابنه جعفر.

No one born among you after the death of the Messenger of God was more virtuous than ʿAlī b. al-Ḥusayn. After him, no one among you was like his son Muḥammad b. ʿAlī, nor like his son Jaʿfar (Ibn ʿAbd Rabbih, *al-ʿIqd al-farīd*, 5:82–83; Mubarrad, *Kāmil*, 4:119; Ṭabarī, *Taʾrīkh* 7:569–70).

The letter was written before 145 and thus during the lifetime of Jaʿfar al-Ṣādiq, who passed away in 148. See also how the caliph received Jaʿfar when he was brought to the caliph's presence by his order, as reported by one of the caliph's close associates:

رُزام مولى خالد بن عبد الله القسري قال: وجّهني [المنصور] في حمل جعفر بن محمّد بن علي بن الحسين بن علي بن أبي طالب فحملته. فلمّا صرنا على باب المنصور وقيل: «جعفر بن محمّد!» فما هو إلّا أن سمع به أمر بالأبواب ففُتحت، والسُتور فرُفعت، وخرج المنصور يستقبله إلى صحن الدار، فعانقه وأخذ بيده يمشي معه إلى صدر فراشه وقد جعل يده على صدره وحنا عليه، فأجلسه معه على فراشه.

[Ruzām, client of Khālid b. ʿAbd Allāh al-Qasrī:] Manṣūr sent me to bring Jaʿfar b. Muḥammad b. ʿAlī b. al-Ḥusayn b. ʿAlī b. Abī Ṭālib to him, so I did. When we arrived at Manṣūr's doorstep and [the name of] "Jaʿfar b. Muḥammad" was announced, he [Manṣūr] upon hearing the name immediately ordered the doors to be opened and the curtains to be raised and came out to the front yard to welcome him, [where he] embraced him, took him by the hand, then led him to the upper part of his sitting place, and had him sit with him on his seat while [Manṣūr] had his hand upon his chest and inclined towards him (Raqqām al-Baṣrī, *al-ʿAfw waʾl-iʿtidhār*, 2:568–69).

And the caliph's comments when he received news of Jaʿfar's death:

إنّ جعفرًا كان ممّن قال الله فيه: ﴿ثُمَّ أَوْرَثْنَا الْكِتَابَ الَّذِينَ اصْطَفَيْنَا مِنْ عِبَادِنَا﴾ وكان ممّن اصطفى الله وكان من السابقين بالخيرات.

Jaʿfar was among those about whom God said, "Then We allowed the Book to be inherited by those of Our servants whom We chose." He was among those whom God chose and of "those who took the lead in good deeds" (Yaʿqūbī, *Taʾrīkh*, 2:383; the quotation is from Qurʾān 35:32).

See also the following comments about him:

لكنّ الله قد قدّم لك فضلاً ليس لأحد من قومك.

God granted you an excellence that no one among your family shares with you (Kulaynī, *Kāfī*, 1:358–59 quoting ʿAbd Allāh b. al-Ḥasan, father of the abovementioned Muḥammad b. ʿAbd Allāh al-Nafs al-Zakiyya).

the Shīʿa—shorthand for an earlier name, Shīʿat ʿAlī—and who held specific theological doctrines and historical views about the past. Others[6] also believed that Jaʿfar had a better claim to the caliphate than his contemporary caliphs did. Even though he never claimed the position for himself, the Shīʿa considered him to be the legitimate ruler of the Muslim community as heir and successor to the Prophet, not only as the bearer of true knowledge of religion but also as the rightful leader of the community. The absolute majority of the Shīʿa thus venerate him as the sixth Imam of their doctrine, following ʿAlī, his two sons Ḥasan and Ḥusayn, Ḥusayn's son ʿAlī Zayn al-ʿĀbidīn, and the latter's son Muḥammad al-Bāqir.

Certain supporters of the House of the Prophet had esoteric inclinations[7] and attributed supernatural qualities to Jaʿfar al-Ṣādiq and other Imams, including unlimited knowledge and knowledge of the unseen. He consistently condemned these claims in the strongest possible terms. Such supporters wrote, but ascribed to him, numerous books and reports on the

---

عمرو بن أبي المقدام قال: كنت إذا نظرت إلى جعفر بن محمّد علمت أنّه من سلالة النبيّين.

[ʿAmr b. Abī al-Miqdām:] Whenever I looked at Jaʿfar b. Muḥammad, I knew that he was a descendant of the prophets (Ibn ʿAdī, *Kāmil*, 2:556; thence, Mizzī, *Tahdhīb al-Kamāl*, 5:78; Dhahabī, *Siyar aʿlām al-nubalāʾ*, 6:257).

كان أفضل الناس وأعلمهم بدين الله.

He was the best of people and the most knowledgeable about God's religion (Yaʿqūbī, *Taʾrīkh*, 2:381).

سمعت أبي يقول: جعفر بن محمّد ثقة، لا يُسأل عن مثله.

I heard my father say "Jaʿfar b. Muḥammad is reliable. One does not ask about the likes of him" (Ibn Abī Ḥātim, *al-Jarḥ wa'l-taʿdīl*, 2:487).

كان من سادات أهل البيت فقهًا وعلمًا وفضلاً.

He was one of the masters of the House of the Prophet in religious law, knowledge, and excellence (Ibn Ḥibbān, *Thiqāt*, 6:131).

كان سيّد بني هاشم في زمانه.

He was master of the Banū Hāshim in his time (Dhahabī, *ʿIbar*, 1:209).

أحد الأئمّة الأعلام، بَرٌّ صادق كبير الشأن، سيّد بني هاشم.

One of the leading luminaries, pure, virtuous, great in stature, and master of the Banū Hāshim (Dhahabī, *Mīzān al-iʿtidāl*, 1:414, 192).

6 For later periods, see, for instance, Dhahabī, *Siyar aʿlām al-nubalāʾ*, 13:120 where he says:

جعفر الصادق كبير الشأن، من أئمّة العلم، كان أولى بالخلافة من أبي جعفر المنصور.

Jaʿfar al-Ṣādiq, great in stature, one of the leaders in knowledge. He had a greater right to the caliphate than [the caliph of his time] Abū Jaʿfar al-Manṣūr.

And Dhahabī, *Taʾrīkh al-Islām*, 3:833, where he says of Jaʿfar:

كان يصلح للخلافة لسُؤدده وفضله وعلمه وشرفه.

He was qualified for the caliphate because of his sublime status, merits, knowledge, and family honor.

7 See Modarressi, *Crisis and Consolidation*, 21–32.

natural sciences, alchemy, geomancy, dream interpretation, and augury, as well as Sufism and other esoteric genres. It is obvious, however, that all of this literature is misattributed. This topic has also attracted a good number of treatments in different languages.

For the mainstream of the Shīʿa, the Imam was and remained the source of correct religious knowledge and the bearer of the legacy of the House of the Prophet. The oldest definition of Shīʿism, by a prominent scholar of Kūfa in the early second century, Abān b. Taghlib (d. 141),[8] neatly explains this point: "The Shīʿa are those who follow the opinion of ʿAlī when reports from the Prophet are contradictory, and the opinion of Jaʿfar b. Muḥammad [al-Ṣādiq] when reports from ʿAlī are contradictory."[9]

As noted above, Jaʿfar al-Ṣādiq was a highly esteemed jurist in his time, and his mastery of Islamic religious law was a matter of unanimous agreement in the Muslim society of his time. This mastery is well documented in Islamic sources, some of which will be quoted in the first chapter of the present work. The following story, describing an alleged meeting between Abū Ḥanīfa, the eponym of the Ḥanafī school of Islamic law, and Jaʿfar al-Ṣādiq in the presence of the Abbasid caliph Manṣūr (r. 136–58), as quoted by some early Ḥanafī sources on the authority of Abū Ḥanīfa's student Ḥasan b. Ziyād al-Luʾluʾī, shows how the Muslim community remembered Jaʿfar al-Ṣādiq in its early centuries:[10]

8 On him and his works see Modarressi, *Tradition and Survival*, 1:107–16.

9 Najāshī, *Rijāl*, 12.

10 For the first time in more than twelve centuries, the authority of this report has come under doubt by the editor of the 2003 Beirut edition of Dhahabī's *Taʾrīkh al-Islām* (3:830) on three grounds: (1) Abū Ḥanīfa was not on good terms with the Abbasid caliphate, to the extent that he died in Manṣūr's prison, and he was thus an unlikely candidate to be chosen by the caliph for this task. (2) The caliph respected Jaʿfar al-Ṣādiq to the point that he wept when he received the news of Jaʿfar's death (Yaʿqūbī, *Taʾrīkh*, 2:383). (3) The ultimate source of the report, Ibn ʿUqda, Abū al-ʿAbbās Aḥmad b. Muḥammad b. Saʿīd al-Kūfī (d. 332), a major source of *ḥadīth* (*ḥāfiẓ*) in Kūfa in the late third to early fourth century, was commonly known as a Shīʿī during his lifetime and after, and hence it is possible that sectarian bias might have played a role in the making of the report as a whole or in part. For the present purpose, however, it suffices that the report was in circulation in the early fourth century, as attested by the fact that it is quoted in Ibn ʿAdī (d. 365), *Kāmil* (2:556), and cited in early Ḥanafī works on Abū Ḥanīfa. Furthermore, the arguments made by the editor of Dhahabī's *Taʾrīkh al-Islām* fail to take note of important facts: (1) The nature of politics is that people are favored and fall out of favor in response to changing circumstances, especially if one keeps in mind that Abū Ḥanīfa allegedly fell out with the caliph late in his life during Nafs al-Zakiyya's rebellion in 145, some ten years after the beginning of Manṣūr's caliphate. This was the same time that the government began to prosecute the ʿAlids, including Jaʿfar, whom the caliph would no longer treat with the high degree of respect depicted in this story. The episode must have therefore occurred during the years when Abū Ḥanīfa was still favored by the government.

سمعت أبا حنيفة وسُئِل من أفقه من رأيت؟ قال: ما رأيت أحدًا أفقه من جعفر بن محمّد. لمّا أقدمه المنصور الحيرة بعث إليّ فقال: يا أبا حنيفة! إنّ الناس قد فُتِنوا بجعفر بن محمّد فهيّىء له من مسائلك الصعاب. فهيّأت له أربعين مسألة ثمّ أتيت أبا جعفر [المنصور] وجعفرٌ جالسٌ عن يمينه. فلما بصرتُ بهما دخلني لجعفر من الهيبة ما لم يدخلني لأبي جعفر. فسلّمت وأُذن لي فجلست. ثمّ التفتَ إلي جعفر فقال: يا أبا عبد الله! تعرف هذا؟ قال: نعم! هذا أبو حنيفة – ثمّ أتبعها: قد أتانا. ثمّ قال: يا أبا حنيفة! هات من مسائلك تسأل أبا عبد الله. فابتدأت أسأله، فكان يقول في المسألة: أنتم تقولون فيها كذا وكذا، وأهل المدينة يقولون كذا وكذا، ونحن

---

(2) There are reports in major historical and biographical sources (among the earliest being Zubayr b. Bakkār, *Muwaffaqiyyāt*, 149; Ṭabarī, *Taʾrīkh*, 7:603; Ibn ʿAbd Rabbih, *al-ʿIqd al-farīd*, 3:224–25), some of which were edited by the same editor in the past (Mizzī, *Tahdhīb al-Kamāl*, 5:95–97; Dhahabī, *Siyar aʿlām al-nubalāʾ*, 6:266–97), in which the caliph openly threatens, at times swearing by the name of God, to kill Jaʿfar al-Ṣādiq. The reported reaction of the caliph to Jaʿfar's death thus sounds like government propaganda to preempt any suspicion of a possible role of the government in his death. As noted in Chapter 1 below, the community was aware that the caliph was not on good terms with Jaʿfar and that he looked forward to the latter's death as a means of relieving himself of some anxiety. (3) The fact that although Ibn ʿUqda was indeed a Shīʿī (see the entry on him in *Encyclopaedia of Islam* II, 12 [suppl.]: 400–401 [Wilferd Madelung]), he was known as a Zaydī Shīʿī (see Najāshī, *Rijāl*, 94; Ṭūsī, *Fihrist*, 28: both mentioning among his works *Kitāb man rawā ʿan Zayd b. ʿAlī*, and Ṭūsī also mentioning a *Kitāb Yaḥyā b. al-Ḥusayn b. Zayd wa-akhbārih*) like his father (Khaṭīb al-Baghdādī, *Taʾrīkh Baghdād*, 6:150), and as such should have had no special sentiment for Jaʿfar al-Ṣādiq or Imāmī Shīʿism. Needless to say, an Imāmī would not consider knowledge of the diversity of opinions to be a great merit for an Imam. As is well known to students of the history of Islam, Zaydīs supported the cause of the Ḥasanī branch of the ʿAlids and were not on good terms with Jaʿfar al-Ṣādiq (see, for instance, Kulaynī, *Kāfī*, 5:19; Abū Manṣūr al-Ṭabarsī, *Iḥtijāj*, 2:292–93; ʿAlī al-Ṭabrisī, *Mishkāt al-anwār*, 2:75) nor his followers (see, for instance, Kashshī, *Rijāl*, 221; Ṭūsī, *Tahdhīb*, 4:53). In a report in Mufīd, *Amālī*, 33, a contemporary to the Zaydīs' revolts in the lifetime of Jaʿfar al-Ṣādiq expresses a general concern among Jaʿfar's followers at the time:

> إن ظفر زيدٌ وأصحابه فليس أحدٌ أسوأ حالاً عندهم منّا، وإن ظفر بنوأمية فنحن عندهم بتلك المنزلة.
>
> If Zayd and his companions are victorious, nobody will be in a worse situation than us with them. If the Umayyads are victorious, we will have the same status with them too.

A younger contemporary of Ibn ʿUqda, Ibn Bābawayh (d. 381), tells us in his *Kamāl al-dīn* (a book that he wrote only a few decades after Ibn ʿUqda) that "the Zaydīs are the harshest of the people against us [that is, the Imāmīs]" (Ibn Bābawayh, 126). A few decades later, Abū Ḥayyān al-Tawḥīdī refers in his *al-Imtāʿ wa'l-muʾānasa* to the then-existing hostility between these two branches of Shīʿism as an example of deep animosity between two religious groups (Abū Ḥayyān al-Tawḥīdī, 2:188).

Abū Ḥanīfa was certainly not less favored by the Zaydīs than was Jaʿfar al-Ṣādiq. Ibn ʿUqda, in particular, wrote a book titled *Kitāb Akhbār Abī Ḥanīfa wa-musnadih* (Najāshī, *Rijāl*, 94; Ṭūsī, *Fihrist*, 28). He thus seems to have quoted this story, as he did with thousands of other reports that he cited in his works or recited to his students, with no specific sectarian bias.

نقول كذا وكذا. فربما تابعنا، وربما تابع أهل المدينة، وربما خالفنا جميعًا، حتّى أتيتُ على أربعين مسألة، ما أخرم منها مسألة. ثمّ قال أبوحنيفة : أليس قد رُوينا أنّ أعلم الناس أعلمهم باختلاف الناس؟[11]

I heard Abū Ḥanīfa [when he was] asked who was the person most knowledgeable in religious law he had ever seen. He replied: I have never seen anyone more knowledgeable in religious law than Jaʿfar b. Muḥammad [al-Ṣādiq]. When Manṣūr brought him to Ḥīra [near Kūfa, the seat of the Abbasid government in its early years], he sent for me and said, "O Abū Ḥanīfa! The people are enchanted by Jaʿfar b. Muḥammad, so prepare for him some of your hardest questions." I prepared [a list of] forty questions and went before Abū Jaʿfar [al-Manṣūr] while Jaʿfar was sitting on his right. When I saw the two, the awe that I felt for Jaʿfar was well above that which I felt for Abū Jaʿfar [al-Manṣūr]. I offered my greetings and was given permission to sit down. Then Abū Jaʿfar [al-Manṣūr] turned to Jaʿfar and said, "O Abū ʿAbd Allāh! Do you know this man?" Jaʿfar said, "Yes, this is Abū Ḥanīfa," and added, "He has been to see us before." Then [Manṣūr] said, "O Abū Ḥanīfa! Present your questions so that we may ask Abū ʿAbd Allāh." So I started asking him questions and he would say in his answer to every question, "You [in the school of Iraq] say such-and-such [about this question], and the people of Medina [that is, the jurists of the school of the Ḥijāz] say such-and-such, and we [in the tradition of the House of the Prophet] say such-and-such." His opinions agreed at times with ours, at times with those of the people of Medina,[12] and at times with none, until I finished all forty of my ques-

11 Ibn ʿAdī, *Kāmil*, 2:556; Muwaffaq b. Aḥmad al-Makkī, *Manāqib Abī Ḥanīfa*, 1:137 (possibly from *Kashf al-āthār al-sharīfa fī manāqib Abī Ḥanīfa* by Abū Muḥammad ʿAbd Allāh b. Muḥammad al-Ḥārithī [d. 340], a major source of reports in Muwaffaq al-Makkī's book); Abū al-Muʾayyad al-Khwārazmī, *Jāmiʿ masānīd Abī Ḥanīfa*, 1:251; Mizzī, *Tahdhīb al-Kamāl*, 5:79–80; Dhahabī, *Siyar aʿlām al-nubalāʾ*, 6:257–58; Dhahabī, *Taʾrīkh al-Islām*, 3:830. See also Ibn Shahrāshūb, *Manāqib Āl Abī Ṭālib*, 4:255, who quotes the story from a *Musnad Abī Ḥanīfa*; Dhahabī, *Tadhkirat al-ḥuffāẓ*, 1:157, where the key sentence from the report is quoted.

12 This point is well attested, especially in the opinions quoted from him in Sunnī works of law. Compare, for instance, Ibn Qudāma, *Mughnī*, 5:148—in which Jaʿfar al-Ṣādiq is reported to have supported the opinion of his maternal grandfather, Qāsim b. Muḥammad b. Abī Bakr, one of the Seven Jurists of Medina, on the unlawfulness of a special kind of fragrant food for a pilgrim to Mecca who is in the state of pilgrim sanctity (*iḥrām*)—with Tirmidhī, *Sunan*, 1:84 (under *ḥadīth* no. 34), where Jaʿfar is said to have agreed with the opinion of the jurists of Iraq on the number of times that a Muslim was supposed to wipe his head in ritual ablution (*wuḍūʾ*). In Ibn Qudāma (13:290) Jaʿfar's opinion on naming God when slaughtering an animal sides with that of the jurists of Mecca, but he agrees primarily with the Iraqis, both Kūfans and Baṣrans, on the lawfulness of a person who has not yet performed his own *ḥajj* obligation substituting for someone else in the same ritual (Ibn Qudāma, 5:42).

tions. He did not leave a single question unanswered. Commenting on the story, Abū Ḥanīfa then said, "Are we not told that the most knowledgeable of the people is the one who knows best the differences of opinion among the people?"[13]

Mālik b. Anas, the eponym of the Mālikī school of Islamic law, was a student of Jaʿfar al-Ṣādiq and transmitted *ḥadīth* from him. The following report conveys how Mālik remembered his time with Jaʿfar al-Ṣādiq:

سمعت مالك بن أنس فقيه المدينة يقول: كنت أدخل على الصادق جعفر بن محمّد فيقدّم لي مخدّة ويعرف لي قدرًا ويقول: يا مالك! إنّي أحبّك. فكنت أسرّ بذلك وأحمد الله تعالى عليه. قال: وكان لا يخلو من إحدى ثلاث خصال: إمّا صائمًا، وإمّا قائمًا، وإمّا ذاكرًا. وكان من عظماء العبّاد وأكابر الزهّاد الّذين يخشون الله، وكان كثير الحديث طيّب المجالسة كثير الفوائد. فاذا قال: «قال رسول الله» إخضرّ مرّةً واصفرّ أخرى حتّى يُنكره من كان يعرفه. ولقد حججت معه سنةً فلمّا استوت به راحلته عند الإحرام كان كلّما همّ بالتلبية انقطع الصوت في حلقه وكاد أن يخرّ من راحلته. فقلت: قُل يابن رسول الله! فلا بدّ لك من أن تقول. فقال: يابن أبي عامر! كيف أجسر أن أقول: «لبّيك اللّهمّ لبّيك»، وأخشى أن يقول لي: «لا لبّيك ولا سعديك!»[14]

I heard Mālik b. Anas, the jurist of Medina, say: I used to visit al-Ṣādiq Jaʿfar b. Muḥammad. He would offer me a cushion and honor me and say, "O Mālik! I like you!" That would make me happy, and I would praise God the Exalted for that. He was always engaged in one of three practices: fasting, prayer, or remembrance of God. He was among the greatest of worshippers and self-deniers who feared God. He was also

13 Jaʿfar al-Ṣādiq's extensive knowledge of the differences of opinion among the jurists of different regions is well attested in his answers to questions, as will be further documented in Chapter 2. When someone who was not a follower of his asked him a legal question, he would quote the diversity of opinions of the jurists of different regions (Kashshī, *Rijāl*, 253; see, for example, Kulaynī, *Kāfī*, 4:236, where he refers to the opinion of the jurists of Mecca with whom he disagreed). At times, he also noted their points of consensus, as in, for instance, Ibn Bābawayh, *ʿIlal al-sharāʾiʿ*, 1:18, where he says, "The jurists of the Ḥijāz have not disagreed with the jurists of Iraq on this point."

14 Quoted from Muṣʿab b. ʿAbd Allāh al-Zubayrī (d. 236) in Abū al-Qāsim al-Jawharī (d. 381), *Musnad al-Muwaṭṭaʾ*, 286–87 (whence Ibn ʿAbd al-Barr, *Tamhīd*, 2:67; Ibn Khalfūn, *Asmāʾ shuyūkh Mālik*, 135; Qāḍī ʿIyāḍ, *Shifā*, 2:142; Ibn Farḥūn, *Irshād al-sālik*, 1:201); Ibn Ḥajar, *Tahdhīb al-Tahdhīb*, 7:306; and through a Shīʿī chain of transmission in Ibn Bābawayh, *Amālī*, 432 (see also his *ʿIlal al-sharāʾiʿ*, 1:224, and *Khiṣāl*, 167).

full of pleasant speech, and his company was plentiful in benefits. When he said, "The Messenger of God said," he would turn sometimes green, sometimes yellow, such that even those who knew him could not recognize him.[15] One year, I performed *ḥajj* with him. When his mount stopped in order for him to enter the state of pilgrim sanctity, every time he would resolve to say the *talbiya*, his voice would choke up, and he would almost fall off his mount. I said, "Say it, O son of the Messenger of God! You must say it." He said, "O son of Abū ʿĀmir![16] How can I dare to say, 'Here I am, My Lord, here I am,' when I fear that He may say to me, 'You are not welcome!'"

A brief remark about the sources for this study seems merited. As expected, there is an enormous number of quotations from, as well as reports and information about, Jaʿfar al-Ṣādiq in the collections of religious reports and compendia of law, as well as in works on biography and literature, by adherents of various doctrinal and sectarian tendencies in the general Islamic tradition.[17] Some of that material is spurious or pure fabrication. In Sunnī *ḥadīth*, attempts can frequently be observed by late Umayyad and early Abbasid transmitters to rebuff rivals by putting statements in the mouths of leaders of the opposing group, which was a well-attested tactic in the sectarian milieu of the early Muslim centuries. In Shīʿī *ḥadīth*, the hand of various esoteric groups and individuals who pretended to have affection

---

15 A report in Kulaynī, *Kāfī*, 6:39 further attests to the utmost respect that members of the House had for the memory of the Prophet (see also 5:114):

عن أبي هارون مولى آل جعدة قال: كنت جليساً لأبي عبد الله بالمدينة، ففقدني أيّامًا، ثمّ إنّي جئت إليه فقال: لم أرك منذ أيّام يا أبا هارون! فقلت: ولد لي غلام. فقال: بارك الله لك! فما سمّيته؟ قلت: سمّيتُه محمّدًا. فأقبل بخدّه نحو الأرض وهو يقول: محمّد محمّد محمّد، حتّى كاد يلصق خدّه بالأرض. ثمّ قال: نفسي ووُلدي وأهلي وأبويّ وأهل الأرض كلّهم جميعًا فداءٌ لرسول الله. لا تسبّه ولا تضربه ولا تُسىء إليه.

[Abū Hārūn, client of Āl Jaʿda:] I used to sit in the company of Abū ʿAbd Allāh [Jaʿfar al-Ṣādiq] in Medina. He missed me for a few days. The next time I went to him, he said, "I have not seen you for some days, O Abū Hārūn!" I said, "A child was born to me." He said, "May God bless you! What did you name him?" I said, "I named him Muḥammad." He bent with his face toward the floor, saying "Muḥammad, Muḥammad, Muḥammad," until his face almost touched the floor. Then he said, "Myself, my children, my family, my parents, and all the people of the earth altogether be ransomed for the Messenger of God. Do not insult him [your child], beat him, or mistreat him."

16 Mālik was the son of Anas b. Mālik b. Abī ʿĀmir al-Aṣbaḥī.

17 A work by Muḥammad Kāẓim al-Qazwīnī, *Mawsūʿat al-Imām Jaʿfar al-Ṣādiq*, attempts to collect the reports from or about the Imam, mostly those recorded in Imāmī Shīʿī sources. It is organized thematically and thus serves as an easy starting point for research on any aspect of Jaʿfar al-Ṣādiq's life, thought, and teachings.

for and affiliation with the House of the Prophet,[18] although many of them may not have even believed in God or Islam,[19] can clearly be seen behind many texts that do not match the language and conventions of the Imams.[20] Some of that material was nevertheless received favorably among the uneducated or unsophisticated masses.[21] There were also *ḥadīth* fabricators in both camps who boldly improvised lies on behalf of Jaʿfar al-Ṣādiq with no specific doctrinal agenda, simply because of the popularity of his name as a leading authority on religious teachings.[22] There is, however, a large

18 The esoterics usually had no education or social or family distinction. Their esotericism and exaggeration were only stratagems to acquire distinction in the community and set themselves up as devoted supporters and advocates of the Shīʿī cause (see Kashshī, *Rijāl*, 138, 148, and passim). They were ready and happy to create tension, hatred, and animosity between people only to assert themselves as notables in the community. Much of the material that they forged and ascribed to the Imams could have potentially put the lives of the Imams and those of their disciples and transmitters in danger, or the community of the supporters and well-wishers of the House of the Prophet in deep shame and disgrace, if the Imams had actually said this or the alleged transmitters reported it at the time. This is a clear indication that such material, with its claimed authority and chains of transmission, was blatant fabrication.

19 See Modarressi, *Crisis and Consolidation*, 35–36.

20 Such were many of the fabrications told about Jaʿfar al-Ṣādiq by the esoterics, which could easily be distinguished by their tone and content as neither in line with his widely transmitted statements nor comparable to his style of speech, personal character, or family and class culture. As attested in numerous examples, the close disciples of the Imam who were familiar with his language would immediately recognize the true from the false as soon as they received a statement ascribed to him (see Chapter 1 below).

21 A very common practice by the esoterics was to *edit* narratives and paraphrase words, putting the new versions into the mouths of the Imam or his prominent disciples and then into vast circulation in the Shīʿī community of the time. With a small edit, a straightforward statement could take on a very different meaning by the time it reached Kūfa. Many of the Shīʿa of Kūfa had recollections of some phonetically similar statements from the Imams (see, for instance, Modarressi, *Tradition and Survival*, 1:90), a fact that helped the forgers succeed in their edits. Human inclination toward wonders, make-believe, imagination, and exaggeration about their spiritual leaders always led uneducated masses to fall victim to the traps set by the esoterics, to believe in their claims and ascriptions, and to act as a type of free-of-charge mass media to spread each new fabrication.

22 These three categories of lies and liars will be discussed in greater detail in Chapter 1. See also the intelligent observation of a prominent scholar of *ḥadīth*, Abū Ḥātim Muḥammad b. Idrīs al-Rāzī (d. 277), in Ibn Abī Ḥātim, *al-Jarḥ wa'l-taʿdīl*, 9:25. It shows that the government and its supporters were happy with, and presumably encouraged, fabrications about and misattributions to Jaʿfar al-Ṣādiq, as these would taint the image of the Imam and the House of the Prophet in the eyes of the religious masses, and especially of the scholars of *ḥadīth*, by casting them as "weak transmitters" of false material:

> كتب الفضل بن الربيع إلى أبي فقال: لا تُحدّث عن جعفر بن محمّد. فقلت لأبي: هذا أبو البختري ببغداد يحدّث عن جعفر بن محمّد بالأعاجيب ولا يُنهى. قال: يا بُنيّ! أمّا من يكذب على جعفر بن محمّد فلا يُبالون به، وأمّا من يصدق على جعفر فلا يُعجبهم!
>
> Al-Faḍl b. al-Rabīʿ wrote to my father, saying, "Do not transmit *ḥadīths* from Jaʿfar b. Muḥammad." I said to my father, "Here is Abū al-Bakhtarī in Baghdad transmitting fantastical *ḥadīths* from Jaʿfar b. Muḥammad but not getting forbidden." He said,

body of material that sounds authentic or can reasonably be assumed to be so. As for the provenance of the material, there is naturally much more in Shīʿī sources, especially those of the Jaʿfarī school.

The present study uses all material that corresponds to the language and character of Jaʿfar al-Ṣādiq, as known through both historical and biographical accounts, and as such can reasonably be deemed reliable. The same is true with those reports that are supported by internal or external[23] evidence, including the language and style of legal discourse in his time.[24] Sectarian tendencies and doctrinal affiliations play no role in

---

"O my son! They do not care about one who attributes lies to Jaʿfar b. Muḥammad, but they do not like the one who transmits truthfully from Jaʿfar!"

Al-Faḍl b. al-Rabīʿ and his father served the Abbasid caliphate as top officials for many decades, al-Faḍl as *ḥājib* (the doorkeeper or chamberlain) for Manṣūr and his successors, and as vizier for Hārūn al-Rashīd (after the fall of the Barmakids) and his son, Amīn. Al-Faḍl died in 208. For Abū al-Bakhtarī, see below, Chapter 1.

23 External evidence includes corroboration of the dates given for historical events through records in early chronological works. In a report in Kulaynī, *Kāfī*, 2:346–47, for instance, a follower of Jaʿfar al-Ṣādiq tells him that after his previous meeting with the Imam a number of years earlier, his entire family was wiped out in the plague outbreak of the year 31 (that is, 131 AH). He was clearly referring to a well-documented plague that started in the month of Rajab in 131 AH and ended in Shawwāl of the same year. It is said that during the plague, one thousand people died every day in Baṣra alone. See Conrad, "Plague in the Early Medieval Near East"; Modarressi, *Tradition and Survival*, 1:104.

24 A well-known example is the use of the formulas "I said . . . he said . . ." and *araʾayta* ("imagine/consider/what do you think about?"), which are frequently attested in the surviving material from the earliest periods of Islamic legal discourse. The second formula is clearly a linguistic convention from pre-Islamic Arabic and is repeatedly used in the Qurʾān (including the variations *araʾaytaka*, *araʾaytakum*, and *araʾaytum*), in the Sunna of the Prophet (with numerous examples that should be easy to find with a simple online/digital search in *ḥadīth* and *fiqh* databases such as al-Shāmila and al-Waqfiyya for Sunnī sources, and Noor Digital Library for Shīʿī works), and in legal and theological writings of the time (abundantly in legal works, such as those by Mālik, Shaybānī, and Shāfiʿī [see also Calder, *Studies in Early Muslim Jurisprudence*, 9, 10, 45–47, 52–53], but also in early theological treatises; for one example, see ʿAbd Allāh b. Yazīd al-Fazārī [late second century AH], *Tawḥīd*, 203, 205, 207, 208, 210, 211, 212, 213, 218, 219). Contrary to the assumption of some Western scholars of Islamic law, this second formula had nothing to do with the concept of *raʾy*—the use of personal preference or arbitrary decision-making (but cf. Dārimī, *Sunan*, 1:281, 285; Kulaynī, *Kāfī*, 1:58). The formula is very common in early Shīʿī material. Examples should be easy to find with an online/digital search. Here are just a few examples in reports from Jaʿfar al-Ṣādiq in the collection of material that I have selected for the present study from Kulaynī alone: 1:53, 54, 58; 2:81, 173, 213, 219, 264, 266, 280, 281, 450, 475, 488; 3:197, 209, 355, 435, 459, 517, 520, 525, 528; 4:27, 109, 137, 146, 248, 311, 333, 337, 362, 523, 539; 5:13, 23–26, 38, 44, 77, 100, 130, 185, 197, 200, 209, 220, 235, 258, 259, 264, 286, 290, 391, 407, 448, 464, 468, 473, 481, 482, 525; 6:4, 116, 146, 148, 162, 163, 184; 7:34, 35, 38, 45, 57, 130, 131, 147, 150, 160, 161, 162, 176, 178, 208, 214, 219, 221, 227, 248, 252, 258, 266, 267, 357, 361, 362, 387, 397, 418, 431, 433, 473, 697; 8:99, 146. Many more can be found in Ṭūsī, *Tahdhīb*, e.g., 1:364; 2:7, 365; 3:288, 290; 4:33, 155, 161; 6:135, 345; 7:28, 41, 57, 128, 176, 180, 205, 227, 235, 244, 248, 261, 264, 269, 426; 8:87, 228, 315; 9:133, 154; 10:16, 80, 233, and other early Shīʿī *ḥadīth* collections.

my acceptance or rejection of any individual item, whether a historical or a religious report.[25]

There are three further points to note:

First, the word "Shīʿī" is used in this work as an adjective in respect for the publisher's preference. This is a break from my thirty-year-long practice of using the word "Shīʿite."

Second, unless otherwise specified, all dates in this book are according to the Islamic *hijrī* calendar, except for publication dates, which refer to the Common Era.

Third, the editions used of the sources cited in the work are those specified in the bibliography at the end of the book. The reader will notice that at times I use a different edition, as specified in each citation. This is a reminder of a time during which libraries were closed because of a pandemic, resulting in the author having no access to the specific editions used throughout a work, and requiring him to be content with whatever he could find online.

And finally, it is a pleasant duty to thank Michael Cook and Intisar Rabb who read an earlier draft of this work and offered invaluable suggestions for its improvement. My thanks are also due to the anonymous peer reviewers for their very helpful comments and corrections, to Rami Koujah for helping in various ways as my research assistant, and to Hanna Siurua and Stuart Brown for their careful and thorough copyediting of this volume.

25 No particular attention will be paid to the chains of transmission (*isnāds*) that could easily be forged and put into circulation together with any text of the forger's choice. See Chapter 3 below, n. 58 on p. 255 to n. 60 on p. 256, and the accompanying text.

CHAPTER 1
Life

Abū ʿAbd Allāh Jaʿfar b. Muḥammad al-Ṣādiq ("the truthful")[1] was born in the year 80[2] or 83[3] in Medina, where he also died and was buried in 148. His father, Abū Jaʿfar Muḥammad al-Bāqir, was a son of ʿAlī Zayn al-ʿĀbidīn, son of Ḥusayn, son of ʿAlī and Fāṭima al-Zahrāʾ (daughter of the Prophet). On his maternal side, Jaʿfar al-Ṣādiq was a descendant of Abū Bakr, the first caliph; Jaʿfar's mother was a daughter of a prominent jurist of Medina in the late first to early second century, Qāsim b. Muḥammad b. Abī Bakr (d. 107). In the Sunnī works on the Qurʾān, *ḥadīth*, and religious law, he is commonly referred to as Jaʿfar b. Muḥammad and in the Shīʿī works as Abū ʿAbd Allāh.

I. His Father

Jaʿfar al-Ṣādiq's father, Muḥammad al-Bāqir (57–114 AH), was a highly respected scholar of the Qurʾān, *ḥadīth*, and religious law in his time. Muḥammad al-Bāqir was the most distinguished member of the House of the Prophet at the turn of the first century[4] and as such was regarded

1 On the use of this epithet for him in his lifetime, see, inter alia, Kulaynī, *Kāfī*, 3:144 (cf. Ṭūsī, *Tahdhīb*, 1:292); Ibn Bābawayh, *ʿIlal al-sharāʾiʿ*, 1:224; Ṭūsī, *Tahdhīb*, 1:313. There is also a hagiographical explanation for this in a report in Ibn Bābawayh, *ʿIlal al-sharāʾiʿ*, 1:224.

2 Bukhārī, *Taʾrīkh*, 2:199; Ibn Ḥibbān, *Thiqāt*, 6:131; Ibn Ḥibbān, *Mashāhīr ʿulamāʾ al-amṣār*, 156; Mizzī, *Tahdhīb al-Kamāl*, 5:97, and numerous other Sunnī sources of his biography listed in the editor's footnote in Mizzī, 5:74.

3 This is the date preferred by most Shīʿī sources of his biography, such as Kulaynī, *Kāfī*, 1:472; Mufīd, *Irshād*, 271; Ibn Abī al-Thalj, *Taʾrīkh al-Aʾimma*, 10; and Faḍl b. Ḥasan al-Ṭabrisī, *Iʿlām al-warā*, 271. See also Ibn al-Khashshāb, *Taʾrīkh mawālīd al-Aʾimma wa-wafayātihim*, 185 (year 80 or 83); Ibn Shahrāshūb, *Manāqib Āl Abī Ṭālib*, 4:280 (year 83 or 86); Ibn al-Muṭahhar, *Mustajād*, 176.

4 See the introduction, n. 5 on p. 3. This was clearly why some people thought that the Prophet's mule was in Muḥammad al-Bāqir's possession, a rumor that he categorically denied saying that he had never seen the animal (Abū Ṭālib al-Hārūnī, *Amālī*, 520). A report of Kaysānī provenance, however, has the mule transferred after ʿAlī to his son Ḥasan, then Ḥusayn, and then to a third son of ʿAlī, Muḥammad Ibn al-Ḥanafiyya (Ibn Nāṣir al-Dīn, *Jāmiʿ al-āthār*, 6:3627; this was most likely meant by "Muḥammad b. ʿAlī" in the original version of the former narrative too). Either way, by the time of Muḥammad b. al-Ḥanafiyya and Muḥammad al-Bāqi, the poor

as the spiritual leader by the pro-ʿAlid communities in Iraq[5] who hoped that someday he might challenge the Umayyads and establish a moral government.[6] This he never ventured to do. He is recognized by the Imāmī Shīʿa as their fifth Imam.

There is a fair amount of information about him in the standard biographical works[7] as well as in monographs and encyclopedia entries[8] in different languages. Additional information on his life and character can be found in collections of early Shīʿī *ḥadīth*.

We are told, for example, that as a child, Muḥammad was very attached to ʿAbd Allāh b. ʿAbbās,[9] the first cousin of the Prophet and one of the most

animal would have already passed well beyond the maximum age of longevity for its kind. To the ordinary people of the time, having the mule of the Prophet in one's possession meant close affiliation with him. So, a report in Naṣr b. Muzāḥim, *Waqʿat Ṣiffīn*, 403 (see also Ibn ʿAsākir, *Taʾrīkh madīnat Dimashq*, 4:231) had ʿAlī ride the horse and mule of the Prophet in the Battle of Ṣiffīn in the year 37 (both would have been of considerable age at the time, if they even lived that long, and likely not fully dependable—and the mule in particular not even suitable—for a battle scene). Another, in Abū al-Shaykh, *Akhlāq al-Nabī*, 464, finds him riding the mule in the Battle of Nahrawān in the year 38. Four others, in Balādhurī, *Ansāb al-ashrāf*, 2:102; Barqī, *Maḥāsin*, 477, Qāḍī Nuʿmān, *Daʿāʾim al-Islām*, 2:536, and Ṭūsī, *Tahdhīb*, 9:3, 5 make him ride it in the markets of Kūfa. Yet another, in Maqrīzī, *Imtāʿ*, 1:358, has ʿAbbās b. ʿAbd al-Muṭṭalib, the uncle of the Prophet and forefather of the Abbasid caliphs, riding the mule to the leaders of Mecca right before the conquest of the town in the year 8, to inform them of the Muslims' imminent arrival. It should also be noted that some sources ascribe more than one mule to the Prophet (e.g., Ibn Sayyid al-Nās, *ʿUyūn al-āthār*, 2:422; Maqrīzī, *Imtāʿ*, 7:220), including one that was killed by the owner of a reed grove into which the animal intruded (Ibn Bābawayh, *Faqīh*, 4:126; Maqrīzī, *Imtāʿ*, 7:222). Further information about the mule of the Prophet can be found in the collections of *ḥadīth* (e.g., Bukhārī, *Ṣaḥīḥ*, nos. 2873–74; Bayhaqī, *Sunan*, 10:45; Bayhaqī, *Dalāʾil al-nubuwwa*, 7:278), and works on history (e.g., Ṭabarī, *Taʾrīkh*, 3:174; Abū Nuʿaym, *Dhikr akhbār Iṣbahān*, 2:54, 183), as well as those on the biography of the Prophet, some of which devote special chapters to the animal (e.g., Abū al-Shaykh, *Akhlāq al-Nabī*, 2:460–68). Much of this literature is now accessible on the internet under بغلة النبي.

5 See Ibn ʿAsākir, *Taʾrīkh madīnat Dimashq*, 54:279, where the caliph Hishām b. ʿAbd al-Malik (r. 105–25) refers to him as "the one that the people of Iraq are in love with," and ʿAlī b. Ibrāhīm, *Tafsīr*, 2:284, where someone describes Muḥammad al-Bāqir to Hishām as "the prophet of the people of Kūfa." See also Kulaynī, *Kāfī*, 1:342.

6 See Saʿd b. ʿAbd Allāh al-Ashʿarī, *Maqālāt*, 75; Kulaynī, *Kāfī*, 1:342, 536, 8:80, 341; Ibn Samka, *ʿAbbāsī*, 169; Nuʿmānī, *Ghayba*, 167–68, 169, 215, 216, 237; Ibn Bābawayh, *Kamāl al-dīn*, 325; Ibn ʿAsākir, *Taʾrīkh madīnat Dimashq*, 54:291.

7 For long lists of many of these sources, see the editors' footnotes in Mizzī, *Tahdhīb al-Kamāl*, 26:136–37 and Dhahabī, *Taʾrīkh al-Islām*, volume for the years 101–20 of the Beirut, 1987 edition, 462. See also Rifāʿī, *Muʿjam*, 8:251–77.

8 E.g., *Encyclopaedia of Islam* II, 7:397–400 [Etan Kohlberg]; *Encyclopaedia Iranica*, 3:725–26 [Wilferd Madelung]. See also Modarressi, *Tradition and Survival*, 1:37–38.

9 Kashshī, *Rijāl*, 57, where his son, Jaʿfar, says of Ibn ʿAbbās:

كان أبي يحبّه حبًّا شديدًا، وكانت أمّه تلبسه ثيابه وهو غلام فينطلق إليه في غلمان بني عبد المطّلب.

> My father loved him very dearly. His mother would dress him when he was a boy, and he would go to him [Ibn ʿAbbās] with other boys of the descendants of ʿAbd al-Muṭṭalib.

See further Madelung, "ʿAbd Allāh b. ʿAbbās," 13–25.

learned members of the first generation of Muslims. He reportedly met and quoted a number of other Companions of the Prophet,[10] including Jābir b. ʿAbd Allāh al-Anṣārī[11] and ʿAbd Allāh b. ʿUmar,[12] the learned son of the second caliph. He also quoted ʿĀʾisha,[13] the wife of the Prophet, obviously through an intermediary as he was too young when she died to quote her directly. As expected, however, his main source of *ḥadīth* was his father, ʿAlī b. al-Ḥusayn Zayn al-ʿĀbidīn.

In terms of character, Muḥammad al-Bāqir was peace-loving and rejected violence.[14] He boldly contradicted the scholars of his town, Medina, when he thought their established standpoints were wrong,[15] but for obvious reasons he would not openly challenge the government on matters of lifestyle that he considered unlawful. Here is an example: Following the opinion of ʿAlī, Muḥammad al-Bāqir maintained that only specially trained dogs, and no other animals, could lawfully be used for hunting. However, because hunting with falcons was a very popular pastime of the caliphs and their entourages, he did not issue a *fatwā* against it.[16]

He was respected and recognized by his contemporaries as an eminent jurist.[17] Ḥakam b. ʿUtayba, a prominent jurist of Kūfa in his time (d. 115), said that he had never seen a person as quick to apprehend and answer delicate legal questions as Muḥammad al-Bāqir.[18] For his part, Muḥammad also treated his fellow jurists and their opinions with due respect. In an instance in which he disagreed with other jurists on a case, he explained to the person seeking his opinion that the divergent opinion of his peers was also based on an interpretation of a statement by the Prophet.[19] The Umayyad caliphs occasionally[20] consulted him about matters on which the Syrian jurists disagreed among themselves.[21] At times, he attended the court of the governor of Medina[22] and the judicial sessions of its judges, where he would also note their mistakes.[23]

---

10 See a list of these Companions in Mizzī, *Tahdhīb al-Kamāl*, 26:137–38. The list is based on appearances of Muḥammad al-Bāqir's name as an intermediary in the chains of transmission of reports in Sunnī *ḥadīth* collections. To what extent one can depend on these chains and reports is a different question.

11 Kashshī, *Rijāl*, 43; for an example, see Kulaynī, *Kāfī*, 7:113.

12 E.g., Ibn al-Ashʿath, *Ashʿathiyyāt*, 62 (whence Ḥimyarī, *Qurb al-isnād*, 89); Kulaynī, *Kāfī*, 6:61.

13 E.g., Kulaynī, *Kāfī*, 6:137.

14 See, for instance, Barqī, *Maḥāsin*, 260.

15 Kulaynī, *Kāfī*, 5:247.

16 Kulaynī, *Kāfī*, 6:207, 208, with a variant in ʿAyyāshī, *Tafsīr*, 2:11.

17 There are also references to his public *ḥadīth* sessions in which he quoted religious reports to a general audience. See, for instance, Ṭūsī, *Tahdhīb*, 5:20.

18 See the story behind his admiration of Muḥammad al-Bāqir in Kulaynī, *Kāfī*, 7:24, 167.

19 Kulaynī, *Kāfī*, 5:174–75.

20 E.g., Kulaynī, *Kāfī*, 7:228; Ibn ʿAsākir, *Taʾrīkh madīnat Dimashq*, 54:278–79.

21 Kulaynī, *Kāfī*, 7:228.

22 Kulaynī, *Kāfī*, 3:433.

23 Kulaynī, *Kāfī*, 5:290; Ibn Bābawayh, *Faqīh*, 3:21–22.

In his personal life, Muḥammad al-Bāqir is attested to have purchased land[24] and engaged in trade.[25] A conversation between him and Muḥammad b. al-Munkadir, a well-known ascetic of Medina (d. 130) who tells the story, shows Muḥammad al-Bāqir's stance on managing his personal life:

خرجت إلى بعض نواحي المدينة في ساعة حارّة فلقيني أبو جعفر محمّد بن علي، وكان رجلاً بادنًا ثقيلاً، وهو متّكئ على غلامين أسودين (أو مَولَيَين)، فقلت في نفسي: سبحان الله! شيخ من أشياخ قريش في هذه الساعة على هذه الحال في طلب الدنيا؟ أما لأعظنّه. فدنوت منه فسلّمت عليه فردّ عليّ السلام بِبُهر وهو يتصابّ عرقًا. فقلت: أصلحك الله! شيخ من أشياخ قريش في هذه الساعة على هذه الحال في طلب الدنيا؟ أرأيت لو جاء أجلك وأنت على هذه الحال ما كنت تصنع؟ فقال: لو جاءني الموت وأنا على هذه الحال جاءني وأنا في طاعة الله عزّ وجلّ، أكُفّ بها نفسي وعيالي عنك وعن الناس. وإنّما كنت أخاف أن لو جاءني الموت وأنا على معصية من معاصي الله. فقلت: صدقتَ يرحمك الله! أردت أن أعظك فوعظتَني.[26]

I went to one of the districts of Medina during a hot part of the day and ran into Abū Jaʿfar Muḥammad b. ʿAlī. He was a corpulent, heavy man, and he was leaning on two black slaves (or two servants). I said to myself, "Praise be to God! An elder of the Quraysh in pursuit of worldly life at this hour and in this condition? I will counsel him." I approached and greeted him, and he returned the greeting with labored breathing while dripping with sweat. I said, "May God put you on the right path! An elder of the Quraysh in pursuit of worldly life at this hour and in this condition? What do you think you would do if death came to you in this condition?" He said, "If death came to me in this condition, it would come while I was in obedience to God, the Mighty and Majestic, keeping myself and my family free of need to seek help from you or other people. I would fear death's coming to me while I were in a state of disobedience to God." I said, "You have spoken the truth. May God have mercy on you! I wanted to counsel you, but you counseled me."

---

24 Barqī, *Maḥāsin*, 538; Kulaynī, *Kāfī*, 3:524 (two variants of the same report), 5:171 (with variants in Kulaynī and in Ṭūsī, *Tahdhīb*, 7:20; see also Aḥmad b. ʿĪsā, *Amālī*, 3:160 for a possibly related report from Jaʿfar al-Ṣādiq). Muḥammad al-Bāqir also owned a public bathhouse in Medina (Kulaynī, 6:497).

25 Kulaynī, *Kāfī*, 5:73, 177; see also 5:197, where a case of trade with some Egyptian merchants is attributed variously to him or to his son, Jaʿfar al-Ṣādiq, in what appear to be two versions of the same report.

26 Kulaynī, *Kāfī*, 5:73–74.

He thus appears to have led a reasonably comfortable life, even if he was not rich by the standards of the time.[27] At the time of his death, he owned sixty slaves, one third of whom, determined by casting lots, were to be set free in his will.[28]

He was considerably overweight,[29] to the extent that walking was a challenge for him.[30] The problem might have been caused by his diet, which always included a lot of meat,[31] something he greatly liked.[32] His diet also included dates[33] and occasionally cheese,[34] among other foods.[35]

In his marital life, he seems to have been an agreeable and loving spouse.[36] At home, he lived and dressed in the way that his wife demanded, to the astonishment of his admirers, who did not expect him to inhabit a luxurious home, or to wear cheerful colors.[37] If asked, he would explain to them that the house belonged to his wife.[38] He told a group of visitors that he dyed his beard[39] to please his women.[40] He would keep his beard light

---

27 See Ibn Bābawayh, *Thawāb al-aʿmāl*, 219.

28 Barqī, *Maḥāsin*, 624; Kulaynī, *Kāfī*, 7:18, 55 (cf. 7:56).

29 Kulaynī, *Kāfī*, 5:73 (see also 3:410); Qāḍī Nuʿmān, *Daʿāʾim al-Islām*, 1:237; Ṭūsī, *Tahdhīb*, 1:62, 91. On his other health problems, see Kulaynī, 3:58; Ṭūsī, 1:256.

30 Kulaynī, *Kāfī*, 5:73, 171, 172. He needed two men at his side while walking (Kulaynī, 5:73) and a servant to help him get up for prayer (ʿAyyāshī, *Tafsīr*, 1:400). His son Jaʿfar made his bed every night (Kulaynī, 3:323).

31 Barqī, *Maḥāsin*, 462.

32 Barqī, *Maḥāsin*, 462 (*mā kāna yaṣbiru ʿan al-laḥm*); Kulaynī, *Kāfī*, 6:308, 309. The amount of money that he had in his possession at the time of his death was either thirty or seventy dirhams (one number being a corruption of the other in Arabic script), which he had kept aside to buy meat for the meal of what turned out to be his last day (Barqī, 460 [thirty or seventy dirhams]; Kulaynī, 6:308 [thirty dirhams]).

33 Barqī, *Maḥāsin*, 531, 538; Kulaynī, *Kāfī*, 6:345, 346.

34 Barqī, *Maḥāsin*, 496–97; Ḥimyarī, *Qurb al-isnād*, 19; Kulaynī, *Kāfī*, 6:339.

35 He is reported to have had a special fondness for pomegranates over other fruits. See Barqī, *Maḥāsin*, 541.

36 See also Kulaynī, *Kāfī*, 5:511, where Jaʿfar al-Ṣādiq reports that his father had a wife who constantly caused him distress but whom he always forgave.

37 Kulaynī, *Kāfī*, 6:446–48, 477.

38 Kulaynī, *Kāfī*, 6:447, 448, 477.

39 He said that the Prophet, too, dyed his beard "and here is his hair with us" (Ibn Bābawayh, *Faqīh*, 1:69). The Family also held the shirt in which ʿAlī was killed. Muḥammad al-Bāqir showed it to a disciple and Jaʿfar al-Ṣādiq to another. See Kulaynī, *Kāfī*, 6:457.

40 Kulaynī, *Kāfī*, 6:480–81. He said "I am a man who likes women" (إنّي رجلٌ يحبّ النساء), a reminder of the Prophet's alleged statement: حُبّبَ إليّ من دنياكم النساء والطيب (ʿAbd al-Razzāq, *Muṣannaf*, 4:321; Nasāʾī, *Sunan*, no. 8836; and other sources cited in the editors' footnote in Aḥmad b. Ḥanbal, *Musnad*, 19:304–7). See further Aḥmad b. Muḥammad b. ʿĪsā al-Ashʿarī (attr.), *Nawādir*, 114–15; Ḥimyarī, *Qurb al-isnād*, 20; Ṭabarī, *Jāmiʿ al-bayān*, 5:99–100 (also Qāḍī Nuʿmān, *Daʿāʾim al-Islām*, 2:201–2; Dāraquṭnī, *Sunan*, 4:320–21; Bayhaqī, *Sunan*, 7:288–89; Ibn ʿAsākir, *Taʾrīkh madīnat Dimashq*, 54:291–92); Kulaynī, 5:366, 569; Ibn Bābawayh, *Khiṣāl*, 161; Ṭūsī, *Tahdhīb*, 7:368, 466–7. Also a spurious story in Ṭabarī, *Jāmiʿ al-bayān*, 5:99–100 (quoted also in Qāḍī Nuʿmān, 2:201–2; Dāraquṭnī, 4:320–21; Bayhaqī, 7:288–89; Ibn ʿAsākir, 54:291–92).

and round[41] and dye it, usually black[42] but occasionally with henna[43] and/or *wasma* (woad, an herbal dye that produced an azure blue color).[44] The use of the latter, he thought, had gradually made his teeth loose,[45] so he had to fasten them with gold and chew a special kind of gum.[46] He once married a wife[47] from the Arab tribe of Thaqīf whom he loved dearly but eventually had to divorce as she adhered to the doctrine of the Khawārij and would not stop cursing ʿAlī.[48] However, the separation from her left him sad and suffering, a situation that noticeably affected his health.[49]

In his daily life, he was described by his son Jaʿfar as follows:

كان أبي كثير الذكر. لقد كنت أمشي معه وإنّه ليذكر الله، وآكل معه الطعام وإنّه ليذكر الله، ولقد كان يحدّث القوم وما يشغله ذلك عن ذكر الله. وكنت أرى لسانه لاذقًا بحنكه يقول لا اله إلّا الله.[50]

My father frequently recited the name of God. I used to walk with him while he kept reciting the name of God and have my meals with him while he continued to recite the name of God. He used to talk to people but that did not distract him from remembering God. I would see him as if his tongue were stuck in his palate constantly saying "There is no deity save God."

---

41 Kulaynī, *Kāfī*, 6:448, 486–87.

42 Kulaynī, *Kāfī*, 6:480.

43 Ibn Saʿd, *Ṭabaqāt*, 7:317; Kulaynī, *Kāfī*, 6:481, 482.

44 Ibn Saʿd, *Ṭabaqāt*, 7:317; Kulaynī, *Kāfī*, 6:482–83; Ibn ʿAsākir, *Taʾrīkh madīnat Dimashq*, 54:283.

45 Kulaynī, *Kāfī*, 6:482, 483 (see also 3:262); Ibn ʿAsākir, *Taʾrīkh madīnat Dimashq*, 54:283.

46 Kulaynī, *Kāfī*, 6:482–83.

47 She was called Umm ʿAlī (Kulaynī, *Kāfī*, 6:477, 5:351) and Muḥammad al-Bāqir had a son with her named Ibrāhīm (Kulaynī, 5:351). At the time of his wedding to this wife, her female servants took him and dyed his beard with woad (Kulaynī, 6:482).

48 Kulaynī, *Kāfī*, 6:55, 447, 477.

49 Kulaynī, *Kāfī*, 5:351. His father, ʿAlī Zayn al-ʿĀbidīn, faced a similar predicament with his beloved wife from the Arab tribe of Shaybān who was also a Khārijī and cursed ʿAlī all the time. That marriage ended in divorce too (Kulaynī, 5:351, 7:435). There is of course the possibility that one of these two marriage stories was adapted from the other. For ʿAlī Zayn al-ʿĀbidīn's conciliatory gesture toward the Khawārij, see Ṭūsī, *Tahdhīb*, 5:484, where it is reported that he offered a portion of his sacrifice to them. (A report in Kulaynī, 4:499 says that ʿAlī b. al-Ḥusayn and his son Muḥammad al-Bāqir used to share their sacrifice with neighbors, members of their family, and those in need.) See further Modarressi, "Mutual Understanding and Harmonious Relations," 34, and the accompanying endnote, n. 37.

50 Kulaynī, *Kāfī*, 2:499. See also 2:363; Kashshī, *Rijāl*, 178.

He left a will with details of his wishes for his funeral,[51] including the designation of eight hundred dirhams from his inheritance to be spent on his memorial.[52] He made a special endowment for eulogizers to eulogize him for ten successive years after his death[53] in the desert of Minā, outside of Mecca, during the annual *ḥajj*, which he used to attend every year. For thirty-four years after his death, as long as his son Jaʿfar was alive, a light burned every night in the room in which he had lived.[54]

II. Personal Life

As mentioned earlier, Jaʿfar al-Ṣādiq was born in Medina in the year 80 or 83. He lost his mother in his childhood.[55] The sources contain some scattered material on his marital and private life.[56]

---

51 Kulaynī, *Kāfī*, 3:140, 144. See further Ibn Saʿd, *Ṭabaqāt*, 7:317; Ṭūsī, *Tahdhīb*, 1:449; Ibn Shahrāshūb, *Manāqib Āl Abī Ṭālib*, 4:278.

52 Kulaynī, *Kāfī*, 3:217.

53 Kulaynī, *Kāfī*, 5:117.

54 Kulaynī, *Kāfī*, 3:251 (also Ibn Bābawayh, *Faqīh*, 1:97–98; Ṭūsī, *Tahdhīb*, 1:28).

55 Kulaynī, *Kāfī*, 5:528.

56 E.g., Kulaynī, *Kāfī*, 4:104, 5:320–22, 335, 569; Kashshī, *Rijāl*, 292; Ibn Bābawayh, *Faqīh*, 1:305, 3:362; Ṭūsī, *Tahdhīb*, 1:134, 3:13–14, 8:302. See also his advice on marital life in ʿAyyāshī, *Tafsīr*, 1:364, 445; Kulaynī, 5:324, 325, 335, 401. See also Kulaynī, 7:17 on the death of his wife, Fāṭima, the daughter of his uncle Ḥusayn b. ʿAlī Zayn al-ʿĀbidīn and the mother of two of his sons, Ismāʿīl and ʿAbd Allāh (Ibn Saʿd, *Ṭabaqāt*, 7:543; Mufīd, *Irshād*, 284; Faḍl b. Ḥasan al-Ṭabrisī, *Iʿlām al-warā*, 291–92; on this wife, see also Ṭūsī, *Tahdhīb*, 1:134). See also Kulaynī, 7:55, in which his handmaiden Sālima is mentioned; Kashshī, 366, where his other handmaiden Saʿīda is mentioned; and Barqī, *Maḥāsin*, 625, where Jaʿfar asks two of his associates to find him a handmaiden to take care of his daughter Umm Farwa:

أطلبوا لي جارية من هذا الّذي يسمّونها « كَدبانوجة»، مسلمة، تكون مع أمّ فروة.

See also Ḥimyarī, *Qurb al-isnād*, 44 and Kulaynī, 6:232, in which a servant of his daughter Umm Farwa named Saʿīda, most probably the same as above, is mentioned. On his daughter Umm Farwa, see Ibn Saʿd, 7:543, in which she is identified as the full sister of Ismāʿīl and ʿAbd Allāh; Kulaynī, 4:293–94, 6:197, 8:216; Ibn al-Khashshāb, *Taʾrīkh mawālīd al-Aʾimma wa-wafayātihim*, 187; as well as Kulaynī, 4:398, 428 and Kashshī, 370, in which the editor misidentified her in the footnote. See also Iṣbahānī, *Maqātil al-Ṭalibiyyīn*, 464, where Yaḥyā b. ʿAbd Allāh b. al-Ḥasan is said to have been brought up by Jaʿfar after Yaḥyā's father, ʿAbd Allāh, and older brothers, Nafs al-Zakiyya and Ibrāhīm, were killed. Ḥusayn, son of Zayd b. ʿAlī b. al-Ḥusayn, was also brought up by Jaʿfar after his father was killed when Ḥusayn was only four years old (see Modarressi, *Tradition and Survival*, 1:280–83 and the many sources cited therein). See further Ṭūsī, 7:461, where it is said that a governor of Medina, Muḥammad b. Ibrāhīm, was Jaʿfar's son-in-law. Ibn Saʿd, 7:544, and Irbilī, *Kashf al-ghumma*, 2:378, identify this person as the Abbasid Muḥammad b. Ibrāhīm b. Muḥammad b. ʿAlī b. ʿAbd Allāh b. al-ʿAbbās; he must be the same as the individual named in two reports in Ṭūsī, 5:115–16 in the context of the *ḥajj*. See also Aḥmad b. Muḥammad b. ʿĪsā, *Nawādir*, 104 (on Jaʿfar's father's giving him a handmaiden); Kulaynī, 6:55 (on the marriage he arranged for his son, Mūsā); Barqī, 622 (on relations between him and his brother ʿAbd Allāh). In Barqī, 624–25, there is an interesting exchange between two of Jaʿfar's sons, ʿAbd Allāh and Mūsā. ʿAbd Allāh asks an associate to get him a righteous assistant, one who believes in the truth of the Shīʿī doctrine,

The location of his house in Medina was known from his time until some thirty-five years ago. Ibn Shabba (d. 262), the author of the oldest, partially surviving local history of the town, gave the exact location of the house as lying to the southeast of the Prophet's mosque, next to the house ascribed to the prominent Companion Abū Ayyūb al-Anṣārī (d. 52).[57] The two houses still stood next to each other in exactly the same spot at the end of the fourteenth century, at the beginning of a lane named after ʿĀrif Ḥikmat, the prominent judge and *shaykh al-Islām* of the Ottoman empire (d. 1275), who established the biggest library in Medina in this same lane in the thirteenth century.[58] The house of Jaʿfar al-Ṣādiq was visited by pilgrims as a shrine,[59] but in more recent times it served as the residence of the *imām* of the Prophet's mosque,[60] until around 1406/1985, when it was demolished by the Saudi government in the course of the project to expand the Prophet's mosque.

Like his forefathers, Jaʿfar al-Ṣādiq was commonly addressed by people as the son of the Prophet (*yā ʾbna Rasūl Allāh*).[61] He diligently adhered to the practice of the Prophet as remembered by the members of his House[62] and those associated with it. This practice occasionally differed from what others at the time considered the practice of the Prophet.[63]

People thought that he was wealthy.[64] He said that the rumors of his wealth did not bother him, and he pointed out that his forefathers similarly did not like to be called poor.[65] He said to one of his followers, "I am one of the richest among the people of Medina."[66] He reportedly declined a gift of money from the caliph Manṣūr, saying that "I am [a man] of wealth, sufficiency, and bounty."[67] He once gave the entire amount of a gift of money

---

to work for him on his farm. Mūsā immediately intervenes: "Leave his righteousness and belief to himself. Get this man a strong laborer who can make his farm thrive!" ʿAbd Allāh then says to the associate, "Do what this man tells you to do!"

57 Ibn Shabba, *Taʾrīkh al-Madīna al-munawwara*, 1:259.

58 See ʿAbd al-Quddūs al-Anṣārī, *Āthār al-Madīna*, 38.

59 Ibn al-Mashhadī, *Mazār*, 102; Majlisī, *Biḥār al-anwār*, 99:335–36, 100:160.

60 ʿAbd al-Quddūs al-Anṣārī, *Āthār al-Madīna*, 38.

61 There are too many examples to cite, and one should be able to find many of them with a digital search of early Islamic sources, both Sunnī and Shīʿī. In Muslim, *Ṣaḥīḥ*, no. 1622, a transmitter refers to Muḥammad al-Bāqir as "Muḥammad b. Fāṭima bt. Rasūl Allāh."

62 See, for instance, the many details that Jaʿfar al-Ṣādiq cited about the Prophet's practice at the dinner table in Barqī, *Maḥāsin*, 456–58; Kulaynī, *Kāfī*, 6:270–72, 297.

63 E.g., Barqī, *Maḥāsin*, 442; Kulaynī, *Kāfī*, 6:271. At times, he quoted the practice of the Prophet in his daily life, but then added that one might no longer be able to follow it in all its details (Barqī, 458; Kulaynī, 6:272).

64 Kulaynī, *Kāfī*, 6:439; Ṭūsī, *Amālī*, 677.

65 Kulaynī, *Kāfī*, 6:439–40.

66 إنّي لَمِن أكثر أهل المدينة مالاً (Kulaynī, *Kāfī*, 1:538; see also 5:166, where he says إنّ الله يعلم أنّي واجد).

67 أنا في غنى و كفاية وخير كثير (Ibn Bisṭām, *Ṭibb al-Aʾimma*, 115; see also Kulaynī, *Kāfī*, 2:563, 4:6, 9, 260).

sent to him by Manṣūr to someone who had complained to him about his difficult life.[68] However, he lived a modest life. He hosted a generous table for guests[69] but himself ate simple food in moderation.[70]

Following the lead of his father, Jaʿfar was engaged in trade[71] and in farming.[72] He was very much in favor of investment in real estate,[73] and he kept his investments diversified so that if one lost value, another would do well and compensate for the loss:[74]

أتى رجل جعفرًا شبيهًا بالمتنصّح[75] له فقال له: يا أبا عبد الله! كيف صرت اتّخذت الأموال قِطَعًا متفرّقة ولو كانت في موضع واحد كانت أيسر لمعونتها وأعظم لنفعها. فقال أبو عبد الله: اتّخذتُها متفرّقة فإن أصاب هذا المال شيء سَلُم هذا المال.[76]

A man approached Jaʿfar seeming like a person who would give him advice, and said to him, "O Abū ʿAbd Allāh! How did it come about that you put your money in different businesses? If it were all in a single place, it would be more cost effective and beneficial." Abū ʿAbd Allāh said, "I put it in different businesses so that if something goes wrong with this part of my money, the other money will be secure."

He said that he liked for God to see him managing his life well[77] and working for his daily bread so that he would not need people:

عبد الأعلى مولى آل سام قال: إستقبلت أبا عبد الله في بعض طرق المدينة في يوم صايف شديد الحرّ، فقلت: جعلت فداك! حالك عند الله عزّ وجل وقرابتك من رسول الله – صلّى الله عليه وآله وسلّم – وأنت تجهد نفسك في مثل هذا اليوم؟ فقال: يا عبد الأعلى! خرجت في طلب الرزق لأستغني عن أمثالك.[78]

68 Kulaynī, *Kāfī*, 4:21; Kashshī, *Rijāl*, 183–84.
69 Kulaynī, *Kāfī*, 3:385.
70 See Barqī, *Maḥāsin*, 440; Kulaynī, *Kāfī*, 6:328. In this, he followed the practice of his grandfather, ʿAlī Zayn al-ʿĀbidīn; see Barqī, 440–41.
71 Kulaynī, *Kāfī*, 5:74, 76–77. See also 5:161–62, 289, 304.
72 Kulaynī, *Kāfī*, 3:566, 4:6, 5:76–77; Kashshī, *Rijāl*, 292. He employed workers (Kulaynī, 5:289) and contractors (Kulaynī, 5:269).
73 Kulaynī, *Kāfī*, 5:91–92.
74 Kulaynī, *Kāfī*, 5:91.
75 The word is corrupted in the edition of the source used in this work to المستنصح.
76 Kulaynī, *Kāfī*, 5:91.
77 Kulaynī, *Kāfī*, 5:166 (see also 5:87).
78 Kulaynī, *Kāfī*, 5:74.

[ʿAbd al-Aʿlā, client of Āl Sām:] I met Abū ʿAbd Allāh on a street in Medina on a very hot summer day. I said, “May I be made your ransom! With your status before God, the Mighty and Majestic, and your relationship to the Messenger of God (may God's prayer and peace be upon him and his Family), you exert yourself on a day like this?” He said, “O ʿAbd al-Aʿlā! I came out to earn my daily bread so that I would not have to depend on the likes of you.”

أبو عمرو الشيباني قال: رأيت أبا عبد الله وبيده مسحاة وعليه إزار غليظ يعمل في حائط له والعرق يتصابّ عن ظهره، فقلت: جعلت فداك! أعطني أكفّك. فقال لي: إنّي أحبّ أن يتأذّي الرجل بحرّ الشمس في طلب المعيشة.[79]

[Abū ʿAmr al-Shaybānī:] I saw Abū ʿAbd Allāh holding a spade and wearing a coarse cloth around his waist, working in his orchard. The sweat was dripping from his back. I said, “May I be made your ransom! Let me take over from you.” He said to me, “I like for a man to suffer under the heat of the sun in pursuit of a livelihood.”

الفضل بن أبي قرّة قال: دخلنا على أبي عبد الله وهو يعمل في حائط له، فقلنا: جُعلنا فداك! دعنا نعمل لك أو تعمله الإخوان. قال: لا! دعوني! فإنّي أشتهي أن يراني الله عزّ وجل أعمل بيدي وأطلب الحلال في أذى نفسي.[80]

[Al-Faḍl b. Abī Qurra:] We came upon Abū ʿAbd Allāh while he was working in his orchard. We said, “May we be made your ransom! Let us work for you, or let the brothers do it.” He said, “No! Leave me! I wish for God, the Mighty and Majestic, to see me working with my own hands, and pursuing what is licit through my own toil.”

أبو بصير قال: سمعت أبا عبد الله يقول: إنّي لأعمل في بعض ضياعي حتّى أعرق، وإنّ لي ما يكفيني، ليعلم الله أنّي أطلب الرزق الحلال.[81]

[Abū Baṣīr:] I heard Abū ʿAbd Allāh saying “I work on some of my estates until I sweat, even though I have enough to suffice me, so that God knows that I pursue a licit livelihood.”

79 Kulaynī, *Kāfī*, 5:76.
80 Ibn Bābawayh, *Faqīh*, 3:99.
81 Kulaynī, *Kāfī*, 5:77.

معتّب قال: قال لي أبو عبد الله وقد تزيّد السعر بالمدينة: كم عندنا من طعام؟ قلت: عندنا ما يكفينا أشهر كثيرة. قال: أخرجه وبعه. قلت له: وليس بالمدينة طعام! قال: بعه. فلمّا بعته قال: اشتر من الناس يومًا بيوم. وقال: يا معتب! اجعل قوت عيالي نصفًا شعيرا ونصفا حنطة.[82] [أنّا نكره أن نأكل جيّدًا ويأكل الناس رديًّا.][83]

[Muʿattib:][84] Once, when there was a price hike in Medina, Abū ʿAbd Allāh said to me, "How much food do we have?" I said, "We have enough for many months." He said, "Take it out and sell it." I said to him, "But there is no food in Medina!" He said, "Sell it." When I sold it, he said, "Buy [food] from the people day by day." And he said, "O Muʿattib! Make half of my family's provisions barley and half wheat. We hate to eat high quality [food] while people are eating inferior quality."

As a businessman, he was professional and serious. He would scrutinize his agents and take them to task. In response to an excuse by an agent who had mishandled the Imam's assets but defended himself by swearing that he had not misappropriated the funds, the Imam answered:

---

82 Kulaynī, *Kāfī*, 5:166.

83 The sentence between the brackets is from a variant of the report in Kulaynī, *Kāfī*, 5:166.

84 The best of Jaʿfar al-Ṣādiq's ten servants (Kashshī, *Rijāl*, 250; see also Ibn Saʿd, *Ṭabaqāt*, 7:544; Kulaynī, *Kāfī*, 371; Dhahabī, *Mīzān al-iʿtidāl*, 4:158; Ibn Ḥajar, *Lisān al-Mīzān*, 8:105, and numerous other sources listed in the editor's footnote therein) who was killed by Manṣūr (Ibn Saʿd, 7:544). He is credited with a number of transmissions from Jaʿfar al-Ṣādiq in Shīʿī *ḥadīth* collections, which are listed mostly in Khuʾī, *Muʿjam rijāl al-ḥadīth*, 18:226–27, 453–54 (see also Ibn Bābawayh, *Khiṣāl*, 494 and *ʿIlal al-sharāʾiʿ*, 2:174 for another instance), but also in Sunnī works such as Ibn Kathīr, *Tafsīr*, 1:355 (on Qurʾān 1:102), where his name is corrupted to Mughīth (عن مغيث عن مولاه جعفر بن محمّد), corrected by Ibn Ḥajar in *Lisān al-Mīzān*, 8:105, 127. Early sources offer no further biographical information on this servant. A recent work, which calls him Muʿattib b. ʿAbd Allāh, clearly uses ʿAbd Allāh in its lexicographical sense of "a servant of God" and not as a personal name of the man's father. This was a common practice in the Muslim biographical tradition to identify anyone whose father's name was unknown as "son of a servant of God," as in the case of all Mamlūk kings and other notables who were originally brought into Egypt and greater Syria as slaves. See further Ziriklī, *Aʿlām*, 8:260, col. 1, n. 1; Modarressi, *Maktab*, 116, n. 2. Just as one example, see the list of the biographical entries in Ibn Taghrībirdī, *al-Manhal al-ṣāfī*, vol. 13, under all Turkic names. All of the 37 former slaves and later notables of the Mamlūk period with the name Sūdūn; 61 Āybaks, Bardbaks, Bīlbaks, Jānbaks, Tunbaks, Uzbaks, Yushbaks, and Baktimurs; 59 Āqbughās, Āljbughās, Āltanbughās, Ārbughās, Aranbughās, Baybughās, Quṭlūbughās, Kimīshbughās, Mankulībughās, Timurbughās, and Yalbughās; 32 Āydimurs, Azdīmurs, Asnadīmurs, and Bīdīmurs; 26 Āqbays, Āqbirdīs, Aqṭāys, Āqṭuwās, Āqṭuwāns, and Āqūshes; 14 Īnāls; 13 Sunqurs, Āqsunqurs, and Qarāsunqurs; 12 Sanjars; 12 Arghūns; 12 Baybarses; 11 Bahādurs; 10 Taghrībirdīs and Taghrībirmishes; 9 Qānībays; and hundreds of others with less frequently used (eight cases or fewer) Turkic names as well as all 21 with standard slave names, such as Luʾluʾa, Yāqūt, Jawhar, Khushqadam, and Khushgaldī, are uniformly identified as "ibn ʿAbd Allāh," as were ʿIkrima, *mawlā* Ibn ʿAbbās, and countless others.

يا هذا! خيانتك وتضييعك مالي سواء إلّا أنّ الخيانة شرّهما عليك.[85]

Your misappropriation or mismanagement of my money are the same to me, but dishonesty is the greater evil of the two for yourself.

However, he always kept within legal and ethical boundaries:

أبو جعفر الفزاريّ قال: دعا أبو عبد الله مولىً له يقال له مصادف فأعطاه ألف دينار وقال له: تجهّز حتّى تخرج إلى مصر فإنّ عيالي قد كثروا. قال: فتجهّز بمتاع وخرج مع التجّار إلى مصر. فلمّا دنوا من مصر استقبلتهم قافلة خارجة من مصر فسألوهم عن المتاع الّذي معهم ما حاله في المدينة، وكان متاع العامّة، فأخبروهم أنّه ليس بمصر منه شيء. فتحالفوا وتعاقدوا على أن لا ينقصوا متاعهم من ربح الدينار دينارًا. فلمّا قبضوا أموالهم وانصرفوا إلى المدينة دخل مصادف على أبي عبد الله ومعه كيسان في كلّ واحد ألف دينار، فقال: جعلت فداك! هذا رأس المال وهذا الآخر ربح. فقال: إنّ هذا الربح كثير ولكن ما صنعته في المتاع؟ فحدَّثه كيف صنعوا وكيف تحالفوا. فقال: سبحان الله! تحلفون على قوم مسلمين ألّا تبيعوهم إلّا ربح الدّينار دينارًا؟ ثمَّ أخذ أحد الكيسين فقال: هذا رأس مالي ولا حاجة لنا في هذا الربح.[86]

[Abū Jaʿfar al-Fazārī:] Abū ʿAbd Allāh summoned a client of his named Muṣādif, gave him one thousand dinars, and said, "Prepare yourself to go to Miṣr [that is, Miṣr al-Fusṭāṭ] because my family has grown." He [Muṣādif] loaded some goods and traveled with the traders to Miṣr. When they got close to Miṣr, they were met by a caravan leaving Miṣr, so they asked them about the conditions in town regarding the goods they had with them, which were goods used by the general public. They [the members of the caravan] told them [the traders] that none of it was available in Miṣr. They [the traders] then made a pact and agreement among themselves that they would not reduce the price of their goods below profiting a dinar for every dinar [that is, their minimum prices would be double the cost of the goods]. When they collected their money and went back to Medina, Muṣādif came to Abū ʿAbd Allāh with two bags, each filled with one thousand dinars. He said, "May I be made your ransom! This is the principal, and this is the profit." Abū ʿAbd Allāh said, "This profit is too much; what did you do with the goods?" He told him about what they had done and their pact.

85 Kulaynī, *Kāfī*, 5:304.
86 Kulaynī, *Kāfī*, 5:161–62.

He [Abū ʿAbd Allāh] said, "Praise be to God! You make a pact against a group of Muslims to not sell them anything unless it is at a profit of a dinar for a dinar?" He then took one of the bags and said, "This is my principal, and we have no need for this profit."

He was also a hard bargainer, to the point that it attracted attention and criticism.[87] His reaction to such criticism was to say that it would not please God if he were defrauded of his money[88] and that someone who is cheated is neither praised nor rewarded.[89]

Examples of his generosity abound.[90] As previously noted, he once gave the entirety of a gift of money sent to him by the caliph to someone in difficulty.[91] After the failure of Zayd b. ʿAlī's uprising, he gave one thousand dinars to one of his disciples to distribute among the families of those killed in the fighting.[92] At harvest time, he would order his servants to dismantle the walls around his orchard at ʿAyn Abī Ziyād[93] on the outskirts of Medina, so that people could come through and take the fruits for free. He would thus make, at best, an annual profit of ten percent on the orchard, amounting to something like four hundred dinars on the equivalent of four thousand dinars worth of produce.[94] He designated a section of his gardens as charity for passersby.[95] His dinner receptions for guests were always generous and even extravagant, but within reason.[96] He bequeathed one third[97] of his estate to family members and others, including an individual who had attempted to kill him with a broadsword when Jaʿfar rejected his invitation to join the rebellion of Nafs al-Zakiyya in 145.[98] The text of two documents

87 Kulaynī, *Kāfī*, 4:494, 546; Khaṭīb al-Baghdādī, *Taʾrīkh Baghdād*, 5:346.

88 وما لله من الرضا أن أُغبَن في مالي؟ (Kulaynī, *Kāfī*, 4:546).

89 المغبون لا محمود ولا مأجور (Kulaynī, *Kāfī*, 4:496; Khaṭīb al-Baghdādī, *Taʾrīkh Baghdād*, 5:346; cf. Ibn Bābawayh, *Faqīh*, 3:122, where the same statement is also quoted from Muḥammad al-Bāqir).

90 E.g., Barqī, *Maḥāsin*, 502; Kulaynī, *Kāfī*, 3:501, 4:8–9, 21, 49, 5:138, 480, 6:278–79; Kashshī, *Rijāl*, 335, 369; Abū Nuʿaym, *Ḥilyat al-awliyāʾ*, 3:194; Ṭūsī, *Amālī*, 281, 677; Ibn Shahrāshūb, *Manāqib Āl Abī Ṭālib*, 4:236. See further Ḥimyarī, *Qurb al-isnād*, 43. However, like in everything else, he was moderate and reasonable in his charitable spending (e.g., Kulaynī, 3:566, 569), giving priority to the essential interests of religion and the Muslim community (e.g., Ṭūsī, *Tahdhīb*, 5:447).

91 Kulaynī, *Kāfī*, 4:21; Kashshī, *Rijāl*, 183–84.

92 Ibn Bābawayh, *Amālī*, 275. See also Kashshī, *Rijāl*, 338.

93 A large estate belonging to Jaʿfar that was later seized on the caliph Manṣūr's orders after the revolt of Nafs al-Zakiyya. See below.

94 Kulaynī, *Kāfī*, 3:569.

95 Ḥimyarī, *Qurb al-isnād*, 22; Kulaynī, *Kāfī*, 4:59.

96 Barqī, *Maḥāsin*, 400, 413–14; Kulaynī, *Kāfī*, 1:385, 6:278–80, 328, 8:164; Qāḍī Nuʿmān, *Daʿāʾim al-Islām*, 2:107.

97 Kulaynī, *Kāfī*, 7:55.

98 ʿAyyāshī, *Tafsīr*, 2:386; Kulaynī, *Kāfī*, 7:55.

of manumission for slaves written by him have been preserved.[99] His son Mūsā al-Kāẓim reported that his father continued until the end of his life to encourage Mūsā to be generous.[100]

He occasionally accepted gifts and charitable donations from his followers and admirers[101] but reminded them that he personally did not need their gifts.[102] There are reports of cases in which he accepted large gifts but then returned them to the donors as his own gift.[103] For charitable monies, his initial response was to ask the donors or their representatives to use the funds personally for appropriate purposes.[104]

He was strongly opposed to superstitious beliefs and practices embraced by people in his time, including amulets,[105] astrology,[106] and other notions.[107] A disciple once told him that he, the disciple, had become captivated by astrology to the point that he would cancel important trips because the horoscope or the position of celestial objects deemed them inauspicious. The Imam advised him to burn his astrological books.[108]

He also cautioned against the theological and sectarian debates of the time (known at the time as *khuṣūma* or *mukhāṣama*), which normally involved unhealthy levels of controversy and antagonism.[109] Should one be drawn into such a debate, the Imam advised, one should engage in it only to the extent necessary and use the Qurʾān as one's main—and indeed only—point of reference.[110] However, he allowed certain able disputants and theologians in his entourage to participate in theological debates for the purpose of defending the truth.[111]

His legal opinions would not vary depending on whether the involved party was a follower of his or whether the issue at hand affected the cause of the House of the Prophet. Once, for instance, he reiterated the common

---

99 Kulaynī, *Kāfī*, 6:181.

100 Kulaynī, *Kāfī*, 4:39. See further Jaʿfar's remarks on generosity in Ḥimyarī, *Qurb al-isnād*, 72–73; Kulaynī, 4:40, 41–42.

101 Kulaynī, *Kāfī*, 4:9 (see also 2:512), 7:58, 62; Kashshī, *Rijāl*, 200; Ṭūsī, *Tahdhīb*, 9:233.

102 ʿAyyāshī, *Tafsīr*, 1:321.

103 E.g., Kulaynī, *Kāfī*, 1:408, where he accepted a gift of 80,000 dirhams from a follower of his, but immediately returned it to the donor (cf. Kashshī, *Rijāl*, 200; Ṭūsī, *Tahdhīb*, 4:137).

104 E.g., Kulaynī, *Kāfī*, 7:15. (See also 7:14; cf. 7:58, where he refused to accept charitable bequests made for the House of the Prophet.)

105 Ibn Bisṭām, *Ṭibb al-Aʾimma*, 48.

106 E.g., Kulaynī, *Kāfī*, 4:6; 8:351–52.

107 E.g., Kulaynī, *Kāfī*, 6:6–7; Ṭūsī, *Tahdhīb*, 7:475.

108 Ibn Bābawayh, *Faqīh*, 2:175.

109 ʿAyyāshī, *Tafsīr*, 2:295; Kulaynī, *Kāfī*, 1:156, 2:213; Qāḍī Nuʿmān, *Sharḥ al-akhbār*, 3:476; Ibn Bābawayh, *Tawḥīd*, 456, 458, 460; Abū Nuʿaym, *Ḥilyat al-awliyāʾ*, 3:184, 198 (whence Mizzī, *Tahdhīb al-Kamāl*, 5:86; Dhahabī, *Siyar aʿlām al-nubalāʾ*, 6:264, Dhahabī, *Tadhkirat al-ḥuffāẓ*, 1:158; Dhahabī, *Taʾrīkh al-Islām*, 3:833).

110 Ibn Bābawayh, *Tawḥīd*, 347.

111 See further Modarressi, *Crisis and Consolidation*, 109–15.

reservation in the Muslim tradition against reciting poetry instead of the Qur'ān or prayers during the month of Ramaḍān. When his son Ismāʿīl asked whether it would make a difference if the poetry glorified the House of the Prophet, Jaʿfar said that it would not change the situation.[112] When a woman willed a sum of money either to be spent on enabling someone to make the *ḥajj* pilgrimage on her behalf or to be distributed among needy descendants of Fāṭima al-Zahrā', the daughter of the Prophet, Jaʿfar's response was that the money should be spent on *ḥajj* rather than the descendants of Fāṭima.[113] In yet another example, the daughter of Ḥumrān b. Aʿyan, one of Jaʿfar's closest and most favored associates,[114] imposed specific conditions on her husband in the marriage contract that Jaʿfar considered legally invalid, and he explicitly said so. He prefaced his opinion with this remark:

إنّ لأبيها حُمران لَحَقًّا ولا يحملنا ذلك على أن لا نقول الحقّ.[115]

Her father, Ḥumrān, has a right [over us], but that does not prevent us from speaking the truth.

He followed the same principle in matters related to himself. Consider the following example. In the year 142, the *ḥajj* procession was headed by the current governor of Mecca, Ismāʿīl b. ʿAlī b. ʿAbd Allāh b. al-ʿAbbās. As the procession from ʿArafāt to Muzdalifa began, Jaʿfar fell from his mule:

رأيت أبا عبد الله وقد حجّ ووقف الموقف، فلمّا دفع الناس منصرفين سقط أبو عبد الله عن بغلة كان عليها، فعرفه الوالي الّذي وقف بالناس تلك السنة - وهي سنة [اثنتين و]أربعين ومائة [وكان الّذي وقف بالناس تلك السنة إسماعيل بن علي بن عبد الله بن العبّاس] - فوقف على أبي عبد الله [حتّى يركب]. فقال له أبو عبد الله [ورفع رأسه إليه]: لا تَقِف! إنّ الإمام إذا دفع بالناس لم يكن له أن يقف [إلّا بالمزدلفة. فلم يزل إسماعيل يتقصّد حتّى ركب أبو عبد الله ولحق به.][116]

112 Ṭūsī, *Tahdhīb*, 4:195.

113 Ṭūsī, *Tahdhīb*, 5:447. See also Kulaynī, *Kāfī*, 7:17.

114 See Kashshī, *Rijāl*, 10, 176–81; Mizzī, *Tahdhīb al-Kamāl*, 7:306–7 and the many sources cited in the editor's footnote therein. See also Modarressi, *Tradition and Survival*, 1:239.

115 Kulaynī, *Kāfī*, 5:403, where the word لأبيها is corrupted to لابنة (also in Ibn Bābawayh, *Faqīh*, 3:270). Corrected on the basis of Ṭūsī, *Tahdhīb*, 7:371.

116 Ḥimyarī, *Qurb al-isnād*, 13–14 with inserts from a variant of the report at 161. See also Kulaynī, *Kāfī*, 4:541, where an abridged version of the report is quoted. The date appears in both sources as 140. I have corrected it to 142 as that was the year in which Ismāʿīl b. ʿAlī headed the *ḥajj* procession (Fasawī, *al-Maʿrifa wa'l-ta'rīkh*, 1:134; Ṭabarī, *Ta'rīkh*, 7:514). He also led the *ḥajj* in the year 137 (Fasawī, 1:118). In the year 140, the caliph Manṣūr led the *ḥajj* (Fasawī, 1:122; Ṭabarī, 7:504).

I saw Abū ʿAbd Allāh, who had come for the *ḥajj* and attended the gathering [in ʿArafāt]. When the people started to descend [from ʿArafāt toward Minā], Abū ʿAbd Allāh fell from the mule he was on. The governor leading the procession that year recognized him. (It was the year 142. The official who led the procession that year was Ismāʿīl b. ʿAlī b. ʿAbd Allāh b. al-ʿAbbās.) He stopped so that Abū ʿAbd Allāh could mount again. Abū ʿAbd Allāh, raising his head to him, said, "Do not stop! When the leader [of the procession] begins to drive the people [from ʿArafāt], he may not stop until he reaches Muzdalifa." So Ismāʿīl proceeded slowly until Abū ʿAbd Allāh mounted and caught up with him.

He took the same course in matters of social etiquette:

كنّا نمشي مع أبي عبد الله وهو يريد أن يعزّي ذا قرابة له بمولود له، فانقطع شسع نعل أبي عبد الله، فتناول نعله من رجله ثمّ مشى حافياً. فنظر إليه ابن أبي يعفور، فخلع نعل نفسه من رجله وخلع الشسع منها وناوله أبا عبد الله، فأعرض عنه كهيئة المغضِب، ثمّ أبى أن يقبله. ثمّ قال: ألا إنّ صاحب المصيبة أولى بالصبر عليها. فمشى حافياً حتّى دخل على الرجل الّذي أتى ليعزّيه.[117]

We were walking with Abū ʿAbd Allāh as he was going to offer condolences to a relative on the loss of his child. The strap of Abū ʿAbd Allāh's sandal broke, so he removed the sandal from his foot and walked barefoot. Ibn Abī Yaʿfūr[118] saw him, removed his own sandal, removed the strap from it, and gave it to Abū ʿAbd Allāh. He looked the other way, seeming annoyed, and refused to accept the strap. Then he said, "Indeed, it is more appropriate for the one who suffers a calamity to endure it patiently." He then continued to walk barefoot until he reached the man whom he had gone to console.

A non-Shīʿī who used to frequent Jaʿfar al-Ṣādiq's meetings described them as follows:

كنت أجالس أبا عبد الله فلا والله ما رأيت مجلساً أنبل من مجلسه.[119]

I used to sit in the company of Abū ʿAbd Allāh and, by God, I never saw a more noble company than his.

---

117 Kulaynī, *Kāfī*, 6:464.

118 ʿAbd Allāh b. Abī Yaʿfūr al-ʿAbdī al-Kūfī (d. 131), a close disciple of Jaʿfar al-Ṣādiq. On him, see Modarressi, *Tradition and Survival*, 1:103–5 and the sources cited therein.

119 Kulaynī, *Kāfī*, 2:657.

An Egyptian adherent of the doctrine of the Khawārij asked Jaʿfar a Qurʾānic question through a friend who was going on the *ḥajj*. He was impressed by the answer and said to the intermediary:

لولا ما أهرق جدُّه من الدماء ما اتّخذت إمامًا غيره![120]

Had his grandfather not shed that much blood, I would not follow any other *imām*![121]

Jaʿfar underwent several major illnesses in his life.[122] In the last two years of his life, he suffered from loosening of, and discomfort in, his teeth.[123] Traveling, even the annual pilgrimage to Mecca, became a challenge.[124] Earlier, he had been seriously ill for more than two years[125] with a pain in his stomach,[126] and he subsequently attributed his recovery to a change of his eating habits to include rice.[127] He once said to a Kūfan disciple, "The most favorable things that I receive from your region are rice and the viola flower."[128]

He expressed a wish to be in Iraq for its natural blessings: to immerse himself in the Furāt (Euphrates) once a day and to enjoy a Sūrānī pomegranate

120 ʿAyyāshī, *Tafsīr*, 2:124–25, and a variant in Kulaynī, *Kāfī*, 4:492.

121 This is a reference to the Battle of Nahrawān, where ʿAlī fought the first generation of the Khawārij.

122 See Kulaynī, *Kāfī*, 1:379, 2:246, 4:422; Ibn Bābawayh, *Faqīh*, 2:251; Mufīd, *Amālī*, 32; Ṭūsī, *Amālī*, 281, 676; Ṭūsī, *Tahdhīb*, 1:198–99. See further Durust b. Abī Manṣūr, *Kitāb*, 295 (also Kulaynī, 4:324; Ṭūsī, *Tahdhīb*, 4:292, 5:57).

123 Ibn Bābawayh, *ʿIlal al-sharāʾiʿ*, 1:278. See also Kulaynī, *Kāfī*, 4:293 and Ṭūsī, *Tahdhīb*, 5:28. He was also once diagnosed with ophthalmia (inflammation of the conjunctiva or the eyeball). See Bazanṭī, *Jāmiʿ*, 114; Ibn Bisṭām, *Ṭibb al-Aʾimma*, 84 (whence Ḥasan b. Faḍl al-Ṭabrisī, *Makārim al-akhlāq*, 2:269).

124 Kulaynī, *Kāfī*, 1:359 (a report from the year 145).

125 A report in Ṭūsī, *Tahdhīb*, 4:251 says that he was ill and could not fast in three successive Ramaḍāns. These were presumably the ones for which he ordered his son, ʿAbd Allāh, to make up fasts for him after his death, as mentioned below (Aḥmad b. ʿĪsā, *Amālī*, 2:342).

126 Barqī, *Maḥāsin*, 502–3; Kulaynī, *Kāfī*, 6:341–42 (see further Mufīd, *Amālī*, 18 for a case from the year 120). He seems to have suffered from digestive problems due to his insistence on following the modest diet of average people in his time and place, which relied on oil and vinegar (see Kulaynī, 4:256, 6:327–28—still better than bread and salt, which seems to have been the diet of the very poor, as in Ṭūsī, *Tahdhīb*, 5:442). His health once deteriorated on the way to the *ḥajj* because of this diet, but he recovered when he ate a chicken ordered by his handmaiden Ḥumayda (Kulaynī, 4:260). This servant was the mother of his son, Mūsā (Kulaynī, 1:385, 477; see also 4:260, 301; Ibn Abī al-Thalj, *Taʾrīkh al-Aʾimma*, 25; Faḍl b. Ḥasan al-Ṭabrisī, *Tāj al-mawālīd*, 46; Ibn al-Khashshāb, *Taʾrīkh mawālīd al-Aʾimma wa-wafayātihim*, 189; and see further on Ḥumayda, Kulaynī, 1:310, 4:301), who, together with Jaʿfar's daughter Umm Farwa represented him in the mourning sessions of Medinan women for deaths in their families (Kulaynī, 3:217).

127 Barqī, *Maḥāsin*, 502–3; Kulaynī, *Kāfī*, 6:341–42. This might have been the same illness as that mentioned in Kulaynī, 2:246 as above.

128 Barqī, *Maḥāsin*, 502; Kulaynī, *Kāfī*, 6:341.

once a day.[129] He had visited the region a number of times during his trips to the Abbasid court and was aware of its nature, customs, and culture.[130] Every part of it reminded him of his grandfather ʿAlī, his children and descendants, and their associates who lived and died on Iraqi soil. As attested by a large number of reports,[131] he visited all of the cities that were connected to his family and asked the local communities for their memories of the lives, sufferings, and tragedies of the members of the House of the Prophet who lost their lives in Iraq.[132] On these same trips[133] he also visited Christian churches, praising their cleanliness.[134]

---

129 Barqī, *Maḥāsin*, 540. For his special interest in the water of Furāt, see further Kulaynī, *Kāfī*, 6:388–89; Ibn Qūlawayh, *Kāmil al-ziyārāt*, 47; Ṭūsī, *Tahdhīb*, 6:38–39. For his praise of the Sūrānī pomegranate, most likely an attribution to Sūra, a region in Bābil, see also Barqī, 544; Kulaynī, 6:356; Ibn Bābawayh, *Khiṣāl*, 249.

130 E.g., Barqī, *Maḥāsin*, 426; Ḥimyarī, *Qurb al-isnād*, 170–71; Kulaynī, *Kāfī*, 1:351, 3:283, 284, 4:490, 6:341, 351, 416 (see also 4:80, 81, 5:552); Ibn Bābawayh, *Faqīh*, 1:317.

131 For a good number of these reports, some of which sound genuine and others spurious, see Majlisī, *Biḥār al-anwār*, 97:385–434.

132 He asked, for instance, about the last hours of the life of his uncle, Zayd b. ʿAlī, before he was killed in Kūfa:

> عبد الله بن أبان قال: دخلنا على أبي عبد الله فسألَنا: أفيكم أحد عنده علم من عمّي زيد بن علي؟ فقال له رجل من القوم: أنا عندي علم من عمّك. كنّا عنده ذات ليلة في دار معاوية بن إسحاق الأنصاري إذ قال: انطلقوا بنا نصلّي في مسجد السهلة. فقال أبو عبد الله: وفعل؟ فقال: لا! جاءه أمر فشغله عن الذهاب. فقال: أما والله لو استعاذ الله به حولاً لأعاذه.
>
> [ʿAbd Allāh b. Abān:] We went to Abū ʿAbd Allāh and he asked us, "Do any of you have knowledge about my uncle, Zayd b. ʿAlī?" One of us said to him, "I have knowledge about your uncle. We were with him one night in the house of Muʿāwiya b. Isḥāq al-Anṣārī, when he said, 'Let us go pray in the mosque of Sahla.'" Abū ʿAbd Allāh said, "Did he do so?" He said, "No! Something came up that preoccupied him [and kept him] from going." He said, "By God, had he gone there and sought refuge in God for a full year, He would have granted him refuge" (Kulaynī, *Kāfī*, 3:494).
>
> عبد الرحمن بن كثير عن أبي عبد الله قال: سمعته يقول لأبي حمزة الثمالي: يا أبا حمزة! هل شهدت عمّي ليلة خرج؟ قال: نعم! قال: فهل صلّى في مسجد سهيل؟ قال: وأين مسجد سهيل؟ لعلّك تعني مسجد سهلة؟ قال: نعم! أما إنّه لو صلّى فيه ركعتين ثمّ استجار بالله لأجاره سنةً.
>
> [ʿAbd al-Raḥmān b. Kathīr:] I heard Abū ʿAbd Allāh say to Abū Ḥamza al-Thumālī, "O Abū Ḥamza! Did you see my uncle the night he started his uprising?" He said, "Yes!" He said, "Did he pray in the mosque of Suhayl?" He said, "Where is the mosque of Suhayl? Perhaps you mean the mosque of Sahla?" He said, "Yes! Had he prayed two *rakʿa*s of prayer in it and sought refuge in God, God would have granted him refuge for a full year" (Ṭūsī, *Tahdhīb*, 6:37).

Abū Ḥamza al-Thumālī, Thābit b. Dīnār (d. 148–50) was a respected Kūfan scholar and *ḥadīth* transmitter known to both Sunnī and Shīʿī communities in Kūfa. On him, see Modarressi, *Tradition and Survival*, 1:377–79 and the sources cited therein. Masjid Sahla was one of the oldest mosques of Kūfa; it had been built in the first century. It was a Shīʿī hub since its inception and, as such, a highly respected mosque among the Shīʿa, then and now (see Majlisī, *Biḥār al-anwār*, 97:434–55; see further Haider, *Origins of the Shīʿa*, 238–39).

133 ʿAyyāshī, *Tafsīr*, 3:80, where he tells a Kūfan disciple who has asked him about the legality of a Muslim's praying in churches, "Pray there! How clean they are! I saw them when I was with you."

134 ʿAyyāshī, *Tafsīr*, 3:80; Ṭūsī, *Tahdhīb*, 2:222.

He especially liked dates[135] and had good knowledge of their various kinds.[136] On one of his trips to Iraq on the orders of the caliph Manṣūr, some of his disciples met him in Ḥīra near Kūfa. He praised the quality of the Kūfan dates to them.[137] He identified the types produced in the Ḥijāz, too, mentioned the names under which they were known there, and asked about their corresponding names in Iraq.[138] He said that specific Iraqi dates were better than Ḥijāzī ones but noted that overall the dates of the Ḥijāz were better than those of Iraq.[139]

Other characteristics and practices that the sources attribute to him include his fondness for perfume, a preference he shared with his great-grandfather, the Prophet. The place in which he prayed was recognizable by his sweet smell.[140] Like his father,[141] he had one or two ivory combs that he used,[142] and, like him, he dyed his beard with a light coat of henna.[143] He liked domestic pigeons and had them at home.[144]

135 Barqī, *Maḥāsin*, 535, 538–39. He said that sugar was his favorite among edible things (Kulaynī, *Kāfī*, 4:61).
136 Barqī, *Maḥāsin*, 533–37.
137 Kulaynī, *Kāfī*, 6:351.
138 Barqī, *Maḥāsin*, 535–37; Kulaynī, *Kāfī*, 6:348.
139 Barqī, *Maḥāsin*, 538; Kulaynī, *Kāfī*, 6:348.
140 Kulaynī, *Kāfī*, 6:511.
141 Kulaynī, *Kāfī*, 6:489.
142 Kulaynī, *Kāfī*, 6:488.
143 Fasawī, *al-Maʿrifa wa'l-ta'rīkh*, 2:649.
144 Kulaynī, *Kāfī*, 6:547, 548.

A report says that he used to repeat the expression *Wa'llāh*[145] in conversations.[146] He knew and enjoyed Arabic poetry;[147] he reportedly composed verse himself[148] and occasionally recited lines of it in his everyday exchanges.[149] Finally, for riding around town, he preferred a donkey—the modest, lower-class means of transportation—over the mule,[150] which signified higher social rank. He used mules for the *ḥajj* pilgrimage and other long trips.[151]

---

145 That is, "By God." Legally speaking, this statement can be made in three different contexts, each with different legal consequences: (1) A simple swearing by the name of God to emphasize a point, which does not give rise to any obligation, is allowed according to Qur'ān 2:225 and 5:89, but disfavored in trade according to a report attributed to the Prophet in Ibn Bābawayh, *Faqīh*, 3:97. A report in ʿAyyāshī, *Tafsīr*, 1:208 suggests that the formulas *Lā wa'llāh* (لا والله) and *Balā wa'llāh* (بلى والله) were endorsed under Islam as a replacement for the Arabs' pre-Islamic *Jāhilī* practice to swear by their fathers. Muḥammad b. ʿAlī al-Jawād, a descendant of Jaʿfar al-Ṣādiq and the ninth Imam of the Imāmī Shīʿa, who once used the expression *Wa'llāh* (والله) in a letter to deny a false ascription to himself, commented on his own action: "I hate to say 'By God' but it made me sad that matters be said about [that is, be ascribed to] me that did not actually happen" (Ṭūsī, *Tahdhīb*, 8:290). (2) An oath taken in the name of God to support a testimony in court is a major sin if false and disfavored if accurate, according to a number of reports from Jaʿfar al-Ṣādiq, including one citing ʿĪsā (Jesus) and another citing the Prophet (Kulaynī, *Kāfī*, 7:434). (3) An oath taken in the name of God to pledge one to a certain course of action has legal consequences if broken, and these can include financial liability.

146 Aḥmad b. Muḥammad b. ʿĪsā, *Nawādir*, 52. There are many examples of his statements that confirm this report, including Barqī, *Maḥāsin*, 146, 156, 347, 504, 581; Tirmidhī, *Sunan*, 1:26; ʿAyyāshī, *Tafsīr*, 2:244; Kulaynī, *Kāfī*, 1:53, 179, 200, 2:73, 77, 97, 123, 190, 242, 243, 342, 636, 3:100, 130, 415, 4:83, 259, 292 (four cases), 343, 5:19, 106, 108, 138, 260, 552, 6:271, 299, 383, 445, 7:423, 442, 8:34–36, 292, 383; Kashshī, *Rijāl*, 145–46, 147, 179, 180, 209 (قال بأيمان ثلاثة = said with a triple oath, that is, والله، بالله، تالله), 227, 228, 230, 250, 273, 292, 298, 299, 331, 341, 400, 401, 427–28; Qāḍī Nuʿmān, *Sharḥ al-akhbār*, 3:454; Ibn Bābawayh, *Faqīh*, 3:228, 279; Ibn Bābawayh, *ʿIlal al-sharāʾiʿ*, 1:17, 18, 2:277; Ibn Bābawayh, *Maʿānī al-akhbār*, 154, 217, 388; Ibn Bābawayh, *Thawāb al-aʿmāl*, 73, 136; Ṭūsī, *Amālī*, 158; Ṭūsī, *Tahdhīb*, 1:225, 2:98, 104, 3:100, 4:199, 5:29, 31, 9:4; Abū Manṣūr al-Ṭabarsī, *Iḥtijāj*, 2:293.

147 See, for instance, Ṭūsī, *Amālī*, 281. See further Kashshī, *Rijāl*, 206, where Jaʿfar suggests an alternative to a word in a line of poetry by Kumayt, the well-known poet of the Umayyad period (d. 126), in his presence.

148 Ibn Bābawayh, *Amālī*, 578; Tanūkhī, *Faraj baʿd al-shidda*, 5:88; Ibn Shahrāshūb, *Manāqib Āl Abī Ṭālib*, 4:273–77, where eight pieces of poetry are quoted from earlier sources as if composed by Jaʿfar himself, though he might have quoted them from others. See also Zamakhsharī, *Rabīʿ al-abrār*, 4:322.

149 E.g., Muḥammad b. al-Muthannā al-Ḥaḍramī, *Kitāb*, 259, 275; Ibn ʿAbd Rabbih, *al-ʿIqd al-farīd*, 6:113; Ibn Abī al-Dunyā, *Ishrāf*, 230 (also in Bayhaqī, *Shuʿab al-īmān*, 7:207); Kulaynī, *Kāfī*, 1:360 (from Akhṭal in his *Dīwān*, 250), 2:224, 4:21, 24, 25 (attributed to ʿAlī in his *Dīwān*, 80), 5:323; Kashshī, *Rijāl*, 94 (from Abū al-Ṭufayl ʿĀmir b. Wāthila al-Kinānī in his *Dīwān*, 65); Ibn Bābawayh, *Amālī*, 309 and *Kamāl al-dīn*, 74 (from Abū Khirāsh al-Hudhalī in his *Dīwān*, 15); Tanūkhī, *Faraj*, 5:295–96; Ṭūsī, *Tahdhīb*, 5:444 (also 462); Ibn Shahrāshūb, *Manāqib Āl Abī Ṭālib*, 4:277 (attributed in this source to Dhū al-Rumma, a corruption of Umm Salama as in Kulaynī, 5:117); Zamakhsharī, *Rabīʿ al-abrār*, 4:322; ʿAlī b. al-Muṭahhar, *al-ʿUdad al-qawiyya*, 153.

150 Kulaynī, *Kāfī*, 2:243; Kashshī, *Rijāl*, 215, 288, 332. Cf. Barqī, *Maḥāsin*, 352; Kulaynī, 8:276, where a similar preference is quoted from his father.

151 Ḥimyarī, *Qurb al-isnād*, 13, 45, 161; Kulaynī, *Kāfī*, 4:541, 6:445, 537–38 (see also 6:521); Kashshī, *Rijāl*, 257, 311.

Late in his life, he lost three of his children in successive years.[152] The last of the three was his eldest son,[153] Ismāʿīl, who predeceased his father by one or two years and whose death left the father in deep grief.[154] Jaʿfar then ordered his next-oldest son, ʿAbd Allāh, a full brother of Ismāʿīl, to make up on Jaʿfar's behalf after he died the fasts that Jaʿfar could not observe himself because of a long illness.[155]

He died in Medina in 148.[156] He was shrouded in the two garments that he wore on his pilgrimage trips to Mecca[157] and buried next to the graves of his father, grandfather, and grand-uncle Ḥasan al-Mujtabā in the main cemetery of the town, Baqīʿ al-Gharqad, where the site of his grave is still known.[158] Some half a century after his death, an old associate of his who no

152 Ibn Bābawayh, *Kamāl al-dīn*, 73. See also Kulaynī, *Kāfī*, 3:225, 226; Ṭūsī, *Tahdhīb*, 1:289.

153 See, for instance, ʿAyyāshī, *Tafsīr*, 1:406, 2:327 (the latter also in Kashshī, *Rijāl*, 374); Ṭūsī, *Tahdhīb*, 6:336 (also 9:194). On Ismāʿīl, see further Barqī, *Maḥāsin*, 417; Kulaynī, *Kāfī*, 4:571, 587, 5:196, 511, 6:547, 548, 551, 7:388–89, 432–33, 8:223–24; Kashshī, 377; Ibn Bābawayh, *Faqīh*, 3:135; Ibn Bābawayh, *ʿIlal al-sharāʾiʿ*, 2:87; Ibn Bābawayh, *ʿUyūn akhbār al-Riḍā*, 2:234; Ṭūsī, *Tahdhīb*, 4:70. There is a report in Kulaynī, 5:299–300, in which the Imam advises Ismāʿīl not to trust a person who is known to drink wine. A shorter report in Ḥimyarī, *Qurb al-isnād*, 315 ascribes major elements of that report to a conversation between the Imam and another son of his. One version is clearly a redaction of the other. See also Ṭūsī, *Tahdhīb*, 9:194, where it is reported that Jaʿfar willed a part of his inheritance to the son of Ismāʿīl, Muḥammad.

154 Kulaynī, *Kāfī*, 2:75, 92, 3:193–94, 204; Ibn Bābawayh, *Amālī*, 309; Ibn Bābawayh, *Kamāl al-dīn*, 71–74; Ibn Bābawayh, *Faqīh*, 1:98; Ṭūsī, *Tahdhīb*, 1:429.

155 Aḥmad b. ʿĪsā, *Amālī*, 2:342.

156 The current presumption in the Imāmī Shīʿī community that he died on the twenty-fifth day of Shawwāl (the tenth month of the Arabic lunar year) is not attested in the early sources, although the month of Shawwāl is one of the two alternatives named as the month of his death (Kulaynī, *Kāfī*, 1:472; Mufīd, *Irshād*, 284; Faḍl b. Ḥasan al-Ṭabrisī, *Iʿlām al-warā*, 271; Faḍl b. Ḥasan al-Ṭabrisī, *Tāj al-mawālid*, 43; Ibn Shahrāshūb, *Manāqib Āl Abī Ṭālib*, 4:280; the other date given is Monday, the fifteenth of Rajab [the seventh month of the Islamic lunar year]). The date of 25 Shawwāl was first suggested in early twelfth-century Iran (Imāmī Khātūnābādī, *Jannāt al-khulūd*, 29), most likely on the basis of a kind of mathematical calculation. The date of death of Jaʿfar's son Mūsā al-Kāẓim is recorded as 25 Rajab, 183, and Mūsā is said to have survived his father by thirty-five years and nine months. As is common in such contexts, the latter date was most probably approximate (see, as just one example of such approximate dates, Ibn Ṭāwūs, *Luhūf*, 87, where Jaʿfar al-Ṣādiq is quoted as saying that ʿAlī b. al-Ḥusayn Zayn al-ʿĀbidīn wept for forty years over the killing of his father, Ḥusayn. Ḥusayn was, however, killed on 10 Muḥarram in the year 61, and ʿAlī Zayn al-ʿĀbidīn died on 12 or 25 Muḥarram in 95, so the time between the two dates was only thirty-four years and a few days, not forty years). For the purpose of determining the date of Jaʿfar's death, however, the thirty-five years and nine months that Mūsā is said to have survived his father was assumed to be accurate. Using this calculation of thirty-five years and nine months from 25 Rajab 183, Mūsā's death date, yields 25 Shawwāl 148 for Jaʿfar's death date.

157 Kulaynī, *Kāfī*, 1:396, 3:149.

158 His tomb survived until 1344/1926, when it was demolished by the Saudi government. For a picture of the old building, see the image of it taken by an unknown photographer before its destruction, reproduced on the cover of this book.

There is also a shrine in Cairo near the mosque of al-Azhar and the shrine of Ḥusayn, known as Maqām Jaʿfar al-Ṣādiq, which locals respect and visit as the tomb of the Imam. See,

longer lived in Medina would still be allowed to be buried in the same cemetery as "a client of Abū ʿAbd Allāh who lived in Iraq," in contravention of the long-established tradition of the people of Medina not to allow anybody but locals to be buried in that cemetery.[159]

Two poets, Abū Hurayra al-ʿIjlī[160] and Mālik b. Aʿyan al-Juhanī,[161] both well known for their sentiments toward the House of the Prophet, eulogized him.[162] Pieces of these elegies have survived.[163] As had happened in the case of his father, Muḥammad al-Bāqir, a light burned every night in the room in which Jaʿfar had lived by order of his son Mūsā (al-Kāẓim) for some thirty-odd years until around 180, when the latter was arrested and moved to Baghdad on the order of the caliph Hārūn al-Rashīd (r. 170–93).[164]

---

for instance, the report published in *al-Yawm al-sābiʿ* (22 Jul. 2014), available at http://www.youm7.com/story/2014/7/22/1786516/زيارة.

Taqī al-Dīn al-Maqrīzī, the historian of Egypt (d. 845), suggested that the tomb belonged to a Fatimid emir named Jaʿfar whom the Cairenes misidentified as Jaʿfar al-Ṣādiq (Maqrīzī, *Khiṭaṭ*, 2:48–49). Until more recent times, Cairenes observed an annual gathering at the site with special rituals (Mubārak, *Khiṭaṭ*, 2:86). As part of the Chinese government's efforts to boost tourism in the country in the past two decades, a local government developed a small shrine in the territory of the Uyghurs (in the middle of the Taklamakan Desert, some sixty miles north of the town of Niya, Minfeng) into a more attractive building as Mazār Jaʿfar al-Ṣādiq. For more information and pictures of this building, see the collections under the handle *centralasiatraveler*, available at http://www.flickr.com/photos/centralasiatraveler/1261901056 (dated 19 Nov. 2006) and http://www.flickr.com/photos/centralasiatraveler/sets/72157601726736264/ (undated).

159 Kashshī, *Rijāl*, 386–87.

160 On him, see Ibn Shahrāshūb, *Maʿālim al-ʿulamāʾ*, 149. He also composed poems in praise of Muḥammad al-Bāqir (Balādhurī, *Ansāb al-ashrāf*, 3:307; Marzubānī, *Muʿjam al-shuʿarāʾ*, 366; Ibn Shahrāshūb, *Manāqib Āl Abī Ṭālib*, 4:212).

161 A Baṣran Shīʿī (Kashshī, *Rijāl*, 216) and a transmitter from Jaʿfar al-Ṣādiq (see Khuʾī, *Muʿjam rijāl al-ḥadīth*, 12:156–59). On him, see further Marzubānī, *Muʿjam al-shuʿarāʾ*, 239; Ibn Abī Ḥātim, *al-Jarḥ waʾl-taʿdīl*, 8:206; Ibn Shahrāshūb, *Maʿālim al-ʿulamāʾ*, 152. Marzubānī, 239 (whence Ibn ʿAsākir, *Taʾrīkh madīnat Dimashq*, 54:271; Dhahabī, *Siyar aʿlām al-nubalāʾ*, 4:404) also quotes a poem by him in praise of Muḥammad al-Bāqir.

162 Both poets are, however, said to have died before Jaʿfar al-Ṣādiq. For Abū Hurayra al-ʿIjlī, see Ibn Shahrāshūb, *Maʿālim al-ʿulamāʾ*, 149 and Ibn al-Muṭahhar, *Khulāṣat al-aqwāl*, 191 (unless the person named in these two sources is a different individual); for Mālik b. Aʿyan al-Juhanī, see Ṭūsī, *Rijāl*, 302.

163 Abū Hurayra al-ʿIjlī's eulogy in Ibn ʿAyyāsh, *Muqtaḍab al-athar*, 52 and Ibn Shahrāshūb, *Manāqib Āl Abī Ṭālib*, 4:278, and that of Mālik b. Aʿyan al-Juhanī in Marzubānī, *Muʿjam al-shuʿarāʾ*, 239; Mizzī, *Tahdhīb al-Kamāl*, 5:97 (both quoting Zubayr b. Bakkār); Ibn Shahrāshūb, 4:277–78.

164 Kulaynī, *Kāfī*, 3:251 (also Ibn Bābawayh, *Faqīh*, 1:98; Ṭūsī, *Tahdhīb*, 1:289).

III. Political Stance

Few people in Mecca[165] or Baṣra[166] were supporters of the House of the Prophet in Jaʿfar's time. But Iraq in general,[167] and in particular Kūfa,[168] the town in which ʿAlī spent the last years of his time as caliph, was home to the largest concentration of Jaʿfar's followers anywhere.[169] It is said that the majority of the people of Kūfa during his lifetime were his followers.[170] Other reports estimate the number of his followers there at fifty thousand[171] or more.[172]

This community was under constant suspicion and surveillance by the caliphate, which considered it a potential threat. In some periods during the lifetime of Jaʿfar al-Ṣādiq, the community was so afraid of government persecution that its members did not even greet one another in the mosque lest they be identified by government agents and harassed.[173]

When it came to politics, Jaʿfar al-Ṣādiq was very much like his father: non-participating, peaceful, and against violence.[174] His peaceful disposition is exemplified by his comment on a report according to which the Prophet said that anybody killed defending his own property is a martyr.[175]

---

165 For background, see Kashshī, *Rijāl*, 246, 389. Generally speaking, the majority of the residents of Mecca and Medina at the time were not on friendly terms with the ʿAlids. See Kulaynī, *Kāfī*, 2:409, 410.

166 Ḥimyarī, *Qurb al-isnād*, 128; Kulaynī, *Kāfī*, 5:349, 8:93; Ṭūsī, *Tahdhīb*, 3:27. See further Mizzī, *Tahdhīb al-Kamāl*, 5:77–78. There was, however, a community of his followers there. A report in Barqī, *Maḥāsin*, 478–79 says that a Baṣran brought a shrimp to show it to Jaʿfar and ask him about the lawfulness of eating it. In posing his question to the Imam, he mentions that "our community" is divided over the lawfulness of shrimp "with some regarding it as lawful and others as unlawful."

167 Kulaynī, *Kāfī*, 2:242; Ṭūsī, *Amālī*, 698 (quoting Jaʿfar al-Ṣādiq as thanking God for locating most of his followers in Iraq).

168 Kulaynī, *Kāfī*, 8:81:

ما من بلدة من البلدان أكثر محبًّا لنا من الكوفة.

No town has more well-wishers for us than Kūfa.

See also Qāḍī Nuʿmān, *Sharḥ al-akhbār*, 3:459; Ibn Qūlawayh, *Kāmil al-ziyārāt*, 314.

169 Other regions in which he had followers included Medina (Kulaynī, *Kāfī*, 3:118), Khurāsān (Ṭabarī, *Taʾrīkh*, 7:503; Kulaynī, 2:637; Ibn Samka, *ʿAbbāsī*, 204; Ṣūrī, *Qaḍāʾ ḥuqūq al-muʾminīn*, 28), Bāb al-Abwāb (Ṭūsī, *Tahdhīb*, 6:135), Sijistān (Kashshī, *Rijāl*, 385; Mufīd [attr.], *Ikhtiṣāṣ*, 203), and Jibāl in central Iran (Ṭūsī, 9:66), including Ray (Kulaynī, 5:115) and the Arab immigrants in Qum (Kashshī, 332–33), who made up the largest group of his followers in any locality outside Kūfa.

170 See, for instance, Ibn Qūlawayh, *Kāmil al-ziyārāt*, 168; Mufīd, *Amālī*, 142.

171 Ibn Bābawayh, *Ṣifāt al-Shīʿa*, 203.

172 Kulaynī, *Kāfī*, 2:242.

173 Irbilī, *Kashf al-ghumma*, 2:227 (quoting ʿAbd Allāh b. Jaʿfar al-Ḥimyarī's currently missing *Kitāb al-Dalāʾil*). At times, they did not greet even the Imam, by his own order. See Kulaynī, *Kāfī*, 2:219.

174 See, for instance, Kulaynī, *Kāfī*, 8:87.

175 This statement is quoted from the Prophet in all six canonical books of Sunnī *ḥadīth* (Bukhārī, *Ṣaḥīḥ*, no. 2480; Muslim, *Ṣaḥīḥ*, no. 226; Ibn Mājah, *Sunan*, no. 2580; Abū Dāwūd, *Sunan*, no.

Quoting that statement from the Prophet, Jaʿfar al-Ṣādiq commented, "But if I were there, I would leave the thief alone and would not fight him."[176] He would disassociate himself from anyone who used violence. He even did so with one of his close, learned associates, Ḥarīz b. ʿAbd Allāh al-Azdī, when the latter got involved in armed struggle against the Khawārij in Sijistān. Jaʿfar said to a companion of his who tried to intercede for Ḥarīz:[177]

ويحك! إنّ حريزًا شهر السيف وليس منّي من شهر السيف.

> Beware! Ḥarīz has taken up arms, and whoever takes up arms is not mine.

To a follower who asked him about joining the revolt of Muḥammad b. ʿAbd Allāh al-Nafs al-Zakiyya in the year 145, Jaʿfar responded:

أسكنوا ما سكنت السماء والأرض.[178]

> Remain tranquil as long as the sky and the earth remain tranquil.

And he counseled another follower:

يا سدير! ألزم بيتك وكن حِلسًا من أحلاسه واسكن ما سكن الليل والنهار.[179]

> O Sadīr! Stay in your home, and be like one of its fixtures, and remain tranquil as long as the night and the day remain tranquil.

Many people of the time believed in the right of the House of the Prophet to lead the Muslim community.[180] Criticizing the practices of the government, Jaʿfar also commented at times, "Were we in charge [we would do

4772; Tirmidhī, *Sunan*, nos. 1438–40; Nasāʾī, *Sunan*, nos. 3533–44) as well as in many other *ḥadīth* works cited in the editors' footnotes in Aḥmad b. Ḥanbal, *Musnad*, 11:74–75 and on other instances in this work where the statement is repeated.

176 ʿAlāʾ b. Razīn al-Qallāʾ, *Kitāb*, 367; Kulaynī, *Kāfī*, 5:52. The statement is attributed to Muḥammad al-Bāqir in Kulaynī, 7:296 and Qāḍī Nuʿmān, *Daʿāʾim al-Islām*, 1:398, and to him or his son Jaʿfar in Ibn Bābawayh, *Faqīh*, 4:68. In view of Muḥammad al-Bāqir's physical conditions, his fighting with a thief would not be conceivable. The transmitter of the report was not one of the former disciples of Muḥammad al-Bāqir's father, ʿAlī Zayn al-ʿĀbidīn, a fact that makes it unlikely that the report refers to an earlier stage in Muḥammad al-Bāqir's life when he might have been more fit. The attribution to Jaʿfar al-Ṣādiq seems, therefore, more plausible.

177 Kulaynī, *Kāfī*, 7:370. See also Kashshī, *Rijāl*, 336, 384.

178 Ibn Bābawayh, *ʿUyūn akhbār al-Riḍā*, 1:310; Ibn Bābawayh, *Maʿānī al-akhbār*, 266.

179 Kulaynī, *Kāfī*, 8:264.

180 See, for instance, Barqī, *Maḥāsin*, 154.

such-and-such]."[181] However, he was very careful not to put his own life or that of others in danger. There were a good number of instances in which he acted against what he said was required by the strict dictates of the law in order to protect lives.[182] The Zaydīs criticized him. They asserted that they had no disagreement with him except on the point that he did not believe in *jihād*.[183] He rejected this accusation and noted that there were specific conditions for the obligatoriness of the duty of *jihād* that the Zaydīs did not know or care about.[184]

He visited both Abū al-ʿAbbās al-Saffāḥ[185] and Abū Jaʿfar al-Manṣūr, the first and second Abbasid caliphs, in Iraq. In the case of Saffāḥ, the purpose of the visit was presumably to congratulate him on his accession.[186] Jaʿfar's visit to Manṣūr, at the beginning of the latter's reign, was probably for the

181 لو كان الأمرُ إلينا. See, for instance, Ṭūsī, *Tahdhīb*, 8:99. See also Qāḍī Nuʿmān, *Daʿāʾim al-Islām*, 2:256: لو وليتُ أمرَ الناس.

182 E.g., Aḥmad b. Muḥammad b. ʿĪsā, *Nawādir*, 37 (and Ṭūsī, *Tahdhīb*, 7:372); ʿAyyāshī, *Tafsīr*, 3:25–26; Kulaynī, *Kāfī*, 4:83, 6:449. He would even attend the funeral of an anti-ʿAlid Umayyad, presumably for the same reason (Kulaynī, 3:190).

183 Kulaynī, *Kāfī*, 5:19. See also 1:357, and Khazzāz al-Qummī, *Kifāyat al-athar*, 301, quoting the same group as saying:

> ليس الإمام من جلس في بيته وأغلق بابه وأرخى ستره.
>
> The Imam is not someone who remains in his home, closes his door, and lowers his curtains.

184 Kulaynī, *Kāfī*, 5:19.

185 Barqī, *Maḥāsin*, 588; Kulaynī, *Kāfī*, 3:493, 4:83, 5:108 (the last report does not specify the time, but Dāwūd b. ʿAlī, who is mentioned in it as being alive and in office at the time, was appointed as the governor of Kūfa and then Medina very late in 132 and died early in 133, both events occurring during the caliphate of Saffāḥ), 6:449, 7:378; Ibn Qūlawayh, *Kāmil al-ziyārāt*, 37, 48; Ibn Bābawayh, *Sifāt al-Shīʿa*, 204; Ṭūsī, *Tahdhīb*, 6:38–39. See also Ḥimyarī, *Qurb al-isnād*, 170, and see ʿAlī b. Asbāṭ, *Nawādir*, 353 and Kulaynī, 8:208 (the last two reports belong to the legacy of the esoteric groups, but the initial references to Jaʿfar al-Ṣādiq's presence in Ḥira during the time of Saffāḥ may refer to a common memory). Most references to Jaʿfar's undated visit to Ḥīra, where he was met by many of his local followers, and to Kūfa are most likely from this first trip; see, for instance, Ibn Qūlawayh, 34; Kulaynī, 2:43, 4:571–72, 6:268, 537, 8:87; Kashshī, *Rijāl*, 245, 257, 288, 311; Ibn Bābawayh, *Faqīh*, 2:351–52; Ṭūsī, 2:208 (cf. Ibn al-Mashhadī, *Mazār*, 122), 4:222, 6:35, 36, also Ḥimyarī, 170–71. There are also reports about his presence in Ḥīra in the time of Manṣūr (e.g., Kulaynī, 6:268; Rāwandī, *Kharāʾij*, 2:642 [a report of esoteric provenance]).

186 One of Jaʿfar's meetings with Saffāḥ in Ḥīra took place at the beginning of Ramaḍān (Kulaynī, *Kāfī*, 4:83). For this meeting, and possibly for most other meetings with the Abbasids, he had to wear a black overgarment in accordance with the etiquette of the Abbasid court, but he said to a disciple who was present, "I am wearing this but know that it is the clothing of the people of the Fire" (Kulaynī, 6:449). That black is the color of the clothes worn by the denizens of the Fire is also mentioned in Kulaynī, 3:403. On a second trip to Kūfa during the time of Manṣūr, however, he reportedly wore white clothes when he went to meet the caliph (Kulaynī, 6:445). Privately, he would wear a shining white garment (Kulaynī, 5:65), and a black coat and shoes (Ibn Bābawayh, *ʿIlal al-sharāʾiʿ*, 2:36, reading *khuff* for *khazz*, as in footnote 2 therein), and occasionally red shoes on trips (Barqī, *Maḥāsin*, 378; Kulaynī, 6:466) with no problems.

same reason,[187] but one or more times he was summoned or brought to the caliph for interrogation.[188] Manṣūr also summoned him in Mecca or Medina on occasion during the caliph's *ḥajj* trips.[189] At one time, when Manṣūr left Mecca after a visit, Jaʿfar had to accompany him along the road to say goodbye to him.[190]

Two episodes in Jaʿfar al-Ṣādiq's life brought him face to face with politics and its consequences. Early in the fourth decade of the second century, when the anti-Umayyad revolution began under the banner of ending oppression of the House of the Prophet, there were major expectations that Jaʿfar al-Ṣādiq, as the most revered member of the House, would take the lead. A passionate follower told him that "half of the world" supported his claim to the leadership of the Islamic state.[191] The people of Kūfa allegedly waited only for his order to seize the city from its garrison.[192] Many leaders of society,[193] even the Abbasids who eventually took the reins of power, reportedly looked to him in the early days of the insurrection as one of their first choices for the spiritual leadership of the movement.[194] To the dismay and disappointment of some of his Kūfan followers and admirers,[195] Jaʿfar remained quiet and did not embark on any political activity.[196] He also forbade his followers to engage in politics[197] or join any armed group.[198] Until 145, as explained below, the Abbasid governors of Medina usually treated Jaʿfar with great respect. For his part, he occasionally visited them when they held court.[199]

187 Kulaynī, *Kāfī*, 4:540, 6:268, 8:87; Ibn Qūlawayh, *Kāmil al-ziyārāt*, 36; Ibn Bābawayh, *Thawāb al-aʿmāl*, 118; Ṭūsī, *Tahdhīb*, 5:425 (cf. Kulaynī, 4:540).

188 Kulaynī, *Kāfī*, 6:445; Muwaffaq b. Aḥmad al-Makkī, *Manāqib Abī Ḥanīfa*, 148. Ibn Ṭāwūs, in *Muhaj al-daʿawāt*, 220–364, lists nine times that Jaʿfar was brought to Manṣūr, twice in or near Medina and the other times in Iraq for interrogation. The list sounds ahistorical, at times taking different reports pertaining to the same trip as references to different trips.

189 E.g., Kulaynī, *Kāfī*, 2:559–60, 563 (see also 8:383); Ṭūsī, *Amālī*, 480–81; Zubayr b. Bakkār, *Muwaffaqiyyāt*, 149–50. See also Balādhurī, *Ansāb al-ashrāf*, 3:221, who does not specify the time. The last meeting between Jaʿfar and Manṣūr took place in late 147 when Manṣūr led the *ḥajj* (Fasawī, al-*Maʿrifa wa'l-ta'rīkh*, 1:131; Ṭabarī, *Ta'rīkh*, 8:26).

190 Ṭūsī, *Tahdhīb*, 5:475.

191 Kulaynī, *Kāfī*, 2:242. See also Ibn Shahrāshūb, *Manāqib Āl Abī Ṭālib*, 3:362.

192 Kulaynī, *Kāfī*, 8:331; Kashshī, *Rijāl*, 353–54.

193 Kulaynī, *Kāfī*, 8:331.

194 Tanūkhī, *Faraj*, 275–76; Shahristānī, *Milal*, 1:179; Ibn Shahrāshūb, *Manāqib Āl Abī Ṭālib*, 4:229 (quoting earlier sources). See also Kulaynī, *Kāfī*, 8:274.

195 Kulaynī, *Kāfī*, 2:242 (see also 1:368); Nuʿmānī, *Ghayba*, 198, 288, 294, 330; Ṭūsī, *Ghayba*, 262, 263, 265.

196 See Ṭabarī, *Ta'rīkh*, 7:603; Kulaynī, *Kāfī*, 1:378; Kashshī, *Rijāl*, 362, 365; Iṣbahānī, *Maqātil al-Ṭālibiyyin*, 273.

197 See Kulaynī, *Kāfī*, 8:264–65; Ibn Bābawayh, *ʿUyūn akhbār al-Riḍā*, 1:310.

198 See Kulaynī, *Kāfī*, 8:264; Kashshī, *Rijāl*, 336, 383–84; Najāshī, *Rijāl*, 144–45; Ibn Bābawayh, *ʿIlal al-sharāʾiʿ*, 577.

199 Kulaynī, *Kāfī*, 7:269 (with ʿAbd al-ʿAzīz b. ʿUmar), 375 (with Dāwūd b. ʿAlī b. ʿAbd Allāh b. al-ʿAbbās), 233 (with Muḥammad b. Khālid al-Qasrī; see also 3:507), 4:564, 5:395, 7:266–67 (with Ziyād b. ʿUbayd Allāh al-Ḥārithī), 363 (with ʿĪsā b. Mūsā).

Some twelve years later, in 145, he resisted strong pressures,[200] including even acts of disrespect and threats to his life,[201] from those who supported the uprising led by a member of the more active and politically ambitious Ḥasanid branch of the House, Muḥammad b. ʿAbd Allāh al-Nafs al-Zakiyya,[202] whose revolt Jaʿfar did not support.[203] He even left Medina to avoid the event.[204] However, he did not support the government against the rebellion either. In fact, he occasionally confirmed that the government was unjust but said that the timing and unprofessional planning of the uprising would doom the attempt to remove the oppressors.[205]

In the eyes of the government, however, the revolt was an act of the ʿAlids against the Abbasids. It did not matter much whether Jaʿfar al-Ṣādiq did or did not endorse the rebellion. After the movement's failure, Manṣūr sent a new governor to Medina and ordered that all properties belonging to the ʿAlids in Medina be seized unless they showed up to welcome his designated governor for the town. Jaʿfar al-Ṣādiq did not appear for the purpose and his estate at ʿAyn Abī Ziyād was seized.[206] Later, when he asked Manṣūr to return the estate to him, the caliph refused and said it had been "your [that is, the ʿAlids'] *Mahdī*" (the title that Nafs al-Zakiyya assumed for himself)[207] who had taken control of it.[208] The estate remained in government hands and was not returned to Jaʿfar during his lifetime. Years later, Manṣūr's son and successor, Mahdī (r. 158–69), returned it to Jaʿfar's heirs.[209]

The young Abbasid government, which had been established on the strength of Muslim sentiment in favor of the House of the Prophet, was now engaged in a bloody battle with the descendants of the Prophet. It realized the sensitivity of the conflict and thus tried to strike a quick and decisive blow against the rebels. Jaʿfar al-Ṣādiq was respected by the Muslim community as

200 These pressures included arguments by leading scholars of the time urging him to join the uprising, as his participation would add considerable weight. See, for instance, Kulaynī, *Kāfī*, 5:23–27 (a text that might have been somewhat edited in later times):

وقد أحببنا أن نعرض ذلك عليك فتدخل معنا فلا غنى عن مثلك لموضعك وكثرة شيعتك.

We wanted to present this to you so that you can join us. We cannot do without the likes of you, because of your stature and the large number of your followers.

201 See, for details, Kulaynī, *Kāfī*, 1:359–60, 362–64, 7:55. See also ʿAyyāshī, *Tafsīr*, 2:386; Iṣbahānī, *Maqātil al-Ṭālibiyyin*, 140, 172.

202 On him, see the entry in *Encyclopaedia of Islam* II, 7:388–89 [F. Buhl]; see also Elad, *Rebellion of Muḥammad al-Nafs al-Zakiyya*.

203 See Balādhurī, *Ansāb al-ashrāf*, 2:407; Kulaynī, *Kāfī*, 1:242, 358, 8:398; Kashshī, *Rijāl*, 214; Ibn Bābawayh, *ʿUyūn akhbār al-Riḍā*, 1:310; also Ibn Bābawayh, *Maʿānī al-akhbār*, 266.

204 Irbilī, *Kashf al-ghumma*, 2:162.

205 This line of argument continued in Zaydī-Imāmī discourse for quite a while. See, for instance, Ibn Qiba al-Rāzī, *Naqḍ kitāb al-Ishhād*, 194, 200.

206 For other properties seized after this failed revolt, see Rabb, "Curious Case of Bughaybigha."

207 See Iṣbahānī, *Maqātil al-Ṭālibiyyīn*, 237–45.

208 Ṭabarī, *Taʾrīkh*, 7:579.

209 Ṭabarī, *Taʾrīkh*, 7:603. See also Ibn Shabba, *Taʾrīkh al-Madīna al-munawwara*, 1:222.

the most prominent member of the Family, and that fact by itself was enough to make him an object of the caliph's jealousy, concern, and revenge. Even though he did not join or support the rebellion, the government considered him a serious potential threat. There is a report that Manṣūr ordered Jaʿfar's house to be burnt. This was reportedly attempted, but the fire did not spread beyond the door and the entrance.[210] If the episode actually happened, that was perhaps as much as the government intended.

During his first trip to Medina after the crackdown on the ʿAlids, late in 147, the year that he led the pilgrimage ceremonies,[211] the caliph ordered Jaʿfar al-Ṣādiq, who had failed to appear among those welcoming the caliph to town and had not attended prayer with him, to be brought into his presence.[212] When he arrived, the caliph accused him of harboring sympathy for the rebels, an accusation that Jaʿfar categorically denied. He reminded the caliph that if he had any political ambitions, he would have used the momentum fifteen years earlier when he was younger and the conditions were ripe and more suitable. The caliph knew what Jaʿfar had done at that time but was not moved by the reminder. A report claims that Manṣūr openly threatened to kill him[213] and that Jaʿfar responded to the threat by saying that he would not live much longer anyway. Additionally, he noted that the caliph should be assured that Jaʿfar would never bother him with anything, nor would he bother the caliph's successor should it happen that Jaʿfar outlived the caliph.[214] Jaʿfar was released and allowed to go home but remained under suspicion and surveillance.[215] This was the last meeting between the two, as the Imam passed away a few months later.[216]

While as a matter of principle, Jaʿfar al-Ṣādiq did not participate in or support any political uprising against the established order, he was very much opposed to any support for, or involvement with, unjust rulers, even at the level of working for them in a construction or farming project.[217]

---

210 Kulaynī, *Kāfī*, 1:473.

211 Ṭabarī, *Taʾrīkh*, 8:26.

212 Zubayr b. Bakkār, *Muwaffaqiyyāt*, 149–50 (whence Tanūkhī, *Faraj*, 1:313–18, and others).

213 Zubayr b. Bakkār, *Muwaffaqiyyāt*, 145; Ṭabarī, *Taʾrīkh*, 7:603; Ibn ʿAbd Rabbih, *al-ʿIqd al-farīd*, 2:159–60, 3:224–25.

214 Ṭabarī, *Taʾrīkh*, 7:603; Iṣbahānī, *Maqātil al-Ṭālibiyyīn*, 273.

215 See Tanūkhī, *Faraj*, 1:318–20; Irbilī, *Kashf al-ghumma*, 3:172–73.

216 Zubayr b. Bakkār, *Muwaffaqiyyāt*, 151.

217 Kulaynī, *Kāfī*, 5:107. There are a couple of statements ascribed to Jaʿfar al-Ṣādiq that specifically condemn the Abbasids. This genre sounds like a later contribution, even if not very late. See, for instance, Kulaynī, 8:341 and Nuʿmānī, *Ghayba*, 291, against the *Banū Mirdās* (the offspring of Mirdās), clearly a reference to Banū al-ʿAbbās (using, for precautionary reasons, an analogy between the name of ʿAbbās b. ʿAbd al-Muṭṭalib, the forefather of the Abbasids, and the name of a well-known poet and Companion of the Prophet ʿAbbās b. Mirdās al-Sulamī). Other anti-Abbasid reports and literature at times use allusions such as وُلد س ا ب ع (سابع being the reverse of عبّاس), as in Ibn Qūlawayh, *Kāmil al-ziyārāt*, 198 (cf. Kulaynī, 4:575, where the reference is decoded as وُلد العبّاس); وُلد سابع, as in Ṭūsī, *Tahdhīb*, 6:329; بنو السباع, as in ʿAlī b. Ibrāhīm, *Tafsīr*, 2:242;

He quoted the Prophet's warning to religious scholars who associated with rulers:

> الفقهاء أمناء الرسل ما لم يدخلوا في الدنيأ. قيل: يا رسول الله! وما دخولهم في الدنيأ؟ قال: اتّباع السلطان، فإذا فعلوا ذلك فاحذروهم على دينكم.[218]

> "The Muslim jurists are the trustees of the prophets as long as they do not get involved in worldly matters." He was asked, "O Messenger of

---

and *Banū Nutayla*, as in a piece of poetry, most likely from the late third or fourth century, that is preserved in Nuṣayrī literature and cited in Rakīnī, *Jabal ʿĀmil fī qarn*, 105 (the name obviously refers to the name of ʿAbbās b. ʿAbd al-Muṭṭalib's mother, Nutayla bt. Janāb [or Khabāb] b. Kulayb, from Banū Namr b. Qāsiṭ b. Rabīʿa). *Bakriyya wa-Ibāḍiyya* in Ibn Qiba al-Razī, *Naqḍ kitāb al-Ishhād*, 179, is clearly an intentional "customization" of Bakriyya and ʿAbbāsiyya (cf. Bāqillānī, *Tamhīd*, 169). There is a whole history with many parallels to this kind of naming. When mentioning a break of tradition by the second caliph, ʿUmar b. al-Khaṭṭāb, presumably through his use of the discretionary authority of the leader of the Muslim community, early Shīʿī sources at times referred to him by the phonetically similar name Zufar (e.g., Sayyārī, *Qirāʾāt*, 201, 289; ʿAlī b. Ibrāhīm, *Tafsīr*, 2:359; Ḥimyarī, *Qurb al-isnād*, 57, 60; Kulaynī, 5:465), or as رمع, which is the reverse of عمر, as in Ibn Bābawayh, *Faqīh*, 3:64: أوّل من ردّ شهادة المملوك رمع (cf. Kulaynī, 7: 390: أوّل من ردّ شهادة المملوك عمر), 4: 188: أوّل من أعال الفرائض رمع (and cf. Kulaynī, 7: 80: أوّل من أعال الفرائض عمر).These two cases, and the abovementioned instance of وُلد العبّاس, indicate that later copies of Kulaynī's *Kāfī* underwent minor edits once old precautionary measures were no longer necessary. See also Ṭurayḥī, *Majmaʿ al-baḥrayn*, 4:340. The first case, however, concerns Shurayḥ, the judge of Kūfa, who rejected the testimony of ʿAlī's slave in a specific case (Ibn Bābawayh, 3:64). It therefore seems that the replacement of a name by a symbol was not specifically intended in this case, but began with the corruption of the name شريح to رمع in an early text. It should also be noted that ʿUmar was occasionally referred to by early Muslims as Ibn Ḥantama in reference to his mother, Ḥantama bt. Hāshim b. al-Mughīra Dhū al-Rumḥayn (see, for instance, Zubayr b. Bakkār, *Muwaffaqiyyāt*, 496; Ṭabarī, *Taʾrīkh*, 4:211; Kulaynī, 1:428; Khaṭīb al-Baghdādī, *Taʾrīkh Baghdād*, 15:21). Likewise, the first caliph, Abū Bakr, is at times referred to in early Sunnī and Shīʿī (e.g., Kulaynī, 8:204) sources as Abū al-Faṣīl, clearly because of the closely connected meanings of the two words *bakr* and *faṣīl* in Arabic, each referring to a baby camel of a different age. He occasionally also appears as Abū Rakb, *rakb* (ركب) being the reverse of *bakr* (بكر), as in a poem by the mid-third-century poet ʿAbd Allāh b. ʿAmmār al-Barqī in Ibn Shahrāshūb, *Mathālib al-Nawāṣib*, 3:76. The third caliph, ʿUthmān, was also occasionally referred to as Ibn Arwā in reference to his mother, Arwā bt. Kurayz (e.g., Masʿūdī, *Murūj al-dhahab*, 3:92; Ibn Bābawayh, *Faḍāʾil al-Shīʿa*, 315; Ibn Bābawayh, *Faqīh*, 1:195; Ibn al-Athīr, *Kāmil*, 4:235; Ibn Abī al-Ḥadīd, *Sharḥ Nahj al-balāgha*, 1:270; Ibn Namā, *Sharḥ al-thār*, 381; also in a piece of poetry by Kuthayyir ʿAzza [*Dīwān*, 222 from Marzubānī, *Akhbār shuʿarāʾ al-Shīʿa*, 70] or Sayyid al-Ḥimyarī [*Dīwān*, 427 from Iṣbahānī, *Aghānī*, 7:276]. There were many similar nicknames that people used in the early centuries to refer to those in power. One of the best known was *Banū al-Zarqāʾ* for Banū Marwān (e.g., Nuʿaym b. Ḥammād, *Fitan*, 72; Abū Dāwūd, *Sunan*, nos. 4646–47; Tirmidhī, *Sunan*, no. 2236; Balādhurī, *Ansāb al-ashrāf*, 5:255, 257; Ibn ʿAsākir, *Taʾrīkh madīnat Dimashq*, 70:278; Ibn al-Athīr, 4:194; also a poem by Diʿbil in Marzubānī, 99) in reference to Zarqāʾ bt. Mawhib, the grandmother of Marwān b. al-Ḥakam. The name was pejorative in this case as Zarqāʾ is said to have been known in her time as a prostitute (Hishām al-Kalbī, *Mathālib al-ʿArab*, 77; Ibn al-Athīr, 4:194). *Waʾllāhu aʿlam*.

218 Kulaynī, *Kāfī*, 1:46, with a variant in Abū Nuʿaym, *Ḥilyat al-awliyāʾ*, 3:194 (whence Dhahabī, *Siyar aʿlām al-nubalāʾ*, 6:262; Dhahabī, *Taʾrīkh al-Islām*, 3:833).

> God! What is [the meaning of] their involvement in worldly matters?" He said, "Following the rulers. When they do that, be vigilant about your religion."

Jaʿfar advised his followers against going to unjust rulers even to defend their own legitimate rights.[219]

Living with constant suspicion and harassment on the part of the government was naturally challenging, especially in the last years of Jaʿfar's life. He is reported to have said to a group, most probably of Kūfan visitors:

> أشكوا إلى الله وحدتي وتقلقلي بين أهل المدينة حتّى تقدموا وأراكم وآنس بكم، فليت هذا الطاغية أذن لي فاتّخذت قصرًا في الطائف فسكنته وأسكنتكم معي وأضمّن لهم أن لا يجيئ من ناحيتنا مكروه أبدًا.[220]
>
> I grieve before God for my loneliness and anxiety among the people of Medina until you come and I see you and get companionable with you. If only this tyrant would allow me to take up residence in Ṭāʾif to live there. I would put you up with me. I would guarantee them that nothing odious would ever come from our side.

And to another transmitter he said,

> لَوَددت أنّي وأصحابي في بلدة من الأرض حتّى نموت أو يأتي الله بالفرج.[221]
>
> I wish I could live with my disciples in a remote town until we die, or until God finds us a way out [of this difficult situation].

219 Kulaynī, *Kāfī*, 1:54, 7:411–12, and for the community's following that advice, see, for instance, Ṭūsī, *Tahdhīb*, 10:127. In the *Maqbūla* of ʿUmar b. Ḥanẓala, quoted in full in Chapter 3, the Imam advised his Kūfan followers to choose a judge among themselves and refer their disputes to him as *qāḍī al-taḥkīm* (as opposed to the *qāḍī al-manṣūb*, as discussed in works on the Islamic justice system). They still could, and at times had to and actually did, go to the caliphal court to defend themselves against unjust claims, but they did not appeal to the court to gain anything.

220 Kulaynī, *Kāfī*, 8:215; Kashshī, *Rijāl*, 365, with a variant at 362 where he is quoted as saying to two of his Kūfan visitors: "I wish that you and I lived in Ṭāʾif... we would guarantee them [the rulers] that we would never make trouble for them" (reading نُضَمِّن لهم ألّا نُحَرِّج عليهم).

221 Ṭūsī, *Amālī*, 2:272.

IV. As Jurist

Abū Ḥanīfa's description of Jaʿfar al-Ṣādiq's knowledge of the diversity of opinions among the different schools, quoted earlier, is confirmed by a large number of reports in which Jaʿfar asks his questioners about what judges and jurists in different localities thought and said about various questions of law.[222] At times, he also asked contemporary scholars about the *ḥadīths* they had heard on a subject.[223] Typically, many of his clients began their inquiries by telling him what the jurists of their regions said or the local community upheld, and then asked whether he agreed or disagreed with those positions.[224] Such exchanges naturally kept him up to date on the range of opinions in the legal circles of his time, and he occasionally quoted these opinions in his legal responses.[225]

His name and fame as an authority on religious law were recognized beyond the community of the admirers of the House of the Prophet in Medina, Mecca,[226] and Iraq.[227] As a preeminent jurist of Medina, he attracted questioners from various groups,[228] and he responded to their questions according to what the law required.[229] When the questioner was a follower of a different school, Jaʿfar would quote the opinion of that school to him.[230]

---

222 E.g., Ḥimyarī, *Qurb al-isnād*, 128–29; Kulaynī, *Kāfī*, 4:267, 7:166, 245, 278, 397, 404, 8:93; Ibn Bābawayh, *Faqīh*, 3:48; Ṭūsī, *Tahdhīb*, 6:214–15, 281, 7:43, 8:189.

223 E.g., Kulaynī, *Kāfī*, 7:404; Ibn Bābawayh, *Maʿānī al-akhbār*, 296; Ṭūsī, *Tahdhīb*, 5:40–41, 7:241.

224 E.g., ʿAyyāshī, *Tafsīr*, 1:18, 400, 3:18; Kulaynī, *Kāfī*, 2:40, 3:37, 98, 307, 322, 5:23, 103, 174, 202, 255, 6:167, 185, 203, 384, 433, 7:21, 112, 247 (cf. 248), 309; Qāḍī Nuʿmān, *Daʿāʾim al-Islām*, 2:383; Ibn Bābawayh, *Faqīh*, 3:30, 48, 75; Ibn Bābawayh, *ʿIlal al-sharāʾiʿ*, 2:137; Ṭūsī, *Tahdhīb*, 1:139, 164, 2:45, 326, 3:277, 4:316, 7:155, 188, 10:309.

225 E.g., ʿAyyāshī, *Tafsīr*, 1:138, 3:18; Kulaynī, *Kāfī*, 2:226, 4:206, 236, 523, 5:27, 6:185, 247, 296, 7:429; Ibn Bābawayh, *Faqīh*, 3:337; Ṭūsī, *Tahdhīb*, 7:92.

226 See ʿAlī b. Jaʿfar, *Masāʾil*, 270; Ḥimyarī, *Qurb al-isnād*, 240 (with a variant in Kulaynī, *Kāfī*, 4:479–80), about a group of pilgrims who had gathered and crowded around Jamarat al-ʿAqaba in Minā when the announcement was made:

إنّ جعفر بن محمّد يقول: ليس هذا موضع وقوف فارموا وامضوا.

Jaʿfar b. Muḥammad says, "This is not a place to stop [as a ritual of the pilgrimage]. Throw your pebbles and leave."

227 See Kulaynī, *Kāfī*, 5:103, where a Kūfan follower of the Imam tells him that the (Sunnī) jurists of his town considered the profit drawn from a premodern version of a certificate of deposit unlawful even if it was not earned as interest. The Imam answers that it is lawful if there is no prior contract to make the profit a regular interest payment given to the owner of the money. And for the opposite opinion of the local jurists, he tells the questioner:

إذا قدمت العراق فقل: جعفر بن محمّد أفتاني بهذا.

When you return to Iraq, say that Jaʿfar b. Muḥammad advised me on this.

228 Ṭūsī, *Tahdhīb*, 2:90.

229 E.g., Kulaynī, *Kāfī*, 5:201.

230 Kashshī, *Rijāl*, 253.

He advised the jurists among his disciples to do the same.[231] His opinions were known to contemporary judges and jurists, many of whom had studied with him. The judge of Kūfa asked a follower of Jaʿfar al-Ṣādiq who came to him for litigation, "Whose opinion do you want me to judge you by? That of your master or someone else?" The man replied, "My master!" The judge then decided the case on the basis of what he had heard from the Imam on the issue at hand.[232]

As a preeminent jurist of Medina, Jaʿfar al-Ṣādiq was consulted by governmental officials when they needed a legal opinion on a matter in dispute. Manṣūr, too, consulted Jaʿfar in a number of cases, either directly[233] or through the governors of Medina[234] such as Ziyād b. ʿUbayd Allāh al-Ḥārithī[235] and Muḥammad b. Khālid al-Qasrī.[236] The latter once asked him about the details of the rites of *istisqāʾ* (praying for rain). Jaʿfar advised the governor on how to conduct the rites.[237] When the governor performed them correctly, the people of Medina said it must have been Jaʿfar who taught him how to perform them.[238] Ziyād b. ʿUbayd Allāh once asked Jaʿfar to attend court to give his opinion on a matter of law. Jaʿfar first asked the other local jurists who were already present and challenged them on their opinions. The governor said, "Leave them alone, O Abū ʿAbd Allāh! If we wanted them, we would not have asked you to come." He then followed Jaʿfar's opinion.[239] (There was, however, at least one other case in which he did not follow Jaʿfar's opinion.)[240] Other governors of Medina likewise sought Jaʿfar's opinion, including ʿAbd al-ʿAzīz b. ʿUmar, who asked him to come to the court and give a verdict in a criminal case,[241] and Dāwūd b. ʿAlī b. ʿAbd Allāh b. al-ʿAbbās, who consulted

231 Kashshī, *Rijāl*, 253, 330.

232 Kulaynī, *Kāfī*, 5:173.

233 E.g., ʿAyyāshī, *Tafsīr*, 1:323; Kulaynī, *Kāfī*, 7:287–88, 348–49. The case in ʿAyyāshī, 1:323 is about the owners of the houses adjacent to the sanctuary in Mecca who did not want to sell their houses to accommodate the expansion of the sanctuary. The Imam responded:

إن كانوا هم نزلوا قبل البيت فلهم أفنيتهم وإن كان البيت قديمًا قبلهم فله فناؤه.

> If the neighbors resided there before the sanctuary was built, they have full rights over their properties, but if the sanctuary was there before them, then it has a priority right over its surroundings.

His son Mūsā al-Kāẓim reportedly repeated his father's answer when asked by the Abbasid caliph Mahdī about a similar project for further expansion of the mosque (ʿAyyāshī, *Tafsīr*, 1:323–24). As in some similar cases, one of the two stories may be a redaction of the other.

234 E.g., ʿAyyāshī, *Tafsīr*, 1:266.

235 E.g., Kulaynī, *Kāfī*, 7:203, 266–67.

236 E.g., Kulaynī, *Kāfī*, 3:507, 538.

237 Kulaynī, *Kāfī*, 3:462; Ṭūsī, *Tahdhīb*, 3:148.

238 Kulaynī, *Kāfī*, 3:462.

239 Kulaynī, *Kāfī*, 7:266–67.

240 Kulaynī, *Kāfī*, 5:395. For relations between this governor and Jaʿfar, see further Ibn Bābawayh, *Faqīh*, 3:108.

241 Kulaynī, *Kāfī*, 7:269.

him on two other legal questions.[242] Similarly, ʿĪsā b. Mūsā, Shaykh al-Dawla, the governor of Kūfa who was sent by Manṣūr to Medina to crack down on the uprising of Nafs al-Zakiyya, asked Jaʿfar for advice.[243] Jaʿfar once sent his servant to the judge, apparently of Medina, to remind him of the Sunna of the Prophet in a specific case involving marriage.[244]

During the annual rites of the *ḥajj*, Jaʿfar al-Ṣādiq was a source of religious information for the pilgrims,[245] including the religious scholars.[246] One pilgrim asked ʿAbd Allāh b. al-Ḥasan, father of Nafs al-Zakiyya, about a matter relating to the *ḥajj*. ʿAbd Allāh answered, "There is Jaʿfar b. Muḥammad, who has devoted himself (*naṣaba nafsah*) to these matters. Go and ask him."[247] When someone received from Jaʿfar an answer to a question on the *ḥajj* that differed from the answer given by ʿAbd Allāh b. al-Ḥasan, the latter advised the questioner to follow the opinion of Jaʿfar, saying that "he received the answer from his forefathers."[248] Zurāra b. Aʿyan, one of Jaʿfar al-Ṣādiq's most prominent and learned disciples,[249] marveled at Jaʿfar's knowledge of the laws concerning *ḥajj* rituals:

جعلني الله فداك! أسألك عن الحجّ منذ أربعين عامًا فتفتيني.[250]

> May I be made your ransom! I have been asking you questions about the *ḥajj* for forty years now, and you continue to answer me.

As a jurist, Jaʿfar was very careful about the specifics of each case. When posed a legal question, he did not hesitate to ask further factual questions to clarify the situation and would sometimes ask the questioner to repeat his question so that he could get a full sense of it:

---

242 Kulaynī, *Kāfī*, 4:237; 7:375. The same governor also arranged for the killing of Muʿallā b. Khunays, an aide to Jaʿfar al-Ṣādiq, although he later claimed that he had not ordered the killing. See Kulaynī, 2:372, 513 (also 5:94); Kashshī, *Rijāl*, 377–81. See also Modarressi, *Tradition and Survival*, 1:326.

243 Ḥimyarī, *Qurb al-isnād*, 98; Kulaynī, *Kāfī*, 5:130.

244 Kulaynī, *Kāfī*, 5:399.

245 Kulaynī, *Kāfī*, 2:160, 4:257; Ṭūsī, *Tahdhīb*, 5:218.

246 Barqī, *Maḥāsin*, 210.

247 ʿAyyāshī, *Tafsīr*, 2:107–8. See also Kashshī, *Rijāl*, 360, where another prominent member of the House from among the Zaydīs explains Jaʿfar's superiority in knowledge by saying that "he had free time whereas we were engaged [in combat]."

248 Kulaynī, *Kāfī*, 4:236.

249 On him, see Modarressi, *Tradition and Survival*, 1:404–5.

250 Ibn Bābawayh, *Faqīh*, 2:306.

عمر بن يزيد قال: قلت لأبي عبد الله: الدراهم بالدراهم مع أحدهما الرصاص وزنًا بوزن؟ قال: أعِد، فأعدت، ثمّ قال: أعِد، فأعدت عليه. فقال: لا أرى به بأسًا.[251]

['Umar b. Yazīd:] I said to Abū ʿAbd Allāh, "[What is your position on] the exchange of dirhams for dirhams, each of the same weight, except that one has lead in it?" He said, "Say it again," so I repeated [the question]. Then he repeated, "Say it again," so I repeated [the question] to him. Then he said, "I do not think there is anything wrong with that."

سعيد بن يسار قال: قلت لأبي عبد الله: جُعلت فداك! امرأة دفعت إلى زوجها مالاً ليعمل به وقالت له حين دفعته إليه: أنفق منه، فإن حدث بي حدثٌ فما انفقت منه فلك حلالٌ طيّب. قال: أعِد يا سعيد المسألة . . .[252]

[Saʿīd b. Yasār:] I said to Abū ʿAbd Allāh, "May I be made your ransom! A woman gives money to her husband so that he can trade with it, and when she gives it to him, she says, 'Spend from it. If something happens to me, then whatever you spent from it will be lawful for you.'" He said, "O Saʿīd! Repeat the question." [Then he gave the answer.]

شعيب العَقَرقوفي قال: سألت أبا عبد الله عن الرجل يكون له الجارية يقع عليها يطلب ولَدَها فلم يرزق منه ولدًا فوهبها لأخيه أو باعها فولدت له أولادًا. أيزوّج ولَدَه من غيرها ولَدَ أخيه منها؟ فقال: أعِد عليّ. فأعدت عليه. فقال: لا بأس به.[253]

[Shuʿayb al-ʿAqarqūfī:] I asked Abū ʿAbd Allāh about a man who had a slave woman and slept with her in order to have children, but did not succeed. He therefore gifted or sold her to his brother, and then she bore children [for the second man]. Can he [the first man] marry his children from another woman to the children that his brother had with this [slave] woman? Abū ʿAbd Allāh said, "Say it again." I repeated [the question] to him. He said, "There is nothing wrong with that."[254]

251 Ṭūsī, *Tahdhīb*, 7:114.
252 ʿAyyāshī, *Tafsīr*, 1:365–56; Kulaynī, *Kāfī*, 5:136.
253 Kulaynī, *Kāfī*, 5:399.
254 The daughters of a man's former wife with whom he consummated the marriage are not lawful marriage partners for him, whether born before or after his marriage with the mother (Qur'ān 4:23). This rule applies also to the children of a slave woman with whom the owner had sexual relations (see Kulaynī, *Kāfī*, 5:433). In the text at hand, the questioner asks whether stepsiblings can legally marry. The Imam says yes. In this case, they are also first cousins, but marriage between first cousins is allowed in Islamic family law.

عبد الله بن سنان قال: قلت لأبي عبد الله: أخبرني عن القوّاد ما حدّه؟ قال: لا حدّ على القوّاد. أليس إنّما يعطى الأجر على أن يقود؟ قلت: جعلت فداك! إنّما يجمع بين الذكر والأنثى حرامًا! قال: ذاك المؤلّف بين الذكر والأنثى حرامًا؟ فقلت: هو ذاك! قال يُضرب ثلاثة أرباع حدّ الزاني – خمسة وسبعين سوطًا – وينفى من المصر الّذي هو فيه.[255]

[ʿAbd Allāh b. Sinān:] I said to Abū ʿAbd Allāh, "Tell me about what the *ḥadd* punishment is for the *qawwād*." He said, "There is no *ḥadd* punishment for the *qawwād*. Is he not given money in order to guide?" I said, "May I be made your ransom! He is someone who arranges for men and women to meet unlawfully!" He said, "He is the one who brings about unlawful unions between men and women?" I said, "That is him!" He said, "He should be given three-quarters of the lashes prescribed as the *ḥadd* punishment for fornication—seventy-five lashes—and he should be banished from the town he is in."[256]

موسى بن سَعدان عن بعض رجاله قال: كنت عند أبي عبد الله فأتاه رجل فقال له: جعلت فداك! ما ترى في شابّين كانا [مصطحبين] فوُلد لهذا غلام وللآخر جارية، أيتزوّج ابن هذا ابنة هذا؟ قال: فقال: نعم! سبحان الله! لِمَ لا يحلّ؟ قال له: إنّه كان صَديقًا له. قال: سبحان الله! وإن كان، فلا بأس. [قال: إنّه كان يكون بينهما ما يكون بين الشباب. قال: لا بأس.] قال: إنّه كان يفعل به. قال: فأعرض بوجهه ثمّ أجابه وهو مستتر بذراعيه فقال: إن كان الّذي منه دون الإيقاب فلا بأس أن يتزوّج، وإن كان قد أوقب فلا يحلّ له أن يتزوّج.[257]

[Mūsā b. Saʿdān:] I was with Abū ʿAbd Allāh when a man came to him and said, "May I be made your ransom! What is your position on two young men who kept 'close company,' and to one was born a boy and to the other a girl. Can the son of the former marry the daughter of the latter?" The Imam said, "Yes! Praise be to God! Why would it not be permissible?" The man said to him, "Because he was his 'friend.'" The Imam said, "Praise be to God! Even so, there is nothing wrong with

255 Kulaynī, *Kāfī*, 7:262.

256 A *ḥadd* punishment is a fixed punishment prescribed in the Qurʾān; that for fornication is a hundred lashes (Qurʾān 24:2). *Qawwād* means a procurer, but the Arabic word derives from a root that means "to guide," and this is why the word was obscure to the Imam.

257 Kulaynī, *Kāfī*, 5:417–18, with a variant in Ṭūsī, *Tahdhīb*, 7:310, used here to complete a lacuna and correct an error in the edition of Kulaynī's *Kāfī* used in this work.

that." The man said, "There was between them what goes on between young men." The Imam said, "There is nothing wrong with that." The man said, "He had sexual relations with him." The Imam turned his face away [in embarrassment]. Then he said, covering his face with his arms, "If what occurred was less than intercourse, there is nothing wrong with the marriage. But if he had intercourse, then it is not lawful for him to marry her."[258]

عبد الرحمن بن الحجّاج: قلت له: فإن جعل مكان الذهب فلوسًا؟ قال: ما أدرى ما الفلوس.[259]

[ʿAbd al-Raḥmān b. al-Ḥajjāj:] I said to him [as a follow-up to a question], "What if *fulūs*[260] are substituted for gold?" He said, "I do not know what *fulūs* are."

مفضّل بن عمر قال: ألقى أليّ درهمًا فقال: أيش هذا؟ فقلت: ستّوق. فقال: وما الستّوق؟[261]

[Mufaḍḍal b. ʿUmar:] He [Jaʿfar al-Ṣādiq] threw a dirham to me and said, "What is this?" I said, "A *suttūq*." He said, "What is *suttūq*?"[262]

عبد الرحمن بن الحجّاج قال: سألته عن الصرف فقلت له: الرُفقة ربما عجلت فخرجت فلم نقدر على الدمشقيّة والبصريّة. فقال: وما الرُفقة؟[263]

258 The text of the report poses a problem. While the prohibition of marriage in cases of prior sexual relations of this nature is the standard view in Jaʿfarī law, supported by other statements of the Imam (see Ḥurr al-ʿĀmilī, *Wasāʾil al-Shīʿa*, 20:444–45), the law applies to marriage of the one who commits the act with the immediate daughter or sister of the passive partner, not to marriage involving the next generation. No one, including those who cited this report in their works, ever extended the prohibition of marriage to bar the children of the two friends from marrying each other. This may indicate further lacunas or corruption in the text of the report.

259 Ṭūsī, *Tahdhīb*, 7:105. There are similar reports of instances in which the nature of different kinds of local currency had to be explained to Jaʿfar or his father before they could issue opinions on the legality of exchanging money in those cases. E.g., Ṭūsī, 7:108 (a question asked of Muḥammad al-Bāqir by someone from Sijistān regarding a kind of local currency called *darāhim shāhiyya*).

260 Copper coins. For the history of this coin, see especially Maqrīzī, *Ighāthat al-umma*, 141, 144–46; Maqrīzī, *Shudhūr al-ʿuqūd*, 36–39, 84–88.

261 Ṭūsī, *Tahdhīb*, 7:109.

262 *Suttūq* was a fake, silver-coated copper coin, as explained later in the report by the questioner, who characterizes it as containing layers of silver on the upper and lower surfaces but copper in the middle.

263 Kulaynī, *Kāfī*, 5:642; Ibn Bābawayh, *Faqīh*, 3:185; Ṭūsī, *Tahdhīb*, 7:104 with minor variations.

['Abd al-Raḥmān b. al-Ḥajjāj:] I asked him[264] about exchanging money and said, "The *rufqa*[265] occasionally leaves in a hurry before we are able to find the Damascene and Baṣran currencies [that is, the specific currencies we need]." He said, "What is *rufqa*?"

عبيد الله ومحمّد الحلبي قالا: قدم لأبي عبد الله متاعٌ من مصر فصنع طعامًا ودعا له التجّار فقالوا: نأخذه بده دوازده.[266] قال: وكم يكون ذلك؟ قالوا: في كلّ عشرة آلاف ألفين. قال: فإنّي أبيعكم هذا المتاع باثنى عشر ألف.[267]

['Ubayd Allāh and Muḥammad al-Ḥalabī:] A consignment arrived for Abū 'Abd Allāh from Egypt. He prepared a meal and invited the traders over. They said, "We buy it at ten-for-twelve" [using the Persian expression]. He said, "How much is that?" They said, "Two thousand for every ten thousand" [using the Arabic equivalent]. He said, "I am selling you this consignment for twelve thousand."

عبد الرحمن بن الحجّاج قال: سألت أبا عبد الله عن الحميل، فقال: وأيّ شيء الحميل؟[268]

['Abd al-Raḥmān b. al-Ḥajjāj:] I asked Abū 'Abd Allāh about *ḥamīl*.[269] He said, "What is *ḥamīl*?"

---

264 This means Ja'far al-Ṣādiq, who refers later in the text to his father's answer to the objection of the "people" (that is, the jurists) of Medina to his *fatwā* on the subject. Ja'far narrates that story in more detail in a report in Kulaynī, *Kāfī*, 5:247.

265 A caravan or convoy, as explained later in the text.

266 A Persian expression meaning sale at a profit of twenty percent. This was an Iranian method that the merchants of Kūfa adopted in their trades (see Ibn Abī Shayba, *Muṣannaf*, 7:435, quoting Ibn 'Abbās as calling it *bay' al-a'ājim*) and that then spread to other localities. The method was endorsed by early jurists such as Shurayḥ, Ḥasan al-Baṣrī (cf. Raqqām, *al-'Afw wa'l-i'tidhār*, 2:580; 'Aynī, *'Umdat al-qārī* [Cairo: Munīriyya, 1930], 12:16), Ibn Sīrīn, Ibrāhīm al-Nakha'ī, and Sufyān al-Thawrī (Ibn Abī Shayba, 7:436; 'Abd al-Razzāq, *Muṣannaf*, 8:232); but frowned on by others such as Ibn 'Umar, Ibn 'Abbās (Aḥmad b. 'Īsā, *Amālī*, 3:165), Sa'īd b. Jubayr (quoting Ibn 'Abbās but also independent of him), and Masrūq ('Abd al-Razzāq, 8:232; Ibn Abī Shayba, 7:435–37).

267 Ibn Bābawayh, *Faqīh*, 3:135; Ṭūsī, *Tahdhīb*, 7:54 (also Kulaynī, *Kāfī*, 5:197, no. 4); cf. Kulaynī, 5:197, no. 2, with a similar *isnād*, but here Ja'far reports the story as something that happened between the merchants and his father. Several other reports in Kulaynī, 5:197, 204 and Ṭūsī, 7:55 quote Ja'far as denying the legality of that method of sale, and one (Ḥimyarī, *Qurb al-isnād*, 29–30; Ṭūsī, 7:54) portrays him as being in favor of it (see further Kulaynī, 5:203).

268 Kulaynī, *Kāfī*, 7:165, 166.

269 The word is defined in the same quote and others in the same chapter of Kulaynī's *Kāfī* as a slave's acknowledgment of another person as his or her relative (see also below, Chapter 4, text 100 on p. 407).

سلمة بن محُرز قال: قلت لأبي عبد الله: إنّ رجلاً أرمانيًّا مات وأوصى إليّ. فقال لي: وما الأرمانيّ؟[270]

[Salama b. Muḥriz:] I said to Abū ʿAbd Allāh, "An *armānī*[271] man died and appointed me as executor of his will." The Imam said to me, "What is *armānī*?"

محمّد بن الفيض: [عن أبي عبد الله] قال: . . . ما تسمّون هذا الحذو؟ قلت: الممسوح.[272]

[Muḥammad b. al-Fayḍ was asked by Abū ʿAbd Allāh:] "What do you call this footwear?" I said, "*Mamsūḥ*."[273]

سأل رجل أبا عبد الله عن الرجل يتقلّد السيف أيُصلّي فيه؟ قال: نعم. فقال الرجل: إنّ فيه الكيمخت. فقال: وما الكيمخت؟[274]

Abū ʿAbd Allāh was asked about a man who carries a sword: can he pray with it? He said, "Yes." The man said, "But there is *kīmukht* in it." The Imam said, "What is *kīmukht*?"[275]

علي بن حنظلة قال: سألت أبا عبد الله عن الربيثاء، فقال: قد سألني عنها غير واحد واختلفوا في صفتها. قال: فرجعت فأمرت بها فجعلت في وعاء ثمّ حملتها إليه فسألته عنها، فردّ علي مثل الّذي ردّ. فقلت: قد جئتك بها! فضحك، فأريتها إيّاه. فقال: ليس به بأس.[276]

[ʿAlī b. Ḥanẓala:] I asked Abū ʿAbd Allāh about [a fish called] *rubaythā*ʾ. He said, "I was asked about it by more than one person, and they differed on its description." I went back, ordered one to be put in a vessel, and carried it to him, and asked him [again] about the fish, and he gave me the same answer. I said, "I brought it to you!" He laughed and I showed it to him. He said, "There is no problem with it."

270 Kulaynī, *Kāfī*, 7:86.
271 Possibly Armenian.
272 Kulaynī, *Kāfī*, 6:463.
273 *Mamsūḥ* was a flat shoe without heel, commonly used by the Jews at the time (Kulaynī, *Kāfī*, 6:463 [no. 4], 464 [no. 9]).
274 Ṭūsī, *Tahdhīb*, 2:368.
275 *Kīmukht* was the dead animal skin that was used for the leather sheath of a sword.
276 Barqī, *Maḥāsin*, 478.

محمّد بن مسلم قال: سألت أبا عبد الله عن الجرّيث، فقال: والله ما رأيته قطّ ولكن وجدناه في كتاب علي حرامًا.[277]

[Muḥammad b. Muslim:] I asked Abū ʿAbd Allāh about *jirrīth*.[278] He said, "By God, I have never seen it, but we found it [described as] unlawful in the book of ʿAlī."[279]

عبد الله بن بكير قال: سألت أبا عبد الله عن الرجل يشيّع إلى القادسيّة، أوَ يُقصّر؟ قال: كم هي؟ قلت: الّتي رأيت. قال: نعم. يقصّر.[280]

[ʿAbd Allāh b. Bukayr:] I asked Abū ʿAbd Allāh about a man who goes to Qādisiyya to say farewell [to someone(s)]; should he shorten his prayer [by half, like a traveler]? He said, "What is the distance?" I said, "What you saw." He said, "Yes, he should shorten his prayer."[281]

In the same way, he would tell his addressee explicitly if he did not have a specific answer to a question:

عيص بن القاسم قال: سألت أبا عبد الله عن رجل واقع امرأته وهي طامث. قال: لا يلتمس فعل ذلك فقد نهى الله أن يقربها. قلت: فإن فعل أعليه كفّارة؟ قال: لا أعلم فيه شيئًا. يستغفر الله تعالى.[282]

---

277 Ṭūsī, *Tahdhīb*, 9:4.

278 A fish from the eel family. See Cook, "Early Islamic Dietary Law," 240–42.

279 Muḥammad al-Bāqir, too, said to Zurāra b. Aʿyan, who asked him about the lawfulness of the same fish, "What is *jirrīth*?" (Ṭūsī, *Tahdhīb*, 9:5).

280 Ḥimyarī, *Qurb al-isnād*, 170–71.

281 The phrase "what you saw" clearly refers to Jaʿfar's presence in town as mentioned before. The distance between the two towns today is indeed a couple of miles longer than the minimum distance required by the Jaʿfarī school to shorten prayers by half. However, in reply to a question from his disciple ʿAbd al-Raḥmān b. al-Ḥajjāj in Ṭūsī, *Tahdhīb*, 4:222, the Imam confirmed that he had seen Qādisiyya and noted that the distance between it and Kūfa did not allow for the shortening of prayers. With the old town being located almost at the borderline of the legal distance for the shortening of prayers, the two questions might have concerned different sides of Qādisiyya, a town that also grew considerably over the following centuries, possibly causing the town center to shift southward, away from Kūfa, and thus adding to the distance between the two towns as is the case in our times.

282 Ṭūsī, *Tahdhīb*, 1:164. This is what Tirmidhī, *Sunan*, no. 137, quotes from Saʿīd b. Jubayr and others:

> قال ابن المبارك: يستغفر ربّه ولا كفّارة عليه. وقد رُوى نحو قول ابن المبارك عن بعض التابعين، منهم سعيد بن جبير وابراهيم النخعى، وهو قول عامّة علماء الأمصار.
>
> Ibn al-Mubārak said, "He repents to his Lord and he does not owe an expiation." A similar opinion was reported from some of the Successors (*tābiʿūn*, the religious

[ʿĪṣ b. al-Qāsim:] I asked Abū ʿAbd Allāh about a man who had intercourse with his wife while she was menstruating. He said, "He may not solicit that action; God forbade him to approach her." I said, "If he did it, does he owe an expiation?" He said, "I do not know anything specific about this. He should ask God, the Exalted, for forgiveness."

إسماعيل بن الفضل قال: سألت أبا عبد الله عن القنوت وما يقال فيه، فقال: ما قضى الله على لسانك، ولا أعلم له شيئًا مؤقّتًا.[283]

[Ismāʿīl b. al-Faḍl:] I asked Abū ʿAbd Allāh about the *qunūt* [in prayer] and what should be said in it. He said, "Whatever God puts on your tongue. I do not know of anything prescribed for it."

He did not always answer questions right away but occasionally took time to reflect on them first, as in these examples:

أبو بصير قال: قلت لأبي عبد الله: جُعلت فداك! إنّ صاحبيَّ هذين جهلا أن يقفا بالمزدلفة. فقال: يرجعان مكانهما فيقفان بالمشعر ساعةً. قلت: فإنّه لم يُخبرهما أحدٌ حتّى كان اليوم وقد نفر الناس. قال: فنكس رأسه ساعةً ثمّ قال: أليسا قد صلّيا الغداة بالمزدلفة؟ قلت: بلى! فقال: أليسا قد قنتا في صلاتهما؟ قلت: بلى! فقال: تمّ حجّهما. ثمّ قال: المشعر من المزدلفة والمزدلفة من المشعر وإنّما يكفيهما اليسير من الدُعاء.[284]

[Abū Baṣīr:] I said to Abū ʿAbd Allāh, "May I be made your ransom! These two companions of mine failed to stand at Muzdalifa." He said, "They should return to their place there and stand at the Mashʿar for a while." I said, "Nobody informed them until today, and the people have already left the site." He lowered his head for a while and then said, "Did they not pray the morning prayer in Muzdalifa?" I said, "Yes!" He said, "Did they not perform the *qunūt* in their prayer?" I

scholars among the second generation of Muslims), and it is the majority opinion among the scholars of the provinces.

According to other reports, however, Jaʿfar recommended the expiatory payment of one dinar (Ṭūsī, 1:163, as also in a report from the Prophet in Tirmidhī, no. 135), half a dinar (Ṭūsī, 1:163, also Tirmidhī, no. 136), a quarter-dinar, or a combination depending on whether the violation occurred early in the woman's menstrual period, when it should have been easier for the man to restrain himself, or toward the middle or end of it (Ṭūsī, 1:164). A simpler version of this opinion, cited in a report attributed to Ibn ʿAbbās, was supported by a number of early jurists as in Tirmidhī, no. 137, and was also attributed to Jaʿfar al-Ṣādiq by a disciple (Ṭūsī, 1:163).

283 Kulaynī, *Kāfī*, 3:340.

284 Kulaynī, *Kāfī*, 4:472.

said, "Yes!" He said, "Their *ḥajj* is complete." Then he said, "Mashʿar is Muzdalifa, and Muzdalifa is Mashʿar,[285] and it is sufficient to perform a short supplication."

يونس بن يعقوب قال: قلت لأبي عبد الله: إنّ أهل مكّة يذبحون البقرة في اللَبَب فما ترى في أكل لحومها؟ قال: فسكت هُنيهةً ثمّ قال: قال الله تعالى: ﴿فَذَبَحُوهَا وَمَا كَادُوا يَفْعَلُونَ﴾. لا تأكل إلّا ما ذُبح من مذبحه.[286]

[Yūnus b. Yaʿqūb:] I said to Abū ʿAbd Allāh, "The people of Mecca slaughter cattle in the upper part of the chest; what is your position about eating their meat?" He kept silent for a moment, then said, "God, the Exalted, said, 'They slaughtered it but would hardly do it.'[287] Do not eat anything but that which has been slaughtered at the [proper] point of slaughtering."[288]

أبو بصير عن أبي عبد الله قال: سألته عن الرجل يجتمع عنده من الزكاة الخمسمائة والستمائة، أيشترى بها نسمة ويعتقها؟ فقال: إذًا يظلم قومًا آخرين حقوقهم. ثمّ مكث مليًّا ثم قال: إلّا أن يكون عبدًا مسلمًا في ضرورة، فيشتريه ويعتقه.[289]

[Abū Baṣīr:] I asked Abū ʿAbd Allāh about a man who has accumulated five hundred or six hundred [dirhams] as *zakāt*. Can he use it to buy a slave to manumit?[290] The Imam said, "If he does so, he does an injustice against the rights of other people [among the beneficiaries of *zakāt*]." He was silent for a while and then said, "Unless it is a Muslim slave in a situation of necessity, [in which case] he can buy and manumit him."

285 A reference to Qurʾān 2:198: "When you depart ʿArafāt, remember God at the sacred Mashʿar." The Prophet stayed in Mashʿar (that is, Muzdalifa), overnight on his way from ʿArafāt to Minā, so all pilgrims do likewise. In the case at hand, the two men passed through Mashʿar, performed their morning prayer there, and offered the *qunūt*, the supplication in prayer in which one asks God for His blessings. They thus satisfied the requirement set by the Qurʾān of passing through the desert of Mashʿar and remembering God there, even if not to the perfect standard set by the Prophet.

286 ʿAyyāshī, *Tafsīr*, 1:138.

287 Qurʾān 2:71.

288 The question concerns the equivalence between *dhabḥ* (cutting the throat) specified in the Qurʾānic passage, and *naḥr* (stabbing the upper part of the animal's chest) as done in the case at hand.

289 Kulaynī, *Kāfī*, 3:557.

290 The Qurʾān did not allow Muslims to take the prisoners of war as slaves. It ordered them to free the prisoners of war either graciously or on ransom: ﴿فَإِمَّا مَنًّا بَعْدُ وَإِمَّا فِدَاءً﴾ (Qurʾān 47:4). Over the course of time, however, Muslim governments adopted what was the rule of conduct between states in premodern times: reciprocity, "I treat you the same way that you treat me."

That was also the normal practice of the Arabs before the advent of Islam, when slaves from Africa and elsewhere were also brought to and sold in Mecca.

The market value of slaves in premodern times varied according to the condition and qualities of the slave as well as according to the specific time and place. However, in pre-Islamic and early Islamic Arabia and its vicinity, the base price of a slave was around 700 dirhams or 70 dinars (according to the nominal exchange rate between the two currencies, 1 dinar equaled 10 dirhams, later modified by ʿUmar to 12 dirhams, as will be explained later in this chapter). This amount was what ʿAlī had saved right before his assassination, for the purpose of buying a slave (Ibn Saʿd, *Ṭabaqāt*, 3:37). It is also what Khadīja, the first wife of the Prophet, reportedly paid for Zayd b. Ḥāritha (Ibn Abī Shayba, *Muṣannaf*, 13:232, quoted also in Ibn ʿAsākir, *Taʾrīkh madīnat Dimashq*, 19:352; Dhahabī, *Siyar aʿlām al-nubalāʾ*, 1:223; Maqrīzī, *Imtāʿ*, 6:303; a different report in Ibn Saʿd, 3:39, quoted also in Ibn ʿAbd al-Barr, *Istīʿāb*, 2:543; Ibn Ḥajar, *Iṣāba*, 2:598; Maqrīzī, 6:302 has the figure as 400 dirhams, with the alternative figure of 600 in the last work, possibly indicating that both of these figures may have originated from corruptions of 700 in the Arabic script). This sum is also what Muḥammad al-Bāqir paid for Ḥumayda, a Berber handmaiden (and, later, mother of Mūsā al-Kāẓim, the future Imam), whom he bought for his son Jaʿfar al-Ṣādiq (Kulaynī, *Kāfī*, 1:476–77; the report specifies seventy dinars), and it is what a slave in the lifetime of Jaʿfar al-Ṣādiq asked his owner to sell him for in the market (Kulaynī, 5:219–20, also quoted below, Chapter 4, text 71 on p. 383).

The price could, however, be as low as 500 or 600 dirhams, as in the report quoted above (Kulaynī, 3:557; see also Kulaynī, 6:107, 108 [both 500 dirhams for an old slave], 7:22, 26–27 [altogether three cases at 600 dirhams]). A slave with secretarial and accounting knowledge was sold in Kūfa for 60 dinars = 600 dirhams in the year 105 (Ṭabarī, *Taʾrīkh*, 7:28, with a variant in Iṣbahānī, *Aghānī*, 15:124). The Companion Zayd b. Arqam bought back for 600 dirhams a slave that he had sold in the same session for 800 dirhams in a contract of *ʿayna*, a sham credit sale with the intention of circumventing the legal prohibition on receiving interest on a loan (Ibn ʿAbd al-Barr, *Istidhkār*, 19:24, and other sources cited in the editor's footnote). A slave could even be traded for less than 500 dirhams (Kulaynī, 7:19) and, occasionally, for a mere 30 dinars (Kulaynī, 7:18), that is, 300 dirhams according to the most common exchange rate in the Kūfan market at the time. This was about the price that Abū Bakr paid for Bilāl b. Rabāḥ, the muezzin of the Prophet (Ibn Saʿd, 9:389; Ibn Abī Shayba, 11:199). This was also the price paid for a slave bought in Baṣra in the mid-third century (Ibn al-Jawzī, *Akhbār al-ẓurrāf*, 90–91; Dhahabī, *Mīzān al-iʿtidāl*, 7:447). The annual tribute that ʿAbd Allāh b. Ṭāhir (d. 230), ruler of Khurāsān in the early third century, had to pay to the caliphate in Baghdad in lieu of the *kharāj* of Kabul included two thousand Turkic slaves for the total value of 600,000 dirhams, that is, 300 dirhams each (Ibn Khurdādhbih, *al-Masālik wa'l-mamālik*, 37, 39). In the market of Medina in the mid-second century, a male slave from Axum (today Eritrea and a part of northern Ethiopia) who was deemed "good enough to lead a blind man" could be had for 30 dinars (or around 300 dirhams); a slave girl from Spain "who would bear handsome children" could be bought for 25 dinars (250 dirhams) (Kulaynī, 5:480); and a handmaiden could cost as little as 20 dinars (200 dirhams) (ʿAyyāshī, *Tafsīr*, 2:142). The lower-class (*wakhsh*) women slaves used by Andalusian families as servants were usually sold in the market of Cordoba for 28 dinars (Abū al-Aṣbagh, *Dīwān al-aḥkām*, 2:670, 675), corresponding to about 330 dirhams at the exchange rate of 1 dinar = 12 dirhams, the rate favored by the Mālikīs that most probably prevailed in fifth-century Cordoba. Eunuchs had a higher value, as they were in high demand, whereas older slaves naturally fetched a lower price (Mālik, *Muwaṭṭaʾ* [recension of Abū Muṣʿab al-Zuhrī], 7:391).

The price could also exceed 700 dirhams. For example, 800 dirhams were paid for a slave in the time of the Prophet in Medina (Bukhārī, *Ṣaḥīḥ*, nos. 6716 and 7186; Muslim, *Ṣaḥīḥ*, no. 997; and other sources cited in the editor's footnotes in Abū Dāwūd, *Sunan*, 6:89–90). Other recorded prices included 1,000 dirhams (Kulaynī, 3:557, 5:209–10, Ṭūsī, *Tahdhīb*, 8:302),

125 dinars = 1,250 dirhams (Kulaynī, 7:66), or 61 dinars of Carmona, near Seville, corresponding to 100 regular dinars, paid in fifth-century Andalusia for a black slave girl, obviously of high quality (Abū al-Aṣbagh, 2:667). In the mid-fourth century, a geographer noted that the highest market price for slaves throughout the lands that he visited was 3,000 dinars paid for Turkic slaves, boys and girls alike, in Khurāsān (Ibn Ḥawqal, *Ṣurat al-arḍ*, 376). That obviously referred to very exceptional cases, as noted below.

Such was also the market value of slaves in Egypt and greater Syria in the early centuries. The Ikhshīdid Kāfūr (d. 357) was bought at a young age by Muḥammad b. Ṭughuj, ruler of Egypt (r. 323–34), for 18 dinars (Ibn Khallikān, *Wafayāt al-aʿyān*, 4:100; Ibn Taghrībirdī, *al-Nujūm al-zāhira*, 4:3). Later in the time of the Mamlūks, the market price of the *mamlūks* as a particular category of slaves who would eventually join the military could be around the average rate mentioned above or much higher, depending on personal conditions or social and political circumstances, as well as the supply in the market. Baybars (r. 658–76), for instance, was allegedly sold at the age of fourteen in Damascus for 800 dirhams, and Qaytbay (r. 872–901) was sold to Barsbay (r. 824–41) in 839 as part of a group of slave boys of his age for 50 dinars each (Ibn Iyās, *Badāʾiʿ al-ẓuhūr*, 3:3), which would have been around 500 or 600 dirhams, whereas five hundred *mamlūks* of Khushqadam (r. 865–72) were sold after his death for 10,000 dirhams each (Ibn Iyās, 3:18). The emir Yashbuk al-Sūdūnī al-Mushidd (d. 849) was originally sold to Ṭaṭar (r. 824) for 200 dinars, then bought back by Barsbay for 1,000 dinars, and freed (Sakhāwī, *al-Ḍawʾ al-lāmiʿ*, 10:277–78). Similarly, the *atabegs* Fāris al-Dīn Aqṭāy (d. 652) and Manṣūr Qalāwūn (r. 678–89) were each bought at a young age for 1,000 dinars (Dhahabī, *Taʾrīkh al-Islām*, 14:722 and 15:640, respectively; Ibn Taghrībirdī, *al-Manhal al-ṣāfī*, 9:91 for Manṣūr Qalāwūn). See also Ashtor, *Histoire des prix et des salaires*, 463, 504; *Encyclopaedia Iranica*, 3:771–72.

Highly valued and precious slaves, normally girls but also men of musical and other talents (see Bayhaqī, *Sunan*, 10:380; Ibn Ḥawqal, 377; Ibn Qudāma, *Mughnī*, 14:160–61) could be priced at 500 dinars = 5,000 dirhams in Iraq (Kulaynī, 4:545). This was the amount allegedly offered by the caliph Manṣūr to the jurist Rabīʿat al-Raʾy to buy a handmaiden for himself (Dhahabī, *Siyar aʿlām al-nubalāʾ*, 6:90, 92). The price of a slave could be 5,000 dirhams or more, as mentioned in a question of criminal law posed to Jaʿfar al-Ṣādiq (Kulaynī, 7:302); 700 dinars = 7,000 dirhams, as paid by the caliph Muʿtaṣim for a slave girl who originally belonged to the poet Maḥmūd al-Warrāq (Khaṭīb al-Baghdādī, *Taʾrīkh Baghdād*, 15:103); 10,000 dirhams or more (Kulaynī, 7:304 [إن كان نفيساً]; Ibn Bābawayh, *Faqīh*, 4:96); 20,000 dirhams (Kulaynī, 7:305, 308) in hypothetical questions posed to Jaʿfar al-Ṣādiq; 2,000 dinars for a handmaiden offered to Maʾmūn (Ibn ʿAsākir, 33:330); and in very exceptional cases, even 30,000 dirhams (Kulaynī, 5:497 [for a جاريةٌ فارهة]; Raqqām, *al-ʿAfw wa'l-iʿtidhār*, 1:205 [for a singing girl]; Iṣbahānī, *Maqātil al-Ṭālibiyyīn*, 124–25 [for a handmaiden whom Mukhtār al-Thaqafī gifted to ʿAlī b. al-Ḥusayn Zayn al-ʿĀbidīn and who bore him his son Zayd]). Muʿāwiya is said to have paid 40,000 dirhams for a handmaiden whom he bought for ʿAqīl b. Abī Ṭālib (Ibn Abī al-Ḥadīd, *Sharḥ Nahj al-balāgha*, 1:251). Yazīd b. ʿAbd al-Malik paid 3,000 and 4,000 dinars for his two singing girls, Sallāma (Masʿūdī, *Murūj al-dhahab*, 3:196) and Ḥabāba (Ṭabarī, *Taʾrīkh*, 7:23), respectively. An unusual case in this range is that of the *ḥadīth* transmitter ʿIkrima [d. 105], who was allegedly bought by Khālid b. Yazīd b. Muʿāwiya for 4,000 dinars (Ibn Saʿd, 7:282–83; Ibn ʿAsākir, 41:84–85, and other sources cited in the editor's footnote therein), but the figure sounds wrong. The figure of 40,000 dirhams appears also in a contract of manumission in Ibn Rushd, *al-Bayān wa'l-taḥṣīl*, 18:457 (from *al-ʿUtbiyya*, a third-century work of Mālikī law).

The round figure of 1,000 dinars as the price of a slave, which is mentioned in works of *ḥadīth* (e.g., ʿAyyāshī, *Tafsīr*, 2:142) and law (e.g., Mālik, *Mudawwana*, 15:6–7; ʿAynī, *Bināya*, 7:496; *al-Fatāwā al-Hindiyya*, 3:674–90) when discussing hypothetical cases, sounds hypothetical, too. Similarly, some of the extremely high figures alleged to have been paid by caliphs, rulers, and princes, as well as other notables—usually for singing girls—sound

There were also questions that Jaʿfar declined to address immediately but answered later[291] or sent an answer through an intermediary.[292] Some of these questions might have related to burning issues of the time on which he did not want to take a clear position,[293] or matters that were sensitive for one reason or another, in which case his goal was to save the questioner from getting into trouble with his community.

عبد الله بن بكير قال: دخل زرارة على أبي عبد الله فقال: إنكم قلتم لنا [صلّوا] في الظهر والعصر على ذراع وذراعين، ثمّ قلتم أبردوا بها في الصيف، فكيف الإبراد بها؟ وفتح ألواحَه ليكتب ما يقول. فلم يُجبه أبو عبد الله. فأطبق ألواحَه وقال: إنّما علينا أن نسألكم وأنتم أعلم بما عليكم، وخرج. ودخل أبو بصير على أبي عبد الله، فقال:

---

mythical and ahistorical; others might be true. Examples of this genre by the Umayyads and in the pre-Umayyad times include 100,000 dirhams for a handmaiden whom Muʿāwiya allegedly bought and gifted to Ḥusayn (Ibn ʿAsākir, 70:196); the 10,000 dinars that Hishām b. ʿAbd al-Malik is said to have paid for a slave girl (Ibn Ḥamdūn, *Tadhkira*, 2:347); and the 20,000 dinars that were reportedly paid by ʿUbayd Allāh b. Maʿmar al-Qurashī (d. 29), ruler of Makrān and chief of the army sent by ʿUthmān to conquer the region of Istakhr in southwestern Iran, for a singing girl (Yāfiʿī, *Mirʾāt al-jinān*, 1:73, from Marzubānī's *al-Muqtabas*). Among the Abbasids, there are many examples in which the caliphs or their crown princes are said to have offered or bought their favorite singing girls for very high prices. Many of these latter cases are collected in a recent monograph: Sulāf Faḍl Allāh Ḥasan, *Dawr al-jawārī wa'l-qahramānāt fī dār al-khilāfa al-ʿAbbāsiyya* (Damascus, 2013). The Būyid ruler, ʿIzz al-Dawla (r. 356–67), allegedly rejected an offer to buy his singing slave girl for 100,000 dirhams (Miskawayh, *Tajārib al-umam*, 5:430). In Mamlūk Cairo, the emir Bashtak al-Nāṣirī (d. 744) bought a slave girl for 6,000 dinars (Ṣafadī, *Wāfī*, 10:42; whence Ibn Taghrībirdī, 3:468). An extreme case of this genre is that of Isḥāq b. Ayyūb al-Taghlibī, ruler of Mosul (d. 287), who allegedly offered 100,000 dinars for the singing girl Bidʿa. The offer was rejected by her owner (Ibn al-Sāʿī, *Nisāʾ al-khulafāʾ*, 64).

There is also a related issue mentioned in Islamic criminal law: Someone who had caused the death of a fetus was required to compensate the mother or her family through the offer of a white slave child, male or female, of seven or eight years (*ghurra*) with a minimum value of 500 dirhams (Abū Dāwūd, no. 4580), as Abū Ḥanīfa maintained, or 50 dinars = 600 dirhams, as Mālik suggested, reflecting the difference of opinion between the two jurists about the nominal exchange rate of the two currencies (Qurṭubī, *al-Jāmiʿ li-aḥkām al-Qurʾān*, 7:21–22). Ibn Qudāma, 12:66 explains that the required compensation was originally set at five camels, but when paid in cash it became subject to the dispute concerning the nominal exchange rate, as will be further explained later in the present chapter. He also quotes and rejects the view that the slave child must be white, a view based solely on the original meaning of the Arabic word *ghurra*. See also Nawawī, *Sharḥ Muslim*, 11:188, who claims unanimous agreement among all Muslim jurists that whiteness was not a requirement.

And finally, for a peculiar case of a price change in the case of slave boys, see Ibn Qudāma, 7:375. (I wrote this long footnote for Shaun Marmon.)

291 E.g., Kulaynī, *Kāfī*, 2:24–25, 170; Kashshī, *Rijāl*, 193.

292 E.g., Ḥimyarī, *Qurb al-isnād*, 44; Kashshī, *Rijāl*, 143–44; Ṭūsī, *Tahdhīb*, 2:22.

293 E.g., Kulaynī, *Kāfī*, 2:387.

إنّ زرارة سألني عن شيء فلم أجبه، وقد ضقتُ من ذلك، فاذهب أنت رسولي إليه فقل [له]: صلّ الظهر في الصيف إذا كان ظلّك مثلك، والعصر إذا كان مثليك.[294]

['Abd Allāh b. Bukayr:] Zurāra came to Abū ʿAbd Allāh and said, "You told us to pray noon and afternoon prayers when [one's shadow] is one and two *dhirā*ʿs (arm cubits[295]) long [respectively]; then you told us to delay it until it cools down during the summer; so how much are they to be delayed for cooling down?" Zurāra then opened his notebook to write down what he [the Imam] would say, but Abū ʿAbd Allāh did not answer him. He closed his notebook and said, "It is our duty to ask you, and you know your duty best." And he left. Then Abū Baṣīr came to Abū ʿAbd Allāh, and he [the Imam] said, "Zurāra asked me about something but I did not answer him, and I feel uneasy about it. Go to him as my messenger and say to him, 'Pray the noon prayer during the summer when your shadow is as long as you are, and the afternoon prayer when your shadow is twice as long as you are.'"

Numerous Sunnī judges and jurists of the time used to attend his audience. They included notables such as Rabīʿa b. Farrukh, better known as Rabīʿat al-Ra'y (d. 136),[296] whose *fatwā* sessions Jaʿfar also occasionally attended;[297] Ibn Abī Laylā, Muḥammad b. ʿAbd al-Raḥmān al-Anṣārī (d. 148), who served as judge of Kūfa for thirty-three years and whose high respect for Jaʿfar[298] and his opinions[299] is attested in numerous reports; Yaḥyā b. Saʿīd al-Anṣārī (d. 143), a student of Jaʿfar and a leading jurist of Medina in his time who later in life moved to Iraq and served as judge of Hāshimiyya; ʿAbd Allāh b. Shubruma al-Ḍabbī (d. 144), a noted jurist and judge of Kūfa;

294 Kashshī, *Rijāl*, 143–44.

295 An arm cubit is equivalent to about eighteen inches.

296 Kulaynī, *Kāfī*, 2:634.

297 Kulaynī, *Kāfī*, 7:409. ʿAbd Allāh b. al-Ḥasan, too, used to frequent Rabīʿa's sessions. See Khaṭīb al-Baghdādī, *al-Faqīh wa'l-mutafaqqih*, 1:380.

298 E.g., Kulaynī, *Kāfī*, 7:35; Kashshī, *Rijāl*, 164; Ṭūsī, *Tahdhīb*, 3:22.

299 See, for instance, Ṭūsī, *Tahdhīb*, 6:292, where Ibn Abī Laylā is quoted as saying that he deferred to the opinion or judgment of no other scholar but Jaʿfar b. Muḥammad:

> نوح بن درّاج قال: قلت لابن أبي ليلى: أكنت تاركًا قولاً قلتَه أو قضاءً قضيته لقول أحد؟ قال: لا! إلّا رجل واحد. قلت: من هو؟ قال: جعفر بن محمّد.
>
> [Nūḥ b. Darrāj:] I said to Ibn Abī Laylā, "Have you ever backtracked from an opinion you held or judgment you made based on the opinion of someone else?" He said, "No! Except for one man." I said, "Who is he?" He said, "Jaʿfar b. Muḥammad."

See further Kashshī, *Rijāl*, 164; Kulaynī, *Kāfī*, 5:215–16, 7:35 (see also Ibn Bābawayh, *Faqīh*, 4:182, for a report from Jaʿfar with a reference to an order of the Prophet; however, a variant of the report in Kulaynī, 7:34–35 and Ibn Bābawayh, 4:181 ascribes the quote to Muḥammad al-Bāqir with reference to a judgment by ʿAlī); Ibn Bābawayh, *Maʿānī al-akhbār*, 219; Ṭūsī, *Tahdhīb*, 3:22; see also Zarkashī, *al-Baḥr al-muḥīṭ*, 6:70.

and Ḥafṣ b. Ghiyāth (d. 194), a judge first of the eastern part of Baghdad and then of Kūfa and a young companion of and frequent transmitter from Jaʿfar, whom he used to call Khayr al-Jaʿāfir[300] or Sayyid al-Jaʿāfira.[301]

There are numerous reports of debates between Jaʿfar and other prominent scholars of his time over legal matters. Many of these debates may have actually occurred, but some of their details may not be historical. Generally speaking, it seems that he and other scholars treated each other with mutual respect. This is illustrated by the following example, an anecdote told by Muʿāwiya b. ʿAmmār al-Duhnī (d. 175), a respected *ḥadīth* transmitter and jurist in Kūfa,[302] and author of a monograph on *ḥajj* that has fully survived in later works:[303]

أوصت إليّ امرأة من أهلي بثلث مالها فأمرت أن يُعتَق ويُحَجّ ويُتصدَّق عنها، فلم يبلغ ذلك، فسألت أبا حنيفة عنها فقال: يجعل أثلاثًا: ثلثٌ في العتق وثلثٌ في الحجّ وثلثٌ في الصدقة. فدخلت على أبي عبد الله فقلت: إنّ امرأة من أهلي ماتت وأوصت إليّ بثلث مالها وأمرت أن يُعتق عنها ويُتصدّق ويُحجّ عنها، فنظرتُ فيه فلم يبلغ. فقال: إبدأ بالحجّ فإنّه فريضة من فرائض الله تعالى، وتَجعل ما بقي طائفةً في العتق وطائفةً في الصدقة. فأخبرتُ أبا حنيفة بقول أبي عبد الله. فرجع عن قوله وقال بقول أبي عبد الله.[304]

A woman of my family passed away and bequeathed a third of her estate for the manumission [of a slave], the performance of the *ḥajj*, and general charity on her behalf, but the value of the estate was insufficient. I asked Abū Ḥanīfa [about this] and he said, "Divide the money into three parts [and spend] one third on the manumission, one third on the *ḥajj*, and one third on general charity." I then visited Abū ʿAbd Allāh and told him [about the case]. He said, "Start with the *ḥajj*, because the *ḥajj* is an obligation. Spend what remains [on the supererogatory acts], partly on manumission and partly on general charity." I informed Abū Ḥanīfa of what Abū ʿAbd Allāh had said. He renounced his [original] opinion and adopted that of Abū ʿAbd Allāh.

300 E.g., Ibn Bābawayh, *Amālī*, 315.

301 E.g., Ṭūsī, *Amālī*, 581.

302 On him, see Yaḥyā b. Maʿīn, *Ta'rīkh*, 2:573; Ibn al-Junayd, *Su'ālāt Ibn al-Junayd*, 161; Bukhārī, *Ta'rīkh*, 7:335–36; Ibn Ḥibbān, *Thiqāt*, 9:167; Najāshī, *Rijāl*, 411; Mizzī, *Tahdhīb al-Kamāl*, 28:202–4, and many other sources cited in the editor's footnote therein.

303 See Modarressi, *Tradition and Survival*, 1:327–29.

304 Kulaynī, *Kāfī*, 7:19, with a variant in Ṭūsī, *Tahdhīb*, 5:407–8.

Here are a couple of other examples:

عبد الرحمن بن الحجّاج عن أبي عبد الله، قال: سألته عن بيت وقع على قوم مجتمعين فلا يُدرى أيّهم مات قبل؟ قال: فقال: يورِث بعضهم من بعض. قلت: فإنّ أبا حنيفة أدخل فيها شيئًا. قال: وما أدخل؟ قلت: رجلين أخوين أعجميّين ليس لهما وارثٌ إلّا مواليهما، أحدهما له مائة ألف درهم والآخر ليس له شيء، ركبا في السفينة فغرقا فلم يدر أيّهما مات أوّلاً، فقال يُدفع المال إلى موالي الّذي ليس له شيء. قال [أبو عبد الله]: ما أُنكر ما أدخل فيها. صَدَق. وهو هكذا. ثمّ قال: يُدفع المال إلى موالي الّذي ليس له شيء، ولم يكن للأخر مالٌ يرثه موالي الآخر.[305]

[ʿAbd al-Raḥmān b. al-Ḥajjāj:] I asked Abū ʿAbd Allāh about [a scenario in which] a house has collapsed on a group of people gathered together, and it is not known in what order they died. He said, "They inherit from one another." I said, "Abū Ḥanīfa added something to this [hypothetical scenario]." He said, "What did he add?" I said, "[Suppose there are] two non-Arab brothers who had no heirs other than their patrons.[306] One has one hundred thousand dirhams and the other has nothing. They take a trip on a ship and drown, and it is not known which of them died first. He [Abū Ḥanīfa] said, 'The money is given to the patron of the one who had nothing.'" The Imam said, "I am not against what he added to the case; he spoke the truth, and it is so." Then he said, "The money is given [as inheritance] to the patrons of the one who had nothing, and the [one who had nothing] had no money for the patrons of the other to inherit."

الحسين بن المختار قال: قال أبو عبد الله لأبي حنيفة: ما تقول في بيت سقط على قوم وبقي منهم صبيّان، أحدهما حرّ والآخر مملوك لصاحبه، فلم يُعرف الحرّ من المملوك؟ فقال أبو حنيفة: يُعتق نصف هذا ويُعتق نصف هذا ويقسّم المال بينهما. فقال أبو عبد الله: ليس كذلك، ولكن يُقرع بينهما فمن أصابته القرعة فهو الحرّ، ويُعتق هذا فيُجعل مولى له.[307]

305 Kulaynī, *Kāfī*, 7:137.

306 This refers to an old Arab institution in which non-Arabs who wanted to live in the Arab land would enter into a contract with a member of an Arab tribe, becoming a client of the tribesman. The non-Arab would be protected as a client of the tribe. In return, the tribe member who offered protection to him would inherit from the client if the latter died without issue.

307 Kulaynī, *Kāfī*, 7:138.

[Ḥusayn b. al-Mukhtār:] Abū ʿAbd Allāh said to Abū Ḥanīfa, "What is your position regarding a house that collapses upon some people and only two minor boys survive, one of whom is free and the other is a slave of the free one, but it is not known who is free and who is the slave." Abū Ḥanīfa said, "Half of each of them is manumitted, and the money is divided between them." Abū ʿAbd Allāh said, "That is not so. Rather, lots are cast between them, and whoever wins is free, and the other is manumitted and made his client."[308]

عبد الملك بن عتبة قال: سألت أبا حنيفة فقلت: إنّي لا أزال أدفع المال مضاربةً إلى الرجل فيقول قد ضاع أو قد ذهب؟ قال: فادفع إليه أكثره قرضًا والباقي مضاربةً. فسألت أبا عبد الله عن ذلك فقال: يجوز.[309]

[ʿAbd al-Malik b. ʿUtba:] I asked Abū Ḥanīfa, "I continue to pay a man money to act on a sleeping partnership agreement, and he [occasionally] says that the money got lost or is gone." He said, "Pay most of it to him as a loan, and the remainder as part of the sleeping partnership agreement." I asked Abū ʿAbd Allāh about this and he said, "This is permissible."

قال أبو حنيفة لأبي عبد الله: تجيزون شهادة واحد ويمين؟ قال: نعم! قضى به رسول الله – صلّى الله عليه وآله وسلّم – وقضى به عليٌّ عندكم.[310]

Abū Ḥanīfa said to Abū ʿAbd Allāh, "Do you accept the testimony of one individual with an oath?" He said, "Yes! The Messenger of God (may God's prayer and peace be upon him and his Family) judged on that basis, and ʿAlī judged on that basis [while he was] with you [in Iraq]."

عبد الرحمن بن الحجّاج قال: سألت أبا عبد الله عمّا اختلف فيه ابن أبي ليلى وابن شُبرُمة في السواد وأرضه فقلت: إنّ ابن أبي ليلى قال إنّهم إذا أسلموا فهم أحرار وما في أيديهم من أرضهم لهم، وأمّا ابن شُبرُمة فزعم أنّهم عبيد وأنّ أرضهم الّتي بأيديهم

308 Jaʿfar's opinion followed a practice of the Prophet (Muslim, *Ṣaḥīḥ*, no. 1668) and a judicial decision of ʿAlī during his time in Yemen (Kulaynī, *Kāfī*, 7:137). For similar decisions by Mālik in similar cases, see his *Mudawwana*, 15:3, 32–33.

309 Ṭūsī, *Tahdhīb*, 7:188.

310 Ḥimyarī, *Qurb al-isnād*, 359; Ṭūsī, *Tahdhīb*, 6:296, with a variant in Tirmidhī, *Sunan*, no. 1344 and numerous other Sunnī *ḥadīth* collections. See the long lists in the editor's footnotes in Ibn al-Qayyim (who is in favor of this opinion), *al-Ṭuruq al-ḥukmiyya* [Jeddah, 1428 [2007]], 1:169–71, 353–54, 357–58. See also Mālik, *Mudawwana*, 15:24.

ليست لهم. فقال في الأرض بما قال ابن شُبرُمة وقال في الرجال بما قال ابن أبي ليلى أنّهم إذا أسلموا فهم أحرار.[311]

[ʿAbd al-Raḥmān b. al-Ḥajjāj:] I asked Abū ʿAbd Allāh about the dispute between Ibn Abī Laylā[312] and Ibn Shubruma[313] regarding the Sawād [Mesopotamia] and its land. I said, "Ibn Abī Laylā said that if they [that is, the original, non-Muslim inhabitants of the land] convert to Islam, they are free and the land they possess belongs to them, but Ibn Shubruma thought that they were slaves [of the Muslims who conquered the land] and the land they possess does not belong to them." Abū ʿAbd Allāh agreed with Ibn Shubruma's opinion with respect to the land and with Ibn Abī Laylā with regard to the men—that if they convert to Islam, they are free.

عبد الرحمن بن الحجّاج قال: سألني أبو عبد الله هل يختلف ابن أبي ليلى وابن شُبرُمة؟ فقلت: بلغني أنّه مات مولى لعيسى بن موسى وترك عليه دينًا كثيرًا وترك مماليك يُحيط دَينه بأثمانهم فأعتقهم عند الموت. فسألهما عيسى بن موسى عن ذلك. فقال ابن شُبرُمة: أرى أن تَستسعيهم في قيمتهم فتدفع إلى الغرماء. وقال ابن أبي ليلى: أرى أن تَبيعهم وتدفع أثمانهم إلى الغرماء. فقال [أبو عبد الله]: أما والله إنّ الحقّ لفي ما قال ابن أبي ليلى.[314]

[ʿAbd al-Raḥmān b. al-Ḥajjāj:] Abū ʿAbd Allāh asked me whether Ibn Abī Laylā and Ibn Shubruma disagree [on any question of law]. I said, "I was informed that a client of ʿĪsā b. Mūsā[315] passed away leaving behind a lot of debt as well as slaves, whose combined value equaled his debt, but he manumitted them upon his death. ʿĪsā b. Mūsā asked the two of them [Ibn Abī Laylā and Ibn Shubruma] about the case. Ibn Shubruma said, 'I think he [ʿĪsā] should allow them to work up to their market price and pay their income to the creditors [to settle the debt],' and Ibn Abī Laylā said, 'I think he [ʿĪsā] should sell them and pay their

311 Ṭūsī, *Tahdhīb*, 7:155.

312 The abovementioned Muḥammad b. ʿAbd al-Raḥmān al-Anṣārī, a long-term judge of Kūfa (d. 148).

313 The abovementioned ʿAbd Allāh b. Shubruma al-Ḍabbī, a noted jurist and judge of Kūfa (d. 144).

314 Kulaynī, *Kāfī*, 7:26 (also Qāḍī Nuʿmān, *Daʿāʾim al-Islām*, 2:67–68; Ṭūsī, *Tahdhīb*, 9:217).

315 ʿĪsā b. Mūsā b. Muḥammad b. ʿAlī b. ʿAbd Allāh b. al-ʿAbbās, Shaykh al-Dawla (d. 168), governor of Kūfa (132–47) and chief of the army that Manṣūr sent to Medina to crush the rebellion of Muḥammad b. ʿAbd Allāh al-Nafs al-Zakiyya. The adventure ended with the killing of the latter in 145, as noted earlier.

value to the creditors.'" Abū ʿAbd Allāh said, "By God, the truth is with what Ibn Abī Laylā said."

عبد الرحمن بن الحجّاج قال: سألني أبو عبد الله: يخالف يحيى بن سعيد قضاتكم؟ قلت: نعم! قال: هات شيئًا ممّا اختلفوا فيه. قلت: اقتتل غلامان في الرحبة فعضّ أحدهما على يد الآخر، فعمد المعضوض إلى حجر فضرب به رأسَ صاحبه الّذي عضّه فشجّ فكزّ فمات. فرُفع ذلك إلى يحيى بن سعيد فأقاده. فقال ابن شُبرُمة وابن أبي ليلى لعيسى بن موسى: إنّ هذا الأمر لم يكن عندنا. لا يُقاد عنه بالحجر ولا بالسوط. إنّما هذا الخطأ. فلم يزالوا حتّى وداه عيسى بن موسى من ماله. قال: فقال [أبو عبد الله]: إنّ مَن عندنا يُقيدون بالوكزة. قلت: يزعمون أنّه خطأ وأنّ العمد لا يكون إلّا بالحديد. فقال: إنّما الخطأ أن تريد الشيءَ فتصيب غيرَه. فأمّا كلّ شيء قصدت إليه فأصبته فهو العمد.[316]

[ʿAbd al-Raḥmān b. al-Ḥajjāj:] Abū ʿAbd Allāh asked me, "Does Yaḥyā b. Saʿīd[317] disagree with your judges?" I said, "Yes!" He said, "Give me an example of what they have disagreed on." I said, "Two boys fought in a wide-open space, and one of them bit the hand of the other. The one who was bitten got a rock and hit the one who bit him on the head, causing his skull to fracture; he then stiffened and died. The case was brought to Yaḥyā b. Saʿīd, who ordered him [the perpetrator] to be put to death in retaliation. Ibn Shubruma and Ibn Abī Laylā told ʿĪsā b. Mūsā: 'This decision was unprecedented in our jurisdiction. A killing by a rock or a whip is not subject to the law of retaliation. It is an accident [that is, a case of manslaughter rather than intentional homicide].' They insisted on that until ʿĪsā b. Mūsā paid the blood-money [that is, compensation for wrongful death] from his own wealth." Abū ʿAbd Allāh said, "The [jurists] among us apply retaliation for killing [even] if by a punch." I said, "They believe a case like this is an accident, and that intentional homicide occurs only when metal is used."[318] He said, "An accident is when you intend to hit something but hit something else.[319] But anything you intended to hit and actually did hit entails intentional homicide."

316 ʿAyyāshī, *Tafsīr*, 1:427; Kulaynī, *Kāfī*, 7:278–79, with variations.

317 The abovementioned Yaḥyā b. Saʿīd b. Qays al-Anṣārī (d. 143), a transmitter of *ḥadīth* from Jaʿfar al-Ṣādiq and a leading jurist of Medina in his time, who later in life moved to Iraq and served as judge of Hāshimiyya in the south of the region in which Baghdad was subsequently built.

318 See, for instance, ʿAbd al-Razzāq, *Muṣannaf*, 9:271–80; Ibn Abī Shayba, *Muṣannaf*, 9:184–85.

319 See, for instance, ʿAbd al-Razzāq, *Muṣannaf*, 9:274, 277, 280, 281.

عبد الرحمن بن الحجاج قال: سمعت ابن أبي ليلى يقول: كانت الدية في الجاهليّة مائة من الإبل، فأقرّها رسول الله – صلّى الله عليه وآله وسلّم. ثمّ إنّه فرض على أهل البقر مائتي بقرة وفرض على أهل الشاة ألف شاة ثنيّة وعلى أهل الذهب ألف دينار وعلى أهل الورق عشرة آلاف درهم وعلى أهل اليمن الحلل – مائة حلّة. قال عبد الرحمن بن الحجّاج: فسألت أبا عبد الله عمّا روى ابن أبي ليلى، فقال: كان عليّ يقول: الدية ألف دينار – وقيمة الدينار عشرة دراهم، وعشرة آلاف [درهم] لأهل الأمصار وعلى أهل البوادي مائة من الإبل ولأهل السواد مائتا بقرة أو ألف شاة.[320]

[ʿAbd al-Raḥmān b. al-Ḥajjāj:] I heard Ibn Abī Laylā say, "The amount of the blood-money during the Age of Arab Ignorance [that is, the pre-Islamic period] was one hundred camels, and this was affirmed by the Messenger of God (may God's prayer and peace be upon him and his Family). He then imposed [a blood-money amount of] two hundred cattle for the owners of cattle, one thousand two-year-old sheep for the owners of sheep, one thousand dinars for regions where people used gold money [in their transactions], ten thousand dirhams for regions where people used silver money,[321] and one hundred robes upon the people of Yemen, who produced garbs." [ʿAbd al-Raḥmān b. al-Ḥajjāj:] I asked Abū ʿAbd Allāh about what Ibn Abī Laylā transmitted. He said, "ʿAlī used to say: 'The blood-money amount is one thousand dinars and the value of a dinar is ten dirhams.[322] Ten thousand dirhams is owed by

320 Kulaynī, *Kāfī*, 7:280–81.

321 Qurṭubī, *Jāmiʿ*, 7:12 identifies the users of gold money in his time as the people of greater Syria, Egypt, and the Maghrib, and the users of coined money (*wariq*) as the inhabitants of Iraq, Fārs, and Khurāsān.

322 As explained in numerous studies, one of the best being Goitein, *Mediterranean Society*, 1:368–92 (and in traditional Islamic works; see Maqrīzī's *Shudhūr al-ʿuqūd fī dhikr al-nuqūd*), the actual rate of exchange between the two currencies varied, at times dramatically, across time and place, as it depended on the amount and quality of available gold in a dinar and occasionally on the popularity of specific dinar coins. The nominal rate used in Islamic law was either 1 dinar = 10 dirhams or 1 dinar = 12 dirhams, the former being the standard rate adopted by the Shīʿa and the Ḥanafīs and the latter by other Sunnī schools. It is further said that the exchange rate of 1 = 10 was the standard for the financial duties of *zakāt* and *jizya*, whereas 1 = 12 was used in the courts for blood-money and other types of compensation in penal law (Nafrāwī, *al-Fawākih al-dawānī*, 2:34–35). The background to the disagreement over the rate of exchange is said to have been the precedent set by the Prophet in his letter of instructions regarding *zakāt*, mentioned in the report quoted above, which took the market value of a camel to be 10 dinars or 100 dirhams. (The full text of the letter, cited in Ibn Ḥibbān, *Ṣaḥīḥ*, 4:501–10, does not include the reference to the exchange rate, but reports 4542 and 4564 in Abū Dāwūd's *Sunan* do, as do other sources cited in the editor's footnote to the Beirut, 1996 edition of the latter work; see 6:601–2, 621–22.) This exchange rate was subsequently modified by ʿUmar during his caliphate to 1 dinar =12 dirhams because the price of a camel had increased (cf. Barqī, *Maḥāsin*, 638, where a camel was bought for Jaʿfar al-Ṣādiq for

urban people, one hundred camels by desert-dwellers, and two hundred cattle or one thousand sheep by those who live on farmland.'"

حفص بن غياث قال: سمعت أبا عبد الله يقول في رجل أدرك الجمعة وقد ازدحم الناس وكبّر مع الإمام وركع ولم يقدر على السجود، وقام الإمام والناس في الركعة الثانية وقام هذا معهم فركع الإمام ولم يقدر هو على الركوع في الركعة الثانية من الزحام وقدر على السجود، كيف يصنع؟ فقال أبو عبد الله: أمّا الركعة الأولى فهي إلى عند الركوع تامّة، فلمّا لم يسجد لها حتّى دخل في الركعة الثانية لم يكن له ذلك، فلمّا سجد في الثانية فإن كان نوى أنّ هذه السجدة هي للركعة الأولى فقد تمّت له الركعة الأولى، فإذا سلّم الإمام قام فصلّى ركعة يسجد فيها ثمّ يتشهّد ويسلّم، وإن كان لم يَنوِ أن تكون تلك السجدة للركعة الأولى لم تجز عنه الأولى ولا الثانية، وعليه أن يسجد سجدتين وينوي أنّهما للركعة الأولى، وعليه بعد ذلك ركعةٌ تامّة ثانية يسجد فيها.

قال حفص: فسألت عنها ابن أبي ليلى فما طعن فيها ولا قارب. قال: وسمعت بعض مواليهم يسأل ابن أبي ليلى عن الجمعة هل تجب على المرأة والعبد والمسافر؟ فقال ابن أبي ليلى: لا تجب الجمعة على واحد منهم ولا الخائف. فقال الرجل: فما تقول إن حضر واحد منهم الجمعة مع الإمام فصلّاها معه، فهل تجزيه تلك الصلاة عن ظُهر يومه؟ فقال: نعم! فقال له الرجل: وكيف يجزي ما لم يفرضه الله عليه عمّا فرضه الله عليه، وقد قلت إنّ الجمعة لا تجب عليه، ومن لم تجب عليه الجمعة فالفرض عليه أن

eighty dirhams). Later jurists and law schools were thus divided between those who continued to apply the rate derived from the text attributed to the Prophet and those who adopted the alleged modification by ʿUmar. Shāfiʿī, for his part, opted to follow the "spirit" of ʿUmar's decision by allowing the price of a camel to fluctuate. Many Islamic legal sources contain valuable information about the practical situation; see, for instance, Kulaynī, *Kāfī*, 5:197, 245, 248, 249 for second-century Kūfa, where the exchange rate could be even higher than the figures mentioned here—but presumably not as high as the 1 dinar = 18 dirhams mentioned in Kulaynī, 5:247 or the 1 dinar = 19 dirhams given in a variant of the same report in Qāḍī Nuʿmān, *Daʿāʾim al-Islām*, 2:37, both of which sound hypothetical, although there were times in the later Mamlūk period in Egypt when the exchange rate reached 1 dinar = 30 dirhams, as occurred in 801, or 1 dinar = 24 dirhams, as in 803 [Maqrīzī, *Shudhūr al-ʿuqūd*, 86–88]. On the other hand, the rate could also be as low as 1 dinar = 7 dirhams (Kulaynī, 5:245; Ṭūsī, *Tahdhīb*, 7:107–8). Consequently, people had to specify the dirham equivalent of any dinar amount mentioned in a contract; see, for instance, Kulaynī, 5:97, where Jaʿfar al-Ṣādiq says:

يكره أن يُشترى الثوب بدينارٍ غير درهم لأنّه لا يُدرى كم الدرهم من الدينار.

> It is disliked for a garment to be purchased for dinars without [specifying the] dirham [equivalent], because it is not known what the rate of exchange between dirham and dinar is going to be.

يصلّي أربعا، ويلزمك فيه معنىً أنّ الله فرض عليه أربعًا، فكيف اجزأ عنه ركعتان مع ما يلزمك أنّ من دخل فيما لم يفرضه الله عليه لم يجز عنه ممّا فرض الله عليه؟ فما كان عند ابن أبي ليلى فيها جواب. وطلب إليه أن يفسّرها له فأبى.

ثمّ سألته أنا عن ذلك ففسّرها لي فقال: الجواب عن ذلك أنّ الله عز وجل فرض الجمعة على جميع المؤمنين والمؤمنات، ورخّص للمرأة والمسافر والعبد أن لا يأتوها، فلمّا حضروها سقطت الرخصة ولزمهم الفرض الأوّل، فمن أجل ذلك أجزأ عنهم.

فقلت: عمّن هذا؟ فقال: عن مولانا أبي عبد الله.[323]

[Ḥafṣ b. Ghiyāth:] I heard Abū ʿAbd Allāh speak regarding what should be done in the case of a man who attended a crowded Friday prayer, said the *takbīr*, and bowed in tandem with the prayer leader, but was unable to prostrate himself. The prayer leader and the congregation then stood up for the second *rakʿa* and this man stood up with them, and the prayer leader bowed but the man could not bow for the second unit because of the crowd, but he was able to prostrate himself. Abū ʿAbd Allāh said, "As for the first unit, it was complete up to the point of the first bow, so when he did not prostrate himself for it until the second unit, [the second unit] did not count [as complete] for him. When he prostrated himself during the second unit, if he intended the prostration to count toward the first unit, the first unit was thereby completed. When the prayer leader concluded the prayer, the man should have stood and performed another unit during which he prostrated himself and performed the *tashahhud* and concluded the prayer. But if he did not intend that prostration to count toward the first unit, he has fulfilled neither the first nor the second unit, so he must prostrate himself twice and intend them for the first unit, and then he must perform a second complete unit during which he prostrates himself."

[Ḥafṣ:] I asked Ibn Abī Laylā about this and he neither contested nor favored it. [Ḥafṣ further said:] I heard one of their clients ask Ibn Abī Laylā about whether Friday prayer is obligatory for women, slaves, and travelers. Ibn Abī Laylā said, "No! Friday prayer is not obligatory for any of them, nor for the fearful." The man said, "What is your position on one [of those groups of people] attending the Friday prayer and praying it alongside the prayer leader—does it count toward the midday prayer of that day?" He said, "Yes!" The man said, "How can something that God has not obligated him to do count toward something

323 Ṭūsī, *Tahdhīb*, 3:21–22, partially also in Kulaynī, *Kāfī*, 3:430, and Ibn Bābawayh, *Faqīh*, 1:270–71.

that God has obligated him to do? You said that Friday prayer is not obligatory for him, and whoever is not obligated to attend Friday prayer is obligated to pray four [*rakʿa*s of midday prayer]. You must accept that this means that God made four [*rakʿa*s of midday prayer] obligatory for him, so how do two [*rakʿa*s of Friday prayer] suffice, given that you must accept that if a person performs something God has not obligated him to do, it cannot suffice for something God has obligated him to do?" Ibn Abī Laylā did not have an answer. The man asked him to explain it, but he declined.

I later asked him about that, and he explained it to me, saying, "The answer to this is that God made Friday prayer obligatory for all believing men and women, but he granted a dispensation from performing it to women, travelers, and slaves. Hence, when they attend it, the dispensation drops and the original obligation comes into effect. This is why [Friday prayer] suffices for them." I asked, "This [analysis] comes from whom?" He said, "From our master, Abū ʿAbd Allāh."

عيص بن القاسم قال: إنّ ابن شبرمة قال: الطلاق للرجل، فقال أبو عبد الله: الطلاق للنساء. وتبيان ذلك أنّ العبد تكون تحته الحرّة فيكون تطليقها ثلاثًا، ويكون الحرّ تحته الامة فيكون طلاقها تطليقتين.[324]

[ʿĪṣ b. al-Qāsim:] Ibn Shubruma said, "Divorce follows [the personal status of] the man." Abū ʿAbd Allāh said, "Divorce follows [the personal status of] women, and the proof of that is that when a slave man marries a free woman, she is to be divorced three times [before the two are fully separated]. But when a free man marries a slave woman, he can divorce her only twice [before the two are fully separated]."[325]

324 Kulaynī, *Kāfī*, 6:167.

325 This was the position of ʿAlī as recorded in a number of reports. E.g., Kulaynī, *Kāfī*, 6:170:

> أبو أسامة، عن أبي عبد الله قال: قال عمر على المنبر: ما تقولون يا أصحاب محمّد في تطليق الأمة؟ فلم يُجبه أحد. فقال: ما تقول يا صاحب البُرد المَعافِري؟ (يعني أمير المؤمنين [عليًا].) فأشار بيده: تطليقتان.
>
> [Zayd al-Shaḥḥām:] Abū ʿAbd Allāh said, "'Umar said on the pulpit, 'What is your position, O Companions of Muḥammad, regarding divorcing a slave woman?' Nobody answered him. He said, 'What do you say, O wearer of the Maʿāfirī overgarment [meaning ʿAlī]?' ʿAlī indicated with his hand: 'Two divorces.'"

See further Ibn Abī Shayba, *Muṣannaf*, 6:451; Ibn Mājah, *Sunan*, no. 2082; Abū Dāwūd, *Sunan*, no. 2187; Tirmidhī, *Sunan*, no. 1182; Dāraquṭnī, *Sunan*, 4:480; and for the attribution of Maʿāfirī clothes made in Yemen, see Zabīdī, *Tāj al-ʿarūs*, 13:92 and other Arabic dictionaries cited therein. See also Ṭabarānī, *al-Muʿjam al-kabīr*, 12:262.

معاوية بن ميسرة بن شريح قال: شهدت أبا عبد الله في مسجد الخيف وهو في حلقةٍ فيها نحو من مائتي رجل، فيهم عبد الله بن شُبرُمة، فقال: يا أبا عبد الله! إنّا نقضى بالعراق فنقضى بما نعلم من الكتاب والسنّة، ويرد علينا المسألة فنجتهد فيها بالرأى؟ فقال أبو عبد الله: أيُّ رجلٍ كان علي بن أبي طالب؟ فقد كان بالعراق ولَكُم به خُبر. قال: فأطراه ابن شُبرُمة وقال فيه قولاً عظيماً. فقال له أبو عبد الله: فإنّ علياً أبي أن يُدخل في دين الله الرأى وأن يقول في شيء من دين الله بالرأى والمقاييس.[326]

[Muʿāwiya b. Maysara b. Shurayḥ:] I saw Abū ʿAbd Allāh in the Mosque of Khayf[327] sitting in a circle attended by about two hundred men, among whom was ʿAbd Allāh b. Shubruma. He [Ibn Shubruma] said, "O Abū ʿAbd Allāh! We adjudicate in Iraq, and we judge on the basis of what we know from the Book [that is, the Qurʾān] and the Sunna, and from time to time, a case is posed to us that we decide on the basis of our personal opinion."[328] Abū ʿAbd Allāh said, "What sort of a person was ʿAlī b. Abī Ṭālib? He was in Iraq and you have knowledge of him." Ibn Shubruma lauded him [ʿAlī] and gave a magnificent description of him. Abū ʿAbd Allāh said to him, "But ʿAlī refused to allow personal opinion to enter the religion of God or to say anything about the religion of God on the basis of personal opinion or analogy."

إسماعيل بن الفضل الهاشمى قال: سألت أبا عبد الله عن المتعة فقال: إلقِ عبد الملك بن جُرَيج فسَلهُ عنها فإنّ عنده منها علماً. فلقيته فأملى عليّ منها شيئاً كثيراً. فأتيت بالكتاب إلى أبي عبد الله فعرضت عليه فقال: صدق.[329]

[Ismāʿīl b. al-Faḍl al-Hāshimī:] I asked Abū ʿAbd Allāh about *mutʿa* [temporary marriage]. He said, "Meet ʿAbd al-Malik b. Jurayj[330] and ask him about it; he has some knowledge of the matter." I met him and he dictated much to me about it. I brought the notes to Abū ʿAbd Allāh and presented them to him. He said, "He spoke the truth."

326 Barqī, *Maḥāsin*, 210.

327 A mosque in Minā, some three miles to the east of Mecca.

328 Like other jurists in the school of *raʾy*, Ibn Shubruma did not take *ḥadīth* seriously. See his biography in Wakīʿ, *Akhbār al-quḍāt*, 3:37, 117.

329 Kulaynī, *Kāfī*, 5:451.

330 ʿAbd al-Malik b. ʿAbd al-Azīz b. Jurayj (d. 150), head of the school of Mecca in his time. He is said to have been the first to author books on Islamic religious sciences. See the entry on him in *Encyclopaedia of Islam* III [Harald Motzki].

Jaʿfar al-Ṣādiq's legal teachings and responses were issued orally, but his disciples at times jotted them down,[331] with his permission.[332] According to some reports, he urged his followers to record in writing what they heard from him, warning that they would forget unless they wrote it down.[333] At times, he gave written answers to legal questions,[334] occasionally dictated to a scribe.[335]

His legal legacy, including both teachings and practice, has remained the standard manifestation of the Jaʿfarī school of Islamic law ever since his

331 See Kashshī, *Rijāl*, 143–44, where Zurāra b. Aʿyan asks Jaʿfar a question and opens his notebook to write down the answer, as quoted earlier; see also Ṭūsī, *Amālī*, 158. See further Jaʿfar's dictation to Sufyān al-Thawrī in Kulaynī, *Kāfī*, 8:403 (but the report sounds spurious).

332 E.g., ʿAyyāshī, *Tafsīr*, 3:11; Kulaynī, *Kāfī*, 1:164, 2:381.

333 ʿĀṣim b. Ḥumayd al-Ḥannāṭ, *Kitāb*, 160 (whence Kulaynī, *Kāfī*, 1:52), 171 (whence Ṭūsī, *Tahdhīb*, 5:26). This was a break with the emphasis on memorization only a generation earlier, when Muḥammad al-Bāqir was asked by a Kūfan follower to dictate a *ḥadīth* to him so that he could write it down, and the Imam responded, "Where is your memory, you people of Kūfa?" (Ṭūsī, 9:69). See also a statement ascribed to him in Ibn ʿAsākir, *Taʾrīkh madīnat Dimashq*, 54:277: "Memorize it by heart. Do not write it down, as we do not." (See further Cook, "Opponents of the Writing of Tradition"). Even Jaʿfar did not like it when a follower tried to write down a commonly known tenet of the Sunna, as in this example in Ṭūsī, 8:244:

> عبد الله بن سنان قال: سألت أبا عبد الله عن إمرأة ترضع غلامًا لها من مملوكة حتّى تفطمه، أيحلّ لها بيعه؟ قال: لا! حرامٌ عليها ثمنه. أليس قد قال رسول الله – صلّى الله عليه وآله وسلّم: يحرم من الرضاع ما يحرم من النسب؟ أليس قد صار ابنها؟ فذهبت أكتبه فقال أبو عبد الله: ليس مثل هذا يكتب!
>
> [ʿAbd Allāh b. Sinān:] I asked Abū ʿAbd Allāh about a woman who breastfeeds a baby boy from a slave woman of hers until he is weaned—is it lawful for her to sell him? He said, "No! His price is unlawful for her to receive. Did not the Messenger of God (may God's prayer and peace be upon him and his Family) say, 'What is sanctified through breastfeeding is the same as what is sanctified through lineage'? Did he not become her son?" I went to write it down and Abū ʿAbd Allāh said, "Something like this [that is, as obvious as this] is not to be written down!"

334 E.g., Kulaynī, *Kāfī*, 3:250, 546, 4:105, 264–65, 375, 5:191, 226, 227, 231, 6:413, 7:287, 381, 455; Kashshī, *Rijāl*, 143–44, 383, 388; Ṭūsī, *Tahdhīb*, 4:63, 5:54, 6:156, 303, 8:251, 10:309. He also responded in writing to non-legal questions, as in Barqī, *Maḥāsin*, 612; Kulaynī, 1:403, 5:76; Ibn Bābawayh, *Tawḥīd*, 226–29 (partially also in Kulaynī, 1:100 and 2:27–28, which are sections of the same report). See also Kulaynī, 1:164–65.

335 E.g., Kulaynī, *Kāfī*, 4:264–65. There are also cases in which the transmitter specifies that the answer was in the Imam's handwriting. E.g., Kulaynī, 3:450. It is worth noting that a number of old manuscripts of the Qurʾān in various libraries and museums are attributed to his handwriting, usually on the strength of a mention of his name as the scribe in the colophon. These include one in Istanbul (Ziriklī, *Aʿlām*, 2:127), one in Cairo (Habash, *Riḥlat al-Muṣḥaf al-sharīf*, 129), one in the Bodleian Library at Oxford (mentioned in https://www.hamshahri-online.ir/news/315533), one in the Golestan Palace Museum in Tehran (no. 1378), and two in Mashhad (mentioned in https://ejiga.com/w/eUExy20). None of these ascriptions seems authentic. Including a scribe's name in the colophon was most likely not even common in the second century.

time.[336] His son Mūsā al-Kāẓim[337] and his descendants,[338] who succeeded him as the heads of the House of the Prophet, frequently referred to Jaʿfar as the authority in their legal responses.

V. Circle of Disciples

Jaʿfar al-Ṣādiq enjoyed an advantage in that the close circle of disciples who had gathered around his father, Muḥammad al-Bāqir, many of whom were great jurists and *ḥadīth* transmitters, already knew him, appreciated his knowledge, and joined him after his father passed away. They included prominent scholars such as Abān b. Taghlib,[339] Abān b. ʿUthmān,[340] Abū Ḥamza al-Thumālī,[341] Zurāra b. Aʿyan,[342] Muḥammad b. Muslim al-Thaqafī,[343] and Burayd b. Muʿāwiya al-ʿIjlī.[344] Jaʿfar praised the disciples of his father as the trustees of the legacy of the House of the Prophet.[345] Many of those who started their education with Jaʿfar also became notable jurists and scholars.[346] He was proud of both generations of his disciples.[347] Their

336 See, for instance, Ḥimyarī, *Qurb al-isnād*, 357, where the Imam ʿAlī al-Riḍā (d. 201) responds to a question by saying, "By God, this has nothing to do with the religion of Jaʿfar" (لا والله! ما هذا من دين جعفر).

337 E.g., ʿAlī b. Jaʿfar, *Masāʾil*, 274 (whence Ḥimyarī, *Qurb al-isnād*, 238), 287 (whence Ḥimyarī, 298; Kulaynī, *Kāfī*, 7:397); Ḥimyarī, 238 (cf. Kulaynī, 4:303, where the content of the report is ascribed to Muḥammad al-Bāqir), 348; ʿAyyāshī, *Tafsīr*, 1:199; Kulaynī, 1:48, 2:488, 3:293–94 (read: كان أبي جعفر for كان أبو جعفر أو أبي), 4:369 (أما بلغك قولُ أبي عبد الله؟), 442, 524, 566, 5:251, 6:10, 7:55, 307; Ṭūsī, *Tahdhīb*, 1:445, 5:230–31, 426, 483, 8:202, 9:214.

338 E.g., ʿAlī al-Riḍā in Ṭūsī, *Tahdhīb*, 5:391, where he cites an outward discrepancy between the opinions of his predecessors on a matter of law and endorses that of Jaʿfar); 8:171, where he says in response to two questions: أهل المدينة يقولون؛ وكان جعفر يقول; and 9:210, where he responds to a question by saying:

أليس عندكم في ما بلغكم عن جعفر وعن أبي جعفر فيها شيء؟

Is there no opinion on the matter that has reached you from Jaʿfar and his father?

Likewise in Ḥimyarī, *Qurb al-isnād*, 357:

أين التقليد الّذي كانوا يقلّدون [به] جعفرًا وأبا جعفر؟

Where is the adherence to the positions of Jaʿfar and his father that they used to adopt?

See further Kulaynī, *Kāfī*, 5:426.

339 On him, see Modarressi, *Tradition and Survival*, 1:107–16.

340 Modarressi, *Tradition and Survival*, 1:129–31.

341 Modarressi, *Tradition and Survival*, 1:377–79.

342 Modarressi, *Tradition and Survival*, 1:404–5.

343 Modarressi, *Tradition and Survival*, 1:344–45. See also Kashshī, *Rijāl*, 162, 163, 167.

344 Modarressi, *Tradition and Survival*, 1:213–14. See also Kashshī, *Rijāl*, 163.

345 E.g., Kulaynī, *Kāfī*, 8:213; Kashshī, *Rijāl*, 136–37, 161, 213, 331, 403.

346 See, for instance, Kashshī, *Rijāl*, 375.

347 See, for instance, Kulaynī, *Kāfī*, 1:173; Kashshī, *Rijāl*, 277, 330–31, 442.

respect for the Imam was exemplary.[348] But there were certain religious and ethical standards that Jaʿfar expected his disciples to uphold:[349]

عبد الأعلى قال: سمعت أبا عبد الله يقول: أما والله لو كنتم تقولون ما أقول لأقررت أنّكم أصحابي. هذا أبو حنيفة له أصحاب وهذا الحسن البصري له أصحاب. وأنا إمرؤٌ من قريش، قد ولدني رسول الله وعلمت كتاب الله.[350]

[ʿAbd al-Aʿlā b. Aʿyan:] I heard Abū ʿAbd Allāh say, "By God, if you said what I say, I would acknowledge you as my disciples. This Abū Ḥanīfa has disciples, and that Ḥasan al-Baṣrī has disciples. I am a man of Quraysh, born to the Messenger of God, and I know the Book of God . . ."

مفضّل قال: قال أبو عبد الله: إذا أردت أن تعرف أصحابي فانظر إلى من اشتدّ ورعه وخاف خالقه ورجا ثوابه. فإذا رأيت هؤلاء فهؤلاء أصحابي.[351]

[Mufaḍḍal:] Abū ʿAbd Allāh said, "If you wish to know who my disciples are, look to whoever is intensely pious, fears his Lord, and hopes for His reward. If you see such people, they are my disciples."[352]

---

348 See, for instance, Kashshī, *Rijāl*, 383, where it is said that ʿAbd Allāh b. Muskān, one of Jaʿfar's most learned disciples, did not quote directly from him except in a single case, because of the high respect that ʿAbd Allāh had for him. This prevented ʿAbd Allāh from attending the Imam's audience. See also Ḥimyarī, *Qurb al-isnād*, 124 (and Kulaynī, *Kāfī*, 5:117–18), where someone requests that a disciple of the Imam ask him about the lawfulness of the wages paid to a woman eulogizer for her services. The disciple replies:

والله إنّي أعظّم أبا عبد الله أن أسأله عن هذه المسألة.

By God, I regard Abū ʿAbd Allāh too highly to ask him about this matter.

349 In the legal camp of their time, they were known as the disciples of Jaʿfar b. Muḥammad (see also Ibn Khallikān, *Wafayāt al-aʿyān*, 1:434, quoting al-Haytham b. ʿAdī al-Ṭāʾī al-Kūfī [d. 207]). Shāfiʿī refers to them as such in a debate in his *Umm*, 7:483–84, in the context of complaining that none of what his opponents quote from ʿAlī to support their opinions is reliable. Shāfiʿī then adds:

وقد أخبرنا أصحاب جعفر بن محمّد عن جعفر عن أبيه عن علي قال . . . وحديث جعفر عن علي أولى أن يُثبَت من حديث الزعافري عن الشعبي.

The companions of Jaʿfar b. Muḥammad reported to us on the authority of Jaʿfar from his father from ʿAlī. The *ḥadīth* of Jaʿfar from ʿAlī deserves more attention than does that of Zaʿāfirī from Shaʿbī.

350 Kulaynī, *Kāfī*, 2:223.

351 Kulaynī, *Kāfī*, 2:236.

352 See also Qāḍī Nuʿmān, *Sharḥ al-akhbār*, 3:504 (also Kulaynī, *Kāfī*, 2:233) for a redaction of this report:

مفضّل قال: قال أبو عبد الله: من عفّ بطنه وفرجه واشتدّ جهاده وعمل لخالقه ورجا ثوابه وخاف عقابه فاذا رأيت أولئك فَهُم شيعة جعفر.

He advised his disciples and followers on all matters of law, religion, and ethics, as well as the etiquette of personal and social conduct. He also sought their advice when needed.[353] He looked after them and was attentive to both their spiritual well-being and their material needs.[354]

The relationship between Jaʿfar and his learned disciples was that of a jurist and his students. His disciples occasionally asked him to specify the legal basis of his decisions, a common request for jurists of the time from those who consulted them. His answers shed light on his legal methodology and, as such, will be discussed in the next chapter.

Most of his disciples followed his opinions fully and dutifully.[355] Some, however, held independent views on various doctrinal and theological questions, as mentioned in Muslim heresiographical works.[356] Such divergence occasionally caused heated disputes among them.[357] At times, the Imam was asked by some of his followers to intervene, but he refused to do so because he thought that his intervention would not bring the dispute to an end.[358]

The number of those who studied with Jaʿfar over the course of his lifetime was large enough[359] for a late third- to early fourth-century scholar of *ḥadīth* to devote a monograph to their names.[360] Many of Jaʿfar's students recorded what they heard from him, including his responses to their questions, in notebooks, which numbered up to four hundred according to some accounts.[361] Some of these were later compiled into books and monographs on certain legal topics. A few of these works have survived, fully or partially, in their original forms; others are scattered across the

---

[Mufaḍḍal:] Abū ʿAbd Allāh said, "Whoever is virtuous with regard to his stomach and his chastity, works hard, works for the sake of his Creator, hopes for His reward, and fears His punishment—if you see any such people, they are the party of Jaʿfar."

353 E.g., Barqī, *Maḥāsin*, 601; Kulaynī, *Kāfī*, 5:191 (also Ṭūsī, *Tahdhīb*, 7:191, with minor variations).

354 E.g., Kulaynī, *Kāfī*, 3:436, 4:118.

355 See, for instance, Kulaynī, *Kāfī*, 7:81, 97, where Zurāra b. Aʿyan says, "This is what our colleagues have all received from the two Imams, Abū ʿAbd Allāh [al-Ṣādiq] and Abū Jaʿfar [al-Bāqir]." See also Kashshī, *Rijāl*, 184, where Mufaḍḍal b. Qays b. Rummāna tells Jaʿfar al-Ṣādiq, "When our colleagues disagree over a certain question, I say, 'My opinion is whatever Jaʿfar b. Muḥammad says.'"

356 For details, see van Ess, *Theologie und Gesellschaft*, 1:321–403. There were disagreements among them on certain legal points, too (see, for instance, Kulaynī, *Kāfī*, 6:411; Kashshī, *Rijāl*, 248). This point will be discussed further in the next chapter.

357 See Kashshī, *Rijāl*, 279, 498.

358 See, for instance, Kulaynī, *Kāfī*, 8:223.

359 The list of transmitters from Jaʿfar al-Ṣādiq in Ṭūsī, *Rijāl*, 153–328 includes 3,224 names, most of which the author collected from the chains of transmission of reports in Sunnī and Shīʿī sources.

360 *Kitāb man rawā ʿan Jaʿfar b. Muḥammad*, by Ibn ʿUqda, Abū al-ʿAbbās Aḥmad b. Muḥammad b. Saʿīd al-Kūfī (d. 332). See Kohlberg, "Al-Uṣūl al-arbaʿumiʾa," 130; Kohlberg, *Medieval Muslim Scholar at Work*, 315.

361 See Kohlberg, "Al-Uṣūl al-arbaʿumiʾa," 129–30.

early Shīʿī *ḥadīth* collections, as detailed in the first volume of my 2003 book, *Tradition and Survival.*[362]

Some senior disciples of Jaʿfar al-Ṣādiq who accompanied his father as well as himself for many years were very familiar with the legal positions of both on various matters of law. They had heard and memorized the two Imams' responses to legal questions and they were knowledgeable about many of the general principles of law. They would react immediately if they received answers to legal questions that contravened what they expected or had heard previously.[363] The following examples illustrate the reactions that Jaʿfar received from questioners who were surprised by answers that diverged from their expectations:

زرارة عن أبي عبد الله قال: أيّما رجل كان له مالٌ وحال عليه الحول فإنّه يزكّيه. قلت له: فإن هو وهبه قبل حلّه بشهر أو بيوم؟ قال: ليس عليه شيء إذَن. قلت له: إنّ أباك قال لي: من فرّ به من الزكاة فعليه أن يؤدّيها.[364]

[Zurāra:] Abū ʿAbd Allāh said, "Whoever possesses wealth for the duration of a year must pay *zakāt* on it." I said to him, "What if he gifts it one month, or one day, before a year has lapsed?" He said, "Then he owes nothing." I said to him, "Your father said to me, 'Whoever avoids the *zakāt* [by granting a gift] must fulfill it.'"

أبو بصير قال: قلت لأبي عبد الله: متى أصلّي ركعتي الفجر؟ قال: بعد طلوع الفجر. قلت له: إنّ أبا جعفر أمرني أن أصلّيهما قبل طلوع الفجر.[365]

[Abū Baṣīr:] I said to Abū ʿAbd Allāh, "When should I pray the two-*rakʿa* [supererogatory] dawn prayer?" He said, "After daybreak." I said to him, "Abū Jaʿfar ordered me to pray it before daybreak."

أبو بصير قال: سألت أبا عبد الله عن القنوت، فقال: في ما يجهر فيه بالقرائة. قلت له: إنّي سألت أباك عن ذلك فقال: في الخَمس كلّها.[366]

362 Modarressi, *Tradition and Survival*, 1:127–405.

363 For the mentality behind some of these reactions, see Ḥimyarī, *Qurb al-isnād*, 166. See also Kashshī, *Rijāl*, 258.

364 Kulaynī, *Kāfī*, 3:525–26.

365 Ṭūsī, *Tahdhīb*, 2:135.

366 Kulaynī, *Kāfī*, 3:339. In a similar narrative (with a variant in Ṭūsī, *Tahdhīb*, 2:90), another transmitter reports that he, too, asked both Jaʿfar and his father about this issue:

محمّد بن مسلم قال: سألت أبا جعفر عن القنوت في الصلوات الخمس فقال: اقنت فيهنّ جميعًا. قال: [فذكرت ذلك لأبي عبد الله فقال: أمّا ما لا شكّ فيه فما يُجهر فيه بالقرائة.]

[Abū Baṣīr:] I asked Abū ʿAbd Allāh about the *qunūt*. He said, "It is recited in prayers in which the recitation is performed aloud." I said to him, "I asked your father about this, and he said, 'In all five [prayers].'"

شعيب العقرقوفي قال: كنت عند أبي عبد الله ومعنا أبو بصير وأناس من أهل الجبل يسألونه عن ذبائح أهل الكتاب، فقال لهم أبو عبد الله: قد سمعتم ما قال الله في كتابه؟ فقالوا: نُحبّ أن تُخبرنا! فقال: لا تأكلوها. فلمّا خرجنا من عنده قال أبو بصير: كُلها، في عنقي! ما فيها [بأس]، فقد سمعته وسمعت أباه جميعًا يأمران بأكلها. فرجعنا إليه. فقال لي أبو بصير: سَلهُ! فقلت له: جُعلت فداك! ما تقول في ذبائح أهل الكتاب؟ فقال: ألستَ قد شهدتنا بالغداة وسمعت؟! قلت: بلى! فقال: لا تأكلها. فقال لي أبو بصير: في عنقي، كُلها! ثمّ قال لي: سَلهُ ثانية. فقال لي مثل مقالته الأولى. وعاد أبو بصير فقال لي: في عنقي، كُلها! ثمّ قال لي: سَلهُ! فقلت: لا أسأله بعد مرّتين.[367]

[Shuʿayb al-ʿAqarqūfī:] I was with Abū ʿAbd Allāh, and Abū Baṣīr was with us while a group of people from the Jibāl were asking him about meat slaughtered by the People of the Book. Abū ʿAbd Allāh said to them, "Have you not heard what God said in His Book?" They said, "We would like you to inform us!" He said, "Do not eat it." When we left him, Abū Baṣīr said, "Eat it; I take responsibility! I have heard him and his father both order it to be eaten." We went back to him, and Abū Baṣīr said to me, "Ask him!" I said to him, "May I be made your ransom! What do you say regarding meat slaughtered by the People of the Book?" He said, "Were you not with us in the morning and did you not hear [what I said]?" I said, "Yes!" He said, "Do not eat it." Abū Baṣīr said to me, "I take responsibility! Eat it!" Then he said to me, "Ask him again." He said to me what he had said the first time. Abū Baṣīr again said to me, "I take responsibility. Eat it!" Then he said to me, "Ask him." I said, "I will not ask him [again] after doing so twice."

The assumption of the disciples was that the Imams at times gave different answers for a number of reasons, which the disciples placed under the collective rubric of *taqiyya*, precautionary secrecy, even though the answer

---

> [Muḥammad b. Muslim:] I asked Abū Jaʿfar about the *qunūt* in the five prayers. He said, "Recite the *qunūt* in all of them." I mentioned this to Abū ʿAbd Allāh and he said, "What there is no doubt about is that one should recite [the *qunūt*] in prayers in which the recitation is done aloud."

In practice, however, Jaʿfar recited the *qunūt* in all five daily prayers, as did his father (Kulaynī, 3:339).

367 Ṭūsī, *Tahdhīb*, 9:66–67.

might not fall under the strict definition of the term. When they asked the Imams about this, the latter explained the reasons for the differences in their responses, as Jaʿfar al-Ṣādiq did in the following example:[368]

سلمة بن محرز قال: سألت أبا عبد الله عن رجل وقع على أهله قبل أن يطوف طواف النساء، فقال: ليس عليه شيءٌ. فخرجت إلى أصحابنا فأخبرتهم، فقالوا: اتّقاك! هذا مُيسّر قد سأله عن مثل ما سألت فقال له: عليك بَدَنة. قال: فدخلت عليه فقلت: جُعلت فداك! إنّي أخبرت أصحابنا بما أجبتني فقالوا: «اتّقاك! هذا ميسّر قد سأله عمّا سألت فقال له: عليك بَدَنة». فقال: إنَّ ذلك بلغه، فهل بلغك؟ قلت: لا! قال: ليس عليك شيء.[369]

[Salama b. Muḥriz:] I asked Abū ʿAbd Allāh about a man who had intercourse with his wife before the circumambulation (*ṭawāf*) for women.[370] He said, "He is not liable for anything." I went to our companions and informed them. They said, "He gave you that answer out of *taqiyya*. Here is Muyassar [b. ʿAbd al-ʿAzīz al-Nakhaʿī al-Madāʾinī], who asked him the same question and he said to him, 'You owe a sacrifice.'" I went back to him [Jaʿfar al-Ṣādiq] and said, "May I be made your ransom! I informed my companions about your response. They said, 'He gave you that answer out of *taqiyya*. Here is Muyassar who asked him the same question and he said to him, "You owe a sacrifice."'" He [Jaʿfar] said, "He had already received information [about the prohibition of that act]. Had you received that information?" I said, "No!" He said, "You are not liable for anything."

In a similar case in which people told a man that Jaʿfar had given him an answer to a question of inheritance law out of precautionary secrecy, the Imam explained:[371]

368 For some other examples, see Ṭūsī, *Tahdhīb*, 3:27–28.

369 Kulaynī, *Kāfī*, 4:378.

370 This is an additional circumambulation of the Kaʿba that Jaʿfarī law requires the pilgrim to do as a last item of their *ḥajj* in order to leave the state of pilgrim sanctity. After it, everything that is forbidden while in that state becomes lawful again. It is identified in a report from Jaʿfar al-Ṣādiq (Ṭūsī, *Tahdhīb*, 5:253) with the farewell circumambulation that is recommended by all schools of Islamic law as the last rite of the *ḥajj*.

371 The full text of the report will be quoted in the next chapter. As will be explained there in fuller detail, the issue at hand was the difference between Sunnī and Shīʿī inheritance laws. Had the man acted according to the procedures of the latter, he would most probably be ordered by the government to pay the other relatives of the deceased from his own pocket.

فقال [أبو عبد الله]: لا والله! ما اتّقيتك، ولكنّي خفت عليك أن تؤخذ بالنصف. فإن كنت لاتخاف فادفع النصف الآخر الى الابنة.[372]

No, by God! I did not safeguard myself against you. Rather, I feared that you be held responsible for the other half [of the inheritance]. If you have no fear, then give the other half to the daughter [too].

Many of the learned disciples of Jaʿfar al-Ṣādiq were known in their communities as authorities in religious law. They received questions about matters of law and gave answers based on the teachings of the Imam. They often cited him in their responses[373] and in their legal debates among themselves.[374] Some of these senior disciples, however, had their own mind and their own interpretations.[375] A few, though still working within the general framework of the Imam's teachings,[376] adopted independent methodologies not endorsed by him,[377] as the following example demonstrates:

رفاعة عن أبي عبد الله قال: سألته عن رجل طلّق امرأته حتّى بانت منه وانقضت عدّتها ثمّ تزوّجت زوجًا آخر فطلّقها أيضًا، ثمّ تزوّجت زوجها الأوّل، أيهدم ذلك الطلاق الأوّل؟ قال: نعم! قال ابن سماعة: وكان ابن بكير يقول: المطلّقة إذا طلّقها زوجها ثمّ تركها حتّى تبين ثمّ تزوّجها فإنّما هي عنده على طلاق مستأنف. قال ابن سماعة: وذكر الحسين بن هاشم أنّه سأل ابن بكير عنها فأجابه بهذا الجواب، فقال له: سمعت في هذا شيئًا؟ فقال: رواية رفاعة. فقال: إنّ رفاعة روى أنّه إذا دخل بينهما زوج. فقال: زوج وغير زوج عندي سواء. فقلت: سمعت في هذا شيئًا؟ فقال: لا! هذا ممّا رزق الله من الرأي. قال ابن سماعة: وليس نأخذ بقول ابن بكير فإنّ الرواية إذا كان بينهما زوج.[378]

372 Kulaynī, *Kāfī*, 7:87–88, with variants at 7:86–87 and Ṭūsī, *Tahdhīb*, 9:332–33.

373 E.g., Kulaynī, *Kāfī*, 5:512; Ṭūsī, *Tahdhīb*, 6:293–94, 7:373, where Jamīl b. Darrāj names the authority for his opinions as Jaʿfar al-Ṣādiq in the first case, "Jaʿfar or his father" in the second, and "the Imams" in the third; see also Kulaynī, 7:321, where he says that he had not heard anything specific from the Imams about a matter and, thus, offers his own interpretation.

374 E.g., Ṭūsī, *Tahdhīb*, 6:338.

375 E.g., Zurāra b. Aʿyan, particularly on the law of inheritance. See Kulaynī, *Kāfī*, 7:91–92, 93, 97, 100–101, 104, 109; Kashshī, *Rijāl*, 135. Zurāra was considered the most learned scholar in Kūfa in that field, to the point that other scholars in the community checked the reliability of their information with him. See, for instance, Kulaynī, 7:91–92, 94, 100, 103, 104; Ṭūsī, *Tahdhīb*, 9:272, 280, 301.

376 See, for instance, Kulaynī, *Kāfī*, 6:78.

377 See Kulaynī, *Kāfī*, 1:56; Kashshī, *Rijāl*, 212.

378 Kulaynī, *Kāfī*, 6:78.

Rifāʿa reported from Abū ʿAbd Allāh, saying, "I asked him about a man who divorced his wife, after which she separated from him, completed her waiting period, and married another person. [The second man] also divorced her, after which she remarried her first husband. Does this [new marriage] cancel the [legal effect] of the first divorce [so that the first divorce is not counted toward the total of three divorces needed for husband and wife to be completely separated]?" He said, "Yes." Ibn Samāʿa said, "Ibn Bukayr used to say: 'If a woman was divorced by her husband who then left her [until the waiting period had passed and they were fully separated] and then remarried her, she rejoins him with a renewed number of divorces.'" Ibn Samāʿa said, "Ḥusayn b. Hāshim mentioned that he asked Ibn Bukayr about [the likes of] her and he responded to him with this answer, so Ḥusayn said to him, 'Have you heard anything [quoted from the Imams] about this?' Ibn Bukayr said, 'The narration of Rifāʿa.' Ḥusayn said, 'Rifāʿa narrated that report about [a case] in which "a husband intervened between them" [that is, she married someone else before remarrying her first husband].' He [Ibn Bukayr] said, 'It is the same for me, whether or not there was an [intervening] husband.' [Ḥusayn] said, 'Have you heard anything [quoted from the Imams] about this?' He said, 'No! This is a legal decision that was granted by God.'" Ibn Samāʿa said, "We do not follow the opinion of Ibn Bukayr, because the narration [from the Imam] concerns a case in which there was an intervening husband."[379]

As this example indicates, some senior disciples occasionally reached conclusions different from those of the Imam. The Imam, for his part, expected them to refrain from using interpretive methodologies that the Imams did not sanction:

سماعة بن مهران عن أبي عبد الله قال: قلت له: جُعلت فداك! إنّ أناسًا من أصحابك قد لَقوا أباك وجدّك وسمعوا منهما الحديث وقد يرد عليهم الشيءُ ليس عندهم فيه شيءٌ وعندهم ما يُشبهه، فيَقيسوا على أحسنه؟ فقال: ما لكم والقياس؟ إنّما هلك من هلك بالقياس.[380]

[Samāʿa b. Mihrān:] I said to Abū ʿAbd Allāh, "May I be made your ransom! Some of your companions met your father and your grandfather and heard *ḥadīth* from them. Issues are brought to them for

379 For another case that showcases ʿAbd Allāh b. Bukayr's independent opinions, see Kulaynī, *Kāfī*, 6:77–78.

380 Durust b. Abī Manṣūr, *Kitāb*, 292.

which the answer is not found in what they have, but they have similar material. Should they draw an analogy the best they can?" He said, "What do you have to do with analogy? Those who were ruined were ruined by analogy."

محمّد بن حكيم قال: قلت لأبي عبد الله: إنّ قومًا من أصحابنا قد تفقّهوا وأصابوا علمًا ورووا أحاديث، فيَرِد عليهم الشيءُ، فيقولون فيه برأيهم؟ فقال: لا! وهل هلك مَن مضى إلّا بهذا وأشباهه؟[381]

[Muḥammad b. Ḥakīm:] I said to Abū ʿAbd Allāh, "A group of our companions have studied law, acquired knowledge, and transmitted reports. Queries are posed to them. Can they reply on the basis of their personal opinions?" He said, "No! Have those in the past not perished but for this and its like?"

سعيد الأعرج قال: قلت لأبي عبد الله: إنّ مَن عندنا ممّن يتفقّه يقولون: يرد علينا ما لا نعرفه في الكتاب والسنّة فنقول فيه برأينا. قال: كذبوا! ليس بشيء إلّا وقد جاء في الكتاب أو جاءت فيه سنّة.[382]

[Saʿīd al-Aʿraj:] I said to Abū ʿAbd Allāh, "Some of those in our neighborhood who give opinions on legal questions say: 'A matter is brought to us for which we do not find the answer in the Book or the Sunna, so we answer on the basis of our personal opinion.'" He said, "This is not true! There is nothing that has not been addressed in the Book or about which there is no Sunna."

As these examples make clear, Jaʿfar al-Ṣādiq expected his learned disciples and the future generations to be able to derive rulings for specific cases from the legal norms that they had learned. This is how he explained the division of labor between himself and his students:

هشام بن سالم عن أبي عبد الله قال: إنّما علينا أن نُلقي إليكم الأصول وعليكم أن تُفرِّعوا.[383]

[Hishām b. Sālim:] Abū ʿAbd Allāh said, "It is our duty to teach you the principles, and it is your duty to derive legal rules for specific cases."

381 Barqī, *Maḥāsin*, 212.
382 Mufīd (attr.), *Ikhtiṣāṣ*, 281.
383 Bazanṭī, *Jāmiʿ*, 109.

VI. Rejection of Sectarianism

The society in which Jaʿfar al-Ṣādiq was born and lived was one divided by pro-ʿUthmān/pro-Umayyad versus pro-ʿAlī sentiments. Almost a century of rule by the Umayyads, an exclusively Arab dynasty that paid only lip service to Islam, had enormous and enduring effects on Muslim religious culture throughout the lands of the caliphate. For the better part of a century, Muslim society had been bombarded with fierce anti-ʿAlī propaganda, including weekly cursing of ʿAlī from the pulpits of all mosques in Muslim lands. Sentiments in favor of the House of the Prophet persisted in certain pockets in this society, but the official interpretation of Islam and its caliphal practice created a rift in the Muslim community, with resentment between the two tendencies throughout the caliphate.

The two holy cities of Mecca and Medina were at the center of this rift. The people of Medina had some respect for the House of the Prophet, but the pro-ʿUthmān faction had the upper hand in Mecca. The decidedly less than friendly atmosphere toward the ʿAlids in Mecca was the product not only of sustained and vigorous Umayyad propaganda but also that of ʿAbd Allāh b. al-Zubayr, who ruled Mecca from 64 to 73 as a rival to the Umayyad caliphate but, like them, was staunchly anti-ʿAlī. As Jaʿfar al-Ṣādiq visited the town annually for the *ḥajj*, his practice as the chief representative of the House of the Prophet at the time came under periodic scrutiny, and there were always some who complained that he did not act as the previous generations had done. His uniform answer was that he did not care about previous generations but acted according to what religion and law required.[384]

ʿAbbād b. Kathīr (d. 141), a Baṣran ascetic who lived in Mecca, was one of these complainers. Lacking sufficient knowledge of law and tradition to be a religious scholar himself, he nonetheless used to follow and frequently criticize both Muḥammad al-Bāqir and Jaʿfar al-Ṣādiq for their practice if it differed in any way from the community's customary practice. When Jaʿfar performed a certain *ḥajj* ritual differently, ʿAbbād challenged him: "You do that even though you are a source of religious knowledge?"[385] The Imam

384 See, for instance, Barqī, *Maḥāsin*, 442 (also Kulaynī, *Kāfī*, 6:271, 272) for his practice at meals, which came under scrutiny from some people (see further Ḥusayn b. Saʿīd al-Ahwāzī, *Zuhd*, 59; and, for the Prophet's practice in this case, Barqī, 458; Kulaynī, 6:272); Kulaynī, 2:480 for extending his left hand in prayer supplication; 4:194, for praying between the door of the Kaʿba and the Black Stone (see further 4:525; Ibn Bābawayh, *Faqīh*, 2:135).

385 Ṭūsī, *Tahdhīb*, 5:374 (وأنت رجل يؤخذ منك). For this man's other conversations with, and criticisms of, Jaʿfar al-Ṣādiq, see ʿĀṣim b. Ḥumayd al-Ḥannāṭ, *Kitāb*, 172–73 (whence Kulaynī, *Kāfī*, 1:400); Kulaynī, 2:186–87, 222, 293, 439, 6:163, 443, 7:10, 132, 182, 195, 208, 210, 243–44 (read *ʿAbbād*, as in Ibn Bābawayh, *Faqīh*, 4:19 and Ṭūsī, 10:32, for *Yaḥyā b. ʿAbbād*); 8:107; Kashshī, *Rijāl*, 391–92 (read *ʿAbbād*, as in Ibn Bābawayh, *Faqīh*, 4:19 and Ṭūsī, 10:32, for *Yaḥyā b ʿAbbād*), 8:107; Kashshī, *Rijāl*, 391–92 (read *ʿAbbād b. Kathīr* for *ʿAbbād b. Ṣuhayb* in the section title); Ṭūsī, 6:282, 8:202; Ibn Ṭāwūs, *Iqbāl*, 3:87 (referencing a later,

explained to him how his practice followed the Sunna of the Prophet as was known to the scholars of the time.

The jurist Sufyān al-Thawrī (d. 161)[386] and others[387] questioned Jaʿfar's practice during the *ḥajj* on a number of points, most prominently his failure to touch the Black Stone while circumambulating the Kaʿba, a ritual that the Prophet performed as confirmed by Jaʿfar himself.[388] Jaʿfar's response was that the pilgrims would allow the Prophet to approach the stone easily but did not do the same for Jaʿfar, who did not like the unpleasant jostling.[389]

عبد الرحمن بن الحجّاج عن أبي عبد الله قال: كنت أطوف وسفيان الثوريُّ قريب منّي، فقال: يا أبا عبد الله! كيف كان رسول الله – صلّى الله عليه [وآله] وسلّم – يصنع بالحَجَر إذا انتهى إليه؟ فقلت: كان رسول الله – صلّى الله عليه وآله وسلّم – يستلمه في كلِّ طواف فريضة ونافلة. قال: فتخلّف عنّي قليلاً، فلمّا انتهيت إلى الحجر جزتُ ومشيتُ فلم أستلمه، فلحقني فقال: يا أبا عبد الله! ألم تُخبرني أنَّ رسول الله – صلّى الله عليه [وآله] وسلّم – كان يستلم الحجر في كلِّ طواف فريضة ونافلة؟ قلت: بلى! قال: قد مررت به فلم تستلم. فقلت: إنَّ الناس كانوا يرون لرسول الله – صلّى الله عليه وآله وسلّم – ما لا يرون لي فكان إذا انتهى إلى الحجر أفرجوا له حتّى يستلمه [وأنا لا يُفرَج لي]،[390] وإنّي أكره الزحام.[391]

[ʿAbd al-Raḥmān b. al-Ḥajjāj:] Abū ʿAbd Allāh said, "I was circumambulating [the Kaʿba] and Sufyān al-Thawrī was close to me. He said, 'O Abū ʿAbd Allāh! What would the Prophet (may God's prayer and peace be upon him [and his Family]) do with respect to the [Black] Stone when he reached it?' I said, 'The Prophet (may God's prayer and peace be upon him and his Family) would touch it during each obligatory and supererogatory circumambulation.' He then stayed a short distance behind me. When I reached the Stone, I passed it and walked on without touching it, so he joined me and said, 'O Abū ʿAbd Allāh! Did you not tell me that the Prophet (may God's prayer and peace be upon

spurious report that nevertheless may indicate that memory of ʿAbbād's quarreling with Jaʿfar endured). See also Barqī, *Maḥāsin*, 583.

386 Durust b. Abī Manṣūr, *Kitāb*, 294–95; Kulaynī, *Kāfī*, 4:404–5.

387 Kulaynī, *Kāfī*, 4:324, 409, 488–89; Ṭūsī, *Tahdhīb*, 5:57, 104, 202.

388 Kulaynī, *Kāfī*, 4:404.

389 Kulaynī, *Kāfī*, 4:405, 409; Ṭūsī, *Tahdhīb*, 5:104. See also Kulaynī, *Kāfī*, 4:467, where he explains why he was late in leaving ʿArafāt to head toward Mashʿar: "I fear crowds and fear that I may hurt another human being."

390 From the following report in Durust b. Abī Manṣūr, *Kitāb*, 295.

391 Kulaynī, *Kāfī*, 4:404–5.

him [and his Family]) used to touch the Stone during each obligatory and supererogatory circumambulation?' I said, 'Yes!' He said, 'But you passed it and did not touch it.' I said, 'People had consideration for the Prophet (may God's prayer and peace be upon him and his Family) in a way that they do not for me. When he reached the Stone, they would make way for him to touch it, but they do not make way for me, and I dislike crowds.'"

A variant of the report contains additional material in which Jaʿfar explains how his practice, though different from the Prophet's precedent, nonetheless follows the latter's instructions:

عبد الحميد بن سعيد قال: دخل سفيان الثوري على أبي عبد الله فقال: أصلحك الله! بلغني أنّك صنعت أشياءَ خالفتَ فيها النبيّ – صلّى الله عليه [وآله] وسلّم. قال: وما هي؟ قال: بلغني أنّك أحرمت من الجُحفة وأحرم رسول الله – صلّى الله عليه [وآله] وسلّم – من الشجرة، وبلغني أنّك لم تستلم الحجر في طواف الفريضة وقد استلمه رسول الله – صلّى الله عليه [وآله] وسلّم، وبلغني أنّك تركت المنحر ونحرت في دارك. قال: قد فعلتُ! وقال: وما دعاك إلى ذلك؟ فقال: إنّ رسول الله – صلّى الله عليه وآله وسلّم – وقّت الجُحفةَ للمريض والضعيف، وكنت قريبَ العهد بالمرض فأحببت أن آخذ برخص الله. وأمّا استلام الحجر فكان رسول الله – صلّى الله عليه وآله وسلّم – يُفرَّج له وأنا لا يفرّج لي. وأمّا تركي المنحر ونحري في داري فإنّ رسول الله – صلّى الله عليه وآله وسلّم – قال: مكّة كلُّها منحر، فحيث نحرتَ أجزأك.[392]

[ʿAbd al-Ḥamīd b. Saʿīd:] Sufyān al-Thawrī came to Abū ʿAbd Allāh and said, "May God put you on the right path! I heard that you did some things contrary to the [practice of] the Prophet (may God's prayer and peace be upon him [and his Family])." The Imam said, "What are they?" He said, "I heard that you entered the state of pilgrim sanctity (*iḥrām*) in Juḥfa, whereas the Prophet (may God's prayer and peace be upon him [and his Family]) entered the state of pilgrim sanctity in [the Mosque of] Shajara; and I heard that you did not touch the [Black] Stone during the obligatory circumambulation, whereas the Prophet (may God's prayer and peace be upon him [and his Family]) touched it; and I heard that you sacrificed [the requisite animal that is part of the pilgrimage]

392 Durust b. Abī Manṣūr, *Kitāb*, 294–95. See also Kulaynī, *Kāfī*, 4:488–89, where a variant of the last line of the report is quoted through a different transmitter.

in your home rather than at the [ordinary] site of sacrifice." The Imam said, "I did so!" He said, "What made you do that?" He said, "The Prophet (may God's prayer and peace be upon him and his Family) prescribed Juḥfa for the ill and the weak [as a site at which to enter the state of pilgrim sanctity], and I had just recovered from an illness, so I wanted to make use of God's dispensation. As for touching the Stone, people would make room for the Prophet (may God's prayer and peace be upon him and his Family), but they do not make room for me. And as for leaving the site of sacrifice and sacrificing in my home, the Prophet (may God's prayer and peace be upon him and his Family) said, 'Mecca in its entirety is a site of sacrifice.'[393] So wherever you sacrifice, it will suffice."

There were still other conversations of this nature between the two. Here is just one more example:

عبد الرحمن بن الحجّاج عن أبي عبد الله قال: إنّ سفيان فقيهكم أتاني فقال: ما يحملك على أن تأمر أصحابك يأتون الجِعرانة فيُحرمون منها؟ فقلت له: هي وقت من مواقيت رسول الله – صلّى الله عليه وآله وسلّم. فقال: وأيّ وقت من مواقيت رسول الله – صلّى الله عليه [وآله] وسلّم – هي؟ فقلت له: أحرم منها حين قسّم غنائم حنين ومرجعه من الطائف. فقال: إنّما هذا شيء أخذتَه من [رواية] عبد الله بن عمر. فقلت: أليس قد كان عندكم مرضيًّا؟ قال: بلى! ولكن أما علمت أنّ أصحاب رسول الله – صلّى الله عليه [وآله] وسلّم – إنّما أحرموا من المسجد؟ فقلت: إنّ أولئك كانوا متمتّعين في أعناقهم الدماء، وإنّ هؤلاء قطنوا بمكّة فصاروا كأنّهم من أهل مكّة، وأهل مكّة لا متعة لهم، فأحببت أن يخرجوا من مكّة إلى بعض المواقيت وأن يستغبّوا به أيّامًا. فقال لي – وأنا أخبره أنّها وقت من مواقيت رسول الله – صلّى الله عليه وآله وسلّم – : يا أبا عبد الله! فإنّي أرى لك أن لا تفعل. فضحكت وقلت: ولكنّي أرى لهم أن يفعلوا.[394]

['Abd al-Raḥmān b. al-Ḥajjāj:] Abū 'Abd Allāh said, "Sufyān, your [local] jurist, came to me and said, 'What makes you order your followers to go to Ji'rāna to assume the state of pilgrim sanctity there?' I said to him, 'It is one of the *ḥajj* stations assigned by the Messenger of God (may God's prayer and peace be upon him and his Family).' He said, 'Which of the *ḥajj* stations of the Messenger of God (may God's

393 See Ibn 'Abd al-Barr, *Istidhkār*, 12:286, 13:74 (مكّة كلّها مَنحر). See also Ibn Mājah, *Sunan*, no. 8403 (كُلّ فِجاج مكّة طريق ومَنحر).

394 Kulaynī, *Kāfī*, 4:400–401.

prayer and peace be upon him [and his Family]) is it?' I said to him, 'He entered the state of pilgrim sanctity there when he distributed the booty from Ḥunayn on his way back from Ṭā'if.' He said, 'This is something you learned from [the transmission of] ʿAbd Allāh b. ʿUmar.'[395] I said, 'Was he not an admirable person in your view?' He said, 'Yes! But did you not know that the companions of the Messenger of God (may God's prayer and peace be upon him [and his Family]) assumed the state of pilgrim sanctity at the Mosque [of Shajara]?' I said, 'They [the Companions] were performing the *ḥajj* of *tamattuʿ* and had to offer sacrifice [and so were bringing their animals to sacrifice from Medina]. But these people [whom I advise to go to Jiʿrāna] reside in Mecca, so it is as if they are of the people of Mecca, and the people of Mecca do not perform *tamattuʿ*.[396] So I like for them to leave Mecca for one of the *ḥajj* stations and be away from their ordinary life for a few days.' While I was informing him that it was one of the *ḥajj* stations of the Messenger of God (may God's prayer and peace be upon him and his Family), he said to me, 'O Abū ʿAbd Allāh, I think you should not do that!' I laughed and said, 'But I think they should do that!'"

---

395 This event was well known to early authorities on the life of the Prophet, as attested by reports in five of the six canonical Sunnī *ḥadīth* collections (Bukhārī, *Ṣaḥīḥ*, nos. 1778, 1780, 3066, 4148; Muslim, *Ṣaḥīḥ*, no. 1253; Ibn Mājah, *Sunan*, no. 3003; Abū Dāwūd, *Sunan*, no. 1993; Tirmidhī, *Sunan*, nos. 815–16), as well as Aḥmad b. Ḥanbal, *Musnad*, 4:425, and other sources cited in the editor's footnotes in Tirmidhī, 2:169–70. The report quoted here indicates that ʿAbd Allāh b. ʿUmar, too, was known to have assumed that the event occurred. However, ʿAbd Allāh is quoted by his associate Nāfiʿ as denying that the Prophet ever made that pilgrimage trip. In the words of Ibn Kathīr (*al-Bidāya wa-l-nihāya*, 4:492):

> وهذا غريب جدًّا عن ابن عمر وعن مولاه نافع في إنكارهما عمرة الجِعرانة، وقد أطبق النقلة على رواية ذلك [عمرة الجِعرانة] من أصحاب الصحاح والسنن والمسانيد وذكره أصحاب المغازي والسير كلّهم.
>
> It is very strange that Ibn ʿUmar and his client Nāfiʿ denied the [Prophet's] *ʿumra* from Jiʿrāna. The transmitters among the authors of the *ṣiḥāḥ*, the *sunan*, and the *masānīd* have concurrently reported it, as have all the authors of the genre of *maghāzī* and *siyar* [the biographies of the Prophet].

Together with the other two cases mentioned below—in which Nāfiʿ's transmission was challenged—concerning the story of ʿAbd Allāh's triple divorce of his wife during the lifetime of the Prophet and concerning the meaning of Qur'ān 2:223, these cases may cast some doubt on the accuracy of Nāfiʿ's reports from ʿAbd Allāh b. ʿUmar. *Wa'llāhu aʿlam*. It may be worth noting that Nāfiʿ was reportedly one of the four individuals who were chosen by Jaʿfar to witness his father's last will on his deathbed (Kulaynī, *Kāfī*, 1:307). On Nāfiʿ in general, see Juynboll, "Nāfiʿ, the *Mawlā* of Ibn ʿUmar"; Motzki, "*Quo vadis Ḥadīṯ*-Forschung?"

396 Qur'ān 2:196. See also Ibn Abī Shayba, *Muṣannaf*, 5:651–52.

Shabba b. ʿIqāl al-Baṣrī, an Umayyad agent,[397] objected to a legal opinion of Jaʿfar. In response, Jaʿfar pointed out that the opinion was shared by the jurists of the Ḥijāz, and that the Umayyad Walīd b. Yazīd b. ʿAbd al-Malik (r. 125–26), the caliph at the time, preferred their opinion over the opinion of the jurists of Iraq and Syria, following it in a case that involved the caliph and his wife Salāma.[398]

For his part, Jaʿfar, like his predecessors among the Imams of the House of the Prophet, held that people had tampered with much of the Sunna, and he tried to correct the situation wherever he could:

> عبيد بن زرارة عن أبي عبد الله: ما من شيء عليه الناس اليوم إلّا وهو حُرّف عمّا نزل به الوحي.[399]
>
> [ʿUbayd b. Zurāra:] Abū ʿAbd Allāh said, "There is nothing that the people adhere to today that has not been changed from what was revealed [by God]."

> بشير الدهّان عن أبي عبد الله قال: لا والله! ما هم على شيء ممّا جاء به رسول الله – صلّى الله عليه وآله وسلّم – إلّا استقبال الكعبة فقط.[400]
>
> [Bashīr al-Dahhān:] Abū ʿAbd Allāh said, "No, by God! They are not in line with anything that the Messenger of God (may God's prayer and peace be upon him and his Family) conveyed, except in facing the Kaʿba."

The same position had been taken by the Companion Anas b. Mālik (d. 93) a few decades earlier:[401]

---

397 Possibly the same as the one mentioned in Ibn ʿAsākir, *Taʾrīkh madīnat Dimashq*, 73:112–14 as an associate of the caliph Manṣūr in the post-Umayyad period, and not his grandfather, Shabba b. ʿIqāl b. Ṣaʿṣaʿa, whom Ibn ʿAsākir, 73:114–19 and biographical dictionaries of *ḥadīth* transmitters (e.g., Ibn Abī Ḥātim, *al-Jarḥ wa'l-taʿdīl*, 2:385) name as a *ḥadīth* transmitter. In a report in Ṭūsī, *Amālī*, 50–51, a Shabba b. ʿIqāl is mentioned as Manṣūr's governor-designate for Medina (*wallāhu ʿalā ahlihā*) after the failure of Nafs al-Zakiyya's revolt, and he is quoted as giving a harshly worded sermon against ʿAlī and his descendants in his first Friday prayer at the mosque of Medina. The name, however, does not appear in the list of the governors of Medina after the revolt (see Ṭabarī, *Taʾrīkh*, 7:609–10). Balādhurī, *Ansāb al-ashrāf*, 11:71 reports that the children of ʿIqāl b. Shabba, the father of the person in question, were orators (*khuṭabāʾ*), a profession that fits well with the story in Ṭūsī, 50. The phrase *wallāhu ʿalā ahlihā* (Ṭūsī, 50) is possibly to be understood as *wallāhu al-khuṭba*; that is, he was appointed the official *khaṭīb* of Medina, not as the governor.

398 Kulaynī, *Kāfī*, 6:135.

399 Kashshī, *Rijāl*, 140.

400 Barqī, *Maḥāsin*, 156.

401 Attempts were made in later periods to dilute Anas's statement by adding a word or two, or even amending the entire statement to suggest that Anas was upset about a specific

أنس قال: ما أعرف شيئًا اليوم ممّا كنّا عليه على عهد رسول الله – صلّى الله عليه وسلّم.[402]

[Anas:] I do not recognize anything today that we used to follow during the time of the Messenger of God (may God's prayer and peace be upon him).

أنس قال: ما أعرف فيكم اليوم شيئًا كنت أعهده على عهد رسول الله – صلّى الله عليه وسلّم – ليس قولكم لا إله إلّا الله.[403]

[Anas:] I do not recognize today anything that I used to witness during the time of the Messenger of God (may God's prayer and peace be upon him), other than your pronouncement that "There is no deity but God."

أنس قال: ما شيء شهدته على عهد رسول الله – صلّى الله عليه وسلّم – إلّا وقد أنكرته اليوم، إلّا شهادتكم هذه.[404]

[Anas:] There is nothing that I witnessed during the time of the Messenger of God (may God's prayer and peace be upon him) that I recognize today, save this testimony of yours.

A similar statement is quoted from the Companion Abū al-Dardāʾ ʿUwaymir b. Mālik (d. 32), who died too early to witness the Umayyad period. If the report is authentic, it means that the trend had already started by the time of the Umayyads.

عن أبي الدرداء قال: والله ما أعرف فيهم شيئًا من أمر محمّد – صلّى الله عليه وسلّم – إلّا أنّهم يصلّون جميعًا.[405]

[Abū al-Dardāʾ:] By God, I do not recognize any of [the teachings and practice of] Muḥammad (may God's prayer and peace be upon him) among these people except that they pray in congregation.

---

problem—Muslims' failure to pray the five daily prayers at their recommended times or their lack of attention to positioning themselves in even rows in the communal prayers! The original statement is, however, too general and powerful to allow these interpretations.

402 Aḥmad b. Ḥanbal, *Musnad*, 19:39, with a variant at 20:405.

403 Bukhārī, *Ṣaḥīḥ*, no. 529, and other sources cited in the editors' footnotes in Aḥmad b. Ḥanbal, *Musnad*, 21:345.

404 Ibn Rajab, *Fatḥ al-Bārī*, 3:56.

405 Aḥmad b. Ḥanbal, *Musnad*, 36:30, 45:492, with a variant in Bukhārī, *Ṣaḥīḥ*, no. 650.

Other reports confirm the existence of the same mentality among senior members of the Muslim community around the same time and earlier. Consider the following example:

مطرّف عن عمران بن حصين قال: صلّى مع عليّ – رضي الله عنه – بالبصرة فقال: ذكّرنا هذا الرجل صلاةً كنّا نصلّيها مع رسول الله – صلّى الله عليه وسلّم.[406]

[Muṭarraf (b. ʿAbd Allāh):] ʿImrān b. Ḥuṣayn prayed with ʿAlī in Baṣra[407] and said, "This man reminded us of the prayer we used to perform with the Messenger of God (may God's prayer and peace be upon him)."

مطرّف بن عبد الله قال: صلّيت خلف عليّ بن أبي طالب – رضي الله عنه – أنا وعمران بن حصين. فلمّا قضى الصلاة أخذ بيدي عمران بن حصين فقال: قد ذكّرني هذا صلاة محمّد – صلّى الله عليه وسلّم – أو قال: لقد صلّى بنا صلاة محمّد – صلّى الله عليه وسلّم.[408]

[Muṭarraf b. ʿAbd Allāh:] I prayed behind ʿAlī b. Abī Ṭālib with ʿImrān b. Ḥuṣayn. When he finished the prayer, ʿImrān b. Ḥuṣayn took my hand and said, "This reminded me of the prayer of Muḥammad (may God's prayer and peace be upon him)," or he said, "He led us in the prayer of Muḥammad (may God's prayer and peace be upon him)."

These two reports, as well as others,[409] suggest that people at the time did not perform their prayers in the way that the Prophet had done.

Notwithstanding this fact, Jaʿfar al-Ṣādiq constantly urged his followers to maintain harmonious relations and solidarity with other Muslims and to avoid sectarianism.[410] He argued that all Muslims—whom he characterized

406 Bukhārī, *Ṣaḥīḥ*, no. 748.

407 Aḥmad b. Ḥanbal, *Musnad*, 33:75 has "in Kūfa"; cf. the sources cited in the editors' footnote at 33:76–77.

408 Bukhārī, *Ṣaḥīḥ*, no. 286 (see also Aḥmad b. Ḥanbal, *Musnad*, 33:172, 201).

409 E.g., Aḥmad b. Ḥanbal, *Musnad*, 32:251, where a similar statement is quoted from Abū Mūsā al-Ashʿarī (see also 32:244, 466, 494).

410 See his instructions to a group of his Kūfan followers in Mufīd, *Amālī*, 28: "Join the vast crowd of the community" (أدخلوا في دهماء الناس); also 31, where he endorses a report from ʿAlī that praises both camps of Muslims and predicts that they will come together for a common purpose:

الأبدال من أهل الشام والنجباء من أهل الكوفة، يجمعهم الله لشرّ يوم لعدوّنا.

The pious among the people of Shām [greater Syria] and the nobles among the people of Kūfa will be gathered by God on a day that will be the great chagrin of our enemies.

in different reports as those who bear witness to the unity of God,[411] *ahl al-qibla*,[412] or *man kāna ʿalā fiṭrat al-Islām*[413]—will enter Paradise.[414] The long list of his students and transmitters, who display a wide spectrum of sectarian backgrounds,[415] attests to his solidarity-oriented approach.

This stance was in line with Jaʿfar's respect for earlier and contemporary authorities of the Islamic tradition and his justification of their differences of opinion:

---

411 See Ibn Bābawayh, *Khiṣāl*, 408, on the eight gates of paradise:

> إنّ للجنّة ثمانية أبواب: بابٌ يَدخل منه النبيّون والصدّيقون، وبابٌ يدخل منه الشهداء والصالحون، وخمسة أبواب يدخل منها شيعتنا ومحبّونا، وبابٌ يدخل منه سائر المسلمين ممّن شهد أن لا إله إلّا الله.
>
> Paradise has eight gates through which to enter: a gate for the prophets and the truthful, a gate for the martyrs and the righteous, five gates for our followers and well-wishers, and a gate for the rest of the Muslims, who testify that there is no deity but God. [Quite a crowd at one gate, but still better than no gate!]

For background, see *Kitāb Sulaym b. Qays al-Hilālī* (a late Umayyad, anti-ʿUthmānī polemic, the original part of which represents the views of the Kūfan Shīʿa at the time), 2:607–8:

> من وحّد الله وآمن برسول الله ولم يعرف ولايتنا وأخذ بجميع ما ليس بين المختلفين من الأمّة خلاف في أنّ الله عزّ وجلّ أمر به، فهذا ناجٍ. وهذه الطبقة هو أعظم الناس وجُلّهم.
>
> Whoever upholds the oneness of God and believes in God's Messenger, but does not believe in our authority, while accepting the remainder of the elements [of religion] on which the community does not disagree as commanded by God, the Mighty and Majestic—this person will be saved. This class consists of the great majority of people.

412 Ṭūsī, *Tahdhīb*, 5:9. See also Kulaynī, *Kāfī*, 4:271:

> عن أبي عبد الله قال: لا يزال الدين قائمًا ما قامت الكعبة.
>
> This religion will continue as long as the Kaʿba continues to stand.

413 Ibn Bābawayh, *Amālī*, 163 (see also Kulaynī, *Kāfī*, 6:67, where a similar definition is quoted from Jaʿfar's son Mūsā al-Kāẓim, and Ṭūsī, *Tahdhīb*, 9:71, where Muḥammad al-Bāqir declares lawful the meat slaughtered by *man dāna bi-kalimat al-Islām*).

414 Barqī, *Maḥāsin*, 158:

> إنّ الله يُدخِل اولئك الجنّة برحمته.
>
> God will place these people in paradise by His mercy.

See also the following statement about non-Shīʿī Muslims quoted from Muḥammad al-Bāqir in Kulaynī, *Kāfī*, 2:19:

> اولئك المحسن منهم يُدخِله الله الجنّة بفضل رحمته.
>
> God will place the righteous among them in paradise by virtue of His mercy.

See also the reports to this effect from the Prophet in Bukhārī, *Ṣaḥīḥ*, nos. 1396–97; Muslim, *Ṣaḥīḥ*, nos. 13–15, and many other sources listed in the editors' footnotes to Aḥmad b. Ḥanbal, *Musnad*, 14:205–6, 25:217–20, 38:532. See further Rabb, "Islamic Legal Minimalism," 153–56; Modarressi, "Essential Islam," 398–412.

415 See Ṭūsī, *Rijāl*, 153–328 (3,224 names altogether). There is also a list in Mizzī, *Tahdhīb al-Kamāl*, 5:75–76. Both lists include the names of the individuals who appear in the chains of transmission of various reports from Jaʿfar al-Ṣādiq, including those in less reliable sources. One must thus be very careful with both lists, as many of these ascriptions are blatant fabrications, as documented later in this chapter.

منصور بن حازم قال: قلت لأبي عبد الله: أخبرني عن أصحاب رسول الله – صلّى الله عليه وآله وسلّم – صدقوا على محمّد – صلّى الله عليه وآله وسلّم – أم كذبوا؟ قال: بل صدقوا. قال: قلت: فما بالهم اختلفوا؟ قال: أما تعلم أنّ الرجل كان يأتي رسول الله – صلّى الله عليه وآله وسلّم – فيسأله عن مسألة فيجيبه فيها بالجواب، ثمّ يجيئه بعد ذلك ما ينسخ ذلك الجواب، فنسخت الأحاديث بعضها بعضاً.[416]

[Manṣūr b. Ḥāzim:] I said to Abū ʿAbd Allāh, "Tell me about the companions of the Messenger of God (may God's prayer and peace be upon him and his Family)—did they speak the truth or lie about Muḥammad (may God's prayer and peace be upon him and his Family)?" He said, "Nay, they spoke the truth." I said, "Then why did they disagree?" He said, "Do you not know that a man would go to the Messenger of God (may God's prayer and peace be upon him and his Family) and ask him about something, and he would give him an answer, and then the Prophet would receive [a revelation] that abrogated that answer, so some *ḥadīth*s abrogated others."

The Prophetic Sunna was subject to abrogation through changing circumstances.[417] A *ḥadīth*, therefore, could reflect the situation before the emergence of conditions that required the Prophet to issue a new command, whereas another, seemingly contradictory *ḥadīth* pertained to the post-change situation.

And as for the following generations of Muslim jurists:

عمر بن أذينة قال: كتبت إلى أبي عبد الله أسأله عن رواية الحسن البصري يرويها عن علي – عليه السلام – في عين ذات الأربع قوائم: إذا فُقئت ربع ثَمَنها؟ قال: صدق الحسن. قد قال علي ذلك.[418]

[ʿUmar b. Udhayna:] I wrote to Abū ʿAbd Allāh asking him about the report that Ḥasan al-Baṣrī narrated from ʿAlī regarding the restitution of one quarter of [an animal's] value for damage inflicted on the eye of a four-legged animal. He said, "Ḥasan spoke the truth. ʿAlī indeed said that."

416 Kulaynī, *Kāfī*, 1:65.

417 See Muslim, *Ṣaḥīḥ*, no. 344. See also Khaṭīb al-Baghdādī, *al-Faqīh wa'l-mutafaqqih*, 1:331–33.

418 Ṭūsī, *Tahdhīb*, 10:309.

أبو خديجة قال: [قلت لأبي عبد الله] إنّ رجلاً مات وترك أخًا عبدًا وأوصى له بألف درهم فأبى مواليه أن يجيزوا له. فارتفعوا إلى عمر بن عبد العزيز. فقال للغلام: ألك ولد؟ قال: نعم! فقال: أحرار؟ قال: أحرار. فقال: ترضي من جميع المال بألف درهمٍ هم يرثون عمّهم؟ فقال أبو عبد الله: أصاب عمر بن عبد العزيز.[419]

[Abū Khadīja:] I said to Abū ʿAbd Allāh, "A man died, leaving behind a slave brother to whom he bequeathed one thousand dirhams, but his [the brother's] patrons did not permit him to receive it. The two sides took the case to ʿUmar b. ʿAbd al-ʿAzīz. He said to the slave, 'Do you have children?' He said, 'Yes!' He said, '[Are they] free?' He said, '[They are] free.' He said, 'Will you be happy if they inherit the one thousand dirhams from their uncle?'" Abū ʿAbd Allāh said, "ʿUmar b. ʿAbd al-ʿAzīz was correct."[420]

أبان بن تغلب قال: قلت لأبي عبد الله: إبراهيم يزعم أنّ دية اليهودي والنصراني والمجوسي سواء. فقال: نعم! قال الحقّ.[421]

[Abān b. Taghlib:] I said to Abū ʿAbd Allāh, "Ibrāhīm says that the blood money for a Jew, a Christian, and a Magian is the same." He said, "Yes! He has spoken the truth."[422]

الحكم قال: قلت لأبي عبد الله: إنّ والدي تصدّق عليّ بدار ثمّ بدا له أن يرجع فيها، وإنّ قضاتنا يقضون أنّها لي وليس له أن يرجع فيها وقد تصدّق بهاعليّ، ولستُ أدرى هل ما يقضون به عليّ من الصواب أم لا؟ فقال: نِعمَ ما قضت به قضاتكم وبئس ما صنع والدك! إنّما الصدقة لله عزوجل، فما جُعل لله فلا رجعة له فيه.[423]

[Ḥakam:] I said to Abū ʿAbd Allāh, "My father gave me a home as a charitable gift and then wanted to change his mind about it. Our [local] judges hold that it belongs to me and that he cannot change his mind, as he gave it to me out of charity. I do not know whether

419 Ṭūsī, *Tahdhīb*, 9:362–27.

420 This case relates to a situation in which the next of kin, such as a brother, cannot inherit from a decedent because of an obstacle such as slave status, and thereby also blocks his own children from inheriting from the deceased (their uncle in this case). This is an issue known in the Islamic law of inheritance as *ḥajb*. See *al-Mawsūʿa al-fiqhiyya* (Kuwait), 3:45–7, 17:22. See also Coulson, *Succession in the Muslim Family*, 43–45.

421 Kulaynī, *Kāfī*, 7:309.

422 Ibrāhīm b. Yazīd al-Nakhaʿī, the eminent jurist of Iraq (d. 96).

423 Ibn Bābawayh, *Faqīh*, 4:183.

their judgment in my favor is correct or not." He said, "How good is the decision of your judges, and how improper was what your father did! Charity is for God, the Mighty and Majestic, and whatever is done for God cannot be taken back."

زرارة قال: [سألت أبا عبد الله عمّا] يروي الناس أنّ الصلاة في جماعة أفضل من صلاة الرجل وحده بخمسة وعشرين صلاة؟ فقال: صدقوا.[424]

[Zurāra:] I asked Abū ʿAbd Allāh about what people [meaning the majority Sunnīs] report to the effect that prayer in congregation is twenty-five times better than prayer alone. He said, "They have spoken the truth."[425]

عبد الله بن سنان قال: شهدت صلاة المغرب ليلة مطيرة في مسجد رسول الله – صلّى الله عليه وآله وسلّم – فحين كان قريباً من الشفق نادوا وأقاموا للصلاة فصلّوا المغرب، ثمّ أمهلوا الناس حتّى صلّوا ركعتين، ثمّ قام المنادي في مكانه في المسجد فأقام للصلاة فصلّوا العشاء، ثمّ انصرف الناس إلى منازلهم. فسألت أبا عبد الله عن ذلك فقال: نعم! قد كان رسول الله – صلّى الله عليه وآله وسلّم – يعمل هذا.[426]

[ʿAbd Allāh b. Sinān:] I attended the *maghrib* prayer on a rainy evening in the Mosque of the Messenger of God (may God's prayer and peace be upon him and his Family). When dusk drew near, they announced [in the form of the *adhān*] and pronounced the call to prayer [in the form of the *iqāma*] and prayed the *maghrib* prayer. People were then given time to pray two *rakʿa*s [of supererogatory prayer]. The muezzin then stood up in his place in the mosque and pronounced the call to prayer, and they prayed the *ʿishāʾ* prayer. People then went home. I asked Abū ʿAbd Allāh about this, and he said, "Yes! The Messenger of God (may God's prayer and peace be upon him and his Family) used to do that."

Jaʿfar al-Ṣādiq's approach in respect to the Companions of the Prophet and the generation after them was informed by that of Jaʿfar's grandfather, ʿAlī b. al-Ḥusayn Zayn al-ʿĀbidīn, as reflected in his prayers:

---

424 Kulaynī, *Kāfī*, 3:371.

425 Bukhārī, *Ṣaḥīḥ*, no. 646 (cf. no. 645 and Muslim, *Ṣaḥīḥ*, no. 650: twenty-seven times [سبعة وعشرين]; Bukhārī, no. 477 and Muslim, no. 649: twenty-odd times [بضعًا وعشرين], one possibly being a corruption of the other).

426 Kulaynī, *Kāfī*, 3:286.

اَللَّهُمَّ وَأَتْبَاعُ الرُّسُلِ وَمُصَدِّقُوهُمْ مِنْ أَهْلِ الاَرْضِ . . . فِي كُلِّ دَهْر وَزَمَان أَرْسَلْتَ فِيْهِ رَسُولاً، وَأَقَمْتَ لأَهْلِهِ دَلِيلاً، مِنْ لَدُنْ آدَمَ إِلَى مُحَمَّد صَلَّى الله عَلَيْهِ وَآلِهِ . . . فَاذْكُرْهُمْ مِنْكَ بِمَغْفِرَة وَرِضْوَانٍ. اَللَّهُمَّ وَأَصْحَابُ مُحَمَّدٍ خَاصَّةً الَّذِينَ أَحْسَنُوا الصَّحَابَةَ، وَالَّذِينَ أَبْلَوْا الْبَلَاءَ الْحَسَنَ فِي نَصْرِهِ . . . واسْتَجَابُوا لَه . . . فَلَا تَنْسَ لَهُمُ اللّهُمّ مَا تَرَكُوا لَكَ وَفِيكَ، وَأَرْضِهِمْ مِنْ رِضْوَانِكَ . . . أللّهُمَّ وَأوْصِلْ إِلَى التَّابِعِينَ لَهُمْ بِإحْسَان الَّذِينَ يَقُولُونَ: ﴿رَبَّنَا اغْفِرْ لَنَا وَلِإِخْوَانِنَا الَّذِينَ سَبَقُونَا بِالْإِيمَانِ﴾ خَيْرَ جَزَائِكَ.[427]

O God, as for the followers of the messengers and those of the people of the earth who attested to them in every era and time in which you sent a messenger and set up for the people a director, from the period of Adam down to Muḥammad (may God's prayer and peace be upon him and his Family), remember them with forgiveness and good pleasure. And as for the Companions of Muḥammad specifically, those who did well in companionship, who stood the good test in helping him and who responded to him, forget not, O God, what they abandoned for You and in You, and make them pleased with Your good pleasure. O God, give your best reward to all those who did well in following the Companions' road, to all those who say "*Our Lord, forgive us and our brothers who went before us in faith*."[428]

In contrast to some Muslims at the time who would not pray with anyone who did not belong to their own group or harbored different doctrinal tendencies,[429] Jaʿfar al-Ṣādiq attended the Friday prayer with other Muslims[430] and insisted that his followers attend the prayers[431] and participate in the social events of the main body of the Muslim community:

427 ʿAlī b. al-Ḥusayn Zayn al-ʿĀbidīn, *al-Ṣaḥifa al-kāmila al-Sajjādiyya*, prayer no. 4.

428 From Qurʾān 59:10. The translation is adapted with minor changes from William Chittick, *The Psalms of Islam*, 26–28.

429 For early opinions on this question, see Ibn Qudāma, *Mughnī*, 3:17–18.

430 See, for instance, Ṭūsī, *Tahdhīb*, 2:362.

431 There was a tendency in the early community to support this position, as reflected in a *ḥadīth* in Dāraquṭnī, *Sunan*, 2:402 (see also Ṭabarānī, *al-Muʿjam al-kabīr*, 12:447, and other sources quoted in the editor's footnote in Haythamī, *Majmaʿ al-zawāʾid*, 4:500–501):

صلّوا على من قال لا إله إلّا الله وصلّوا خلف من قال لا إله إلّا الله.

Pray over [the body of] anyone who says "There is no deity but God," and pray behind anyone who says "There is no deity but God."

الحسين بن سعيد عن أبي علي قال: قلت لأبي عبد الله: إنّ لنا إماماً مخالفاً وهو يبغض أصحابَنا كلّهم. قال: ما عليك من قوله؟ والله لئن كنتَ صادقاً لأنت أحقّ بالمسجد منه، فكُن أوّل داخل وآخر خارج، وأحسن خُلقك مع الناس وقُل خيراً.[432]

[Ḥusayn b. Saʿīd:] I said to Abū ʿAbd Allāh, "We have a dissenting prayer leader who hates all of our associates." He said, "Why should you care about what he says? By God, if you are truthful, then you have more right to the mosque than him. Be the first to enter [the mosque] and the last to leave, improve your character with the people, and speak nicely."

معاوية بن وهب عن أبي عبد الله قال: سألته عن الرجل يؤمّ القوم وأنت لا ترضى به في صلاة يجهر فيها بالقرائة؟ فقال: إذا سمعت كتاب الله يتلى فأنصت له. قلت: فإنّه يشهد عليّ بالشرك. قال: إن عصى الله فأطع الله. فرددت عليه فأبى أن يرخّص لي.[433]

[Muʿāwiya b. Wahb:] I asked Abū ʿAbd Allāh about a man who leads people in prayer but about whom you have reservations; [what should one do] in a prayer in which he recites aloud?[434] He said, "When you hear the Book of God being recited, keep silent."[435] I said, "He testifies that I associate partners with God." He said, "If he disobeys God, you must obey God." I repeated what I said to him, but he refused to grant me a dispensation.

معاوية بن وهب قال: قلت لأبي عبد الله: كيف ينبغى لنا أن نصنع في ما بيننا وبين قومنا وفي ما بيننا وبين خلطائنا من الناس [ممّن ليسوا على أمرنا]؟ قال: تنظرون إلى أئمّتكم الّذين تقتدون بهم فتصنعون ما يصنعون، فوالله إنّهم ليعودون مرضاهم، ويشهدون جنائزهم، ويقيمون الشهادة لهم وعليهم، ويؤدّون الأمانة إليهم.[436]

432 Ṭūsī, *Tahdhīb*, 3:55.

433 Ṭūsī, *Tahdhīb*, 3:35. Cf. Ibn Bābawayh, *Faqīh*, 1:249:

لا تصلّ خلف من يشهد عليك بالكفر ولا خلف من شهدتَ عليه بالكفر.

Do not pray behind anyone who declares you to be a nonbeliever, nor behind anyone whom you declare to be a nonbeliever.

Different instructions were naturally due to different circumstances.

434 The question at issue is whether one should quietly repeat the recitations of Qurʾānic verses in prayer when the prayer leader misreads them or is not qualified to lead the prayer because of insufficient religiosity, as explained further in the *fiqh* chapters on prayer. See further Kulaynī, *Kāfī*, 3:377.

435 As in Qurʾān 7:204.

436 Kulaynī, *Kāfī*, 2:635, 636 (two slightly different variants of the same text).

[Muʿāwiya b. Wahb:] I said to Abū ʿAbd Allāh, "What should we do with regard to what is between us and our people, and what is between us and people who intermingle with us but who are not in agreement with us [in matters of doctrine]?" He said, "Look to your *imāms* whom you follow, and do what they do. By God, they visit their [opponents'] sick ones, attend their funerals, give testimony [in their support, whether] for something or against something, and return to them what they hold in trust for them."

إسحاق بن عمّار قال: قال لي أبو عبد الله: يا إسحاق! أتصلّي معهم في المسجد؟ قلت: نعم! قال: صلّ معهم فإنّ المصلّى معهم في الصفّ الأوّل كالشاهر سيفه في سبيل الله.[437]

[Isḥāq b. ʿAmmār:] Abū ʿAbd Allāh said to me, "O Isḥāq! Do you pray with these people in the mosque?" I said, "Yes!" He said, "Pray with them, for whosoever prays with them in the first row is like someone who takes up arms in the way of God."

الحلبي عن أبي عبد الله قال: من صلّى معهم في الصفّ الأوّل كان كمن صلّى خلف رسول الله – صلّى الله عليه وآله وسلّم –[438] [في الصفّ الأوّل].[439]

[ʿUbayd Allāh al-Ḥalabī:] Abū ʿAbd Allāh said, "Whoever prays with these people in the first row is like someone who prays behind the Messenger of God (may God's prayer and peace be upon him and his Family) in the first row."

Once, when he noticed that some of his followers left the mosque and did not participate in the prayer with other Muslims, he sent this angry message to them through one of his associates:

عن يونس بن يعقوب قال: قال لي أبو عبد الله: يا يونس! قل لهم: يا مؤلَّفة! قد رأيت ما تصنعون. إذا سمعتم الأذان أخذتم نعالكم وخرجتم من المسجد؟[440]

437 Ṭūsī, *Tahdhīb*, 3:277.
438 Kulaynī, *Kāfī*, 3:380.
439 Ibn Bābawayh, *Amālī*, 449; Ibn Bābawayh, *Faqīh*, 1:250–51.
440 Kashshī, *Rijāl*, 388.

[Yūnus b. Yaʿqūb:] Abū ʿAbd Allāh said to me, "O Yūnus! Say to them, 'O you, *those whose hearts are reconciled*, I saw what you did. When you hear the call to prayer, you take your sandals and leave the mosque?'"[441]

سعيد الأعرج قال: دخلت على أبي عبد الله وهو مُغضب وعنده نفر من أصحابنا وهو يقول: تصلّون قبل أن تزول الشمس؟ وهم سُكوت. فقلت: أصلحك الله! ما نصلّي حتّى يؤذّن مؤذّن مكّة. قال: فلا بأس. أما إنّه إذا أذّن فقد زالت الشمس.[442]

[Saʿīd al-Aʿraj:] I came upon Abū ʿAbd Allāh while he was upset. A group of our companions were sitting with him and he was saying to them, "You pray before the sun has passed its zenith?" They were silent. I said, "May God put you on the right path! We do not pray until the muezzin of Mecca pronounces the call to prayer." He said, "If so, there is no problem. Know that when he pronounces the call to prayer, then the sun has passed its zenith."

ذريح المحاربي قال: قال لي أبو عبد الله: صلّ الجمعة بأذان هؤلاء فإنّهم أشدّ شيءٍ مواظبةً على الوقت.[443]

[Dharīḥ al-Muḥāribī:] Abū ʿAbd Allāh said to me, "Pray the Friday prayer when these people pronounce the call to prayer, for they strictly adhere to the time."

Some of his visiting followers did not participate in congregational prayers in Mecca and Medina, because they shortened their prayers by half as travelers are supposed to do. They were, however, reluctant to break the prayer rows by finishing and leaving early. According to Jaʿfarī law, a Muslim has a choice to pray a full or a shortened prayer in the two sacred precincts of Mecca and Medina. The Imam thus ordered his visiting followers to take the first option and offer the full prayer so they could participate in the communal prayers without problem.

441 That is, المؤلّفة قلوبهم, which is the title used in Qurʾān 9:60 to refer to certain groups of non-Muslims who lived among the Muslim community in the early Islamic period.

442 ʿAyyāshī, *Tafsīr*, 3:72.

443 Ṭūsī, *Tahdhīb*, 2:284 (also Ibn Bābawayh, *Faqīh*, 1:189, without an *isnād*). For a similar case, see Ṭūsī, 5:207, where a follower asks Jaʿfar about buying sheep for sacrifice from non-Shīʿī sellers at ʿArafāt if one cannot be sure that the seller has met the legal requirements of raising and preparing the animal for sacrifice. The Imam answers, "They do not lie. Use the sheep for sacrifice." (See also Kulaynī, *Kāfī*, 4:508 for another case.)

معاوية بن وهب قال: سألت أبا عبد الله عن التقصير في الحرمين والتمام، فقال: لا تتمّ حتّى تجمع على مقام عشرة أيّام. فقلت: إنّ أصحابنا رووا عنك أنّك أمرتهم بالتمام. فقال: إنّ أصحابك كانوا يدخلون المسجد فيصلّون ويأخذون نعالهم ويخرجون والناس يستقبلونهم يدخلون المسجد للصلاة، فأمرتهم بالتمام.[444]

[Muʿāwiya b. Wahb:] I asked Abū ʿAbd Allāh about performing the prayers in full or shortening them [by half] in the two sacred precincts. He said, "[It is preferable that you] do not pray them in full unless you decide to stay for ten days." I said, "Our companions reported that you ordered them to pray in full." He said, "Your companions would enter the mosque, pray, and take their sandals and leave while people were coming to enter into the mosque for prayer, so I ordered them to pray in full."

Muslims in Jaʿfar's time could still accept one another and tolerate diversity within their community, a tendency that persisted to some degree throughout the early Islamic period, especially in Kūfa. A number of reports from Jaʿfar al-Ṣādiq suggest that he encouraged this attitude. To give an example, an Iraqi follower of his met him in Ḥīra, near Kūfa, right after the Abbasid takeover and referred to a discussion that he and his fellow Shīʿa had had about an unnamed Muslim group:

ثمّ جرى ذكر قوم فقلت: جعلت فداك! إنّا نتبرّأ منهم. إنّهم لا يقولون ما نقول. فقال: يتولّونا ولا يقولون ما تقولون، تتبرّؤون منهم؟ قلت: نعم! قال: فهو ذا عندنا ما ليس عندكم فينبغى لنا أن نتبرّأ منكم؟ قلت: لا، جعلت فداك! ما نفعل؟ قال: تولّوهم ولا تتبرّؤوا منهم.[445]

Then a group of people were mentioned, so I said, "May I be made your ransom! We disassociate ourselves from them. They do not hold the positions we do." He said, "They have affection for us but do not adopt your views, so you disassociate yourselves from them?" I said, "Yes!" He said, "Well, I hold views that are different from those you hold, so should I disassociate from you?" I said, "No! May I be made your ransom! What should we do [then]?" He said, "Take them as friends and do not disassociate from them."

444 Ṭūsī, *Tahdhīb*, 5:428 with a variant in Ibn Bābawayh, *ʿIlal al-sharāʾiʿ*, 2:139.
445 Kulaynī, *Kāfī*, 2:43.

A third-century Zaydī-Muʿtazilī scholar of Kūfa, Muḥammad b. Manṣūr al-Murādī, explained this idea in a book called *Kitāb al-Jumla wa'l-ulfa*.[446] In the following passage, he describes the spirit of acceptance of diversity that existed in his town thanks to the teachings and precedent of his predecessors, as well as his own earlier experience with Kūfan scholars:

رأيت أحمد بن عيسى يترحّم على من يقول بخلق القرآن ومن لا يقول به. ورأيت المتفرّقين وعاشرت المختلفين من الخاصّة والعامّة من علماء آل الرسول وأهل الفضل منهم، ومن غيرهم من أهل العلم والفضل من الشيعة الموجِبين لإنكار المنكر وحياطة الدين، فما رأيتهم يكفّر بعضهم بعضًا ولا يستحلّون ذلك ولا يتبرّأ بعضهم من بعض، بل قد رأيت بعضهم يتولّى بعضًا ويترحّم عليه بعد المعرفة منهم بمخالفة بعضهم لبعض. وقد عاشرت رؤساء المعتزلة ومن لا أحصى منهم ممّن يقول بهذا القول (يعني خلق القرآن)، منهم جعفر بن حرب وجعفر بن مبشّر الثقفي ومحمّد بن عبد الله الإسكافي، فما سألني أحد منهم قطّ عمّا يختلف الناس فيه ولا كاشفوني عن شيئ من ذلك. وكذلك سمعنا عن إبراهيم بن عبد الله أنّه سُئل عن معنى ما يختلف الناس فيه على مذاهب، فلم يجبه وقال: أعينوني على ما اجتمعنا عليه حتّى نتفرّغ فيه لما اختلفنا. ورُوي عن جعفر الصادق أنّه قال: ألزم ما اجتمع عليه المتفرّقون.[447]

I saw Aḥmad b. ʿĪsā[448] asking God to bless with His mercy those who argued that the Qurʾān was created as well as those who rejected this view. And I saw people who were divided and disagreed [with one another] among both the elect and the common scholars of the House of the Prophet as well as the people of merit among them, and other people of knowledge and merit among the Shīʿa, who believed in the obligatoriness of forbidding wrong and protecting the religion. I did not, however, see them declare one another disbelievers or deem doing so to be permissible, nor did they disassociate themselves from one another. Instead, I saw them support each other and each ask God to bless the other with His mercy while knowing of disagreement among them. And I kept company with the leaders of the Muʿtazilīs and countless others who held this view [that is, that the Qurʾān was created] such as Jaʿfar b. Ḥarb, Jaʿfar b. Mubashshir al-Thaqafī, and Muḥammad

446 The work itself has not survived in its complete form, but the bulk of its contents is said to have been quoted by an early fifth-century scholar of Kūfa, Abū ʿAbd Allāh al-ʿAlawī, in a supplement to his *al-Jāmiʿ al-kāfī*.

447 Ibn al-Wazīr, *Tarjīḥ asālīb al-Qurʾān*, 27–31.

448 Aḥmad b. ʿĪsā b. Zayd b. ʿAlī b. al-Ḥusayn, a major authority of Zaydī *ḥadīth*. He died in 247.

b. ʿAbd Allāh al-Iskāfī.[449] None of them ever asked me about what people disagreed over, nor ever attempted to uncover my belief about any of that. We also heard as much about Ibrāhīm b. ʿAbd Allāh,[450] who was once asked about the nature of that about which people disagreed in the different schools, but he did not answer and said, "Support me on matters on which we all agree until we find free time for matters about which we disagree." And it is reported from Jaʿfar al-Ṣādiq that he said, "Adhere to what the differing groups agree on."[451]

VII. On *Ḥadīth* Fabrication

A widespread phenomenon in the sectarian milieu of the first two centuries of Islam was the fabrication of reports on the Prophet and early authorities of the Islamic tradition—a problem that has plagued the field of *ḥadīth* since its birth.[452] Fabricated *ḥadīths* made their way into religious culture and many entered the *ḥadīth* collections.[453] Jaʿfar al-Ṣādiq, like his father, constantly complained about and condemned this phenomenon. Here are a few reactions from Jaʿfar:

قيل لأبي عبد الله: إنّ الناس يقولون إنّ القرآن نزل على سبعة أحرف، فقال: كذبوا.
نزل حرفٌ واحد من عند ربٍّ واحد على نبيٍّ واحد.[454]

---

449 These were three of the leading theologians in the Muʿtazilī community of Baghdad in the first half of the third century. Jaʿfar b. Ḥarb died in 236, Jaʿfar b. Mubashshir in 234, and Iskāfī in 240.

450 Ibrāhīm b. ʿAbd Allāh b. al-Ḥasan, brother of Nafs al-Zakiyya, who also led a revolt against the Abbasid Manṣūr. He was killed in 145.

451 For the report from Jaʿfar al-Ṣādiq at the end of the excerpt, see further his advice to one of his close disciples, Jamīl b. Darrāj al-Nakhaʿī (on whom, see Modarressi, *Tradition and Survival*, 1:307–8), cited in Kashshī, *Rijāl*, 251:

يا جميل! لا تحدّث أصحابنا بما لم يجمعوا عليه.

O Jamīl! Do not talk to our companions about what they have not all agreed upon.

452 The phenomenon began very early in the life of the Muslim community. See, for instance, the introduction to Muslim, *Ṣaḥīḥ* (ed. Muḥammad Fu'ād ʿAbd al-Bāqī, Cairo, [1955]), 13, where Muslim quotes Ibn ʿAbbās as follows:

إنّا كنّا نحدّث عن رسول الله – صلّى الله عليه وسلّم – إذ لم يكن يكذَب عليه، فلمّا ركب الناس الصعب والذلول تركنا الحديث عنه.

We used to narrate on the authority of the Messenger of God (may God's prayer and peace be upon him) at a time when one would not lie about him. However, when the people began to look everywhere [for anything attributed to him], we abandoned quoting *ḥadīth* on his authority.

453 See, inter alia, Ibn ʿAbd al-Barr, *Tamhīd*, 1:44–55, where he estimates that some twelve thousand false *ḥadīths* were fabricated, attributed to the Prophet, and circulated among the people.

454 Sayyārī, *Qirā'āt*, 6, with a variant in Kulaynī, *Kāfī*, 2:630.

It was said to Abū ʿAbd Allāh, "People say that the Qurʾān was revealed in seven forms." He said, "They lied. Only one form was revealed by one Lord to [this] one Prophet."

الفضل بن أبي قرّة قال: قلت لأبي عبد الله: هؤلاء يقولون إنّ كسب المعلّم سحت. فقال: كذبوا أعداءُ الله! إنّما أرادوا أن لا يعلّموا [أولادَهم] القرآن. ولو أنّ رجلاً أعطى المعلّم دية ولده لكان للمعلّم حلالاً.[455]

[Al-Faḍl b. Abī Qurra:] I said to Abū ʿAbd Allāh, "These people say that the payment a teacher receives for his teaching is ill-gotten." He said, "The enemies of God lied! They wish to avoid teaching their children the Qurʾān. Were someone to give a teacher even the [value of] the blood-money compensation for his child, it would be lawful for the teacher to take it."

عبد الرحمن بن أبي عبد الله قال: قلت لأبي عبد الله: إنّ ناسًا من هؤلاء القصّاص يقولون إذا حجّ الرجل حجّةً ثمّ تصدّق ووصل كان خيرًا له. قال: كذبوا. لو فعل هذا الناس لعُطّل هذا البيت. إنّ الله جعل هذا البيت ﴿قِيَامًا لِلنَّاسِ﴾.[456]

[ʿAbd al-Raḥmān b. Abī ʿAbd Allāh:] I said to Abū ʿAbd Allāh, "Some of these storytellers [street preachers] say that if a man performs the *ḥajj* once and then donates and gives money [to others], it is better for him [than performing the *ḥajj* again would be]." He said, "They lied. If people did that, this House [of God] would be abandoned. God made this House 'an establishment for humankind.'"[457]

عبد الأعلى قال: سألت أبا عبد الله عن الغناء وقلت: إنّهم يزعمون أنّ رسول الله – صلّى الله عليه وآله وسلّم – رخّص في أن يقال: «جئناكم جئناكم، حيّونا حيّونا نحيّيكم». فقال: كذبوا. إنّ الله عزّ وجلّ يقول: ﴿وَمَا خَلَقْنَا السَّمَاءَ وَالْأَرْضَ وَمَا بَيْنَهُمَا لَاعِبِينَ﴾.[458]

[ʿAbd al-Aʿlā b. Aʿyan:] I asked Abū ʿAbd Allāh about singing and said, "They claim that the Messenger of God (may God's prayer and peace be

455 Kulaynī, *Kāfī*, 5:121, and with adaptations from a slightly different version in Ibn Bābawayh, *Faqīh*, 3:99.
456 Ibn Bābawayh, *ʿIlal al-sharāʾiʿ*, 2:137.
457 The concluding phrase is from Qurʾān 5:97.
458 Kulaynī, *Kāfī*, 6:433.

upon him and his Family) permitted people to sing the song 'We have come to you / we have come to you / greet us / greet us / we greet you.'" He said, "They lied. God, the Mighty and Majestic, says, 'We did not create the heavens and earth and what is between them in jest.'"[459]

عثمان بن عيسى عن شيخ من أهل المدينة قال: سألت أبا عبد الله عن الرجل يشرب الماء فلا يقطع نفَسه حتّى يروى؟ قال: وهل اللّذة إلّا ذاك؟ قلت: فانّهم يقولون إنّه «شرب الهيم». قال: كذبوا. إنّما «شرب الهيم» ما لم يذكر اسم الله عزّ وجلّ عليه.[460]

['Uthmān b. 'Īsā:] I asked Abū 'Abd Allāh about a man who gulps water without stopping until his thirst is quenched. He said, "Isn't that pleasant?" I said, "They say it is 'ecstatic drinking' [condemned[461] in Qur'ān 56:55]." He said, "They lied. 'Ecstatic drinking' is when one does not mention the name of God, the Mighty and Majestic, upon drinking."

محمّد بن الفيض قال: قلت لأبي عبد الله: إنّ هؤلاء يقولون إنّ العدس قدّس عليه ثمانون نبيًّا. قال: كذبوا.[462]

[Muḥammad b. al-Fayḍ:] I said to Abū 'Abd Allāh, "These people say that eighty prophets blessed lentils as sacred."[463] He said, "They lied."

عبد الصمد بن بشير قال: ذُكر عند أبي عبد الله بدء الأذان وأنّ رجلاً من الأنصار رأى في منامه الأذان فقصّه على رسول الله – صلّى الله عليه وآله وسلّم – وأمره رسول الله – صلّى الله عليه وآله وسلّم – أن يعلّمه بلالاً. فقال: كذبوا.[464]

['Abd al-Ṣamad b. Bashīr:] The origin of the call to prayer was mentioned in the presence of Abū 'Abd Allāh along with [the report] that a man from the Anṣār had a dream about it that he then mentioned to the Messenger of God (may God's prayer and peace be upon him and his Family), and the Messenger of God (may God's prayer and peace

459 Qur'ān 21:16.

460 Kulaynī, *Kāfī*, 6:384.

461 For early opinions against this practice, see Ibn Abī Shayba, *Muṣannaf*, 8:159.

462 Barqī, *Maḥāsin*, 504; Kulaynī, *Kāfī*, 4:344 (cf. Barqī, 505; Kulaynī, 6:342).

463 For Sunnī reports on this case, which normally mention seventy prophets rather than eighty, including one that claims the authority of Ja'far al-Ṣādiq (!), see Ibn al-Jawzī, *Mawḍū'āt*, 3:113–14; Fattanī, *Tadhkirat al-mawḍū'āt*, 147, and the early collections of *ḥadīth* cited in these two works.

464 'Ayyāshī, *Tafsīr*, 1:285.

be upon him and his Family) told him to teach it to Bilāl. He [Jaʿfar al-Ṣādiq] said, "They lied."[465]

سيابة عن أبي عبد الله قال: سأله رجل فقال له: جُعلت فداك! أسمع قومًا يقولون إنّ الزراعة مكروهة. فقال له: ازرعوا واغرسوا، فلا والله ماعمل الناس عملاً أحلّ ولا أطيب منه.[466]

[Sayāba b. Ayyūb:] A man questioned Abū ʿAbd Allāh, saying, "May I be made your ransom! I hear a group of people saying that farming is disfavored." He said to him, "Cultivate and plant, for by God there is no work that is more lawful and pleasant than it."[467]

عمرو بن سفيان الجرجاني رفعه إلى أبي عبد الله قال: سأل أحدَ مواليه فقال: ما لك لا تخرج؟ قال: اليوم الأحد. قال: وما للأحد؟ قال: للحديث الّذي جاء عن النبي – صلّى الله عليه وآله وسلّم: «إحذروا حدّ الأحد فإنّ له حدًّا مثل هذا السيف». قال: كذبوا! كذبوا! ما قال ذلك رسول الله.[468]

[ʿAmr b. Sufyān al-Jurjānī:] Abū ʿAbd Allāh asked one of his associates, "Why are you not leaving on your travels?" He said, "Today is Sunday." He said, "And what is wrong with Sunday?" He said, "Because of the *ḥadīth* reported from the Prophet (may God's prayer and peace be upon him and his Family), 'Beware of the sharpness of Sunday, for it is sharp like this sword.'"[469] He said, "They lied! They lied! The Messenger of God did not say that."

---

465 See also the statement from Jaʿfar al-Ṣādiq in Kulaynī, *Kāfī*, 3:482, where he blames those who ascribe the *adhān* to a dream, saying, "The religion of God is too honorable for it to be dreamed of in one's sleep." The point will be discussed further in Chapter 3.

466 Kulaynī, *Kāfī*, 5:260.

467 See Yaḥyā b. Ādam, *Kharāj*, 80; Shaybānī, *Iktisāb*, 36–37; Bukhārī, *Ṣaḥīḥ*, no. 6912; Abū Dāwūd, *Sunan*, no. 3462. See also Ibn Ḥazm, *Muḥallā*, 8:210; Sarakhsī, *Uṣūl*, 1:108, 2:292; Dhahabī, *Mīzān al-iʿtidāl*, 4:336.

468 Ibn Bābawayh, *Khiṣāl*, 383.

469 As is clear to those who know Arabic, this proposition was based on the phonetic similarity of the Arabic words *ḥadd* (sharpness) and *aḥad* (Sunday).

عبيد بن زرارة قال: قلت لأبي عبد الله: إنّ الناس يروون أنّ عليًا كتب إلى عامله بالمدائن أن يشترى له جارية فاشتراها وبعث بها إليه، وكتب أنّ لها زوجًا، فكتب إليه علي أن يشترى بُضعها، فاشتراه. قال: كذبوا على علي. أعلي يقول هذا؟[470]

['Ubayd b. Zurāra:] I said to Abū 'Abd Allāh, "People relate that 'Alī wrote to his governor in Ctesiphon asking him to buy him ['Alī] a [certain] slave woman. He [the governor] did, sent her to 'Alī, and wrote to him that she had a husband. 'Alī then wrote to him to purchase sexual access to her. He [the governor] purchased that." He said, "They lied about 'Alī. Would 'Alī say that?"[471]

عمرو بن شمر قال: قلت لجعفر بن محمّد: جعلت فداك! إنّا نتحدّث بالعراق أنّ عليًا صلّى على سهل بن حنيف فكبّرعليه ستًّا. فقال جعفر: إنّه لم يكن كذا ولكنّه كبّر عليه خمسًا.[472]

['Amr b. Shimr:] I said to Ja'far b. Muḥammad, "May I be made your ransom! We keep mentioning among ourselves in Iraq that 'Alī prayed [the funeral prayer] over Sahl b. Ḥunayf,[473] saying six *takbīrs* over his body."[474] Ja'far said, "That was not so; he rather said five *takbīrs* over him."

رباح بن أبي نصر قال: قلت لأبي عبد الله: إنّا نُروى بالكوفة أنّ عليًا قال: إنّ من تمام حجّك إحرامك من دُويرة أهلك. فقال: سبحان الله! لو كان كما يقولون لِمَ استمتعَ رسول الله بثيابه إلى الشجرة؟[475]

---

470 Kulaynī, *Kāfī*, 5:483–84.

471 See 'Abd al-Razzāq, *Muṣannaf*, 7:281–82; Sa'īd b. Manṣūr, *Sunan*, 4:63 (nos. 1949–50); Ibn Abī Shayba, *Muṣannaf*, 6:457 for three variants of this narrative. None of these variants, however, suggested that 'Alī himself requested the purchase of sexual access to the slave woman. The full story as cited above is attributed to 'Umar in Sa'īd b. Manṣūr, 4:64 (no. 1951) (partially also in Ibn Abī Shayba, 6:456).

472 Ṭūsī, *Tahdhīb*, 3:317.

473 A companion of the Prophet who attended the Battle of Badr with him, and an associate of 'Alī whom 'Alī appointed governor of Medina and then Baṣra. He died in Kūfa in 38.

474 'Abd al-Razzāq, *Muṣannaf*, 3:480–81; Ibn Abī Shayba, *Muṣannaf*, 4:501–2.

475 'Āṣim b. Ḥumayd al-Ḥannāṭ, *Kitāb*, 152 (also Kulaynī, *Kāfī*, 4:322; Ṭūsī, *Tahdhīb*, 5:59, both with variations). A report in Ibn Bābawayh, *Ma'ānī al-akhbār*, 382 ascribes a variant of this to Muḥammad al-Bāqir with this ending:

> إنّ رسول الله – صلّى الله عليه وآله وسلّم – كان من أهل المدينة ووقته من ذي الحليفة وإنّما كان بينهما ستّة أميال. ولو كان فضلاً لأحرم رسول الله – صلّى الله عليه وآله وسلّم – من المدينة.
>
> The Messenger of God (may God's prayer and peace be upon him and his Family) was one of the people of Medina, and his station [for entering the state of pilgrim sanctity] was Dhū al-Ḥulayfa, and between them was six miles. Had it been

[Rabāḥ b. Abī Naṣr:] I said to Abū ʿAbd Allāh, "We keep hearing in Kūfa that ʿAlī said, 'Part of the perfection of your *ḥajj* is to enter the state of pilgrim sanctity in your family home.'" He said, "Praise be to God! If it were as they say, why did the Prophet keep his [usual] clothes on until he reached [the Mosque of] Shajara?"

أبو بصير عن أبي عبد الله قال: دخل عليّ أناس من أهل البصرة فسألوني عن مال اليتيم هل عليه زكاةٌ؟ قال: قلت لهم: لا! فقالوا: إنّا نتحدّث عندنا أنّ عمر سأل عليّاً عن مال أبي رافع، فقال: أنفد به الزكاة. فقلت لهم: لا، وربّ الكعبة! ما ترك أبو رافع يتيماً.[476]

[Abū Baṣīr:] Abū ʿAbd Allāh said, "Some people from Baṣra came to me and asked whether the property of an orphan is subject to *zakāt*. I said to them, 'No!' They said, 'But we report among ourselves that ʿUmar asked ʿAlī about the wealth of Abū Rāfiʿ and ʿAlī replied, "*Zakāt* finished it off."' I said to them, 'No, by the Lord of the Kaʿba! Abū Rāfiʿ did not leave behind any orphan.'"[477]

عبد الرحمن بن الحجّاج قال: قلت لأبي عبد الله: إنّي أدخل سوق المسلمين فأشترى منهم الفراء للتجارة فأقول لصاحبها: أليس هي ذكيّة؟ فيقول: بلى! فهل يصلح لي أن أبيعها على أنّها ذكيّة؟ قال: لا! قلت: وما أفسد ذلك؟ قال: إستحلال أهل العراق للميتة فزعموا أنّ دباغ جلد الميتة ذكاته، ثمّ لم يرضوا إلّا أن يكذبوا في ذلك على رسول الله.[478]

[ʿAbd al-Raḥmān b. al-Ḥajjāj:] I said to Abū ʿAbd Allāh, "I go to the market of the Muslims and buy from them fur cloaks for trade. I ask the seller: 'Are they not ritually clean?' He says, 'Yes, indeed!' Is it all right if I sell the cloaks as ritually clean?" He said, "No!" I said, "What makes this illicit?" He said, "The reason is that the people of Iraq consider carrion lawful to use, as they maintain that tanning the hide of carrion makes it ritually clean. And they are not satisfied [with anything] short of attributing this lie to the Messenger of God."

meritorious, the Messenger of God (may God's prayer and peace be upon him his Family) would have entered the state of pilgrim sanctity in Medina.

476 ʿĀṣim b. Ḥumayd al-Ḥannāṭ, *Kitāb*, 171.

477 For similar responses from Muḥammad al-Bāqir and Zayd b. ʿAlī b. al-Ḥusayn, see Zayd b. ʿAlī, *Musnad*, 138; Aḥmad b. ʿĪsā, *Amālī*, 2:297 (partially also in Ṭūsī, *Tahdhīb*, 4:27).

478 Kulaynī, *Kāfī*, 3:398.

معاوية بن وهب قال: قلت لأبي عبد الله: إنّ الناس يروون عن رسول الله – صلّى الله عليه وآله وسلّم – أنّ الصدقة لا تحلّ لغنيّ ولا لذى مرّةٍ سويّ. فقال: قد قال «لغنيّ» ولم يقل «لذى مرّةٍ سويّ».[479]

[Muʿāwiya b. Wahb:] I said to Abū ʿAbd Allāh, "People narrate that the Messenger of God (may God's prayer and peace be upon him and his Family) said, '*Zakāt* is not lawful [to receive] for either a wealthy person or a strong, healthy individual.'"[480] He said, "He [the Prophet] said 'for a wealthy person,' but he did not say 'for a strong, healthy individual.'"

أبو العبّاس قال: قلت لأبي عبد الله: حرّم رسول الله – صلّى الله عليه وآله وسلّم – المدينة؟ قال: نعم! حرّم بريدًا في بريد، غضاها. قلت: صيدها؟ قال: لا! يكذب الناس.[481]

[Faḍl b. ʿAbd al-Malik al-Baqbāq, Abū al-ʿAbbās:] I said to Abū ʿAbd Allāh, "Did the Messenger of God (may God's prayer and peace be upon him and his Family) declare Medina to be a sacred precinct?" He said, "Yes! He declared sacred the shrubs of Medina within a some twelve-mile radius." I said, "[What about] hunting?" he said, "No; people lie."

سعيد الأعرج قال: سمعت أبا عبد الله يقول: طلّق ابن عمر امرأته ثلاثًا. فسأل عمر رسول الله – صلّى الله عليه وآله وسلّم – فأمره أن يراجعها. فقلت: إنّ الناس يقولون إنّما طلّقها واحدة وهي حائض. قال: فلأيّ شيء سأل رسولَ الله – صلّى الله عليه وآله وسلّم – إذا كان هو أملك برجعتها؟ كذبوا. ولكنّه طلّقها ثلاثًا فأمره رسول الله – صلّى الله عليه وآله وسلّم – أن يراجعها.[482]

[Saʿīd al-Aʿraj:] I heard Abū ʿAbd Allāh say, "Ibn ʿUmar divorced his wife in a triple divorce, so ʿUmar asked the Messenger of God (may God's prayer and peace be upon him and his Family) about it, and he ordered him [Ibn ʿUmar] to take her back." I said, "People say that he divorced her once while she was menstruating."[483] He said, "So why

479 Ibn Bābawayh, *Faqīh*, 3:109, with a variant in Kulaynī, *Kāfī*, 3:563.

480 Abū Dāwūd, *Sunan*, no. 4361; Tirmidhī, *Sunan*, no. 652; Nasāʾī, *Sunan*, no. 2596.

481 Kulaynī, *Kāfī*, 4:365.

482 Kulaynī, *Kāfī*, 6:59; see also variants at 6:60–61; Ibn Bābawayh, *Faqīh*, 3:320.

483 See especially Dāraquṭnī, *Sunan*, 5:14–22, who has collected the largest number of Sunnī reports on the event.

then did he ask the Messenger of God (may God's prayer and peace be upon him and his Family) if he had an [indisputable] right to take her back? They lied. He divorced her in a triple divorce, so the Messenger of God (may God's prayer and peace be upon him and his Family) ordered him to take her back."

In the last case, Jaʿfar was following his father's precedent by taking a tough stance against those he believed were misleading the community with their false testimonies:

عن زرارة قال: كنت عنده (يعني أبا جعفر) إذ مرّ به نافع مولى ابن عمر فقال له أبو جعفر: أنت الّذي تزعم أنّ ابن عمر طلّق إمرأته واحدة وهي حائض فأمر رسول الله – صلّى الله عليه وآله وسلّم – عمر أن يأمره أن يراجعها؟ قال: نعم! فقال له: كذبتَ – والله الّذي لا إله إلّا هو – على ابن عمر. أنا سمعت ابن عمر يقول: طلّقتُها على عهد رسول الله – صلّى الله عليه وآله وسلّم – ثلاثًا فردّها رسول الله – صلّى الله عليه وآله وسلّم – عليّ وأمسكتها بعد الطلاق. فاتّق الله يا نافع، ولاتَرْوِ على ابن عمر الباطل.[484]

[Zurāra:] I was with him [Abū Jaʿfar Muḥammad al-Bāqir] when Nāfiʿ, the client of Ibn ʿUmar, passed by. Abū Jaʿfar said to him, "Are you the one who claims that Ibn ʿUmar divorced his wife once while she was menstruating, and that the Messenger of God (may God's prayer and peace be upon him and his Family) ordered ʿUmar to order him [that is, his son] to take her back?" He said, "Yes!" He [Muḥammad al-Bāqir] said to him, "By God who is the only god, you attributed a falsehood to Ibn ʿUmar. I heard Ibn ʿUmar say: 'I divorced her during the time of the Messenger of God (may God's prayer and peace be upon him and his Family) in a triple divorce, and the Messenger of God (may God's prayer and peace be upon him and his Family) returned her to me and I remained with her after the divorce.' Fear God, O Nāfiʿ, and do not report falsely on the authority of Ibn ʿUmar."[485]

---

484 Kulaynī, *Kāfī*, 6:61.

485 For another instance in which Nāfiʿ was accused of quoting ʿAbd Allāh b. ʿUmar incorrectly by such distinguished jurists as Saʿīd b. Jubayr, Sālim b. ʿAbd Allāh b. ʿUmar, and ʿAbd Allāh b. ʿAbd al-Raḥmān b. Zayd b. al-Khaṭṭāb, see Ṭabarī, *Jāmiʿ al-bayān*, 2:405–6; Ṭaḥāwī, *Sharḥ mushkil al-āthār* (in Rabāṭ, *Tuḥfat al-akhyār*, 3:602); ʿUqaylī, *Duʿafāʾ*, 4:159; Ibn ʿAsākir, *Taʾrīkh madīnat Dimashq*, 61:438–39 (see also Dhahabī, *Siyar aʿlām al-nubalāʾ*, 5:100). A further case

This report exemplifies Muḥammad al-Bāqir's consistent reaction to transmissions that he considered fake. The same attitude is also evident in the following example. A group of his Kūfan followers, who had traveled to the Ḥijāz for the *ḥajj*, came to visit him. He asked one of them:

من أين أحرمت؟ قال: من الكوفة. قال: ولِمَ أحرمت من الكوفة؟ فقال: بلغني عن بعضكم أنّه قال: ما بَعُدَ من الإحرام فهو أعظم للأجر. فقال: ما بلّغك هذا إلّا كذّاب.[486]

"Where did you enter the state of pilgrim sanctity?" He said, "In Kūfa." He said, "Why did you enter the state of pilgrim sanctity in Kūfa?" He said, "I was told on the authority of one of you that he said, 'The farther away one enters the state of pilgrim sanctity, the greater the reward.'" He said, "Only a liar informed you of this."

And a couple of further examples:

زرارة عن أبي جعفر قال: قلت له: ما تقول في رجل قال لامرأته: أنتِ عليّ حرام، فإنّا نُروى بالعراق أنّ عليًا جعلها ثلاثًا. قال: كذبوا! لم يجعلها طلاقًا.[487]

[Zurāra:] I said to Abū Jaʿfar, "What is your position regarding a man who says to his wife, 'You are forbidden to me'? Reports are circulating among us in Iraq that ʿAlī considered this a triple divorce." He said, "They lied! He did not consider it a divorce."

زرارة عن أبي جعفر قال: قلت له: أصلحك الله! رجلٌ طلّق امرأته على طهر من غير جماع بشهادة عدلين؟ قال: إذا دخلت في الحيضة الثالثة فقد انقضت عدّتها. قلت له:

---

was mentioned earlier in connection with the Prophet's *ʿumra* from Jiʿrāna. See also Aḥmad b.ʿĪsā, *Amālī*, 4:299 for another instance of disagreement between Muḥammad al-Bāqir and Nāfiʿ:

> محمّد بن قيس قال: كان نافع يُفتى أهل مكّة في الصيد يُصاد في الحلّ فيدخل الحرم، قال: لا بأس به. فأرسل أبو جعفر فنهاهم، فكان لا يفتيهم وكفّ.
>
> [Muḥammad b. Qays:] Nāfiʿ used to issue *fatwā*s to the people of Mecca about game that had been shot in the non-sacred lands but that then enters the sacred precinct. He said, "There is nothing wrong with it." Abū Jaʿfar sent a message to them [that is, the people of Mecca] and forbade them [to eat such game], so he [Nāfiʿ] ceased giving them *fatwā*s.

486 Ṭūsī, *Tahdhīb*, 5:52.

487 Kulaynī, *Kāfī*, 6:135.

أصلحك الله! إنّ أهل العراق يروون عن علي أنّه قال: «هو أحقّ برجعتها ما لم تغتسل من الحيضة الثالثة». قال: كذبوا.[488]

[Zurāra:] I said to Abū Jaʿfar, "May God put you on the right path! A man divorced his wife when she was in a state of purity, without having had intercourse [with her during that period], and in the presence of two upright witnesses." He said, "When she commences her third menstrual cycle, her waiting period is concluded." I said to him, "May God put you on the right path! The people of Iraq narrate that ʿAlī said, 'He has a greater right to take her back so long as she has not performed the full-body ablution after her third menses.'"[489] He said, "They lied."

محمّد بن مسلم قال: قلت لأبي جعفر: إنّ أهل الكوفة يروون عن علي أنّه كان يأمر بالوضوء قبل الغسل من الجنابة. قال: كذبوا على علي. ما وجدنا ذلك في كتاب علي. قال الله تعالى: ﴿وَإِنْ كُنْتُمْ جُنُبًا فَاطَّهَّرُوا﴾.[490]

[Muḥammad b. Muslim:] I said to Abū Jaʿfar, "The Kūfans report that ʿAlī used to order people to perform ablution before taking a bath to cleanse ritual impurity." He said, "They attribute this falsely to ʿAlī. We did not find this in the book of ʿAlī. God, the Exalted, said, 'If you are in a state of ritual impurity, purify yourselves.'"[491]

أبو الورد قال: قلت لأبي جعفر: إنّ أبا ظبيان حدّثني أنّه رأى عليًا أراق الماء ثمّ مسح على الخفّين. قال: كذب أبو ظبيان. أما بلغك قول علي فيكم: «سبق الكتاب الخفّين»؟[492]

[Abū al-Ward:] I said to Abū Jaʿfar, "Abū Ẓabyān [Ḥusayn b. Jundab al-Janbī] told me that he saw ʿAlī pour water and wipe over his boots." He said, "Abū Ẓabyān lied. Did the statement of ʿAlī [when he was] among you [in Iraq] not reach you: 'The Book [that is, the Qurʾān] outlawed [the practice of wiping over] boots'?"

488 ʿAyyāshī, *Tafsīr*, 1:229; Kulaynī, *Kāfī*, 6:87.

489 See Ibn Abī Shayba, *Muṣannaf*, 6:579 quoting this statement from *Jaʿfar ʿan abīh ʿan ʿAlī* (!); Ṭabarī, *Jāmiʿ al-bayān*, 4:507–8.

490 Ṭūsī, *Tahdhīb*, 1:139.

491 Qurʾān 5:6.

492 Ṭūsī, *Tahdhīb*, 1:362.

Jaʿfar himself was a victim of fabrications of all kinds, first and foremost from those who sought to rebuff the followers of the House of the Prophet by falsely quoting from its senior members, ʿAlī and Jaʿfar in particular, statements that contradicted the well-known and established positions of the House of the Prophet and supported the standpoints of their opponents. This was a very common tactic in the sectarian milieu of late Umayyad/early Abbasid times. Examples abound across discussions of law and theology, as well as in reports on events in early Islamic history, for which the account offered by the House of the Prophet differed from those promoted and sanctified as indisputably correct history by the Umayyads and the early Abbasids, and their respective entourages. The fabricators went as far as portraying the Imams quoting the Sunna of the Prophet from some of the archenemies of his Family.[493]

A report cited by a disciple of Jaʿfar and recorded in an early work on *ḥadīth* transmitters provides an interesting example of the vast genre of fabrications in his name:

> ميمون بن عبد الله قال: أتى قوم أبا عبد الله يسألونه الحديث من الأمصار وأنا عنده. فقال لي: أتعرف أحدًا من القوم؟ قلت: لا! قال: فكيف دخلوا عليّ؟ قلت: هؤلاء قوم يطلبون الحديث من كلّ وجه، لا يبالون ممّن أخذوا الحديث. فقال لرجل منهم: هل سمعت من غيري من الحديث؟ قال: نعم! قال: فحدّثني ببعض ما سمعت. قال: إنّما جئت لأسمع منك، لم أجيء أحدّثك. قال: وتتفضّل أن تحدّثني ما سمعت؟ أجعل الّذي حدّثك حديثه أمانةً لا تحدّث به أحدًا؟ قال: لا! قال: فأسمِعنا بعض ما اقتبست من العلم حتّى نفيدك إن شاء الله! قال: حدّثني سفيان الثورى عن جعفر بن محمّد قال: النبيذ كلّه حلال إلّا الخمر. ثمّ سكت. فقال أبو عبد الله: زدنا! قال: حدّثني سفيان عمّن حدّثه عن محمّد بن علي أنّه قال: من لا يمسح على خفّيه فهو صاحب بدعة، ومن لا يشرب النبيذ فهو مبتدع، ومن لا يأكل الجرّيث وطعام أهل الذمّة وذبايحهم فهو ضالّ. أمّا النبيذ فقد شربه عمر، نبيذ زبيب فرشحه بالماء، وأمّا المسح على الخفّين فقد مسح عمر على الخفّين ثلاثًا في السفر ويومًا وليلةً في الحضر، وأمّا الذبايح فقد أكلها علي وقال: كلوها فانّ الله تعالى يقول: ﴿الْيَوْمَ أُحِلَّ لَكُمُ الطَّيِّبَاتُ وَطَعَامُ الَّذِينَ أُوتُوا الْكِتَابَ حِلٌّ لَكُمْ وَطَعَامُكُمْ حِلٌّ لَهُمْ﴾. ثمّ سكت. فقال أبو عبد الله: زدنا! قال: قد حدّثتك بما سمعت. قال: أكلّ الّذي سمعت هذا؟ قال: لا. قال: زدنا! قال:

493 E.g., Ibn ʿAdī, *Kāmil*, 2:557; Abū Ṭāhir al-Silafī, *Muʿjam al-safar*, 448.

حدّثنا عمرو بن عبيد عن الحسن قال: أشياء صدّق الناس بها وأخذوا بها وليس في الكتاب لها أصل. منها عذاب القبر، ومنها الميزان، ومنها الحوض، ومنها الشفاعة، ومنها النيّة، ينوي الرجل من الخير والشرّ فلا يعمله فيثاب عليه، ولا يثاب الرجل إلّا بما عمل، إن خيرًا فخيرًا وإن شرًّا فشرّا. قال: فضحكت من حديثه، فغمزني أبو عبد الله أن كفّ حتّى نسمع. قال: فرفع [الرجل] رأسه إليّ فقال: ما يُضحكك؟ من الحقّ أو من الباطل؟ قلت له: أضحك الله وأبكى! وإنّما يُضحكني منك تعجّبًا كيف حفظت هذه الأحاديث! فسكت.

فقال أبو عبد الله: من أيّ البلاد أنت؟ قال: من أهل البصرة. قال: فهذا الّذي تحدّث عنه وتذكر اسمه جعفر بن محمّد، تعرفه؟ قال: لا! قال: فهل سمعت منه شيئًا قطّ؟ قال: لا! قال: فهذه الأحاديث عندك حقّ؟ قال: نعم! قال: متى سمعتها؟ قال: لا أحفظ، إلّا أنّها أحاديث أهل مصرنا منذ دهر لا يمترون فيها. قال له أبو عبد الله: لو رأيت هذا الرجل الّذي تحدّث عنه فقال لك هذه الّتي ترويها عنّي كذب لا أصل لها ولا أعرفها ولم أحدّث بها هل كنت تصدّقه؟ قال: لا! قال: لِمَ؟ قال: لأنّه شهد على قوله رجال لو شهد أحدهم على عنق رجل لجاز قوله.[494]

[Maymūn b. ʿAbd Allāh:] A group of people from the provinces came to Abū ʿAbd Allāh while I was with him, seeking *ḥadīth*. He asked me, "Do you know any of these people?" I said, "No!" He added, "So what are they doing in here?" I said, "These people seek *ḥadīth* from anywhere; they do not care from whom they receive *ḥadīth*." He asked one of them, "Have you heard *ḥadīth* from anyone other than me?" He said, "Yes!" He [Jaʿfar] said, "Tell me some of what you have heard." He said, "I came to hear from you, not to report to you." He said, "Would you go ahead and tell me some of what you heard? Did the person who related *ḥadīth*s to you give them to you as a trust commended [on the condition that] you not pass it on to anyone?" He answered, "No!" He replied, "Then let us hear some of the knowledge you acquired so we can be of benefit to you, God willing!" He said, "Sufyān al-Thawrī reported to me on the authority of Jaʿfar b. Muḥammad that he said, 'All *nabīdh* is lawful except for [grape] wine.'" He then fell silent. Abū ʿAbd Allāh said, "Tell us more!" He said, "Sufyān reported to me, from someone who informed him, that Muḥammad b. ʿAlī [al-Bāqir] said, 'Whoever does not wipe over his boots is a heretic, and whoever does not drink *nabīdh* is a heretic; whoever does not eat *jirrīth* and the

494 Kashshī, *Rijāl*, 393–96.

food of the *dhimmīs* and their slaughter is errant. As for *nabīdh*, ʿUmar drank grape *nabīdh* diluted with water. As for wiping over the boots, ʿUmar wiped over his boots for three days while traveling, and one day and one night while not traveling. As for the slaughtered animals [of *dhimmīs*], ʿAlī ate them and said, "Eat them, for God, the Exalted, says: 'This day all good foods have been made lawful for you, and the food of the People of the Book is lawful for you, and your food is lawful for them.'"'"[495] Then he fell silent. Abū ʿAbd Allāh said, "Tell us more!" He said, "I have reported to you what I heard." He said, "Is that all you have heard?" He said, "No!" He said, "Tell us more!" He said, "'ʿAmr b. ʿUbayd reported to us that Ḥasan [al-Baṣrī] said, 'There are things people believe in and rely on that have no basis in the Book. Among them are the punishment of the grave, the Scale, the Pool, intercession, and the intention, so that when a man intends to do good or bad but does not actually do it, his intention is still recompensed. A man is recompensed only for what he does; if it is good, then good, and if it is bad, then bad.'" I laughed at his reporting. Abū ʿAbd Allāh signaled to me to refrain so we could hear [more]. [The man] lifted his head to me and said, "What makes you laugh? Something true or something false?" I said to him, "God causes laughter and crying![496] It was amazement at how you memorized all these *ḥadīths* that made me laugh." He fell silent.

Abū ʿAbd Allāh asked, "What region are you from?" He said, "I am from the people of Baṣra." He said, "This person you narrate from and whose name you mention as Jaʿfar b. Muḥammad—do you know him?" He said, "No!" He said, "Have you heard anything about him?" He said, "No!" He said, "So you consider these *ḥadīths* to be true?" He said, "Yes!" He said, "When did you hear them?" He said, "I do not remember, except that they are the *ḥadīths* of the people of our town since time immemorial that they do not dispute." Abū ʿAbd Allāh said to him, "If you were to meet this man from whom you transmit and he were to say to you, 'These things that you narrate from me are false, without basis; I do not recognize them, and I did not transmit them,' would you believe him?" He said, "No!" He said, "Why?" He said, "Because those who testified to his sayings were men whose word would be accepted were they to testify with regards to the neck [that is, life] of a man."[497]

495 Qurʾān 5:5.

496 A reference to Qurʾān 53:43: "And it is He Who causes laughter and weeping."

497 The idea that unmasking the supposed source of a false statement does not affect the authority of the statement was a common position among the *ahl al-ḥadith*. See, for instance, Ibn Qudāma, *Mughnī*, 9:345–46:

لنا أنّ النبي – صلّى الله عليه وسلّم – قال : لا نكاح إلّا بولي . . . فان قيل : فانّ الزهري راويه وقد أنكره. قال ابن جريج : سألت الزهري عنه فلم يعرفه. قلنا . . . لوثبت هذا لم يكن حجّة لأنّه قد نقله ثقات عنه ، فلو نسيه الزهري لم يضرّه لأن النسيان لم يعصم منه إنسان. قال النبي – صلّى الله عليه وسلّم – نسي آدم فنسيت ذرّيته.

The argument in our favor is that the Prophet (may God's prayers and peace be upon him) said, "There is no marriage except with a guardian." If it is said "This [statement] is quoted on the authority of Zuhrī, but he denied it—Ibn Jurayj said, 'I asked Zuhrī about it and he did not know it,'" we would respond: Even if that is true, it is not a valid argument because reliable transmitters narrated it from him. If Zuhrī forgot it, that does not discredit it, because nobody is immune from forgetfulness. The Prophet (may God's prayers and peace be upon him) said, "Adam forgot, so his descendants forget!"

Also Zarkashī, *al-Baḥr al-muḥīṭ*, 4:321, 323–24:

[مسألة – إنكار الشيخ ما حدّث به:] نسيان [الراوي] الأصل لا يسقط العمل بما فيه. قال ابن القشيري: أطلق الشافعي القول بقبول الحديث وإيجاب العمل به. وذهب الكرخي والرازي وأكثر الحنفية إلى أنّه لا يقبل، ولهذا ردّوا خبر «أيّما امرأة نكحت بغير إذن وليّها [فنكاحها باطل]» لأنّ راويه الزهري قال لا أذكره . . . لنا أنّ الراوي عدل جازم بالرواية فيجب العمل [بها] لحصول اليقين. وتوقّف الشيخ [المروي عنه] ليس بمعارض، بل يجب على الشيخ أن يقول: «حدّثني فلان عنّي» ويعمل به!

[On the question of the source denying that he had ever transmitted the report:] If the [alleged] original transmitter [of a report] does not remember it, that does not discredit the report. Ibn al-Qushayrī said, "Shāfiʿī said that all *ḥadīths*, with no exception, should be accepted and acted upon. [Abū al-Ḥasan] al-Karkhī, [Fakhr al-Dīn] al-Rāzī, and most Ḥanafīs held that [such a] report is not accepted. That is why they rejected the statement [ascribed to the Prophet] that 'The marriage of any woman who marries without the permission of her guardian is null and void,' because its [alleged] source, Zuhrī, said 'I do not remember it.'" The argument in our favor is that the transmitter [from Zuhrī] was a righteous person and certain of his transmission, so acting upon it is obligatory because of the certainty that it produces. The fact that the source did not know of it does not controvert the report's authority. Rather it is obligatory upon the source to say, "This person transmitted to me on my authority," and to act upon it!

The prime engine for fabrications of this sort were the Quṣṣāṣ ("storytellers"),[498] the popular street preachers.[499] They were members of an institution reportedly established by Muʿāwiya[500] to publicize the Umayyad caliphate's positions in their propaganda war against ʿAlī and his supporters.[501] In late Umayyad and post-Umayyad times, however, the storytellers changed their approach and began exploiting the popularity of the House of the Prophet by ascribing their own fabrications to them. The Quṣṣāṣ were known for making statements and ascribing them to

498 Here are a few comments made about this group and its role in composing and spreading false reports:

أكذب الناس على رسول الله السُؤّال والقُصّاص.

> More than anybody else, the storytellers and beggars made false attributions to the Messenger of God (Ibn Mufliḥ, *al-Ādāb al-sharʿiyya*, 2:87, quoting Aḥmad b. Ḥanbal).

القُصّاص ومعظم البلاء (في وضع الحديث) منهم يجري.

> ... the Storytellers, and most calamities [with respect to the forgery of *ḥadīth*] come from them (Ibn al-Jawzī, *Mawḍūʿāt*, 1:29; see also Ibn ʿAbd al-Barr, *Tamhīd*, 1:55).

However, a report in Ibn Mufliḥ, 2:83 quotes Aḥmad b. Ḥanbal praising the Quṣṣāṣ for their public tales, despite the fact that their stories were riddled with falsities:

قال أحمد في رواية إسحاق بن إبراهيم: ما أنفعهم للعامّة وإن كان عامّة ما يتحدّثون به كذبًا!

> According to a report by Isḥāq b. Ibrāhīm, Aḥmad said, "How beneficial they [the Quṣṣāṣ] are for the laity, even if most of what they report is untrue!"

See also Dhahabī, *Siyar aʿlām al-nubalāʾ*, 11:170.

499 For this description, see, for instance, Kashshī, *Rijāl*, 215, where Saʿd b. Ṭarīf al-Iskāf, an early second-century *qāṣṣ*-preacher (see Modarressi, *Tradition and Survival*, 1:118), tells Muḥammad al-Bāqir (clearly in the last decades of the Umayyad rule) that he sat preaching and mentioned the rights and merits of the Family of the Prophet. The Imam answers that he wishes there were preachers like him every thirty *dhirāʿ*s (arm cubits):

سعد الإسكاف قال : قلت لأبي جعفر: إنّي أجلس فأقصّ وأذكر حقّكم وفضلكم. قال: وددت أنّ على كلّ ثلاثين ذراعًا قاصًّا مثلك.

500 Maqrīzī, *Khiṭaṭ*, 2:253. Numerous works in different languages have been written about this institution. See the entry on *ḳāṣṣ* in *Encyclopaedia of Islam* II, 4:733–35 for a list of some recent studies.

501 Accordingly, numerous statements from the Imams condemned the Quṣṣāṣ. See, for instance, the statement attributed to Jaʿfar al-Ṣādiq in Ibn Bābawayh, *Iʿtiqādāt*, 84:

ذُكر القصّاصون عند الصادق فقال: لعنهم الله! إنّهم يشنّعون علينا.

> The Storytellers were mentioned in the presence of [Jaʿfar] al-Ṣādiq. He said, "May God curse them! They disgrace us."

religious authorities even in their presence.[502] There were also many other individuals who were active in this field. An infamous case was that of the judge Abū al-Bakhtarī Wahb b. Wahb (d. 199 or 200),[503] judge of Baghdad under Hārun al-Rashīd, who openly improvised fabrications and attributed them to Jaʿfar al-Ṣadiq.[504] To make his fabrications appear more acceptable, he claimed to have a close familial relationship with the Imam through his mother, whom he asserted the Imam had married. The story was altogether false.[505]

Jaʿfar al-Ṣādiq constantly complained about those who fabricated statements in his name:

عن أبي عبد الله: إنّ الناس أولعوا بالكذب علينا.[506]

Another report quotes Jaʿfar as saying that the derogatory word *ḥāʾik*—which means "weaver" and was a common insult in Arabic to denote a worthless person—does not mean a professional weaver of fabrics, but a person who "weaves falsehoods about God and the Prophet" (Kulaynī, *Kāfī*, 2:340). The Arabs did not like the profession of fabric-weaving, a curious attitude that has long puzzled students of the Arabs' social history. In the early Islamic centuries, the disgrace associated with weavers was occasionally applied even to tailors, as can be seen in the eulogy of the Khārijī poet Ḥabīb b. Khudra for Zayd b. ʿAlī; he calls those who abandoned Zayd *awlād darza*, sons of tailors (Mubarrad, *Kāmil*, 3:1371). A report in Hishām al-Kalbī, *Mathālib al-ʿArab*, 36, suggests that the derogatory attitude may have originated from the phonetic similarity between the Arabic word *ḥāʾik* and a Persian word for a rogue, *hāhik*. The latter word appears in a story of a conversation between the caliph Manṣūr and a member of the Banū Sāma b. Luʾayy b. Ghālib, a tribe that considered itself part of the Quraysh but that was ranked lower than other Qurashī tribes because of doubts about its affiliation. In the story, Manṣūr asks the tribesman which clan of Quraysh he belongs to:

قال: أمِن بني هاشم؟ قال: لا! قال: أفمِن بني أميّة؟ قال: لا! قال: فمَن أنت؟ قال: مِن بني سامة بن لؤي.
قال: هؤلاء قريش الحاحكين. وهذه اللفظة فارسيّةٌ تضربها الفرس وتعني بها السفلة.

He [the caliph] said, "From Banū Hāshim?" He said, "No!" He said, "Then from Banū Umayya?" He said, "No!" He said, "Then who are you?" He said, "[I am] from Banū Sāma b. Luʾayy." He said, "They are the *ḥāḥika* of the Quraysh." [The author comments:] This is a Persian word by which Persian-speakers mean "the lowly."

502 Ibn Ḥibbān, *Majrūḥīn*, 1:85. See for an example Ibn ʿAdī, *Kāmil*, 3:1173 (whence Bayhaqī, *Shuʿab al-īmān*, 5:102; Ibn al-Jawzī, *Mawḍūʿāt*, 1:43, 3:114).

503 On him, see Modarressi, *Tradition and Survival*, 1:389–92 and the sources cited therein.

504 See his biography in Khaṭīb al-Baghdādī, *Taʾrīkh Baghdād*, 15:627–33. The man is in fact the first in Ibn al-Jawzī's list of *ḥadīth* forgers (*Mawḍūʿāt*, 1:35). Ibn Dāwūd al-Ḥillī, in his *Rijāl*, 283 describes him as *akdhab al-bariyya* (the foremost fabricator of lies among human beings).

505 Kashshī, *Rijāl*, 310. The man may never have met Jaʿfar al-Ṣādiq in person. See Ibn Abī Ḥātim, *al-Jarḥ waʾl-taʿdīl*, 9:25:

عمر بن حفص بن غياث قال: قلت لأبي: زعم أبو البختري أنّه رآك عند جعفر بن محمّد. قال: ما رآني. ما رأيته.

[ʿUmar b. Ḥafṣ b. Ghiyāth:] I said to my father, "Abū al-Bakhtarī claimed that he saw you with Jaʿfar b. Muḥammad." He said, "He did not see me; I did not see him."

506 Kashshī, *Rijāl*, 136.

Abū ʿAbd Allāh: "People have enthusiastically made false attributions to us."

ابن سِنان قال: قال أبو عبد الله : إنّا أهل بيت صادقون لا نخلو من كذّاب يكذب علينا فيسقط صدقنا بكذبه علينا عند الناس.[507]

[ʿAbd Allāh b. Sinān:] Abū ʿAbd Allāh said, "We are people of a truthful household, but we do not lack fabricators who falsely attribute things to us and thus tarnish our reputation for truthfulness among people with their lies."

There was an added factor that further encouraged these fabrications. During the Umayyad period, the pro-ʿUthmān faction worried very little about ʿAlī, as he was officially regarded as an outcast by the government and was, as noted earlier, regularly cursed from the pulpit of every mosque throughout the caliphate. It was later in the Umayyad reign, and then in early Abbasid times, that the pro-ʿAlī tendency found an opportunity to manifest itself. That trend culminated in the early third century, to a great extent thanks to efforts by Aḥmad b. Ḥanbal to make ʿAlī's name the fourth in the list of the "rightly guided" caliph-successors to the Prophet. This was also the time in which mainstream Islamic orthodoxy, with its specific interpretations of the historical past and of the doctrinal and legal present, was taking shape. There was thus an urgent need to "tame" and reshape ʿAlī's image as orthodox in order to present the orthodoxy as uniform and homogeneous, and to eliminate any elements that splinter groups could use to attack the orthodoxy and to bolster their own propositions and arguments. This was the stage on which the role of *ḥadīth* transmitters was vitally important, because their many contributions, placed mostly, though not solely, in the mouth of Jaʿfar al-Ṣadiq, presented ʿAlī as someone who fully agreed with the orthodox teachings on every matter, whether historical, doctrinal, or legal.

A second, similarly active group of fabricators was the Ghulāt, whose members tried to support their own esoteric version of religion by ascribing it to the Imams, and to Jaʿfar al-Ṣādiq in particular. I have discussed this group and their doctrines elsewhere.[508] Volumes have been compiled over the past twelve centuries of the vast amount of material produced by the early Ghulāt. Jaʿfar al-Ṣādiq did his best to disown them, condemn their doctrine and false attributions, and warn his followers of the harm they could

507 Kashshī, *Rijāl*, 305.

508 Modarressi, *Crisis and Consolidation*, 19–49.

cause to the Shīʿī community. Here are a few examples of the Imam's statements on and instructions about the group:[509]

هشام بن سالم عن أبي عبد الله وذكر الغلاة فقال: إنّ فيهم من يكذب حتّى أنّ الشيطان ليحتاج إلى كذبه![510]

[Hishām b. Sālim:] Abū ʿAbd Allāh mentioned the Ghulāt and said, "There are among them those who lie to the extent that Satan is in need of their lies!"

فضيل بن يسار عن أبي عبد الله: إحذروا على شبابكم الغلاة لا يفسدوهم فإنّ الغلاة شرّ خلق الله، يصغّرون عظمة الله ويدعون الربوبيّة لعباد الله.[511]

[Fuḍayl b. Yasār:] Abū ʿAbd Allāh said, "Beware that the Ghulāt do not corrupt your youth, for the Ghulāt are the most evil of God's creation. They belittle God's magnificence and attribute divinity to the servants of God."

عن مرازم قال: قال أبو عبد الله: قل للغالية: توبوا إلى الله فإنّكم فسّاق كفّار مشركون.[512]

[Murāzim b. Ḥukaym:] Abū ʿAbd Allāh said, "Say to the Ghulāt, 'Repent before God, for you are immoral, disbelievers, and polytheists.'"

خلف بن حمّاد عن رجل عن أبي عبد الله قال: لا تصلّ خلف الغالي وإن كان يقول بقولك.[513]

[Khalaf b. Ḥammād:] Abū ʿAbd Allāh said, "Do not pray behind any of the Ghulāt, even if he professes what you profess."[514]

509 There are also statements by the Imam against "those who tell lies among the Shīʿa" (e.g., Kashshī, *Rijāl*, 299, 307), referring clearly to a group known at the time as *Mufawwiḍa*. The members of this group tried to identify themselves as ordinary Shīʿa, but their esoteric worldview was very similar to that of the Ghulāt (see Modarressi, *Crisis and Consolidation*, 21–29, 32–49). On the Ghulāt, *see* further Kashshī, 223–25, 294, 297 (also Kulaynī, *Kāfī*, 1:257), 302.

510 Kashshī, *Rijāl*, 297.

511 Ṭūsī, *Amālī*, 650.

512 Kashshī, *Rijāl*, 297.

513 Ṭūsī, *Tahdhīb*, 3:31.

514 The last part of the report confirms my earlier point—that certain members of the Ghulāt identified themselves as ordinary Shīʿa. This is an obvious reference to the *Mufawwiḍa* as described in Modarressi, *Crisis and Consolidation*, 21–29.

Sharīk b. ʿAbd Allāh al-Nakhaʿī, a judge in Kūfa (d. 177), made the following comment about the effect of the false attributions of the second group of fabricators—the Ghulāt—but is understandably silent on the first—the Quṣṣāṣ and other *ḥadīth* fabricators:

يحيى بن عبد الحميد الحمّاني في كتابه، قال: قلت لشريك إنّ اقوامًا يزعمون أنّ جعفر بن محمّد ضعيف في الحديث، فقال: أخبرك القصّة: كان جعفر بن محمّد رجلاً صالحًا مسلمًا ورعًا، فاكتنفه قوم جهّال يدخلون عليه ويخرجون من عنده ويقولون «حدّثنا جعفر بن محمّد» ويحدّثون بأحاديث كلّها منكرات كذب موضوعة على جعفر، يستأكلون الناس بذلك ويأخذون منهم الدراهم. والله ما قال جعفر شيئًا من هذا قطّ. كان جعفر أتقى لله وأورع من ذلك. فضعّفوه. ولو رأيت جعفرًا لعلمت أنّه أوحد[515] الناس.[516]

[Yaḥyā b. ʿAbd al-Ḥamīd al-Ḥimmānī:] I said to Sharīk, "Some people claim that Jaʿfar b. Muḥammad was a weak [that is, unreliable] *ḥadīth* transmitter."[517] He said, "Let me tell you the story: Jaʿfar b. Muḥammad was a righteous and pious man. He was surrounded by a group of ignorant people who would visit him and then come out and say, 'Jaʿfar b. Muḥammad told us . . .' and they would transmit *ḥadīth*s that were all unacceptable lies and fabrications attributed to Jaʿfar. They

515 In the edition of the source used here (Mashhad, 1970): واحد.

516 Kashshī, *Rijāl*, 324–25.

517 See Aḥmad b. Ḥanbal, *al-ʿIlal wa-maʿrifat al-rijāl: Riwāyat al-Marrūdhī wa-Ṣāliḥ b. Aḥmad wa'l-Maymūnī*, 57, 164; Dhahabī, *Siyar aʿlām al-nubalāʾ*, 6:91. Compare with Ḥākim al-Naysābūrī's judgment in his *Maʿrifat ʿulūm al-ḥadīth*, 228:

> أصحّ أسانيد أهل البيت – رضي الله عنهم – جعفر بن محمّد عن أبيه عن جدّه عن علي، إذا كان الراوي عن جعفر ثقة.
>
> The most sound [and reliable] chains of transmission by the members of the Family of the Prophet are [the ones through] Jaʿfar b. Muḥammad, from his father, from his grandfather, from ʿAlī, provided that the transmitter from Jaʿfar is reliable.

The fact that Bukhārī did not quote Jaʿfar al-Ṣādiq in his *Ṣaḥīḥ* may be influenced by the claim mentioned above that Jaʿfar was a weak transmitter. Much has, however, been said about or against Bukhārī's approach in this case (see, for instance, Muḥammad b. ʿAqīl al-Ḥaḍramī, *al-Naṣāʾiḥ al-kāfiya*, 155; Ḥaḍramī, *al-ʿAtb al-jamīl*, 59–60). I have found Salah al-Din al-Idlibi's conclusion in his article, "Asbāb ʿudūl al-imām al-Bukhārī ʿan al-takhrīj li'l-Imām Jaʿfar al-Ṣādiq fī Ṣaḥīḥih," 66–68 sound and balanced. He argues that Jaʿfar al-Ṣādiq was primarily a jurist, even if one whose legal thought was based on the Qurʾān and Sunna, and not a transmitter of *ḥadīth*s as such. *Ḥadīth* transmission was a distinct discipline, pursued mostly, though not exclusively, by people whose interests and mentality differed from those of the jurists. People who viewed (and still view) *ḥadīth* transmission as the only or the most meritorious act would frown at the legal profession and disapprove of the jurists' dismal contribution to the transmission of *ḥadīth*s—an attitude they also displayed vis-à-vis Abū Ḥanīfa and his followers.

would defraud people with them to take their money. By God, Jaʿfar said none of that. Jaʿfar was more pious and God-fearing than that. They besmirched him. Had you seen Jaʿfar, you would know that he was unique among people."

Heirs to both groups of fabricators still abound in Muslim communities. They continue their predecessors' legacy, repeating and publicizing old fabrications falsely attributed to the Imams.

The widespread phenomenon of introducing false reports and attributing them to Jaʿfar al-Ṣādiq and his father prompted Jaʿfar and Muḥammad al-Bāqir to set standards for their followers as well as others. Their aim was to help people distinguish between truth and falsehood in the citations that they received from transmitters of religious reports, street preachers, and other networks that had been set up to propagate the caliph's points of view throughout the lands of the caliphate:

عبد الله بن بُكير عن رجل عن أبي جعفر قال: دخلنا عليه جماعة فقلنا: يابن رسول الله! إنّا نريد العراق فأوصنا. فقال: إذا جائكم عنّا حديث فوجدتم عليه شاهدًا او شاهدين من كتاب الله فخُذوا به والاّ فقِفوا عنده ثمّ ردّوه إلينا حتّى يستبين لكم.[518]

[ʿAbd Allāh b. Bukayr:] Abū Jaʿfar [al-Bāqir] said, "If a *ḥadīth* attributed to us reaches you, and you find one or two corroborations for it in the Book of God, accept it. Otherwise, suspend judgment and refer it to us until it is clarified for you."

عبد الله بن أبي يعفور عن أبي عبد الله قال: إذا ورد عليكم حديث فوجدتم له شاهدًا من كتاب الله أو من قول رسول الله – صلّى الله عليه وآله وسلّم – [فخُذوا به] وإلّا فالّذي جاءكم به أولى به.[519]

[ʿAbd Allāh b. Abī Yaʿfūr:] Abū ʿAbd Allāh said, "If you come across a *ḥadīth* and find something in the Book of God or the sayings of the Messenger of God (may God's prayer and peace be upon him and his Family) corroborating it, then accept it; otherwise it is more appropriate for the one who brought it to you to keep it!"

518 Kulaynī, *Kāfī*, 2:222.
519 Kulaynī, *Kāfī*, 1:69.

يونس بن عبد الرحمن قال: حدّثني هشام بن الحكم أنّه سمع أبا عبد الله يقول: لا تقبلوا علينا حديثًا إلّا ما وافق القرآن والسنّة أو تجدون معه شاهدًا من أحاديثنا المتقدّمة. فاتّقوا الله ولا تقبلوا علينا ما خالف قول ربّنا تعالى وسنّة نبيّنا – صلّى الله عليه وآله وسلّم.[520]

[Yūnus b. ʿAbd al-Raḥmān:] Hishām b. al-Ḥakam told me that he heard Abū ʿAbd Allāh say, "Do not accept a statement attributed to us unless it accords with the Qurʾān and Sunna, or you find one of our earlier statements corroborating it. Do not accept anything attributed to us that contradicts the word of our Lord, the Exalted, or the Sunna of our Prophet (may God's prayer and peace be upon him and his Family)."

VIII. Views on Religious Ethics

As noted earlier, Jaʿfar al-Ṣādiq was moderate in his thought, practice, and remarks. He advised his followers to restrain their affection for the Family of the Prophet:

إتّقوا الله، وأحبّوا أهلَ بيت نبيّكم حُبًّا مقتصدًا.[521]

Be conscious of God, and love the Family of your Prophet in moderation.

He did not like exaggeration even in such essential components of Shīʿī religious practice as visitation of the tomb of Ḥusayn in Karbalāʾ:

حنان بن سدير قال: قلت لأبي عبد الله: ما تقول في زيارة قبر الحسين فإنّه بلغنا عن بعضكم أنّه قال: تعدل حجّة وعمرة؟ فقال: ما أصعب هذا الحديث! ما تعدل هذا كلّه، ولكن زوروه ولا تجفوه، فإنّه سيّد الشهداء وسيّد شباب أهل الجنة وشبيه يحيى بن زكريّا وعليهما بكت السماء والأرض.[522]

[Ḥanān b. Sadīr:] I said to Abū ʿAbd Allāh, "What is your opinion on visiting the grave of Ḥusayn, because we have heard that some of you said it is equivalent to a *ḥajj* and an *ʿumra*?" He said, "How difficult this *ḥadīth* is! It does not equate all of that; but visit him and do not neglect him. He is the leader of the martyrs, he is the leader of the youth of

520 Kashshī, *Rijāl*, 224.

521 Ḥimyarī, *Qurb al-isnād*, 139, 159.

522 Ḥimyarī, *Qurb al-isnād*, 99–100; Ibn Qūlawayh, *Kāmil al-ziyārāt*, 91.

the people of paradise, and he resembled Yaḥyā b. Zakariyyā, and the heavens and earth wept for both of them."

He usually appeared well dressed in public,[523] including during the *ḥajj*, attracting criticism from ascetics and impostors who would tell him that ʿAlī or "your forefathers" used to wear rough, casual clothes. His uniform answer was that their times required what they did, but that their times were different. He said to the Baṣran ʿAbbād b. Kathīr:

كان علي في زمان يستقيم له ما لبس فيه، ولو لَبستُ مثل ذاك اللباس في زماننا لقال الناس: هذا مُراءٍ مثل عبّاد![524]

In his time, what ʿAlī wore was appropriate for him. If I wear the same clothes in our times, people would say, "He is ostentatious like ʿAbbād!"[525]

He said to Sufyān al-Thawrī (as variously quoted):

إنّ آبائي كانوا في زمانٍ مُقفِرٍ مُقتِّرٍ وهذا زمان قد أرخت الدنيا عزاليها فأحقّ أهلها بها أبرارهم.[526]

My forefathers lived in a barren and impoverished era, but the present is a time in which the world has brought forth its riches. The most entitled to those riches among its people are the righteous ones.

إنّ علياً كان في زمان ضيّق. فإذا اتّسع الزمان فأبرار الزمان أولى به.[527]

ʿAlī lived during an era of hardship. If the era becomes more prosperous, the righteous people of that era are the most entitled to [that prosperity].

---

523 See, for instance, Ḥimyarī, *Qurb al-isnād*, 13; Kulaynī, *Kāfī*, 6:444, 452, 462; Kashshī, *Rijāl*, 432; Ṭūsī, *Tahdhīb*, 1:289. The length of his dress would naturally conform to general Islamic norms: not too long, as also emphasized by his father, Muḥammad al-Bāqir (Kulaynī, 6:457; see further 6:456). Jaʿfar's ring was bought for seven dinars after his death (Kulaynī, 6:470).

524 Kulaynī, *Kāfī*, 6:443 (with a variant at 6:443–44); Qāḍī Nuʿmān, *Daʿāʾim al-Islām*, 2:154.

525 On ʿAbbād's ostentatious style, see further Kulaynī, *Kāfī*, 2:293.

526 Kashshī, *Rijāl*, 392–93 (with a variant in Kulaynī, *Kāfī*, 6:442); Abū Nuʿaym, *Ḥilyat al-awliyāʾ*, 3:213 (whence Mizzī, *Tahdhīb al-Kamāl*, 5:86; Dhahabī, *Siyar aʿlām al-nubalāʾ*, 6:262; Dhahabī, *Tadhkirat al-ḥuffāẓ*, 1:158).

527 Kashshī, *Rijāl*, 392.

He reportedly said to a third person:

إنّ علي بن أبي طالب كان يلبس ذلك في زمان لا يُنكَر ولو لَبس [أحدٌ] مثل ذلك اليوم لَشَهر به، فخيرُ لباس كلّ زمان لباسُ أهله.[528]

ʿAlī b. Abī Ṭālib used to wear that [kind of clothes] at a time when doing so was not unusual. If someone wore something like that today, he would be seen as odd. The best clothing for each era is the clothing of its people.

And in response to disciples who had worn good clothes and wondered if doing so was acceptable, he said,

إلبس وتجمّل فإن الله جميل يحبّ الجمال.[529]

Dress and adorn yourself, for God is beautiful and loves beauty.[530]

إذا أنعم الله على عبده بنعمة أحبّ أن يراها عليه لأنّه جميل يحبّ الجمال.[531]

If God bestows favor upon His servant, He likes to see it on him[532] because He is beautiful and loves beauty.[533]

﴿مَنْ حَرَّمَ زِينَةَ اللهِ الَّتِي أَخْرَجَ لِعِبَادِهِ وَالطَّيِّبَاتِ مِنَ الرِّزْقِ؟﴾ إنّ الله إذا أنعم على عبد نعمةً أحبّ أن يراها عليه.[534]

Who outlawed the adornment of God and the delights of wealth that He bestowed upon His servants?[535] When God bestows favor upon a servant, He likes to see it on him.[536]

528 Kulaynī, *Kāfī*, 6:444.

529 Kulaynī, *Kāfī*, 6:442.

530 The last sentence is a statement quoted from the Prophet in Muslim, *Ṣaḥīḥ*, no. 91; Tirmidhī, *Sunan*, no. 1999; and other sources cited in the editors' footnotes in Aḥmad b. Ḥanbal, *Musnad*, 6:338–39 and 28:438. See also Suyūṭī, *Jāmiʿ al-uṣūl*, 2:269–70. Ibn ʿAbbās (Kulaynī, *Kāfī*, 6:442; Qāḍī Nuʿmān, *Daʿāʾim al-Islām*, 2:153), and Ḥasan al-Mujtabā (ʿAyyāshī, *Tafsīr*, 2:143) also used this statement in their responses.

531 Kulaynī, *Kāfī*, 6:483. See also Ṭūsī, *Amālī*, 275.

532 A similar statement is quoted from the Prophet in Sunnī *ḥadīth*. See, for instance, Ibn Mājah, *Sunan*, no. 3605; Tirmidhī, *Sunan*, no. 2819.

533 The whole text is quoted also from ʿAlī in Kulaynī, *Kāfī*, 6:438.

534 Kulaynī, *Kāfī*, 6:444.

535 Qurʾān 7:32.

536 The last sentence is also found in the Sunnī sources, as mentioned above.

إظهار النعمة أحبّ إلى الله من صيانتها، فايّاك أن تُرَينّ إلّا في أحسن زيّ قومك.[537]

Displaying one's favors is more beloved of God than is safeguarding them. Beware of being seen except with the best dress of your people.

بَيِّض قلبك والبس ما شئت.[538]

Purify your heart and wear whatever you wish.[539]

Other statements from Jaʿfar provide a window onto some of his views about Muslim religious life and the nature of Islamic teachings:

أبو بصير عن أبي عبد الله قال: مرّ بي أبي وأنا بالطواف، وأنا حَدَث وقد اجتهدت في العبادة، فرآني وأنا أتصابّ عرقًا فقال لي: يا جعفر! يا بُنَيّ! إنّ الله إذا أحبّ عبدًا رضى عنه باليسير.[540]

[Abū Baṣīr:] Abū ʿAbd Allāh said, "My father passed by me while I was circumambulating [the Kaʿba]. I was young and exerting myself in worship. He saw me dripping with sweat. He said to me, 'O Jaʿfar! O my son! When God loves a servant, He will be satisfied with something easy from him.'"[541]

إسماعيل بن يسار قال: سمعت أبا عبد الله يقول: إنّ ربّكم رحيم يشكر القليل.[542]

---

537 Kulaynī, *Kāfī*, 6:440.

538 Ibn Bābawayh, *ʿIlal al-sharāʾiʿ*, 2:36.

539 Jaʿfar said this in response to some of his followers who asked him about wearing black clothes—a color that could indicate sympathy with the Abbasids, who assumed black as their official color.

540 Kulaynī, *Kāfī*, 2:86, 87.

541 For the background of this idea, see Muslim, *Ṣaḥīḥ*, no. 2593 (also Abū Ṭālib, *Amālī*, 456), quoting the Prophet:

إنّ الله تعالى رفيق يحبّ الرفق، يعطي عليه ما لا يعطي على العنف.

God is gentle and loves that which is gentle. He rewards gentle acts with what He may not reward for hard acts.

And Ṭūsī, *Tahdhīb*, 5:52, where Muḥammad al-Bāqir is quoted as saying:

لا يُعرَض لي بابان كلاهما حلال إلّا أخذت باليسير، وذلك لأنّ الله يسير يحبّ اليسير ويعطي على اليسير ما لا يعطي على العنف.

Whenever two lawful options are available to me, I choose the easier of the two. That is because God is easy and loves that which is easy. He rewards simple matters with what He may not reward for hard acts.

542 Ṭūsī, *Tahdhīb*, 2:238.

[Ismāʿīl b. Yasār:] I heard Abū ʿAbd Allāh say, "Your God is merciful; He lauds even something little."

أبو عبيدة الحذّاء قال: سألت أبا عبد الله عن رجل نذر أن يمشي إلى مكّة حافيًا، فقال: إنّ رسول الله – صلّى الله عليه وآله وسلّم – خرج حاجًّا فنظر إلى امرأة تمشى بين الإبل، فقال: من هذه؟ فقالوا: أخت عقبة بن عامر، نذرت أن تمشي إلى مكّة حافية. فقال رسول الله – صلّى الله عليه وآله وسلّم: يا عقبة! إنطلق إلى أختك فمُرها فلتركب فإنّ الله غني عن مشيها وحفاها. قال: فرَكِبَت.[543]

[Abū ʿUbayda al-Ḥadhdhāʾ:] I asked Abū ʿAbd Allāh about a man who vowed to walk to Mecca barefoot. He said, "The Messenger of God (may God's prayer and peace be upon him and his Family) went out to perform the *ḥajj* and saw a woman walking amid the camels. He said, 'Who is this?' They told him, 'The sister of ʿUqba b. ʿĀmir. She vowed to walk to Mecca barefoot.' The Messenger of God (may God's prayer and peace be upon him and his Family) said, 'O ʿUqba! Go to your sister and order her to ride. God has no need of her walking and being barefoot.' So she rode."[544]

سيف التمّار قال: قلت لأبي عبد الله: أيّ شيء أحبّ إليك، نمشي أو نركب [في الحجّ]؟ قال: تركبون أحبّ إليّ، فإنّ ذلك أقوى على الدعاء والعبادة.[545]

[Sayf al-Tammār:] I said to Abū ʿAbd Allāh, "Which do you prefer we do [during the *ḥajj*]: walk or ride?" He said, "I prefer that you ride, for that preserves your strength for supplication and worship."

زرارة قال: قلت لأبي عبد الله: علّمني دعاءً! فقال: إن أفضل الدعاء ما جرى على لسانك.[546]

[Zurāra:] I said to Abū ʿAbd Allāh, "Teach me a supplication!" He said, "The best supplication is what flows [from your mind] to your tongue."

543 Ṭūsī, *Tahdhīb*, 5:14.

544 The story is reported in several variants also in Bukhārī, *Ṣaḥīḥ*, no. 1866; Muslim, *Ṣaḥīḥ*, no. 1664; Ibn Mājah, *Sunan*, no. 2134; Abū Dāwūd, *Sunan*, nos. 3293–304; Tirmidhī, *Sunan*, no. 1544; Nasāʾī, *Sunan*, no. 4757; and numerous other sources cited in the editors' footnotes in Aḥmad b. Ḥanbal, *Musnad*, 28:523, 540–42, 603, 610–11, 29:331.

545 Ṭūsī, *Tahdhīb*, 5:12.

546 Ibn Ṭāwūs, *Amān*, 19.

عبد الرحمن بن الحجّاج قال: كنت عند أبي عبد الله إذ دخل عليه عبد الملك القمّي فقال له: أصلحك الله! أشرب الماء وأنا قائم؟ فقال له: إن شئت. قال: فأشرب بنفسٍ واحد؟ قال: إن شئت. قال: أسجد ويديّ في ثوبي؟ فقال: إن شئت. ثمّ قال: إنّي والله ما من هذا وشِبهه أخاف عليكم.[547]

['Abd al-Raḥmān b. al-Ḥajjāj:] I was with Abū ʿAbd Allāh when ʿAbd al-Malik al-Qummī came to him and said, "May God put you on the right path! May I drink water while standing?"[548] He said, "If you wish." He said, "May I drink it all continuously?"[549] He said, "If you wish." He said, "May I prostrate [in prayer] with my hands in my garment?"[550] He said, "If you wish." Then he [Jaʿfar] said, "By God, I am not worried for you on account of matters of this kind."

موسى بن بكر قال: قلت لأبي عبد الله: إنّ أصحابنا يقولون إنّما يؤخذ الشارب والأظفار يوم الجمُعة. قال: سبحان الله! خذها إن شئت في يوم الجمُعة وإن شئت في ساير الأيّام.[551]

[Mūsā b. Bakr:] I said to Abū ʿAbd Allāh, "Our companions say that mustaches and nails should be trimmed on Friday."[552] He said, "Praise be to God! If you wish, do it on Friday; if you wish, on any other day."

حمّاد بن عثمان قال: قلت لأبي عبد الله: أيُكرَه السفر في شيء من الأيّام المكروهة مثل الأربعاء وغيره؟ قال: افتتح سفرك بالصدقة واخرج إذا بدا لك.[553]

[Ḥammād b. ʿUthmān:] I said to Abū ʿAbd Allāh, "Is traveling on any of the disapproved days, such as Wednesday or the like, religiously discouraged?" He said, "Start your trip by giving charity and depart [on your trip] whenever you wish."[554]

---

547 Barqī, *Maḥāsin*, 581 (whence Kulaynī, *Kāfī*, 6:383 and, partially, 3:408). All three acts that the man asked about were practices that many Muslims considered, then and even now, to be disavowed and disapproved of by Islamic religious ethics.

548 For early opinions against this practice, see Ibn Abī Shayba, *Muṣannaf*, 8:151–52; Barqī, *Maḥāsin*, 580–81.

549 For opinions against this, see Ibn Abī Shayba, *Muṣannaf*, 8:159; Barqī, *Maḥāsin*, 575–76.

550 For this practice, see Ṭūsī, *Tahdhīb*, 2:326, 356.

551 Ibn Bābawayh, *Faqīh*, 1:74.

552 Ibn Bābawayh, *Khiṣāl*, 39, 391, 392; Ibn Bābawayh, *Thawāb al-aʿmāl*, 22. Among non-Shīʿī works, see, for instance, ʿAbd al-Razzāq, *Muṣannaf*, 3:197; Ibn Abī Shayba, *Muṣannaf*, 2:630.

553 Ibn Bābawayh, *Faqīh* 2:175 (and a variant in Barqī, *Maḥāsin*, 348; Kulaynī, *Kāfī*, 4:283).

554 For the "disapproved days" to initiate a trip, see Barqī, *Maḥāsin*, 346–48.

جميل بن درّاج قال: سألت أبا عبد الله عن قتل الخطّاف أو إيذاؤهنّ في الحرم فقال: لا يُقتلن، فإنّي كنت مع علي بن الحسين فرآني وأنا أوذيهنّ فقال لي: يا بُنَيّ! لاتقتلهنّ ولا تؤذهنّ فإنّهنّ لا يُؤذين شيئًا.[555]

[Jamīl b. Darrāj:] I asked Abū ʿAbd Allāh about killing or harming swallows in the sacred precinct. He said, "They may not be killed. I was [as a child] with [my grandfather] ʿAlī b. al-Ḥusayn [Zayn al-ʿĀbidīn] and he saw me harassing them, so he said to me: 'O my son! Do not kill or harass these [birds], for they do not harm anything.'"

عمّار بن موسى عن أبي عبد الله قال: سألته عن الخطّاف فقال :لا بأس به، هو ممّا يحلّ أكله، لكن كره لأنّه استجار بك ووافي منزلك. وكلُّ طير يستجير بك فأَجِره.[556]

[ʿAmmār b. Mūsā:] I asked Abū ʿAbd Allāh about [the lawfulness of eating the flesh of] the swallows. He said, "There is nothing wrong with that; it is lawful to eat, but it is discouraged because it seeks refuge with you and comes to your house. Give protection to any bird that seeks refuge with you."

عن أبي عبد الله: من أقرّ عند تجريد أو تخويف أو حبس أو تهديد فلا حدّ عليه.[557]

Abū ʿAbd Allāh said, "*Ḥadd* punishments do not apply to someone who admits [wrongdoing] in the face of [bodily] exposure, fear, imprisonment, or threat."

معاوية بن عمّار قال: سألت أبا عبد الله عن الثياب السابريّة يعملها المجوس. ألبسها ولا أغسلها وأُصلّي فيها؟ قال: نعم! قال معاوية: فقطعت له قميصًا ورداءً من السابري ثمّ بعثت بها إليه في يوم جمُعة حين ارتفع النهار. فكأنّه عرف ما أُريد فخرج فيها إلى الجمُعة.[558]

[Muʿāwiya b. ʿAmmār:] I asked Abū ʿAbd Allāh about *sāburī* clothes,[559]

555 Kulaynī, *Kāfī*, 6:224.

556 Ṭūsī, *Tahdhīb*, 9:81.

557 Kulaynī, *Kāfī*, 7:216 (see also Ḥimyarī, *Qurb al-isnād*, 54).

558 Ṭūsī, *Tahdhīb*, 2:362.

559 An attribution to either Nīshāpūr, the town in Khurāsān (Thaʿālibī, *Thimār al-qulūb*, 540), or Shāpūr in Fārs in the south of Iran (Jāḥiẓ, *Tabaṣṣur bi'l-tijāra*, 32; Ibn Ḥawqal, *Ṣūrat al-arḍ*, 2:264, formally called Bīshapūr but still known to the locals as Shāpūr), where these clothes were made from thin fabrics (see further Samʿānī, *Ansāb*, 7:4; Majd al-Dīn Ibn al-Athīr, *Nihāya*, 2:334; Ibn Ḥajar, *Tabṣīr*, 712). A report in Ibn Bābawayh, *Faqīh*, 3:185 (partially quoted earlier) by ʿAbd al-Raḥmān b. al-Ḥajjāj, himself a trader in *sāburī* clothes (see Modarressi,

made by Magians, as to whether I may wear them without washing them and then pray in them. He said, "Yes!" [Muʿāwiya said:] I cut a shirt and cloak for him from *sāburī* [cloth] and sent them to him on a Friday in the late morning. It was as if he noted what I meant and came out wearing them to the Friday prayer.

سفيان بن خالد عن أبي عبد الله: أنّه كان يصلّي ذات يوم إذ مرّ رجل قدّامه وابنه موسى جالس، فلمّا انصرف قال له ابنه: يا أبه! ما رأيت الرجل مرّ قدّامك؟ فقال: يا بُنيّ! إنّ الّذي أصلّي له أقرب إليّ من الّذي مرّ قدّامي.[560]

[Sufyān b. Khālid:] Once when Abū ʿAbd Allāh was praying, a man passed in front of him while his son Mūsā was sitting there. When [Abū ʿAbd Allāh] finished, his son said to him, "O father! Did you not see the man pass in front of you?"[561] He said, "O my son! The One I pray to is closer to me than the one who passed in front of me."

جميل بن درّاج قال: سمعت أبا عبد الله يقول: إذا تزوّج العبد الحرّة فولده أحرار وإذا تزوّج الحرّ الأمة فولده أحرار.[562]

[Jamīl b. Darrāj:] I heard Abū ʿAbd Allāh say, "If a slave marries a free woman, his children are free; and if a free man marries a slave woman, his children are free."[563]

Tradition and Survival, 1:169) may be assumed to support the first account, as he tells the Imam about his trips for trade to Nishāpūr:

عبد الرحمن بن الحجّاج قال: سألته عن الصرف فقلت له: الرُفقة ربما عجلت فخرجت فلم نقدر على الدمشقيّة والبصريّة وإنّما يجوز بنيسابور الدمشقيّة والبصريّة.

[ʿAbd al-Raḥmān b. al-Ḥajjāj:] I asked [the Imam] about money exchange, saying, "The group occasionally leaves in a hurry before we are able to find Damascene and Baṣran coins, the only currencies that are used in Nīshāpūr."

However, the same report is quoted in Kulaynī, *Kāfī*, 5:642 (whence Ṭūsī, *Tahdhīb*, 7:104) with the town named as Sābūr, where Damascene and Baṣran coins were used in trade. This may point to the town in Fārs, which was much closer to Baṣra and as such a more plausible location for the use of Baṣran coins.

560 Ṭūsī, *Tahdhīb*, 2:323.

561 This refers to the majority opinion among Muslim jurists at the time, according to which a praying person must stop others from passing in front of him. See Ibn Qudāma, *Mughnī*, 3:91–94; *al-Mawsūʿa al-fiqhiyya* (Kuwait), 37:36–39.

562 Kulaynī, *Kāfī*, 5:394.

563 There are variants of this report, as well as other statements to this effect quoted from Jaʿfar al-Ṣādiq, in Kulaynī, *Kāfī*, 5:492–93. In Sunnī law, a child born of a mixed marriage between a free person and a slave assumes the status of the mother, whether she is the free partner or the slave. See *al-Mawsūʿa al-fiqhiyya* (Kuwait), 23:13.

عبد الله بن سنان قال: سمعت أبا عبد الله يقول: كان أمير المؤمنين يقول: إنَّ الناس كلّهم أحرار إلّا من أقرّ على نفسه بالعبوديّة وهو مُدرِك، مِن عبد أو أمة، ومن شُهِد عليه بالرقّ صغيرًا كان أو كبيرا.[564]

['Abd Allāh b. Sinān:] I heard Abū 'Abd Allāh say "The Commander of the Faithful ['Alī] used to say, 'All human beings are free[565] except someone, male or female, who acknowledges, while of legal capacity, that he or she is a slave and someone, whether a child or an adult, who is legally proven to be a slave through witness testimony.'"

بكر بن محمّد الأزدي قال: دخلت على أبي عبد الله ومعي علي بن عبد العزيز، فقال لي: من هذا؟ فقلت: مولى لنا. فقال: أعتقتموه أو أباه؟ فقلت: بل أباه. فقال: ليس هذا مولاك. هذا أخوك وابن عمّك. وإنّما المولى هو الّذي جرت عليه النعمة، فإذا جرت على أبيه فهذا أخوك وابن عمّك.[566]

[Bakr b. Muḥammad al-Azdī:] I came upon Abū 'Abd Allāh with 'Alī b. 'Abd al-'Azīz. The Imam said to me, "Who is this?" I said, "A client of ours." He said, "Did you manumit him or his father?" I said, "His father." He said, "This is not your client. He is your brother and cousin. A client is one who received the favor [of manumission], but if it was his father who received the favor [of manumission], then this one is your brother and cousin."

---

564 Kulaynī, *Kāfī*, 6:195.

565 A similar statement is attributed to 'Umar, who allegedly said to his governor in Egypt:

منذ كم تعبّدتم الناس وقد ولَدَتهم أمهاتُهم أحرارًا؟

> Since when did you enslave people even though they were born of their mothers free people? (Ibn 'Abd al-Ḥakam, *Futūḥ Miṣr*, 195; Ibn al-Jawzī, *Manāqib Amīr al-Mu'minīn 'Umar*, 382).

The statement is a part of a report that today's Sunnī *ahl al-ḥadīth* strongly reject as unreliable, as in the following links:
http://al-maktaba.org/book/31615/17769;
http://islamqa.info/ar/answers/279025/;
http://www.khaledabdelalim.com/home/play-2008.html;
http://sites.google.com/site/islamfacilepourtous/hommes/sahaba/chobha/btlan-qste-mty-astbdtm-alnas-wqd-wldthm-amhathm-ahrara-snda-wmtna.

566 Ḥimyarī, *Qurb al-isnād*, 41–42 (also Kulaynī, *Kāfī*, 6:199; Ibn Bābawayh, *Faqīh*, 3:78–79).

سماعة قال: قال أبو عبد الله: إنّ الله عزّ وجلّ فوّض إلى المؤمن أموره كلّها ولم يفوّض إليه أن يذلّ نفسه. أما تسمع قول الله عزّو جلّ يقول: ﴿وَلِلَّهِ الْعِزَّةُ وَلِرَسُولِهِ وَلِلْمُؤْمِنِينَ﴾؟ فالمؤمن ينبغي أن يكون عزيزًا ولا يكون ذليلاً.[567]

[Samāʿa b. Mihrān:] Abū ʿAbd Allāh said, "God, the Mighty and Majestic, delegated to the believer authority over all his own affairs, but He did not give him authority to humiliate himself. Did you not hear God, the Mighty and Majestic, say, 'Honor belongs to God and to His Messenger and the believers'?[568] A believer should be honorable, not humiliated."

ابن أبي يعفور عن أبي عبد الله قال: قلت له: إنّي أريد أن أتزوّج إمرأةً وإنّ أبويّ أرادا غيرها. قال: تزوّج الّتي هويت ودع الّتي يهوى أبواك.[569]

[Ibn Abī Yaʿfūr:] I said to Abū ʿAbd Allāh, "I want to marry a [certain] woman, but my parents want someone else [for me]." He said, "Marry the one that you fancy and leave alone the one that your parents like."

مصادف عن أبي عبد الله قال: رُبّ إمرأة خير من رجل.[570]

[Muṣādif:] Abū ʿAbd Allāh said, "Many a woman is better than a man."

حبيب الخثعمي قال: سمعت ابا عبد الله يقول: أحبّوا للناس ما تحبّون لأنفسكم.[571]

[Ḥabīb al-Khathʿamī:] I heard Abū ʿAbd Allāh say, "Love for others what you love for yourself."[572]

---

567 Kulaynī, *Kāfī*, 5:36, 64, with a variant at 5:63.

568 Qurʾān 63:8.

569 Kulaynī, *Kāfī*, 5:104.

570 Kulaynī, *Kāfī*, 4:306; Ṭūsī, *Tahdhīb*, 5:413.

571 Kulaynī, *Kāfī*, 2:170, 635 (see also 2:146).

572 As is commonly known, this is the Golden Rule, which is quoted in Shīʿī *ḥadīth* also from the Prophet (e.g., Abū Ṭālib, *Amālī*, 455; Ṭūsī, *Amālī*, 507; Ibn Shuʿba al-Ḥarrānī, *Tuḥaf al-ʿuqūl*, 19) and ʿAlī (e.g., *Nahj al-balāgha*, letter no. 31 [ed. Ṣubḥī al-Ṣāliḥ, 397]; Ibn Bābawayh, *Amālī*, 478 [also Ṭūsī, 435]). Sunnī sources quote a variant of the statement from the Prophet. However, whereas the Shīʿī version advocates this as the accepted pattern of behavior with the entire humanity (*al-nās*), the version quoted in the most authoritative Sunnī sources advises it as recommended behavior between Muslims (*li-akhīk*, *li-akhīh*). See Bukhārī, *Ṣaḥīḥ*, no. 13; Muslim, *Ṣaḥīḥ*, no. 45; Ibn Mājah, *Sunan*, no. 66; Tirmidhī, *Sunan*, no. 2515; Nasāʾī, *Sunan*, no. 5017, and many other works cited in the editor's footnote in the Beirut, 1996 edition of Tirmidhī, 4:284. (Cf., for instance, Bayhaqī, *Shuʿab al-īmān* [Riyadh, 2003], 2:99).

عجلان بن صالح قال أبو عبد الله: أَنصِف الناس من نفسك وواسِهِم من مالك وارضِ لهم ما ترضى لنفسك.[573]

[ʿAjlān b. Ṣāliḥ:] Abū ʿAbd Allāh said, "Treat people in the same way that you deem fair for yourself; help them with your money, and be happy for them with what you are happy with for yourself."

Finally, a couple of witty responses from Jaʿfar that illustrate his sense of humor:[574]

أبو بصير قال: قلت لأبي عبد الله إنّ عيسى بن أعين يشكّ في الصلاة فيعيدها. فقال: هل يشكّ في الزكاة فيعطيها مرّتين؟[575]

[Abū Baṣīr:] I reported to Abū ʿAbd Allāh that ʿĪsā b. Aʿyan has doubts about [his correct performance of] his prayers, so he often repeats them. He said, "Does he ever have doubts about his *zakāt* and pay it twice?!"[576]

محمّد بن مسلم قال: قلت لأبي عبد الله: في كم يُقطَع السارق؟ قال: في ربع دينار. قال: قلت له: في درهمين؟ فقال: في ربع دينار، بلغ الدينار ما بلغ. فقلت له: أرأيت من سرق أقلّ من ربع دينار هل يقع عليه حين سرق اسم السارق؟ وهل هو عند الله سارق في تلك الحال؟ فقال: كلّ من سرق من مسلم شيئًا قد حواه وأحرزه فهو يقع عليه اسم السارق وهو عند الله سارق، ولكن لا يُقطَع إلّا في ربع دينار أو أكثر. ولو قُطِعت أيدي السُرّاق في ما هو أقلّ من ربع دينار لألفيت عامّة الناس مُقطَعين.[577]

[Muḥammad b. Muslim:] I said to Abū ʿAbd Allāh, "What is the [minimum] amount [of a stolen good] for which the thief incurs amputation?" He said, "A quarter of a dinar." I said to him, "How about two dirhams?" He said, "For a quarter of a dinar, whatever the dinar is worth." I said to him, "What is your position on someone who steals

573 Ḥusayn b. Saʿīd, *Zuhd*, 19; Kulaynī, *Kāfī*, 2:144–45 (with variations); Ibn Bābawayh, *Faqīh*, 4:12, 282, 290. See also Ibn Abī Shayba, *Muṣannaf*, 12:162 and Abū Ṭālib, *Amālī*, 444, where variants of this statement are quoted through Muḥammad al-Bāqir from the Prophet.

574 See Qāḍī ʿIyāḍ, *Shifā*, 2:94, where the author describes Jaʿfar al-Ṣādiq as a man "of good humor and smile." See also Bazanṭī, *Jāmiʿ*, 115 (also Kulaynī, *Kāfī*, 2:663). For another example of this kind, see an alleged, though unlikely, conversation between Jaʿfar al-Ṣādiq and Abū Ḥanīfa in Kushājim, *al-Maṣāyid wa'l-matārid*, 202–3.

575 Muḥammad b. ʿAlī b. Maḥbūb, *Nawādir al-Muṣannaf*, 109.

576 ʿĪsā b. Aʿyan was a wealthy member of the Shīʿī family of Āl Aʿyan in Kūfa. See Kulaynī, *Kāfī*, 3:556.

577 Kulaynī, *Kāfī*, 4:313.

less than a quarter of a dinar: Is he to be called a thief for stealing? And is he a thief before God in such circumstances?" He said, "Anyone who steals something from a Muslim that is owned and protected is called a thief and is a thief before God. However, he is not subject to amputation of the hand except for a quarter of a dinar or more. If the hands of thieves were amputated for less than a quarter of a dinar, then you would find almost everyone with amputated hands!"

يونس بن يوسف قال: كنت مع أبي عبد الله في الحِجر فاستسقى فأُتى بقدح من صُفر، فقال له رجلٌ إنّ عبّاد بن كثير يكره الشرب في صُفر. فقال: ألا سألته ذهبٌ هو أم فضّة؟![578]

[Yūnus b. Yūsuf:] I was with Abū ʿAbd Allāh in the *ḥijr* [of Ismāʿīl, a space adjacent to the Kaʿba where the pilgrims sit]. He asked for water and was brought some in a cup made of brass. A man told him that ʿAbbād b. Kathīr disliked drinking from brass. He said, "Did you not ask him whether brass is gold or silver?!"[579]

حمّاد بن عثمان قال: بعثني عمر بن يزيد إلى أبي جعفر الأحول بدراهم وقال قل له: إن أراد أن يحجّ به فليحجّ وإن أراد أن ينفقها فلينفقها. قال: فأنفقها ولم يحجّ. فذكر ذلك أصحابنا لأبي عبد الله فقال: وجدتم الشيخ فقيهًا![580]

[Ḥammād b. ʿUthmān:] ʿUmar b. Yazīd sent me to Abū Jaʿfar al-Aḥwal[581] with some money and told me tell him he has a choice to use it either for the *ḥajj* or for himself. He used the money for himself and did not perform the *ḥajj*. Our companions mentioned this to Abū ʿAbd Allāh, who said, "You found the *shaykh* to be intelligent!"

578 Barqī, *Maḥāsin*, 583; Kulaynī, *Kāfī*, 6:385.

579 The point at issue here is that only gold and silver vessels are prohibited in Islamic law. ʿAbbād's reaction to a brass vessel went, as usual for him, beyond the religious injunctions.

580 Kulaynī, *Kāfī*, 4:313.

581 Abū Jaʿfar Muḥammad b. ʿAlī b. al-Nuʿmān al-Bajalī, Ṣāḥib al-Ṭāq, a prominent Shīʿī *mutakallim* of the mid-second century. On him, see Modarressi, *Tradition and Survival*, 1:338–39.

CHAPTER 2

The Legal School

أبو أُسامة عن أبي عبد الله قال: ما من شيء يحتاج إليه أحد من وُلد آدم إلّا وقد جرت فيه من الله ومن رسوله – صلّى الله عليه وآله وسلّم – سنّةٌ، عرفها من عرفها وأنكرها من أنكرها.[1]

[Abū Usāma:] Abū ʿAbd Allāh said, "None of the children of Adam is in need of anything for which a standard has not already been established by God and His Messenger (may God's prayer and peace be upon him and his Family). Let whoever knows it know it, and whoever is ignorant of it ignore it."

حنان بن سَدير عن أبي عبد الله قال: سألني ابن شُبرُمة: ما تقول في القَسامة في الدم؟ فأجبته بما صنع النبي – صلّى الله عليه وآله وسلّم. فقال: أرأيت لو أنّ النبي – صلّى الله عليه وآله وسلّم – لم يصنع هكذا كيف كان يكون القول فيه؟ قال: فقلت له: أمّا ما صنع النبي – صلّى الله عليه وآله وسلّم – فقد أخبرتك به، وأمّا ما لم يصنع فلا علم لي به.[2]

[Ḥanān b. Sadīr:] Abū ʿAbd Allāh said, "Ibn Shubruma asked me, 'What is your position on *qasāma*[3] in cases of homicide?' I answered him with reference to the practice of the Prophet (may God's prayer and peace be upon him and his Family). He said, 'Had the Prophet (may God's prayer and peace be upon him and his Family) not done that, what do you think the answer would be?' I said to him, 'As for what the Prophet (may God's prayer and peace be upon him and his Family) did, I have already told you about it. As for what he did not do, I have no knowledge of that.'"

---

1 Kulaynī, *Kāfī*, 3:69.

2 Ḥimyarī, *Qurb al-isnād*, 97; Kulaynī, *Kāfī*, 7:362 (see also 1:58, no. 21, which may refer to the same conversation). For the background of the conversation, see Ibn Bābawayh, *Faqīh*, 4:72.

3 See the section on *ḳasāma* in the entry on *ḳasam* in *Encyclopaedia of Islam* II, 4:689–90 [J. Pedersen and Y. Linant de Bellefonds], for a brief description of the concept.

منصور بن حازم قال: كنت عند أبي عبد الله فأتاه رجل فسأله عن رجل تزوّج امرأة. . . قلت: جُعلت فداك! ما تفخر الشيعة إلّا بقضاء عليٍّ في هذه. فما تقول فيها؟ قال: يا شيخ! تخبرني أنّ عليّاً قضى بها وتسألني ما تقول فيها؟![4]

[Manṣūr b. Ḥāzim:] I was with Abū ʿAbd Allāh when someone approached him asking about [an issue regarding] a man who married a woman . . . [He answered it]. I said, "May I be made your ransom! The Shīʿa have always taken pride in ʿAlī's judgment in this case. So what is your position on it?" He said, "O *shaykh*! You tell me of ʿAlī's judgment in this case and then ask for my position on it?!"

أبان بن تغلب: الشيعة هم الّذين إذا اختلف الناس عن رسول الله – صلّى الله عليه وآله وسلّم – أخذوا بقول علي، وإذا اختلف الناس عن علي أخذوا بقول جعفر بن محمّد.[5]

[Abān b. Taghlib:] The Shīʿa are those who follow the opinion of ʿAlī when reports from the Prophet (may God's prayer and peace be upon him and his Family) are contradictory, and who follow the opinion of Jaʿfar b. Muḥammad when reports from ʿAlī are contradictory.

These short statements exemplify the nature and principal characteristics of the specific tradition of law and legal interpretation to which Jaʿfar al-Ṣādiq, and his father Muḥammad al-Bāqir, belonged. This tradition was characterized by a focus on the text, and nothing but the text, of the Qurʾān and the Sunna of the Prophet as the source of the law, and on the transmission, interpretation, and practice of ʿAlī, as known to and transmitted by the learned among his descendants, as the interpretive model for everything Islamic. This is what was called the legal legacy of the Family of the Prophet, which was known to differ in its sources and approaches from the other main legal schools of early Muslim history, referred to conventionally as the schools of the Ḥijāz and Iraq.[6]

In the legal works of both the Jaʿfarī and Zaydī schools, references to the legacy of the Family of the Prophet abound. Here are just a few examples:

4 Aḥmad b. Muḥammad b. ʿĪsā, *Nawādir*, 99; ʿAyyāshī, *Tafsīr*, 1:382; Kulaynī, *Kāfī*, 5:422.
5 Najāshī, *Rijāl*, 12, as also quoted in the introduction.
6 Kulaynī, *Kāfī*, 5:145.

أبو خالد الواسطي قال: سألت زيد بن علي عن مال اليتيم، أفيه زكاةٌ؟ فقال: لا! قلت: إنّ بني أبي رافع يروون عن أمير المؤمنين[7] أنّه زكّى مالَهم. فقال: نحن أهل البيت نُنكر هذا.[8]

[Abū Khālid (ʿAmr b. Khālid) al-Wāsiṭī:] I asked Zayd b. ʿAlī about the property of an orphan—is *zakāt* owed on it? He said, "No!" I said, "The descendants of Abū Rāfiʿ report that the Commander of the Faithful [ʿAlī] paid *zakāt* on their wealth." He said, "We, members of the Family of the Prophet, deny that."[9]

قاسم بن إبراهيم في الركعتين الأخيرتين: يسبّح فيهما أو يقرأ بفاتحة الكتاب؟ قال: الّذي رأيت عليه مشايخ آل الرسول التسبيح.[10]

Regarding the question whether one should recite *tasbīḥ* or the opening *sūra* of the Qurʾān in the last two *rakʿa*s of prayer, Qāsim b. Ibrāhīm[11] said, "What I found the elders of the Family of the Prophet always recite was *tasbīḥ*."

---

7 This is a common reference to ʿAlī in Shīʿī literature, but it was also used by many Sunnīs in the early periods, especially those from Persianate cultural backgrounds. See, for instance, Bayhaqī, *Shuʿab al-īmān*, 12:394 (whence Ibn ʿAsākir, *Taʾrīkh madīnat Dimashq*, 42:514):

> الأحنف بن قيس قال: ما سمعت بعد كلام رسول الله – صلّى الله عليه وسلّم – أحسن من كلام أمير المؤمنين – رضى الله عنه – حيث يقول: إنّ للنكبات نهايات لابدّ لأحد إذا نكب من أن ينتهى إليها، فينبغي للعاقل إذا أصابته نكبة أن ينام لها حتّى تنقضى مدّتها فإنّ في رفعها قبل انقضاء مدّتها زيادة في مكروهها.
>
> [Aḥnaf b. Qays:] "After the speech of the Messenger of God (may God's prayer and peace be upon him), I never heard words better than those of the Commander of the Faithful (may God be pleased with him) when he said, "Misfortunes have ends, so anyone who suffers a misfortune should reach its end. The intelligent person, if afflicted with a misfortune, should keep calm until it passes, for trying to end it before it has run its course increases its ill effects."

As is well known to students of early Arabic literature, this statement is by ʿAlī (see Quḍāʿī, *Dustūr maʿālim al-ḥikam*, 304).

8 Zayd b. ʿAlī b. al-Ḥusayn, *Musnad*, 138.

9 This is confirmed by a report from Muḥammad al-Bāqir in Aḥmad b. ʿĪsā, *Amālī*, 2:297 (partially also in Ṭūsī, *Tahdhīb*, 4:27), and by another from Jaʿfar al-Ṣādiq in ʿĀṣim b. Ḥumayd al-Ḥannāṭ, *Kitāb*, 152.

10 Aḥmad b. ʿĪsā, *Amālī*, 1:113.

11 Qāsim b. Ibrāhīm al-Ḥasanī al-Rassī (d. 246), Imam of the Zaydī Shīʿa in his time and author of numerous works. See the entry on him in *Encyclopaedia of Islam* II, 8:453–54 [Wilferd Madelung].

أجمع آل رسول الله على أن يقولوا في الأذان والإقامة: حيّ على خير العمل.[12]

The Family of the Messenger of God unanimously included "Come for the best of deeds" in the [calls to prayer, both] *adhān* and *iqāma*.

أجمع آل رسول الله على الجهر ببسم الله الرحمن الرحيم.[13]

The Family of the Messenger of God unanimously recited aloud [in the beginning of their prayer] "In the name of God, the Beneficent, the Merciful."[14]

رُوينا عن رسول الله – صلّى الله عليه وآله وسلّم – وعن علي والحسن والحسين وعلي بن الحسين ومحمّد بن علي وجعفر بن محمّد أنّهم كانوا يجهرون ببسم الله الرحمن الرحيم في ما يُجهر فيه من الصلوات. وقال علي بن الحسين: أجتمعنا وُلد فاطمة على ذلك.[15]

We have been told about the Prophet (may God's prayer and peace be upon him and his Family), ʿAlī, Ḥasan, Ḥusayn, ʿAlī b. al-Ḥusayn, Muḥammad b. ʿAlī, and Jaʿfar b. Muḥammad that they used to recite [the opening formula] "In the name of God, the Beneficent, the Merciful" aloud in any prayer in which the recitation is made aloud. ʿAlī b. al-Ḥusayn said, "We, the children of Fāṭima, have all agreed on this matter."

رفاعة بن موسى قال: سألت أبا عبد الله عن متمتّع لا يجد هديًا. قال: يصوم ثلاثة أيّام بعد النفر. والله تعالى يقول: ﴿ثَلَاثَةِ أَيَّامٍ فِي الْحَجِّ﴾. قلت: قول الله في ذي الحجّة؟ قال: نحن أهل البيت نقول في ذي الحجّة.[16]

[Rifāʿa b. Mūsā:] I asked Abū ʿAbd Allāh about a pilgrim who is performing *ḥajj al-tamattuʿ* and cannot find an animal to sacrifice. He said, "He should fast three days following his departure, as God, the Majestic and Exalted, says: 'Three days during the *ḥajj*.'"[17] I said, "Did

12 ʿAlawī, *Adhān bi-ḥayya ʿalā khayr al-ʿamal*, 91, quoting Ḥasan b. Yaḥyā b. al-Ḥusayn b. Zayd b. ʿAlī.

13 ʿAlawī, *al-Jāmiʿ al-kāfī*, 2:101.

14 Beyond these examples, the agreement of the Family—اجماع العترة or الّذي عليه العلماء من آل الرسول—is frequently mentioned in Zaydī law as a decisive factor, as is well known to students of that legal system.

15 Qāḍī Nuʿmān, *Daʿāʾim al-Islām*, 1:193.

16 Ṭūsī, *Tahdhīb*, 5:232, with a variant in Kulaynī, *Kāfī*, 4:506–7.

17 Qurʾān 2:196.

God mean the month of Dhū al-Ḥijja?" He said, "That is what we, the People of the Family [of the Prophet], say."

سفيان بن عيينة عن الزهري قال: قال لي علي بن الحسين: وأمّا صوم السفر والمرض فإنّ العامّة قد اختلفت في ذلك. وأمّا نحن فنقول: يُفطِرُ في الحالين جميعًا. فانّ الله عزّ وجلّ يقول: ﴿فَمَنْ كَانَ مِنْكُمْ مَرِيضًا أَوْ عَلَىٰ سَفَرٍ فَعِدَّةٌ مِنْ أَيَّامٍ أُخَرَ﴾.[18]

[Sufyān b. ʿUyayna, quoting Zuhrī:] ʿAlī b. al-Ḥusayn said to me, "As for the question of fasting when one is traveling or ill, the majority differ on this matter [on whether refraining from fasting is optional or obligatory]. As for us, our position is that one is to break one's fast in both cases, for God, the Mighty and Majestic, says: 'Whoever of you is ill or traveling, [make up the fast with] a number of other days.'"[19]

عن أبي جعفر قال: إنّا آل محمّد نلبس المعصفر.[20]

Abū Jaʿfar said, "We, the Family of the Prophet, wear that which is dyed with saffron."

عن علي قال: إنّا أهل بيت لا نشرب المسكر ولا نأكل الجرّي ولا نمسح على الخفّين.[21]

ʿAlī said, "We are members of a Family who do not drink intoxicants, do not eat *jirrī*,[22] and do not wipe over boots [when performing ablution]."

عيسى بن عبد الله العلوي عن أبيه عبد الله بن محمّد بن عمر بن علي بن أبي طالب قال: خلط علي قوم من أصحابنا في شيء من أمر الحجّ فاستأذنتُ على جعفر بن محمّد فأُدخلت عليه فقلت [له]: إنّ قومًا من أصحابنا خلطوا على شيء من أمر الحجّ. قال لي: أليس قد أدركتَ أباك وسمعتَ منه؟ قلت: بلى! قال: ورأيت خالك زيد بن علي وسمعت منه؟ – وعدّد علي رجالاً من أهلنا – قلت: بلى! فقال لي: فانظر إلى ما سمعت منهم فخُذ به، وما سمعت من غيرهم فارمِ به تهتَد.[23]

18 Kulaynī, *Kāfī*, 4:83, 86.
19 Qurʾān 2:184.
20 Ibn Abī Shayba, *Muṣannaf*, 8:268.
21 Ibn Bābawayh, *Faqīh*, 4:298.
22 The same as *jirrīth*, mentioned in the previous chapter and in a number of reports in the present chapter; a fish from the eel family.
23 Aḥmad b. ʿĪsā, *Amālī*, 1:237.

[ʿĪsā b. ʿAbd Allāh al-ʿAlawī, quoting his father, ʿAbd Allāh b. Muḥammad b. ʿUmar b. ʿAlī b. Abī Ṭālib:][24] A group of our companions were confused about some matters relating to the *ḥajj*, so I asked permission from Jaʿfar b. Muḥammad to visit him and was allowed to be in his presence. I said [to him], "A group of our companions are confused about some matters relating to the *ḥajj*." He said to me, "Did you not meet your father and hear from him?" I said, "Yes!" He said, "And you saw your [maternal] uncle[25] Zayd b. ʿAlī and heard from him?"—and he counted a number of other men from our family. I said, "Yes!" He said to me, "Look to what you heard from them and apply it, and discard whatever you heard from others. That will put you on the right path."

I. ʿAlī: Father of the Legal Legacy of the House of the Prophet

From a very young age, reportedly from around age five, ʿAlī was brought up by the Prophet, who in turn had been brought up by ʿAlī's father, Abū Ṭālib, who had taken custody of Muḥammad when the latter lost both of his parents as well as his grandfather, ʿAbd al-Muṭṭalib. Thereafter ʿAlī lived with the Prophet, became the first male to embrace Islam at the age of ten, married the Prophet's daughter, and accompanied the Prophet until the end of his life. He thus witnessed at close hand what the Prophet said and did during the course of his life as a prophet, and was as such considered a major authority on the Prophet's Sunna:[26]

أبصر عمر بن الخطّاب على عبد الله بن جعفر ثوبين مضرّجين وهو مُحرِمٌ فقال: ما هذه الثياب؟ فقال علي بن أبي طالب: ما أخال أحدًا يعلّمنا السنّة. فسكت عمر.[27]

ʿUmar b. al-Khaṭṭāb saw ʿAbd Allāh b. Jaʿfar wearing two red garments while in the state of pilgrim sanctity. He said, "What are these clothes?" ʿAlī b. Abī Ṭālib said, "I would not think that anyone [would try to] teach us[28] the Sunna." ʿUmar kept silent.

24 On the father and the son, see Modarressi, *Tradition and Survival*, 1:294–98.

25 ʿAbd Allāh b. Muḥammad b. ʿUmar b. ʿAlī's mother was a daughter of ʿAlī Zayn al-ʿĀbidīn and a sister of Zayd b. ʿAlī. ʿAbd Allāh was thus Zayd's nephew. See Modarressi, *Tradition and Survival*, 1:294.

26 See various reports from early Islamic authorities on this in Ibn ʿAsākir, *Taʾrīkh madīnat Dimashq*, 42:401–10.

27 Shāfiʿī, *Umm*, 5:52. Also Bayhaqī, *Sunan*, 5:94, with a variant at 5:97 that identifies the parties to the story as Muḥammad, son of ʿAbd Allāh b. Jaʿfar, and ʿUthmān (and gives the background to the story). The final comment is by ʿAlī in both variants.

28 ʿAbd Allāh was the son of Jaʿfar b. Abī Ṭālib, an older brother of ʿAlī, who was also among the very early Muslims and who was killed in the Battle of Muʾta in the year 8 of the *hijra*. His son, ʿAbd Allāh, was a son-in-law of his uncle ʿAlī.

عن أمّ المؤمنين عائشة، قالت: علي أعلم الناس بالسنّة.[29]

ʿĀʾisha said, "ʿAlī is the most knowledgeable of the people about the Sunna."

عن أبي سعيد الخدري قال: كانت لِعلي من رسول الله دخلةٌ لم تكن لأحد من الناس.[30]

Abū Saʿīd al-Khudrī said, "ʿAlī had an access to the Messenger of God that nobody else shared."

قال علي: كنت إذا سألته (يعني النبي – صلّى الله عليه وآله وسلّم) أنبأني وإذا سكتُّ ابتدأني.[31]

ʿAlī said, "When I asked him—meaning the Prophet—he would inform me, and when I kept silent he would begin speaking to me."

ʿAlī was also recognized for his knowledge of the Qurʾān:

أبو الطفيل قال: شهدت عليًا يخطب وهو يقول: ما من آية إلّا وأنا أعلم بليلٍ نزلت أم بنهار، في سهلٍ أم في جبل.[32]

[Abū al-Ṭufayl:] I saw ʿAlī giving a speech, saying, "There is no passage [of the Qurʾān] of which I do not know whether it was revealed during the night or during the day, on a plain or on a mountain."

As noted earlier, the legal legacy of the Family of the Prophet was faithfully to follow ʿAlī's legal decisions and practice:

عن ابن عبّاس قال: إذا حدّثنا ثقةٌ عن علي بفُتيا لم نعدُها.[33]

[Ibn ʿAbbās:] When a reliable transmitter related to us a legal opinion of ʿAlī, we did not go beyond it.

---

29 Balādhurī, *Ansāb al-ashrāf*, 2:99; also Ibn ʿAsākir, *Taʾrīkh madīnat Dimashq*, 42:804 (علي أعلمكم بالسنّة). See also Nasāʾī, *Sunan*, no. 129. The point is confirmed by a number of reports from other Companions in Ibn ʿAsākir, 42:407, 410.

30 Balādhurī, *Ansāb al-ashrāf*, 2:89.

31 Ibn Saʿd, *Ṭabaqāt*, 2:292; Balādhurī, *Ansāb al-ashrāf*, 2:89.

32 Ibn Saʿd, *Ṭabaqāt*,2:292; Bukhārī, *Taʾrīkh*, 8:165; Balādhurī, *Ansāb al-ashrāf*, 2:89; Ibn ʿAsākir, *Taʾrīkh madīnat Dimashq*, 42:397–98.

33 Balādhurī, *Ansāb al-ashrāf*, 2:90. See further Ibn ʿAsākir, *Taʾrīkh madīnat Dimashq*, 42:407.

Later in the Umayyad period, before the mass fabrication of reports in ʿAlī's name became the norm,[34] Jaʿfar al-Ṣādiq would advise his followers to follow what the proto-Sunnī *ḥadīth* transmitters quoted from ʿAlī, if they could not find any instruction by later Imams on a given question:

إذا نزلت بكم حادثة لا تجدون حكمها في ما رُوي عنّا فانظروا إلى ما رووه عن علي فاعملوا به.[35]

If a case comes up for you and you do not find a ruling for it based on what has been transmitted from us, look to what these people transmit from ʿAlī and act on it.

يونس بن أبي وهب القصري عن أبي عبد الله قال: إعلم أنّ أمير المؤمنين أفضل عند الله من الأئمّة كلّهم وله ثواب أعمالهم، وعلى قدر أعمالهم فُضّلوا.[36]

[Yūnus b. Abī Wahb al-Qasrī:] Abū ʿAbd Allāh said, "Know that the Commander of the Faithful is favored by God above all the Imams; he gets the reward for their [good] deeds, and they are favored according to the measure of their deeds."

عيسى بن عبد الله العلوي قال: إذا سمعتُ حديثين وثبت عندي حديث عن النبي – صلّى الله عليه وآله وسلّم – وحديث عن علي، أخذتُ الحديث الّذي عن علي لأنّه كان أعلم الناس بآخر ما كان عليه النبي – صلّى الله عليه وآله وسلّم.[37]

[ʿĪsā b. ʿAbd Allāh al-ʿAlawī:] If I hear two *ḥadīth*s, and both are reliably reported to me, one from the Prophet and one from ʿAlī, I take the one from ʿAlī because he was the most knowledgeable person about the Prophet's latest practice.

34 Much has been said about this phenomenon in premodern and modern works, with one of the earliest comments being that of Shāfiʿī in his *Umm*, 7:488–89, where he objects to misquotations from ʿAlī on the question of hand amputation as a punishment in criminal law, saying that none of these is authentic:

فقد رويتم عن علي بن أبي طالب في القطع أشياءً منكرة، وكلّ ما رويتم عن علي في القطع غير ثابت عندنا.

You quoted bizarre material from ʿAlī b. Abī Ṭālib regarding amputation [of the hand in punishment], but whatever you quoted from ʿAlī on amputation is not proven to us.

On the phenomenon in general, see especially Ibn al-Jawzī, *Mawḍūʿāt*, 1:20–21, where he quotes a number of fabricators from different groups who acknowledged that when they liked an opinion, they forged a *ḥadīth* to support it: إنّا كنّا إذا رأينا رأيًا جعلنا له حديثًا.

35 Ṭūsī, *ʿUddat al-uṣūl*, 1:379–80.

36 Kulaynī, *Kāfī*, 4:580; Ibn Qūlawayh, *Kāmil al-ziyārāt*, 38; Ṭūsī, *Tahdhīb*, 6:20.

37 Aḥmad b. ʿĪsā, *Amālī*, 1:238.

عبيد بن زرارة عن أبي عبد الله في الرجل يؤخذ وعليه حدود أحدها القتل، قال: كان علي يقيم عليه الحدود ثمّ يقتله. ولا نُخالف عليّاً.[38]

[ʿUbayd b. Zurāra:] On the question of [how to sequence the punishments of] a man arrested and [found] liable to several *ḥadd* punishments, including the death penalty, Abū ʿAbd Allāh said, "ʿAlī used to apply the *ḥadd* punishments [first] and then the capital punishment. And we do not go against ʿAlī's decisions."

محمّد بن مسلم قال: سألت أبا عبد الله عن الثوبين الرديّين بالثوب المرتفع والبعير بالبعيرين والدابّة بالدابّتين؟ فقال: كره ذلك علي فنحن نكرهه.[39]

[Muḥammad b. Muslim:] I asked Abū ʿAbd Allāh about [the permissibility of] trading two garments of lower quality for one of better quality, one camel for two, and one riding animal for two. He said, "ʿAlī disapproved of that, so we disapprove of it."

أبو بصير عن أبي عبد الله في رجل استبدل قوصرتين فيهما بُسر مطبوخ بقوصرة فيها تمر مشقّق، قال: هذا مكروه. قال: أبو بصير: ولِمَ يُكره؟ فقال: كان علي بن أبي طالب يكره أن يُستبدل [وسق من تمر خيبر بوسقين من تمر المدينة].[40] لأنّ تمر المدينة أدونهما. ولم يكن علي يكره الحلال.[41]

[Abū Baṣīr:] Commenting on a man who exchanged two receptacles of cooked, unripe dates for one receptacle of mature dates, Abū ʿAbd Allāh said, "This is cautioned against." Abū Baṣīr said, "Why is that?" He said, "ʿAlī b. Abī Ṭālib disapproved of a load of dates from Khaybar being exchanged for two loads of Medinan dates, because the Medinan dates are the lower quality of the two.[42] And ʿAlī was not one to disapprove of what was lawful."

---

38 Ibn Bābawayh, *Faqīh*, 4:124, with a variant in Kulaynī, *Kāfī*, 7:250.

39 Ṭūsī, *Tahdhīb*, 7:120.

40 The sentence between brackets appears in the source (Kulaynī, *Kāfī*, 5:881, no. 7) as وسق من تمر المدينة بوسقين من تمر خيبر, which does not go well with the justification mentioned immediately after as لأنّ تمر المدينة أدونهما, corrected on the basis of two shorter variants of the report in the same source (Kulaynī, 5:881, no. 8; also Ṭūsī, *Tahdhīb*, 7:97, no. 413) and Ṭūsī, 7:94, no. 400.

41 Kulaynī, *Kāfī*, 5:881.

42 The point at issue is the unlawfulness of the exchange of dates of different weights in order to block a possible sham sale contract with the intention of circumventing the legal prohibition on receiving interest on a loan.

عبد الله بن سنان قال: سألت أبا عبد الله عن رجل كانت تحته أمة فطلّقها على السنّة فبانت منه، ثمّ اشتراها بعد ذلك قبل أن تنكح زوجًا غيره؟ قال: أليس قد قضى علي في هذه؟[43]

['Abd Allāh b. Sinān:] I asked Abū 'Abd Allāh about a man who was married to a slave woman and then divorced her according to the Sunna, after which she was separated from him. But then he purchased her before she married another man.[44] He said, "Did 'Alī not issue a judgment on this matter?"[45]

الحكم بن أبي عقيل قال: قلت لأبي عبد الله: إنّ لي خصمًا يتكثّر عليَّ بالشهود الزور وقد كرهت مكافاته مع أنّي لا أدرى أيصلح لي ذلك أم لا؟ قال: فقال لي: أما بلغك عن أمير المؤمنين أنّه كان يقول: لا تؤسروا أنفسكم وأموالكم بشهادات الزور؟ فما على امرئ من وكف في دينه ولا مأثم من ربّه إن يدفع ذلك عنه.[46]

[Ḥakam b. Abī 'Aqīl:] I said to Abū 'Abd Allāh, "I have an adversary who brings a lot of false witnesses against me, and I hate to retaliate. Moreover, I do not even know whether doing so is lawful for me." He said to me, "Did you not hear that the Commander of the Faithful used to say, 'Do not make yourselves and your properties prisoners to false testimony? A man suffers neither a deficiency in his religion nor is he held blameworthy by his Lord if he repels such an adversary away from himself.'"

عبيد بن زرارة عن أبي عبد الله في الرجل يسافر في شهر رمضان، يصوم أو يُفطر؟ قال: إن خرج قبل الزوال فليفطر، وإن خرج بعد الزوال فليَصم. قال: يُعرف ذلك بقول عليّ: «أصوم وأفطر حتّى إذا زالت الشمس عزم عليّ» (يعني الصيام).[47]

['Ubayd b. Zurāra:] On the question whether a man traveling during the month of Ramaḍān should fast or break his fast, Abū 'Abd Allāh said, "If he leaves before noon, he is to break his fast, but if he leaves after the noon, he is to fast." He said, "This is known from the saying of

43 Kulaynī, *Kāfī*, 6:173.

44 The point at issue is whether the woman's change of status from a divorced wife to a slave would circumvent the Qur'ānic requirement that she subsequently marry another man before the former husband can legally marry her again.

45 'Alī's judgment in the case is quoted at the end of the same report in Kulaynī, *Kāfī*, 6:173.

46 Kulaynī, *Kāfī*, 7:401–2.

47 Kulaynī, *Kāfī*, 4:131.

> ʿAlī: 'I [have the choice to] fast or break my fast until the sun passes its zenith, at which point fasting becomes obligatory for me.'"

The legacy of the Family of the Prophet, manifested in both words and practice, was passed through the family from one generation to the next.[48] There were also written books and documents that Jaʿfar and his father possessed and occasionally referred to,[49] including an early book called *Kitāb ʿAlī*, which contained much of the material that ʿAlī transmitted from the Prophet, both statements and actions, as well as his own juridical decisions during his caliphate.[50] Jaʿfar once showed the book to a disciple of his, Zurāra b. Aʿyan, to document a remark.[51] There are also references to a text on the designated shares of inheritance recorded by ʿAlī from the statements of the Prophet, titled *Ṣaḥīfat al-farāʾiḍ* or *Farāʾiḍ ʿAlī*, which Jaʿfar and his father had in their possession and sometimes showed and read to their associates.[52] These texts were among the oldest records of the Sunna of the Prophet, alongside a text containing the guidelines that the Prophet wrote for ʿAmr b. Ḥazm,[53] a Companion whom he allegedly sent, carrying this text, to the chiefs of Najrān in southwestern Arabia near the border with Yemen to collect religious taxes. The text was preserved in the family of ʿAmr b. Ḥazm until the mid-second century. A couple of *ḥadīth* transmitters

---

48 As noted earlier, people in Mecca and Medina closely watched the practice of the members of the Family and expected them to follow a uniform practice representing that of the Prophet. Consider this example (Kulaynī, *Kāfī*, 4:194):

> أبو بلال المكّي قال: رأيت أبا عبد الله طاف بالبيت ثمّ صلّى في ما بين الباب والحجر الأسود ركعتين، فقلت له: ما رأيت أحدًا منكم صلّى في هذا الموضع؟ فقال: هذا المكان الّذي تيب على آدمَ فيه.
>
> [Abū Bilāl al-Makkī:] I saw Abū ʿAbd Allāh circumambulate the House, then pray two *rakʿas* in the space between the door [of the Kaʿba] and the Black Stone. I said to him, "I have never seen any of you pray in this area." He said, "This is the location where Adam was forgiven."

49 See also the message that ʿAbd Allāh b. al-Ḥasan allegedly sent to Jaʿfar: "You are a man of books" (أنت رجل صحفيّ); that is, you have acquired your knowledge by reading books rather than by studying with teachers, and, as such, your mind is more preoccupied with details mentioned in the books (Kulaynī, *Kāfī*, 8:364, with a variant attributed to Abū Ḥanīfa in a spurious report in Ibn Bābawayh, *ʿIlal al-sharāʾiʿ*, 1:89–90).

50 See Modarressi, *Tradition and Survival*, 1:4–7.

51 Kulaynī, *Kāfī*, 3:397. His father, Muḥammad al-Bāqir, also showed the book to a disciple of his, the Kūfan Muḥammad b. Muslim al-Thaqafī (Kulaynī, 6:219). A report in Ṭūsī, *Tahdhīb*, 8:81–82 by the same disciple quotes Muḥammad al-Bāqir offering an evaluation of a case of divorce on the basis of general pattens in the law of divorce but then immediately saying:

> ولكن كيف أصنع أو أقول هذا وفي كتاب علي أنّ امرأة أتت رسولَ الله – صلّى الله عليه وآله وسلّم . . .
>
> But how can I say this when according to the Book of ʿAlī, [the Prophet decided differently in a similar case]?

52 Kulaynī, *Kāfī*, 7:81, 93, 94–95, 98, 113, 119 (see also 7:125, where the text is called *Kitāb al-Jāmiʿa*).

53 ʿAmr b. Ḥazm al-Anṣārī. He lived until the time of Muʿāwiya (r. 41–60).

of the early second century reported seeing the text in the possession of ʿAmr's grandson, Abū Bakr b. Muḥammad b. ʿAmr b. Ḥazm.[54] In the time of Jaʿfar al-Ṣādiq, it was held by Abū Bakr b. Muḥammad's son, ʿAbd Allāh, with whom Mālik found the document and quoted from it.[55] According to one report, Jaʿfar asked a student of his, the transmitter Abū Maryam,[56] to retrieve the text from ʿAbd Allāh so that Jaʿfar could review it. Abū Maryam went and took the text and brought it to Jaʿfar.[57]

As attested by an extremely large number of references,[58] ʿAlī's transmission of the Prophet's words and practice, as well as his own judicial decisions during his time as caliph, were the foundation of the legal school of Jaʿfar al-Ṣādiq.[59] After ʿAlī, the opinions and practice of his two sons, Ḥasan al-Mujtabā and Ḥusayn, and then of Ḥusayn's son ʿAlī Zayn al-ʿĀbidīn[60] informed the legacy of the Family of the Prophet.[61] It was, however, with

54 Abū Dāwūd, *Marāsīl*, 210; Nasāʾī, *Sunan*, no. 7032.

55 Nasāʾī, *Sunan*, no. 7032.

56 ʿAbd al-Ghaffār b. Qāsim al-Anṣārī, a Kūfan *ḥadīth* scholar in the first half of the second century and a transmitter known to both the Sunnī and Shīʿī communities of his time. On him, see further Modarressi, *Tradition and Survival*, 1:135–37.

57 Ṭūsī, *Tahdhīb*, 10:291 (all pronouns in this report should refer to ʿAbd Allāh, the grandson of ʿAmr b. Ḥazm, who had the document in his possession at this time).

58 There is little point in listing Jaʿfar al-Ṣādiq's countless citations of ʿAlī's statements, as they can be found through a digital search. Here is a select list of instances in two early Shīʿī *ḥadīth* collections in which Jaʿfar used a legal decision, practice, or judicial verdict of ʿAlī to justify his own legal opinion: Kulaynī, *Kāfī*, 3:27, 48, 328, 337, 338, 461, 4:76, 125, 131, 142, 154, 254, 270 (repeated in 271), 280, 322, 329, 347, 369, 389, 479, 394, 522, 5:51, 141, 155, 177, 184, 188, 214–15, 234, 235, 242–43, 284, 295, 296, 407, 6:89, 133, 170, 171, 173, 185, 188, 195, 196, 200, 217, 218, 219, 222, 527, 7:77, 113, 135, 136, 139, 147, 151, 152, 172, 181–82, 231, 250, 263, 265, 318, 321, 325, 327, 328, 332, 333–34, 342, 353, 354, 355, 367, 390, 401–2, 418, 419, 463; Ṭūsī, *Tahdhīb*, 2:88, 325, 337, 4:145, 5:32, 352, 424, 6:199, 240, 319, 393, 7:75, 463, 9:64, 10:108, 121.

59 People were aware of this fact and expected Jaʿfar's opinions to represent those of ʿAlī. See, for instance, Kulaynī, *Kāfī*, 5:215.

60 E.g., Bazanṭī, *Nawādir*, 54; Aḥmad b. Muḥammad b. ʿĪsā, *Nawādir*, 139; Barqī, *Maḥāsin*, 70, 71, 124, 348 (possibly also 349), 360, 639; Muḥammad b. ʿAlī b. Maḥbūb, *Nawādir al-muṣannaf*, 183, 189; Ḥimyarī, *Qurb al-isnād*, 88, 92, 114, 139, 140; Aḥmad b. ʿĪsā, *Amālī*, 1:92; ʿAlī b. Ibrāhīm, *Tafsīr*, 2:450; Ibn al-Ashʿath, *Ashʿathiyyāt*, 164; Kulaynī, *Kāfī*, 3:336, 375, 397, 4:22, 83–87, 256, 264, 304, 369, 417, 434, 497, 499, 535, 5:131, 215, 260, 504, 6:62–63 (a reference by Jaʿfar on this question to "those before us" may refer to the opinion quoted in this report from ʿAlī Zayn al-ʿĀbidīn and to those of ʿAlī as in Ḥimyarī, 104–5, and Muḥammad al-Bāqir as in Kulaynī, 6:63), 224, 236, 450, 577, 7:56, 368; Ibn Bābawayh, *Faqīh*, 1:167, 2:135, 4:14; Ibn Bābawayh, *ʿUyūn akhbār al-Riḍā*, 2:145; Ṭūsī, *Tahdhīb*, 2:267, 4:88, 299, 5:11, 267, 379, 383, 6:289, 337, 7:61, 10:162.

61 There were occasional references to the opinions of ʿAbd Allāh b. ʿAbbās and Zayd b. ʿAlī b. al-Ḥusayn, too. For Ibn ʿAbbās, see, for instance, Aḥmad b. Muḥammad b. ʿĪsā, *Nawādir*, 82; Barqī, *Maḥāsin*, 70; Ḥimyarī, *Qurb al-isnād*, 98 (the same report appears also in Kulaynī, *Kāfī*, 5:130, but the reference to Ibn ʿAbbās is missing), 140–41; ʿAyyāshī, *Tafsīr*, 1:385; Kulaynī, 7:79–80; Ibn Bābawayh, *Faqīh*, 2:204; Ibn Bābawayh, *Maʿānī al-akhbār*, 296; Ṭūsī, *Tahdhīb*, 5:246, 424, 484, 494, 7:191, 9:248. For Zayd, see Furāt b. Ibrāhīm, *Tafsīr*, 151, Ibn al-Ashʿath, *Ashʿathiyyāt*, 59.

Muḥammad al-Bāqir that this legacy assumed a formal shape as a systematic and well-organized tradition.[62]

The main source for Jaʿfar al-Ṣādiq's school after the Qurʾān, the Sunna of the Prophet as quoted by ʿAlī, and ʿAlī's own judgments was thus the teachings and practice of Muḥammad al-Bāqir.[63] This fact is well documented in hundreds of references by Jaʿfar to his father, as recorded in the early sources.[64] It explains his instruction to one of his disciples:

ما سمعت منّي فاروه عن أبي.[65]

Whatever you hear from me, you can quote from my father.[66]

---

62 See ʿAyyāshī, *Tafsīr*, 1:411 (also Kulaynī, *Kāfī*, 2:19); Kashshī, *Rijāl*, 425.

63 See, for instance, Kulaynī, *Kāfī*, 3:84, 86, where Jaʿfar quotes and comments on his father's legal decisions as a text of law. See also references by Jaʿfar to his father as the ultimate authority for his own decisions as, for instance, in Kulaynī, 5:480 (مَنَعني أبي). See further Kulaynī, 5:27, where Jaʿfar says of his father:

كان أبي خير أهل الأرض وأعلمهم بكتاب الله وسنّة نبيه.

> My father was the best human being on earth [in his time] and the most knowledgeable about the Book of God and the Sunna of His Prophet.

See also Kulaynī, 6:469.

64 For references to Muḥammad al-Bāqir's opinions, see, for instance, Ḥusayn b. Saʿīd, *Zuhd*, 10, 95; Barqī, *Maḥāsin*, 212; Ḥimyarī, *Qurb al-isnād*, 31, 142; Aḥmad b. ʿĪsā, *Amālī*, 2:297; ʿAyyāshī, *Tafsīr*, 1:331, 370, 2:128, 295; Ibn al-Ashʿath, *Ashʿathiyyāt*, 21, 48; Kulaynī, *Kāfī*, 1:38, 544, 2:57, 172, 174, 324, 350, 369, 448, 454, 463, 466, 509, 3:21, 83, 189, 190, 432, 525, 566, 4:10, 63, 68, 252, 267, 285, 286, 323, 340, 343, 521, 523, 5:10, 20, 32, 85, 117, 121, 145, 146, 170, 200, 245, 246, 249, 257, 272, 273, 316, 329, 439, 458, 473–74, 480, 488, 550, 567, 6:33, 55, 218, 240, 241, 295, 350, 363, 450, 7:38, 223, 397; Ibn Bābawayh, *Faqīh*, 2:481; Ibn Bābawayh, *Khiṣāl*, 532–33; Ṭūsī, *Tahdhīb*, 1:7, 237, 419, 4:8, 27, 72, 223, 5:27, 223, 248, 447, 6:197, 250, 530, 7:87, 105, 223, 350, 8:53, 9:182, 392, 10:206.

For references to his practice, see, for instance, Muʿāwiya b. ʿAmmār, *Kitāb*, 38; Jaʿfar al-Ḥaḍramī, *Kitāb*, 222, 231; Muḥammad b. ʿAlī b. Maḥbūb, *Nawādir al-muṣannaf*, 189; Barqī, *Maḥāsin*, 202, 297, 351, 461, 496, 599; Ḥimyarī, *Qurb al-isnād*, 19; Aḥmad b. ʿĪsā, *Amālī*, 4:488; ʿAyyāshī, *Tafsīr*, 1:400, 2:11, 3:27; Kulaynī, *Kāfī*, 1:544, 3:327, 331, 332, 410, 446, 453, 461 (see also Ibn Bābawayh, *Faqīh*, 1:322), 4:9, 303, 330, 344, 346, 355, 408, 417, 418, 434, 499, 510, 520, 545, 5:117, 170, 177, 197, 200, 242, 249, 254, 257, 313, 316, 6:189, 206, 207, 309, 381, 450, 464, 469, 502, 551, 7:55, 8:291; Ibn Bābawayh, *Faqīh*, 1:238, 284, 293, 2:221, 265, 281; Ibn Bābawayh, *ʿUyūn akhbār al-Riḍā*, 2:45; Ṭūsī, *Tahdhīb*, 1:62, 91, 332, 2:15, 127, 301, 367, 3:232, 292, 4:269, 299, 5:189, 211, 248, 275, 7:87, 105, 210, 271.

65 Kulaynī, *Kāfī*, 1:51.

66 However, there were occasional discrepancies between the positions of the two. E.g., Kulaynī, *Kāfī*, 2:339 (with a variant in Ṭūsī, *Tahdhīb*, 2:90), 3:339, 543, 5:241–42 (but there seems to be some confusion in this last report, and the views of the two might have been similar; cf. Kulaynī, 5:244; Ibn Bābawayh, *Faqīh*, 3:161; Ṭūsī, 7:220), 6:207–8; Kashshī, *Rijāl*, 134; Ṭūsī, 2:28, 4:70–71 (the latter is possibly a redaction of a conversation between Jaʿfar and his son, Ismāʿīl, recorded in the same source at 4:70, no. 6), 8:53 (other reports at 8:54 and 59 may explain the legal background of and reconcile the two opinions in this case). The discrepancies were at times due to the fear of government that led one or the other to take a precautionary position, but mostly they reflect changing times and circumstances, as in, for

II. Foundational Sources

A. *Qur'ān as Text and Criterion*

In the legal legacy of the Family of the Prophet,[67] the Qur'ān was not only the principal source and the ultimate recourse for defining Islam,[68] but also the criterion by which to test the validity of everything else:

قال سفيان سمعت جعفرًا يقول: إنّ على كلّ حقٍّ حقيقة وعلى كلّ صواب نورًا، فما وافق كتاب الله فخُذوه وما خالفه فدَعوه.[69]

> [Sufyān b. Saʿīd al-Thawrī:] I heard Jaʿfar say, "There is a sign of truthfulness above every truth and a light above everything that is right. So accept what conforms with the Book of God and reject what does not."

Variants of the latter part of this statement are quoted from the Prophet in several *ḥadīth* collections.[70] Among Sunnī scholars, the Ḥanafīs approved of the statement,[71] whereas the *ahl al-ḥadīth* strongly disapproved of it.[72] Under-

---

instance, Kulaynī, 6:187, where Jaʿfar explains that the reason behind his different decision in a certain case lies in the new practice and mentality of the marketplace:

> إنّ الناس كانوا لا يشترطون، والآن هم يشترطون، والمسلمون عند شروطهم.
>
> People were not used to doing conditional contracts. Now they are and Muslims should stand by their commitments.

67 See, for instance, Kulaynī, *Kāfī*, 5:300, where Muḥammad al-Bāqir says: إذا حدثتكم بشيء فاسألوني عن كتاب الله.

68 ما خالف كتابَ الله رُدَّ إلى كتاب الله (Ibn Bābawayh, *Faqīh*, 3:320); كلّ شيء خالف كتاب الله فهو ردّ إلى كتاب الله (Kulaynī, *Kāfī*, 6:60–61): Whatever contravenes the Book of God should be referred back to the Book of God.

69 Yaʿqūbī, *Ta'rīkh*, 2:381. See also ʿAyyāshī, *Tafsīr*, 1:83, where the statement is quoted by Jaʿfar from ʿAlī; Kulaynī, *Kāfī*, 1:69, where it is quoted by Jaʿfar from the Prophet.

70 Shāfiʿī, *Risāla*, 224; Barqī, *Maḥāsin*, 221; Kulaynī, *Kāfī*, 1:69; Ṭabarānī, *al-Muʿjam al-kabīr*, 2:97, 12:244; Dāraquṭnī, *Sunan*, 5:371.

71 See Sarakhsī, *Uṣūl*, 1:364. The Shāfiʿī jurist, Abū Isḥāq al-Shīrāzī, too, rejected any religious report that disagreed with the Qur'ān, even if the report was transmitted by reliable individuals. See his *Lumaʿ*, 215. See also Shāfiʿī's comment in his *Umm*, 10:255–56:

> كان علي بن أبي طالب لا يقبل الحديث عن رسول الله، والرواية تزداد كثرةً ويخرج منه الألوف ولا يعرفه أهل الفقه ولا يوافق الكتاب والسنّة. فايّاك وشاذّ الحديث وعليك بما . . . يوافق الكتاب والسنّة. فما خالف القرآن فليس عن رسول الله وإن جاءت به الرواة.
>
> ʿAlī b. Abī Ṭālib would not accept a *ḥadīth* on the authority of the Messenger of God, but reports [from the Prophet] proliferated; thousands of them appeared, but the jurists did not recognize them and they did not accord with the Book and the Sunna. Beware of such odd *ḥadīths* and cleave to what accords with the Book and the Sunna. Whatever disagrees with the Qur'ān is not from the Messenger of God, even if it is reported by transmitters.

72 ʿAbd al-Raḥmān b. Mahdī (d. 198), an early scholar of *ḥadīth*, accused the atheists and the Khawārij of having fabricated the statement: الزنادقة والخوارج وضعوا ذلك الحديث. See Ibn ʿAbd

standing the concept of agreement as complying with a verbal parallel in the Qurʾān, the latter thought that the statement left no room for *ḥadīth.* Should a report have a parallel text in the Qurʾān, the report would be redundant; if it lacked such a parallel, it would be null and void.[73] This argument misses the point that a report is not necessarily expected to agree with a specific parallel text in the Qurʾān. The opening sentence of Jaʿfar's statement quoted above shows that the intended meaning is general patterns of values and countervalues—the spirit of the Qurʾān, so to speak, and not exact parallels. This is the understanding that also underpins a number of other reports from Jaʿfar al-Ṣādiq requiring a *ḥadīth* to be confirmed by the Qurʾān:

> ايّوب بن الحرّ قال: سمعت أبا عبد الله يقول: كلّ حديث لا يوافق كتاب الله فهو زخرف.[74]
>
> [Ayyūb b. al-Ḥurr:] I heard Abū ʿAbd Allāh say, "Any *ḥadīth* that does not conform with the Book of God is false."
>
> كُليب الأسدي قال: سمعت أبا عبد الله يقول: ما أتاكم عنّا من حديث لا يصدّقه كتاب الله فهو باطل.[75]
>
> [Kulayb al-Asadī:] I heard Abū ʿAbd Allāh say, "Any *ḥadīth* that you receive on our authority that is not supported by the Book of God is void."

The text of the Qurʾān, understood within its context but not restricted by later interpretations and practice, was thus the ultimate source in Jaʿfar al-Ṣādiq's legal thought.

---

al-Barr, *Jāmiʿ bayān al-ʿilm wa-faḍlih*, 2:1191. One is tempted to think that الزنادقة might have been a corruption of الرافضة, as atheism had little to do with a denial of the validity of *ḥadīth*s that did not comply with the Qurʾān. After all, the Zanādiqa were not a good match for the Khawārij, whereas the Rāfiḍa were. However, these early scholars of *ḥadīth* perhaps did not have a clear understanding of what the Zanādiqa were up to and thus counted anyone who said something that they did not like among the Zanādiqa. Two other major *ḥadīth* scholars in the early third century, Yaḥyā b. Maʿīn (d. 233) (cf. Ibn al-Jawzī, *Mawḍūʿāt*, 1:421), and ʿAlī b. al-Madīnī (d. 234) (Ibn Baṭṭa, *Ibāna*, 2:265–66) also blamed the Zanādiqa for fabricating the statement.

73 E.g., Shāfiʿī, *Risāla*, 224; Ibn Ḥazm, *Iḥkām fī uṣūl al-aḥkām*, 1:187–202; Bayhaqī, *Maʿrifat al-sunan*, 1:116–18; Ibn ʿAbd al-Barr, *Jāmiʿ bayān al-ʿilm wa-faḍlih*, 2:1183–84, 1187, 1191. There were also those who approved of the statement but held that it was not a general instruction but only an attempt to define a standard for distinguishing true from false in cases of contradictory reports.

74 Barqī, *Maḥāsin*, 221; ʿAyyāshī, *Tafsīr*, 1:83; Kulaynī, *Kāfī*, 1:69.

75 Barqī, *Maḥāsin*, 221; ʿAyyāshī, *Tafsīr*, 1:83.

Examples of Jaʿfar's statements affirming the primacy of the Qurʾān include the following:

الحلبي قال: سألت أبا عبد الله عن الحجّ فقال: تمتّع. ثمّ قال: إنّا إذا وقفنا بين يدي الله تعالى قلنا: يا ربّنا أخذنا بكتابك، وقال الناس رَأَينا رأيَنا، فيفعل الله بنا وبهم ما أراد.[76]

[ʿUbayd Allāh al-Ḥalabī:] I asked Abū ʿAbd Allāh about the *ḥajj*. He said, "Perform *tamattuʿ*." Then he said, "When we stand before God, the Exalted, we will say, 'O our Lord! We held onto Your Book,' and [the other] people will say, 'We judged by our personal judgment.' God will then do what he wants with us and with them."

عبد الأعلى مولى آل سام قال: قلت لأبي عبد الله: عثرت فانقطع ظفري فجعلت على إصبعي مرارة فكيف أصنع بالوضوء؟ قال يُعرَف هذا وأشباهه من كتاب الله: ﴿مَا جَعَلَ عَلَيْكُمْ فِي الدِّينِ مِنْ حَرَجٍ﴾. إمسح عليه.[77]

[ʿAbd al-Aʿlā, client of Āl Sām:] I said to Abū ʿAbd Allāh, "I tripped and my nail became detached, so I put balm on my toe. How should I perform ablution?" He said, "This and similar cases are known from the Book of God: 'He did not place any difficulty upon you in religion.'[78] Wipe over it."

محمّد بن مسلم قال: سألت أبا عبد الله عن الرجل أو المرأة يذهب بصره فيأتيه الأطبّاء فيقولون نُداويك شهرًا أو أربعين ليلة مستلقيًا، أكذلك يصلّي؟ فرخّص في ذلك وقال: ﴿فَمَنِ اضْطُرَّ غَيْرَ بَاغٍ وَلَا عَادٍ فَلَا إِثْمَ عَلَيْهِ﴾.[79]

[Muḥammad b. Muslim:] I asked Abū ʿAbd Allāh about a man or a woman who becomes blind and is visited by physicians, who say they will treat the patient for one month or forty nights while the patient lies supine. Does the patient pray like that? He offered a dispensation for it and recited, "Whoever is compelled by necessity, without disobeying or transgressing, there is no sin on him."[80]

---

76 Ṭūsī, *Tahdhīb*, 5:26.
77 Kulaynī, *Kāfī*, 1:33.
78 Qurʾān 22:78.
79 Kulaynī, *Kāfī*, 3:014.
80 Qurʾān 2:173.

محمّد بن مسلم قال: سألت أبا عبد الله عن الجرّي والمارماهي والزمير وما ليس له قشر من السمك، أحرامٌ هو؟ فقال لي: يا محمّد! إقرأ هذه الآية التي في الأنعام: ﴿قُل لَّا أَجِدُ فِي مَا أُوحِيَ إِلَيَّ مُحَرَّمًا عَلَىٰ طَاعِمٍ يَطْعَمُهُ﴾ - إلى آخر الآية. إنّما الحرام ما حرّم الله في كتابه، ولكنّهم كانوا يَعافون أشياءً فنحن نَعافها.[81]

[Muḥammad b. Muslim:] I asked Abū ʿAbd Allāh about [specific categories of fish] and fish that do not have scales—are they unlawful? He said to me, "O Muḥammad! Read this passage in [the *sūra* of] *Anʿām*: 'Say: I do not find in that which is revealed to me anything forbidden to one who eats thereof'—to the end of the passage.[82] The unlawful is that which God has deemed unlawful in His Book,[83] but people used to dislike things, so we [too] dislike those [things]."[84]

81 Ṭūsī, *Tahdhīb*, 9:6 with a number of corruptions corrected above on the basis of a variant in ʿAyyāshī, *Tafsīr*, 2:126, which is ascribed to Muḥammad al-Bāqir.

82 Qurʾān 6:145.

83 The Prophet reportedly gave the same answer to a similar question as recorded in Ibn Mājah, *Sunan*, no. 1117; Tirmidhī, *Sunan*, no. 1726 (and other sources cited in the editor's footnote therein, 3:340):

> سلمان الفارسي قال: سُئل رسول الله - صلّى الله عليه وسلّم - عن السَمن والجُبْن والفِراء فقال: «الحلال ما أحلّ الله في كتابه والحرام ما حرّم الله في كتابه».
>
> [Salmān al-Fārisī:] The Messenger of God (may God's prayer and peace be upon him) was asked about fat, cheese, and fur. He said, "The lawful is what God has made lawful in His Book, and the unlawful is what God has made unlawful in His Book."

See also the following report by Shāfiʿī in his *Umm*, 10:256:

> حدّثنا الثقة عن رسول الله - صلّى الله عليه وسلّم - أنّه قال في مرضه الّذي مات فيه: «إنّي أحرّم ما حرّم القرآن».
>
> A reliable person reported to us that the Messenger of God (may God's prayer and peace be upon him), during his terminal illness, said, "I forbid only what the Qurʾān forbids."

See also the comment by Suyūṭī in his *Itqān*, 4:24:

> قال الإمام الشافعي: جميع ما حكم به النبي - صلّى الله عليه وسلّم - فهو ممّا فهمه من القرآن. قلت: ويؤيّد هذا قوله - صلّى الله عليه وسلّم - «إنّي لا أحلّ إلّا ما أحلّ الله ولا أحرّم إلّا ما حرّم الله في كتابه».
>
> Imam al-Shāfiʿī said, "All legal decisions by the Prophet—may God's prayer and peace be upon him—were matters that he understood from the Qurʾān." I say that this point is confirmed by his statement "I do not declare anything lawful except what God declared lawful, nor do I declare anything unlawful except what God declared unlawful in His Scripture."

84 There are several other reports from Jaʿfar al-Ṣādiq on this question in which he gave the same answer and used the same Qurʾānic passage. Some of these reports will be quoted in Chapter 4.

زرارة عن أحدهما[85] قال: أكل الغراب ليس بحرام. إنّما الحرام ما حرّم الله في كتابه. ولكنّ الأنفس تتنزّه عن كثير من ذلك تفزّزًا.[86]

[Zurāra:] Eating crows is not unlawful. What is unlawful is what God has made unlawful in His Book. But people by their nature refrain from many of that kind as they feel revulsion.[87]

حُمران قال سمعت أبا عبد الله يقول في ذبيحة[88] اليهودي: قال: لا تأكل ذبيحته حتّى تسمعه يذكر اسم الله. أما سمعت قول الله: ﴿وَلَا تَأْكُلُوا مِمَّا لَمْ يُذْكَرِ اسْمُ اللَّهِ عَلَيْهِ﴾؟[89]

[Ḥumrān b. Aʿyan:] I heard Abū ʿAbd Allāh say about meat slaughtered by a Jew, "Do not eat what he slaughters until you hear him invoke the name of God. Did you not hear what God said? 'Do not eat that on which the name of God was not invoked.'"[90]

قال الصادق: أيُّ قضيّة أعدل من القرعة إذا فُوّض الأمر إلى الله؟ أليس الله يقول: ﴿فَسَاهَمَ فَكَانَ مِنَ الْمُدْحَضِينَ﴾؟[91]

[Jaʿfar] al-Ṣādiq said, "What is a more just basis than drawing lots if the matter is left to God? Does God not say, 'And he drew lots and was among the losers'?"[92]

85 This formula, repeated frequently in early Shīʿī *ḥadīth*, means "either Muḥammad al-Bāqir or Jaʿfar al-Ṣādiq." It indicates that the report was taken from a notebook in which the author recorded what he had heard from the two Imams but did not specify the exact source of each individual report.

86 Ṭūsī, *Tahdhīb*, 9:81.

87 In another report by the same transmitter in ʿAyyāshī, *Tafsīr*, 3:4, a hermeneutical argument is offered to explain why the flesh of horses, mules, and donkeys is disfavored. The argument is based on a juxtaposition of Qurʾān 6:145 and 16:8:

> عن زرارة قلت له: أليس لحمها حلالاً؟ قال: أليس قد بيّن الله لكم: ﴿وَالْخَيْلَ وَالْبِغَالَ وَالْحَمِيرَ لِتَرْكَبُوهَا وَزِينَةً﴾؟
>
> [Zurāra:] I said to him, "Is their meat not lawful?" He said, "Did God not make it clear for you: 'And [created] horses, mules, and donkeys for you to ride and take as adornment'?"

88 The source also mentions الناصب, which is clearly a later addition as the context as well as the singular pronoun in the next sentence indicate.

89 ʿAyyāshī, *Tafsīr*, 2:116.

90 Qurʾān 6:121.

91 Ibn Bābawayh, *Faqīh*, 3:52, with a variant in Barqī, *Maḥāsin*, 603.

92 Qurʾān 37:141.

صالح بن الحكم قال: سمعت أبا عبد الله يقول – وقد سُئِل عن الصلاة في البِيَع والكنائس – فقال: صلّ فيها. قلت: أصلّي فيها وهم يصلّون فيها؟ قال: صلّ إلى قبلتك ودعهم يصلّون [إلى] حيث شاءوا. أما تقرأ القرآن: ﴿قُلْ كُلٌّ يَعْمَلُ عَلَىٰ شَاكِلَتِهِ فَرَبُّكُمْ أَعْلَمُ بِمَنْ هُوَ أَهْدَىٰ سَبِيلًا﴾؟[93]

[Ṣāliḥ b. al-Ḥakam:] I heard Abū ʿAbd Allāh say when he was asked about praying in synagogues and churches, "Pray in them." I said, "Shall I pray while they pray in it?" He said, "Pray in the direction of your *qibla* and let them pray toward whatever they wish. Do you not read in the Qurʾān, 'Say: Everyone acts according to his disposition, for your Lord knows best who is best guided on the path'?"[94]

أبو بصير قال: قلت لأبي عبد الله: إنّ عمر بن رياح زعم أنّك قلت لا طلاق إلّا ببيّنة؟ فقال: ما أنا قلته، بل الله تبارك وتعالى يقوله.[95]

[Abū Baṣīr:] I said to Abū ʿAbd Allāh, "ʿUmar b. Riyāḥ [or Rabāḥ] claimed that you said that divorce is not valid without witnesses." He said, "I did not say that; rather God, the Blessed and Exalted, said so."[96]

الحلبي عن أبي عبد الله قال: سُئل عن الرجل يكون له دينٌ إلى أجل مسمّى فيأتيه غريمه فيقول: أنقدني كذا وكذا وأضع عندك بقيّته، أو يقول: أنقدني بعضه وأمدّ لك في الأجل فيما بقي عليك. قال: لا أرى به بأسًا. إنّه لم يزدد على رأس ماله. قال الله عزّ وجلّ: ﴿فَلَكُمْ رُءُوسُ أَمْوَالِكُمْ لَا تَظْلِمُونَ وَلَا تُظْلَمُونَ﴾.[97]

[ʿUbayd Allāh al-Ḥalabī:] Abū ʿAbd Allāh was asked[98] about a man who owes a debt due on a certain date, but his creditor comes and says, "Pay me such-and-such now and I leave the rest with you." Or he says, "Pay me some of it right now and I will give you more time for the remainder." The Imam said, "I do not see anything wrong with that. He does not add anything to the principal. God, the Mighty and Majestic, said, 'You shall have your principal, and you shall neither act unjustly nor be treated unjustly.'"[99]

---

93 From two variants in ʿAyyāshī, *Tafsīr*, 3:80; one also in Ibn Bābawayh, *Faqīh*, 1:157.

94 Qurʾān 17:84.

95 ʿAyyāshī, *Tafsīr*, 2:59.

96 This is a reference to Qurʾān 65:2: ﴿وَأَشْهِدُوا ذَوَيْ عَدْلٍ مِنْكُمْ﴾ ("Call to witness two righteous men from among you").

97 Kulaynī, *Kāfī*, 5:259.

98 The conversation is attributed to Muḥammad al-Bāqir in Ibn Bābawayh, *Faqīh*, 3:21.

99 Qurʾān 2:279.

عبد الله بن سنان عن أبي عبد الله في رجل قال امرأته طالقٌ ومماليكه أحرارٌ إن شرب حرامًا أو حلالًا من الطلا أبدًا، فقال: أمّا الحرام فلا يقربه أبدًا إن حلف وإن لم يحلف. وأمّا الطلا فليس له أن يحرّم ما أحلّ الله. قال الله عزّ وجلّ: ﴿يَا أَيُّهَا النَّبِيُّ لِمَ تُحَرِّمُ مَا أَحَلَّ اللَّهُ لَكَ﴾. فلا يجوز يمين في تحريم حلال ولا في تحليل حرام ولا في قطيعة رحم.[100]

['Abd Allāh b. Sinān:] On the question whether a man who said that his wife would be divorced and his slaves manumitted if he ever drank *ṭilā* [that is, grape juice boiled down to a third of its original volume], lawfully or unlawfully, Abū 'Abd Allāh said, "As for what is unlawful, he should never go near it whether or not he swore [an oath]. As for *ṭilā*, he cannot forbid what God has made lawful. God, the Mighty and Majestic, said, 'O Prophet, why do you forbid what God made lawful for you?'[101] Thus, it is not permissible to vow to make lawful what is unlawful, or to make unlawful what is lawful, or to cut ties with kin."

محمّد بن مسلم عن أبي عبد الله قال: سألته عن ظبي دخل الحرم. قال: لا يؤخذ ولا يُمَسّ. إنّ الله تعالى يقول: ﴿وَمَنْ دَخَلَهُ كَانَ آمِنًا﴾.[102]

[Muḥammad b. Muslim:] I asked Abū 'Abd Allāh about a gazelle that enters the sacred precinct. He said, "It cannot be captured or touched. God, the Exalted, says, 'Whosoever enters it is safe.'"[103]

أبو هلال عن أبي عبد الله في الّتي يموت عنها زوجها، قال: تخرج إلى الحجّ والعمرة، ولا تخرج الّتي تُطلّق، لأنّ الله يقول: ﴿وَلَا يَخْرُجْنَ﴾. إلّا أن تكون طُلّقت في سفر.[104]

[Abū Hilāl:] Regarding a woman whose husband dies, Abū 'Abd Allāh said, "She can go out to perform *ḥajj* and *'umra*, but a divorced woman may not, because God said, 'They should not leave [their homes]'[105] unless she is divorced while traveling."

عمّار الساباطي عن أبي عبد الله قال: سألته عن رجل حلق قبل أن يذبح؟ قال: يذبح ويعيد الموسى. لأن الله تعالى يقول: ﴿وَلَا تَحْلِقُوا رُءُوسَكُمْ حَتَّىٰ يَبْلُغَ الْهَدْيُ مَحِلَّهُ﴾.[106]

100 Ibn Bābawayh, *Faqīh*, 3:321.
101 Qur'ān 66:1.
102 Ṭūsī, *Tahdhīb*, 5:362.
103 Qur'ān 3:97.
104 Ṭūsī, *Tahdhīb*, 5:401–2.
105 Qur'ān 65:1.
106 Ṭūsī, *Tahdhīb*, 5:485.

> [ʿAmmār al-Sābāṭī:] I asked Abū ʿAbd Allāh about a man who shaved his hair before offering his sacrifice [thus reversing the order of the two final components of the *ḥajj*]. He said, "He must offer his sacrifice and [symbolically] draw a razor over the scalp, because God, the Exalted, says, 'Do not shave your heads until the sacrificial animal has reached the place of slaughter.'"[107]

B. The Sunna of the Prophet

Muslims are called by the Qurʾān to take the Prophet as their role model and to follow his example:

> ﴿لَقَدْ كَانَ لَكُمْ فِي رَسُولِ اللهِ أُسْوَةٌ﴾.[108]
>
> You have a good model to follow in the Messenger of God.

In the legal legacy of the Family of the Prophet, the Sunna, that is, the statements, practice, and endorsements of the Prophet,[109] as remembered and preserved in full detail by his Family, was therefore next to the Qurʾān in importance. The following examples illustrate how this worked:

> مرازم بن حكيم قال: سمعت أبا عبد الله يقول: من خالف سنّة محمّد – صلّى الله عليه وآله وسلّم – فقد كفر.[110]
>
> [Murāzim b. Ḥukaym:] I heard Abū ʿAbd Allāh say, "Whoever contravenes the Sunna of Muḥammad (may God's prayer and peace be upon him and his Family) is a disbeliever."

> حفص بن البختري عن أبي عبد الله: المتعة [إلى الحجّ] والله أفضل، وبها نزل القرآن وجرت السنّة [من رسول الله – صلّى الله عليه وآله وسلّم].[111]
>
> [Ḥafṣ b. al-Bakhtarī:] Abū ʿAbd Allāh said, "By God, the *ḥajj* of *mutʿa* is preferred. It was revealed in the Qurʾān and established by the Sunna."

107 Qurʾān 2:196.
108 Qurʾān 33:21.
109 Ibn Bābawayh, *Maʿānī al-akhbār*, 155.
110 Barqī, *Maḥāsin*, 220.
111 Ṭūsī, *Tahdhīb*, 4:292. The phrase between brackets is from a similar report in Ṭūsī, 5:26.

أبو بصير عن أبي عبد الله في الرجل يقذف الرجل بالزنا، قال: يُجلد هو على كتاب الله وسنّة نبيّه – صلّى الله عليه وآله وسلّم.[112]

[Abū Baṣīr:] Regarding a man who slanders another man about committing fornication, Abū ʿAbd Allāh said, "He will be lashed on the basis of the Book of God and the Sunna of His Prophet (may God's prayer and peace be upon him and his Family)."

عمر بن أذينة قال: رأيت أبا عبد الله يطرح التراب على الميّت فيمسكه ساعة في يده ثمّ يطرحه ولا يزيد على ثلاثة أكُفّ، فسألته عن ذلك فقال: هكذا كان يفعل رسول الله – صلّى الله عليه وآله وسلّم – وبه جرت السنّة.[113]

[ʿUmar b. Udhayna:] I saw Abū ʿAbd Allāh throw soil on a dead body [laid in a grave]. He would hold it for a period in his hand and then throw it, and he would not exceed three handfuls. I asked him about this, and he said, "This is what the Messenger of God (may God's prayer and peace be upon him and his Family) used to do, and this is the established practice."

جميل بن صالح عن أبي عبد الله قال: كنت أطوف بالبيت فإذا رجل يقول: ما بال هذين الركنين يُستلمان ولا يُستلم هذان؟ فقلت: إنّ رسول الله – صلّى الله عليه وآله وسلّم – استلم هذين ولم يتعرّض لهذين، فلا تعرّض لهما إذ لم يتعرّض لهما رسول الله – صلّى الله عليه وآله وسلّم.[114]

[Jamīl b. Sāliḥ:] Abū ʿAbd Allāh said, "I was circumambulating the House [of God, the Kaʿba] when a man said, 'Why are these two corners [of the Kaʿba] touched but those two are not?' I said, 'The Messenger of God (may God's prayer and peace be upon him and his Family) touched these two but not those two, so do not touch those since the Messenger of God (may God's prayer and peace be upon him and his Family) did not do it.'"

112 Kulaynī, *Kāfī*, 7:205.
113 Kulaynī, *Kāfī*, 3:198. For a Sunnī parallel, see Ibn Mājah, *Sunan*, no. 1565.
114 Kulaynī, *Kāfī*, 4:048.

معاوية بن عمّار قال: قال أبو عبد الله: إذا غربت الشمس فأفض مع الناس. واقتصدوا في السير فانّ رسول الله – صلّى الله عليه وآله وسلّم – كان يَكف بناقته حتّى كان يصيب رأسها مقدّم الرحل. فسنّة رسول الله – صلّى الله عليه وآله وسلّم – تتّبع.[115]

[Muʿāwiya b. ʿAmmār:] Abū ʿAbd Allāh said, "When the sun sets [on the ninth day of Dhū al-Ḥijja], leave [ʿArafāt toward Muzdalifa] along with the people and move moderately, for the Messenger of God (may God's prayer and peace be upon him and his Family) would restrain his camel until its head would hit the front of the saddle. The Sunna of the Messenger of God (may God's prayer and peace be upon him and his Family) is to be followed."

إبراهيم الكرخي قال: قلت لأبي عبد الله: إنّي أقدر أن أتوجّه نحو القبلة في المحمل. فقال: ما هذا الضيق؟ أما لكم في رسول الله أسوة؟[116]

[Ibrāhīm al-Karkhī:] I said to Abū ʿAbd Allāh, "I am able to face the *qibla* in the carriage while traveling." He said, "What is this hardship? Do you not have in the Messenger of God an example to follow?"[117]

عبد الله بن سنان عن أبي عبد الله قال: سئل وأنا حاضر عن امرأة أرضعت غلامًا مملوكًا لها من لبنها حتّى فطمته، هل لها أن تبيعه؟ فقال: لا! هو ابنها من الرضاعة. ثمّ قال: أليس رسول الله – صلّى الله عليه وآله وسلّم – قال: يحرم من الرضاع ما يحرم من النسب.[118]

[ʿAbd Allāh b. Sinān:] Abū ʿAbd Allāh was asked, while I was present, about a woman who breastfed a slave boy of hers from her own milk until he was weaned—may she sell him? He said, "No! He is her son by fosterage." Then he said, "Did the Messenger of God (may God's prayer and peace be upon him and his Family) not say, 'What is proscribed through lineage is proscribed through fostering'?"

رفاعة قال: سألت أبا عبد الله عن الرجل يطوف الطواف الواجب بعد العصر، أيصلّي الركعتين حين يفرغ من طوافه؟ قال: نعم! أما بلغك قول رسول الله – صلّى

115 Ṭūsī, *Tahdhīb*, 5:187–88.
116 Ibn Bābawayh, *Faqīh*, 1:285.
117 For the Prophet's precedent, see Ṭūsī, *Tahdhīb*, 3:228.
118 Kulaynī, *Kāfī*, 5:446 (as also cited, from Ṭūsī, with slight differences in wording, in Chapter 1, n. 333 on p. 68).

الله عليه وآله وسلّم: يا بني عبد المطّلب! لا تمنعوا الناس من الصلاة بعد العصر فتمنعوهم من الطواف.[119]

[Rifāʿa:] I asked Abū ʿAbd Allāh about a man performing the obligatory circumambulation [of the Kaʿba] after the afternoon prayer—is he to pray two *rakʿa*s after concluding his circumambulation? He said, "Yes! Did you not hear that the Messenger of God (may God's prayer and peace be upon him and his Family) said, 'O you children of ʿAbd al-Muṭṭalib! Do not prevent people from praying after the afternoon prayer, or you will prevent them from circumambulating'?"[120]

أبو يحيى الواسطي عن بعض أصحابنا، قال: سُئل أبو عبد الله عن المجوس أكان لهم نبي؟ قال: نعم! أما بلغك كتاب رسول الله – صلّى الله عليه وآله وسلّم – إلى أهل مكّة؟ [121]

[Abū Yaḥyā al-Wāsiṭī:] Abū ʿAbd Allāh was asked about whether the Magians had a prophet. He said, "Yes! Did you not hear of the letter of the Messenger of God (may God's prayer and peace be upon him and his Family) to the people of Mecca?"[122]

محمّد بن الطيّار قال: سألت أبا عبد الله عمّا يجب فيه الزكاة فقال: في تسعة أشياء: الذهب والفضّة والحنطة والشعير والتمر والزبيب والإبل وا لبقر والغنم، وعفا رسول الله – صلّى الله عليه وآله وسلّم – عمّا سوى ذلك. فقلت: أصلحك الله! فإنّ عندنا حبًّا كثيرًا. قال: وما هو؟ قلت: الأرز. قال: نعم! ما أكثره! فقلت: أفيه الزكاة؟ قال:

119 Kulaynī, *Kāfī*, 4:424.

120 A prayer of two *rakʿa*s is required after each circumambulation. Preventing people from praying would thus virtually prevent them from circumambulating. In Sunnī sources, the *ḥadīth* appears with the following text:

> يا بني عبد مناف! لا تمنعوا أحدًا طاف بهذا البيت وصلّى أيّة ساعة شاء من الليل والنهار.
>
> O Banū ʿAbd Manāf! Do not prevent anyone from circumambulating this House or from praying at any hour of the night or day that they want (Ibn Mājah, *Sunan*, no. 1254; Abū Dāwūd, *Sunan*, no. 1894; Tirmidhī, *Sunan*, no. 868; and many other sources cited in the editor's footnote to the Beirut, 1996 edition of this source, 2:210).

The reference in this version to "the children of ʿAbd Manāf" instead of "the children of ʿAbd al-Muṭṭalib" had a political implication, as the first referred exclusively to the Banū Hāshim while the latter included the Banū Umayya, too.

121 Kulaynī, *Kāfī*, 3:567.

122 The text of the letter, which affirms prophethood among the Magians, is quoted later in the same report (Kulaynī, *Kāfī*, 3:567–68).

فزبرني وقال: أقول لك إنّ رسول الله – صلّى الله عليه وآله وسلّم – عفا عمّا سوى ذلك وتقول لي إنّ عندنا حبًّا كثيرًا أفيه الزكاة؟[123]

[Muḥammad b. al-Ṭayyār:] I asked Abū ʿAbd Allāh about the [items] on which *zakāt* is due. He said, "On nine things: gold, silver, wheat, barley, dates, raisins, camels, cattle, and sheep. The Messenger of God (may God's prayer and peace be upon him and his Family) excused everything else." I said, "May God put you on the right path! We have one grain in abundance." He said, "What is it?" I said, "Rice." He said, "Yes! How abundant it is!" I said, "Is *zakāt* owed on it?" He yelled at me and said, "I tell you that the Messenger of God (may God's prayer and peace be upon him and his Family) excused everything else, and you tell me that you have grain in abundance and ask if *zakāt* is owed on it?"

معاوية بن عمّار عن أبي عبد الله [في الوقوف بعرفة] قال: قِف في مَيسرة الجبل، فانّ رسول الله – صلّى الله عليه وآله وسلّم – وقف بعرفات في مَيسرة الجبل.[124]

[Muʿāwiya b. ʿAmmār:] [Addressing the proper way of standing at ʿArafāt during the *ḥajj*] Abū ʿAbd Allāh said, "Stand on the left side of the mountain, for the Messenger of God (may God's prayer and peace be upon him and his Family) stood at ʿArafāt on the left side of the mountain."

سعيد الأعرج قال: قلت لأبي عبد الله: جعلت فداك! معنا نساءٌ فأفيض بهنّ بليل؟ قال: نعم! تريد أن تصنع كما صنع رسول الله – صلّى الله عليه وآله وسلّم؟ قلت: نعم! قال: أفض بهنّ بليل.[125]

[Saʿīd al-Aʿraj:] I said to Abū ʿAbd Allāh, "May I be made your ransom! We have women [pilgrims] in our [*ḥajj*] group. Shall I take them [from Muzdalifa toward Minā] at night?" He said, "Yes! Do you want to do as the Messenger of God (may God's prayer and peace be upon him and his Family) did?" I said, "Yes!" He said, "Take them there at night."

إسحاق بن الفضل سأل أبا عبد الله عن السجود على الحُصر والبواري فقال: لا بأس، وأن يُسجد على الأرض أحبّ إليّ، فإنّ رسول الله – صلّى الله عليه وآله وسلّم – كان

123 Ṭūsī, *Tahdhīb*, 4:4.
124 Kulaynī, *Kāfī*, 4:463.
125 Kulaynī, *Kāfī*, 4:474–75.

يحبّ ذلك، أن يُمكّن جبهته من الأرض، فأنا أُحبّ لك ما كان رسول الله – صلّى الله عليه وآله وسلّم – يحبّه.[126]

[Isḥāq b. al-Faḍl:] I asked Abū ʿAbd Allāh about prostrating on straw mats. He said, "There is nothing wrong with that, but I prefer that one prostrates on the earth. The Messenger of God (may God's prayer and peace be upon him and his Family) used to prefer that, placing his forehead firmly on the earth, so I prefer for you what the Messenger of God (may God's prayer and peace be upon him and his Family) preferred."

علي بن أبي حمزة قال سألت أبا عبد الله عن لباس الفِراء والصلاة فيها فقال: لا تصلّ فيها. [و]لا بأس بالسنجاب فإنّه دابّةٌ لا تأكل اللحم وليس هو ممّا نهى عنه رسول الله – صلّى الله عليه وآله وسلّم – إذ نهى عن كلّ ذي ناب ومخلب.[127]

[ʿAlī b. Abī Ḥamza:] I asked Abū ʿAbd Allāh about praying in clothing made from fur. He said, "Do not pray in it, but there is nothing wrong with [clothing made from the skins of] squirrels, for it is a creature that does not eat meat, and it is not something that the Messenger of God (may God's prayer and peace be upon him and his Family) forbade when he forbade that which has fangs and claws."

عامر بن عميرة قال: قلتُ لأبي عبد الله: بلغني عنك أنّك قلت لو أنّ رجلاً مات ولم يحجّ حجّة الإسلام فحجّ عنه بعض أهله أجزأ ذلك عنه؟ فقال: نعم! أشهد على أبي أنّه حدّثني أنّ رسول الله – صلّى الله عليه وآله وسلّم – أتاه رجل فقال: يا رسول الله! إنّ أبي مات ولم يحجّ. فقال له رسول الله – صلّى الله عليه وآله وسلّم: حجّ عنه فإنّ ذلك يُجزئ عنه.[128]

[ʿĀmir b. ʿUmayra:] I said to Abū ʿAbd Allāh, "I have heard that you said that if a man dies without performing the *ḥajj*, but some members of his family then perform the *ḥajj* on his behalf, it counts for him." He said, "Yes! I testify that my father reported to me that the Messenger of God (may God's prayer and peace be upon him and his Family) was approached by a man who said, 'O Messenger of God! My father died without performing the *ḥajj*.' The Messenger of God (may God's prayer

126 Ṭūsī, *Tahdhīb*, 2:311.
127 Kulaynī, *Kāfī*, 3:397–98 (see also Ṭūsī, *Tahdhīb*, 2:203).
128 Kulaynī, *Kāfī*, 4:277.

and peace be upon him and his family) said to him, 'Perform the *ḥajj* on his behalf, for that counts for him.'"[129]

رفاعة قال: سأل رجلٌ أبا عبد الله: الركوب [في الحجّ] أفضل أم المشي؟ فقال: الركوب أفضل من المشي لأنّ رسول الله – صلّى الله عليه وآله وسلّم – ركب.[130]

[Rifāʿa:] Someone asked Abū ʿAbd Allāh whether riding or walking [while performing the *ḥajj*] was better. He said, "Riding is better than walking because the Messenger of God (may God's prayer and peace be upon him and his Family) rode."

Much of what was quoted in these reports from the Prophet was shared by all Muslims across the board. There were, however, details that members of the Family of the Prophet remembered that would be important in understanding what the Prophet had meant in given cases. Consider this example:

علي بن إبراهيم قال: سألت امرأةٌ أبا عبد الله فقالت: إنّي كنت أقعد في نفاسي عشرين يوما حتّى أفتوني بثمانية عشر يومًا. فقال أبو عبد الله: ولم أفتوك بثمانية عشر يومًا؟ فقالت: للحديث الّذي روى عن رسول الله – صلّى الله عليه وآله وسلّم – أنه قال لأسماء بنت عميس حين نفست بمحمّد بن أبي بكر [فقالت: يا رسول الله! كيف أصنع؟ فقال لها: اغتسلي واحتشي وأهلّي بالحجّ. فاغتسلت واحتشت ودخلت مكّة ولم تطف ولم تسع حتّى تقضى الحجّ. فرجعت إلى مكّة فقالت: يا رسول الله! أحرمت ولم أطف ولم أسع. فقال لها رسول الله – صلّى الله عليه وآله وسلّم: وكم لكِ اليوم؟ فقالت: ثمانية عشر يومًا. فقال: فاخرجي الساعة فاغتسلي واحتشي وطوفي واسعي]. فقال أبو عبد الله: إنّ أسماءَ سألت رسول الله – صلّى الله عليه وآله وسلّم – وقد أتى بها ثمانية عشر يومًا، ولو سألَته قبل ذلك [وأخبرَته] لأمَرَها [بما أمَرَها به].[131]

129 A variant of the report from the Prophet is quoted in Ibn Abī Shayba, *Muṣannaf*, 5:560 and Nasāʾī, *Sunan*, no. 2638, and a different version (in which "father" is replaced with "mother," one being possibly a corruption of the other) in Bukhārī, *Ṣaḥīḥ*, nos. 1852, 6699, 7315, and numerous other sources cited in the editors' footnote in Aḥmad b. Ḥanbal, *Musnad*, 4:43.

130 Ṭūsī, *Tahdhīb*, 5:12.

131 Kulaynī, *Kāfī*, 3:98–99. The sentences between brackets are from a variant of the report, attributed to Muḥammad al-Bāqir, in *Kitāb al-Aghsāl* by Aḥmad b. Muḥammad b. ʿAyyāsh al-Jawharī (d. 401), as quoted in Ḥasan b. Zayn al-Dīn al-ʿĀmilī, *Muntaqā al-jumān*, 1:235.

> [ʿAlī b. Ibrāhīm:] A woman asked Abū ʿAbd Allāh, "I used to observe a period of [restrictions with] postpartum bleeding for twenty days, until they [that is, the local jurists] gave me a legal opinion [requiring only] eighteen days [of restrictions]." Abū ʿAbd Allāh said, "Why did they give you a legal opinion specifying eighteen days?" She said, "Because of the *ḥadīth* transmitted from the Prophet (may God's prayer and peace be upon him and his Family) about what he said to Asmāʾ bt. ʿUmays when she had postpartum bleeding after delivering Muḥammad b. Abī Bakr [during the Prophet's Farewell Pilgrimage]. She [Asmāʾ] said, 'O Messenger of God! What should I do?' He said to her, 'Take a bath, wear a sanitary pad, and perform the *talbiya*.' She bathed, wore the pad, and entered Mecca without circumambulating [the Kaʿba] or performing the *saʿy* [that is, walking to and fro between the two mounds of Safā and Marwa] until she had completed the *ḥajj*. She then returned to Mecca and said, 'O Messenger of God! I assumed a state of pilgrim sanctity and did not circumambulate [the Kaʿba] or perform *saʿy*.' The Messenger of God (may God's prayer and peace be upon him and his family) said to her, 'How many days has the postpartum been?' She said, 'Eighteen days.' He said, 'Go now and bathe, wear a sanitary pad, circumambulate, and perform the *saʿy*.'" Abū ʿAbd Allāh said, "Asmāʾ [happened to] ask the Messenger of God (may God's prayer and peace be upon him and his Family) when eighteen days had passed. Had she asked and informed him before that, he would have ordered her to do the same."

A report recorded in a number of major Sunnī *ḥadīth* collections grants the practice of the Prophet's "rightly guided" successors the same status as that enjoyed by the Sunna of the Prophet himself.[132] ʿAlī might have never heard of that report. He was allegedly offered the caliphate by the council that ʿUmar set up on his deathbed to choose his successor. The offer came with the condition that he follow the practice of the Prophet as well as that of the two former caliphs, but ʿAlī refrained from committing himself to the *sunna* of anyone other than the Prophet.[133] Following his lead, the Imams among his descendants, including Jaʿfar al-Ṣādiq, recognized only the Sunna of the Prophet as valid precedent.[134] Many people in the early period,

132 Ibn Mājah, *Sunan*, nos. 43, 420; Abū Dāwūd, *Sunan*, no. 4607; Tirmidhī, *Sunan*, no. 2676; Aḥmad b. Ḥanbal, *Musnad*, 28:367, 373, 375 (and the many other sources cited in the editors' footnotes at 28:367–71, 373–76). For an evaluation of this report, see Ibn Ḥazm, *Iḥkām*, 6:76–78.

133 Yaʿqūbī, *Taʾrīkh*, 2:162; Ṭabarī, *Taʾrīkh*, 4:233; Ibn al-Athīr, *Kāmil*, 3:66.

134 The practice of a Companion of the Prophet during his lifetime in matters related to law was considered valid, as it was assumed to have come to the Prophet's attention and received his endorsement. See, for instance, Ṭūsī, *Tahdhīb*, 7:298:

however, would call any common practice among the people *sunna*.[135] The Imams were careful to differentiate what was Sunna from what was not:

محمّد بن مسلم عن أبي جعفر قال: سألته عن نكاح اليهوديّة والنصرانيّة فقال: لا بأس به. أما علمت أنّه كانت تحت طلحة بن عبيد الله يهوديّة على عهد النبي – صلّى الله عليه وآله وسلّم؟

[Muḥammad b. Muslim:] I asked Abū Jaʿfar [Muḥammad al-Bāqir] about marrying a Jewish or Christian woman. He said, "There is nothing wrong with that. Do you not know that Ṭalḥa b. ʿUbayd Allāh had a Jewish wife during the time of the Prophet (may God's prayer and peace be upon him and his Family)?"

There were also those who considered the statements and practice of individual Companions in matters of religion to go back to a Prophetic order, reasoning that the Companions would not have said or done such things otherwise. This conclusion disregards the possibility of the practice being a personal choice by a Companion on matters on which the law was silent. It is also based on an assumption of the Companions' righteousness. Other Sunnī scholars, however, understood this assumption to relate to the Companions' reliability in transmission from the Prophet or to the status of the majority of the Companions:

متى كان الغالب العدالة أُلحِق المجهول بقسم العدول، ولذلك اتّفق المحدّثون على ترك البحث عن أحوال الصحابة. لأنّ قرن الصحابة غلب فيه العدالة فأجروا الحكم في [الجميع] وقبلوا الحديث عن كلّ من يثبت له الصحبة.

When righteousness is widespread, the unknown individual is counted as an upright individual. That is why the *ḥadīth* authorities agreed to refrain from researching the reliability of the Companions, because during the age of the Companions, righteousness was the norm. Hence, they deemed all of them alike, and they accepted *ḥadīth* from anyone who was verified to be a Companion (Wansharīsī, *al-Miʿyār al-muʿrib*, 10:203–4).

There were also arguments based on a statement ascribed to the Prophet that said,

خير الناس قرني ثمّ الّذين يلونهم.

The best of the people are those of my generation, then those following them (Bukhārī, *Ṣaḥīḥ*, no. 2652; Muslim, *Ṣaḥīḥ*, no. 2533; and many other sources cited in the editor's footnotes to Tirmidhī, *Sunan*, 6:167–68 and Aḥmad b. Ḥanbal, *Musnad*, 6:76–77, 7:200, 235).

But there was also a report from the Prophet, quoted in two variants, that had a different tone:

مثل أمّتي مثل المطر (أو كالغَيث) لا يُدرى أوّله خير أم آخره.

My community is like rain; it is not known whether its beginning is better or its end (Tirmidhī, *Sunan*, no. 2869 and other sources cited in the editor's footnote in Tirmidhī, 4:550; Ibn Abī al-Dunyā, *Maṭar*, 66).

أمّتي أمّة مباركة لا يُدرى أوّلها خير أو آخرها.

My community is a blessed community; it is not known whether its beginning is better or its end (Ibn ʿAsākir, *Taʾrīkh madīnat Dimashq*, 26:286; ʿAjlūnī, *Kashf al-khifāʾ*, 1:328).

135 See, for instance, Abū Yūsuf, *Radd ʿalā Siyar al-Awzāʿī*, 11, where he says:

وأهل الحجاز يقضون بالقضاء فيقال لهم: عمّن؟ فيقولون: بهذا جرت السنّة. وعسى أن يكون قضى به عامل السوق أو عامل مّا من الجهات.

The people of the Ḥijāz adjudicate, and when it is said to them, "On what authority?" they say, "This is according to the established *sunna*." It was possibly a

عبد الله بن سِنان عن أبي عبد الله قال: خِتان الغُلام من السُنّة[136] وخَفض الجواري ليس من السُنّة.[137]

['Abd Allāh b. Sinān:] Abū 'Abd Allāh said, "Circumcising boys is from the Sunna, but circumcising girls is not from the Sunna."

الحلبي قال: سألت أبا عبد الله عن الغسل إذا رمى الجمار فقال: ربما اغتسلتُ، فأمّا من السُنّة فلا، ولكن من الحرّ والعَرَق.[138]

['Ubayd Allāh al-Ḥalabī:] I asked Abū 'Abd Allāh about bathing after one throws pebbles on the columns [in Minā as part of the *ḥajj*]. He said, "I occasionally bathe, but not because of a *sunna*; rather because of heat and sweat!"

---

practice of the government official in charge of the market or another official within the government.

Shāfiʿī said the following in his critique of Abū Yūsuf's abovementioned work (*Umm*, 10:252):

وقد زعم أبو يوسف أنّ السنّة جرت على ما قال، وعاب الأوزاعي أن يقول: «قد جرت السنّة» بغير بداية ثابتة مفسّرة. ثمّ ادّعاه بغير بداية [في الأصل: «رواية»] ثابتة ولا خبر ثابت.

Abū Yūsuf claimed that the *sunna* was established according to what he said, and he censured Awzāʿī for saying "the *sunna* was established" with no solid, clear origin. Yet he himself put forward a similar claim with no solid origin or sound report.

See also Sarakhsī, *Uṣūl*, 1:380, quoting Shāfiʿī as saying:

لا ينصرف السنّة إلى سنن رسول الله – صلّى الله عليه وسلّم – لاحتمال أن يكون المراد بها سنّة البلدان أو الرؤساء – حتّى قال: – في كلّ موضع قال مالك – رحمه الله: السنّة ببلدنا كذا ، فإنّما أراد سنّة سليمان بن بلال الّذي كان عريفاً بالمدينة.

[The word] *sunna* does not necessarily mean a *sunna* of the Messenger of God (may God's prayer and peace be upon him) because of the possibility that it may refer to the practice of towns or of government officials [in different localities] . . . Everywhere that Mālik said "the *sunna* of our town is such," he meant the *sunna* of Sulaymān b. Bilāl, who was a local government official in Medina.

Sulaymān b. Bilāl (d. 172), a contemporary of Mālik and *ḥadīth* transmitter, was in charge of the *kharāj* (land tax) administration in Medina (Ibn Saʿd, *Ṭabaqāt*, 7:598; Dhahabī, *Siyar aʿlām al-nubalāʾ*, 7:426).

Confusing the two senses of *sunna* would occasionally lead to ridiculous outcomes. An Andalusian Muslim, for instance, performed the procedures for the most unpleasant practice of mutual cursing (*liʿān*) with his wife in the grand mosque of Córdoba in the year 388 "to revive a *sunna* that had been forgotten!" (Wansharīsī, *Miʿyār*, 4:76).

136 For the diversity of opinion among the schools on this matter, see, for instance, Isnawī, *Tamhīd*, 331.

137 Kulaynī, *Kāfī*, 6:37, no. 2. A similar statement is quoted from Muḥammad al-Bāqir (Kulaynī, 6:37, no. 1):

أبو بصير عن أبي جعفر قال: السنّة في الختان على الرجال وليس على النساء.

[Abū Baṣīr:] Abū Jaʿfar said, "The Sunna of circumcision is for men and not women."

138 Kulaynī, *Kāfī*, 4:482 (two slightly different variants of the same report).

حريز قال: سألت أبا عبد الله عن المُحرِم أيَشُمّ الريحان؟ قال: لا! قلت: فالصائم؟ قال: لا! قلت له: أيَشُمّ الصائم الغالية؟ قال: نعم! قلت: فكيف جاز له أن يشُمّ الطيب ولا يشُمّ الريحان إذا كان صائمًا؟ فقال: لأنّ الطيب سنّة والريحان بدعة للصائم.[139]

[Ḥarīz:] I asked Abū ʿAbd Allāh whether a person in a state of pilgrim sanctity can sniff a fragrant plant. He said, "No!" I said, "What about a fasting person?" He said, "No!" I said to him, "Can a fasting person smell perfume?" He said, "Yes!" I said, "Why can a person sniff perfume but not a fragrant plant when fasting?" He said, "Because [sniffing] perfume is from the Sunna, whereas [sniffing] a fragrant plant is a *bidʿa* for someone who is fasting."[140]

The Imams were also careful not to allow anyone to take their actions as Sunna.[141] To them, this was a status bestowed exclusively on the Messenger of God:

سالم عن أبي عبد الله قال: أوصى علي إلى الحسن والحسين. فدخل رجل يوم عرفة على الحسن وهو يتغدّى والحسين صائم. ثمّ جاء بعد قبض الحسن فدخل على الحسين يوم عرفة وهو يتغدّى. فقال له الرجل: إنّي دخلتُ على الحسن يتغدّى وأنت صائم، ثمّ دخلت عليك وأنت مفطر؟ فقال: إنّ الحسن كان إمامًا فأفطر لِئَلّا يُتّخذ صومُه سنّةً

139 Barqī, *Maḥāsin*, 318.

140 On the last point in the report, see further Kulaynī, *Kāfī*, 4:112:

محمّد بن الفيض قال: سمعت أبا عبد الله ينهى عن النرجس [للصائم] فقلت: جعلت فداك! لِمَ ذلك؟ فقال: لأنّه ريحان الأعاجم.

[Muḥammad b. al-Fayḍ:] I heard Abū ʿAbd Allāh advising against [sniffing] narcissus for one who is fasting. I said, "May I be made your ransom! Why is that?" He said, "Because it is the fragrant flower that [non-Muslim] Persians sniff [in their rituals]."

Kulaynī, who lived in a land formerly inhabited by Zoroastrians, added (4:113):

وأخبرني بعض أصحابنا أنّ الأعاجم كانت تشمّه إذا صاموا.

Some of my colleagues informed me that the [non-Muslim] Persians used to sniff it while fasting.

See also Ṭūsī, *Istibṣār*, 2:94. For the diversity of opinion on this topic among the early generations and Jaʿfar al-Ṣādiq's strict position in some instances, see Ibn Qudāma, *Mughnī*, 5:148. Jaʿfar's opinion on a pilgrim's inhaling the fragrance of a flower while in the state of pilgrim sanctity, quoted above, agreed with that of the Companion Jābir b. ʿAbd Allāh al-Anṣārī and, to some extent, with that of ʿAbd Allāh b. ʿUmar, which was later adopted by the Shāfiʿīs. See further Bayhaqī, *Sunan*, 5:92; *al-Mawsūʿa al-fiqhiyya* (Kuwait), 26:210–11.

141 For a parallel, see Mālik, *Muwaṭṭa'*, no. 114; ʿAbd al-Razzāq, *Muṣannaf*, 1:370–71, quoting ʿUmar as saying, when he refused to wash his clothes that were contaminated with semen:

واللهِ لو فعلتُها لكانت سُنّة.

By God, had I done that, it would become a *sunna*.

يتأسّى به الناس، فلمّا أن قُبض كنت أنا الإمام فأردت أن لا يُتّخذ صومي سنّةً يتأسّى الناس بي.[142]

[Sālim b. Mukram:] Abū ʿAbd Allāh said, "ʿAlī appointed Ḥasan and Ḥusayn as his successors. A man went to Ḥasan on the Day of ʿArafa while the latter was having lunch, but Ḥusayn was fasting. After Ḥasan passed away, he went to Ḥusayn on the same Day of ʿArafa while the latter was having lunch. The man said to him, 'I went to Ḥasan [while he was] having lunch and you were fasting; then I came to you and you are having lunch?' Ḥusayn said, 'Ḥasan was the Imam, so he broke his fast so that his fast would not be taken as a *sunna* that people follow. When Ḥasan passed away I became the Imam, so I did not want my fast to be adopted as a *sunna* that people follow.'"

Notwithstanding his emphasis on the validity of the Sunna of the Prophet alone, Jaʿfar al-Ṣādiq's preference was that the long-standing practices and customs of the Muslim community should be allowed to continue whenever they did not contravene the practice of the Prophet and the first generation of Muslims:[143]

142 Ibn Bābawayh, *Faqīh*, 2:53; Ibn Bābawayh, *ʿIlal al-sharāʾiʿ*, 2:73. Later Imams, too, continued to vary in their practices on this issue, clearly for the same reason as that stated by Ḥusayn. ʿAlī Zayn al-ʿĀbidīn and Muḥammad al-Bāqir did not fast on the Day of ʿArafa (Ṭūsī, *Tahdhīb*, 4:299). According to a report, Muḥammad al-Bāqir said that the Prophet, too, stopped fasting on that day once the fast of Ramaḍān had been made obligatory (Kulaynī, *Kāfī*, 4:146). Jaʿfar al-Ṣādiq, however, used to fast on that day (Ṭūsī, 4:298).

143 A long-standing practice or custom of the Muslim community may indeed represent a part of its collective memory from the community of the Prophet and the first generation of Muslims—a memory that may not always have been transmitted in words. Consider the following statement (ʿAbd al-Razzāq, *Muṣannaf*, 1:332):

معمر عن الزهري قال: الحائض تقضى الصوم. قلت: ممّن؟ قال: هذا ما اجتمع الناس عليه وليس في كل شيء نجد الإسناد.

[Maʿmar b. Rāshid:] Zuhrī said, "The menstruating woman should make up for the fasts that she misses." I said, "On whose authority [do you assert this]?" He said, "This is what all people have agreed upon. We cannot find a chain of transmission for everything."

However, a practice or custom may at times represent a non-religious, cultural mentality, as in the following example (Ibn Qudāma, *Mughnī*, 9:395):

جاء في حديث: «العرب بعضهم لبعض أكفاء إلّا حائكًا أو حجّامًا». قيل لأحمد: «كيف تأخذ به وأنت تضعّفه؟» قال: «العمل عليه». يعني أنّه ورد موافقًا لأهل العرف.

It is reported in a *ḥadīth* that "Arabs are equal to one another, except for one who is a weaver or a cupper." It was said to Aḥmad, "How do you rely on this [report] when you deem it weak?" He said, "The communal practice conforms with it," meaning, [the statement] was made in agreement with the customary practice of people.

For a Muslim evaluation of the collective and historical memory of a community or a large group of people, see Modarressi, "Facts or Fables?"

طلحة بن زيد عن أبي عبد الله قال: جرت السنّة أن لا تؤخذ الجزية من المعتوه ولا من المغلوب على عقله.[144]

[Ṭalḥa b. Zayd:] Abū ʿAbd Allāh said, "The established *sunna* is that the *jizya* [poll tax] should not be taken from the mentally impaired or the insane."

عبد الرحمن بن الحجّاج عن أبي عبد الله قال: قلت له: كم أدنى ما تُقصَّر فيه الصلاة؟ قال: جرت السنّة ببياض يوم.[145]

[ʿAbd al-Raḥmān b. al-Ḥajjāj:] I asked Abū ʿAbd Allāh, "What is the minimum distance required of a trip to allow a traveler to shorten prayers by half?" He said, "The established *sunna* is a full day [of traveling]."

محمّد الورّاق قال: عرضت على أبي عبد الله كتابًا فيه قرآن مختّم معشّر بالذهب وكُتب في آخره سورةٌ بالذهب، فأريته إيّاه فلم يعب فيه شيئًا إلّا كتابة القرآن بالذهب وقال: لا يُعجبني أن يُكتب القرآن إلّا بالسواد كما كُتب أوّل مرّة.[146]

[Muḥammad al-Warrāq:] I presented to Abū ʿAbd Allāh a volume with a copy of the Qurʾān that was decorated with gold and the final *sūra* written in gold. I showed it to him and he did not censure anything about it, except for the writing of the Qurʾān in gold. He said, "I do not

144 Kulaynī, *Kāfī*, 3:567.

145 Ṭūsī, *Tahdhīb*, 4:222. This expression recurs repeatedly in the sources, as in the following few examples:

الزهرى في رجل تزوّج امرأة: مضت السنّة أن لا يدخل بها حتّى يعطيها شيئًا.

[Zuhrī:] The prevailing *sunna* for a man who marries a woman is that he give her [a gift] before he becomes intimate with her (Ibn Abī Shayba, *Muṣannaf*, 6:101).

دفن الميّت في التراب أفضل من دفنه في التوابيت. بهذا جرت السنّة.

Burying a dead person in soil is better than burying him in a coffin. This is established by the *sunna* (Mufīd, *Aḥkām al-nisāʾ*, 63).

ولكنّ المؤمنين شهداء الله في الأرض فيشهدون بوفاته على الملّة. وعلى هذا جرت السنّة.

The Believers are God's witnesses on earth, so they testify that the deceased died as a Muslim. This is an established *sunna* (Kāsānī, *Badāʾiʿ al-ṣanāʾiʿ*, 2:196).

على هذا جرت السُنّة بعد الفراغ من الصلاة بالدعوات الكثيرة.

The *sunna* is established that one should follow prayer with profuse supplications (Fakhr al-Dīn al-Rāzī, *Tafsīr*, 5:202).

السنّة في القبر التسطيح، وهو أولى على الراجح من مذهب الشافعي.

The *sunna* about graves is to level them, and this is preferable according to the more supported opinion in the Shāfiʿī school (Qāḍī Ṣafad, *Raḥmat al-umma*, 1:88).

146 Kulaynī, *Kāfī*, 2:629.

like for the Qurʾān to be written in anything but black [ink], as it was written the first time."

روح بن عبد الرحيم عن أبي عبد الله قال: سألته عن شراء المصاحف وبيعها فقال: إنّما كان يوضع الورق عند المنبر، وكان بين المنبر والحائط قدر ما تمرّ الشاة أو رجل منحرف، فكان الرجل يأتي ويكتب من ذلك، ثمّ إنّهم اشتروا بعد [ذلك]. قلت: فما ترى في ذلك؟ قال لي: أشتري أحبّ إليّ من أن أبيعه. قلت: فما ترى إن أُعطى على كتابته أجرًا؟ قال: لا بأس، ولكن هكذا كانوا يصنعون.[147]

[Rawḥ b. ʿAbd al-Raḥīm:] I asked Abū ʿAbd Allāh about buying and selling copies of the Qurʾān. He said, "Pages [of the Qurʾān] used to be set at the pulpit [in the Mosque of the Prophet in Medina], with a narrow passage between the pulpit and the wall, enough for a sheep or a man walking sideways to pass through. A man would come and copy from [the copy of the Qurʾān] there. After that, they began to buy [and sell] the Qurʾān." I said, "What is your position on that?" He said to me, "I would prefer to buy it more than I would to sell it." I said, "What would be your position be if I were to pay [someone] to write it down?" He said, "There is nothing wrong with that, but I [wanted to tell you] how they used to do it at the time."

As seen in the last two examples, Jaʿfar al-Ṣādiq at times used language that was also used by the adherents of *ḥadīth* in the early periods. It employed phrases such as the following:

أرى[148] / لا أرى / أُحِبّ / أَحَبُّ إليّ / لا أُحِبّ / أكره / لا يُعجبني / أتّقي ذلك / أرجو ألّا يأثم / ما أزعم / أخشى

In my opinion . . . / It is not my opinion . . . / I prefer . . . / It is preferable to me . . . / I do not prefer . . . / I dislike . . . / It does not strike me as sound . . . / I worry about that / I hope that does not entail committing a sin / I do not believe . . . / I fear . . .

This tendency to express rulings in terms of preferences and discouragement was in accordance with Qurʾān 16:116, which advised against passing categorical judgment on a question on which there was no clear permission or prohibition from God. In Mālik's words:

147 Kulaynī, *Kāfī*, 5:122.

148 As mentioned in the introduction, n. 24 on p. 11, in the present context this word has nothing to do with the concept of *raʾy* as personal preference or arbitrary decision-making.

لم يكن من أمر الناس ولا مَن مضى من سلفنا ولا أدركت أحدًا أقتدي به يقول في شيءٍ: هذا حلال وهذا حرام. ما كانوا يجترؤون على ذلك [في ما لا نصّ فيه]، وإنّما كانوا يقولون: نكره هذا، ونرى هذا حسنًا، ونتّقي هذا، ولا نرى هذا، ولا يقولون حلال ولا حرام. الحلال ما أحلّه الله ورسوله والحرام ما حرّمه الله ورسوله.[149]

It was not a practice of the people, nor of those of our forebears past, nor of anyone I can take as a role model, to say about anything "This is lawful and that is unlawful." They never dared to [make such categorical statements] on matters on which there was no specific text. Rather, they used to say, "We dislike this; we think this is good; we avoid this; we do not suggest this." They did not say "lawful" or "unlawful." The lawful is what is deemed lawful by God and His Messenger, and the unlawful is what is deemed unlawful by God and His Messenger.

Examples of the usage of such language abound in Jaʿfar's responses.[150]

149 Ibn ʿAbd al-Barr, *Jāmiʿ bayān al-ʿilm wa-faḍlih*, 2:1075.

150 The following examples come from the relatively small selection of material that I have collected for the present study; more should be easy to find with a digital search:

أرى: ʿAyyāshī, *Tafsīr*, 1:189; Kulaynī, *Kāfī*, 2:106, 4:300, 5:172, 185, 209, 259, 286, 291, 380, 7:38, 64, 172, 206, 208, 286, 294 (see also 4:524 and 6:400); Ibn Bābawayh, *Faqīh*, 4:126–27, 172; Ṭūsī, *Tahdhīb*, 6:199, 7:51, 8:53.

لا أرى: Kulaynī, 3:67, 4:337, 416, 509, 5:259, 337, 418, 422, 6:125–26, 7:180 (see also 4:524); Ibn Bābawayh, 2:202; Ṭūsī, 4:146, 5:247, 248, 7:51, 114, 137, 10:118.

أحبُّ: Ṭūsī, 4:232, 6:350, 376, 380, 7:192, 8:313.

أحبُّ إليَّ: ʿAyyāshī, 2:68, 70; Kulaynī, 3:65, 457 (أحبّ إليّ ولا أرى بالّذي فعلتَ بأسًا), 4:81, 270, 301, 326, 333, 341 (لا أقول إنّه حرام ولكن تطهيره أحبّ إليّ), 456, 482, 490, 515, 539, 5:121, 353, 396, 515, 6:72 (أحبّ إليّ ولا أرى بما فعله بأسًا); 194, 7:17, 71; Qāḍī Nuʿmān, *Daʿāʾim al-Islām*, 2:102; Ibn Bābawayh, 1:331, 2:271; Ṭūsī, 2:62, 136, 246, 311, 3:307, 5:9, 78, 198 (لايضرّك والطُهرُ أحبّ إليّ), 206, 242, 248, 374, 7:17, 137.

لا أحبّ: Kulaynī, 4:333, 405, 416, 433, 496, 5:223, 224, 231, 247, 369, 440, 495, 6:347, 517, 520; Ibn Bābawayh, 2:168, 250 (ما أحبّ ذلك وما أرى به بأسًا); Ṭūsī, 2:51, 205, 5:356, 6:350, 380, 7:448,483, 9:63, 83.

أكره / كرهه: Aḥmad b. Muḥammad b. ʿĪsā, *Nawādir*, 42, 132, 170; Barqī, *Maḥāsin*, 629; Kulaynī, 3:369, 4:490, 5:157, 181, 193, 273, 419, 480; Qāḍī Nuʿmān, 1:246; Ṭūsī, 4:260, 5:359, 399, 6:380, 7:147, 299, 463.

يُعجبني / لا يُعجبني: ʿAyyāshī, 2:69; Kulaynī, 2:451, 629, 4:439, 503, 5:152, 223, 224, 7:37, 302; Ṭūsī, 5:78, 300, 309, 313, 7:37, 157, 234.

أتّقي ذلك: Kulaynī, 5:555 (for a Sunnī parallel, see Dārimī, *Sunan*, 2:1080).

أرجو ألّا يأثم: Ṭūsī, 6:188.

ما أزعم: Kulaynī, 4:301 (ما أزعم أنّ ذلك ليس له لو فعل، وكان الإهلال أحبّ إليّ), 5:478 (ما أزعم أنّه حرام).

أخشى: Ṭūsī, 5:420.

نحنُ نحتاط: Kulaynī, 5:424.

لا آمُر: Kulaynī, 3:65; Ṭūsī, 4:40.

أنا ناهٍ عنها نفسي ووُلدي: Kulaynī, 5:474, 6:173.

إن شئتَ أخبرتك بما آمُرُ به تفسي ووُلدي: Ṭūsī, 4:245.

III. Interpretation

As demonstrated by the examples quoted above, Jaʿfar al-Ṣādiq's legal approach was to understand the text in its context by using lexical semantics, and to apply hermeneutics to turn a ruling issued for a specific case into a general principle and thereby allow it to cover all cases that share a clear common denominator with the original ruling.

For Jaʿfar al-Ṣādiq, the plain meaning of a text was the valid one. This was what the text stood for, what the speaker meant to say, and the message that he intended to convey. Any claim to a different meaning had to establish beyond doubt why the speaker used language in a way that did not correspond with its plain meaning.

قيل لأبي عبد الله: رُوِيَ عنكم أنّ الخمر والمَيسِر والأنصاب والأزلام رجال؟ فقال: ما كان الله ليخاطب خلقه بما لا يعقلون.[151]

It was said to Abū ʿAbd Allāh that it has been reported that you [members of the House of the Prophet] hold that *khamr*, *maysir*, *anṣāb*, and *azlām* [the sins and evils mentioned in Qurʾān 5:90] are [references to certain] people. He replied, "God would not address His creation with what they could not comprehend."

As for Jaʿfar's use of semantic and hermeneutic techniques, the following examples are illuminating. The first one concerns Qurʾān 4:23, which sets the rule regarding those within the prohibited degree of affinity for marriage: "Forbidden to you are . . . the mothers of your wives and your stepdaughters who are under your care from your wives with whom you have consummated marriage." Here, the Imam argues with respect to an unqualified word in the passage:

إسحاق بن عمّار عن جعفر بن محمّد: الربائب عليكم حرام مع الأُمّهات اللاتي قد دخلتم بهنّ. هُنّ في الحجور وغير الحجور سواء. والأُمّهات مبهمات: دُخل بالبنات أم لم يُدخل بهنّ. فحَرِّموا وأبهِموا ما أبهم الله.[152]

[Isḥāq b. ʿAmmār:] Jaʿfar b. Muḥammad said, "Stepdaughters from mothers with whom you have consummated marriage are unlawful

151 ʿAyyāshī, *Tafsīr*, 2:75; Kashshī, *Rijāl*, 291.

152 ʿAyyāshī, *Tafsīr*, 1:383 (also Ṭūsī, *Tahdhīb*, 7:273). The same opinion and argument are attributed to Ibn ʿAbbās in the Sunnī tradition. See Ibn Qudāma, *Mughnī*, 9:515 and the sources cited in the editor's footnote therein.

to you regardless of whether they are in your care. As for the 'mothers [of your wives],' however, the word is unqualified; [the prohibition applies] regardless whether you have consummated marriage with the daughters. So, consider mothers [of wives] forbidden altogether. Leave vague what God has left vague."

The point is further explained in a statement from Jaʿfar's father:

أبو حمزة الثمالي قال: سألت أبا جعفر عن رجلٍ تزوّج امرأةً وطلّقها قبلَ أن يدخل بها، أتحلّ له ابنتُها؟ قال: لا بأس به. إنّ الله يقول: ﴿وَرَبَائِبُكُمُ اللَّاتِي فِي حُجُورِكُمْ مِنْ نِسَائِكُمُ اللَّاتِي دَخَلْتُمْ بِهِنَّ فَإِنْ لَمْ تَكُونُوا دَخَلْتُمْ بِهِنَّ فَلَا جُنَاحَ عَلَيْكُمْ﴾. ولو تزوّج الابنة ثمّ طلّقها قبلَ أن يدخلَ بها لم تحلّ له أُمُّها. قلت: أليس هما سواء؟ قال: لا! ليس هذه مثل هذه. إنّ الله يقول: ﴿وَأُمَّهَاتُ نِسَائِكُمْ﴾، لم يستثن في هذه كما اشترط في تلك. هذه هنا مبهمة ليس فيها شرط، وتلك فيها شرط.[153]

[Abū Ḥamza al-Thumālī:] I asked Abū Jaʿfar about a man who marries a woman and divorces her before consummating the marriage with her. Is her daughter lawful for him? He said, "There is nothing wrong with that.[154] God, the Exalted, says: '[Among women not lawful as marriage partners are] the stepdaughters in your care, born of your wives with whom you have consummated marriage, but if you have not consummated marriage with them, there is no blame on you.' But if he marries the daughter and then divorces her before consummating marriage with her, her mother is not lawful for him." I said, "Are they not the same?" He said, "No! The one thing is not like the other. God says, 'The mothers of your wives.' He did not make an exception in this case like He imposed a condition in the other. This case is unqualified; it does not have a condition, whereas the other case does have a condition."

زرارة عن أبي عبد الله قال: لا يرجع الرجل فيما يهب لامرأته ولا المرأة فيما تهب لزوجها، حيز أم لم يُحز. أليس الله تبارك وتعالى يقول: ﴿وَلَا يَحِلُّ لَكُمْ أَنْ تَأْخُذُوا مِمَّا

153 ʿAyyāshī, *Tafsīr*, 1:381–82.

154 That is to say, she is not forbidden to him as a daughter of a wife, because the wife was divorced before the consummation of the marriage. However, if the child was brought up by the husband as in a case where marriage continued for years without consummation, the girl should be forbidden to the man as indicated by the implied rationale in a report from Jaʿfar al-Ṣādiq in Kulaynī, *Kāfī*, 5:448 and Ibn Bābawayh, *Faqīh*, 3:259 on a nanny who raised a baby boy: إن قبلت وربّت حرمت عليه (see further Ḥurr al-ʿĀmilī, *Wasāʾil al-Shīʿa*, 20:500–502). The same rationale clearly applies to an adopted child, too.

آتَيْتُمُوهُنَّ شَيْئًا﴾ وقال: ﴿فَإِنْ طِبْنَ لَكُمْ عَنْ شَيْءٍ مِنْهُ نَفْسًا فَكُلُوهُ هَنِيئًا مَرِيئًا﴾؟ وهذا يدخل في الصداق والهبة.[155]

[Zurāra:] Abū ʿAbd Allāh said, "A man should not take back what he gifts to his wife, nor a woman what she gifts to her husband, whether or not the gift is already possessed by the other. Did God, the Blessed and Exalted, not say, 'It is unlawful for you to take anything [back] of what you have given them,'[156] and He said, 'If they give up anything of it to you willingly then take it in satisfaction and ease'?[157] This applies to both bridal gifts and ordinary gifts."

زرارة عن أبي عبد الله أنّه قال في الصيد: ما خلا الكلاب ممّا يصيد – الفهود والصقور وأشباه ذلك – فلا تأكلَنّ من صيده إلّا ما أدركتَ ذكاته، لأنّ الله عزّ وجلّ قال: ﴿مُكَلِّبِينَ﴾ فما خلا الكلب فليس صيده بالّذي يؤكل إلّا أن تدرك ذكاته.[158]

[Zurāra:] Regarding hunting, Abū ʿAbd Allāh said, "As for things besides dogs that hunt—lynxes, hawks, and the like—what they hunt cannot be eaten unless you are able to slaughter it [according to Islamic ritual law], because God, the Mighty and Majestic, speaks of 'trained dogs.'[159] So what is hunted by anything other than a dog cannot be eaten, unless it is slaughtered."

عبيد بن زرارة قال: قلت لأبي عبد الله: قول الله عزّ وجلّ: ﴿فَمَنْ شَهِدَ مِنْكُمُ الشَّهْرَ فَلْيَصُمْهُ﴾؟ قال: ما أبيَنَه! من شهد فليَصُمه ومن سافر فلا يَصُمه.[160]

[ʿUbayd b. Zurāra:] I said to Abū ʿAbd Allāh, "[Tell me about] the statement of God, the Mighty and Majestic: 'Whosoever among you is present during the month must fast it.'"[161] He said, "How clear it is! Whoever is present when the month begins should fast it, and whoever is traveling should not fast it."

155 Kulaynī, *Kāfī*, 7:30 (also Ṭūsī, *Istibṣār*, 4:110; Ṭūsī, *Tahdhīb*, 9:152).
156 Qurʾān 2:229.
157 Qurʾān 4:4.
158 ʿAyyāshī, *Tafsīr*, 2:11 (with a variant in Kulaynī, *Kāfī*, 6:205). See also Kulaynī, 6:203–4 for a couple of other reports on the topic with the same argument.
159 Qurʾān 5:4.
160 Kulaynī, *Kāfī*, 4:126.
161 Qurʾān 2:185.

عن أبي عبد الله قال: إذا دخل شهر رمضان فلله فيه شرط. قال الله تعالى: ﴿فَمَنْ شَهِدَ مِنْكُمُ الشَّهْرَ فَلْيَصُمْهُ﴾. فليس للرجل إذا دخل شهر رمضان أن يخرج إلّا في حجّ أو عمرة أو مال يخاف تلفه أو أخ يخاف هلاكه.[162]

Abū ʿAbd Allāh said, "When the month of Ramaḍān commences, God made for it a [specific] condition. God, the Exalted, says, 'Whosoever among you who is present during the month must fast it.'[163] Thus, once the month of Ramaḍān commences, a man may not travel unless it is to perform a *ḥajj* or *ʿumra*, to pursue money that he fears may be wasted, or [to aid] a brother who he fears may die."

مسعدة بن صدقة عن [جعفر بن محمّد][164] قال: سمعته يقول – وسُئل عن الأمر بالمعروف والنهي عن المنكر، أواجبٌ هو على الأمّة جميعًا؟ فقال: لا! فقيل له: ولِمَ؟ قال: إنّما هو على القوي المطاع العالم بالمعروف من المنكر، لا على الضعيف الّذي لا يهتدي سبيلاً. والدليل على ذلك كتاب الله عزّ وجلّ: قوله ﴿وَلْتَكُنْ مِنْكُمْ أُمَّةٌ يَدْعُونَ إِلَى الْخَيْرِ وَيَأْمُرُونَ بِالْمَعْرُوفِ وَيَنْهَوْنَ عَنِ الْمُنْكَرِ﴾، فهذا خاصٌّ غير عامّ، كما قال الله عزّ وجلّ: ﴿وَمِنْ قَوْمِ مُوسَىٰ أُمَّةٌ يَهْدُونَ بِالْحَقِّ وَبِهِ يَعْدِلُونَ﴾، ولم يقل «على أمّة موسى» ولا على كلّ قومه، وهم يومئذٍ أمم مختلفة. والأمّة واحد فصاعدًا، كما قال الله عزّ وجلّ: ﴿إِنَّ إِبْرَاهِيمَ كَانَ أُمَّةً قَانِتًا لِلَّهِ﴾.[165]

[Masʿada b. Ṣadaqa:] Jaʿfar b. Muḥammad was asked whether enjoining right and forbidding wrong was a universal obligation for the community, and I heard him say, "No!" It was said to him, "Why not?" He said, "It is [a duty] for the strong individual, who is to be obeyed [by virtue of the ability to use force] and who is knowledgeable of the right and the wrong. It is not for the weak, who has no way [to enforce it]. The proof for this is the Book of God, the Mighty and Majestic, where He says, 'Let there be among you a community calling to the good, enjoining good, and forbidding wrong.'[166] This is specific, not general. It is like when God, the Mighty and Majestic, says, 'And among

162 Ṭūsī, *Tahdhīb*, 4:216.

163 Qurʾān 2:185.

164 Ibn Bābawayh, *Khiṣāl*, 6, quoting a part of this report. This is also how this transmitter usually mentions Jaʿfar al-Ṣādiq (Modarressi, *Tradition and Survival*, 1:320). In Kulaynī, *Kāfī*, 5:59, however, the authority of the report appears as عن أبي عبد الله; presumably a later emendation by either the author or a copyist.

165 Kulaynī, *Kāfī*, 5:59–60.

166 Qurʾān 3:104.

the people of Moses is a community that guides by the truth and does justice thereby.'[167] He did not say, 'Upon the community of Moses,' nor upon all his people, and at that time they were composed of several communities. A 'community' means one or more people, as God, the Mighty and Majestic, says, 'Truly Abraham was a community, devoutly obedient to God.'"[168]

عبيد بن زرارة قال: سألت أبا عبد الله عن رجل طاف بالبيت أُسبوعًا طواف الفريضة ثمّ سعى بين الصّفا والمروة أربعة أشواط ثمّ غمزه بطنه فخرج فقضى حاجته ثمّ غشي أهله. قال: يغتسل ثمّ يعود فيطوف[169] ثلاثة أشواط ويستغفر ربّه ولا شيء عليه. قلت: فإن كان طاف بالبيت طواف الفريضة فطاف أربعة أشواط ثمّ غمزه بطنه فخرج [فقضى] حاجته فغشي أهله؟ فقال: أفسد حجّه وعليه بَدَنة ويغتسل ثمّ يرجع فيطوف أُسبوعًا ثمّ يسعى ويستغفر ربّه. قلت: كيف لم تجعل عليه حين غشي أهله قبل أن يفرغ من سعيه كما جعلت عليه هديًا حين غشي أهله قبل أن يفرغ من طوافه؟ قال: إنّ الطواف فريضة وفيه صلاة، والسعي سنّةٌ من رسول الله – صلّى الله عليه وآله وسلّم. قلت: أليس الله يقول: ﴿إِنَّ الصَّفَا وَالْمَرْوَةَ مِنْ شَعَائِرِ اللهِ﴾؟ قال: بلى! لكن قد قال فيهما: ﴿وَمَنْ تَطَوَّعَ خَيْرًا فَإِنَّ اللهَ شَاكِرٌ عَلِيمٌ﴾. فلو كان السعي فريضةً لم يقل: «فمن تطوّع خيرًا».[170]

['Ubayd b. Zurāra:] I asked Abū 'Abd Allāh about a man who performs [as part of the *ḥajj*] the obligatory circumambulation around the House [of God, the Kaʿba] seven times [as required]. He then performs the *saʿy* between the mounds of Ṣafā and Marwa four times. His stomach then signals to him, so he goes to answer the call of nature and then engages his wife. He said, "He must undertake a full-body washing, resume the *saʿy* for three cycles, and ask his Lord for forgiveness, and he is not liable for anything." I said, "What if he performed four cycles of the obligatory circumambulation around the House, and then his stomach signaled to him, so he went to answer the call of nature and then engaged his wife?" He said, "His *ḥajj* is invalidated; he must offer

167 Qur'ān 7:159.

168 Qur'ān 16:120. On this report, see especially Cook, *Commanding Right and Forbidding Wrong*, 256–57, and the accompanying notes.

169 That is, he walks to and fro between the two mounds of Ṣafā and Marwa, a Qur'ānic usage (2:158), although the common term for this act, as also used elsewhere in this text, is *saʿy*, not *ṭawāf*.

170 Kulaynī, *Kāfī*, 4:379–80 (also Ṭūsī, *Tahdhīb*, 5:321–22).

a sacrifice, undertake a full-body washing, resume circumambulation for seven rounds, perform the *saʿy*, and ask his Lord for forgiveness." I said, "How is it that you do not require him to offer a sacrifice when he engages his wife before finishing the *saʿy*, but you require him to offer a sacrifice when he engages his wife before completing the circumambulation?" He said, "The circumambulation is an obligation and there is a prayer attached to it, but *saʿy* is a rite established by the Messenger of God (may God's prayer and peace be upon him and his Family)." I said, "Does God not say, 'Ṣafā and Marwa are among the rituals set by God'?"[171] He said, "Yes, but He says about them, 'And whoever does good voluntarily, then God is Thankful, Knowing.' If the *saʿy* were obligatory, He would not say, 'whoever does good voluntarily.'"[172]

أبو أيّوب قال: قلت لأبي عبد الله: إنّا نريد أن نتعجّل السير – وكانت ليلة النفر حين سألته – فأيّ ساعة ننفر؟ فقال: لا تنفروا في اليوم الثاني حتّى تزول الشمس، فأمّا اليوم الثالث فإذا ابيضّت الشمس فانفروا على بركة الله. فإنّ الله جلّ ثناؤه يقول: ﴿فَمَنْ تَعَجَّلَ فِي يَوْمَيْنِ فَلَا إِثْمَ عَلَيْهِ﴾ فلو سكت لم يبقَ أحدٌ إلّا تعجّل ولكنّه قال: ﴿وَمَنْ تَأَخَّرَ فَلَا إِثْمَ عَلَيْهِ﴾.[173]

[Abū Ayyūb Ibrāhīm al-Khazzāz:] I said to Abū ʿAbd Allāh, "We want to leave early [at the end of the *ḥajj*]"—and when I asked him it was the Night of Departure—"so what time should we depart?" He said, "Do not depart on the second day until the sun has passed its zenith. As for the third day, depart when the sun rises, with God's blessing. God, Whose praise is magnified, says, 'Whosoever hastens on after two days, no sin shall be upon him.'[174] Had He not said anything else, anybody who stayed would have rushed [to leave], but He said, 'And whosoever delays, no sin shall be upon him.'"

إسماعيل الهاشمي عن أبي عبد الله: عن امرأة زنت فأتت بولد وأقرّت عند إمام المسلمين بأنّها زانية وأنّ ولدها ذلك من الزنا، وأنّ ذلك الولد نشأ حتّى صار رجلاً، فافترى عليه رجلٌ فكم يُجلد من افترى عليه؟ قال: يُجلد ولا يُجلد. قلت: كيف يُجلد ولا يُجلد؟ قال: من قال «يا ولد الزنا» لا يُجلد، إنّما يُعزَّر، وهو دون الحدّ، ومن قال «يابن

171 Qurʾān 2:158.

172 The argument is based on the differences between two categories of obligation, *farḍ* and *wājib*, as explained in works on *uṣūl al-fiqh*.

173 ʿAyyāshī, *Tafsīr*, 1:210 with a variant in Kulaynī, *Kāfī*, 4:250.

174 Qurʾān 2:203.

الزانية» جُلد الحدّ تامًّا. قلت: وكيف صار هكذا؟ قال: لأنّه إذا قال «يا ولد الزنا» فقد صدق فيه، وإذا قال «يابن الزانية» جُلد الحدّ تامًّا لفريته عليها بعد اظهارها التوبة وإقامة الإمام عليها الحدّ.[175]

[Ismāʿīl al-Hāshimī:] Regarding the situation of a woman who fornicated and then gave birth to a child, and admitted to the ruler of the Muslims that she is a fornicator and that her child was the product of fornication; the child then grows up to become a man and someone slanders him—how many lashes should the slanderer receive? Abū ʿAbd Allāh said, "He will be lashed and he will not be lashed." I said, "How is he both lashed and not lashed?" He said, "Whoever says, 'O child of fornication,' is not lashed, but is given a discretionary punishment that is less than the *ḥadd* punishment [of eighty lashes]. And whoever says 'O child of a fornicator' is lashed according to the full *ḥadd* punishment." I said, "How is that so?" He said, "Because if he says, 'O child of fornication,' he has spoken the truth [and thus is not punished with the *ḥadd*]. But if he says, 'O child of a fornicator,' he is lashed according to the full *ḥadd* punishment because he has slandered her [that is, the mother] after she manifested her repentance and the ruler applied the *ḥadd* punishment to her."[176]

Jaʿfar's father, Muḥammad al-Bāqir, applied the same methods—using semantic and hermeneutic techniques—in his legal interpretation, as the following examples demonstrate:

زرارة قال: قلت لأبي جعفر: ألا تخبرني من أين علمت وقلت إنّ المسح ببعض الرأس وبعض الرجلين؟ فقال: يا زرارة! قاله رسول الله – صلّى الله عليه وآله وسلّم – ونزل به الكتاب من الله. لأنّ الله عزّ وجلّ قال: ﴿فَاغْسِلُوا وُجُوهَكُمْ﴾ فعرفنا أنّ الوجه كلّه ينبغي أن يغسل، ثمّ قال: ﴿وَأَيْدِيَكُمْ إِلَى الْمَرَافِقِ﴾ فوَصَل اليدين إلى المرفقين بالوجه فعرفنا أنّه ينبغي لهما أن يُغسلا إلى المرفقين، ثمّ فصّل الكلام فقال: ﴿وَامْسَحُوا بِرُءُوسِكُمْ﴾ فعرفنا حين قال ﴿ بِرُءُوسِكُمْ﴾ أنّ المسح ببعض الرأس، لمكان الباء، ثمّ وَصَل الرجلين بالرأس – كما وصل اليدين بالوجه – فقال: ﴿وَأَرْجُلَكُمْ إِلَى الْكَعْبَيْنِ﴾

175 Barqī, *Maḥāsin*, 306.

176 The point here is that the word "fornicator" is commonly understood to refer to the current status of its subject, whereas illegitimacy refers to the child's status at birth. The fact that the child was illegitimate at birth was already established by the mother's acknowledgment, but the mother had thereafter repented and was thus no longer considered a fornicator.

فعرفنا حين وصلها بالرأس أنّ المسح على بعضها. ثمّ فسّر ذلك رسول الله – صلّى الله عليه وآله وسلّم – للناس فضيّعوه.[177]

[Zurāra:] I said to Abū Jaʿfar, "Will you tell me from where you learned to say that wiping [in ritual ablution] applies to part of the head and part of the feet?" He said, "O Zurāra! The Messenger of God (may God's prayer and peace be upon him and his Family) said it, and it was revealed by God in the Book. God, the Mighty and Majestic, said, 'Wash your faces,'[178] so we learned that the entirety of the face must be washed. Then He said, 'and your hands up to your elbows,' and he linked the arms up to the elbows to the face, so we learned that they must be washed up to the elbows. Then there is a disconnect in the speech; He said, 'and wipe *over* your heads,' so we learned when he said '*over* your heads' that wiping applied to part of the head due to the "over" (*bā*ʾ) preposition.[179] He linked the feet to the head, just as he linked the arms to the face, saying, 'and your feet up to the ankles.' By linking feet to the head, we learned that wiping applied to part of them. This was explained by the Messenger of God (may God's prayer and peace be upon him and his Family) to the people, but they forgot it."

---

177 ʿAyyāshī, *Tafsīr*, 2:18–19. Also Kulaynī, *Kāfī*, 3:30; Ibn Bābawayh, *Faqīh*, 1:56–57.

178 Qurʾān 5:6.

179 The letter *bā*ʾ appended to the start of a noun usually functions as a preposition meaning "by" or "with"; however, in some instances it can mean "a part of" (this use is known in Arabic grammar as الباء للتبعيض). Shāfiʿī (*Umm*, 1:111) held the same opinion on the basis of the implication of the Qurʾānic passage that a partial wiping of the front of the head is good enough for *wuḍūʾ*:

معنى الآية أنّ من مسح شيئًا من رأسه أجزاه.

> The Qurʾānic passage means that wiping over any part of the head will suffice.

His followers followed suit. See, for instance, Ibn Abī al-Khayr, *Bayān*, 1:125:

دليلنا قوله تعالى: ﴿وَامْسَحُوا بِرُءُوسِكُمْ﴾ والباء للتبعيض.

> Our basis is the word of God, the Exalted: "And wipe over your heads." [The letter] *bā*ʾ [preceding "heads" in the Arabic] is to signify a part [of its subject].

And Māwardī, *Ḥāwī*, 1:137:

دليلنا قوله تعالى: ﴿وَامْسَحُوا بِرُءُوسِكُمْ﴾. دلّ على دخولها للتبعيض. مرادًا بها «بعض رؤوسكم».

> Our basis is the word of God, the Exalted: "And wipe over your heads." This indicates that the letter *bā*ʾ is added to signify a part [of its subject], meaning "a part of your heads."

The idea was also confirmed by Shīrāzī, *Lumaʿ*, 184–85; Shīrāzī, *Tabṣira*, 1:237; Fakhr al-Dīn al-Rāzī, *Maḥṣūl*, 1:379; Nawawī, *Majmūʿ*, 1:441, and other Shāfiʿī authors, as well as some Ḥanafīs (e.g., Jaṣṣāṣ, *al-Fuṣūl fī al-uṣūl* [Kuwait, 1994], 1:94; Sarakhsī, *Mabṣūṭ* [Beirut, 1993], 1:63). However, the validity of that linguistic principle has been disputed by a few Arab linguists. See, for instance, Ibn Sīda, *Muḥkam*, 10:569. See also Ibn al-ʿArabī, *Aḥkām al-Qurʾān*, 2:571; Ibn Jinnī, *Sirr ṣināʿat al-iʿrāb*, 1:123; Juwaynī, *Burhān*, 1:180.

زرارة ومحمّد بن مسلم قالا: قلنا لأبي جعفر: ما تقول في الصلاة في السفر؟ كيف هي وكم هي؟ قال: إنّ الله تعالى يقول: ﴿وَإِذَا ضَرَبْتُمْ فِي الْأَرْضِ فَلَيْسَ عَلَيْكُمْ جُنَاحٌ أَنْ تَقْصُرُوا مِنَ الصَّلَاةِ﴾، فصار التقصير في السفر واجبًا كوجوب التمام في الحضر. قلنا: إنّما قال: ﴿فَلَيْسَ عَلَيْكُمْ جُنَاحٌ﴾ ولم يَقُل: «افعلوا». فكيف أوجب ذلك كما أوجب التمام في الحضر؟ قال: أوَ ليس قد قال في الصفا والمروة: ﴿فَمَنْ حَجَّ الْبَيْتَ أَوِ اعْتَمَرَ فَلَا جُنَاحَ عَلَيْهِ أَنْ يَطَّوَّفَ بِهِمَا﴾؟ ألا ترى أنّ الطواف بهما واجب مفروض؟ قلنا: فمن صلّى في السفر أربعًا أيُعيد أم لا؟ قال: إن كان قد قُرئت عليه آية التقصير وفُسّرت له فصلّى أربعًا أعاده ، وإن لم يكن قُرئت عليه ولم يعلمها فلا إعادة عليه.[180]

[Zurāra and Muḥammad b. Muslim:] We said to Abū Jaʿfar, "What is your opinion about prayer during travel? How is it performed and how many [*rakʿas*] is it?" He said, "God, the Exalted, says, 'When you travel upon the earth, there is no blame upon you for shortening prayer [by half].'[181] Hence, praying half while traveling is obligatory, just like it is obligatory to pray in full when in residence." We said, "He said, 'there is no blame upon you'; He did not say, 'do.' So how [do you say that] He made this obligatory like He made the full prayer obligatory when in residence?" He said, "Did He not say regarding Ṣafā and Marwa, 'Whosoever performs the *ḥajj* to the House, or makes the *ʿumra*, there is no blame on him in going to and fro between them'?[182] Do you not see that walking the distance between them is obligatory?" We said, "Whoever prays four *rakʿas* while traveling, should they repeat their prayer or not?" He said, "If the Qurʾānic passage on praying half was recited and explained to him and he still prayed four, he must repeat it. If it was not recited to him and he did not know about it, he does not have to repeat it."

حُمران قال: قلت لأبي جعفر: أرأيت المؤمن له فضلٌ على المسلم في شيء من المواريث والقضايا والأحكام حتّى يكون للمؤمن أكثر ممّا يكون للمسلم في المواريث أو غير ذلك؟ قال: لا! هما يجريان في ذلك مجرىً واحدًا إذا حكم الإمام عليهما. ولكن للمؤمن فضلاً على المسلم في أعمالهما وما يتقرّبان به إلى الله. قلت: أليس الله يقول: ﴿مَنْ جَاءَ بِالْحَسَنَةِ فَلَهُ عَشْرُ أَمْثَالِهَا﴾ وزعمتَ أنّهم مجتمعون على الصلاة والزكاة والصوم والحجّ

180 ʿAyyāshī, *Tafsīr*, 1:436.
181 Qurʾān 4:101.
182 Qurʾān 2:158.

مع المؤمن؟ فقال: أليس الله قد قال: ﴿وَاللَّهُ يُضَاعِفُ لِمَنْ يَشَاءُ﴾؟ فالمؤمنون هم الّذين يُضاعف الله لهم الحسنات.[183]

[Ḥumrān:] I said to Abū Jaʿfar, "Do you think a true believer is favored above an ordinary Muslim with respect to any matter of inheritance, adjudication, or the like, so that a true believer gets more than an ordinary Muslim in inheritance and otherwise?" He said, "No! They are treated alike as they are both subjects of the *imām* [of the Muslim community]. However, true believers are favored above ordinary Muslims with respect to their deeds and what they do to draw closer to God." I said, "Does God not say, 'Whosoever does a good deed shall have ten times the like thereof,'[184] and you believe that the ordinary Muslim shares with the true believer the duties of praying, paying *zakāt*, fasting, and performing the *ḥajj*?" He said, "Did God not say, 'And God multiplies for whomsoever He wills'?[185] The true believers are those whose deeds are multiplied."

زرارة عن أبي جعفر قال: لا ينبغي نكاح أهل الكتاب. قلت: جُعلت فداك! وأين تحريمه؟ قال: قوله [تعالى]: «ولا تُمسكوا بعِصَم الكوافر».[186]

[Zurāra:] Abū Jaʿfar said, "One should not marry the People of the Book." I said, "May I be made your ransom! Where is the prohibition stated?" He said, "His, the Exalted, saying, 'And hold not to the ties of disbelievers.'"[187]

IV. Venture Beyond Text[188]

That Jaʿfar al-Ṣādiq, his father, and the Imams among their descendants rejected the validity of forming legal opinions independently of texts through personal preference or arbitrary decision-making (*ra'y*)[189] and of reasoning by analogy (*qiyās*), as the two concepts were known and practiced at the time, is well known in the Islamic legal tradition and attested to by numerous reports from them and their close associates. Their language and reasoning

183 ʿAyyāshī, *Tafsīr*, 1:270.
184 Qur'ān 6:160.
185 Qur'ān 2:261.
186 Kulaynī, *Kāfī*, 5:358.
187 Qur'ān 60:10.
188 This subtitle is borrowed from the title of Chapter 4 of Weiss, *Spirit of Islamic Law*.
189 The lexicographical sense of *ra'y* is opinion in general, and that was meant when, for instance, Ḥafṣ al-Aʿwar said to Jaʿfar al-Ṣādiq ما رأيك فيها؟ ("What is your position on this?") (Ṭūsī, *Tahdhīb*, 7:177, with a variant in Ibn Bābawayh, *Faqīh*, 4:241; cf. Kulaynī, *Kāfī*, 7:153, where it is "Khaṭṭāb al-Aʿwar" who posed the question to Mūsā al-Kāẓim).

are very familiar, and similar to those employed by other opponents of arbitrary decision-making and reasoning by analogy at that time and after. Here are a few statements attributed to Jaʿfar al-Ṣādiq about *ra'y*:

مسعدة بن صدقة قال: قال لي جعفر بن محمّد: من أفتى الناس برأيه فقد دان بما لا يعلم.[190]

[Masʿada b. Ṣadaqa:] Jaʿfar b. Muḥammad said, "Whoever gives people legal opinions on the basis of his own personal preference has committed himself in matters of religion to that which he does not know."

عبد الرحمن بن الحجّاج قال: سألت أبا عبد الله عن مجالسة أصحاب الرأي فقال: جالسهم، وإيّاك وخصلتين تهلك فيهما الرجال: أن تفتي الناس برأيك أو تدين بما لا تعلم.[191]

[ʿAbd al-Raḥmān b. al-Ḥajjāj:] I asked Abū ʿAbd Allāh about sitting in the company of the partisans of *ra'y*. He said, "Sit with them, but beware of two traits that ruin men: issuing opinions to people on the basis of your personal preference, and committing yourself in matters of religion to that which you do not know."

محمّد بن بشر الأسلمي قال: كنت عند أبي عبد الله وورقة يسأله، فقال له أبو عبد الله: أنتم قوم تحملون على السنّة ونحن قوم نتّبع الأثر.[192]

[Muḥammad b. Bishr al-Aslamī:] I was with Abū ʿAbd Allāh when Waraqa was questioning him. Abū ʿAbd Allāh said to him, "You are a people who impose [your personal opinions] on the Sunna, while we are a people who follow the Sunna."

And here are some of his statements about *qiyās*:

أبو شيبة قال: سمعت أبا عبد الله يقول: إنّ دين الله لا يصاب بالمقاييس.[193]

[Abū Shayba al-Khurāsanī:] I heard Abū ʿAbd Allāh say, "God's religion cannot be attained through analogies."

190 Ḥimyarī, *Qurb al-isnād*, 12.
191 Barqī, *Maḥāsin*, 205, with variants at 204; Kulaynī, *Kāfī*, 1:42.
192 Barqī, *Maḥāsin*, 214.
193 Barqī, *Maḥāsin*, 211; Kulaynī, *Kāfī*, 1:56 (see also 57).

أبان بن تغلب عن أبي عبد الله قال: إنّ السنّة إذا قيست محق الدين.[194]

[Abān b. Taghlib:] Abū ʿAbd Allāh said, "When analogy is applied to the Sunna, the religion is effaced."

عبد الله بن سِنان عن أبي عبد الله قال: السنّة لا تقاس.[195]

[ʿAbd Allāh b. Sinān:] Abū ʿAbd Allāh said, "The Sunna cannot be analogized from."

ابن شُبرُمة قال: ما ذكرتُ حديثًا سمعته من جعفر بن محمّد إلّا كاد أن يتصدّع قلبي. قال: حدّثني أبي عن جدّي عن رسول الله – صلّى الله عليه وسلّم – (قال ابن شُبرُمة: وأُقسم بالله ما كذب أبوه على جدّه ولا جدّه على رسول الله – صلّى الله عليه وسلّم): من عمل بالمقاييس فقد هلك وأهلك، ومن أفتى بغير علم. فقد هلك وأهلك.[196]

[Ibn Shubruma:] I do not remember a *ḥadīth* I heard from Jaʿfar b. Muḥammad without having my heart almost break. He said, "My father told me, from my grandfather, from the Messenger of God (may God's prayer and peace be upon him)"—Ibn Shubruma added, "I swear by God that his father did not lie about his grandfather, and his grandfather did not lie about the Messenger of God (may God's prayer and peace be upon him)"—"[that the Messenger of God said,] 'Whoever engages in analogy [in matters of religion] will cause ruin and fall into ruin, and whoever gives legal opinions without knowledge will cause ruin and fall into ruin.'"

الحسن بن راشد قال: قلت لأبي عبد الله: الحائض تقضي الصلاة؟ قال: لا! قلت: تقضي الصوم؟ قال: نعم! قلت: من أين جاء ذا؟ قال: إنَّ أوَّل من قاس إبليس! قلت: والصّائم يستنقع في الماء؟ قال: نعم! قلت: فيبلُّ ثوبًا على جسده؟ قال لا! قلت: من أين جاء ذا؟ قال: من ذاك![197]

[Ḥasan b. Rāshid:] I asked Abū ʿAbd Allāh, "Does a menstruating woman have to make up [missed] prayers?" He said, "No!" I said, "Does she have to make up [missed] fasts?" He said, "Yes!" I said, "On

194 Barqī, *Maḥāsin*, 214; Kulaynī, *Kāfī*, 1:57 (also 7:299–300).
195 Kulaynī, *Kāfī*, 1:57, 4:134. See also Ḥimyarī, *Qurb al-isnād*, 359.
196 Barqī, *Maḥāsin*, 206; Kulaynī, *Kāfī*, 1:43.
197 Kulaynī, *Kāfī*, 4:113.

what basis?" He said, "The first person who did *qiyās* was Iblīs!"[198] I said, "Can a fasting person stay in water to cool himself down?" He said, "Yes!" I said, "Can he wet the clothes that he is wearing [for the same purpose]?" He said, "No!" I said, "On what basis?" He said, "On that same basis [that the first to do *qiyās* was Iblīs]."[199]

سماعة بن مهران عن أبي عبد الله قال: إنّما هلك من هلك بالقياس. قلت: أصلحك الله! ولِمَ ذاك؟ قال: لأنّه ليس من شيء إلّا وجرى به كتابٌ أو سنّة، وإنّما ذاك إليكم إذا ورد عليكم شيء أن تقولوا.[200]

[Samāʿa b. Mihrān:] Abū ʿAbd Allāh said, "Those who were ruined were ruined by *qiyās*." I said, "May God put you on the right path! Why is that?" He said, "Because there is nothing that is not addressed by the Book and the Sunna, and your duty is [simply] to quote what is there when a question comes up to you."

[محمّد بن] عبد الرحمن بن أبي ليلى قال: حججت في السنة الّتي حجّ فيها أبو حنيفة إلى مكّة، فكنّا في الطريق حتّى أتينا المدينة، فلمّا صرنا إلى المدينة قال لي أبو حنيفة: أُحبّ أن أدخل على هذا الرجل فأسلّم عليه – يريد جعفر بن محمّد بن علي بن الحسين بن علي بن أبي طالب رضى الله عنه – وأسأله، وأخاف أن لا يأذن لي. قال [محمّد بن] عبد الرحمن بن أبي ليلى: فقلت له: أخلَقُ به إن عَلِم بمكانك أن لا يأذن لك، ولكن كُن معي فإن أذن لي دخلتَ معي. قال: فمضينا إلى بابه فقلت لغلامه: إقرئه السلام وقُل له: [محمّد بن] عبد الرحمن بن أبي ليلى ورجل من أهل الكوفة. قال: فرجع إلينا بالإذن، فدخلنا عليه فرحّب بنا وقرّب، حتّى إذا اطمأنّا أقبل عليّ وقال: من هذا الرجل؟ فقلت بأبي أنت وأمّي! هذا أبو حنيفة! فقيه أهل الكوفة. قال: فأقبل عليه وقال: أنت النعمان بن ثابت؟ قال: نعم! بأبي أنت وأمّي! قال: أنت الّذي تقيس الدين برأيك؟ قال: بأبي أنت وأمّي! إنّما أقول ذلك في النازلة (أو الحادثة) تحدث ليس لها في كتاب الله خبر

198 This is a reference to Qur'ān 7:11–12 (also 38:76 and 17:61), describing how Iblīs disobeyed God's command to prostrate himself before Adam, arguing that he was made of a better material than Adam was: "God said, 'What prevented you from prostrating yourself when I commanded you to [do so]?' He [Iblīs] said, 'I am better than he is; You created me from fire, whereas You created him from clay.'"

199 In other words, the human mind is incapable of deciphering the mind of God. Any attempt to explain the wisdom behind the laws of the *sharīʿa* is doomed to fail and thus not allowed.

200 Durust b. Abī Manṣūr, *Kitāb*, 292.

ولا في سنّة رسول الله – صلّى الله عليه وسلّم – ولا في إجماع المسلمين ولا في الخبر المتّصل حجّةٌ، فان كان ذلك نظرنا إلى أشبه الأشياء بها فقِسناها عليه. قال: فتبسّم ثمّ قال: ويحك يا نعمان! ما لم يكن له في كتاب الله ولا في سنّة رسول الله ولا في إجماع المسلمين ولا في الخبر المتّصل حجّة فقد زال عنك حكمه ووضع عنك فرضه. فلا تتكلّف ما لم تؤمر.[201] [إتّق الله ولا تقِس الدين برأيك.][202]

[Muḥammad b. ʿAbd al-Raḥmān b. Abī Layla:] I went on the *ḥajj* in the same year that Abū Ḥanīfa went to Mecca. We were on the road until we reached Medina. When we arrived in Medina Abū Ḥanīfa said to me, "I would like to visit this man to greet him"—he was referring to Jaʿfar b. Muḥammad b. ʿAlī b. al-Ḥusayn b. ʿAlī b. Abī Ṭālib—"and to question him, but I fear that he may not permit me." I said to him, "If he knows your situation, it is more likely that he will not permit you. But remain with me, so if he permits me, you can enter with me." We went to his door and I said to his servant, "Convey greetings to him, and tell him it is [Muhammad b.] ʿAbd al-Raḥmān b. Abī Laylā and a man from Kūfa." He [the servant] came back to us with permission, so we entered and he greeted us and ushered us close to himself. When we felt comfortable, he turned to me and said, "Who is this man?" I said, "May my father and mother be made your ransom! This is Abū Ḥanīfa! [He is] the jurist of the people of Kūfa." He turned to him and said, "You are Nuʿmān b. Thābit?" He said, "Yes! May my father and mother be made your ransom!" He said, "You are the one who analogizes the religion using your personal opinion?" He said, "May my father and mother be made your ransom! I do that in novel cases that occur without there being any mention of it in the Book of God, nor a basis in the Sunna of the Messenger of God (may God's prayer and peace be upon him), the consensus of the Muslims, or a report that goes all the way up [to the Prophet]. If that is the case, we consider the most similar case to the matter and analogize." He smiled, then said, "Beware, O Nuʿmān! Whatever is not covered by a firm basis (*ḥujja*) in the Book of God, the Sunna of the Messenger of God, the consensus of the Muslims, or a report that goes all the way [to the Prophet] does not have a ruling for you and the obligation respecting it is canceled for you. Do not assume responsibility for

201 Balawī (d. 604), *Alif-bāʾ*, 2:305.

202 The phrase between the brackets is from a variant of the report in Zubayr b. Bakkār, *Muwaffaqiyyāt*, 76–78.

what you have not been commanded.[203] Fear God, and do not analogize the religion using your personal judgment."

A key problem with analogical reasoning was that it ignored essential details that would render the legal disposition of particular cases different, even if they were similar in some respects. A conversation between the Imam and one of his learned disciples explains the point well:

عبد الرحمن بن الحجّاج قال: سألني أبو عبد الله هل يختلف ابن أبي ليلى وابن شُبرُمة؟ فقلت: بلغني أنّه مات مولى لعيسى بن موسى وترك عليه دينًا كثيرًا وترك مماليك يحيط دينه بأثمانهم، فأعتقهم عند الموت. فسألهما عيسى بن موسى عن ذلك. فقال ابن شبرمة: أرى أن تستسعيهم في قيمتهم فتدفعها إلى الغرماء فإنّه قد أعتقهم عند موته، وقال ابن أبي ليلى: أرى أن تبيعهم وتدفع أثمانهم إلي الغرماء فإنّه ليس له أن يعتقهم عند موته وعليه دينٌ يحيط بهم. وهذا أهل الحجاز اليوم، يعتق الرجل عبده وعليه دينٌ كثيرٌ فلا يجيزون عتقه إذا كان عليه دين كثير. فرفع ابن شُبرمة يده إلى السماء وقال: سبحان الله! يا ابن أبي ليلى! متى قلت بهذا القول؟ والله ما قلتَه إلّا طلب خلافي. فقال أبو عبد الله: فعن رأي أيّهما صدر؟ قال: قلت: بلغني أنّه أخذ برأي ابن أبي ليلى، وكان له في ذلك هوى، فباعهم وقضى دينه. قال: فمع أيّهما مَن قِبَلكم؟ قلت له: مع ابن شُبرمة، وقد رجع ابن أبي ليلى إلى رأي ابن شُبرمة بعد ذلك. فقال: أما والله إنّ الحقَّ لفي الّذي قال ابن أبي ليلى وإن كان قد رجع عنه. فقلت له: هذا ينكسر عندهم في القياس. فقال: هات قايِسني! فقلت: أنا أُقايِسك؟! فقال: لتقولنّ بأشدّ ما يدخل فيه من القياس!

فقلت له: رجل مات وترك عبدًا، لم يترك مالاً غيره، وقيمة العبد ستّمائة درهم ودَينه خمسمائة درهم فأعتقه عند الموت. كيف يصنع؟ قال: يباع العبد فيأخذ

203 On this last point, see also the statement variously, and with minor variations, attributed to the Prophet (e.g., Ṭabarānī, *al-Muʿjam al-awsaṭ*, 7:265–66; Dāraquṭnī, *Sunan*, 5:538) or ʿAlī (*Nahj al-balāgha*, no. 105 [ed. Ṣubḥī al-Ṣāliḥ, 487]; Āmidī, *Ghurar al-ḥikam*, 189):

إنّ الله سبحانه فرض عليكم فرائضَ فلا تُضيّعوها وحدّ لكم حدودًا فلا تعتدوها ونهاكم عن أشياء فلا تنتهكوها وسكت عن أشياء – ولم يدعها نسيانًا – فلا تتكلّفوها.

God (Glory be to Him) imposed obligations upon you, so do not abandon them. He placed limits on you, so do not transgress them. He forbade things, so do not violate them. And He kept silent about things, but He did not omit them out of forgetfulness, so do not burden yourselves with them.

الغرماء خمسمائة درهم ويأخذ الورثة مائة درهم. فقلت: أليس قد بقي من قيمة العبد مائة درهم عن دَينه؟ فقال: بلى! قلت: أليس للرجل ثلثه يصنع به ما يشاء؟ قال: بلى! قلت: أليس قد أوصى للعبد بالثلث من المائة حين أعتقه؟ فقال: إنّ العبد لا وصيّة له، إنّما ماله لمواليه. فقلت له: فإذا كانت قيمة العبد ستّمائة درهم ودينه أربعمائة درهم؟ قال: كذلك. يباع العبد فيأخذ الغرماء أربعمائة درهم ويأخذ الورثة مائتين، فلا يكون للعبد شيء. قلت له: فإنّ قيمة العبد ستّمائة درهم ودَينه ثلاثمائة درهم؟ فضحك وقال: من ههنا أوتي أصحابك. جعلوا الأشياء شيئًا واحدًا ولم يعلموا السنّة. إذا استوى مال الغرماء ومال الورثة، أو كان مال الورثة أكثر من مال الغرماء، لم يتّهم الرجل على وصيّته وأُجيزت وصيّته على وجهها. فالآن يوقَف هذا العبد فيكون نصفه للغرماء ويكون ثلثه للورثة ويكون له السدس.[204]

[ʿAbd al-Raḥmān b. al-Ḥajjāj:] Abū ʿAbd Allāh asked me whether Ibn Abī Laylā and Ibn Shubruma disagree [on any legal issue]. I said, "I was informed that a client of ʿĪsā b. Mūsā[205] passed away, leaving behind a lot of debt as well as slaves, whose combined value equaled his debt, but he manumitted them upon his death. ʿĪsā b. Mūsā asked the two of them about the case. Ibn Shubruma said, 'I think you should allow them to work up to their market price and pay their income to the creditors [to settle the debt], because he [the client] manumitted them upon his death.' Ibn Abī Laylā said, 'I think you should sell them and pay their value to the creditors, because he [the client] could not manumit them upon his death while carrying a debt that covered them [that is, their market value]. These people of the Ḥijāz today do not allow a person to manumit his slave if he owes a large debt.' Then Ibn Shubruma raised his hand to the sky and said, 'Praise be to God! O Ibn Abī Laylā! When was it that you picked up this opinion? I swear you did not say it except to disagree with me.'" Abū ʿAbd Allāh said, "Which of the two opinions did he [ʿĪsā] adopt?" I said, "I heard that he adopted the opinion of Ibn Abī Laylā. He had a personal interest in the case, so he sold them and repaid the debt." Abū ʿAbd Allāh said, "With whose opinion do those in your region [that is, the jurists of Kūfa] align?" I said to him, "With Ibn Shubruma, and [even] Ibn Abī Laylā finally went back to the opinion of Ibn Shubruma." He said, "By God, the truth is with what Ibn Abī Laylā said, even if he went back on

204 Kulaynī, *Kāfī*, 7:26–27; Ṭūsī, *Tahdhīb*, 9:217–18.
205 ʿĪsā b. Mūsā b. Muḥammad b. ʿAlī b. ʿAbd Allāh b. al-ʿAbbās, Shaykh al-Dawla (d. 168), governor of Kūfa in 132–47, as also mentioned in Chapter 1.

it." I said to him, "For them [the jurists], that [opinion] fails through analogy." He said, "Come, challenge me with analogy!" I said, "Me, challenge you with analogy?" He said, "Challenge me with the hardest of analogies that can be presented here!"

I said, "A man dies and leaves behind a slave with no other wealth. The value of the slave is six hundred dirhams, and the debt he owes is five hundred dirhams, and he manumitted the slave upon his death. What should be done?" He said, "The slave is to be sold and the creditors are to take five hundred dirhams and the heirs one hundred dirhams." I said, "Is there not one hundred dirhams left over of the slave's price after paying the debt?" He said, "Yes!" I said, "Can the man not do what he wishes with one-third of his inheritance?" He said, "Yes!" I said, "Did he not [virtually] bequeath one-third of the one hundred [dirhams] when he manumitted him?" He said, "Bequests cannot be made to a slave. His [the slave's] money belongs to his masters." I said to him, "What if the value of the slave is six hundred dirhams and the debt is four hundred dirhams?" He said, "Likewise. The slave is sold, the creditors take four hundred dirhams, the heirs take two hundred, and nothing remains for the slave." I said to him, "What if the value of the slave is six hundred dirhams and the debt is three hundred dirhams?" Then he laughed and said, "This is the point that led your companions into their mistake. They treated [different] things alike and did not know the Sunna. If the shares owed to the creditors and the heirs are equal, or the share of the heirs is more than the share owed to the creditors, the [deceased] man is not under suspicion [of having intended to harm the creditors] for his bequest. His bequest is permissible on its face. Thus, the slave is set apart; half of him goes to the creditors, one-third goes to the heirs, and he gets one-sixth [manumitted]."

Another example:

أبو المغرا عن أبي عبد الله في الرجل يستأجر الأرض ثمّ يؤاجرها بأكثر ممّا استأجرها؟ قال: ليس به بأس. [إنّ الأرض ليست بمنزلة البيت والأجير. إنّ فضل البيت حرام وفضل الأجير حرام.][206]

[Abū al-Maghrā:] Abū ʿAbd Allāh said with regard to a man who leases land and then subleases it for a higher price than he leased it for, "There is nothing wrong with that. Land is not the same as a home or a hired laborer. The profit earned through the sublet of a house

206 Kulaynī, *Kāfī*, 5:272, with two variants at 5:271–72.

> is unlawful, and the profit earned through the sub-hiring of a hired laborer is unlawful."[207]

However, when the operative cause of a law is explicitly mentioned in the Qur'ān or the Sunna, or the text is applicable to the case at hand a fortiori, or two or more cases share a common denominator that determines their shared legal status, the law is extended from a case regarding which the law is already defined by the text to another case that remains undefined.[208] The following examples illustrate this process:

> الحلبي قال: سألت أبا عبد الله عن رجل أُهِلّ بالحجّ والعمرة جميعًا ثمّ قدم مكّة والناس بعرفات فخشى إن هو طاف وسعى بين الصفا والمروة أن يفوته الموقف. فقال: يدع العمرة فإذا أتمّ حجّه صنع كما صنعت عائشة ولا هَدى عليه.[209]

> ['Ubayd Allāh al-Ḥalabī:] I asked Abū 'Abd Allāh about a man who said the *talbiya* for the *ḥajj* and the *'umra* together [that is, for *ḥajj tamattu'*], then arrived in Mecca while the people were at 'Arafāt, so

207 For similar ideas in the Sunnī tradition, see, for instance, 'Abd al-Razzāq, *Muṣannaf*, 8:222–23.

208 The procedure is known in Muslim jurisprudence as *ilghā' khuṣūṣiyyat al-mawrid*, at times expressed also as *al-mawrid laysa bi-mukhaṣṣiṣ*, both denoting disregard of specific details and conditions that are not essential to the law. Similarity per se cannot serve as the basis for extending a law from one case to another. It can only serve as a pedagogical method to make the argument more understandable to a student. In a conversation between Ja'far al-Ṣādiq and one of his disciples in Ibn Bābawayh, *Faqīh*, 2:168–69, and Ibn Bābawayh, *'Ilal al-sharā'i'*, 2:139 (with variants in Ṭūsī, *Tahdhīb*, 5:360, and with a different ascription in Kulaynī, *Kāfī*, 4:234), the Imam mentions a similar case to support his argument, and the disciple says, "People call this *qiyās*!" (هذا القياس عند الناس). The Imam said, "I likened one thing to another so that you could understand it" (إنما شبّهت لك شيئًا بشيء لِتَعرفه). His response recalls the title of Chapter 12 of Book 96 of Bukhārī's *Ṣaḥīḥ* (containing *ḥadīths* 7314–15):

> باب من شبّه أصلاً معلومًا بأصلٍ مبيّن قد بيّن الله حكمَهما ليُفهم السائل.

> The chapter on the one who likens a known subject to a subject whose ruling has been made clear by God, to help the questioner understand it.

A commentator on Bukhārī (Muḥammad b. 'Abd al-Hādī al-Sindī, *al-Hāshiya 'alā al-Bukhārī*, 4:227) explained this sense of comparison:

> المطلوب تشبيه المجهول على المخاطب بالمعلوم عنده، مع أنّ كلًّا منهما معلوم عند المتكلّم بدون هذا التشبيه، وإنّما يشبّه لتفهيم السائل المخاطب والتوضيح عنده لا لاثبات الحكم كما يقول به أهل القياس.

> The objective is to liken that which the addressee does not know to what he does know; meanwhile, both are known to the one who does the comparison, without his needing to liken them to each other. He likens them to one another in order to help the questioner who is being addressed understand and to illustrate it to him, but not in order to derive a rule, as is the view of the people of analogy.

Muḥammad al-Bāqir, too, occasionally used the same method in explaining his positions to his disciples. See, for instance, Ṭūsī, 2:133.

209 Ṭūsī, *Tahdhīb*, 5:174.

he feared that if he circumambulated and performed the *saʿy* between Ṣafā and Marwa [so as to perform his *ʿumra* first, as one is supposed to do in *ḥajj tamattuʿ*], he would miss the standing at ʿArafāt [for his *ḥajj*]. The Imam said, "He should forgo the *ʿumra*, and when he completes his *ḥajj* he should do what ʿĀʾisha did,[210] and he does not owe a sacrificial animal."

Here, the case of the man was very different from the case of ʿĀʾisha, but the two shared a clear common denominator, the time constraint, which was obviously the reason behind the permissibility of ʿĀʾisha's postponing some of the *ḥajj* rituals. This approach, rooted in an essential shared element, is also apparent in the following examples:

زرارة عن أبي عبد الله: أيّما رجل كان له مالٌ وحال عليه الحول فانّه يزكّيه. قلت له: فإن هو وهبه قبل حلّه بشهر أو بيوم؟ قال: ليس عليه شيء إذَن. وقال [في من يَهبه بعد الحول]: إنّما هذا بمنزلة رجل أفطر في شهر رمضان يومًا في إقامته، ثمّ خرج في آخر النهار في سفر، أراد بسفره ذلك إبطال الكفّارة الّتي وجبت عليه. إنّه حين رأى الهلال الثاني عشر وجبت عليه الزكاة ولكنّه لو كان يوهبها قبل ذلك لجاز ولم يكن عليه شيء، بمنزلة من خرج ثمّ أفطر. إنّما لا يمنع ما حال عليه [الحول]، وأمّا ما لم يحلّ فله منعه. قلت له: إنّ أباك قال لي: من فرّ به من الزكاة فعليه أن يؤدّيها. قال: صدق أبي! عليه أن يؤدّي ما وجب عليه، وما لم يجب عليه فلا شيء عليه فيه. أرأيت لو أنّ رجلاً أُغمي عليه يومًا ثمّ مات وقد مات قبل أن يؤدّيها، أعليه شيء؟ قلت: لا! إلّا أن يكون أفاق من يومه. ثمّ قال: لو أنّ رجلاً مرض في شهر رمضان ثمّ مات فيه أكان يصام عنه؟ قلت: لا! قال: فكذلك الرجل، لا يؤدّي عن ماله إلّا ما حال عليه الحول.[211]

[Zurāra:] Abū ʿAbd Allāh said, "Whoever possesses wealth for the duration of a year must pay *zakāt* on it." I said to him, "What if he gifts it one month, or one day, before a year has lapsed?" He said, "Then he owes nothing." And he said [regarding a person who makes such a gift after a year has lapsed], "He is like a man who breaks his fast for a day during the month of Ramaḍān while he is at his residence, then leaves

210 This is a reference to a story about ʿĀʾisha, wife of the Prophet, on a *ḥajj* trip. She could not perform some of the rituals of the *ḥajj* because of menstruation and was advised by the Prophet to skip them and perform them later. The story is quoted in Bukhārī, *Ṣaḥīḥ*, no. 1560, and the other five canonical Sunnī *ḥadīth* collections, as well as in many other early works cited in the editor's footnote to Beirut, 1998 edition of Ibn Mājah's *Sunan*, 4:446.

211 Kulaynī, *Kāfī*, 3:525–26; Ibn Bābawayh, *ʿIlal al-sharāʾiʿ*, 2:62–63, with minor variations.

at the end of the day on a journey, thinking that by traveling, he will negate the expiation that has become obligatory for him. Actually, as soon as the man [in the original case] sees the twelfth crescent [of the year], the *zakāt* becomes due for him. But if he gifts it before that, that is permissible and he owes nothing. He is like someone who traveled and then broke his fast. He cannot avoid [paying *zakāt*] on that which he has possessed for a year, but on that which has not been in his possession for a year he can avoid it." I said to him, "Your father said to me, 'Whoever avoids the *zakāt* [by granting a gift] must fulfill it.'" He said, "My father spoke the truth. The man must fulfill what is obligatory for him, and he owes nothing for what is not obligatory for him." Then he said, "What do you think about a man who falls unconscious one day and then dies, not having paid *zakāt*—did he have the responsibility to do it?" I said, "No! Unless he recovers the same day." Then he said, "If a man falls ill during the month of Ramaḍān and then dies during it, is the fast [for the day of his death] to be made up on his behalf?" I said, "No!" He said, "It is the same for this man; he owes nothing on his wealth except on that which has been a year in his possession."

محمّد بن عذافر قال: قلت لأبي عبد الله [رجل] يكون في وقت فريضة لا تمكّنه الأرض من القيام عليها ولا السجود عليها من كثرة الثلج والماء والمطر والوحل، أيجوز له أن يصلّي في المحمل؟ قال: نعم! هو بمنزلة السفينة. إن أمكنه قائمًا وإلّا قاعدًا.[212]

[Muḥammad b. ʿUdhāfir:] I said to Abū ʿAbd Allāh, "A man finds himself in the time for an obligatory prayer, but the ground does not permit him to stand or prostrate upon it because of an abundance of snow, water, rain, or mud. Is it permissible for him to pray in the carriage?" He said, "Yes! It is like being on a ship. [He should pray] standing, if he can, or else seated."[213]

212 Ṭūsī, *Tahdhīb*, 3:232.

213 We came across another example of this kind in the previous chapter in a conversation between Jaʿfar al-Ṣādiq and Sufyān al-Thawrī about the *ḥajj* station for a group of non-Meccans who resided in Mecca. Jaʿfar defended the correctness of his advice to them, saying:

إنّ هؤلاء قطنوا بمكّة فصاروا كأنّهم من أهل مكّة، وأهل مكّة لا متعة لهم.

> These people [whom I advised to go to Jiʿrāna to assume the status of pilgrim sanctity] reside in Mecca, so it is as if they are of the people of Mecca, and the people of Mecca do not perform *tamattuʿ*.

محمّد بن مسلم عن أبي عبد الله قال: سألته عن رجل أجنب في السفر ولم يجد إلّا الثلج أو ماءً جامدًا، فقال: هو بمنزلة الضرورة. يتيمّم ولا أرى [له] أن يعود إلى هذه الأرض الّتي توبق دينه.[214]

[Muḥammad b. Muslim:] I asked Abū ʿAbd Allāh about a man who becomes ritually impure with a major impurity but can find nothing [with which to perform the ritual full-body ablution] other than ice or frozen water. He said, "[His situation] is like one of necessity. He should perform the dry ablution with earth, and I do not believe that he should ever return to that land that endangers his religion."

أبو ولّاد عن أبي عبد الله قال: لا بأس بأجر السمسار. إنّما يشترى للناس يومًا بعد يوم بشيء مسمّى. إنّما هو بمنزلة الأُجَراء.[215]

[Abū Wallād:] Abū ʿAbd Allāh said, "There is nothing wrong with paying a middleman. He buys things for people day after day for a specified payment. He is like a hired laborer."

معاوية بن عمّار عن أبي عبد الله في رجل توفّي وأوصى أن يُحَجَّ عنه. قال: إن كان صرورة فمن جميع المال. إنّه بمنزلة الدَّين الواجب. وإن كان قد حجَّ فمن ثلثه. ومن مات ولم يحجّ حجّة الإسلام ولم يترك إلّا قدر نفقة الحمولة وله ورثة، فهم أحقُّ بما ترك. فإن شاؤوا أكلوا وإن شاؤوا حجّوا عنه.[216]

[Muʿāwiya b. ʿAmmār:] Regarding a man who dies and stipulates in his will that a *ḥajj* be performed on his behalf, Abū ʿAbd Allāh said, "If he has never performed the *ḥajj*, then [the expenses for] the *ḥajj* will be charged to the entirety of his estate. It is like an obligatory debt.[217] If he has performed *ḥajj* before, then [the *ḥajj* is paid for] from a third [of his estate]. Whoever dies and has never performed the Islamic *ḥajj* and leaves behind only enough for transportation [for performing the *ḥajj*] but has heirs, they are more entitled to what he leaves behind. If they wish they can use it [for themselves] and if they wish they can perform the *ḥajj* [with it] on his behalf."

214 Kulaynī, *Kāfī*, 3:67.
215 Kulaynī, *Kāfī*, 5:196 (repeated at 5:285).
216 Kulaynī, *Kāfī*, 4:305.
217 On this point, see also Ibn Abī Shayba, *Muṣannaf*, 5:559–60; Bukhārī, *Ṣaḥīḥ*, no. 6699, and other sources cited in the editors' footnote in Aḥmad b. Ḥanbal, *Musnad*, 4:43.

عبد الرحمن بن الحجّاج قال: سألت أبا عبد الله عن رجل رمى صيدًا في الحلّ وهو يؤمّ الحرم في ما بين البريد والمسجد، فأصابه في الحلّ فمضى برميته حتّى دخل الحرم فمات من رَميَته، هل عليه جزاءٌ؟ فقال: ليس عليه جزاءٌ. إنّما مَثَل ذلك مَثَل من نَصب شركًا في الحلِّ إلى جانب الحرم فوقع فيه صيد فاضطرب حتّى دخل الحرم فمات [فيه] فليس عليه جزائه، لأنّه نصب حين نصب وهو له حلال ورمى حيث رمى وهو له حلال، فليس عليه في ما كان بعد ذلك شيء.[218]

[ʿAbd al-Raḥmān b. al-Ḥajjāj:] I asked Abū ʿAbd Allāh about a man who shot at game while he was outside the sacred precinct [of Mecca] on the way toward it, somewhere between the milestone of the precinct and the mosque. He shot at it outside of the precinct but [the game] continued with the arrow in it until it entered the sacred precinct and died from the arrow. Does he owe a penalty? He said, "He owes no penalty. He is like someone who sets a trap outside the sacred precinct next to it, and game falls into it and is bewildered and then enters the sacred precinct and dies. There is no penalty because he [the second man] set up [the trap] where he did and it was permissible for him, and [likewise] he [the first man] shot where he shot and it was permissible for him, so he is not liable for what happened after that."

علي بن أبي حمزة قال: سألت أبا عبد الله عن رجلٍ بدأ بالمروة قبل الصفا؟ قال: يعيد. ألا ترى أنّه لو بدأ بشماله قبل يمينه في الوضوء [يعيد الوضوء].[219]

[ʿAlī b. Abī Ḥamza:] Abū ʿAbd Allāh was asked about a [pilgrim] man who began [his *saʿy*] with Marwa rather than Ṣafā [with which he is supposed to begin it]. He said, "He must repeat it. Do you not see that if he began with his left side before his right when performing the ablution, he would have to repeat the ablution?"

عبيد الله بن علي الحلبي عن أبي عبد الله [في] رجلٍ فجر بامرأةٍ ثمّ بدا له أن يتزوّجها [قال:] أوّله سفاح وآخره نكاح. مَثَله مَثَل النخلة أصاب الرجل من ثمرها حرامًا ثمّ اشتراها بعد فكانت له حلالاً.[220]

---

218 Ibn Bābawayh, *Faqīh*, 2:168–69; Ibn Bābawayh, *ʿIlal al-sharāʾiʿ*, 2:139, with two variants in Ṭūsī, *Tahdhīb*, 5:360 and Kulaynī, *Kāfī*, 4:234 (attributed to Mūsā al-Kāẓim in the latter source).

219 Kulaynī, *Kāfī*, 4:436.

220 Kulaynī, *Kāfī*, 5:356.

[ʿUbayd Allāh al-Ḥalabī:] Abū ʿAbd Allāh said, regarding a man who fornicated with a woman and then wanted to marry her, "It started as fornication but ended as marriage. This is like a palm tree whose dates a man acquires unlawfully, but which he later purchases, so they become lawful for him."

Jaʿfar followed the same approach in cases in which the law applied to a second case a fortiori:

حفص بن غياث قال: سألت أبا عبد الله: أخبرني عن النساء كيف سَقَطت الجزية عنهنّ ورُفِعَت عنهنّ؟ فقال: لأنّ رسول الله – صلّى الله عليه وآله وسلّم – نهى عن قتل النساء والولدان في دار الحرب إلّا أن يقاتِلن. فلمّا نهى عن قتلهنّ في دار الحرب كان ذلك في دار الإسلام أولى.[221]

[Ḥafṣ b. Ghiyāth:] I said to Abū ʿAbd Allāh, "Tell me how the *jizya* was dropped and removed from women." He said, "[It was] because the Messenger of God (may God's prayer and peace be upon him and his Family) forbade killing women and children in the abode of war, unless they fight. Since it is forbidden to fight them in the abode of war, that applies a fortiori in the abode of Islam."

Likewise, common sense, public interest, and blocking what might lead to unlawful acts (*sadd al-dharīʿa*, as it is known in Sunnī jurisprudence) were essential elements of his legal thought.[222] Here are a few examples of each:

داود بن فرقد عن أبي عبد الله قال: سألني داود بن علي عن رجل كان يأتي بيت رجل فنهاه أن يأتي بيته فأبى أن يفعل، فذهب إلى السلطان فقال السلطان: إن فعل فاقتله،

221 Barqī, *Maḥāsin*, 327–28 (whence Kulaynī, *Kāfī*, 5:28–29).

222 A report from Jaʿfar al-Ṣādiq suggests that the Prophet, too, considered these elements in his legal directives (Ṭūsī, *Tahdhīb*, 6:281):

داود بن الحصين عن أبي عبد الله قال: إنّ الله أمر في الطلاق بشهادة رجلين عدلين. والنكاح لم يجيء عن الله فيه عزيمة فسنّ رسول الله – صلّى الله عليه وآله وسلّم – في ذلك شاهدين تأديبًا ونظرًا لئلّا يُنكر الولد والميراث.

[Dāwūd b. al-Ḥuṣayn:] Abū ʿAbd Allāh said, "God ordered that two righteous men bear witness to divorce but did not impose any such obligation for marriage, so the Messenger of God (may God's prayer and peace be upon him and his Family) ordered the presence of two witnesses as a matter of discipline and in consideration for the child and for inheritance so that neither can be disavowed."

See also Ibn Qudāma, *Mughnī*, 9:348.

فقتَلَه، فما ترى فيه؟ فقلت: أرى [أنّه قد أقرّ بقتل رجل مسلم فاقتله].[223] إنّه إن استقام هذا ثمّ شاء أن يقول كلّ انسان لعدوّه دخل بيتي فقتلتُه [لفعل].[224]

[Dāwūd b. Farqad:] Abū ʿAbd Allāh said, "Dāwūd b. ʿAlī [governor of Medina] asked me about a man who used to go to another man's house. The [latter] man forbade him to go to his house, but he did not stop doing so. He [the owner of the house] went to the government and the government said to him, 'If he does that, kill him.' So he killed him—'What is your position on this?' I said to him, 'I believe you should kill him because he confessed that he killed a Muslim man [with no legal excuse].[225] If this becomes an acceptable norm and everyone who wants to say that his enemy entered his house so he killed him will do so.'"

سماعة قال: سألت أبا عبد الله عن مسلم قتل ذمّيًّا، فقال: هذا شيء شديد لا يحتمله الناس. فليُعط أهلُ [الذمّيّ ديةَ المسلم ثمّ يُقتل به المسلم] ، حتّى يُنكل عن قتل أهل السواد وعن قتل الذمّي. ثمّ قال: لو أنّ مسلمًا غضب على ذمّي فاراد أن يقتله ويأخذ أرضه ويؤدّي إلى أهله ثمانمائة درهم، إذًا يكثر القتل في الذمييّن، ومن قتل ذمّيًّا ظلمًا فإنّه ليَحرُم على المسلم أن يقتل ذمّيًّا حرامًا.[226]

[Samāʿa:] I asked Abū ʿAbd Allāh about a Muslim who kills a *dhimmī*. He said, "This is something sensitive that the people cannot tolerate.

---

223 From a variant of the report in Kulaynī, *Kāfī*, 7:375.

224 Ibn Bābawayh, *Faqīh*, 4:126–27.

225 In the more detailed version of the report in Kulaynī, *Kāfī*, 7:375, the man claimed that he had been given permission to kill the intruder by the previous rulers—that is, the Umayyad agents in Medina—as Dāwūd b. ʿAlī, who is mentioned in the text, was the first governor named by the newly established Abbasid caliphate after the overthrow of the Umayyads, as also mentioned in Chapter 1. He was appointed by Abū al-ʿAbbās al-Saffāḥ very late in 132, held that office for three months, and died in Rabīʿ al-Awwal, 133 (Ṭabarī, *Taʾrīkh*, 7:459). The man's claim had no legal value, as the government had no authority to allow one person to kill another on a mere claim and without the case's having gone through the court system. In his reply in Kulaynī, 7:375, Jaʿfar al-Ṣādiq refers to the story of a Companion who asked the Prophet whether a man who sees someone in bed with his wife could kill him. The Prophet answered that the issue had to be proved by the testimony of four witnesses as required by the Qurʾān (Muslim, *Ṣaḥīḥ*, no. 1498). Even on a purely administrative basis, the man's claim to possess the government's permission for the killing could no longer be substantiated, since the former government and its officials were by then all gone. The key fact was the man's confession that he had killed another human being, the legal effect of which would be the application of the law of retaliation: a life for a life (Deuteronomy 19:21, endorsed by Qurʾān 5:45).

226 Ṭūsī, *Tahdhīb*, 10:188.

The family of the *dhimmī* should pay the blood-money of a Muslim,[227] and then the Muslim should be killed in retaliation for his killing of the *dhimmī*.[228] This is so to prevent people from killing the people of the Sawād (Mesopotamia) and from killing *dhimmī*s." Then he said, "If a Muslim became angry with a *dhimmī* and wanted to kill him, take his land, and give to his family eight hundred dirhams, the killing of *dhimmī*s would proliferate. Whoever kills a *dhimmī* unjustly, [he commits a murder as] it is unlawful for a Muslim to kill a *dhimmī* unjustly."

زرارة قال: قلت لأبي عبد الله: رجلٌ دفع إلى رجل مالاً قرضًا، على من زكاته؟ على المُقرض أو على المقترض؟ قال: زكاته إن كان موضوعًا عنده حولاً على المقترض. قلت: فليس على المُقرض زكاةً؟ قال: لا يزكّى المال من وجهين في عام واحد، وليس على الدافع شيء لأنّه ليس في يده. إنّما المال في يد الآخذ. فمن كان المال في يده زكّاه. قلت: أفيزكّي غيره من ماله؟ قال: إنّه مالُه مادام في يده وليس ذلك المال لأحد غيره. ثمّ قال: يا زرارة! أرأيت وضيعة ذلك المال وربحه لمن هو وعلى من؟ قلت: للمقترض. قال: فله الفضل وعليه النقصان. أله أن ينكح ويلبس منه ويأكل منه، ولا ينبغي له أن يزكّيه؟![229]

[Zurāra:] I said to Abū ʿAbd Allāh, "A man gave a cash loan to another person; who owes the *zakāt* on it? The creditor or the debtor?" He said, "The *zakāt* is owed by the debtor if it [the money] has been with him for one year." I asked, "The creditor does not owe *zakāt* on it?" He said, "The *zakāt* is not paid twice in one year, and the lender does not owe anything because it was not in his possession. The money was in

227 More precisely, the family should pay the difference between the blood-money of a Muslim and that of a non-Muslim, as specified in two other reports from Jaʿfar al-Ṣādiq (Ṭūsī, *Tahdhīb*, 10:189). In two further reports (Ṭūsī, 10:187), however, Jaʿfar is quoted as saying that the blood-money of a Muslim and that of a non-Muslim who is protected by Islam (*dhimmī*) are the same (a view supported by a number of early jurists as quoted in, for instance, Ibn Abī Shayba, *Muṣannaf*, 9:138–39).

> أبان بن تغلب عن أبي عبد الله قال: دية اليهودي والنصراني والمجوسي دية المسلم.
>
> [Abān b. Taghlib:] Abū ʿAbd Allāh said, "The blood-money of a Jew, a Christian, or a Magian is the same as the blood-money of a Muslim."
>
> زرارة عن أبي عبد الله قال: من أعطاه رسول الله ذمّةً فديته كاملة (يعني دية المسلم). قال زرارة: فهؤلاء؟ قال: وهؤلاء ممّن أعطاهم ذمّة.
>
> [Zurāra:] Abū ʿAbd Allāh said, "The blood-money of anyone to whom the Messenger of God granted protection is paid in full [that is, like the blood money of a Muslim]." Zurāra said, "What about these people [non-Muslims currently living in Muslim lands]?" He said, "These people are among those to whom he granted protection."

228 This view was also supported by a number of other early jurists. See, for instance, Ibn Abī Shayba, *Muṣannaf*, 9:141–44.

229 Kulaynī, *Kāfī*, 3:520.

the possession of the recipient. Whoever has possession of the money pays *zakāt* on it." I said, "Does one pay *zakāt* on someone else's money from his own money?" He said, "It is his money as long as it is in his possession, and that money does not belong to anyone else." Then he said, "O Zurāra! Who do you think is liable for a loss of value on that money and who gets its profit?" I said, "The debtor." He said, "He gets the excess and suffers the loss. Could he marry, dress, and eat from it, but not pay *zakāt* on it?"

إسحاق بن عمّار عن أبي عبد الله في رجل مات وترك أبويه وإخوة لأمّ، قال: الله سبحانه أكرم من أن يزيدها في العيال وينقصها من الميراث الثلث.[230]

[Isḥāq b. ʿAmmār:] Abū ʿAbd Allāh said about a man who died and left behind his parents and maternal siblings, "God, praised be He, is too gracious to add to her burden while reducing her share of inheritance."[231]

إسماعيل بن عبد الخالق قال: سألت أبا عبد الله عن النوم في المسجد الحرام، فقال: هل للناس بُدٌّ من أن يناموا في المسجد الحرام؟ لا بأس به.[232]

[Ismāʿīl b. ʿAbd al-Khāliq:] I asked Abū ʿAbd Allāh about sleeping in the Sacred Mosque [in Mecca]. He said, "Do the people have another option but to sleep in the Sacred Mosque? There is nothing wrong with it."

---

230 Ṭūsī, *Tahdhīb*, 9:284.

231 This is a question of *ḥajb* in the Muslim law of inheritance. Qurʾān 4:11 assigns one-third of the inheritance to a mother if her child dies without issue, but one-sixth if the deceased had siblings. The siblings thus block the mother from getting a full share of inheritance, that is, one-third, and reduce it by half, to one-sixth. The above report suggests, however, that *maternal* siblings do not block the mother in this way. See further Ibn Taymiyya, *Majmūʿat fatāwā*, 5:343–44, where the author reaches a similar conclusion on siblings of all kinds through a different legal analysis:

> هي (أي الأُمّ) بالثلث أولى، فإنّها إذا أخذت الثلث مع الأب فمع غيره من العصبة أولى، فدلّ القرآن على أنّه إن لم يرثه إلّا الأمّ والأب أو عصبة سوى الابن فلأُمّه الثلث.
>
> A mother is more entitled to the third. If she takes a third along with the father, then she is even more entitled to take it along with another agnate. The Qurʾān indicates that if the deceased does not leave any heirs but the mother and the father, or any agnates other than a son, then the mother gets one-third.

232 Ḥimyarī, *Qurb al-isnād*, 127. See also Kulaynī, *Kāfī*, 3:370.

زرارة بن أعين قال: سُئل أبو عبد الله عن الرجل يتزوّج المرأة بغير شهود، فقال: لا بأس بتزويج البتّة فيما بينه وبين الله. إنّما جعل الشهود في تزويج البتّة من أجل الولد. لولا ذلك لم يكن به بأس.[233]

[Zurāra b. Aʿyan:] Abū ʿAbd Allāh was asked about a man who marries a woman without witnesses. He said, "There is nothing wrong with that in principle in a stable, permanent marriage as far as what is between himself and God is concerned. Witnesses were, however, added to the requirement for a stable, permanent marriage for the sake of the child. Were it not for that, there would be nothing wrong with this case."

يعقوب بن شعيب عن أبي عبد الله قال: سألته عن الرجل يبيع للقوم بالأجر [و]عليه ضمان مالهم، فقال: إذا طابت نفسه بذلك. إنّما أخاف أن يغرموه أكثر ممّا يصيب منهم.[234] فإذا طابت نفسه فلا بأس.[235]

[Yaʿqūb b. Shuʿayb:] I asked Abū ʿAbd Allāh about [the legality of] a man's selling on behalf of others on commission, on the condition that he be responsible for their property. He said, "Only if he is happy with that. I fear that they may fine him more than he makes from them. But if he is happy with that, there is nothing wrong with it."

عبد الله بن محرز قال: سألت أبا عبد الله عن رجل أوصى إليّ وهلك وترك ابنةً، فقال: أعط الابنة النصف واترك للموالى النصف. فرجعت. فقال أصحابنا: لا والله! ما للموالى شيء [وإنّما اتّقاك]. فرجعت إليه من قابل وقلت له: إنّ أصحابنا قالوا: ليس للموالى شيء وإنّما اتّقاك. فقال: لا والله! ما اتّقيتك، ولكنّي خفت عليك أن تؤخذ بالنصف. فإن كنت لا تخاف فادفع النصف الآخر إلى الابنة.[236]

[ʿAbd Allāh b. Muḥriz:] I asked Abū ʿAbd Allāh about a man who entrusted me with the execution of his will and then died and left behind a daughter. He said, "Give the daughter half, and leave half for the paternal relatives." I went back, and our companions said, "No, by God! The paternal relatives do not get anything. He safeguarded

233 Kulaynī, *Kāfī*, 5:387.

234 In the edition of the source used in this study, the word منهم appears as عليهم, which seems to be a corruption.

235 Ṭūsī, *Tahdhīb*, 7:157.

236 Ṭūsī, *Tahdhīb*, 7:87–88, with two variants at 7:86–87.

himself against you [that is, he gave you that answer out of precautionary secrecy]." I went back to him the next year and said, "Our companions say, 'The paternal relatives do not get anything. He safeguarded himself against you [and gave you that answer out of precautionary secrecy].'" He said, "No, by God! I did not safeguard myself against you. Rather, I feared that you be held responsible for the other half. If you have no fear, then give the other half to the daughter [too]."[237]

يعقوب بن شعيب قال: سألت أبا عبد الله عن الحُليّ أيُزكّى؟ قال: إذًا لا يبقى منه شيء.[238]

[Yaʿqūb b. Shuʿayb:] I asked Abū ʿAbd Allāh whether *zakāt* is payable on jewelry. He said, "If it were, nothing of it would remain."

عيص بن القاسم عن أبي عبد الله في الزكاة قال: ما أخذ منكم بنو أميّة فاحتسبوا به. فإنّ المال لا يبقى على هذا إن تزكّيه مرّتين.[239]

[ʿĪṣ b. al-Qāsim:] Abū ʿAbd Allāh said in regard to *zakāt* [collected by an unjust government], "[In calculating your remaining *zakāt* liability,] consider whatever the Umayyads collected from you as already paid, for wealth will not remain if *zakāt* is paid twice on it."

237 The point at hand is the difference between the systems of inheritance in Shīʿī and Sunnī law. In this case, Shīʿī law would assign the entire inheritance to the daughter, but Sunnī jurists would give her half and give the rest to her male relatives through the paternal line. In the present case, had the paternal male relatives come to know about the inheritance, they would have claimed their half, potentially taking the executor of the will to the authorities, who would order him to pay the other half to them from his own pocket. For a similar case, see Ṭūsī, *Tahdhīb*, 7:372, where the Imam said that although a woman who took an oath to manumit her slave if she were to marry after the death of her husband was not legally bound by her oath, the Imam worried that she might nonetheless be held responsible for it by the government, so he advised her to sell her slave before the government learned about the case:

> منصور بن حازم عن أبي عبد الله قال: سألته عن امرأة حلفت لزوجها بالعتاق والهدي إن هو مات لا تتزوّج بعده أبدًا، ثمّ بدا لها أن تتزوّج. قال: تبيع مملوكها. إنّي أخاف عليها السلطان. وليس عليها في الحقّ شيء.
>
> [Manṣūr b. Ḥāzim:] I asked Abū ʿAbd Allāh about a woman who swore to her husband, on pain of her slave getting automatically freed or of having to offer a sacrifice, that she would never marry again after his death, but now wants to remarry. He said, "She should sell her slave, as I fear for her with respect to the government [that it would take her slave from her if they learn about her previous commitment]. Legally speaking, she is not liable for anything [if she breaks her word and remarries]."

238 Kulaynī, *Kāfī*, 3:518.

239 Kulaynī, *Kāfī*, 3:543.

يونس بن يعقوب قال: كنت عند أبي عبد الله فدخل عليه رجل من القمّاطين فقال: جعلت فداك! تقع في أيدينا الأرباح والأموال وتجارات نعرف أنّ حقّك فيها ثابت وإنّا عن ذلك مقصّرون. فقال أبو عبد الله: ما أنصفناكم إن كلّفناكم اليوم.[240]

[Yūnus b. Yaʿqūb:] I was with Abū ʿAbd Allāh when one of the swaddle-makers came to him and said, "May I be made your ransom! We receive profits, money, and businesses to which we know you to have an established right,[241] but we are negligent of it." Abū ʿAbd Allāh said, "We would not be fair to you if we held you responsible today."

بعض أصحابنا عن أبي عبد الله قال: قلت له: الرجل يمرّ على قِراح الزرع، أيأخذ منه السنبلة؟ قال: لا! قلت: أيّ شيء السنبلة؟ قال: لو كان كلّ من يمرّ به يأخذ سنبلةً كان لا يبقى شيء![242]

I said to Abū ʿAbd Allāh, "A man comes across ears of grain. May he take a spike of grain?" He said, "No!" I said, "What [significance] is a spike of grain?" He said, "If everyone who came across it took a spike of grain, nothing of it would remain!"

Jaʿfar's legal positions took into account changes in social circumstances that required amending earlier laws:[243]

عن أبي عبد الله قال: لا ينبغي أن يتزوّج الرجل الحُرّ المملوكة اليوم. إنّما كان ذلك حيث قال الله عزّ وجلّ: ﴿وَمَنْ لَمْ يَسْتَطِعْ مِنْكُمْ طَوْلاً [أَنْ يَنْكِحَ الْمُحْصَنَاتِ الْمُؤْمِنَاتِ فَمِنْ مَا مَلَكَتْ أَيْمَانُكُمْ مِنْ فَتَيَاتِكُمُ الْمُؤْمِنَاتِ]﴾. والطَول المَهر، ومَهر الحُرّة اليوم مَهر الأمة أو أقلّ.[244]

Abū ʿAbd Allāh said, "A free man should not marry a slave woman today. That was permitted when God, the Mighty and Majestic, said, 'And whosoever among you has not the *means* to marry free, believing

240 Ṭūsī, *Tahdhīb*, 4:138.

241 This is a reference to Qurʾān 8:41 on the Islamic financial duty of *khums* that Shīʿī law applies to all kinds of income, rather than war booty alone. See the entry on *khums* in *Encyclopaedia of Islam* II, 12 (suppl.): 531–35 [A. Zysow and R. Gleave].

242 Ṭūsī, *Tahdhīb*, 6:385.

243 See also the report in Chapter 1, where Jaʿfar al-Ṣādiq justified differences between the Companions' reports from the Prophet as reflecting executive orders issued by the Prophet in different circumstances.

244 Kulaynī, *Kāfī*, 5:360.

women, then [let him marry] believing maidens among those whom your right hands possess.'[245] The *means* [mentioned in the Qur'ānic passage] is the dower, and the dower of a free woman today is the same as or less than that for a slave woman."

جميل بن درّاج قال: سألت أبا عبد الله عن حبس لحوم الأضاحى فوق ثلاثة [أيّام] بمِنى. قال: لا بأس بذلك اليوم. إنّ رسول الله – صلّى الله عليه وآله وسلّم – إنّما [نهى عن] ذلك لأنّ الناس كانوا يومئذٍ مجهودين،[246] فأمّا اليوم فلا بأس.[247]

[Jamīl b. Darrāj:] I asked Abū ʿAbd Allāh about detaining the meat of sacrificial animals in Minā for more than three days. He said, "There is nothing wrong with that today. The Messenger of God (may God's prayer and peace be upon him and his Family) forbade it because the people were poor at the time [and needed it]. But today, there is nothing wrong with that."

معاوية بن عمّار عن أبي عبد الله قال: كنّا نقول لا بدّ أن يُستفتح بالحَجَر ويُختم به، وأمّا اليوم فقد كثر الناس[248] [فلا].[249]

[Muʿāwiya b. ʿAmmār:] Abū ʿAbd Allāh said, "We used to say that one must begin and end [circumambulation around the Kaʿba] with [touching of] the Black Stone, but not any longer as there is such a big crowd now."

عمّار بن موسى عن أبي عبد الله قال: إنّما يكره قطع السدر بالبادية لأنّه بها قليل، وأمّا ههنا فلا بأس.[250]

[ʿAmmār b. Mūsā:] Abū ʿAbd Allāh said, "Cutting lote trees in the desert is disliked[251] because they are rare there, but here there is nothing wrong with that."

245 Qur'ān 4:25.
246 Or, as in a variant of the report in Kulaynī, *Kāfī*, 4:500: كنّا نقول: لا يُخرج منها شيء لحاجة الناس إليه.
247 Barqī, *Maḥāsin*, 320.
248 Kulaynī, *Kāfī*, 4:404.
249 From Ṭūsī, *Tahdhīb*, 5:399.
250 Kulaynī, *Kāfī*, 5:264.
251 This is a reference to numerous reports from the Prophet in the Sunnī tradition against the cutting of lote trees. See the monograph by Suyūṭī (d. 911) on the topic, *Rafʿ al-khidr ʿan qaṭʿ al-sidr*, in his *Ḥāwī*, 2:51–55.

بكر بن محمّد عن أبي عبد الله قال: سأله رجل وأنا حاضر فقال: يكون لي غلام. أريد عتقه فهل عتقه أحبّ إليك أو أبيعه وأتصدّق بثمنه؟ فقال: إنّ العتق في بعض الزمان أفضل وفي بعض الزمان الصدقة أفضل. إذا كان الناس حسنة حالهم فالعتق أفضل وإذا كانوا شديدة حالهم فالصدقة أفضل.[252]

[Bakr b. Muḥammad:] A man said to Abū ʿAbd Allāh while I was present, "I have a male slave whom I want to manumit. Is it better to manumit him or to sell him and donate the proceeds?" He said, "Sometimes manumission is preferable, sometimes donation is preferable. If the people are in a good condition, manumission is preferred, but if they are in a poor condition, donation is preferred."

This approach follows ʿAlī's precedent, as in the following example:

سُئل علي – عليه السلام – عن قول النبي – صلّى الله عليه وآله وسلّم: «غيّروا الشيب ولا تتشبّهوا باليهود» فقال : إنّما قال – صلّى الله عليه وآله وسلّم – ذلك والدين قُلّ، فأمّا الآن وقد اتّسع نِطاقه وضرب بِجِرانه فامرؤ وما اختار.[253]

ʿAlī was asked about the saying of the Prophet (may God's prayer and peace be upon him and his Family): "Change your gray hair and do not resemble the Jews."[254] He said, "He [the Prophet] (may God's prayer and peace be upon him and his family) said that when the religion [of Islam] was in the minority. Now it has become widespread and established. So one goes with one's preference."

Culture and social realities were also important factors in Jaʿfar al-Ṣādiq's legal methodology:

عبد الرحمن بن الحجّاج عن أبي عبد الله: لولا أنّ خروج النساء شهرة لأمرت الصرورة منهنّ أن تخرج [إلى الميقات لتُحرم منها بالحجّ].[255]

[ʿAbd al-Raḥmān b. al-Ḥajjāj:] Abū ʿAbd Allāh said, "Were women's going out not considered bad by society, I would order those among them who were performing the *ḥajj* for the first time to go to the *mīqāt*

252 Kulaynī, *Kāfī*, 6:194–95.

253 *Nahj al-balāgha*, *ḥikam* no. 17 (ed. Ṣubḥī al-Ṣāliḥ, 471).

254 Tirmidhī, *Sunan*, no. 1752, and other sources cited in the editors' footnotes in Aḥmad b. Ḥanbal, *Musnad*, 3:32, 12:507–8.

255 Kulaynī, *Kāfī*, 4:301.

[that is, the *ḥajj* station] to assume the state of pilgrim sanctity for the *ḥajj* there."

أبان بن تغلب قال: سأل أبا عبد الله أخي وأنا حاضر عن الثوب يكون مصبوغًا بالعصفر ثمّ يُغسل، ألبسه وأنا محرم؟ قال: نعم! ليس العصفر من الطيب. ولكن أكره أن تلبس ما يشهرك بين الناس.[256]

[Abān b. Taghlib:] Abū ʿAbd Allāh was asked by my brother in my presence about a garment that was dyed with safflower and then washed—can I wear it while I am in a state of pilgrim sanctity? He said, "Yes! Safflower is not perfume. However, I do not like you to wear what makes you stand out among people."

معلّي بن خنيس عن أبي عبد الله قال: كان علي عندكم فأتى البزّازين[257] واشترى ثلاثة أثواب بدينار: القميص إلى فوق الكعب، والإزار إلى فوق الساق، والرداء من بين يديه إلى ثدييه ومن خلفه إلى إليتيه. ثمّ رفع يده إلى السماء فلم يزل يحمد الله على ما كساه حتّى دخل منزله. ثمّ قال: هذا اللباس الّذي ينبغي للمسلمين أن يلبسوه. قال أبو عبد الله: ولكن لا يقدرون أن يلبسوه هذا اليوم، ولو فعلناه لقالوا: مجنون! ولقالوا: مُراءٍ.[258]

[Muʿallā b. Khunays:] Abū ʿAbd Allāh said [speaking to a group of Kūfan visitors], "ʿAlī was with you when he went to clothes-sellers and bought three garments for one dinar: a shirt that stopped above the ankles, an *izār* that stopped at the shin, and a *ridāʾ* that covered the front of his body to his chest and from his back to his rear. He then lifted his hand to the sky, continuously praising God for what He had dressed him in until he entered his home. Then he said, 'These are the clothes that Muslims should wear.'" Abū ʿAbd Allāh said, "However, today they cannot wear that. If we did so, they would say 'He is crazy!' and 'He is ostentatious!'"

256 Ṭūsī, *Tahdhīb*, 7:157. See also Kulaynī, *Kāfī*, 4:342, with a minor variation and through a different chain of transmission.

257 From Ḥasan b. Faḍl al-Ṭabrisī, *Makārim al-akhlāq*, 127. The word is corrupted to بني ديوان in Kulaynī, *Kāfī*, 6:455.

258 Kulaynī, *Kāfī*, 6:455–56.

داود بن سرحان قال: مات أبو عبيدة الحذّاء وأنا بالمدينة فأرسل إليّ أبو عبد الله بدينار وقال: اشتر بهذا حَنوطًا. واعلم أنّ الحَنوط هو الكافور، ولكن إصنع كما يصنع الناس.[259]

[Dāwūd b. Sarḥān:] Abū ʿUbayda al-Ḥadhdhāʾ[260] passed away when I was in Medina, so Abū ʿAbd Allāh sent me a dinar and said, "Buy *ḥanūṭ* with this [to apply to the corpse before burial]. Know that *ḥanūṭ* is camphor, but do as the people do."

عبد الله بن يحيى الكاهلي قال: سألت أبا عبد الله عن قوم مسلمين حضرهم رجل مجوسيّ، أيدعونه إلى طعامهم. قال: أمّا أنا فلا أؤاكل المجوسي، وأكره أن أُحرِّم عليكم شيئًا تصنعونه في بلادكم.[261]

[ʿAbd Allāh b. Yaḥyā al-Kāhilī:] I asked Abū ʿAbd Allāh about a group of Muslims to whom a Magian man has come. Should they invite him to their meals? He said, "For my part, I do not eat with Magians, but I would hate to forbid you to do something which you do in your lands."

سيف بن عميرة عن أبي عبد الله قال: لا تدخل القبر وعليك نعل ولا قلنسوة ولا عمامة. قلت: فالخُفّ؟ قال: لا بأس بالخُفّ فانّ في خلع الخُفّ شناعة.[262]

[Sayf b. ʿAmīra:] Abū ʿAbd Allāh said, "Do not enter a grave wearing sandals, head caps, or turbans." I said, "What about boots?" He said, "There is nothing wrong with boots, for there is a distastefulness to removing one's boots."

محمّد بن شريح قال: سألت أبا عبد الله عن شراء الأرض من أرض الخراج فكرهه وقال: إنّما أرض الخراج للمسلمين. فقالوا له: فإنّه يشتريها الرجل وعليه خراجها. فقال: لا بأس. إلّا أن يستحيي من عيب ذلك.[263]

[Muḥammad b. Shurayḥ:] I asked Abū ʿAbd Allāh about the purchase of a piece of *kharāj* land. He disliked it and said, "*Kharāj* land belongs to all Muslims." [Other people in attendance] told him that the buyer

259 Kulaynī, *Kāfī*, 3:146; Kashshī, *Rijāl*, 368.

260 Abū ʿUbayda Ziyād b. ʿĪsā, a *ḥadīth* transmitter and disciple of Jaʿfar al-Ṣādiq and his father. On him, see Kashshī, *Rijāl*, 368; Muḥammad Taqī al-Tustarī, *Qāmūs al-rijāl*, 4:507–11.

261 Barqī, *Maḥāsin*, 452–53; Kulaynī, *Kāfī*, 6:263.

262 Ṭūsī, *Tahdhīb*, 1:313.

263 Ṭūsī, *Tahdhīb*, 7:148.

would [continue to] pay *kharāj* on the land. He said, "Then there is no problem [with the purchase], unless he feels embarrassed by the contempt attached to it."[264]

ثعلبة وعبد الله بن هلال عن أبي عبد الله في الرجل يتزوّج ولد الزنا، قال: لا بأس. إنّما يُكره ذلك مخافةَ العار.[265] [إن لم يخف العيب على ولده فلا بأس].[266]

[Thaʿlaba b. Maymūn and ʿAbd Allāh b. Hilāl:] Regarding a man who marries a woman of illegitimate birth, Abū ʿAbd Allāh said, "There is no problem [with the marriage]. It is disliked because of a possible contempt attached to it. If he does not think that his children [from the woman] may fall victim to such contempt, there is nothing [legally] wrong [with the marriage]."[267]

حنان بن سدير قال: دخلنا على أبي عبد الله ومعنا فرقد الحجّام، فقال له: جُعلت فداك! إنّي أعمل عملاً وقد سألت عنه غير واحد فزعموا أنّه عمل مكروه، وأنا أُحبّ أن أسألك عنه فإن كان مكروهًا انتهيت عنه وعملت غيره من الأعمال، وإنّي منتهٍ في ذلك إلى قولك. قال: وما هو؟ قال: حجّام. قال: كُل من كسبك يا ابن أخ! وتصدّق وحجّ منه وتزوّج، فإنّ النبي – صلّى الله عليه وآله وسلّم – قد احتجم وأعطى الأجر،

264 That is, to holding and working on non-Muslim land that the Muslims conquered by war. For the legal and social problems involved with this, see Modarressi, *Kharāj in Islamic Law*, 124–31.

265 Ibn Bābawayh, *Faqīh*, 3:271.

266 The sentence between the brackets is from a report on the same subject in Kulaynī, *Kāfī*, 5:353.

267 This explains why in answer to a similar question by another transmitter in Kulaynī, *Kāfī*, 5:353, Jaʿfar al-Ṣādiq allowed the marriage but advised against having children from it:

> عبد الله بن سنان قال: قلت لأبي عبد الله: ولد الزنا يُنكَح؟ قال: نعم! ولا يُطلبُ ولدُها.
>
> [ʿAbd Allāh b. Sinān:] I asked Abū ʿAbd Allāh, "Can one marry an illegitimate child?" He said, "Yes! But one should try not to have children by her."

In Deuteronomy 23:2, the illegitimate child, *mamzer*, shall not enter into the congregation of the Lord even to his tenth generation. A redaction of this statement, attributed to Jaʿfar al-Ṣādiq, appears in Kulaynī, *Kāfī*, 5:225 and Ṭūsī, *Tahdhīb*, 7:78; it reduces the number of generations to seven. (The Hebrew word *mamzer* in this report is variously corrupted in different manuscripts, as also noted by the editor of Kulaynī, 5:225, n. 2.) Cf. another report from Jaʿfar al-Ṣādiq in Kulaynī, 8:238, which says that God judges people by their deeds and not their lineage:

> ولد الزنا إن عَمل خيرًا جُزى به، وإن عَمل شرًّا جُزى به.
>
> For an illegitimate child: if he does good, he will be rewarded for it; if he does bad, he will be punished for it.

See further Kohlberg, "Position of the *Walad Zinā*," 237–66.

ولو كان حرامًا ما أعطاه. قال: جعلني الله فداك! إنّ لي تيسًا أُكريه فما تقول في كسبه؟ فقال: [إنّ العرب لتعاير به ولا بأس.][268]

> [Ḥanān b. Sadīr:] We went to Abū ʿAbd Allāh with Farqad the cupper accompanying us. He [Farqad] said to him [Jaʿfar al-Ṣādiq], "May I be made your ransom! I work in an occupation about which I asked more than one person and they said that it is disapproved. I would like to ask you about it. If it is disapproved, I will quit and find other work. I will act in this matter according to your opinion." He said, "What is it?" He said, "[I am] a cupper." He said, "Eat from what you earn, O son of a brother! Donate, perform the *ḥajj*, and marry with it. The Prophet (may God's prayer and peace be upon him and his Family) was cupped and paid for the service. If it were forbidden, he would not have paid." He said, "May God make me your ransom! I have a stallion that I lend for breeding—what do you say about profiting from it?"[269] He said, "The Arabs look upon [the practice] with contempt, but there is nothing [legally] wrong with it."

Jaʿfar was keenly attuned to social sensitivities, as can be seen in the following story. It so happened that a black slave of his, together with someone else, killed a person. The victim's family asked the governor of Medina, Muḥammad b. Khālid al-Qasrī, to kill the perpetrators in retaliation. The governor asked Jaʿfar al-Ṣādiq for his permission as the owner of the slave, but he kept silent, because his legal position was that two people could not be put to death for the killing of one person. The governor refrained from taking action out of respect for Jaʿfar. The people of Medina told the family that the only way they could convince the governor was to pursue Jaʿfar and put pressure on him. They did so. Jaʿfar withdrew his protection and allowed the governor to act according to their request.[270]

There are many similar instructions from Jaʿfar's father, whose emphasis on giving priority to the best interests of the Muslim community set an example for his son. Here is an example:

---

268 Kulaynī, *Kāfī*, 5:115–16. The phrase between brackets is from another report from Jaʿfar al-Ṣādiq on the same subject in Kulaynī, 5:116 and Ṭūsī, *Tahdhīb*, 6:355.

269 This question is referred to in Islamic legal works as *ḍirāb al-faḥl*, stud breeding. Many jurists disapproved of lending stallions for breeding if it was done for profit. See Ibn Qudāma, *Mughnī*, 8:130–31.

270 Kulaynī, *Kāfī*, 7:373–74, where it is also said that the slave was not a Muslim (according to a report in Ḥimyarī, *Qurb al-isnād*, 66 and Kulaynī, 6:182; ʿAlī, too, had a Christian slave who did not become a Muslim as long as he was a slave). Jaʿfar's opinion would not have made a difference at the end, as the government had established policies for cases like this one.

زرارة قال: حضر أبو جعفر جنازة رجل من قريش وأنا معه وكان فيها عطاء فصرخت صارخة، فقال عطاء: لتسكتنّ أو لنرجعنّ. فلم تسكت فرجع عطاء. قال: فقلت لأبي جعفر: إنّ عطاء قد رجع! قال: ولِمَ؟ قلت: صرخت هذه الصارخة فقال لها: لتسكتنّ أو لنرجعنّ، فلم تسكت فرجع. فقال: إمض بنا! فلو أنّا إذا رأينا شيئًا من الباطل مع الحقّ تركنا له الحقّ، لم نقض حقّ مسلمٍ.[271]

[Zurāra:] Abū Jaʿfar attended the funeral of a man from the Quraysh and I accompanied him. ʿAṭāʾ[272] [too] attended the funeral. A wailer wailed, so ʿAṭāʾ said, "She must be quiet or we will go back." She did not quiet down, so ʿAṭāʾ went back. I said to Abū Jaʿfar, "ʿAṭāʾ went back!" He said, "Why?" I said, "A wailer wailed, and he said 'She must be quiet or we will go back,' but she did not quiet down, so he went back." He said, "Let us carry on! If every time we saw something false alongside something right we left the right because of the false, we would never fulfill our duty toward the Muslims."

And at times, he acted to protect the standing of the Family of the Prophet in the community:

زرارة قال: رأيت ابنًا لأبي عبد الله في حياة أبي جعفر، يقال له عبد الله، فطيم قد درج. فأُخرج في سفط إلى البقيع، فخرج أبو جعفر. فلمّا انتهى إلى البقيع تقدّم أبو جعفر فصلّى عليه وكبّر عليه أربعًا، ثمّ أمر به فدُفن. ثمّ أخذ بيدي فتنحّى بي ثمّ قال: إنّه لم يكن يصلّى على الأطفال. إنّما كان أمير المؤمنين – عليه السلام – يأمر بهم فيُدفنون من وراء، ولا يصلّى عليهم، وأنّما صلّيت عليه من أجل أهل المدينة، كراهية أن يقولوا [إنّ بني هاشم][273] لا يصلّون على أطفالهم.[274]

[Zurāra:] I saw a son of Abū ʿAbd Allāh's during the lifetime of Abū Jaʿfar who was named ʿAbd Allāh and who was weaned but died. He was taken in a casket to [the cemetery of] Baqīʿ. Abū Jaʿfar went out and, when he reached Baqīʿ, went forth, prayed over him, said four *takbīr*s, and then ordered him to be buried. He then took my hand and took me aside and said, "It used to be that children were not prayed over. The Commander of the Faithful [ʿAlī] would order that they be taken

271 Kulaynī, *Kāfī*, 3:171–72.

272 ʿAṭāʾ b. Abī Rabāḥ Aslam b. Ṣafwān (d. 114), the *muftī* of Mecca in his time.

273 Added from a variant in Ibn Bābawayh, *Faqīh*, 1:105; Ibn Bābawayh, *Tawḥīd*, 393.

274 Kulaynī, *Kāfī*, 3:206–7.

into the cemetery from the back door to be buried and not be prayed over. But I prayed over him for the sake of the people of Medina, as I would hate for them to say that the Banū Hāshim do not pray over their children."

V. Legal Analysis

Besides drawing on general ethical and social considerations, the method that Jaʿfar al-Ṣādiq and his father used in their legal interpretation in cases in which neither a specific nor a generalizable relevant text was available was to define the applicable rules on the basis of general patterns in the law. Some examples of this style of legal analysis have already been given in Chapter 1. Here are a few others:

هشام بن سالم قال: قلت لأبي عبد الله: إنّ الناس يكلّمونا ويردّون علينا قولنا أنّه لا يصلّى على الطفل لأنّه لم يصلّ، فيقولون: لا يصلّى إلّا على من صلّى؟ فنقول: نعم! فيقولون: أرأيتم لو أنّ رجلاً نصرانيًّا أو يهوديًّا أسلم ثمّ مات من ساعته فما الجواب فيه؟ فقال: قولوا لهم: أرأيتم لو أنّ هذا الّذي أسلم الساعة ثمّ افترى على إنسان ما كان يجب عليه في فريته؟ فانّهم سيقولون يجب عليه الحدّ. فإذا قالوا هذا قيل لهم: فلو أنّ هذا الصبى الّذي لم يصلّ افترى على إنسان هل كان يجب عليه الحدّ؟ فإنّهم سيقولون لا! فيقال لهم: صدقتم! إنّما يجب أن يصلّى على من وجبت عليه الصلاة والحدود، ولا يصلّى على من لم تجب عليه الصلاة والحدود.[275]

[Hishām b. Sālim:] I said to Abū ʿAbd Allāh, "People speak to us and criticize our position that an infant is not prayed over when he dies because he did not pray. They say, 'So only people who pray are prayed over?'[276] We say, 'Yes!' They say, 'What do you think of a Christian or Jewish man who became Muslim and died shortly after [before he could pray even once, but we have to pray over him nonetheless]?' What is the answer to this question?" He said, "Say to them, 'What do you think: If this person who became Muslim immediately slandered someone—what is prescribed for his slander?' They will say, 'The fixed punishment [for slander] is to be applied to him.' If they say that, say to them, 'If this boy who does not [yet] pray slanders someone, is the fixed punishment applicable to him?' They will say, 'No!' So it will be said to them, 'You have spoken the truth! It is obligatory to

275 Kulaynī, *Kāfī*, 3:209.
276 See Barqī, *Maḥāsin*, 313–14.

pray over those for whom prayer and fixed punishments have become obligatory, but it is not obligatory to pray over those for whom prayer and fixed punishments have not become obligatory.'"

عمر بن يزيد قال: سألت أبا عبد الله عن رجل أراد أن يعتق مملوكًا له، وقد كان مولاه يأخذ منه ضريبة فرضها عليه في كلّ سنة فرضي بذلك المولى ورضي بذلك المملوك، فأصاب المملوك في تجارته مالاً سوى ما كان يعطي مولاه من الضريبة. فقال: إذا أدّى إلى سيّده ما كان فرض عليه فما اكتسب بعد الفريضة فهو للمملوك. ثمّ قال أبو عبد الله: أليس قد فرض الله عزّ وجلّ على العباد فرائض إذا أدُّوها إليه لم يسألهم عمّا سواها؟ قلت له: فما ترى للمملوك أن يتصدّق ممّا اكتسب ويعتق، بعد الفريضة الّتي كان يؤدّيها إلى سيّده؟ قال: نعم! واجب ذلك له. قلت: فإن أعتق مملوكًا ممّا اكتسب سوى الفريضة، لمن يكون ولاء المعتَق؟ قال: يذهب فيتوالي إلى من أحبّ، فإذا ضمّن جريرته وعقله كان مولاه وورثه. قلت له: أليس قال رسول الله – صلّى الله عليه وآله وسلّم: الولاء لمن أعتق؟ فقال: هذا سائبة لا يكون ولاؤه لعبد مثله. قلت: فإن ضمّن الّذي أعتقه جريرته وحدثه، أيلزمه ذلك ويكون مولاه ويرثه؟ قال: لا يجوز ذلك، ولا يرث عبدٌ حرّا.[277]

[ʿUmar b. Yazīd:] I asked Abū ʿAbd Allāh about a man who wanted to manumit his slave, and he imposed on the slave an annual payment, to which both the master and the slave agreed. The slave earned money in trade over and above what he would give to his master as regular payment. He [Jaʿfar al-Ṣādiq] said, "If he gives his master what he is required to give, then anything he earns in addition to it belongs to the slave." Then Abū ʿAbd Allāh said, "Did not God, the Mighty and Majestic, impose obligations upon His servants, [such] that if they performed them, He would not ask anything else of them?" I said to him, "What is your position on the slave's donating from what he earns and manumitting [a slave], after paying what he owes to his master?" He said, "Yes! That takes legal effect." I said, "If he manumits a slave from [the money] he earns in addition to what he owes, to whom does the clientage of the freed slave belong?" He said, "He can become the client of whomever he prefers. If that person assumes liability for his offenses and restitutions, he [the former slave] is his client and the latter inherits from him." I said to him, "Did not the Messenger of God

277 Kulaynī, *Kāfī*, 6:190.

(may God's prayer and peace be upon him and his Family) say, 'Clientship goes to whoever manumits'? He said, "This is a *sāʾiba* [that is, a freed slave who no longer has any bond with the former master],[278] who cannot be a client of a slave like him." I said, "What if the slave who manumits him assumes liability for his offenses and actions? Does he become obligated to fulfill it, and does he become his patron and inherit from him?" He said, "That is not permissible, and a slave cannot inherit from a free person."

عبد الرحمن بن الحجّاج قال: قلت لأبي عبد الله: الرجل يجيئني يطلب المتاع فأقاوله على الربح ثمّ أشتريه فأبيعه منه؟ فقال أليس إن شاء أخذ وإن شاء ترك؟ قلت: بلى! قال: لا بأس به. قلت: فإنّ من عندنا يفسده! قال: ولِمَ؟ قلت: باع ما ليس عنده. قال: فما يقول في السَلَم قد باع صاحبه ما ليس عنده؟ قلت: بلى! قال: فإنّما صَلُح من أجل أنهم يُسمّونه سَلَمًا. إنّ أبي كان يقول: لا بأس ببيع كلّ متاع كنت تجده في الوقت الّذي بعته فيه.[279]

[ʿAbd al-Raḥmān b. al-Ḥajjāj:] I said to Abū ʿAbd Allāh, "A man comes to me seeking a commodity. I negotiate with him over the price, then buy the commodity, and sell it to him." He said, "Is it not the case that he can take it if he wants and refuse it if he wants?" I said, "Yes!" He said, "There is nothing wrong with this." I said, "The [jurists] in our region say it is invalid." He said, "Why?" I said, "Because he sells what he does not possess." He said, "What do they say about the future sale contract, in which one sells what one does not yet possess?" I said, "True!" He said, "It is considered valid [by them] only because they call it a 'future sale contract.' My father used to say 'There is nothing wrong with selling any commodity that you can find at the time you conclude the sale for it.'"

---

278 This was a common legal concept in the early Islamic period. See, for instance, Mālik, *Muwaṭṭaʾ* [recension of Yaḥyā b. Yaḥyā al-Laythī], no. 2281 (2:340–41 of Beirut, 1997 edition); Bukhārī, *Ṣaḥīḥ*, no. 6372; Ibn ʿAbd al-Barr, *Istidhkār*, no. 1497; and in Shīʿī sources, Kulaynī, *Kāfī*, 7:171, where Jaʿfar al-Ṣādiq defines the term as follows:

أبو الربيع قال: سُئل أبو عبد الله عن السائبة فقال: هو الرجل يعتق غلامه ثمَّ يقول له: اذهب حيث شئت، ليس لي من ميراثك شيء ولا عليّ من جريرتك شيء، ويُشهد على ذلك شاهدين.

[Abū al-Rabīʿ Khalīd b. Awfā:] Abū ʿAbd Allāh was asked about the *sāʾiba*. He said, "It is when a man manumits his slave and says to him, 'Go wherever you please; I have no claim to any of your inheritance nor am I liable for your offenses.' And he gets two witnesses to observe this."

279 Kulaynī, *Kāfī*, 5:200.

عبد الرحمن بن الحجّاج قال: سألت أبا عبد الله عن العينة[280] فقلت: يأتيني الرجل فيقول: اشتَرِ المتاع واربَح فيه كذا وكذا، فأرضيه على الشيء من الربح فنتراضى به ثمّ ينطلق، فأشترى المتاع من أجله لولا مكانه لم أُرده، ثمّ آتيه به فأبيعه؟ قال: ما أرى بهذا بأسًا. لو هلك منك المتاع قبل أن تبيعه إيّاه كان من مالِك، وهو عليك بالخيار: إن شاء اشتراه منك بعد ما تأتي به وإن شاء ردّه، فلست أرى به بأسًا.[281]

[ʿAbd al-Raḥmān b. al-Ḥajjāj:] I asked Abū ʿAbd Allāh about [the legal status of] brokerage. I said, "A man comes to me and says, 'Buy the goods and make a profit of such-and-such on them.' I agree to the profit, we conclude an agreement, and he leaves. I then buy for his sake the goods, which I would not want were it not for him, and I take them to him and sell them." He said, "I do not think there is anything wrong with this. If the goods perished before you sold them to him, [the loss] would come out of your wealth. He has a choice: If he wishes he can buy them from you after you present them or if he wishes he can refuse them. So I do not think there is anything wrong with this."

خالد بن نجيح قال: قلت لأبي عبد الله: الرجل يجيئني فيقول اشترِ هذا الثوب وأربحك كذا وكذا؟ فقال أليس إن شاء أخذه وإن شاء ترك؟ قلت: بلى! قال: لا بأس به. إنّما يحلّل الكلام ويحرّم الكلام.[282]

[Khālid b. Najīḥ:] I said to Abū ʿAbd Allāh, "A man comes to me and says, 'Buy this garment and I will give you a profit [in the amount of] such-and-such.' He said, "Is it not the case that he can take it or leave it, as he wishes?" I said, "Yes!" He said, "There is nothing wrong with that. It is the statement [of specific conditions made in the contract] that makes things lawful or unlawful."

إسحاق بن عمّار قال: قلت لأبي عبد الله: يكون للرجل عندي الدراهم الوَضَح فيلقاني فيقول: كيف سعر الوَضَح اليوم؟ فأقول له: كذا وكذا. فيقول لي: حَوّلها إلى دنانير بهذا السعر وأثبتها لي عندك. فما ترى في هذا؟ فقال لي: إذا كنت قد

280 Brokerage, a common practice in second-century Kūfa (see Kulaynī, *Kāfī*, 5:203: إنّ عامّة تجارنا اليوم يعطون العينة). The term is also used, though not intended in this report, in the sense of a sham buy-back sale to circumvent the legal prohibition on receiving interest on a loan (see, for instance, ʿAbd al-Razzāq, *Muṣannaf*, 8:184; Ibn Abī Shayba, *Muṣannaf*, 6:526–27; Kulaynī, 5:202–5; see also *al-Mawsūʿah al-fiqhiyya* [Kuwait], 9:95–97).

281 Ṭūsī, *Tahdhīb*, 7:51.

282 Kulaynī, *Kāfī*, 5:201.

استقصيت له السعر يومئذ فلا بأس بذلك. فقلت: إنّي لم أوازنه ولم أناقده. إنّما كان كلام بيني وبينه. فقال: أليس الدراهم من عندك والدنانير من عندك؟ قلت: بلى! قال: فلا بأس بذلك.[283]

[Isḥāq b. ʿAmmār:] I said to Abū ʿAbd Allāh, "A man had deposited some authentic dirhams with me. He then met me and asked, 'What is the price of authentic [dirhams] today?' I said to him, 'Such-and-such.' He then instructed me, 'Exchange them for dinars at this price, and write it down in your books for me.' What is your position on this?" He said to me, "If you covered all the details of the price for him on that day, there is nothing wrong with that." I said, "I did not weigh or convert [the dirhams into dinars, physically] for him. It was merely a conversation between the two of us." He answered, "Are not the dirhams and the dinars coming from you?" I said, "Yes!" He said, "Then there is nothing wrong with that."

الحلبي قال: قلت لأبي عبد الله: أتقبّل الأرض بالثلث أو الربع فأقبّلها بالنصف؟ قال: لا بأس به. قلت: فأتقبّلها بألف درهم فأقبّلها بألفين؟ قال: لا يجوز. قلت: كيف جاز الأوّل ولم يجز الثاني؟ قال: لأنّ هذا مضمون وذلك غير مضمون.[284]

[ʿUbayd Allāh al-Ḥalabī:] I said to Abū ʿAbd Allāh, "I have a contract for tax farming[285] [with the government] on a piece of land in exchange for the payment of a third or a fourth [of its produce]; can I subcontract it to someone else in exchange for the payment of half [of its produce]?" He said, "There is nothing wrong with that." I said, "[Suppose] I contract it for one thousand dirhams; can I subcontract it [to someone else] for two thousand?" He said, "That is not permissible." I said, "How is the first permissible but not the second?" He said, "Because [the amount] is fixed and guaranteed in this [latter] case, but not in that [former] case."[286]

283 Kulaynī, *Kāfī*, 5:245.

284 Kulaynī, *Kāfī*, 5:272.

285 The concept discussed in the report was known as *qibāla*, which in the usage of early Muslim administration could mean either a tax-farming contract, as here (see Kulaynī, *Kāfī*, 5:269–70), or an arrangement similar to a rental in which a person uses a piece of land belonging to a private owner or the government in exchange for the payment of a share of its crop on an annual basis (see Kulaynī, 5:248, and further, Modarressi, *Kharāj in Islamic Law*, 6).

286 The point at issue is the risk involved. In the first case, in which the tenure of the land is transferred against a share of the crop, the new tenant has no obligation if there is no crop because of natural causes. In the second case, however, he is subject to the payment obligation even if the crop is damaged by, for instance, a natural calamity, as the payment obligation does not depend on the crop, as further explained in another report from Jaʿfar in Kulaynī, *Kāfī*, 5:273 (cf. 5:264).

الحسن بن صالح قال: سألت جعفر بن محمّد عن رجل طلّق امرأته وهو غائب في بلدة أخرى وأشهد على طلاقها رجلين، ثمّ إنّه راجعها قبل انقضاء العدّة ولم يشهد على الرجعة، ثمّ إنّه قدم عليها بعد انقضاء العدّة وقد تزوّجت رجلاً فأرسل إليها أنّي قد كنت راجعتك. قال: لا سبيل له عليها، لأنّه قد أقرّ بالطلاق وادّعى الرجعة بغير بيّنة فلا سبيل له عليها.[287]

[Al-Ḥasan b. Ṣāliḥ:] I asked Jaʿfar b. Muḥammad about a man who divorced his wife while he was away in another town, and two men bore witness to his divorce. He then revoked [the divorce] before the conclusion of the waiting period, but he did not have witnesses attest to that. He then went to her after the conclusion of the waiting period and [found that] she had married another man, so he sent a message to her that he had revoked the divorce. He said, "He has no access to her, because he acknowledged the divorce and [then] claimed to have revoked it without proof, so now he has no access to her."

مسعدة بن صدقة قال: سمعت جعفر بن محمّد وسُئل: ما بال الزاني لا تسمّيه كافرًا وتارك الصلاة قد تسمّيه كافرًا؟ وما الحجّة في ذلك؟ فقال: لأنّ الزاني وما أشبهه إنّما يفعل ذلك لمكان الشهوة فإنّها تغلبه، وتارك الصلاة لا يتركها إلّا استخفافًا بها. وإذا وقع الاستخفاف وقع الكفر.[288]

[Masʿada b. Ṣadaqa:] I heard Jaʿfar b. Muḥammad being asked, "Why do you not call the fornicator a disbeliever, when you call someone who abandons prayer a disbeliever? What is the argument for that?" He said, "Because the fornicator, or a person like him, acts out of lust that overtakes him. The one who abandons prayer does so only because he belittles it, and when belittling occurs, so does disbelief."

حكم بن حكيم الصيرفي قال: قلت لأبي عبد الله: ما تقول في الكلب يصيد الصيد فيقتله [ويأكل منه]؟ قال: لا بأس بأكله. قلت: فإنّهم يقولون إنّه إذا قتله وأكل منه فإنّما أمسك على نفسه فلا تأكله؟ فقال: كُل! أوَ ليس قد جامعوكم على أنّ قتله ذكاته؟ قلت: بلى! قال: فما يقولون في شاة ذبحها رجل، أذكّاها؟ قلت: نعم! قال: فان السَبُع جاء بعد ما ذكّاها فأكل منها بعضها، أيؤكل البقيّة؟ قلت : نعم! قال: فإذا

287 Kulaynī, *Kāfī*, 6:80.
288 Ḥimyarī, *Qurb al-isnād*, 47.

أجابوك إلى هذا فقُل لهم: كيف تقولون: إذا ذكّى ذلك وأكل منه لم تأكلوا، وإذا ذكّاها هذا وأكل أكلتم؟[289]

[Ḥakam b. Ḥakīm al-Ṣayrafī:] I said to Abū ʿAbd Allāh, "What is your opinion regarding [the legality of eating game caught by] a dog that hunts game and kills it but then eats from it?" He said, "There is nothing wrong with eating it." I said, "These people [that is, the jurists among the Sunnī majority] say that if it kills it and eats from it then it has reserved it for itself, so you should not eat it." He said, "Eat! Do they not agree with you that if [the dog] kills the game, it [the game] has been legally slaughtered?" I said, "Yes!" He said, "What do they say about a man who butchers a sheep; has he slaughtered it ritually?" I said, "Yes!" He said, "If a predator comes after it was slaughtered and eats some of it, can the rest be eaten?" I said, "Yes." He said, "If they give you this answer, say to them, 'How can you say that if [the dog] slaughters and [then] eats from it you should not eat it, but if [the man] slaughters it and [the predator] eats from it you can eat it?'"

إسحاق بن عمّار قال: قلت لأبي عبد الله: رجلٌ طاف بالكعبة ثمّ خرج فطاف بين الصفا والمروة، فبينما هو يطوف إذ ذكر أنّه قد ترك من طوافه بالبيت؟ قال: يرجع إلى البيت فيتمّ طوافه ثمّ يرجع إلى الصفا والمروة فيتمّ ما بقى. قلت: فإنّه بدأ بالصفا والمروة قبل أن يبدأ بالبيت؟ فقال: يأتي البيت فيطوف به، ثمّ يستأنف طوافه بين الصفا والمروة. قلت: فما الفرق بين هذين؟ قال: لأنّ هذا قد دخل في شيء من الطواف وهذا لم يدخل في شيء منه.[290]

[Isḥāq b. ʿAmmār:] I said to Abū ʿAbd Allāh, "A man circumambulates the Kaʿba and then goes to walk the distance between Ṣafā and Marwa. In the midst of this, he remembers that he did not finish his circumambulation of the House [of God, the Kaʿba]." He said, "He must return to the House and complete his circumambulation, and then go back to Ṣafā and Marwa and complete what is left." I said, "What if he began with Ṣafā and Marwa before the House?" He said, "He is then to go to the House and circumambulate it, then start his walk between Ṣafā and Marwa anew." I said, "What is the difference between the two?" He said, "It is that [in the first case] he did some of the circumambulation but in the other he did not."

289 Kulaynī, *Kāfī*, 6:204.
290 Kulaynī, *Kāfī*, 4:421.

رفاعة بن موسى قال: سألت أبا عبد الله عن المتمتّع لا يجد الهدي، فقال: يصوم قبل التروية بيوم ويوم التروية ويوم عرفة. قلت: فإنّه قدم يوم التروية [وهو لا ينبغي أن يصوم بمنى أيّام التشريق؟ قال: فإذا رجع إلى مكّة صام. قلت: فإن أعجله أصحابه وأبوا أن يقيموا بمكّة؟] قال: يصوم يوم الحصبة وبعده يومين. قلت: وما الحصبة؟ قال: يوم نَفرِه. قلت: يصوم وهو مسافر؟ قال: نعم! أليس هو يوم عرفة مسافرًا؟[291]

[Rifāʿa b. Mūsā:] I asked Abū ʿAbd Allāh about a pilgrim who is performing *ḥajj tamattuʿ* and cannot find an animal to sacrifice. He said, "He should fast the day before the Day of Tarwiya [the Day of Quenching the Thirst, the eighth day of Dhū al-Ḥijja, when the pilgrims leave Mecca for ʿArafāt], the Day of Tarwiya, and the Day of ʿArafa [the ninth day of Dhū al-Ḥijja]." I said, "What if he arrived on the Day of Tarwiya and he is not supposed to fast in Minā during the days of *tashrīq* [the eleventh through thirteenth days of Dhū al-Ḥijja]?" He said, "Then he is to fast when he returns to Mecca." I said, "What if his companions rush him and refuse to stay in Mecca?" He said, "He is then to fast the Day of Ḥaṣba [the end of the pilgrimage when the pilgrims leave Minā] and two days after it." I said, "What is the Day of Ḥaṣba?" He said, "The day of his departure." I said, "He is to fast while traveling?" He said, "Yes! Is he not a traveler on the Day of ʿArafa?"

منصور بن حازم قال: سألت أبا عبد الله عن المضطرّ إلى الميتة وهو يجد الصيد، فقال: الصيد! قلت: إنّ الله قد أحلّ الميتة إذا اضطّر إليها ولم يحلّ له الصيد؟ قال: تأكل من مالِك أحبّ إليك أو ميتة؟ قلت: من مالى! قال: هو من مالِك، لأنّ عليك الفدية من مالك.[292]

[Manṣūr b. Ḥāzim:] I asked Abū ʿAbd Allāh about someone [in the state of pilgrim sanctity] who is desperate to the point that he can legally eat carrion, but he can also find game. [Which one should he eat?] He said, "He should eat the game." I said, "God permitted him the carrion if he is in need, but He did not permit game for him." He said, "Would you prefer to eat from your wealth or carrion?" I said, "From my wealth." He said, "It [the game] is from your wealth because you are required to pay compensation for it [as expiation]."

291 Kulaynī, *Kāfī*, 4:506–7. The sentence between the brackets is from Ṭūsī, *Tahdhīb*, 4:231, a variant of the same report quoted by a different transmitter.

292 Barqī, *Maḥāsin*, 317, with a variant in Kulaynī, *Kāfī*, 4:383, and Ṭūsī, *Tahdhīb*, 5:368.

إسحاق بن عمّار قال: سألته عن الرجل يموت فيوصي بحَجّة فيُعطَي رجلٌ دراهمَ يحجّ بها عنه فيموت قبل أن يحجّ ثمّ أُعطِي الدراهمُ غيره، فقال: إن مات في الطريق أو بمكّة قبلَ أن يقضيَ مناسكَه فإنّه يُجزى عن الأوّل. قلت: فإن ابتلى بشيءٍ يُفسِد عليه حجّه حتّى يصير عليه الحجّ من قابل، أيُجزى عن الأوّل؟ قال: نعم! قلت: لأنّ الأجير ضامن للحجّ؟ قال: نعم![293]

[Isḥāq b. ʿAmmār:] I asked him about a man who dies and entrusts the performance of a *ḥajj* [on his behalf to an agent], and a man is accordingly given money to perform the *ḥajj* on his behalf but dies before doing so, after which the money is given to someone else. He said, "If he dies during the journey or in Mecca before performing the *ḥajj* rites, the obligation of the first man has been satisfied." I said, "What if he is afflicted with something that invalidates his *ḥajj* such that he would have to perform *ḥajj* anew the following year; would that suffice for the first [man]?" He said, "Yes!" I said, "Because the hired agent is a guarantor for the *ḥajj*?" He said, "Yes!"[294]

داود بن الحُصَين عن أبي عبد الله قال: سألته عن شهادة النساء في النكاح بلا رجل معهنّ إذا كانت المرأة منكرة. قال: لا بأس به. ثمّ قال لي: ما يقول في ذلك فقهاؤكم؟ قلت: يقولون: لا يجوز إلّا شهادة رجلين عدلين. فقال: إنّ الله أمر في الطلاق بشهادة رجلين عدلين فأجازوا الطلاق بلا شاهد واحد، والنكاح لم يجيء عن الله فيه عزيمة فسنّ رسول الله – صلّى الله عليه وآله وسلّم – في ذلك الشاهدين تأديبًا ونظرًا لئلّا يُنكَر الولد والميراث، وقد ثبت عقدة النكاح واستحلّ الفرج بلا أن يُشهد. وكان أمير المؤمنين – عليه السلام – يجيز شهادة أمرأتين في النكاح عند الإنكار ولا يجيز في الطلاق إلّا شاهدين عدلين. قلت: فإنّى ذكر الله تعالى وقوله: ﴿رَجُلٌ وَامْرَأَتَانِ﴾؟ قال: ذلك في الدَيْن، إذا لم يكن رجلان فرجل وامرأتان، أو رجل واحد ويمين المدّعي إذا لم تكن امرأتان. قضى بذلك رسول الله – صلّى الله عليه وآله وسلّم – وأمير المؤمنين – عليه السلام – بعده عندكم.[295]

[Dāwūd b. al-Ḥuṣayn:] I asked Abū ʿAbd Allāh about the [admissibility of] women's testimony in the absence of men, with respect to

293 Kulaynī, *Kāfī*, 4:306.

294 This is a case of "transfer of obligation," as elaborated in works of Islamic law in the chapter on sureties.

295 Ṭūsī, *Tahdhīb*, 6:281–82.

> marriage if the woman denies [marriage]. He said, "There is nothing wrong with it." Then he asked me, "What do the jurists [among the Sunnī majority] in your region say about this?" I said, "They [the Sunnī jurists] say that only the testimony of two righteous men is permitted." He said, "Regarding divorce, God ordered that two righteous men bear witness[296] and they [the jurists] permit divorce without a single witness. But for marriage, God did not impose any such obligation, so the Messenger of God (may God's prayer and peace be upon him and his Family) ordered [the presence of] two witnesses as a matter of discipline and in consideration for the child and for inheritance so that neither can be disavowed. But [in principle] the marriage contract is established and intercourse becomes lawful without witnesses. The Commander of the Faithful [ʿAlī] would allow the testimony of two women for marriage in the case of a denial, but for divorce, two righteous [male] witnesses are required." I said, "Did God not mention 'a man and two women'?"[297] He said, "That is with respect to loans; if there are not two men, then a man and two women. If there are not two women, then one man and an oath by the claimant. The Messenger of God (may God's prayer and peace be upon him and his Family) judged accordingly, and so did the Commander of the Faithful [ʿAlī] after the Prophet [when he was] among you [in Iraq]."[298]

VI. Legal Presumptions

Many of Jaʿfar al-Ṣādiq's decisions were based on the application of general rules to specific cases. As is well known to students of Islamic law, many of these rules are general to all or several chapters of the law, while others are specific to particular chapters. The first category is known as *qawāʿid* (legal canons) and the second as *ḍawābiṭ* (legal criteria). Jaʿfar al-Ṣādiq's legal legacy contains many references to both categories and elucidates their application in various cases. The following examples illustrate his use of these rules.

---

296 Qurʾān 65:2.

297 Qurʾān 2:282.

298 As noted earlier, the last sentence, on the Prophet's and ʿAlī's practice of issuing judgments on the basis of the testimony of a single witness combined with an oath by the claimant, is also quoted on the authority of Jaʿfar al-Ṣādiq in numerous Sunnī *ḥadīth* collections.

A. Presumption of Lawfulness

كلّ شيء مطلق حتّى يرد فيه نهي.[299]

Everything is unrestricted unless some [legal impediment] arises to prohibit it.

كلّ شيء فيه حلال وحرام فهو لك حلال حتّى تعرف الحرام منه بعينه فتدعه.[300]

Anything that contains both lawful and unlawful varieties is lawful for you until you know the exact variety of it that is unlawful, which you should then avoid.

كلّ شيء لك حلال حتّى تعلم أنّه حرام بعينه فتدعه. والأشياء كلّها على هذا حتّى يستبين لك غير ذلك أو تقوم به البيّنة.[301]

Everything is lawful for you until you know what is specifically unlawful, so you avoid it. Everything is on this basis until it becomes clear to you that it is otherwise, or evidence is established to that effect.

كلّ شيء لك حلال حتّى يجيئك شاهدان يشهدان عندك أنّ فيه ميتة.[302]

Everything is lawful to you [to eat] until two witnesses testify to you that it contains carrion.[303]

زرارة قال: سألت أبا عبد الله[304] عن الجرّيث فقال: وما الجرّيث؟ فنعتّه له. فقال: ﴿قُلْ لَا أَجِدُ فِي مَا أُوحِيَ إِلَيَّ مُحَرَّمًا عَلَىٰ طَاعِمٍ يَطْعَمُهُ﴾ – إلى آخر الآية. ثمّ قال: لم يحرّم الله شيئًا من الحيوان في القرآن إلّا الخنزير بعينه.[305]

[Zurāra:] I asked Abū ʿAbd Allāh about [a fish called] *jirrīth*. He asked, "What is *jirrīth*?" I described it to him. He recited, "Say 'I do not find in that which is revealed to me anything forbidden to one who [wants

299 Ibn Bābawayh, *Faqīh*, 1:208.

300 Ḥasan b. Maḥbūb, *Mashyakha*, 153 (see also 147); Kulaynī, *Kāfī*, 5:313–14.

301 Kulaynī, *Kāfī*, 5:313.

302 Kulaynī, *Kāfī*, 6:339.

303 He said this in answer to someone who asked him about the rennet used to make cheese, commonly believed at the time to come occasionally from the stomach of an animal not ritually slaughtered. See Cook, "Magian Cheese."

304 As in the manuscript of Ṭūsī, *Tahdhīb*, used by Ḥurr al-ʿĀmilī in his *Wasāʾil al-Shīʿa*, 24:135. The edition of Ṭūsī used in the present work has the name as Abū Jaʿfar, that is, Muḥammad al-Bāqir.

305 Ṭūsī, *Tahdhīb*, 9:5.

to] eat thereof'—to the end of the passage."[306] Then he said, "God did not make any animals unlawful by their nature in the Qur'ān except for swine."[307]

B. Presumption of Cleanliness

كلّ ماء طاهر إلّا ما عُلم أنّه قذر.[308]

All water is [ritually] pure except for what is known to be ritually impure.

كلّ شيء نظيف حتّى تعلم أنّه قذر.[309]

Everything is [ritually] clean until you know it to be ritually unclean.

C. Presumption of Righteousness

كلّ من كان على فطرة الإسلام جازت شهادته.[310]

The testimony of anyone who follows the original disposition of Islam is permitted.

D. Presumption of Continuity

عبد الله بن سنان قال: سأل أبي أبا عبد الله وأنا حاضر: إنّي أُعير الذمّي ثوبي وأنا أعلم أنّه يشرب الخمر ويأكل لحم الخنزير، فيردّه عليّ. أفأغسله قبل أن أصلّي فيه؟ فقال أبو

306 Qur'ān 6:145.

307 He gave the same response to a number of similar questions, as in the following example ('Ayyāshī, *Tafsīr*, 2:125):

> حريز عن أبي عبد الله قال: سُئل عن سباع الطير والوحش. فقال: ليس الحرام إلّا ما حرّم الله في كتابه. اقرأ هذه الآية: ﴿قُلْ لَا أَجِدُ فِي مَا أُوحِيَ إِلَيَّ مُحَرَّمًا عَلَىٰ طَاعِمٍ يَطْعَمُهُ﴾ – إلى آخر الآية.
>
> [Ḥarīz:] Abū 'Abd Allāh was asked about birds and beasts of prey. He said, "Nothing is unlawful except what God made unlawful in His Book. Read this verse: 'Say: I do not find in that which is revealed to me anything forbidden to one who [wants to] eat thereof'—to the end of the passage."

308 Kulaynī, *Kāfī*, 1:1.

309 Ṭūsī, *Tahdhīb*, 1:285.

310 Ibn Bābawayh, *Amālī*, 163. See further Ibn Bābawayh, *Faqīh*, 3:28 (also Ṭūsī, *Tahdhīb*, 6:283):

> عن أبي الحسن الرضا في رجل طلّق امرأته وأشهد شاهدين ناصبيّين، قال: كلّ من وُلد على الفطرة وعُرف بالصلاح في نفسه جازت شهادته.
>
> Regarding a man who divorced his wife in the presence of two anti-'Alī witnesses, Abū al-Ḥasan ['Alī] al-Riḍā [the eighth Imam of Imāmī Shī'ism] said, "Whoever was born in the original disposition [of Islam] and is known to be a good person, their testimony is accepted."

عبد الله: صلّ فيه ولا تغسله من أجل ذلك، فإنّك أعرته إيّاه وهو طاهر ولم تستيقن أنّه نجّسه، فلا بأس أن تصلّي فيه حتّى تستيقن أنّه نجّسه.[311]

['Abd Allāh b. Sinān:] My father asked Abū 'Abd Allāh while I was present, "I lent a *dhimmī* my garment, knowing that he drinks wine and eats swine. He then returned it to me. Should I wash it before praying in it?" Abū 'Abd Allāh said, "Pray in it and do not wash it for that reason. You loaned it to him when it was pure, and you are not certain that he made it impure. There is nothing wrong with praying in it until you are certain that he made it impure."

زرارة قال: قلت له: الرجل ينام وهو على وضوء. أتوجب الخفقة والخفقتان عليه الوضوء؟ قال: لا! حتّى يستيقنَ أنّه قد نام حتّى يجيء من ذلك أمرٌ بيّن، وإلّا فإنّه [كان] على يقين من وضوئه، ولا ينقض اليقين أبدًا بالشك ولكنّه ينقضه بيقين آخر.[312]

[Zurāra:] I said to him, "A man sleeps while in the state of [having performed] ritual ablution. Does dozing off once or twice require him to redo his ablution?" He said, "No! Until he is certain that he slept and the matter is proven beyond doubt. Otherwise, he was certain that he was in the state of [having performed] ritual ablution; and certainty is not negated by doubt, but only by another certainty."

زرارة قال: قلت له: أصاب ثوبي دم رعاف أو غيره. وحضرت الصلاة ونسيت أنّ بثوبي شيئًا وصلّيت، ثمّ إنّي ذكرت بعد ذلك. قال: تغسله وتعيد الصلاة. قلت: فإن ظننت أنّه قد أصابه ولم أتيقّن ذلك فنظرت فلم أر شيئًا، ثمّ صلّيت فرأيت فيه. قال: تغسله ولا تعيد الصلاة. قلت: لِمَ ذلك؟ قال: لأنّك كنت على يقين من طهارتك ثمّ شككت، فليس ينبغي لك أن تنقض اليقين بالشكّ أبدًا.[313]

[Zurāra:] I said to him, "My garment got blood on it from a nosebleed or something else. I attended the prayer but had forgotten that there was something on my garment, so I prayed but remembered it afterward." He said, "Wash it and repeat the prayer." I said, "What if I thought that it got blood on it but I was not certain of it; I looked and saw nothing, then prayed, and then saw it?" He said, "Wash it but do not repeat the prayer." I said, "Why is that?" He said, "Because you had certainty that

311 Ṭūsī, *Tahdhīb*, 2:361.
312 Ṭūsī, *Tahdhīb*, 1:8.
313 Ṭūsī, *Tahdhīb*, 1:421–22.

it was ritually clean, and then you had doubt. You should never negate your certainty with doubt."

E. Presumption of No Hardship

الفضيل بن يسار عن أبي عبد الله في الرجل الجنب يغتسل فينضح من الماء في الإناء؟ فقال: لا بأس. ﴿مَا جَعَلَ عَلَيْكُمْ فِي الدِّينِ مِنْ حَرَجٍ﴾.[314]

[Al-Fuḍayl b. Yasār:] Regarding a man in a state of major ritual impurity who performs a full-body ablution [bath] but some drops of the water that he has used fall into the water container, Abū ʿAbd Allāh said, "There is no problem. 'He imposed no difficulty upon you in religion [Qurʾān 22:78].'"

محمّد بن الميسّر قال: سألت أبا عبد الله عن الرجل الجنب ينتهي إلى ماء قليل في الطريق ويريد أن يغتسل منه وليس معه إناء يغرف به ويداه قذرتان؟ قال: يضع يده ويتوضأ ثمّ يغتسل.[315] هذا ممّا قال الله تعالى: ﴿مَا جَعَلَ عَلَيْكُمْ فِي الدِّينِ مِنْ حَرَجٍ﴾.[316]

[Muḥammad b. al-Muyassar:] I asked Abū ʿAbd Allāh about a man in a state of major ritual impurity who finds a small amount of water on the road and wishes to make a full-body ablution with it, but does not have a container to draw out the water and his hands are dirty. He said, "He should put in his hand to wash it and then bathe. This is referred to in the statement of God, the Exalted, 'He imposed no difficulty upon you in religion [Qurʾān 22:78].'"

F. Presumption of No Harm

عقبة بن خالد عن أبي عبد الله قال: قضى رسول الله – صلّى الله عليه وآله وسلّم – بالشفعة بين الشركاء في الأرضين والمساكن، وقال: «لا ضرر ولا ضرار».[317]

---

314 Kulaynī, *Kāfī*, 3:14.

315 فإن الدين ليس بمضيّق: "because religion is not rigid" (Ṭūsī, *Tahdhīb*, 1:417).

316 Kulaynī, *Kāfī*, 3:4, 305. A number of other reports on this and similar topics with the same Qurʾānic argument are quoted in Kulaynī, 3:4, 14, 5:339 and Ṭūsī, *Tahdhīb*, 1:37.

317 Kulaynī, *Kāfī*, 5:280, with another part of the report at 5:294:

> وقضى بين أهل المدينة في مشارب النخل أنّه لا يمنع نَقع الشيء وبين أهل البادية أنّه لا يمنع فضل ماء ليمنع به فضل كلاء.
>
> He [the Prophet] judged between the people of Medina on irrigation of the palm groves: any unneeded [water] should be left available [to others]; and [he judged] between the people of the desert that the extra water should not be blocked [from others] with the intention of denying [others] access to the grass [around it].

[ʿUqba b. Khālid:] Abū ʿAbd Allāh said, "The Messenger of God (may God's prayer and peace be upon him and his Family) ruled that partners in real property and homes have the right to preemption [and ruled between the people of Medina regarding the water canals for irrigating date palms], and he said, 'Do not cause harm or reciprocate harm.'"

عن أبي عبد الله أنّه سُئل عن جدارٍ لرجل – وهو سترة بينه وبين جاره – سقط فامتنع عن بنائه، قال: ليس يُجبر على ذلك إلّا أن يكون وجب ذلك لصاحب الدار الأخرى بحقّ أو بشرط في أصل المِلك. قيل له: فإن كان الجدار لم يسقط ولكنّه هدمه أو أراد هدمه أضرارًا بجاره لغير حاجة منه إلى هدمه. قال: لا يُترك، وذلك أنّ رسول الله – صلّى الله عليه وآله وسلّم – قال: لا ضرر ولا ضرار. فإن هَدَمه كُلّف أن يَبنيه.[318]

Abū ʿAbd Allāh was asked about a wall that belonged to a man and that served as a barrier between him and his neighbor. The wall collapsed and the man did not restore it. He said, "He is not obligated to do so, unless that is an obligation owed to the owner of the other house by virtue of a right or condition related to the basis of his ownership." It was said to him, "What if the wall did not collapse but he tore it down, or intended to tear it down to harm his neighbor, without actually needing to tear it down?" He said, "He is not allowed to do that. This is because the Messenger of God (may God's prayer and peace be upon him and his Family) said, 'Do not cause harm or reciprocate harm.' If he tears it down, he becomes responsible for restoring it."

أبو الصباح الكناني عن أبي عبد الله قال: كلّ من أضرّ بشيء من طريق المسلمين فهو له ضامن.[319]

[Abū al-Ṣabāḥ al-Kinānī:] Abū ʿAbd Allāh said, "One is liable for any damage that one causes on a road that Muslims use."

الحلبي عن أبي عبد الله قال: كلّ شيء يضرّ بطريق المسلمين فصاحبه ضامن لما يصيبه.[320]

[ʿUbayd Allāh al-Ḥalabī:] Abū ʿAbd Allāh said, "Whoever damages a road used by Muslims is liable for repairing it."

318 Qāḍī Nuʿmān, *Daʿāʾim al-Islām*, 2:502.
319 Kulaynī, *Kāfī*, 7:350.
320 Kulaynī, *Kāfī*, 7:349.

G. Effect of Ignorance

حريز عن أبي عبد الله قال: قال رسول الله – صلّى الله عليه وآله وسلّم: رُفع عن أمّتي تسعة: الخطأ، والنسيان، وما لا يعلمون، وما لا يطيقون، وما اضطرّوا إليه، وما أستُكرَهوا عليه، والطيرة، والوسوسة في التفكّر في الخلق، والحسد ما لم يظهر بلسان أو يد.[321]

[Ḥarīz:] Abū ʿAbd Allāh said, "The Messenger of God (may God's prayer and peace be upon him and his Family) said, 'My community has been relieved of [the effects of] nine elements: error, forgetfulness, ignorance, unbearable burdens, necessity, duress, evil omens, doubts caused by speculation about creation, and envy that is not manifested on one's tongue or hand.'"

إسماعيل الجعفي عن أبي عبد الله قال: سمعته يقول: وُضع عن هذه الأمّة. الخطأ، والنسيان، وما استكرهوا عليه، وما لا يعلمون، وما لا يطيقون، وما اضطرّوا إليه.[322]

[Ismāʿīl al-Juʿfī:] I heard Abū ʿAbd Allāh say, "This community has been relieved of [the effects of] error, forgetfulness, duress, ignorance, unbearable burdens, and necessity."

زكريّا بن يحيى عن أبي عبد الله قال: ما حجب الله علمه عن العباد فهو موضوع عنهم.[323]

[Zakariyyā b. Yaḥyā:] Abū ʿAbd Allāh said, "People are not liable for anything of which God has concealed knowledge from His servants."

عبد الرحمن بن الحجّاج عن أبي عبد الله قال: سألته عن الرجل يتزوّج المرأة في عدّتها بجهالة، أهي ممّن لا تحلّ له أبدًا؟ قال: لا! إذا كان بجهالة فليتزوّجها بعد ما تنقضي عدّتها، وقد يُعذر الناس في الجهالة بما هو أعظم من ذلك. قلت: بأيّ الجهالتين يُعذر: بجهالته أن يعلم أنّ ذلك محرّمٌ عليه أم بجهالته أنّها في عدّة؟ قال: إحدى الجهالتين أهون من الأخرى، الجهالة بأنّ الله حرّم ذلك عليه، وذلك لأنّه لا يقدر على الاحتياط معها. قلت: فهو في الأخرى معذور؟ قال: نعم! إذا انقضت عدّتها فهو معذورٌ في أن يتزوّجها. قلت: فإن كان أحدهما متعمّدًا والآخر بجهالة؟ قال: الّذي تعمّد لا يحلّ له أن يرجع إلى صاحبه أبدًا.[324]

---

321 Ibn Bābawayh, *Khiṣāl*, 417, with a variant in Kulaynī, *Kāfī*, 2:463.

322 Aḥmad b. Muḥammad b. ʿĪsā, *Nawādir*, 74.

323 Kulaynī, *Kāfī*, 1:164; Ibn Bābawayh, *Tawḥīd*, 413.

324 Ṭūsī, *Tahdhīb*, 7:306–7, also quoted in Aḥmad b. Muḥammad b. ʿĪsā, *Nawādir*, 110 and Kulaynī, *Kāfī*, 5:427, but as a conversation between ʿAbd al-Raḥmān b. al-Ḥajjāj and Mūsā al-Kāẓim.

[ʿAbd al-Raḥmān b. al-Ḥajjāj:] I asked Abū ʿAbd Allāh about a man who unknowingly marries a woman during her waiting period: "Does she become permanently unlawful to him?" He said, "No! If he did so unknowingly, he can marry her after her waiting period comes to an end. People are excused for their ignorance even in more important matters." I said, "Which of the two types of ignorance is he excused for? Ignorance of the law, that such a marriage is unlawful, or ignorance of the fact that she is in her waiting period?" He said, "One of the [two] types of ignorance has less effect than the other, [namely] ignorance of the law, that God forbade that for him, and that is because this ignorance precludes him from being able to exercise caution." I said, "Is he excused for the latter [that is, ignorance of the fact that she is in her waiting period]?" He said, "Yes! Once her waiting period concludes, he is excused such that he is then able to marry her." I said, "What if one of them acted deliberately [despite their knowledge] and the other out of ignorance?" He said, "The one who acted deliberately cannot ever return to the other."

الحلبي عن أبي عبد الله قال: قلت له: رجل صام في السفر؟ قال: إن كان بلغه أنّ رسول الله – صلّى الله عليه وآله وسلّم – نهى عن ذلك فعليه القضاء، وإن لم يكن بلغه فلا شيء عليه.[325]

[ʿUbayd Allāh al-Ḥalabī:] I said to Abū ʿAbd Allāh, "May a man fast while traveling?" He said, "If he was informed that the Messenger of God (may God's prayer and peace be upon him and his Family) forbade it, he must repeat [the fast done while traveling]. If he was not informed of that, he does not have to do anything."

زرارة قال: سألته عن محرم غشي امرأته وهي مُحرِمة؟ قال: جاهلين أو عالمين؟ قلت: أجِبني في الوجهين جميعًا. قال: إن كانا جاهلَين استغفرا ربّهما ومضيا على حجّهما وليس عليهما شيء، وإن كانا عالمَين فُرّق بينهما من المكان الّذي أحدثا فيه وعليهما بَدَنة [وعليهما] الحجّ من قابل، فإذا بلغا المكان الّذي أحدثا فيه فُرّق بينهما حتّى يقضيا نسكهما ويرجعا إلى المكان الذي أصابا فيه ما أصابا. قلت: فأيُّ الحَجّتين لهما؟ قال: الأولى الّتي أحدثا فيها ما أحدثا، والأخرى عليهما عقوبة.[326]

---

325 Kulaynī, *Kāfī*, 4:128, with two other reports on the same topic. See also Ṭūsī, *Tahdhīb*, 5:486 (also Kulaynī, 4:378; Ṭūsī, 5:322), for a similar case.

326 Kulaynī, *Kāfī*, 4:373 (also Ṭūsī, *Tahdhīb*, 5:317).

[Zurāra:] I asked him about a man in a state of pilgrim sanctity who had engaged his wife who was [also] in a state of pilgrim sanctity. He asked, "Were they ignorant or knowing?" I said, "Give me the answer for both [scenarios]." He said, "If they were ignorant, they should repent to their Lord and continue the *ḥajj*, and they owe nothing. If they were knowing, they have to separate from one another at the point at which the incident occurred and each has to offer a sacrifice [in expiation]. They also have to perform the *ḥajj* again in the future. [Upon doing so], when they reach the place where the incident occurred, they should separate until they have performed the rites and then return to the place where they did what they did." I said, "Which of the two *ḥajj* pilgrimages count for them?" He said, "The first, during which they did what they did; and the second is a punishment for them."

معاوية بن عمّار عن أبي عبد الله قال: سألته عن رجل وقع على امرأته وهو مُحرم، قال: إن كان جاهلاً فليس عليه شيءٌ وإن لم يكن جاهلاً فعليه سوق بَدَنة وعليه الحجّ من قابل، فإذا انتهى إلى المكان الذي وقع بها فُرّق محملُهما فلم يجتمعا في خبأ واحد – ألّا أن يكون معهما غيرُهما – حتّى يبلغ الهديُ مَحِلّه.[327]

[Muʿāwiya b. ʿAmmār:] I asked Abū ʿAbd Allāh about a man who had engaged his wife while in a state of pilgrim sanctity. He said, "If he was ignorant, he does not owe anything. If he was not ignorant, he must offer a sacrifice and must perform the *ḥajj* anew in the future. [Upon doing so], when he [again] reaches the location where he engaged his wife, they are to separate from one another and are not to reunite in a location hidden from view unless there are other people with them until the sacrificial animal reaches the place [of sacrifice]."

عبد الصمد بن بشير قال: جاء رجل يُلبّى حتّى دخل المسجد وهو يُلبّي وعليه قميصه، فوثب إليه أناس. فقالوا: شقّ قميصك وأخرِجه من رجليك فانّ عليك بَدَنة وعليك الحجّ من قابل وحجّك فاسد. فطلع أبو عبد الله فقام على باب المسجد فكبّر واستقبل القبلة، فدنا الرجل من أبي عبد الله وهو ينتف شعرَه ويضرب وجهَه. فقال له أبو عبد الله: أسكن يا عبدَ الله. وكان الرجل أعجميًّا، فقال أبو عبد الله: ما تقول؟ قال: كنت رجلاً أعمل بيدي فاجتمعت لي نفقة فجئت أحجّ، لم أسأل أحدًا عن شيء، فأفتوني هؤلاء أن أشقّ قميصي وأنزعه من قبل رجليّ وأنّ حجّي فاسد وأنّ عليّ بدنة. فقال له:

327 Kulaynī, *Kāfī*, 4:373–74.

متى لبست قميصك؟ أبعد ما لبّيتَ أم قبل؟ قال: قبل أن ألبّي. قال: فأخرجه من رأسك، وإنّه ليس عليك بدنة، وليس عليك الحجّ من قابل. أيُّ رجل ركب أمرًا بجهالة فلا شيء عليه. طف بالبيت سبعًا وصلّ ركعتين عند مقام إبراهيم، واسعَ بين الصفا والمروة، وقصّر من شعرك. فإذا كان يوم التروية فاغتسل وأهلّ بالحجّ واصنع كما يصنع الناس.[328]

> [ʿAbd al-Ṣamad b. Bashīr:] A man came [during the *ḥajj*] uttering the *talbiya* and he entered the mosque uttering it and wearing his shirt. The people jumped at him and said, "Tear your shirt and remove it from under your legs; you must offer a sacrifice and repeat the *ḥajj* in the future, for your *ḥajj* is invalid." Then Abū ʿAbd Allāh appeared and went to the door of the mosque, said the *takbīr*, and faced toward the *qibla*. The man approached Abū ʿAbd Allāh, tearing out his hair and hitting his own face. Abū ʿAbd Allāh said to him, "Calm down, O servant of God!" The man was a non-Arab. Abū ʿAbd Allāh said, "What have you to say?" He said, "I was a man who worked with my hands. I managed to accumulate some money and came to perform the *ḥajj*. I did not ask anyone about anything; now these people told me that I should tear my shirt and remove it from under my legs, that my *ḥajj* is invalid, and that I owe a sacrificial animal." He said to him, "When did you put on your shirt? Before or after you recited the *talbiya*?" He said, "Before the *talbiya*." He said, "Then remove it from over your head. You do not owe a sacrificial animal, and you do not have to repeat the *ḥajj* anew. A man who does something out of ignorance does not owe anything. Circumambulate the House seven times and pray two *rakʿa*s at the station of Ibrāhīm. Perform the *saʿy* between Ṣafā and Marwa and cut your hair. When the Day of Tarwiya arrives, bathe and recite the *talbiya* for the *ḥajj* and do as the people do."

Ignorance of the law mentioned in these reports was certainly prevalent in early Islamic times, before people fully knew the laws of Islam, and it persisted among new converts.[329] But ignorance was not an excuse if the law was of a type that every Muslim was supposed to know or if the person was aware that he or she might have a legal duty in the matter at hand. This principle also applied when the matter was one of strict liability by its nature. Consider the following examples:

328 Ṭūsī, *Tahdhīb*, 5:72–73.
329 Kulaynī, *Kāfī*, 7:248–49; Ibn Bābawayh, *Faqīh*, 4:39.

أبو عبيدة عن أبي عبد الله قال: سألته عن امرأة تزوّجت رجلاً و لها زوج. قال: عليها ما على الزاني المحصن. قلت: فإن كانت جاهلة بما صنعت؟ قال: ما من امرأة اليوم من نساء المسلمين إلّا وهي تعلم أنّ المرأة المسلمة لا يحلّ لها أن تتزوّج زوجين. ولو أنّ المرأة إذا فجرت قالت لم أدر أو جهلتُ أنّ الّذي فعلتُ حرام ولم يُقم عليها الحدّ، إذًا لتعطّلت الحدود.[330]

[Abū ʿUbayda:] I asked Abū ʿAbd Allāh about a woman who married a man while she already had a husband. He said, "She is liable for [the punishment of] a married fornicator." I said, "What if she was ignorant of what she did?" He said, "There is no Muslim woman today who does not know that it is unlawful for a Muslim woman to marry two men." He said, "If a woman commits a licentious deed and says, 'I did not know,' or 'I was ignorant that what I did was unlawful,' and the prescribed punishment is not applied to her, the prescribed punishments would cease to be applied [altogether]."

يزيد الكناسي قال: سألت أبا عبد الله عن امرأة تزوّجت في عدّتها. بجهالة؟ قال: ما من امرأة اليوم من نساء المسلمين إلّا وهي تعلم أنّ عليها عدّة في طلاق أو موت، ولقد كُنّ نساء الجاهليّة يعرفن ذلك. قلت: فإن كانت تعلم أنّ عليها عدّة ولم تدر كم هي؟ قال: إذا علمت أنّ عليها العدّة لزمتها الحجّة، فتسأل حتّى تعلم.[331]

[Yazīd al-Kunāsī:] I asked Abū ʿAbd Allāh about a woman who married, out of ignorance, during her waiting period. He said, "There is no Muslim woman today who does not know that she must observe a waiting period after divorce or [her husband's] death. Even the women of the Age of Arab Ignorance knew that." I said, "What if she knew she must observe a waiting period but she did not know how long it is?" He said, "If she knew that she must observe a waiting period, then she was subject to the rules [of strict liability]. She should have asked until she learned [the rule]."

مسعدة بن زياد عن جعفر عن آبائه عن النبي – صلّى الله عليه وآله وسلّم – أنّه قال: «لا تجامعوا في النكاح على الشبهة. فإنّ الوقوف عند الشبهة خير من الاقتحام في الهلكة».[332]

330 Kulaynī, *Kāfī*, 7:192.

331 Kulaynī, *Kāfī*, 7:192–93.

332 Ṭūsī, *Tahdhīb*, 7:474. See also Ḥusayn b. Saʿīd, *Zuhd*, 19; Barqī, *Maḥāsin*, 215; Kulaynī, *Kāfī*, 1:68. The last sentence (الوقوف عند الشبهة خير من الاقتحام في الهلكة) is attributed to Aktham b.

[Masʿada b. Ziyād:] Jaʿfar quoted from his forefathers, who quoted from the Prophet (may God's prayer and peace be upon him and his Family): "Do not have intercourse in a marriage that involves doubt, for abstention in a case of doubt is better than diving into ruin."

H. Effect of Excuse

موسى بن بكر قال: قلت لأبي عبد الله: الرجل يُغمى عليه اليوم واليومين والثلاثة والأربعة وأكثر من ذلك، كم يقضي من صلاته؟ فقال: ألا أخبرك بما يجمع لك هذا وأشباهه: كلّ ما غلب الله – عزّ وجلّ – عليه من أمر فالله أعذر لعبده.[333]

[Mūsā b. Bakr:] I said to Abū ʿAbd Allāh, "A man falls unconscious for one, two, three, four, or more days. How much of his prayer should he make up?" He said, "Shall I inform you of what will cover this and similar matters? Whatever God, the Mighty and Majestic, overwhelms His servant with, He is best placed to excuse the servant."

مرازم عن أبي عبد الله: قلت: أصلحك الله وجُعلت فداك! مرضت أربعة أشهر لم أُصلّ نافلة. فقال: ليس عليك قضاءٌ. إنّ المريض ليس كالصحيح. كلّ ما غلب الله عليه فالله أولى بالعذر منه.[334]

[Murāzim:] I said to Abū ʿAbd Allāh, "May God put you on the right path and may I be made your ransom! I fell ill for four months without praying any supererogatory prayers." He said, "You do not have to make anything up. The ill person is unlike the healthy person. Whatever God, the Mighty and Majestic, overwhelms [one] with, He is best placed to excuse it."

محمّد بن عذافر قال: قلت لأبي عبد الله: رجل يكون في وقت فريضة لا تمكّنه الأرض من القيام عليها ولا السجود عليها من كثرة الثلج والماء والمطر والوحل. أيجوز له أن يصلّي في المحمل؟ قال: نعم! هو بمنزلة السفينة، إن أمكنه قائمًا وإلّا قاعدًا. وكلّ ما كان من ذلك فالله أولى بالعذر.[335]

Ṣayfī al-Tamīmī (d. 9), the "Sage of the Arabs" (*Ḥakīm al-ʿArab*). See, for example, Thaʿālibī, *al-Tamthīl wa'l-muḥāḍara*, 36; see also Cook, "Early Medieval Christian and Muslim Attitudes."

333 Ibn Bābawayh, *Khiṣāl*, 644, with a variant in Ṭūsī, *Tahdhīb*, 3:302.

334 Kulaynī, *Kāfī*, 3:452 , with a variant in Ṭūsī, *Tahdhīb*, 3:303.

335 Ṭūsī, *Tahdhīb*, 3:232, also cited in part above.

[Muḥammad b. ʿUdhāfir:] I said to Abū ʿAbd Allāh, "At the requisite time for an obligatory prayer, a man finds that the ground does not permit him to stand or prostrate upon it because of an abundance of snow, water, rain, or mud. Is it permissible for him to pray in the carriage?" He said, "Yes! It is like being on a ship. [He should pray] standing, if he can, or else seated. With anything of this nature, God is best placed to excuse."

عبد الله بن سنان عن أبي عبد الله قال: كلّ ما غلب الله عليه فليس على صاحبه شيء.[336]

[ʿAbd Allāh b. Sinān:] Abū ʿAbd Allāh said, "Whatever God overwhelms [one] with, the individual is not liable for anything."

سليمان بن خالد قال: سألت أبا عبد الله عن رجل كان عليه صيام شهرين متتابعين فصام خمسة وعشرين يومًا ثمّ مرض، فإذا برئ أيبني على صومه أم يعيد صومه كلّه؟ فقال: بل يبني على ما كان صام. ثمّ قال: هذا ممّا غلب الله عليه وليس على ما غلب الله عليه شيء.[337]

[Sulaymān b. Khālid:] I asked Abū ʿAbd Allāh about a man who owed a fast of two consecutive months. He fasted twenty-five days and then fell ill. If he recovers, does he build on what he has already fasted or is he to repeat all his fasts together [anew]? He said, "He builds on what he has already fasted." Then he said, "This is something that God overwhelmed [him] with, and whatever [one] is overwhelmed with by God is not subject to any liability."

أبو بصير عن أبي عبد الله قال: إذا كنت في حال لا تقدر إلّا على الطين فتيمّم به، فإنّ الله أولى بالعذر.[338]

[Abū Baṣīr:] Abū ʿAbd Allāh said, "If you are in a situation in which all you have access to is dirt, perform dry ablution with it. God is best placed to excuse."

336 Ṭūsī, *Tahdhīb*, 4:245.
337 Ṭūsī, *Tahdhīb*, 4:284.
338 Kulaynī, *Kāfī*, 3:67.

محمّد بن مسلم عن أحدهما أنّه سئل عن الأضحية فقال: فإذا لم تجدوا من ذلك شيئاً فالله أولى بالعذر.[339]

[Muḥammad b. Muslim:] He was asked about sacrificial slaughter. He said, "If you do not find anything for it, God is best placed to pardon."

معاوية بن عمّار قال: سألت أبا عبد الله عن رجل حجّ ولم يستلم الحجر، فقال: هو من السنّة، فإن لم يقدر فالله أولى بالعذر.[340]

[Muʿāwiya b. ʿAmmār:] I asked Abū ʿAbd Allāh about a man who performed the *ḥajj* but did not touch the [Black] Stone. He said, "It [touching the Stone] is part of the Sunna, but if he is not able to, God is best placed to excuse."

I. Indications of Consent (or Lack Thereof)

معاوية بن وهب قال: جاء رجل إلى أبي عبد الله فقال: إنّي كنت مملوكاً لقوم، وإنّي تزوّجت امرأة حرّة بغير إذن موالي، ثمّ أعتقوني بعد ذلك. أفأجدّد نكاحي إيّاها حين أُعتِقتُ؟ فقال له: أكانوا علموا أنّك تزوّجتَ امرأةً وأنت مملوك لهم؟ قال: نعم! وسكتوا عنّي ولم يعيّروا عليّ. فقال: سكوتهم عنك بعد علمهم إقرارٌ منهم. إثبت على نكاحك الأوّل.[341]

[Muʿāwiya b. Wahb:] A man came to Abū ʿAbd Allāh and said, "I was slave to some people, and I married a free woman without the permission of my masters. They manumitted me thereafter. Should I renew my marriage to her now that I have been manumitted?" He said, "Did they know that you married a woman while you were their slave?" He said, "Yes! And they did not say anything to me or shame me." He said, "Their silence after their knowledge is an acknowledgment on their part. Stay with your original marriage."

علي بن رئاب عن أبي عبد الله قال: الشرط في الحيوان ثلاثة أيّام للمشتري، اشترط أم لم يشترط، فإن أحدث المشتري في ما اشترى حدثًا قبل الثلاثة الأيّام فذلك رضًا منه فلا شرط.[342]

339 Ṭūsī, *Tahdhīb*, 5:205 (see also Kulaynī, *Kāfī*, 4:494).

340 Kulaynī, *Kāfī*, 4:405 , and a variant in Ṭūsī, *Tahdhīb*, 5:104.

341 Kulaynī, *Kāfī*, 5:478.

342 Kulaynī, *Kāfī*, 5:169.

[ʿAlī b. Riʾāb:] Abū ʿAbd Allāh said, "The option [to cancel a sale] with respect to animals lasts three days for the buyer, whether or not it has been stipulated. If the buyer does something to that which he has purchased before the three days have elapsed, he has assented and no longer has the option."

أبو بصير عن أبي عبد الله قال: إذا كابر الرجل المرأة على نفسها ضُرب ضربة بالسيف.[343]

[Abū Baṣīr:] Abū ʿAbd Allāh said, "If a man forces a woman to copulate against her will, he will be struck with a sword."

زرارة عن أحدهما قال في رجل غصب امرأة نفسها: يُقتل،[344] محصناً كان أو غير محصن.[345]

[Zurāra:] Regarding a man who raped a woman by force, he said, "He is to be put to death, whether he was married or unmarried."[346]

J. Time-Bound Obligations

عمر بن يزيد، قلت لأبي عبد الله: الرجل يكون عنده المال، أيزكّيه إذا مضى نصف السنة؟ قال: لا! ولكن حتّى يحول عليه الحول ويحلّ عليه. إنّه ليس لأحد أن يصلّي صلاة إلّا لوقتها، وكذلك الزكاة، ولا يصوم أحد شهر رمضان إلّا في شهره إلّا قضاءً. وكلّ فريضة إنّما تؤدّى إذا حلّت.[347]

[ʿUmar b. Yazīd:] I said to Abū ʿAbd Allāh, "If a man has money, should he pay the *zakāt* on it when half a year has passed?" He said, "No! Only when a year has passed [with the money in his possession]. One may not perform a prayer until its designated time, and the same applies to *zakāt*. Nor may one perform the Ramaḍān fast except in that month, other than to make it up. Each obligation is to be fulfilled when it becomes due."

343 Kulaynī, *Kāfī*, 7:189.

344 Kulaynī, *Kāfī*, 7:189; Ibn Bābawayh, *Faqīh*, 4:29.

345 Ibn Bābawayh, *Faqīh*, 4:30 (as in the manuscript used by Ḥurr al-ʿĀmilī in *Wasāʾil al-Shīʿa*, 28:109).

346 The last sentence indicates that rape is not a category of fornication; the nature of the punishment for fornication is decided by the marital status of the culprit, with leniency granted in certain circumstances. In Jaʿfarī law, rape is a category of *ḥirāba*, that is, fighting against God; it is an instance of high treason, and the punishment thus does not differentiate between married and unmarried perpetrators and is not subject to any rule of leniency, nor to the specific rules of evidence applicable to fornication, as rape can be proven to a judge by knowledge acquired through physical and circumstantial evidence.

347 Kulaynī, *Kāfī*, 3:523–24.

K. Rule of Recognition

إنّ كلّ قوم دانوا بشيء يلزمهم حكمه.[348]

Any people who take something as their religion are bound by its rules.

أبو بصير قال: سمعت أبا عبد الله يقول: نهى رسول الله – صلّى الله عليه وآله وسلّم – أن يقال للاماء: «يا بنت كذا وكذا». فإنّ لكلّ قوم نكاحا.[349]

[Abū Baṣīr:] I heard Abū ʿAbd Allāh say, "The Prophet (may God's prayer and peace be upon him and his Family) forbade people from addressing slave women as the 'daughter of so-and-so,'[350] because all people have their own [forms of] marriage."

عبد الله بن سنان قال: قذف رجل رجلاً مجوسيًّا عند أبي عبد الله فقال: مه! فقال الرجل: إنّه ينكح أمّه وأخته! فقال: ذلك عندهم نكاح في دينهم.[351]

[ʿAbd Allāh b. Sinān:] A man slandered a Magian man in the presence of Abū ʿAbd Allāh. He said, "Hold your tongue!" The man said, "He marries his mother and sister!" He [the Imam] said, "That is marriage in their religion."[352]

اسحاق بن عمّار قال: قال أبو عبد الله: نكاح أهل الشرك جائز،[353] وذلك أنّ رسول الله – صلّى الله عليه وآله وسلّم – قال: لا تسبّوا أهل الشرك فانّ لكلّ قوم نكاحًا.[354]

348 Ṭūsī, *Tahdhīb*, 9:365, or, as put in reports from his descendants at 8:59 (also 9:322):

ألزِموهم بما ألزَموهُ أنفسَهم.

Hold them responsible for what they have made binding upon themselves.

إنّ طلاقكم الثلاث لا يَحلّ لغيركم وطلاقهم يَحلّ لكم، لأنّكم لا ترون الثلاثَ شيئًا وهم يوجبونها.

The wives you divorced thrice are not permissible to others [as the wives are not legally separated from you] but their divorced women are lawful for you, because you do not consider the triple divorce to be valid while they do consider it effective.

A statement quoted from Muḥammad al-Bāqir in Ṭūsī, 9:322 sets the matter straight:

يجوز على أهل كلّ دينٍ ما يستحلّون.

Whatever is permissible for members of a certain religion is legally valid.

349 Ṭūsī, *Tahdhīb*, 7:472.

350 Presumably, something like يا بنت الفاعلة: "O daughter of a prostitute!" (as in Kulaynī, *Kāfī*, 7:240).

351 Kulaynī, *Kāfī*, 5:574; Ṭūsī, *Tahdhīb*, 9:365.

352 For the full story, see Kulaynī, *Kāfī*, 7:240.

353 *Jā'iz* here means that their marriage is considered legally valid in Islamic law.

354 Ṭūsī, *Tahdhīb*, 6:387.

[Isḥāq b. ʿAmmār:] Abū ʿAbd Allāh said, "The marriages of the polytheists are valid, and that is because the Messenger of God (may God's prayer and peace be upon him and his Family) said, 'Do not insult the polytheists [with charges of illegitimacy]. All people have their own [form of] marriage.'"

أبو بصير عن أبي عبد الله قال: كلّ قوم يعرفون النكاح من السفاح فنكاحهم جائز.[355]

[Abū Baṣīr:] Abū ʿAbd Allāh said, "The marriages of any people who distinguish between marriage and fornication are valid."

L. Effects of Unlawful Acts

سعيد بن يسار قال: قلت لأبي عبد الله: رجل فجر بامرأة، أتحلّ له ابنتها؟ قال: نعم! إنّ الحرام لا يحرّم الحلال.[356]

[Saʿīd b. Yasār:] I said to Abū ʿAbd Allāh, "A man fornicates with a woman. Is her daughter lawful [as a marriage partner] for him?" He said, "Yes! The unlawful does not render the lawful unlawful."

عبد الله بن يحيى الكاهلي عن أبي عبد الله: سمعته يقول: سألني بعض هؤلاء عن رجل وقع على امرأة أبيه أو جارية أبيه؟ فقلت: ما أصاب الابن فجورٌ، ولا يُفسِد الحرامُ الحلال.[357]

[ʿAbd Allāh b. Yaḥyā al-Kāhilī:] I heard Abū ʿAbd Allāh say, "Some of these people asked me about a man who slept with the wife or handmaiden of his father. I responded, 'What the son did was licentiousness, but the unlawful does not render the lawful invalid.'"

355 Ṭūsī, *Tahdhīb*, 7:475.

356 See Aḥmad b. Muḥammad b. ʿĪsā, *Nawādir*, 94, with a variant at 95, and another in Ṭūsī, *Tahdhīb*, 7:329 (see also 7:328, where another transmitter testifies that he was present when Saʿīd b. Yasār asked the question and the Imam responded). Two more reports on other instances of this issue, quoted by other transmitters, are recorded in Aḥmad b. Muḥammad b. ʿĪsā, 94 (with a variant in Ibn Bābawayh, *Faqīh*, 3:263) and 96 (also Kulaynī, *Kāfī*, 5:415; see also Yaḥyā al-Hādī, *Aḥkām*, 1:364). The principle (both as الحرام لا يحرّم الحلال and as لا يُحرّم الحرامُ الحلال) was also known to the Sunnī tradition. See ʿAbd al-Razzāq, *Muṣannaf*, 7:198, 201; Ibn Abī Shayba, *Muṣannaf*, 6:83; Ibn Mājah, *Sunan*, no. 2015; Dāraquṭnī, *Sunan*, 4:400–401; Ibn al-ʿArabī, *Aḥkām al-Qurʾān*, 2:387. For the diversity of opinions among Sunnī jurists on this question, see Ibn Qudāma, *Mughnī*, 9:526.

357 Aḥmad b. Muḥammad b. ʿĪsā, *Nawādir*, 501, with two variants through different transmitters at 96; Kulaynī, *Kāfī*, 5:419–02. For a Sunnī version of this expression (in the form of الحلالُ لا يَفسُدُ بالحرام), see Dāraquṭnī, *Sunan*, 4:400.

أبو بصير عن أبي عبد الله قال: سألته عن رجل فجر بامرأة ثمّ بدا له أن يتزوّجها؟ فقال: حلال! أوّله سفاح وآخره نكاح.[358]

[Abū Baṣīr:] I asked Abū ʿAbd Allāh about a man who fornicated with a woman and then decided to marry her. He said, "It is lawful! It started as fornication and ended as marriage."

M. Effect of Conditions

الحلبي عن أبي عبد الله قال في المُكاتَب إذا أدّى بعض مُكاتبته: إنّ الناس كانوا لا يشترطون وهم اليوم يشترطون. والمسلمون عند شروطهم.[359]

[ʿUbayd Allāh al-Ḥalabī:] Regarding the situation of a slave under a written contract of manumission who has already paid off part of his contract, Abū ʿAbd Allāh said, "People used to avoid inserting conditions,[360] but today they do, and Muslims must abide by their commitments."

إسحاق بن عمّار عن جعفر عن أبيه عن علي – عليه السلام: المسلمون عند شروطهم إلّا شرطًا أحلّ حرامًا أو حرّم حلالاً.[361]

[Isḥāq b. ʿAmmār:] Jaʿfar quoted from his father[, who quoted] from ʿAlī: "Muslims must abide by the conditions they stipulate, except for conditions that make something unlawful lawful, or something lawful unlawful."

خالد بن نجيح عن أبي عبد الله قال: إنّما يحلّل الكلام ويحرّم الكلام.[362]

---

358 Kulaynī, *Kāfī*, 5:356 (partially quoted before). For a Sunnī parallel, see Ibn Abī Shayba, *Muṣannaf*, 6:164, 166, 167; Dāraquṭnī, *Sunan*, 4:401:

> سعيد بن جبير قال: سُئل ابن عبّاس عن الرجل والمرأة أصاب كلّ واحد منهما من الآخر حرامًا ثمّ بدا لهما أن يتزوّجا. قال: لا بأس. أوّله سفاح وآخره نكاح.
>
> [Saʿīd b. Jubayr:] Ibn ʿAbbās was asked about a man and a woman who had unlawful intimate relations with one other, after which the man decided to marry the woman. He said, "It is lawful! It started as fornication and ended as marriage."

359 Kulaynī, *Kāfī*, 6:187.

360 This refers to the standard condition at the time that if the slave was unable to pay off the contract in full, he would revert to full slavehood. See Kulaynī, *Kāfī*, 6:185–88, 7:308; Ibn Bābawayh, *Faqīh*, 3:29, 75, 76–78; Ṭūsī, *Tahdhīb*, 8:267, 273. There were also other conditions that the master could impose on the slave's freedom (e.g., Ibn Bābawayh, 3:77; Ṭūsī, 8:270).

361 Ṭūsī, *Tahdhīb*, 7:467, quoted from the Prophet in Abū Dāwūd, *Sunan*, no. 3594; Tirmidhī, *Sunan*, no. 1352; Dāraquṭnī, *Sunan*, 3:426–27; the first sentence also in Ṭūsī, 7:371 (المؤمنون عند شروطهم).

362 Kulaynī, *Kāfī*, 5:201.

[Khālid b. Najīḥ:] Abū ʿAbd Allāh said, "Statements [made as conditions in a contract] render things lawful or unlawful."

عبد الله بن سنان عن أبي عبد الله قال: المسلمون عند شروطهم ما وافق كتاب الله عزّ وجلّ.[363]

[ʿAbd Allāh b. Sinān:] Abū ʿAbd Allāh said, "Muslims must abide by the conditions they stipulate as long as the conditions accord with the Book of God, the Mighty and Majestic."

الحلبي عن أبي عبد الله قال: إن كان شرطًا يخالف كتاب الله عزّ وجلّ فهو ردّ إلى كتاب الله.[364]

[ʿUbayd Allāh al-Ḥalabī:] Abū ʿAbd Allāh said, "If a condition contravenes the Book of God, the Mighty and Majestic, it has to be referred back to the Book of God."

The last sentence appears as a general rule in a number of reports on different cases attributed to Jaʿfar al-Ṣādiq, as in the following examples:

أبو بصير عن أبي عبد الله قال: من خالف كتاب الله رُدَّ إلى كتاب الله عزّ وجلّ.[365]

[Abū Baṣīr:] Abū ʿAbd Allāh said, "Whoever contravenes the Book of God is referred back to the Book of God, the Mighty and Majestic."

صفوان الجمّال عن أبي عبد الله قال: كلّ ما خالف كتاب الله والسنّة فهو يُرَدُّ إلى كتاب الله والسنّة.[366]

---

363 Kulaynī, *Kāfī*, 5:69; also in Ibn Bābawayh, *Faqīh*, 3:127; Ṭūsī, *Tahdhīb*, 7:22 as:

المسلمون عند شروطهم إلّا كلّ شرط خالف كتاب الله عزّ وجلّ فلا يجوز.

> Muslims should abide by the conditions that they stipulate, except conditions that violate the Book of God, the Mighty and Majestic; those have no legal effect.

And in Ṭūsī, 7:67 (with a variant quoted from the Prophet in Bukhārī, *Ṣaḥīḥ*, no. 2729; Muslim, *Ṣaḥīḥ*, no. 1504):

كلّ شرط خالف الكتاب باطل.

> Any condition that violates the Book [of God] is invalid.

364 Kulaynī, *Kāfī*, 5:258.

365 Ṭūsī, *Tahdhīb*, 8:54. See also Ibn Bābawayh, *Faqīh*, 3:320, where Jaʿfar quotes the statement from the Prophet.

366 Ḥimyarī, *Qurb al-isnād*, 61–62.

[Ṣafwān al-Jammāl:] Abū ʿAbd Allāh said, "Whatever contravenes the Book of God and the Sunna will be referred back to the Book of God and the Sunna."

N. Rule of Benefit and Burden

إبراهيم الكرخي قال: سألت أبا عبد الله فقلت له إنّي كنت بعت رجلاً نخلاً بكذا وكذا درهمًا. فانطلق الّذي اشتراه منّي فباعه من رجل آخر بربح، ولم يكن نقدني ولا قبضه منّي، فقال: لا بأس بذلك. أليس قد كان ضمن لك الثمن؟ قلت: نعم! قال: فالربح له.[367]

[Ibrāhīm al-Karkhī:] I questioned Abū ʿAbd Allāh, saying to him, "I sold a palm tree to a man for such-and-such dirhams. The purchaser went and sold it to another man for a profit before paying me and taking possession of it from me." He said, "There is nothing wrong with that. Did he not provide a guarantee to you to pay you the price?" I said, "Yes!" He said, "Then the profit goes to him."

معاوية بن ميسرة قال: سمعت أبا الجارود يسأل أبا عبد الله عن رجل باع دارًا له من رجل وشرط أنّك إن أتيتني بمالي ما بين ثلاث سنين فالدار دارك، فأتاه بماله، قال: له شرطه. قال أبو الجارود: فإنّ ذلك الرجل قد أصاب في ذلك المال في ثلاث سنين؟ قال: هو مالُه. أرأيت لو أنّ الدار احترقت مِن مال مَن كانت تكون الدار؟[368]

[Muʿāwiya b. Maysara:] I heard Abū al-Jārūd[369] asking Abū ʿAbd Allāh about a man who sold a house on behalf of another man and stipulated that "if you bring me my money within three years, the house is yours." The buyer brought him his money. He said, "He is entitled to what he stipulated." Abū al-Jārūd said, "This man made a profit with that money for three years." He said, "It was his money. What would you think if the house burned down—from whose property would it burn?"

إسحاق بن عمّار قال: أخبرني من سمع أبا عبد الله: سأله رجل وأنا عنده فقال له: رجلٌ مسلمٌ احتاج إلى بيع داره فجاء إلى أخيه فقال: أبيعك دارى هذه على أن تشترط

---

367 Kulaynī, *Kāfī*, 5:177–78.

368 Ṭūsī, *Tahdhīb*, 7:176.

369 Ziyād b. al-Mundhir al-Hamdānī al-Khārifī, a Kūfan Shīʿī scholar who transmitted from Muḥammad al-Bāqir and Jaʿfar al-Ṣādiq, later joined the revolt of Zayd b. ʿAlī, and led the Jārūdī branch of Zaydī Shīʿism. On him and Jārūdī Zaydism, see the entry in *Encyclopaedia Iranica*, 1:327–28 [Wilferd Madelung] and van Ess, *Theologie und Gesellschaft*, 1:254–68. See also Modarressi, *Tradition and Survival*, 1:121–25.

لي إن أنا جئتك بثمنها إلى سنة أن تردّ عليّ. فقال: لا بأس بهذا. إن جاء بثمنها إلى سنة ردّها عليه. قلت: فإنّها كانت فيها غلّة كثيرة فأخذ الغلّة، لمن تكون الغلّة؟ فقال: الغلّة للمشتري. ألا ترى أنّها لو احترقت لكانت من ماله؟[370]

[Isḥāq b. ʿAmmār:] Someone once questioned Abū ʿAbd Allāh while I was with him, saying, "A Muslim man needed to sell his house, so he went to his brother and said, 'I will sell you this house of mine, and I prefer that it belong to you rather than someone else, on the condition that if I come to you with the money for it within a year, you will return it to me.'" He said, "There is nothing wrong with that. If he comes with the money for it within a year, he must return it to him." I said, "It contained a lot of produce that he [the buyer] used [during the time he owned the house]; to whom does the produce belong?" He [the Imam] said, "The produce belongs to the buyer. Do you not see that if the house burned down [during that period], it would come out of his wealth?"

O. Prerogatives of State Authority

حفص بن غياث قال: سألت أبا عبد الله: من يقيم الحدود؟ السلطان أو القاضي؟ فقال: إقامة الحدود إلى من إليه الحكم.[371]

[Ḥafṣ b. Ghiyāth:] I asked Abū ʿAbd Allāh, "Who applies the *ḥadd* punishments? The ruler or the judge?" He said, "Applying the *ḥadd* punishments is for the one who rules."

رفاعة عن رجل عن أبي عبد الله قال: دخلت على أبي العبّاس بالحيرة فقال: يا أبا عبد الله! ما تقول في الصيام اليوم؟ فقلت: ذاك إلى الإمام، إن صمت صمنا وإن أفطرت أفطرنا.[372]

[Rifāʿa, reporting from an unnamed narrator:] Abū ʿAbd Allāh said, "I came upon Abū al-ʿAbbās [al-Saffāḥ] at Ḥīra. He said, 'O Abū ʿAbd Allāh! What do you say about fasting today?' I said, 'That is for the *imām* to decide. If you fast, then we fast, and if you break the fast, then we break the fast.'"

370 Kulaynī, *Kāfī*, 5:171.
371 Ibn Bābawayh, *Faqīh*, 4:51; Ṭūsī, *Tahdhīb*, 6:314, 10:155 (see also 6:387 for a similar case).
372 Kulaynī, *Kāfī*, 4:83.

عيسى بن أبي منصور قال: كنت عند أبي عبد الله في اليوم الّذي يُشكّ فيه [أنّه من رمضان]، فقال: يا غلام! اذهب فانظر هل صام الأمير أم لا؟ فذهب ثمّ عاد فقال: لا! فدعا بالغداء فتغدّينا معه.[373]

[ʿĪsā b. Abī Manṣūr:] I was with Abū ʿAbd Allāh on the day that was thought to be the beginning of Ramaḍān [at the end of Shaʿbān]. So he said to his servant, "Go and see whether the governor has fasted or not." He went and came back and said, "No!" [Jaʿfar] then called for lunch to be served and we had lunch with him.

P. The Muslims' Market

حفص بن غياث عن أبي عبد الله قال: قال له رجلّ: أرأيتَ إذا رأيتُ شيئًا في يَدَي رجلٍ، أيجوز لي أن أشهد أنّه له؟ قال: نعم! قال الرجل: أشهد أنّه له؟ فلعلّه لغيره. فقال له أبو عبد الله: أفيحلّ الشراء منه؟ قال: نعم! فقال أبو عبد الله: فلعلّه لغيره، فمن أين جاز لك أن تشتريه ويصير ملكًا لك ثمّ تقول بعد الملك هو لي وتحلف عليه، ولا يجوز أن تنسبه إلى من صار ملكه من قِبَله إليك؟ ثمّ قال أبو عبد الله: لو لم يَجُز هذا لم يَقُم للمسلمين سوق.[374]

[Ḥafṣ b. Ghiyāth:] A man said to Abū ʿAbd Allāh, "What is your position on [a situation in which] I saw something in a man's possession—may I testify that it belongs to him?" He said, "Yes!" The man said, "How can I testify that it belongs to him when it might belong to someone else?" Abū ʿAbd Allāh said to him, "Is it permissible to purchase [it] from him?" He said, "Yes!" Abū ʿAbd Allāh said, "Perhaps it does belong to someone else. So how is it permissible for you to purchase it so that it becomes your property and after you come to own it you say, 'It is mine,' and swear upon it, but it is not permissible to attribute it to the person who owned it before you?" Then Abū ʿAbd Allāh said, "If that is not permissible, then no market will stabilize for the Muslims."

إسحاق بن عمّار عن أبي عبد الله قال: غبن المسترسِل سُحت.[375]

---

373 Ibn Bābawayh, *Faqīh*, 2:79.

374 Kulaynī, *Kāfī*, 7:387.

375 Kulaynī, *Kāfī*, 5:153. See also Ṭabarānī, *al-Muʿjam al-kabīr*, 8:127, as غبن المسترسل حرام; Kulaynī, 5:153 and Ṭūsī, *Tahdhīb*, 7:7 as غبن المؤمن حرام; and Ibn Bābawayh, *Faqīh*, 3:173 for the combination:

> قال الصادق: غبن المسترسِل سُحت وغبن المؤمن حرام.
>
> [What is gained from] cheating a trusting person is ill-gotten, and cheating a faithful person is unlawful.

[Isḥāq b. ʿAmmār:] Abū ʿAbd Allāh said, "[What is gained from] cheating a trusting person is ill-gotten."

عمرو بن جميع عن أبى عبد الله قال: غبن المسترسِل ربا.[376]

[ʿAmr b. Jumayʿ:] Abū ʿAbd Allāh said, "[What is gained from] cheating a trusting person is [tantamount to] usury."

Q. Liability (or Lack Thereof)

الحلبى عن أبي عبد الله قال: كُلّ أجيرٍ يُعطيَ الأجرَ على أن يُصلح فيُفسد فهو ضامن.[377]

[ʿUbayd Allāh al-Ḥalabī:] Abū ʿAbd Allāh said, "Any hired laborer who is paid to fix something but ruins it is liable [for its replacement value]."

زيد الشحّام قال: سألت أبا عبد الله عن رجل قتله القصاص، هل له دية؟ قال: لو كان ذلك لم يقتصّ من أحد، ومن قتله الحدّ فلا دية له.[378]

[Zayd al-Shaḥḥām:] I asked Abū ʿAbd Allāh about a man who was killed by [the application of the Islamic criminal punishment of] retaliation—is blood-money due for him? He said, "If it were, nobody would apply the law of retaliation against anyone. Whoever is killed by a *ḥadd* punishment has no blood-money due."

من اقتصّ منه [فمات][379] فهو قتيل القرآن.[380]

Whoever dies by [the application of the Islamic punishment of] retaliation is killed by [an order of] the Qurʾān.

من قتله القصاص أو الحدّ لم يكن له دية.[381]

Whoever is killed by [the application of the Islamic punishments of] *ḥadd* or retaliation does not have a blood-money due [for his death].

376 Ibn Bābawayh, *Faqīh*, 3:173; quoted from Jaʿfar al-Ṣādiq also in Bayhaqī, *Sunan*, 5:571.
377 Kulaynī, *Kāfī*, 5:241.
378 Kulaynī, *Kāfī*, 7:291 (also at 7:292 through a different transmitter).
379 From the same report in Ṭūsī, *Tahdhīb*, 10:279.
380 Kulaynī, *Kāfī*, 7:377; Ṭūsī, *Tahdhīb*, 10:279.
381 Ṭūsī, *Tahdhīb*, 10:191.

السكوني عن أبي عبد الله قال: قال رسول الله – صلّى الله عليه وآله وسلّم: البئر جُبار، والعجماء جُبار، والمعدن جُبار.[382]

Recompense [for damage and harm] cannot be made against wells, beasts, and mines.

معلّى أبو عثمان عن أبي عبد الله قال: سألته عن رجل غشيته دابّة فأرادت أن تطأه وخشي ذلك منها فزجر الدابّة فنفرت بصاحبها فصرعته فكان جرح أو غيره، فقال: ليس عليه ضمان. إنّما زجر عن نفسه وهى جُبار.[383]

[Muʿallā b. ʿUthmān, Abū ʿUthmān:] I asked Abū ʿAbd Allāh about a man who was overcome by a riding animal that was going to trample him. He was afraid, so he drove the beast away and it ran off with its owner and threw him off, resulting in a wound or the like. He said, "He is not liable. He averted it from himself, and no recompense can be taken for it."

R. Principle of Fait Accompli

زرارة عن ابى عبد الله قال: يا زرارة! إذا خرجت من شيء ودخلت في غيره فشكّك ليس بشيء.[384]

[Zurāra:] Abū ʿAbd Allāh said, "O Zurāra! If you finish something and begin something else, your doubt [about the first act] is inconsequential."

محمّد بن مسلم عن أبي عبد الله قال: إن شكّ الرجل بعد ما صلّى فلم يدر أثلاثًا صلّى أم أربعًا وكان يقينه حين انصرف أنّه قد أتمّ، لم يُعد الصلاة. كان حين انصرف أقرب الى الحقّ منه بعد ذلك.[385]

[Muḥammad b. Muslim:] Abū ʿAbd Allāh said, "If a man feels doubt after completing his prayer, and does not know whether he prayed three or four *rakʿa*s, but when he concluded the prayer he was certain that he had performed it in full, he does not repeat his prayer. When he concluded the prayer, he was closer to reality than he was afterward."

382 Kulaynī, *Kāfī*, 7:377 with a variant in Ibn Bābawayh, *Faqīh*, 4:116. For the Sunnī parallel see, for instance, Bukhārī, *Ṣaḥīḥ*, nos. 1499, 2355, 6912–13; Muslim, *Ṣaḥīḥ*, no. 1710; Abū Dāwūd, *Sunan*, no. 4593; Tirmidhī, *Sunan*, no. 642; Nasāʾī, *Sunan*, nos. 5830–34.

383 Ibn Bābawayh, *Faqīh*, 4:76.

384 Ṭūsī, *Tahdhīb*, 2:352.

385 Ibn Bābawayh, *Faqīh*, 1:231.

S. Law and Spirituality

أبو بصير عن أبي عبد الله قال: كلّ ما فرض الله عزّ وجلّ عليك فإعلانه أفضل من إسراره، وكلّ ما كان تطوّعًا فإسراره أفضل من إعلانه. ولو أنّ رجلاً يحمل زكاة ماله على عاتقه فقسّمها علانيةً كان ذلك حسنًا جميلاً.[386]

[Abū Baṣīr:] Abū ʿAbd Allāh said, "For everything you are obligated to do by God, the Mighty and Majestic, performing it publicly is better than doing so privately. But everything voluntary is better performed privately rather than publicly. If a man carries the *zakāt* from his wealth on his shoulder and distributes it publicly, that is good and beautiful."

T. Law and Symbolism

الحسين بن أبي العلاء قال: سألت أبا عبد الله عن الرجل يمرّ بالرَكيّة وليس معه دلو. قال: ليس عليه أن ينزل الرَكيّة. إنّ ربّ الماء هو ربّ الأرض. فليتيمّم.[387]

[Al-Ḥusayn b. Abī al-ʿAlāʾ:] I asked Abū ʿAbd Allāh about a man who comes across a well and does not have a bucket [to take water for ablution]. He said, "He does not have to descend into the well. Indeed, the Lord of water is the same as the Lord of earth. So he should perform dry ablution with earth."

محمّد بن مسلم قال: سألت أبا عبد الله عن رجل أجنب فتيمّم بالصعيد وصلّى، ثمّ وجد الماء. فقال: لا يُعيد. إنّ ربّ الماء هو ربّ الصعيد.[388]

[Muḥammad b. Muslim:] I asked Abū ʿAbd Allāh about a man who became ritually impure with a major impurity, so he performed ablution with earth and prayed, and thereafter found water. He said, "He will not repeat [the prayer]. The Lord of water is [also] the Lord of earth."

386 Kulaynī, *Kāfī*, 3:501.

387 Kulaynī, *Kāfī*, 3:64.

388 Ṭūsī, *Tahdhīb*, 1:197. See also Kulaynī, *Kāfī*, 3:69:

عنبسة بن مصعب عن أبي عبد الله قال: إذا أتيت البئر وأنت جُنُب ولم تجد دلوًا ولا شيئًا تغرف به فتيمّم بالصعيد فإنّ ربّ الماء وربّ الصعيد واحد.

['Anbasa b. Muṣʿab:] Abū ʿAbd Allāh said, "If you reach a well while you are in a state of major ritual impurity and do not find a bucket, nor anything to ladle with, perform dry ablution with earth. The Lord of water and the Lord of earth are one."

معاوية بن ميسرة قال: سألت أبا عبد الله عن الرجل في السفر لا يجد الماء فتيمّم[389] [و]صلّى، ثمّ أتى الماء وعليه شيء من الوقت، أيَمضى على صلاته أم يتوضّأ ويعيد صلاته؟ قال: يمضي على صلاته. فانّ ربّ الماء هو ربّ التراب.[390]

[Muʿāwiya b. Maysara:] I asked Abū ʿAbd Allāh about a man who is traveling and does not find water, so he performs dry ablution and prays. Later, he comes across water and has some time remaining [to perform the prayer again]. Does he carry on with his prayer as he was doing or does he perform ablution with water and repeat his prayer? He said, "He carries on with his prayer. The Lord of water is [also] the Lord of dirt."

U. Linguistics and Definitions

قال أبو عبد الله: كُلّ ما في القرآن «أَو[/أو]» فصاحبه بالخيار[391] وكُلّ ما كان «فإن لم يَجد» فالأوّل الخيار.[392]

Abū ʿAbd Allāh said, "Whenever the Qurʾān says, '[either] or,' those to whom the passage applies have the freedom to choose, and whenever it says, 'and whoever does not find,' then the first thing mentioned [after it] is to be performed."

389 The word is corrupted to ثمّ in the edition of the source used in this study. Corrected on the basis of Ḥurr al-ʿĀmilī, *Wasāʾil al-Shīʿa*, 3:370.

390 Ṭūsī, *Tahdhīb*, 1:195.

391 This sentence is quoted from Ibn ʿAbbās, ʿAṭāʾ, and ʿIkrima in Bukhārī, *Ṣaḥīḥ*, at the beginning of the chapter on *kaffārāt al-aymān*, right before *ḥadīth* no. 6708.

392 Aḥmad b. Muḥammad b. ʿĪsā, *Nawādir*, 72; ʿAyyāshī, *Tafsīr*, 1:198; Kulaynī, *Kāfī*, 4:358 (all with minor variations). The Sunnī version of this principle is slightly different in wording (e.g., Ibn Abī Shayba, *Muṣannaf*, 5:64; Ṭabarī, *Jāmiʿ al-bayān*, 11:35):

> مجاهد عن ابن عبّاس: كلّ شيء في القرآن «أو[/أو]» فصاحبه مخيّرٌ فيه، وكلّ شيء «فمن لم يجد» فالأوّل ثمّ الّذي يليه.
>
> Mujāhid reported that Ibn ʿAbbās said, "Whenever the Qurʾān says, '[either] or,' those to whom the verse applies have the freedom to choose, and whenever the Qurʾān says, 'and whoever does not find,' the first thing mentioned [is to be performed], or else what follows it."
>
> عكرمة [عن ابن عبّاس]: كلّ ما في القرآن «أو[/أو]» فهو فيه بالخيار، وما كان «فمن لم يجد» فالأوّل ثمّ الّذي يليه.
>
> ʿIkrima reported from Ibn ʿAbbās: "Wherever the Qurʾān says, '[either] or,' one has the freedom to choose; and whenever it says, 'and whoever does not find,' the first thing mentioned [is to be performed], or else what follows it."

حريز عمّن أخبره عن أبي عبد الله قال: كلّ طير يكون في الآجام يبيض في البرّ ويفرخ في البرّ فهو من صيد البرّ، وما كان من صيد البرّ يكون في البرّ ويبيض في البحر ويفرخ في البحر فهو من صيد البحر.[393]

[Ḥarīz:] Reporting from an [unnamed narrator], Abū ʿAbd Allāh said, "Any bird in the thicket that lays eggs on land and hatches [them] on land is [considered] game from the land, and any game that is on land but lays eggs and hatches at sea is [considered] game from the sea."

معاوية بن عمّار عن أبي عبد الله قال: سألته عن دجاج الحَبَش فقال: ليس من الصيد. إنّما الصيد ما طار بين السماء والأرض.[394]

[Muʿāwiya b. ʿAmmār:] I asked Abū ʿAbd Allāh about Abyssinian chicken.[395] He said, "It is not game. Game is what flies between the heavens and the earth."

ابن أبي يعفور قال: كنت عند أبي عبد الله إذ دخل عليه رجلٌ من الخزّازين فقال له: جُعِلتُ فداكَ! ما تقول في الصلاة في الخزّ؟ قال: لا بأس. فقال الرجل: جعلت فداك! [إنّها في بلادي وإنّها هي كلاب تخرج من الماء. فقال أبو عبد الله: إذا خرجت من الماء تعيش خارجة من الماء؟ فقال الرجل: لا!] فقال له أبو عبد الله: فإنّ الله تعالى أحلّها وجعل ذكاتها موتها كما أحلّ الحيتان وجعل ذكاتها موتها.[396]

[Ibn Abī Yaʿfūr:] I was with Abū ʿAbd Allāh when a maker of fur coats came to him. He said to Abū ʿAbd Allāh, "May I be made your ransom! What do you say about praying in a coat made of sea otter fur?" He said, "There is nothing wrong with that." The man said, "May I be made your ransom! They are found in my homeland, and they are dogs that come out of the water." Abū ʿAbd Allāh said, "Do they live out of water when they come out?" The man said, "No!" Abū ʿAbd Allāh said to him,

393 Kulaynī, *Kāfī*, 4:392–93, with a variant in Ṭūsī, *Tahdhīb*, 5:365.

394 Kulaynī, *Kāfī*, 4:232.

395 In a variant of this report in Bazanṭī, *Nawādir*, 56, and Ibn Bābawayh, *Faqīh*, 2:172, the bird is called الدجاج السندي, and described as لايستقلّ بالطيران. *Dujāj al-ḥabash*, as defined in Arabic dictionaries, refers to the guinea fowl, although in some contemporary Arab communities it may refer to a turkey, that is, *dīk rūmī* as it was known in the past. The description given of a bird brought to the Fatimid caliph ʿAzīz (r. 344–86) as cited in Qāḍī Aḥmad Ghaffārī, *Tārīkh-i nigāristān*, 193, from an early history of Egypt, also fits the turkey better. See further the entry on *būqalamūn* in *Encyclopaedia Iranica*, 4:551–53 [Hūshang Aʿlam].

396 Kulaynī, *Kāfī*, 3:399–400, with a variant at 6:451. The text quoted here is adapted from the two variants.

"So God, the Exalted, made them lawful and made their death [out of the water] count as slaughter, just as He made fish lawful and made their death [out of the water] count as slaughter."

CHAPTER 3

Specific Legal Questions

As demonstrated in the preceding chapters, Jaʿfar al-Ṣādiq's legal thought fell very much within the general legal discourse of late Umayyad and early Abbasid times. It was common for the judges and jurists of the period to maintain sharp differences of opinion and to disagree on just about every point. The community had accepted this diversity of opinion alongside a core that all Muslim jurists agreed upon and that formed the essential elements of Islamic religious thought and culture.

As also noted earlier, some of Jaʿfar al-Ṣādiq's legal opinions are quoted in the general sources of Islamic law. They reflect certain characteristics of his school as well as disagreements between him and other jurists of the time. With the advancement of legal "orthodoxy" and the growing popularity of a small number of legal schools, many early opinions, including much that was supported by or attributed to the school of Jaʿfar al-Ṣādiq, gradually disappeared from the legal discourse of the majority Sunnī tradition. In more recent times, certain issues in Jaʿfar al-Ṣādiq's legal legacy have been brought up in sectarian debates and treated in ways that are ahistorical and decontextualized. This chapter examines a few of these issues in an effort to understand them within the historical and legal discourse of their time.

I. "The Masses" versus "the Select"

In the following long conversation between Jaʿfar al-Ṣādiq and one of his followers, the Imam responded to questions on a number of topics, including what to do when reports from the Imams were contradictory:

عمر بن حنظلة قال: سألت أبا عبد الله عن رجلين من أصحابنا بينهما منازعة في دَين أو ميراث فتحاكما إلى السلطان وإلى القضاة، أيحلّ ذلك؟ قال: من تحاكم إليهم في حقّ أو باطل فإنّما تحاكم إلى الطاغوت، وما يحكم له فإنّما يأخذ سحتًا وإن كان حقًّا ثابتًا له لأنّه أخذه بحكم الطاغوت، وقد أمر الله أن يُكفَر به. قال الله تعالى: ﴿يُرِيدُونَ أَنْ يَتَحَاكَمُوا إِلَى الطَّاغُوتِ وَقَدْ أُمِرُوا أَنْ يَكْفُرُوا بِهِ﴾. قلت: فكيف

يصنعان؟ قال: ينظران إلى من كان منكم ممّن قد روى حديثنا ونظر في حلالنا وحرامنا وعرف أحكامنا فليرضوا به حكمًا فإنّي قد جعلته عليكم حاكمًا. فإذا حكم بحكمنا فلم يُقبل منه فإنّما استخفّ بحكم الله وعلينا ردّ. قلت: فإن كان كلُّ رجل اختار رجلاً من أصحابنا فرضيا أن يكونا الناظرَين في حقّهما، واختلفا فيما حكما وكلاهما اختلفا في حديثكم. قال: الحكم ما حكم به أعدلهما وأفقههما وأصدقهما في الحديث وأورعهما، ولا يلتفت إلى ما يحكم به الآخر. قلت: فإنّهما عدلان مرضيّان عند أصحابنا، لا يُفضَّل واحد منهما على الآخر. قال: ينظر إلى ما كان من روايتهم عنّا في ذلك الّذي حَكَما به المجمع عليه من أصحابك فيؤخذ به من حكمنا ويترك الشاذّ الّذي ليس بمشهور عند أصحابك، فإنّ المجمع عليه لا ريب فيه. وإنّما الأُمور ثلاثة: أمرٌ بيّن رشده فيُتّبع، وأمر بيّن غيُّه فيجتنب، وأمرٌ مشكل يردّ علمه إلى الله وإلى رسوله. قال رسول الله – صلّى الله عليه وآله وسلّم: «حلالٌ بيِّن وحرام بيِّن وشبهات بين ذلك، فمن ترك الشبهات نجا من المحرّمات ومن أخذ بالشبهات ارتكب المحرّمات وهلك من حيث لا يعلم». قلت: فإن كان الخبران عنكما مشهورين قد رواهما الثقات عنكم؟ قال: ينظر فما وافق حكمه حكم الكتاب والسنّة وخالف العامّة فيؤخذ به ويترك ما خالف حكمه حكم الكتاب والسنّة ووافق العامّة. قلت: جُعلت فداك! أرأيت إن كان الفقيهان عرفا حكمه من الكتاب والسنّة ووجدنا أحد الخبرين موافقًا للعامّة والآخر مخالفًا لهم، بأيّ الخبرين يؤخذ؟ قال: ما خالف العامّة ففيه الرشاد. قلت: جُعلت فداك! فإن وافقهما الخبران جميعًا؟ قال: ينظر إلى ما هم إليه أميل حكّامهم وقضاتهم، فيترك ويؤخذ بالآخر. قلت: فإن وافق حكّامهم الخبرين جميعًا؟ قال: إذا كان ذلك فارجه حتّى تلقى إمامك، فإنّ الوقوف عند الشبهات خير من الاقتحام في الهلكات.[1]

[ʿUmar b. Ḥanẓala:] I asked Abū ʿAbd Allāh about two people from our community who had a dispute over a loan or an inheritance and brought their case to be adjudicated by the government and [state-appointed] judges. Is that permitted? He said, "Whoever seeks to have his dispute settled by their judgment, whether right or wrong, has sought the judgment of a tyrant. Whatever [gain] the judgment grants him is ill-gotten, even if it is [deemed] his established right, because it is obtained through the judgment of a tyrant. God has

1 Kulaynī, *Kāfī*, 1:67–68.

commanded that the tyrant should be rejected. God, the Exalted, said, 'They wish for a judgment from a tyrant, although they were ordered to reject him.'"[2]

I said, "What should they do, then?" He said, "They should look for someone among you who reports our sayings, has studied what we deem lawful and unlawful, and knows our rulings. They should accept him as a judge, for I have made him a judge over you. If he judges according to our rulings and his judgment is not accepted, then God's judgment has been denigrated and we have been rejected."

I said, "What if each of the two [parties to the dispute] chooses a different person from our community, and they both agree to have these judges look into their claims, but they [the judges] disagree in their judgments and disagree about your sayings?" He said, "The valid judgment is that of the individual who is more upright, legally knowledgeable, truthful in speech, and pious. No heed should be paid to the judgment of the other."

I said, "What if they are both upright and accepted in our community, and neither is preferred over the other?" He said, "Then consider which of their reports from us with respect to the matter at hand is agreed upon by your community. That is what should be taken from our rulings, and any anomalous report that is unknown to your community should be abandoned. What is unanimously agreed upon is not subject to doubt. Matters are of three kinds: matters that are clearly correct, so they are to be followed; matters that are clearly errant, so they are to be avoided; and matters that are ambiguous, so knowledge of them is to be referred to God and His Messenger. The Messenger of God (may God's prayer and peace be upon him and his Family) said, 'The lawful is clear and the unlawful is clear, and between them are doubtful matters. Whoever avoids the doubtful matters is safe from the unlawful, and whoever pursues the doubtful matters commits the unlawful and is ruined without knowing how.'"[3]

I said, "What if two reports attributed to you are well known and reported from you by trustworthy people?" He said, "Look to see which of their rulings matches the rulings in the Book [of God] and the Sunna but contradicts the [opinion of the] masses. That one is to be accepted. For whatever contradicts the Book and the Sunna but aligns with the [opinion of the] masses is to be rejected."

---

2 Qur'ān 4:60.

3 Bukhārī, *Ṣaḥīḥ*, no. 2051; Muslim, *Ṣaḥīḥ*, no. 1599; Abū Dāwūd, *Sunan*, no. 3329, and other sources cited in the editors' footnote to Aḥmad b. Ḥanbal, *Musnad*, 30:290–91.

> I said, "May I be made your ransom! What is your position on [a case in which] two jurists reach their rulings with reliance on the Book and the Sunna, but we find one of the two reports agreeing with the [opinion of the] masses and the other contradicting it: Which of the two reports should we accept?" He said, "The one that contradicts the judgment of the masses has truth and guidance in it."
>
> I said, "May I be made your ransom! What if both reports agree with the practice of the masses?" He said, "Look to see which one their arbitrators and judges lean toward. That one is to be rejected and the other accepted." I asked, "What if their judges agree with both reports?" He said, "If that is the case, then withhold judgment until you meet your Imam. In situations of doubt and ambiguity, holding back is better than falling into ruin."

As explicitly stipulated in the text, the purpose of the instructions is to find a way out of an impasse in the administration of justice when the available evidence regarding the correct ruling is contradictory. Consequently, one must consider all possibilities to determine which reading of the story is more probable. One option is to give priority to the opinion that is prevalent in one's community over an alternative opinion that is less known and represented. This is the approach advised by Jaʿfar al-Ṣādiq in this case: to give preference to the opinion recommended by the legal school of the House of the Prophet over the one supported by the "masses," that is, the pro-caliphate community. The latter opinion represented the views of jurists whose opinions were endorsed and followed by the government.

If the opinion of the Imams agreed with the official position, there was always the possibility that it reflected precautionary considerations. The case of hunting with a falcon, mentioned earlier, illustrates the predicament that Shīʿī jurists faced in the time of the caliphate. Several early jurists thought that hunting with any animal other than a trained dog was not sanctioned by the Qurʾān. However, they could not publicly advocate this opinion, as hunting with falcons was a very popular pastime of the caliphs and their entourage.

> عبيد بن زرارة عن أبي عبد الله قال: ما سمعتَ منّي يشبه قول الناس ففيه التقيّة وما سمعتَ منّي لا يشبه قول الناس فلا تقيّة فيه.[4]
>
> [ʿUbayd b. Zurāra:] Abū ʿAbd Allāh said, "What you heard from me that conformed to popular opinion among the general public was possibly

4 Ṭūsī, *Tahdhīb*, 8:89.

said out of precautionary secrecy, and what you heard from me that did not conform to popular opinion among the general public was not said out of precautionary secrecy."

Many sectarian books written and published in recent times criticize the reference in the long conversation quoted above as an outright anti-Sunnī statement. But this interpretation takes the text out of its original historical context. As noted earlier, the opinions of Jaʿfar al-Ṣādiq frequently agreed with one side or another in the general legal discourse of the time. Thus, as a prominent Shīʿī jurist of the early part of the past century reminded his readers, the Imam's advice to prefer the position that was most popular within one's own community did not entail a rejection of the other side on principle: "We know for certain that many rulings that agree with the popular opinions of the Sunnī schools are not wrong . . . as many of their opinions agree with the truth."[5] Jaʿfar al-Ṣādiq himself explained that his advice had no sectarian implications:

أبو إسحاق الأرّجاني رفعه قال: قال لي أبو عبد الله: أتدري لِمَ أُمِرتم بالأخذ بخلاف ما تقول العامّة؟ فقلت: لا أدري. فقال: إنّ عليًّا لم يكن يدين الله بدين إلّا خالف عليه آل أُميّة[6] إلى غيره، إرادةً لابطال أمره.[7]

Abū ʿAbd Allāh said to me, "Do you know why you were ordered to take the position that is contrary to the masses?" I said, "I do not know." He said, "Anything that ʿAlī advocated in matters of religion, the Umayyads contradicted in the hope of eliminating his influence."[8]

5 Nāʾīnī, *Fawāʾid al-uṣūl*, 4:776–77:

بداهة أنّ كثيرًا من الأحكام الموافقة لرأى العامّة ليست من الباطل. وقد عرفت أنّ كثيرًا من الأحكام الحقّة توافق قول العامّة.

6 The word is corrupted in the source to الأمّة. The last sentence of the text, however, attests to this corruption. For the use of آل أميّة instead of the more common form of بنو أميّة in other reports from Jaʿfar, see, for instance, Ṭūsī, *Amālī*, 667.

7 Ibn Bābawayh, *ʿIlal al-sharāʾiʿ*, 2:218.

8 See further Fakhr al-Dīn al-Rāzī, *Tafsīr*, 1:206, where he says:

إنّ عليًا كان يبالغ في الجهر بالبسملة فلمّا وصلت الدولة إلى بني أميّة سعوا إلى إبطال آثار علي.

ʿAlī used to insist on reciting the *basmala* out loud [in prayer]. When the Umayyads came to power, they worked hard to erase his influence.

The process began with Muʿāwiya. See Ibn Abī al-Ḥadīd, *Sharḥ Nahj al-balāgha*, 11:44–45, quoting the historian Abū al-Ḥasan ʿAlī b. Muḥammad al-Madāʾinī (d. 225) in his *Kitāb al-Aḥdāth*, as noted before. See further the following report in Shāfiʿī, *Umm* [Beirut, 1973],

Thus, no offense was intended to other leading jurists of the time or to their opinions, nor was this approach an attempt to persuade supporters of one school to reject another out of hand. There was, however, no shortage of reactions of the latter kind in the history of the Islamic legal schools. Consider the following two examples. The first comes from Yaʿqūb b. Sufyān al-Fasawī (d. 277), an eminent Sunnī *ḥadīth* scholar:

إذا سُئلت عن شيء ولم يكن عندك شيء فانظر ما ذا قال فيه أبو حنيفة فخالِفه فانّك تُصيب![9]

If you are asked about something and you do not have an answer, look to what Abū Ḥanīfa said about the matter and take the opposite opinion. That way, you will get the right answer!

The second statement is by Ibn al-Ṣalāḥ al-Shahrazūrī (d. 643), a Shāfiʿī scholar and author of one of the most popular works on the *ḥadīth* sciences.[10] He had the following advice for cases of disagreement between Abū Ḥanīfa and Shāfiʿī:

إذا اختلف قولَي الشافعي في مسألة وأحدُ القولين يوافق مذهب أبي حنيفة، قال الشيخ أبو حامد: ما يخالف قول أبي حنيفة أولى لأنّه لولا أنّ الشافعي عرف فيه معنًى خفيًّا لكان لا يخالف أبي حنيفة.[11]

If the two opinions of Shāfiʿī [that is, his "old" and "new" opinions] regarding a matter differ and one of the opinions agrees with that of Abū Ḥanīfa, the Shaykh Abū Ḥāmid[12] said, "Whatever conflicts with

---

1:108; ʿAbd al-Razzāq, *Muṣannaf*, 2:92; Nasāʾī, *Sunan*, no. 3979; Ibn Khuzayma, *Ṣaḥīḥ*, 4:260; Ḥākim al-Naysābūrī, *Mustadrak*, 1:638 (see also Ibn Abī Shayba, *Muṣannaf*, 5:552):

سعيد بن جبير قال: كنّا مع ابن عبّاس بعرفة فقال لي: يا سعيد! ما لي لا أسمع الناس يُلبّون؟ فقلت: يخافون من معاوية! فخرج ابن عبّاس من فسطاطه فقال: لبّيك! اللهمّ لبّيك! فإنّهم تركوا السنّة من بُغض علي.

[Saʿīd b. Jubayr:] We were at ʿArafāt with Ibn ʿAbbās when he said to me, "O Saʿīd! Why do I not hear the people chanting the *talbiya*?" I said, "They fear Muʿāwiya!" Ibn ʿAbbās stormed out of his tent and shouted, "Here I am, my Lord, here I am!" They abandoned the Sunna out of their hatred for ʿAlī!

9 Fasawī, *al-Maʿrifa wa'l-taʾrīkh*, 2:785. See further Juwaynī, *Burhān*, 2:895, 899.

10 Taqī al-Dīn ʿUthmān b. ʿAbd al-Raḥmān al-Mawṣilī. See the entry on him in *Encyclopaedia of Islam* II, 3:927 [T. Leusicki].

11 Ibn al-Ṣalāḥ, *Adab al-muftī wa'l-mustaftī*, 127.

12 Abū Ḥāmid Aḥmad b. Abī Ṭāhir al-Isfarāʾīnī (d. 406), a distinguished jurist and head of the Shāfiʿī school in Baghdad at the turn of the fifth century. On him, see Dhahabī, *Siyar aʿlām al-nubalāʾ*, 17:193–97.

the opinion of Abū Ḥanīfa is preferred, because had Shāfiʿī not noticed a subtle element [meriting a different ruling] in the matter, he would not have contradicted Abū Ḥanīfa."

Similar examples of the interplay of legal diversity and sectarian differences are abundant:

الجرّيُّ رخص فيه علي والحسن ومالك والشافعي وأبو ثور وأصحاب الرأى وساير أهل العلم. قال ابن عبّاس: الجرّي لا تأكله اليهود. ووافقتهم الرافضة ومخالفتهم صواب.[13]

ʿAlī, Ḥasan [al-Baṣrī], Mālik, Shāfiʿī, Abū Thawr, other followers of *raʾy*, and other people of knowledge all declared the *jirrī*/*jirrīth* [an eel-like fish] to be lawful. Ibn ʿAbbās said, "Jews do not eat *jirrī*, and the Rāfiḍa agree with them. What contradicts them is the correct [opinion]."[14]

قال الحافظ العراقي في بيان اسدال طرف العمامة: هل المشروع فيه إرخائه من الجانب الأيسر كما هو المعتاد أو الأيمن لشرفه؟ لم أر ما يدلّ على تعيين الأيمن. ولعلّه (يعني النبي – صلّى الله عليه و سلّم) كان يُرخيها من الجانب الأيمن ثمّ يردّها إلى الجانب الأيسر. إلّا أنّه صار شعارًا للامامیّة فينبغي تجنّبه لترك التشبّه بهم.[15]

Regarding the side of the turban that hangs down—whether one should let the left side hang down, as is customary, or the right, because of that side's privilege—al-Ḥāfiẓ al-ʿIrāqī[16] said, "I do not find anything indicating that it should be on the right side. The Prophet (may God's prayer and peace be upon him) possibly used to let the right side hang down and then move it to the left side, but because that has become a symbol for the Imāmī [Shīʿa] it should be avoided so as not to resemble them."

السنّة في القبر التسطيح، وهو أولى على الراجح من مذهب الشافعي، وقال أبو حنيفة ومالك وأحمد: التسنيم أولى لأنّ التسطيح صار شعارًا للشيعة.[17]

13 Ibn Qudāma, *Mughnī*, 13:347.

14 A number of reports from Muḥammad al-Bāqir and Jaʿfar al-Ṣādiq challenge the validity of this attribution. See ʿAlī b. Jaʿfar, *Masāʾil*, 115; Kulaynī, *Kāfī*, 6:219–20; Ṭūsī, *Tahdhīb*, 9:4–6.

15 ʿAynī, *ʿUmdat al-qārī*, 21:308; Zurqānī, *Sharḥ al-Mawāhib al-ladunniyya*, 5:13.

16 Abū al-Faḍl ʿAbd al-Raḥīm b. Ḥusayn al-ʿIrāqī al-Miṣrī (d. 806), the most eminent *ḥadīth* scholar of his time. On him, see Ziriklī, *Aʿlām*, 3:344–45 and the sources cited therein.

17 Qāḍī Ṣafad, *Raḥmat al-umma*, 1:88. See also Rāfiʿī, *Fatḥ al-ʿAzīz bi-sharḥ al-Wajīz*, 5:231.

> The *sunna* is to flatten the grave, and that is preferable according to the better, supported opinion in the school of Shāfiʿī. Abū Ḥanīfa, Mālik, and Aḥmad [b. Ḥanbal] said that it is better to raise the level of the grave [by heaping loose soil on top of the grave], as flattening the grave has become a symbol for the Shīʿa.

> قال الشافعي وأحمد: المسح على الخفّين أولى من الغسل لما فيه من مخالفة الشيعة.[18]
>
> Shāfiʿī and Aḥmad said that wiping over boots is preferable to washing [the feet][19] because it is against [the opinion or practice of] the Shīʿa.

II. *Taqiyya*: Precautionary Secrecy

The Islamic legal principle of precautionary secrecy (*taqiyya*) is a much written about but often misunderstood topic in the current sectarian disputes among Muslims. It is significant here only to the extent that it features in the legal legacy of Jaʿfar al-Ṣādiq.

The principle of precautionary secrecy has Qurʾānic roots.[20] It stipulates that in matters of religious creed and rituals, one should not disclose one's beliefs if doing so could cause major harm or put one's life in danger. When such situations arise, one should act cautiously in the spirit of compromise to repulse harm and avoid danger in any way possible, short of harming someone else.[21] Other reasons for adopting the principle and holding back one's opinion in a given case might include a wish to avert potential harm from the Muslim community, as explained in many Shīʿī works on *uṣūl*

18 Ibn al-Muṭahhar, *Tadhkirat al-fuqahāʾ*, 1:175. Numerous other practices were discouraged by Sunnī scholars explicitly for the same symbolic reason. Examples include reciting the opening formula (*basmala*) of the *sūras* of the Qurʾān aloud (Lālakāʾī, *Sharḥ*, 1:171; Ibn Baṭṭa, *Ibāna*, 315; Ibn Taymiyya, *Majmūʿat fatāwā*, 22:423; Ibn Taymiyya, *Minhāj al-sunna*, 4:151; see also Rāfiʿī, *Fatḥ al-ʿAzīz*, 2:453); wearing a ring on the right hand (Ibn ʿAbd al-Barr, *Tamhīd*, 6:80–81; Nawawī, *Majmūʿ*, 4:462, quoting ʿAbd al-Raḥmān al-Fūrānī in his *Ibāna*) as against the practice of Muʿāwiya, who wore it on the left (Rāghib al-Iṣbahānī, *Muḥāḍarāt al-udabāʾ*, 4:374; Zamakhsharī, *Rabīʿ al-abrār*, 4:24); pronouncing an honorific for anyone other than the Prophet with the standard formula "peace be upon him" (Ibn al-Qayyim, *Jalāʾ al-afhām*, 550; ʿAlī al-Qārī, *Sharḥ al-Fiqh al-akbar*, 152); saying the *takbīr* five times when praying over the body of a deceased Muslim, rather than four times, as is common among the *ahl al-sunna* (Māzarī, *al-Muʿlim bi-fawāʾid Muslim*, 1:326); eating *jirrī/jirrīth* (see above); making graves flat on top (see above); letting the right side of one's turban hang down (see above); and grieving for Ḥusayn (Ālūsī, *Rūḥ al-maʿānī*, 2:242). See further Modarressi, "Common Ibāḍī-Shīʿite Legacy," 115, n. 64.

19 See below, section VI on p. 285.

20 See Qurʾān 3:28, 16:106, and, for life-threatening cases, 2:173, 195, 5:3, 6:119, 145, 16:115.

21 For this concept, see especially *Mawsūʿat al-fiqh al-Islāmī* (Qum), 31:272–333; *al-Mawsūʿa al-fiqhiyya* (Kuwait), 13:185–200; also *Encyclopaedia of Islam* II, 10:134–36 [R. Strothmann].

al-fiqh and on the general principles of the law, as well as in monographs written on this topic.[22] As such, the principle is in line with general Islamic legal canons that instruct people to give priority to the more important of two considerations (*al-ahamm*)[23] or lesser harm (*al-ḍarar al-akhaff*).[24]

Muslim jurists of different tendencies and schools agree on the outlines of this principle, although most discuss it under the rubrics of *ikrāh* (duress), the other term used in the Qurʾān to address such situations,[25] and *iḍṭirār* (necessity), in cases involving life-threatening danger. For a community such as the supporters of the House of the Prophet, who faced severe repression for their entire history under both the Umayyad and the Abbasid caliphate, practicing precautionary secrecy was naturally essential to survival.

> عن أبي عبد الله قال: التقيّة في كلّ ضرورة، وصاحبها أعلم بها حين تنزل به.[26]
>
> [Abū Isḥāq al-Arrajānī:] Abū ʿAbd Allāh said, "Precautionary secrecy is for situations of no choice, and those who face them know best for themselves when such situations really exist."

> مسعدة بن صدقة عن أبي عبد الله[27] قال: للتقيّة مواضع من أزالها عن مواضعها لم تستقم له. مثل أن يكون قوم سوء، ظاهر حكمهم وفعلهم على غيرحكم الحقّ وفعله، فكلّ شيء يعمل المؤمن بينهم لمكان التقيّة ممّا لا يؤدّي إلى الفساد في الدين فإنّه جائز.[28]
>
> [Masʿada b. Ṣadaqa:] Abū ʿAbd Allāh said, "There are specific occasions for [practicing] precautionary secrecy that make it improper for anyone to do so outside of that context. For example, if there is a group of people who adopt rulings and actions that appear to be contrary to the truth, then any precautionary measure that a believer takes while among them that does not lead to corruption in religion is permissible."

---

22 For a list, see Modarressi, *Introduction to Shīʿī Law*, 117–19.

23 See, for instance, Fayyāḍ, *Muḥāḍarāt fī uṣūl al-fiqh*, 3:77–88; also Ṣaffār, *Fiqh al-maṣāliḥ wa'l-mafāsid*.

24 See, for instance, Suyūṭī, *al-Ashbāh wa'l-naẓāʾir fī qawāʿid wa-furūʿ fiqh al-Shāfiʿiyya*, 87–88; Ibn Nujaym, *al-Ashbāh wa'l-naẓāʾir*, 76–77; Aḥmad al-Zarqā, *Sharḥ al-qawāʿid al-fiqhiyya*, 199–203; Āl Kāshif al-Ghiṭāʾ, *Taḥrīr al-Majalla*, 1:146.

25 Qurʾān 16:106. See further Abou El Fadl, "Law of Duress"; Syed, *Coercion and Responsibility*.

26 Aḥmad b. Muḥammad b. ʿĪsā, *Nawādir*, 73; Ibn Bābawayh, *Faqīh*, 3:230.

27 Possibly عن جعفر بن محمّد, as in other reports quoted by this transmitter from Jaʿfar al-Ṣādiq (Modarressi, *Tradition and Survival*, 1:320). As noted earlier, the formula of عن أبي عبد الله in this and a few other transmissions by this transmitter may be a later addition by either the author of the source or a copyist.

28 Kulaynī, *Kāfī*, 2:168.

سماعة عن أبي عبد الله قال: إذا حلف الرجل تقيّةً لم يضرّه إذا هو أُكره واضطرّ اليه. ليس شيء ممّا حرّم الله إلّا وقد أحلّه لمن اضطرّ اليه.[29]

[Samāʿa:] Abū ʿAbd Allāh said, "If a person swears [to something] out of precautionary secrecy, it is harmless if he was coerced and compelled to do so. God did not prohibit anything without making it lawful for someone who has no choice."

أبو الصباح [الكِناني]عن جعفر بن محمّد قال: ما صنعتم من شيء أو حلفتم عليه من يمين في تقيّة فأنتم منه في سعة.[30]

[Abū Ṣabāḥ al-Kinānī:] Jaʿfar b. Muḥammad said, "If you did or swore to do something out of precautionary secrecy, you are not bound by it."

In cases of severe duress involving an imminent threat to one's life, a report from Jaʿfar al-Ṣādiq forbids one from saving one's own life by putting someone else's life in danger.[31]

أبو حمزة الثمالي قال: قال أبو عبد الله: إنّما جعلت التقيّة ليحقن بها الدم، فإذا بلغت الدم فلا تقيّة.[32]

[Abū Ḥamza al-Thumālī:] Abū ʿAbd Allāh said, "Precautionary secrecy was set up in order to spare blood. If blood is to be spilled, precautionary secrecy does not apply."

The first of the above-quoted statements from Jaʿfar al-Ṣādiq bans the practice of *taqiyya* not only in cases in which it would cause harm to another but also in cases in which it could lead to "corruption in religion." This latter concept is understood to mean serious damage to an essential feature of Islam or the faith of the Muslim community.[33] Extending the logic of these two types of fundamental values, many jurists and schools also ban rape

29 Aḥmad b. Muḥammad b. ʿĪsā, *Nawādir*, 75.

30 Kulaynī, *Kāfī*, 7:442.

31 See *Mawsūʿat al-fiqh al-Islāmī* (Qum), 31:299–301 and the sources cited in the footnotes. See also 31:317–33, where all other proposed exceptions to the general rule of *taqiyya* other than putting someone else's life in danger are listed and disputed. For Sunnī views on the legal status of homicide in situations of *taqiyya*, see especially Ibn Ḥajar, *Fatḥ al-Bārī*, 12:314–15.

32 Ṭūsī, *Tahdhīb*, 6:173.

33 See further Khumaynī, *Risāla fī al-taqiyya*, 177–78.

and fornication under any circumstances,[34] even if the alternative is loss of one's life.[35]

III. *Mutʿa* Marriage

Mutʿa marriage, a time-limited union, has been a hotly debated topic in sectarian disputes between the two main divisions of Islam for the past many centuries. This issue is also addressed here only inasmuch as the study of the legal viewpoints of Jaʿfar al-Ṣādiq is concerned. As in the rest of the book, this study is based on reports deemed reliable by the standards mentioned in the introduction. The opinions and arguments presented here represent the understanding of those reports held by the present author and may or may not agree with the majority opinions of the Jaʿfarī school in its post-formative period.

We begin with Ibn Qudāma's concise description of the differences of opinion on this issue among the Muslim jurists of the first and second centuries:

---

34 The Sunnī schools disagreed among themselves over this question. For a useful summary of their disagreements see *al-Mawsūʿa al-fiqhiyya* (Kuwait), 6:106–7, 108, 110, 119, 13:195. It is reported that the Mālikī jurist Saḥnūn b. Saʿīd (d. 240) allowed copulation with a consentS ing, unmarried woman under duress (*al-Mawsūʿa al-fiqhiyya*, 6:109). Others do not make a clear distinction between rape and fornication as they focus on the criminal consequences of the act in the form of the *ḥadd* punishment that they generally consider to be the same in both cases. On this last point about the *ḥadd* punishment, Mālikīs and Ḥanbalīs are generally more strict and Ḥanafīs and Shāfiʿīs more flexible (*al-Mawsūʿa al-fiqhiyya*, 24:32). Sunnī sources at times also discuss hypothetical alternatives, such as killing the coercer, if possible, or committing suicide in cases in which the victim is coerced to submit to rape; see, for instance, Ibn al-Qayyim, *al-Ṭuruq al-ḥukmiyya* (Jeddah, 1428 [2007]), 1:137–38. (For Sunnī opinions on rape under duress, cf. Ibn al-ʿArabī, *Aḥkām al-Qurʾān*, 3:160.)

35 The Ibāḍīs, in particular, insist that duress does not make rape permissible. See Basyawī, *Jāmiʿ*, 4:203:

> وعنه أيضًا في رجل يأخذه السلطان الجائر فيقول له: أقتل هذا الرجل وإلّا قتلتك أو إزن بهذه المرأة وإلّا قتلتك، قال: هذا غير معذور.
>
> Regarding the situation of a man who is taken by a tyrant who says to him, "Kill this man or I will kill you," or "Rape/have sex with this woman or I will kill you," he said, "This man is not excused."

See also Kindī, *Muṣannaf*, 10:262 (whence with variations, Shiqṣī, *Manhaj al-ṭālibīn*, 2:624):

> فإن كلّفه الزنا وخاف القتل لم يجز له ذلك لأنّ الزنا ظلم للمرأة فليس له ظلم غيره لينجّي نفسه، ولو طاوعته المرأة ورضيت به، لأنّه ظلم لها لما يلحقها من العيب القبيح والإثم العظيم.
>
> If he [the coercer] requires him [the coerced] to rape or have sex with a woman and he fears being killed, it is [still] not permitted for him to do it because it is an injustice against the woman, and he may not, in order to save himself, allow an injustice to be committed against someone else. This is so even if the woman submits and consents, because it is an injustice against her due to the severe disgrace and grave sin that will remain attached to her.

However, the Ibāḍīs, too, refrain from applying the *ḥadd* punishment to someone who violates that prohibition in such extreme circumstances (Basyawī, 4:201; Kindī, 10:263).

معنى نكاح المتعة أن يتزوّج المرأة مدّةً، مثل أن يقول زوّجتك ابنتي شهرًا أو سنةً أو إلى انقضاء الموسم أو قدوم الحاجّ وشبهه، سواء كانت المدّة معلومةً أو مجهولة. فهذا نكاح باطل. نصّ عليه أحمد وقال: نكاح المتعة حرام. وقال أبو بكر: فيها رواية أخرى أنّها مكروهة غير حرام. لأنّ ابن منصور سأل أحمد عنها فقال: يجتنبها أحبّ إليّ. قال: فظاهر هذا الكراهة دون التحريم. وغير أبي بكر من أصحابنا يمنع هذا ويقول في المسألة رواية واحدة في تحريمها. وهذا قول عامّة الصحابة والفقهاء، وممّن روى عنه تحريمها عمر وعلي وابن عمر وابن مسعود وابن الزبير. قال ابن عبد البرّ: وعلى تحريم المتعة مالك وأهل المدينة وأبو حنيفة في أهل العراق، والأوزاعي في أهل الشام، والليث في أهل مصر، والشافعي وسائر أصحاب الآثار. وقال زُفر: يصحّ النكاح ويبطل الشرط. وحُكي عن ابن عبّاس أنّها جائزة. وعليه أكثر أصحابه وعطاء وطاووس.[36] وبه قال ابن جُريج. وحُكي ذلك عن أبي سعيد الخُدري وجابر. وإليه ذهب الشيعة لأنّه قد ثبت أنّ النبى – صلّى الله عليه وسلّم – أذن فيها. ورُوي أنّ عمر قال: متعتان كانتا على عهد رسول الله – صلّى الله عليه و سلّم – أنا أنهى عنهما وأعاقب عليهما: متعة النساء ومتعة الحجّ.[37]

Mutʿa[38] marriage means that a woman is married for a [limited] period. For example, a man may say, "I wed you to my daughter for one month, or one year, or until the end of the [*ḥajj*] season, or until the arrival of the *ḥajj* pilgrims," or the like, whether the duration is known or unknown.[39] This is an invalid marriage. Aḥmad [b. Ḥanbal] stipulated this and said, "*Mutʿa* marriage is unlawful." Abū Bakr [al-Khallāl], however, said, "According to another report, it is reprehensible but not unlawful, because Ibn Manṣūr [Isḥāq al-Marwazī al-Kawsaj] asked Aḥmad about it and he said, 'I prefer that he avoid it.' The apparent meaning of this [statement] is reprehensibility, not unlawfulness." Our colleagues other than Abū Bakr forbid this [type

36 In our edition of the source, this sentence appears as وعليه أكثر أصحاب عطاء وطاووس. I prefer the variant وعليه أكثر أصحابه وعطاء وطاووس, which agrees with three manuscripts of the work, as noted in the source (Ibn Qudāma, *Mughnī*, 10:46), footnote 5.

37 Ibn Qudāma, *Mughnī*, 10:46.

38 According to an Ibāḍī jurist of the sixth century (Kindī, *Muṣannaf*, 9:449, whence Shiqṣī, *Manhaj al-ṭālibīn*, 15:388), this word should be pronounced *mitʿa* in the context of marriage but *mutʿa* in the context of the *ḥajj*. This was perhaps the Omānī dialect at the time, as none of the major Arabic dictionaries that I checked (such as Ibn Manẓūr's *Lisān al-ʿArab* and Zabīdī's *Tāj al-ʿarūs*) confirm it.

39 Supporters of the legality of this type of marriage usually require the exact duration of the contract to be clearly stipulated.

of marriage] and narrate [from Aḥmad] a single opinion prohibiting it. This is the opinion of the overwhelming majority of the Companions and the jurists. Among those who reportedly considered *mutʿa* unlawful were ʿUmar, ʿAlī,[40] Ibn ʿUmar, Ibn Masʿūd, and Ibn al-Zubayr. Ibn ʿAbd al-Barr said, "Mālik and the jurists of Medina maintained the unlawfulness of *mutʿa*,[41] as did Abū Ḥanīfa among the jurists of Iraq, Awzāʿī of the jurists of Syria, Layth of the jurists of Egypt, and Shāfiʿī and the rest of the Traditionists." Zufar said, "The marriage is valid, but the condition [that is, the term stipulated] is void." It was reported that Ibn ʿAbbās held it to be permissible,[42] and this was the view of

---

40 Supporters of the legality of *mutʿa* challenge the authority of this ascription, as will be seen below.

41 The Ḥanafī jurist Abū Bakr al-Sarakhsī (d. 483) in his *Kitāb al-Mabsūṭ* (5:152) and, following him, a number of later Ḥanafī authors (e.g., Marghīnānī, *Hidāya*, 1:195; Zaylaʿī, *Tabyīn al-ḥaqāʾiq*, 2:489; Taftāzānī, *Sharḥ al-Maqāṣid*, 5:283) ascribed the opposite view to Mālik, that is, that *mutʿa* is legal. The ascription was rejected by later Ḥanafīs (e.g., ʿAynī, *Bināya*, 5:63; Ibn al-Humām, *Fatḥ al-Qadīr*, 3:247; Ibn al-Shalabī, *Ḥāshiyat al-Shaykh al-Shalabī*, 2:489) on the grounds that the view is not mentioned in any Mālikī work (ʿAynī, 5:63). It is, however, mentioned as one of Mālik's two opinions on the topic by the prominent Mālikī judge and jurist of the early sixth century, Ibn al-ʿArabī, in his *al-Qabas fī sharḥ Muwaṭṭaʾ Mālik b. Anas* (2:714):

فإذا فعلها أحد رُجم في مشهور المذهب، وفي رواية أخرى عن مالك: لا يُرجم لأنّ نكاح المتعة ليس بحرام.

> One who practices *mutʿa* will be stoned according to the predominant opinion in the [Mālikī] school, but according to another report attributed to Mālik, the person will not be stoned because *mutʿa* marriage is not forbidden.

Abū ʿAbd Allāh al-Qurṭubī, who quoted the statement by Ibn al-ʿArabī in his *Jāmiʿ* (6:220), tried to minimize its significance by pointing to an alleged alternative usage of the term "forbidden" (*ḥarām*) in Mālik's legal vocabulary. Nevertheless, a reference in Najm al-Dīn al-Ṭarsūsī, *Tuḥfat al-Turk*, 90, suggests that the legality of *mutʿa* remained as an opinion among Mālikī jurists until the mid-eighth century. The author advises a ruler to make sure that any Mālikī jurist whom he intends to appoint as a judge does not hold any of a number of opinions known to be supported in Mālikī law:

وإن كان مالكيًّا فينبغي أن ينصّ له في تقليده على أنّه لا يحكم بحلّ نكاح المتعة.

> If [the judge is going to be] a Mālikī, [the ruler] should stipulate in his mandate that [the judge] will not make a decision [on the basis] of the legality of *mutʿa* marriage.

42 This is reported in many early sources. See, as just as one example, Shāfiʿī, *Umm* [Manṣūra, 2001], 10:257.

most[43] of his[44] followers, along with ʿAṭāʾ and Ṭāwūs; it was also the opinion of Ibn Jurayj. [Acceptance of its legality] was also attributed to Abū Saʿīd al-Khudrī and Jābir [b. ʿAbd Allāh al-Anṣārī]. This view was adopted by the Shīʿa because it was established that the Prophet (may God's prayer and peace be upon him) permitted it, but ʿUmar reportedly said, "There were two *mutʿas* during the time of the Messenger of God (may God's prayer and peace be upon him). I forbid both and will punish both: the *mutʿa* of women, and the *mutʿa* of the *ḥajj*."[45]

Ibn Qudāma then quotes several reports suggesting that the legality of *mutʿa* was already abrogated by the Prophet himself later in his life. The main problem with these reports is that they contradict one another when it comes to the timing and occasion of the abrogation; their settings vary from the Battle of Khaybar in the year 7 to the Prophet's Farewell Pilgrimage in the year 10, with other times and events in between also proposed as the context of the abrogation.[46] The title of the chapter on *mutʿa* marriage in Muslim's *Ṣaḥīḥ* attempts to harmonize the contradictory reports:

باب نكاح المتعة وبيان أنّه أُبيح ثمّ نُسخ، ثمّ أُبيح ثمّ نُسخ، واستقرّ تحريمه إلى يوم القيامة.[47]

---

43 Others, however, ascribe this opinion to *all* students of Ibn Abbās. See, for instance, Ibn ʿAbd al-Barr, *Istidhkār*, 16:295:

أصحاب ابن عبّاس من أهل مكّة واليمن كلّهم يرون المتعة حلالاً على مذهب ابن عبّاس.

The companions of Ibn ʿAbbās among the people of Mecca and Yemen all consider *mutʿa* marriage to be permissible, following the opinion of Ibn ʿAbbās.

See also Averroes, *Bidāyat al-mujtahid*, 4:165:

وتبع ابن عبّاس على القول بها أصحابه من أهل مكّة وأهل اليمن.

The companions of Ibn ʿAbbās among the people of Mecca and Yemen followed him in holding this opinion.

44 I prefer the variation noted in Ibn Qudāma, *Mughnī*, 10:46n5, which agrees with three manuscripts of the work; I thus read the phrase as أصحابه وعطاء وطاووس, rather than as أصحاب عطاء وطاووس.

45 The statement quoted from ʿUmar is found in Abū Hilāl al-ʿAskarī, *Awāʾil*, 1:240; Saʿīd b. Manṣūr, *Sunan*, 3:252; Abū ʿAwwāna, *Musnad*, 2:338; Bayhaqī, *Sunan*, 7:335. See further Muttaqī al-Hindī, *Kanz al-ʿummāl*, 16:519, and the sources cited therein. See also a variant in Muslim, *Ṣaḥīḥ*, no. 1249, and other sources mentioned in the editors' footnote in Aḥmad b. Ḥanbal, *Musnad*, 22:365.

46 For details, see Ibn Ḥajar, *Fatḥ al-Bārī*, 19:203–5, who worked hard, though not very convincingly, to reconcile the contradictory reports. See also Ibn ʿAbd al-Barr, *Istidhkār*, 16:289; Qāḍī ʿIyāḍ, *Ikmāl al-muʿlim*, 4:535–37; Nawawī, *Sharḥ Ṣaḥīḥ Muslim*, 9:189–93; Averroes, *Bidāyat al-mujtahid*, 4:165.

47 Muslim, *Ṣaḥīḥ*, "The Book of Marriage," chapter 3, on *mutʿa* marriage (nos. 1404–7). See also Shāfiʿī as quoted in Thaʿlabī, *al-Kashf waʾl-bayān*, 3:288.

Chapter on *mutʿa* marriage and clarification that it was permitted and then abrogated, then permitted and then abrogated, and that its unlawfulness was then established until the Day of Resurrection.

Ibn al-ʿArabī provides a more dramatic evaluation of the case:

نكاح المتعة من أغرب ما ورد في الشريعة، فإنّه نُسخ مرّتين. وليس لها أخت في الشريعة إلّا مسألة القبلة فإنّ النسخ طرأ عليها مرّتين.[48]

Mutʿa marriage is one of the strangest matters to come into the *sharīʿa*, for it was abrogated twice. It has no parallel in the *sharīʿa*, except in the case of the *qibla*, which was [also] abrogated twice.

However, the disparities among the reports were too great to be removed by titular suggestions or comments such as those of Muslim and Ibn al-ʿArabī.[49] As phrased, the reports require a person to believe that *mutʿa* was legalized and prohibited *seven* different times by the Prophet.[50] The Andalusian Mālikī jurist Abū al-ʿAbbās al-Qurṭubī, also known as Ibn al-Muzayyin, comments on this phenomenon:

48 Ibn al-ʿArabī, *Qabas*, 2:713–14 (whence Qurṭubī, *Jāmiʿ*, 6:216, 217). See also Ibn al-ʿArabī, *Aḥkām al-Qurʾān*, 2:389, where he says:

وأمّا متعة النساء فهي من غرائب الشريعة.

As for the *mutʿa* of women, it is one of the strange matters of the *sharīʿa*.

49 See Ibn ʿAbd al-Barr, *Istidhkār*, 16:289:

وأمّا نهيه عن نكاح المتعة ففيه اختلاف واضطراب كثير.

As for his prohibition of *mutʿa* marriage, there is much disagreement and confusion over it.

See also Averroes, *Bidāyat al-mujtahid*, 4:165.

50 Qurṭubī, *Jāmiʿ*, 6:216–18 clearly refers to Ibn al-Muzayyin's conclusion as quoted in the next paragraph above:

وقال غيره ممّن جمع طرق الأحاديث فيها انّها تقتضي التحليل والتحريم سبع مرّات.

Another [scholar] who gathered the different transmissions of the reports regarding *mutʿa* said that they entail that it was permitted and outlawed seven times.

However, Fakhr al-Dīn al-Rāzī is very much against these suggestions in his *Tafsīr*, 10:52:

وقول من قال إنّه حصل التحليل مرارًا والنسخ مرارًا ضعيف لم يقل به أحد المعتبرين إلّا الّذين أرادوا إزالة التناقض عن هذه الروايات.

The opinion of those who held that it [*mutʿa*] was rendered permissible several times and abrogated several times is weak. No one whose opinion is worthy of consideration held this view, except for those who tried to harmonize these contradictory reports.

وقد اختلفت الروايات واضطربت في وقت إباحتها وتحريمها اضطرابًا شديدًا، بحيث يتعذّر فيها التلفيق ولا يحصل معه تحقيق. فعن ابن أبي عَمرة أنّها كانت في أوّل الإسلام. ومن رواية سلمة أنّها كانت عام أوطاس، ومن رواية سَبرة إباحتها يوم الفتح – وهما متقاربان – ثمّ تحريمها حينئذٍ في حديثيهما، ومن رواية علي تحريمها يوم خيبر – وهو قبل الفتح، وفي كتاب مسلم عن علي نهيه – صلّى الله عليه وسلّم – عنها في غزوة تبوك، وقد رَوى أبو داود من حديث الربيع بن سَبرة النهي عنها في حجّة الوداع، ورُوي أيضًا عن الحسن البصري أنّها ما حلّت قطّ إلّا في عُمرة القضاء – ورُوي هذا عن سَبرة أيضًا.[51]

The reports concerning when it [that is, *mutʿa*] was permitted and then declared unlawful are conflicting and very confused, such that they are impossible to reconcile and none can be verified. Ibn Abī ʿAmra said it occurred in the beginning of Islam. But Salama reported that it occurred during the year of [the Battle of] Awṭās. And according to the report from Sabra, it was permitted on the day of the conquest [of Mecca]—the two latter dates being close—and then the prohibition of *mutʿa* occurred on the same occasion in both reports. According to the report attributed to ʿAlī, it was prohibited on the day of Khaybar, which was before the conquest [of Mecca]. Muslim's book attributed a report to ʿAlī according to which the Prophet (may God's prayer and peace be upon him) prohibited it during the Battle of Tabūk. Abū Dāwūd transmitted a report from Rabīʿ b. Sabra that it was prohibited during the Farewell Pilgrimage. It was also reported from Ḥasan al-Baṣrī that it was never made permissible except during the ʿUmrat al-Qaḍāʾ [in the year 7], a report that was attributed to Sabra as well.

Another major problem was that a good number of the early authorities of Islam did not believe that the prohibition came from the Prophet. In Ibn Ḥazm's words:

لا يجوز نكاح المتعة، وهو النكاح إلى أجل، وكان حلالًا على عهد رسول الله – صلّى الله عليه وسلّم – ثمّ نسخها الله تعالى على لسان رسوله نسخًا باتًّا إلى يوم القيامة. وقد ثبت على تحليلها بعد رسول الله – صلّى الله عليه وسلّم – جماعة من السلف – رضي الله عنهم – رواه جابر بن عبد الله عن جميع الصحابة مدّة رسول الله – صلّى الله

51 Ibn al-Muzayyin, *Mufhim*, 4:92.

عليه وسلّم – ومدّة أبي بكر وعمر إلى قرب آخر خلافة عمر. واختُلف في إباحتها عن ابن الزبير، وعن علي فيها توقّف، وعن عمر بن الخطاب أنّه إنّما أنكرها إذا لم يشهد عليها عدلان فقط وأباحها بشهادة عدلين. ومن التابعين: طاووس، وعطاء، وسعيد ابن جبير،[52] وسائر فقهاء مكة – أعزّها الله.[53] وقد تقصّينا الآثار المذكورة في كتابنا الموسوم بالإيصال. وصحّ تحريمها عن ابن عمر وعن ابن أبي عمرة الأنصاري واختلف فيها عن علي وعمر وابن عباس وابن الزبير.[54]

Mutʿa marriage is impermissible, being a marriage with a time limit. It was permissible during the time of the Messenger of God (may God's prayer and peace be upon him), and then God, the Exalted, abrogated it firmly through the words of His Messenger, until the Day of Resurrection. A group of early Muslims (may God be pleased with them) affirmed its permissibility after the time of the Messenger of God (may God's prayer and peace be upon him). Jābir b. ʿAbd Allāh reported [a belief in] its permissibility from all the Companions during the time of the Messenger of God (may God's prayer and peace be upon him), and in the time of Abū Bakr and ʿUmar until late in ʿUmar's caliphate. There is disagreement as to whether Ibn al-Zubayr considered it permissible, and ʿAlī is quoted as having suspended judgment with respect to *mutʿa*. It is said that [even] ʿUmar b. al-Khaṭṭāb censured it only if it was done without two upright witnesses, and he permitted it with the condition of two upright witnesses. Among the Successors, Ṭāwūs, ʿAṭāʾ, Saʿīd b. Jubayr, and the rest of the jurists of Mecca (may God honor it) [allowed *mutʿa*]. We collected all the mentioned reports in our book entitled *al-Īṣāl*. It has been verified as prohibited in the view of Ibn ʿUmar and Ibn Abī ʿAmra al-Anṣārī,

52 وعمران بن حصين وابن عبّاس وبعض الصحابة وطائفة من أهل البيت (Qurṭubī, *Jāmiʿ*, 6:220, quoting Abū Bakr al-Ṭurṭūshī; cf. Thaʿlabī, *al-Kashf waʾl-bayān*, 3:287 where the text reads ابن عبّاس وبعض أصحابه; one of the two forms of بعض الصحابة and بعض أصحابه is most likely a corruption of the other). Ibn Ḥabīb, *Muḥabbar*, 289 adds the name of Zayd b. Thābit as another Companion who supported the legality of *mutʿa*. Quoting a book by the Shāfiʿī jurist and *mutakallim* Ḥusayn b. ʿAlī b. Yazīd al-Karābīsī (d. 248), Shaykh al-Mufīd (d. 413) in his *al-Masāʾil al-Ṣāghāniyya*, 36–37 has a long list of those in favor of *mutʿa* in the first two centuries.

53 See also Ibn Ḥajar, *Talkhīṣ al-ḥabīr*, 3:380 quoting ʿAbd al-Razzāq from Maʿmar [b. Rāshid] on "Qawl ahl Makka fī al-mutʿa." See also Ḥākim al-Naysābūrī, *Maʿrifat ʿulūm al-ḥadīth*, 251, quoting Awzāʿī, "Min qawl ahl al-Ḥijāz al-mutʿa bi al-nisāʾ"; Bayhaqī, *Sunan*, 10:356.

54 Ibn Ḥazm, *Muḥallā*, 9:519–20. See also Tirmidhī, *Sunan*, 2:416 (under *ḥadīth* no. 1121), where he says:

وأمر أكثر أهل العلم مع تحريم المتعة.

The majority of the people of knowledge maintain the unlawfulness of *mutʿa*.

but there is disagreement regarding the views of ʿAlī, ʿUmar, Ibn ʿAbbās, and Ibn al-Zubayr.[55]

It was as if the jurists of Mecca and other students of Ibn ʿAbbās had never heard of the event that the reports claim happened in the lifetime of the Prophet, namely, the abrogation of the legality of *mutʿa*. The nature of the subject, however, required that a large portion of society, not only a few individuals, would have heard about the ban if one had been issued.[56]

---

55 Numerous notables in the post-formative period of Islamic law are mentioned as supporting the continued legality of *mutʿa*. Here are a few examples:

Early in the third century, when Yaḥyā b. al-Aktham (d. 242) was the judge of Baṣra (around the year 202, according to the biographical sources), he met a *shaykh* who held that *mutʿa* was still legal (Rāghib al-Iṣbahānī, *Muḥāḍarāt al-udabāʾ*, 3:214).

In his *Fiṣal* (5:66), Ibn Ḥazm names an older contemporary of his, Ismāʿīl b. ʿAbd Allāh al-Ruʿaynī, with certain unusual ideas of Muʿtazilī provenance in doctrinal matters, who in the early fifth century still supported the legality of *mutʿa*:

> إسماعيل بن عبد الله الرعيني. وكان من المجتهدين في العبادة، المنقطعين في الزهد. أدركته ولكن لم ألقه. وصحّ عندنا أنّه كان يقول بنكاح المتعة. وهذا لا يقدح في إيمانه ولا في عدالته لو قاله مجتهدًا ولم تقم عليه الحجّة بنسخه. وإنّما ذكرنا ذلك عند ما جرى ذكره لغرابة هذا القول اليوم وقلّة القائلين به من الناس.
>
> Ismāʿīl b. ʿAbd Allāh al-Ruʿaynī. He exerted himself in worship and was dedicated to asceticism. I lived at the same time as he did, but never met him. It was verified among us that he used to maintain the permissibility of *mutʿa*, but this does not disparage his faith or uprightness if he had said it as a *mujtahid* and the evidence for its abrogation was not strong enough in his opinion to prove it. We noted this [matter] when we mentioned him because of the rarity of this opinion today, as there are few who support it.

Imam al-Shāfiʿī, too, agreed in his *Kitāb al-Umm* ([Manṣūra, 2001], 7:511) with the point that a belief in the permissibility of *mutʿa* did not undermine one's uprightness:

> المستحلّ لنكاح المتعة والمفتي بها والعامل بها ممّن لا تردّ شهادته.
>
> The testimony of a person who considers *mutʿa* to be lawful, issues *fatwās* [in support of its legality], or practices it [personally] cannot be rejected [in an Islamic court].

Among other groups, the Ibāḍī Rabīʿ b. Ḥabīb al-Azdī al-Farāhīdī (late second century) considered *mutʿa* legal (Ḥārithī, *al-ʿUqūd al-fiḍḍiyya*, 156), as did a number of the school's later jurists:

> يروى ذلك عن ابن عبّاس ومحمّد بن محبوب وأبي صفرة ونبهان بن عثمان وأبي المؤثر وأبي الحواري رحمهم الله، ورأوا أنّ تزويج المتعة حلال جائز. وأخبر أبو الحواري عن عبد الملك بن صفرة أنّه قال: لو أجد تزويج المتعة لفعلت ذلك. وكذلك يروى عن الشيخ أبي الحسن رحمه الله أنّ تزويج المتعة حلال غير منسوخ.
>
> This [opinion] is quoted from Ibn ʿAbbās, Muḥammad b. Maḥbūb, Abū Ṣufra, Nabhān b. ʿUthmān, Abū al-Muʾaththir, and Abū al-Ḥawārī, all of whom held that the marriage of *mutʿa* was lawful. Abū al-Hawārī quoted from ʿAbd al-Malik b. Ṣufra, who said, "If I find [the opportunity for] a marriage of *mutʿa*, I will do it." It is also reported from Shaykh Abū al-Ḥasan that the marriage of *mutʿa* is lawful and not abrogated (Shiqṣī, *Manhaj al-ṭālibīn*, 15:386; see also Kindī, *Muṣannaf*, 19:7, 8–9).

The Zaydīs and the Ismāʿīlīs agreed with the majority Sunnī opinion. For the former, see Yaḥyā al-Hādī, *Aḥkām*, 1:349–51; Aḥmad b. ʿĪsā, *Amālī*, 3:10–15; ʿAlawī, *al-Jāmiʿ al-kāfī*, 4:59–62. For the latter, see Qāḍī Nuʿmān, *Daʿāʾim al-Islām*, 2:226–27.

56 See especially Shīrāzī, *Lumaʿ*, 216.

At the same time, one can clearly observe an attempt by various *ḥadīth* transmitters who were active in the late first and early second centuries and unaware of similar efforts by others to suggest that *mutʿa* had indeed been abrogated already by the Prophet and not, as seems to have been commonly believed at the time,[57] by a decree from ʿUmar. For ʿUmar to have canceled an endorsement of the Prophet would have posed a major doctrinal problem, and that, in turn, would have offered an enormous boost to the anti-orthodox trend in Islam to attack their rivals, a potential that has been used since the early centuries down to our own time. The case of *mutʿa* in fact offers a spectacular example of how *ḥadīth* developed as an effective tool in early sectarian debates[58] of the late Umayyad and

57 See Bayhaqī, *Sunan*, 7:325–38, where the author collects all reports he could find in connection with *mutʿa*, with a good number of them confirming that the practice was banned by ʿUmar.

58 Indeed any kind of debate, even if not sectarian in the real sense of the word. Consider this interesting exchange between Abū Ḥanīfa and Awzāʿī, two well-known Muslim jurists of the second century, as quoted in Abū Muḥammad al-Ḥārithī, *Musnad Abī Ḥanīfa*, 144, and Sarakhsī, *Mabsūṭ*, 1:14:

سفيان بن عيينة قال: اجتمع أبو حنيفة والأوزاعي في دار الخيّاطين بمكّة، فقال الأوزاعي لأبي حنيفة: ما بالكم لا ترفعون أيديكم في الصلاة عند الركوع وعند الرفع منه؟ فقال أبو حنيفة: لأجل أنّه لم يصحّ عن رسول الله – صلّى الله عليه وسلّم – أنّه كان يرفع يديه إذا افتتح الصلاة وعند الركوع وعند الرفع منه. فقال الأوزاعي: كيف لم يصحّ وقد حدّثني الزهري عن سالم عن أبيه [عبد الله] بن عمر أنّ رسول الله – صلّى الله عليه وسلّم – كان يرفع يديه إذا افتتح الصلاة وعند الركوع وعند الرفع منه؟ قال أبو حنيفة: حدّثنا حمّاد عن إبراهيم عن علقمة والأسود عن عبد الله بن مسعود أنّ النبي – صلّى الله عليه و سلّم – كان لا يرفع يديه إلّا عند الافتتاح ثمّ لا يعود. فقال الأوزاعي: أحدّثك عن الزهري عن سالم عن أبيه، وتقول: حدّثني حمّاد عن ابراهيم؟ فقال أبو حنيفة: كان حمّاد أفقه من الزهري، وكان إبراهيم أفقه من سالم، وعلقمة ليس دون ابن عمر. وعبد الله عبد الله. فسكت الأوزاعي.

[Sufyān b. ʿUyayna:] Abū Ḥanīfa and Awzāʿī met in the House of the Tailors in Mecca (Dār al-Khayyāṭīn) [or alternatively Dār al-Ḥannāṭīn, as in Sūq al-Ḥannāṭīn, mentioned in Kulaynī, *Kāfī*, 5:404, possibly, but not necessarily, a corruption of Bāb al-Khayyāṭīn, one of the gates of Masjid al-Ḥarām (see Azraqī, *Taʾrīkh Makka*, 2:92), after which the area around the gate might have been known at the time simply as Khayyāṭīn]. Awzāʿī said to Abū Ḥanīfa, "What is with you not raising your hands during prayer when it comes time to bow and rise up afterward?" Abū Ḥanīfa said, "[I don't do it] because it has not been authentically transmitted that the Messenger of God (may God's prayer and peace be upon him) raised his hands when he commenced prayer, bowed, and rose up afterward." Awzāʿī said, "How has it not been authentically transmitted when Zuhrī reported to me from Sālim, from his father, [ʿAbd Allāh] Ibn ʿUmar, that the Messenger of God (may God's prayer and peace be upon him) used to raise his hands when he commenced prayer, bowed down, and rose up afterward?" Abū Ḥanīfa said, "Ḥammād reported to us from Ibrāhīm, from ʿAlqama [b. Qays] and Aswad [b. Yazīd], from ʿAbd Allāh b. Masʿūd that the Prophet (may God's prayer and peace be upon him) did not raise his hands except when commencing the prayer and would not do it thereafter." Awzāʿī said, "I am reporting [this *ḥadīth*] to you on the authority of Zuhrī, according to Sālim from his father, and you say, 'Ḥammād reported to me from Ibrāhīm?!'" Abū Ḥanīfa said, "Ḥammād was more knowledgeable in law than Zuhrī, Ibrāhīm was more knowledgeable in

early Abbasid period to defend orthodoxy. Simultaneously, another body of material emerged, tailored toward the same end, as *ʿilm rijāl al-ḥadīth*, with the explicit aim of proving the authority and reliability of the transmitters who were active in defending orthodoxy in that period when orthodoxy needed it most.[59]

It is common in sectarian disputes like this to come across unpolished, contradictory reports that look as if they were put together in haste to abort an imminent or ongoing dispute.[60] The simple fact that a good number of these reports put the same message, though with discrepancies in timing and wording, in the mouths of those Companions—ʿAlī and Ibn ʿAbbās in particular—who were commonly believed to have objected to the caliph's decision in this case seems to be a clear attempt to rebuff the caliph's opponents in this matter,[61] and makes one extremely suspicious about the provenance of these reports.[62]

> law than Sālim, and ʿAlqama was no less [knowledgeable] than Ibn ʿUmar. And ʿAbd Allāh was ʿAbd Allāh." Then Awzāʿī fell silent.

Recall also what Ibn al-Jawzī (*Mawḍūʿāt*, 1:20–21) quoted from a number of *ḥadīth* fabricators who acknowledged that when they liked an opinion, they forged a *ḥadīth* to support it (إنّا كنّا إذا رأينا رأيًا جعلنا له حديثًا!).

59 See especially Muslim's introduction to his *Ṣaḥīḥ* (Cairo, [1955]), 15, quoting the Baṣran, Muḥammad b. Sīrīn (d. 110). It is interesting that at the same time that these internal struggles and purges were going on in the Sunnī tradition, a very similar trend in the Shīʿī tradition tried to block the legacy of the Ghulāt from entering mainstream Shīʿism. Many reports were circulated in this period to repudiate esotericism and the esoterics in the Shīʿī community, with a parallel tradition of *ʿilm rijāl al-ḥadīth* aimed at that end. See Modarressi, *Crisis and Consolidation*, 34–42.

60 For two similar cases, see Modarressi, "Early Debates" and "Common Ibāḍī-Shīʿite Legacy" (under the question of wiping over boots [*masḥ ʿalā al-khuffayn*]).

61 In our case, see, for instance, Khaṭṭābī's comment in Ibn Ḥajar, *Fatḥ al-Bārī*, 9:78:

> قال الخطّابي: تحريم المتعة كالإجماع إلّا عن بعض الشيعة، ولا يصحّ على قاعدتهم في الرجوع في المختلفات إلى علي وأهل بيته. فقد صحّ عن علي أنّها نُسخت.
>
> Khaṭṭābī said, "That *mutʿa* is prohibited is agreed upon by almost all [jurists], except by some of the Shīʿa. This does not go well with their principle that matters on which there is disagreement should be considered in light of [the opinions of] ʿAlī and his family. It is verified that ʿAlī held *mutʿa* to have been abrogated."

Also Zaylaʿī, *Tabyīn al-ḥaqāʾiq*, 2:489:

> إليه (يعني جواز المتعة) ذهبت الشيعة وخالفوا عليًا وأكثر الصحابة.
>
> The Shīʿa supported the permissibly of *mutʿa* and went against ʿAlī and most of the Companions.

Needless to say, the Shīʿa did not consider the reports ascribed to ʿAlī on the Prophet's abrogation of *mutʿa* to be reliable. See Aḥmad b. Muḥammad b. ʿĪsā, *Nawādir*, 82, 86; ʿAyyāshī, *Tafsīr*, 1:385.

62 Some of these reports seem to have been specifically designed to counteract similar reports promoted by the other camp. For example, a statement that is widely quoted in many early sources (e.g., ʿAbd al-Razzāq, *Muṣannaf*, 7:497, 500; Ibn Shabba, *Taʾrīkh al-Madīna al-munawwara*, 2:720; Abū Hilāl al-ʿAskarī, *Awāʾil*, 1:240; Ṭabarī, *Jāmiʿ al-bayān*, 8:176–78), as well as later works (e.g., Thaʿlabī, *al-Kashf waʾl-bayān* 3:286; Fakhr al-Dīn al-Rāzī,

Tafsīr, 10:50; and many others, some with minor variations) cited either ʿAlī or Ibn ʿAbbās as saying:

لولا أنّ عمر نهى عن المتعة ما زنى إلّا شقيّ.

Had ʿUmar not banned *mutʿa*, only a rogue would have fornicated.

The report appears in ʿAbd al-Razzāq, *Muṣannaf*, 7:497, as follows:

قال عطاء: سمعت ابن عبّاس يقول: يرحم الله عمر. ما كانت المتعة إلّا رحمة من الله عزّ وجلّ رحم بها أمّة محمّد – صلّى الله عليه وسلّم – فلولا نهيه عنها ما احتاج إلى الزنا إلّا شقيّ. قال: وكأنّي والله أسمع قوله: إلّا شقيّ.

[ʿAṭāʾ b. Abī Rabāḥ:] I heard Ibn ʿAbbās say, "May God have mercy on ʿUmar. *Mutʿa* was a mercy from God, the Mighty and Majestic, for the *umma* of Muḥammad (may God's prayer and peace be upon him). Had he [ʿUmar] not banned it, only a rogue would fornicate." [ʿAṭāʾ added:] By God, it is as if I [still] hear him saying, "only a rogue."

There is an edited version of the report that replaces the most frequently quoted ending of إلّا شقيّ ("only a rogue") with the similarly written phrase إلّا شَفي (whose possible definition follows), as quoted from ʿAbd al-Razzāq:

عبد الرزّاق عن ابن جريج عن عطا عن ابن عبّاس: ما كانت المتعة إلّا رحمة رحم الله بها أمّة محمّد، فلولا نهيه عنها ما احتاج إلى الزنا إلّا شفى.

First, this counterfeit version omits the beginning of the report (يرحم الله عمر), so that the pronoun "he" finds no reference except Muḥammad, to make the phrase imply that it was the Prophet who banned *mutʿa*, rather than ʿUmar, as in the original statement. And the trick worked. This is what Azharī, for instance, concluded from this edited version in his *Tahdhīb al-lugha* (11:424):

قلت: هذا الحديث يدلّ على أنّ ابن عبّاس علم أنّ النبيّ – صلّى الله عليه وسلّم – نهى عن المتعة بعد ما باح باحلالها.

I say: "The *ḥadīth* indicates that Ibn ʿAbbās knew that the Prophet (may God's prayer and peace be upon him) forbade *mutʿa* after having permitted it as lawful."

Second, a clear attempt was made to soften the powerful language of the original statement by taking the sting (إلّا شقيّ) out of it. There were, however, uncertainties about how this word شفى was to be pronounced, and what إلّا شفى meant. Zamakhsharī, *Fāʾiq*, 2:255 and Majd al-Dīn Ibn al-Athīr, *Nihāya*, 2:488 proposed "except a few," implying that some men without sufficient means to pay for a wife's dower while sizzling with lust would possibly storm out and rape the first woman they could find on the street!

قوله : «إلّا شفى (=شَفا)» أي: إلّا خطيئة من الناس لا يجدون شيئًا قليلاً يستحلّون به الفرج!

(Azharī, *Tahdhīb al-lugha*, 11:424; Harawī, *Gharībayn*, 3:279; whence Ibn al-Jawzī, *Gharīb al-ḥadīth*, 1:555; Zabīdī, *Tāj al-ʿarūs*, 38:382–83 [slightly modified]).

Ibn Manẓūr, *Lisān al-ʿArab*, 8:330 made a different suggestion:

«إلّا شفى» أي: إلّا أن يُشفي، أي يُشرف على الزنا. و«أشفى على الهلاك» : إذا أشرف عليه.

Abū Bakr al-Jaṣṣāṣ, *Aḥkām al-Qurʾān*, 3:96 quoted the revised text but without comment. This may indicate that he read and quoted the last word as إلّا شقي, but that the editor of the first edition of the work corrected it to إلّا شُفا on the basis of the dictionaries that he used.

The theory of abrogation used in this case by various transmitters and then authors to support their point of view also deserves special attention. The concept was used so liberally in various contexts that it raised the objection of scholars such as Ibn al-Qayyim (d. 751), who said:

المتأخّرون كلّما استبعدوا شيئًا قالوا منسوخ ومتروك العمل به![63]

> Whenever the later jurists deemed something unusual, they said it was abrogated and not applied in practice.

The sources tell us that temporary marriage was a pre-Islamic institution commonly practiced in Mecca.[64] Arabs from various parts of Arabia came to Mecca for a few months every year to worship their idols and engage in trade. They never took their women with them in order not to expose them to the hardships and dangers of traveling in the desert. But the Arab pilgrims and traders nonetheless needed someone to take care of them and look after their merchandise or possessions while in Mecca during their long stay. So each man would make a contract of temporary marriage with a local woman for the duration of his stay in return for a gift or the advance payment of a full year's or part of a year's maintenance for the woman.[65]

Finally, a similarly worded sentence, using a word with a root resembling that of the إلّا شفا / إلّا شَفى formula, was put together as a counterattack, with attribution to Saʿīd b. al-Musayyib, a late first-century jurist of Medina:

لولا أنّ عمر نهى عن المتعة لفشا الزنى (أو: «صار الزنا جهارًا»).

> Had ʿUmar not banned *mutʿa*, fornication would become widespread (or: would be done openly)! (Ibn Abī Shayba, *Muṣannaf*, 6:219; Ibn Shabba, *Taʾrīkh al-Madīna al-munawwara*, 2:720; Abū Hilāl al-ʿAskarī, *Awāʾil*, 1:240).

63 Ibn al-Qayyim, *al-Ṭuruq al-ḥukmiyya*, 1:228. Likewise, in his discussion of the concept of *ʿawl* (discussed later in this chapter) in *Muḥallā* (9:263), Ibn Ḥazm, who is against that legal theory, had this comment to make:

وبه يقول أبو حنيفة ومالك والشافعي وأحمد. وأصحاب هؤلاء القوم إذا اجتمع أمرهم على شيء كان أسهل شيءٍ عليهم دعوى الإجماع، فإن لم يمكنهم ذلك لم تكن عليهم مؤونة من دعوى أنّه قول الجمهور وأنّ خلافه شذوذ.

> This is the opinion held by Abū Ḥanīfa, Mālik, Shāfiʿī, and Aḥmad. When the followers of these people all agree on a matter, it is the easiest thing for them to claim consensus. If they are unable to do so, it costs them nothing to claim that it is the opinion of the overwhelming majority and so a contrary opinion is errant.

The first part is in line with Aḥmad b. Ḥanbal's statement in his *Masāʾil (Riwāyat ibnih ʿAbd Allāh)*, 439:

من ادّعى الإجماع فهو كاذب، لعلّ الناس قد اختلفوا.

> Whoever claims consensus is a liar; people might have disagreed.

64 Qurṭubī, *Jāmiʿ*, 6:219.

65 See the report from Ibn ʿAbbās about the background of this type of marriage in, for instance, Tirmidhī, *Sunan*, no. 1122; Bayhaqī, *Sunan*, 7:335. For further details, see the entry on *mutʿa* in *Encyclopaedia of Islam* II, 7:757–59 [W. Heffening].

The Prophet endorsed this institution as an accepted form of marriage in the society of his time.

So *mutʿa* was not a type of prostitution or "sex-for-money," so to speak. Otherwise, a Messenger of God would not have instructed his followers to practice it, even for the smallest length of time, in the ethical community of believers that he established. The repeated argument of the opponents of *mutʿa* that it was in effect a form of prostitution allowed by the Prophet as a temporary solution in this or that war because of necessity,[66] drawing on the legal precedent of the lawfulness of eating carrion under necessity, is likewise flawed in its implications.

First, the suggestion that it was in the context of war that the Prophet allowed *mutʿa* is an invention invoked to raise the issue of necessity. What the sources tell us is that the institution was older than Islam and that the Prophet simply allowed it to continue in society; they offer no evidence that the permission was provided in the exceptional circumstances of war. The wording of the statement by ʿUmar, as quoted above by Ibn Qudāma, clearly invalidates the claim that the Prophet legalized *mutʿa* only for a couple of days during a particular war:

> متعتان كانتا على عهد رسول الله.
>
> There were two *mutʿas* during the time of the Messenger of God.

---

66 See ʿAbd al-Razzāq, *Muṣannaf*, 7:506; Bukhārī, *Ṣaḥīḥ*, nos. 4615, 5071, 5075; Muslim, *Ṣaḥīḥ*, no. 1404 (and many other sources cited in the editors' footnote to Aḥmad b. Ḥanbal, *Musnad*, 6:337–38):

> عبد الله بن مسعود قال: كنّا نغزو مع رسول الله – صلّى الله عليه وسلّم – ليس لنا نساء [ونحن شباب]، فقلنا: ألا نستخصي؟ فنهانا عن ذلك، ثمّ رخّص لنا أن ننكح المرأة بالثوب إلى أجل.
>
> [ʿAbd Allāh b. Masʿūd:] We used to go on *jihād* campaigns with the Messenger of God (may God's prayer and peace be upon him) without our women accompanying us, while we were youths. We said [to the Prophet], "Should we not castrate ourselves?" He forbade us to do so, but then provided a dispensation for us to marry women for a [bridal gift of a] garment for a specified period of time.

Bayhaqī, *Sunan*, 7:326 points out that ʿAbd Allāh b. Masʿūd must have been almost forty years old at the time, no longer a youth who might have needed to castrate himself to gain comfort! After all, the solution that the Prophet allegedly offered would not fit the man, as he reportedly wished to live a monastic life by avoiding women altogether, and attempted once more to castrate himself independently from the question of war (Abū al-Shaykh, *Ṭabaqāt*, 3:500: one of the two stories seems to be a redaction of the other; see also Bukhārī, *Ṣaḥīḥ*, nos. 5063, 5073–74; Muslim, *Ṣaḥīḥ*, nos. 1400–1402). In any case, the picture that Sunnī *ḥadīth* tried to draw of helpless Muslim youth was overdramatized, aimed at convincing readers that the Prophet's permission of *mutʿa* was limited to an emergency situation similar to the extreme circumstances in which a Muslim is permitted to eat carrion or pork. As I argue later, however, there was an important difference between the two scenarios: eating carrion or pork would constitute a personal wrong that would not involve others or harm social morality, whereas fornication and prostitution would do both.

Second, the permission to eat carrion in situations of necessity represents a very different category. Eating carrion is a personal act involving no social or ethical harm, and the permission to do so applies when there is no other option short of death by starvation. But how could a prophet ever legalize *prostitution*? How could a prophet allow *fornication* when the choice of the far less evil option[67] of masturbation was available and allegedly often practiced by Muslim soldiers during the *jihād* wars of the caliphate and early Umayyad times?[68] If it was ever allowed by the Prophet, *mutʿa* must have been, in the non-Muslim Arab society of his time and earlier, an acceptable form of legal union between a man and a woman in a personal relationship. If it was allowed, for it to be consistent with the requirements of an Islamic union by definition, it must have entailed a minimum sense of mutual responsibility and protection, together with comfort and affection, as mentioned in the Qurʾān as the ultimate wisdom behind the union of a man and a woman as partners in a personal relationship,[69] even if for a specified span of time. It must have been a contract that embodied the major legal requirements of a marriage as understood at the time, as well as its attendant consequences, such as assignment of paternity for any children born into the marriage and possibly a waiting period for the woman after its termination.

According to one family of reports, the institution remained in effect during the lifetime of the Prophet and Abū Bakr,[70] until sometime in the

67 See the alleged response of Ibn ʿAbbās to a young man's question about masturbation (ʿAbd al-Razzāq, *Muṣannaf*, 7:390–91; Ibn Abī Shayba, *Muṣannaf*, 6:308–9):

نكاح الأمة خيرٌ منه وهو خيرٌ من الزنا.

> Marrying a slave woman is better than it [masturbation], and it [masturbation] is better than fornication.

See further Kulaynī, *Kāfī*, 5:540; Ṭūsī, *Tahdhīb*, 10:64; Ibn ʿĀbidīn, *Radd al-muḥtār*, 3:240; *al-Mawsūʿa al-fiqhiyya* (Kuwait), 4:98. See also Modarressi, "Nawādir-i fiqhī-yi Khawārij wa Muʿtazila," 218–20.

68 See ʿAbd al-Razzāq, *Muṣannaf*, 7:391, 392 (whence Ibn Ḥazm, *Muḥallā*, 11:263):

كانوا يفعلونه في المغازي. قال مجاهد: كان من مضى يأمرون شبابهم بالاستمناء يستعفّون بذلك.

> They [that is, the early Muslims] used to do it when they went on *jihād* campaigns. Mujāhid said, "The former generations would instruct their youth to masturbate in order for them to remain chaste."

69 Qurʾān 30:21. As discussed in works on *uṣūl al-fiqh*, the ultimate wisdom behind a law (*ḥikma* in Muslim legal terminology) is different from its ratio legis (*ʿilla*). The ratio legis produces the law by its very existence, but it is not necessary for a law to fulfill the legislator's ultimate wisdom. However, the wisdom of a law defines the nature and general patterns of a legal concept or commitment.

70 Muslim, *Ṣaḥīḥ*, no. 1405.

caliphate of ʿUmar, variously specified as the beginning,[71] the middle,[72] or the late years of his time.[73] It was banned by ʿUmar, creating a doctrinal dispute over whether a caliph had such authority to ban what the Prophet allowed. Some thought that the endorsement of the Prophet made *mutʿa* valid forever, while others contended that the practice was prohibited, with a majority subsequently being convinced that it was the Prophet himself who had prohibited it.[74] According to Ibn Qudāma in the paragraph cited above, the first opinion—that is, the continuing legality of *mutʿa*—was supported in the first century and the first half of the second century by the school of Ibn ʿAbbās, also known as the school of Mecca,[75] whereas the second opinion was held by a large majority of the schools of Medina and Iraq.

Jaʿfar al-Ṣādiq and his father represented the first tendency:[76]

71 Muslim, *Ṣaḥīḥ*, no. 1217; Ibn Shabba, *Taʾrīkh al-Madīna al-munawwara*, 2:719; Bayhaqī, *Sunan*, 7:335; Aḥmad b. Ḥanbal, *Musnad*, 1:437 (and other sources cited in the editors' footnote therein).

72 Muslim, *Ṣaḥīḥ*, no. 1023.

73 ʿAbd al-Razzāq, *Muṣannaf*, 7:497.

74 Muslim, *Ṣaḥīḥ*, nos. 1406–7.

75 Ibn Ḥazm, *Muḥallā*, 9:519–20; Ibn ʿAbd al-Barr, *Istidhkār*, 16:295; Ibn ʿAbd al-Barr, *Tamhīd*, 10:115. See also Qurṭubī, *Jāmiʿ*, 6:218, who mentions that the people of Mecca used to practice *mutʿa* frequently.

76 See also Ibn ʿAbd al-Barr, *Tamhīd*, 10:113.

أبو مريم عن أبي عبد الله قال: المتعة نزل بها القرآن[77] وجرت بها السنّة من رسول الله – صلّى الله عليه وآله وسلّم.[78]

[Abū Maryam:] Abū ʿAbd Allāh said, "*Mutʿa* was revealed in the Qurʾān and established in the Sunna by the Messenger of God (may God's prayer and peace be upon him and his Family)."

---

77 Qurʾān 4:24. See ʿAbd al-Razzāq, *Muṣannaf*, 7:498; Ṭabarī, *Jāmiʿ al-bayān*, 8:176 (from Suddī and Mujāhid), 177–78 (from Ibn ʿAbbās, Ubayy, Ḥakam [b. ʿUtayba], and Saʿīd b. Jubayr); Bayhaqī, *Sunan*, 7:335; also Averroes, *Bidāyat al-mujtahid*, 4:165, as well as works on different Qurʾānic readings, all reporting that Ibn ʿAbbās read this Qurʾānic passage (4:24) with an addition that specified the subject as temporary marriage:

فما استمتعتم به منهنّ إلى أجلٍ مسمّى.

And for what you enjoyed from those women for a specified time.

Ibn ʿAbd al-Barr, *Tamhīd*, 10:113, claims that Jaʿfar al-Ṣādiq and his father read the passage in the same way as Ibn ʿAbbās did, that is, with the those extra words. The passage appears in this longer form in two reports from Jaʿfar and his father in ʿAyyāshī, *Tafsīr*, 1:385–86; Sayyārī, *Qirāʾāt*, 41 (and other sources cited in the editors' endnotes at 109–10), but it is said that the three extra words represented an explanatory note, as if between brackets, rather than a part of the passage. These reports most probably represent their authors' understanding of the opinion of the Imams as supporting the reading of Ibn ʿAbbās. For that opinion, however, there was no need to accept the reading of Ibn ʿAbbās as valid. The ascription was therefore a misrepresentation of the Imams' position and argument. There are similar misrepresentations in numerous other cases. As just one more example, Qurʾān 5:38 orders a specific punishment for theft. The passage ends with a mention and description of God as "majestic and wise" (والله عزيز حكيم). An old anecdote has it that an illiterate Arab once heard someone recite the passage with the ending of "God is forgiving and merciful" (والله غفور رحيم). He immediately objected that this reading cannot be correct, as mercy and forgiveness have nothing to do with punishment. The people present checked the Qurʾān and found that the correct text was indeed "God is majestic and wise." The Arab who had objected agreed that this formula fitted the context, as majesty and wisdom went well with sanction and punishment (see the story in, for instance, Fakhr al-Dīn al-Rāzī, *Tafsīr*, 11:229; variants of the story reference Qurʾān 2:209 as in, for instance, Qurṭubī, *Jāmiʿ*, 3:395; Suyūṭī, *Itqān*, 3:347). The anecdote was a topos used by Muslim authors to prove that the Qurʾān was a literary miracle as every word was precisely appropriate to its context, pointing to divine authorship of the document. As interesting as the story is, the argument contains an obvious flaw, since only a few pages further in the same *sūra* (5:118), ʿĪsā (Jesus) intercedes for his people before God, and the final sentence describes God as "majestic and wise" (وإن تغفر لهم فإنّك أنت العزيز الحكيم), even though the logic of the anecdote would require a reference to forgiveness and mercy instead, as more appropriate to the situation. To remedy the discrepancy, the Muʿtazilī–Shīʿī statesman, author, and theologian of his time, the vizier Ḥusayn b. ʿAlī al-Maghribī (d. 418), says in his commentary on the Qurʾān (*Maṣābīḥ*, 1:409, also quoted in Ṭūsī, *Tibyān*, 5:496) that when he lived in Egypt (years 381–400, according to his biographers), he saw an inscription on top of the entrance to a house built around the year 70 in which Qurʾān 5:118 was written with the ending of "forgiving and merciful" (وإن تغفر لهم فإنّك أنت الغفور الرحيم). This reference to a personal memory by a Shīʿī individual was obviously aimed at supporting a popular argument for the literary miraculous nature of the Qurʾān, even if this goal was not expressly acknowledged. Few people seem to have noted his intention or used his citation as an alternative record of the passage in question, but the simple mention of it persuaded an early ninth-century author to accuse "the Shīʿa" of corrupting the text of Qurʾān 5:118 to read وأن تغفر لهم فإنّك أنت الغفور الرحيم (Kardarī, *Manāqib*, 288).

78 Kulaynī, *Kāfī*, 5:449.

[محمّد بن] عبد الرحمن بن أبي ليلى قال: سألت أبا عبد الله هل نسخ المتعة شيء؟ قال: لا![79]

[Muḥammad b. ʿAbd al-Raḥmān:] I asked Abū ʿAbd Allāh, "Was *mutʿa* abrogated by anything?" He said, "No!"[80]

Over time, some of those in favor of the legality of *mutʿa* began to interpret the concept too liberally, concluding that a *mutʿa* contract could be for any length of time, even for an hour or two, and solely for a monetary payment. Such conditions would naturally compromise the marital nature of the institution, potentially reducing it in some instances to a mere exchange of sex for money, the legal definition for prostitution.[81] This is an erroneous understanding that is regarded as corrupt and strongly condemned in the reports from Jaʿfar al-Ṣādiq, as in the following examples:

عن جعفر بن محمّد أنّ رجلاً سأله عن نكاح المتعة. قال: صِفه لي. قال: يلقى الرجل المرأة فيقول: أتزوّجك بهذا الدرهم والدرهمين، وقعة أو يوماً أو يومين. قال: هذا زنا.[82]

A man asked Jaʿfar b. Muḥammad about *mutʿa* marriage. He said, "Describe it to me." He said, "A man meets a woman and says, 'I wed you with this dirham or two dirhams, for one encounter, a day, or two.'" He said, "This is fornication."

79 Mufīd, *Risālat al-mutʿa*, as quoted by Ḥurr al-ʿĀmilī, *Wasāʾil al-Shīʿa*, 21:11. See also the following report from Muḥammad al-Bāqir in Kulaynī, *Kāfī*, 5:449:

[متعة النساء] أحلّها الله في كتابه وعلى لسان نبيّه فهي حلال إلى يوم القيامة.

[*Mutʿa* marriage with women] was allowed by God in His Book and by the word of His Prophet. It is thus lawful until the Day of Resurrection.

80 See further Ṭabarī, *Jāmiʿ al-bayān*, 8:176–78, where the same statement is quoted from the jurist Ḥakam b. ʿUtayba.

81 Those who may find this expression unfair in the context at hand cannot take recourse in an analogy with *mahr/ṣadāq* (the dower, nuptial, bridal gift, which may be thought of as a "signing bonus," in a standard [intended-to-be permanent] Islamic marriage) or the argument that the husband's financial responsibility toward his wife is a pillar of marriage and his financial means have thus always been a major consideration in marriages throughout history. There is an obvious distinction, one that common sense can easily grasp, between the two concepts of "living with" (or "being with") someone, even if on a temporary basis, and "sleeping with" someone.

82 Qāḍī Nuʿmān, *Daʿāʾim al-Islām*, 2:226–27. A variant of this report is quoted in Bayhaqī, *Sunan*, 7:338:

بسّام الصيرفي قال: سألت جعفر بن محمّد عن المتعة ووصفتها [له]، فقال لي: ذلك الزنا.

[Bassām al-Ṣayrafī:] I asked Jaʿfar b. Muḥammad about *mutʿa* and I described it. He said, "That is fornication."

هشام بن الحكم عن أبي عبد الله في المتعة، قال: ما يفعلها عندنا إلّا الفواجر.[83]

[Hishām b. al-Ḥakam:] Abū ʿAbd Allāh said regarding *mutʿa*, "Nobody in our society engages in it except the licentious."

عبد الله بن سنان قال: سألت أبا عبد الله عن المتعة فقال: لا تدنّس نفسك بها.[84]

[ʿAbd Allāh b. Sinān:] I asked Abū ʿAbd Allāh about *mutʿa*. He said, "Do not sully yourself with it."

This much suffices for the purpose of the present work. I would, however, like to add a few words about the theological background of this dispute.

A well-known principle in Jaʿfarī law holds that the prescriptions that the Prophet left his community with regarding what was lawful and what was unlawful continue as valid in perpetuity:[85]

عن زرارة عن أبي عبد الله قال: حلال محمّد حلال أبدًا إلى يوم القيامة وحرامه حرام أبدًا إلى يوم القيامة.[86]

[Zurāra:] Abū ʿAbd Allāh said, "What Muḥammad left lawful is lawful forever until the Day of Resurrection, and what he left unlawful is unlawful forever until the Day of Resurrection."

Later decisions by the Companions or by subsequent generations could not challenge the permanent validity of the Sunna of the Prophet. Leaders of the Muslim community had discretionary authority to modify the application of the law, but any such modifications were temporary, valid only as long as the specific conditions requiring the modification existed. Only what the Qurʾān and the Sunna of the Prophet ordered people to do or not to do constituted permanent laws. Likewise, the learned and qualified among the Companions and later generations had their own understandings, and expressed and followed their own interpretations, of the Qurʾān and the Sunna. But those understandings and interpretations were not binding on others, unless they were unanimously agreed upon by the entire

83 Aḥmad b. Muḥammad b. ʿĪsā, *Nawādir*, 87; Kulaynī, *Kāfī*, 5:452.

84 Aḥmad b. Muḥammad b. ʿĪsā, *Nawādir*, 87.

85 There are other understandings of this principle in the Shīʿī tradition. One, for instance, interprets it as a reference to the perpetuity of Islam as a religion—that is, it will never be abrogated by another religion (see Nāʾīnī, *Fawāʾid al-uṣūl*, 4:99; also *Mawsūʿat al-fiqh al-Islāmī* [Qum], 13:215). However, it seems that the principle can also imply the perpetuity of the individual laws that remained in effect at the Prophet's death.

86 Kulaynī, *Kāfī*, 1:58.

Muslim community, a fact that would attest to their Prophetic background. In the legal thought of Jaʿfar al-Ṣādiq, deviations from the Prophet's Sunna, as legitimate as they might have been in their times, do not create a legal precedent, that is, an example to be followed by others in perpetuity.

أبو بصير قال: قال لي أبو عبد الله: يا أبا محمّد![87] كان عندي رهط من أهل البصرة فسألوني عن الحجّ فأخبرتهم بما صنع رسول الله – صلّى الله عليه وآله وسلّم – وبما أمر به، فقالوا لي إنّ عمر قد أفرد الحجّ، فقلت لهم: إنّ هذا رأى رآه عمر، وليس رأى عمر كما صنع رسول الله – صلّى الله عليه وآله وسلّم.[88]

87 As is well known to students of Muslim biographical tradition, there is no conflict between Abū Baṣīr and Abū Muḥammad, the two *kunya*s of this transmitter, Yaḥyā b. al-Qāsim al-Asadī (d. 149–50, as in Kashshī, *Rijāl*, 173). The first was (like Abū al-ʿAynāʾ) a default *kunya* for anyone who was, like this transmitter, blind, and the second was his teknonym, presumably after an elder son named Muḥammad. The default *kunya* was the one by which a person would be generally known except in particular situations, such as when people wanted to indicate closeness to one another as if they had family ties. Many old Arabic names had default *kunya*s, usually after a well-known person in the past with the same name. Certain names thus had occasionally several default *kunya*s when the name was affiliated with different notables in different times and regions. The name Sulaymān, for instance, was associated mostly with the *kunya* Abū Dāwūd in reference to the king/prophet Solomon, son of David, but also with Abū al-Rabīʿ, mostly in North Africa and Egypt, after Rabīʿ b. Sulaymān al-Murādī (d. 270, the disciple of Shāfiʿī and head of his school in Egypt in the middle of the third century, and with Abū Ayyūb, possibly after the Umayyad caliph Sulaymān b. ʿAbd al-Malik (r. 96–99) who was called Abū Ayyūb after his son and successor designate, Ayyūb. Similarly, a Yūsuf is normally Abū Yaʿqūb by default, a reversal of the relation between Jacob and Joseph, but can also be Abū al-Ḥajjāj, after Ḥajjāj b. Yūsuf al-Thaqafī (d. 95), the notorious governor of Kūfa in the Umayyad period, or Abū al-Maḥāsin, after the image of Joseph in the Muslim tradition as an exceptionally handsome young man. A plurality of default *kunya*s could also follow from a name's literal meaning; for example, Abū al-Thanāʾ, Abū al-Maḥāmid, Abū al-Manāqib, and Abū al-Faḍāʾil are all variously assigned to Maḥmūd, which literally means "the praised one." By the same token, Shīrūya/Shīrawayh as a Persian name was assigned the *kunya* of Abū Shujāʿ after its first part, *shīr*, the Persian word for lion. In most other cases, however, there was a single precedent for each name. Here are a few of the best-known default *kunya*s: Ibrāhīm = Abū Isḥāq, Yaʿqūb = Abū Yūsuf, Dāwūd = Abū Sulaymān, Zakariyyā = Abū Yaḥyā, Yaḥyā = Abū Zakariyyā, Muḥammad = Abū ʿAbd Allāh (and Abū Jaʿfar in later periods), Aḥmad = Abū al-ʿAbbās, ʿAlī = Abū al-Ḥasan, Ḥasan = Abū Muḥammad, Ḥusayn = Abū ʿAbd Allāh, ʿUmar = Abū Ḥafṣ, ʿUthmān = Abū ʿAmr, Ḥamza = Abū Yaʿlā, Yāsir = Abū ʿAmmār, ʿAbbās = Abū al-Faḍl, ʿAbd al-Malik = Marwān, and Yazīd = Abū Khālid. Less frequent ones include Mūsā = Abū ʿImrān, ʿĪsā = Abū Mūsā, ʿAbd Allāh = Abū Muḥammad, Zayd = Abū ʿUsāma, and ʿAmr = Abū Umayya or Abū ʿUthmān. There was a parallel tradition of conventional honorific names (*laqab*s). Qalqashandī, *Ṣubḥ al-aʿshā*, 5:488–89 gives a sample list of the most current honorifics before his time: Ibrāhīm = Burhān al-Dīn, Yūsuf = Jamāl al-Dīn, Muḥammad = Shams al-Dīn, Aḥmad = Shihāb al-Dīn, Abū Bakr = Zayn al-Dīn, ʿUmar = Sirāj al-Dīn, ʿUthmān = Fakhr al-Dīn, Ḥamza =ʿIzz al-Dīn, ʿAbd al-Raḥmān = Raḍī al-Dīn, and Sayf al-Dīn for the chiefs of the army. Knowing these defaults helps one not only identify the authors and transmitters mentioned by their *kunya*s but also correct countless errors and typos in the names recorded in manuscripts and prints.

88 Ṭūsī, *Tahdhīb*, 5:26.

> [Abū Baṣīr:] Abū ʿAbd Allāh said to me, "I was visited by a group of people from Baṣra and they asked me about the *ḥajj*, so I told them what the Prophet did [performing *tamattuʿ*, which combines the *ḥajj* and the *ʿumra*] and what he ordered. They said to me, 'But ʿUmar performed the *ḥajj* alone [that is, *ḥajj ifrād*, which is not accompanied with the *ʿumra*].' I said to them, 'This was an opinion that ʿUmar held, and the opinion of ʿUmar did not accord with what the Prophet did.'"

ʿAbd Allāh, the learned son of ʿUmar, had a similar reaction to the same question:

> عن سالم بن عبد الله أنّه سمع رجلاً يسأل عبد الله بن عمر عن التمتّع بالعمرة إلى الحجّ. قال عبد الله بن عمر: هي [يعني متعة الحجّ] حلال! فقال الشامي: إنّ أباك قد نهى عنها! فقال عبد الله بن عمر: أرأيت ان كان أبي نهى عنها وصنعها رسول الله – صلّى الله عليه وسلّم – أأمر أبي يُتّبع أم أمر رسول الله – صلّى الله عليه وسلّم؟ فقال الرجل: بل أمر رسول الله – صلّى الله عليه وسلّم. فقال: لقد صنعها رسول الله – صلّى الله عليه وسلّم.[89]
>
> [Sālim b. ʿAbd Allāh:] A [Syrian] man asked ʿAbd Allāh b. ʿUmar about *tamattuʿ*, in which one combines the *ʿumra* and the *ḥajj*. ʿAbd Allāh b. ʿUmar said, "It is permissible!" The Syrian man said, "Your father forbade it!" ʿAbd Allāh b. ʿUmar said, "If my father forbade it and the Messenger of God (may God's prayer and peace be upon him) performed it, do you think that it is my father's order that is to be followed or the order of the Messenger of God (may God's prayer and peace be upon him)?" The man said, "Rather, the order of the Messenger of God (may God's prayer and peace be upon him) [should be followed]." He said, "Indeed, the Messenger of God (may God's prayer and peace be upon him) performed it."

This was also the response of the Companion Saʿd b. Abī Waqqāṣ in the following episode:

> عن محمّد بن عبد الله بن الحارث بن نوفل أنه سمع سعد بن أبي وقاص والضحاك بن قيس وهما يذكران التمتّع بالعمرة إلى الحجّ، فقال الضحاك بن قيس لا يصنع ذلك إلّا من جهل أمر الله! فقال سعد: بئس ما قلت يا ابن أخي! فقال الضحاك بن قيس: فإنّ

89 Tirmidhī, *Sunan*, no. 824.

عمر بن الخطاب قد نهى عن ذلك. فقال سعد: قد صنعها رسول الله – صلّى الله عليه وسلّم – وصنعناها معه.[90]

[Muḥammad b. ʿAbd Allāh b. al-Ḥārith:] Saʿd b. Abī Waqqāṣ and Ḍaḥḥāk b. Qays were discussing the *tamattuʿ*, in which one combines the *ʿumra* and the *ḥajj*. Ḍaḥḥāk b. Qays said, "Nobody does that except someone who is ignorant of God's command!" Saʿd said, "That is a terrible thing to say, O son of my brother!" Ḍaḥḥāk b. Qays said, "ʿUmar b. al-Khaṭṭāb forbade it." Saʿd said, "The Messenger of God (may God's prayer and peace be upon him) performed it, and we did it with him."

In some cases in which the practice of the Companions seemed to diverge from the Sunna of the Prophet, the apparent discrepancy was caused by reasons that prompted the Companions to act differently. An example is provided by a conversation between Jaʿfar al-Ṣādiq and Sufyān al-Thawrī, already quoted earlier:

عبد الرحمن بن الحجّاج عن أبي عبد الله قال: إنّ سفيان فقيهكم أتاني فقال: ما يحملك على أن تأمر أصحابك يأتون الجِعرانة فيُحرمون منها؟ فقلت له: هي وقت من مواقيت رسول الله – صلّى الله عليه وآله وسلّم. قال: بلى! ولكن أما علمت أنّ أصحاب رسول الله – صلّى الله عليه وآله وسلّم – إنّما أحرموا من المسجد؟ فقلت: إنّ أولئك كانوا متمتّعينَ في أعناقهم الدماء، وإنّ هؤلاء قطنوا بمكّة فصاروا كأنّهم من أهل مكّة، وأهل مكّة لا متعة لهم.[91]

[ʿAbd al-Raḥmān b. al-Ḥajjāj:] Abū ʿAbd Allāh said, "Sufyān, your local jurist, came to me and said, 'What makes you order your followers to go to Jiʿrāna to assume the state of pilgrim sanctity there?' I said to him, 'It is one of the *ḥajj* stations assigned by the Messenger of God (may God's prayer and peace be upon him and his Family).' He said, 'Yes! But did you not know that the Companions of the Messenger of God (may God's prayer and peace be upon him and his Family) assumed the state of pilgrim sanctity at the Mosque [of Shajara]?' I said, 'They were performing the *ḥajj* of *tamattuʿ* and had to offer sacrifice. But these people [whom I advised to go to Jiʿrāna] reside in Mecca, so it is as if they are of the people of Mecca, and the people of Mecca do not perform *tamattuʿ*.'"

90 Tirmidhī, *Sunan*, no. 823.
91 Kulaynī, *Kāfī*, 4:400–401.

A pious leader of the Muslim community would never try to change or cancel the laws of the Qurʾān and the Sunna. Once Islam reached its complete, final status shortly before the death of the Prophet,[92] these laws were meant to be permanent.[93] What a pious leader of the Muslims may legitimately do is to put temporary restrictions on the application of specific laws in response to circumstances that make such a halt necessary at the time to protect a more important interest of the Muslim community. Likewise, he can ban a widespread abuse of law. Consider the following report:

الفضل قال: سمعت أبا عبد الله يقول: بلغ عمر أنّ أهل العراق يزعمون أنّ عمرحرّم المتعة فأرسل فلانًا – قد سمّاه – فقال: أخبِرهم أنّي لم أُحرِّمها، وليس لعمر أن يحرّم ما أحلّ الله، ولكن عمر قد نهى عنها.[94]

[Faḍl b. ʿAbd al-Malik:] I heard Abū ʿAbd Allāh say, "ʿUmar was informed that the people of Iraq [that is, the Muslim immigrants who had just settled in the region] said that ʿUmar had declared *mutʿa* unlawful, so he sent someone—whose name he mentioned—and said, 'Inform them that I did not declare it to be unlawful, and ʿUmar does not have the authority to declare unlawful what God has deemed lawful. Rather, ʿUmar forbade it.'"

This was what the Prophet, too, reportedly did in certain cases, issuing an order that was bound to specific circumstances:

الحلبي قال: سألت أبا عبد الله عن الوباء يكون في ناحية المصر فيتحوّل الرجل إلى ناحية أخرى أو يكون في مصر فيخرج منه إلى غيره؟ فقال: لا بأس. [قلت: بلغنا أنّ رسول الله – صلّى الله عليه وآله وسلّم – عاب قومًا بذلك؟ فقال:][95] إنّما نهى رسول

92 Qurʾān 5:3.

93 The statement quoted from Aḥmad b. Ḥanbal in Ibn ʿAbd al-Barr, *Jāmiʿ bayān al-ʿilm wa-faḍlih*, 2:1095, لا ينسخ القرآن إلّا القرآن, can be understood within the same mentality.

94 Aḥmad b. Muḥammad b. ʿĪsā, *Nawādir*, 82. The language that ʿUmar reportedly used in this case, as in the paragraph quoted earlier from Ibn Qudāma, *Mughnī*, 10:46 (and other sources cited in the footnote therein), may support this explanation:

> متعتان كانتا على عهد رسول الله – صلّى الله عليه وسلّم – وأنا أنهى عنهما وأعاقب عليهما: متعة الحج ومتعة النساء.
>
> There were two *mutʿa*s during the time of the Messenger of God (may God's prayer and peace be upon him). I ban both, and will punish both the *mutʿa* of the *ḥajj* and the *mutʿa* of women.

95 From a variant in Ibn Bābawayh, *ʿIlal al-sharāʾiʿ*, 2:208.

الله – صلّى الله عليه وآله وسلّم – عن ذلك لمكان ربيئة كانت بحيال العدوّ فوقع فيهم الوباء فهربوا منه، فقال رسول الله – صلّى الله عليه وآله وسلّم: «الفارّ منه كالفارّ من الزحف»، كراهيّة أن تخلوا مراكزهم.[96]

['Ubayd Allāh al-Ḥalabī:] I asked Abū ʿAbd Allāh about a scenario in which an epidemic occurs in part of a town and a man relocates to another part, or he leaves the city he is in for another one. He said, "There is nothing wrong with that." I said, "We were informed that the Prophet censured some people for doing that." He said, "The Prophet forbade that in the case of [soldiers at] an observation post that was facing the enemy. Some of them succumbed to an epidemic, so they fled from there. The Prophet said, 'The one who flees from it is like the one who flees from the enemy,'[97] not liking for posts to be abandoned."

حريز عن أبي عبد الله قال: سُئل عن سباع الطير والوحش، حتّى ذُكر القنافذ والوطواط والحمير والبغال والخيل. فقال: ليس الحرام إلّا ما حرّم الله في كتابه، وقد نهى رسول الله – صلّى الله عليه وآله وسلّم – يوم خيبر عن أكل لحوم الحمير، وإنّما نهاهم من أجل ظهرهم أن يُفنوه. وليس الحمير بحرام.[98]

[Ḥarīz:] Abū ʿAbd Allāh was asked about [the meat of] predatory birds and beasts, down to hedgehogs, bats, donkeys, mules, and horses. He said, "Nothing is unlawful except what God made unlawful in His Book.

---

96 Kulaynī, *Kāfī*, 8:108.

97 Aḥmad b. Ḥanbal, *Musnad*, 22:365; Ibn Bābawayh, *Maʿānī al-akhbār*, 254:

> الفرار من الطاعون كالفرار من الزحف.
>
> Fleeing from the plague is like fleeing from a hostile army.

Fleeing from a hostile army while a war is raging is a major sin (Qur'ān 8:15–16). See further *al-Mawsūʿa al-fiqhiyya* (Kuwait), 32:76 and the references cited therein.

98 ʿAyyāshī, *Tafsīr*, 2:125. See also Ibn Bābawayh, *ʿIlal al-sharāʾiʿ*, 2:250, where Jaʿfar quotes the same story from his father:

> أبو الحسن الليثي قال: حدّثني جعفر بن محمّد قال: سُئل أبي عن لحوم الحمر الأهليّة فقال: نهى رسول الله – صلّى الله عليه وآله وسلّم – عن أكلها [يوم خيبر] لأنّها كانت حمولة للناس يومئذ، وإنّما الحرام ما حرّم الله في القرآن.
>
> [Abū al-Ḥasan al-Laythī:] Jaʿfar b. Muḥammad said, "My father was asked about the meat of domestic donkeys. He said, 'The Messenger of God (may God's prayer and peace be upon him and his Family) banned eating it on the day of Khaybar because they were used for carrying loads for people that day. The unlawful is only what God made unlawful in the Qur'ān.'"

The statement quoted from Muḥammad al-Bāqir in this report is attested independently in a couple of reports in ʿĀṣim b. Ḥumayd al-Ḥannāṭ, *Kitāb*, 151; Kulaynī, *Kāfī*, 6:246; Ṭūsī, *Tahdhīb*, 9:41.

The Messenger of God (may God's prayer and peace be upon him and his Family) banned eating the meat of donkeys on the day of Khaybar, but he banned it [as an executive order for that specific time] because the Muslims needed these animals to carry their loads. But donkeys are not unlawful."[99]

الحلبي قال: سُئل أبا عبد الله عن الرجل يشتري الثمرة المسمّاة من أرض فهلك ثمرة تلك الأرض كلّها، فقال: قد اختصموا في ذلك إلى رسول الله – صلّى الله عليه وآله وسلّم – فكانوا يذكرون ذلك، فلمّا رآهم لا يدعون الخصومة نهاهم عن ذلك البيع حتّى تبلغ الثمرة، ولم يُحرّمه ولكن فعل ذلك من أجل خصومتهم.[100]

['Ubayd Allāh al-Ḥalabī:] Abū 'Abd Allāh was asked about [a scenario in which] a man buys a determinate amount of fruit from a tract of land [as a future contract, *salam*], but all of the fruit from that land tract perishes. He said, "Some people brought such a dispute to the Prophet (may God's prayer and peace be upon him and his Family), and they continued to bring it up. When he saw that they would not stop quarreling, he forbade them to make such sales until the fruit ripened. He did not declare it unlawful, but he did that [that is, he forbade it in that specific case] to settle their dispute."

So there is a difference between *taḥrīm*, declaring something unlawful, which falls within God's exclusive jurisdiction, and *nahy*, banning something for a limited period. The latter can be done by the leaders of the Muslim community, who have discretionary authority to issue executive orders on a temporary basis.

There is a story that, if authentic, explains the background of, and motive behind, 'Umar's move to announce a ban on *mut'a*. It is reported in a number of variants, all of which agree on the focal point:

يقال إنّ عمرو بن حريث استمتع من امرأة من بني سعد بن بكر فولدت فجحد ولدها. واستمتع سلمة بن أميّة بن خلف من سلمى مولاة حكيم بن أميّة. فولدت فجحد ولدها. واستمتع عبد الله بن أبي عوف السهمي من بنت أبي لبيبة مولاة هشام بن الوليد بن المغيرة – وكانت تبيع الشراب ويُغشى بيتُها – فولدت له يوسف. فقال له

99 Cf. Kulaynī, *Kāfī*, 3:57:

زرارة، قلت له: أليس لحومها حلالاً؟ قال: بلى! ولكن ليس ممّا جعله الله للأكل.

[Zurāra:] I said to him, "Is the meat of riding animals not lawful?" He said, "Yes! But it is not part of that which God made for eating."

100 Kulaynī, *Kāfī*, 5:571. The story is narrated also in Bukhārī, *Ṣaḥīḥ*, no. 2081.

عمر: أتعترف بهذا الغلام؟ قال: لا! قال: لو قلتَ «نعم» لرجمتك بالحجارة – وكان عمر يعرف هذه المرأة بالسوء – فحرّم المتعة.[101]

It is said that ʿAmr b. Ḥurayth[102] entered a *mutʿa* marriage with a woman from [the tribe of] Banū Saʿd b. Bakr. She gave birth and he denied paternity of the child. Salama b. Umayya b. Khalaf[103] also entered a *mutʿa* marriage with Salmā, a client of Ḥakīm b. Umayya. She gave birth and he denied the child. And ʿAbd Allāh b. Abī ʿAwf al-Sahmī entered a *mutʿa* marriage with the daughter of Abū Labība, the client of Hishām b. al-Walīd b. al-Mughīra—she used to sell wine and her house was frequented [by evildoers]—and she bore him Yūsuf. ʿUmar said to him, "Do you acknowledge this child?" He said, "No!" He said, "If you had said yes, I would have stoned you." (ʿUmar knew that woman was immoral.) So he declared *mutʿa* unlawful.

الأجلح قال: سمعت أبا الزبير يقول في ما يروي عن جابر بن عبد الله: تمتّع عمرو بن حريث من امرأة بالمدينة فحملت، فأتى بها عمر فأراد أن يضربها فقالت: يا أمير المؤمنين! تمتّع منّي عمرو بن حريث. فقال: من شهد نكاحك؟ فقالت: أمّي وأختي. فقال عمر: بغير ولي ولا شهود؟ فأرسل إلى عمرو بن حريث فقام عليه وسأله، فقال: صدقَت. فقال عمر للناس: هذا نكاح فاسد، وقد دخل فيه ما ترون. فرأى عمر أن يحرّمه.[104]

[Al-Ajlaḥ:] I heard Abū Zubayr say, as was reported on the authority of Jābir b. ʿAbd Allāh, "ʿAmr b. Ḥurayth entered a *mutʿa* marriage with a woman in Medina and she became pregnant. ʿUmar went to her, wanting to beat her [in punishment for fornication]. She said, 'O commander of the faithful! ʿAmr b. Ḥurayth entered a *mutʿa* marriage with me.' He said, 'Who witnessed your marriage?' She said, 'My mother and my sister.' ʿUmar said, 'Without the [marriage] guardian and witnesses?'[105] He sent for ʿAmr b. Ḥurayth and stood up to confront him and asked him. He said, 'She has spoken the truth.' Then ʿUmar said to

101 Ibn Shabba, *Taʾrīkh al-Madīna al-munawwara*, 2:719.

102 A Companion and later governor of Kūfa. On him, see Ibn ʿAbd al-Barr, *Istīʿāb*, 3:1172.

103 On him, see Ibn ʿAbd al-Barr, *Istīʿāb*, 2:640.

104 Ibn Shabba, *Taʾrīkh al-Madīna al-munawwara*, 2:716–17; Abū Hilāl al-Askarī, *Awāʾil*, 1:240.

105 This indicates that ʿUmar's objection related to the absence of a *walī* and witnesses, through which he feared a further denial of paternity, rather than to the temporariness of the marriage. This is what Ibn Ḥazm refers to in *Muḥallā*, 9:520, as quoted earlier:

وعن عمر بن الخطاب أنّه إنّما أنكرها إذا لم يشهد عليها عدلان فقط وأباحها بشهادة عدلين.

[It is reported] from ʿUmar b. al-Khaṭṭāb that he denied [the validity of] *mutʿa* only when done without the testimony of two righteous witnesses and allowed it with the testimony of the two righteous witnesses.

the people, 'This is an invalid marriage. You see what it involves.' So 'Umar decided to declare it unlawful."

عن جابر بن عبد الله قال: استمتعت من النساء على عهد رسول الله – صلّى الله عليه وسلّم – وزمن أبي بكر، ثمّ زمن عمر، حتّى كان من شأن عمروبن حريث [ما] الّذي كان، فقال عمر: إنّا كنّا نستمتع ونَفي وإنّي أراكم تستمتعون ولا تفون، فانكحوا ولا تستمتعوا.[106]

[Jābir b. ʿAbd Allāh:] I entered into *mutʿa* marriages with women during the time of the Messenger of God (may God's prayer and peace be upon him), the time of Abū Bakr, and then the time of ʿUmar, until the affair of ʿAmr b. Ḥurayth occurred. Then ʿUmar said, "We used to enter *mutʿa* marriages and stood by our responsibilities, but I see that you enter *mutʿa* marriages but do not stand by your responsibilities, so marry but do not enter *mutʿa* marriages."

So ʿUmar's decision in this case, regardless of the differences in the specific language used by the transmitters, was based on a valid administrative consideration[107] that fell under what Muslim scholars in later periods termed *siyāsa sharʿiyya*, decisions properly within the discretionary authority of the ruler of the Muslim community.[108] Leading jurists in

106 Ibn Shabba, *Taʾrīkh al-Madīna al-munawwara*, 2:717.

107 A Prophetic precedent for this was cited earlier: having witnesses to a marriage was not Qurʾānically mandated, but a quote attributed to Jaʿfar al-Ṣādiq asserts that it was an administrative decision by the Prophet to establish paternity (*nasab*):

داود بن الحصين عن أبي عبد الله قال: النكاح لم يجيء عن الله فيه عزيمة فسنّ رسول الله – صلّى الله عليه وآله وسلّم – في ذلك الشاهدين تأديبًا ونظرًا لئلّا يُنكَر الولد والميراث.

[Dāwūd b. al-Ḥuṣayn:] Abū ʿAbd Allāh said, "For marriage, God did not impose an obligation [for it to be done in the presence of witnesses], so the Messenger of God (may God's prayer and peace be upon him and his Family) ordered [the presence of] two witnesses as a matter of discipline and in consideration for the child and for inheritance, so that neither can be disavowed" (Ṭūsī, *Tahdhīb*, 6:281–82).

هشام بن سالم عن أبي عبد الله قال: إنّما جعلت البيّنات للنسب والمواريث.

[Hishām b. Sālim:] Abū ʿAbd Allāh said, "Witness testimony was established for the sake of lineage and inheritance" (Kulaynī, *Kāfī*, 5:387).

108 More precisely, putting a ban on a widespread pattern of abuse of the law is a duty of the leader of the Muslim community, but choosing a specific method is within his discretionary authority. As almost always, there is more than one solution for any problem, and there is no guarantee that the solution adopted by the ruler will work best. But he is to follow his own judgment according to what he thinks is in the best interest of the Muslim community. In the case at hand, some senior Companions reportedly disapproved of the caliph's decision. They might have advocated enforcement of stricter disciplinary measures on the practice of *mutʿa* by severely punishing those who may have violated its conditions, such as the permission

the late second century maintained that this kind of an executive order remains valid as long as the specified reason behind it continues to apply. Once it lapses, the original law of the Qurʾān or the Sunna of the Prophet again enters into effect.[109]

The situation with regard to *mutʿa* has changed dramatically with the passage of time and place. ʿUmar's concerns were valid and legitimate in their context, with regard to the possibility of a denial of paternity if *mutʿa* was performed with an unchaperoned party and in the absence of witnesses. But the actual situation could vary from time to time and culture to culture. Today, those who have been raised in a Shīʿī community, including the present author, know that the most common reason for an already married man to undertake a valid *mutʿa* marriage is, and has long been, the infertility of the first, permanent wife or, occasionally, the absence of a male child in the family. A man's marrying a second permanent wife is not always an option, whether because of his financial situation, because of particular cultural tastes, because of a desire to avoid jeopardizing love, peace, and happiness in his family, or because of respect and a feeling of indebtedness toward his primary life partner. The birth of a child in the life of a

of the marriage guardian and presence of witnesses, for instance. Such alternatives would prevent the abuse of the law without need for a full-fledged ban that would deprive society of the benefits of the institution. This seems to be what the frequently cited statement from ʿAlī and Ibn ʿAbbās (as noted before) tried to assert: لولا أنّ عمر نهى عن المتعة ما زنى إلّا شقي, objecting to the specific method adopted in this case but not questioning the authority of the caliph to decide. See further Āl Kāshif al-Ghiṭāʾ, *Aṣl al-Shīʿa*, 204–5; Muṭahharī, *Niẓām-i ḥuqūq-i zan*, 60–61.

109 See the earlier discussion of the amount of restitution payable for death or injury to a human being, set by a decree from the Prophet on the basis of the market value of a camel, the most valuable single commodity in Arab society at the time. In the Prophet's time, the price of a camel was ten dinars, equal to one hundred dirhams, but ʿUmar later modified the exchange rate during his caliphate to 1 dinar = 12 dirhams because the price of a camel had increased (see, for instance, Shāfiʿī, *Umm*, 7:274, 380). Later jurists and law schools disagreed on what to do after that. The Ḥanafīs opted to apply the exchange rate specified in the decree attributed to the Prophet, which for them set the fixed rate for all future references from that point onward, but most others continued to implement the rate set by ʿUmar. Shāfiʿī, however, took a middle path, following the criterion set by ʿUmar but not the specific rate that he suggested. This is how he commented on ʿUmar's decision in *Umm*, 7:375, 411–13:

> قال الشافعي: دية الحرّ المسلم مائةٌ من الإبل كما فرضها رسول الله – صلّى الله عليه وسلّم – فإن اعوزت الإبل فقيمتها. فإذا قوّمها عمر قيمة يومها فاتّباعه أن تُقوّم – كلّما وجبت على إنسانٍ – قيمةَ يومها. فتؤخذ الإبل ما وجدت وتقوّم عند الإعواز على ما وصفت.
>
> Shāfiʿī said, "The blood-money of a free Muslim is one hundred camels, as was prescribed by the Messenger of God (may God's prayer and peace be upon him). If one lacks camels, then it is their value. ʿUmar set the value for it on the basis of its value during his lifetime, so following him requires that it [that is, the market value of a camel] be appraised, whenever it becomes someone's duty to pay it, according to the value of its time. So camels are to be used when available, and otherwise their market value [is to be used] when there is a shortage of them, as described."

man whose permanent wife is infertile is a blessing that he receives with the greatest joy, pride, and gratitude—making for a situation very different from the culture of Medina in the time of ʿUmar, as reflected in the anecdotes quoted above. However, the occasional cases of paternity denials, which still occur *when the marriage is not registered* (even with ordinary or "permanent" marriages), continue to be a source of concern, analogous to the situation in Medina of his time.

I wish to make three additional points before finishing with this subject and moving on to the next topic.

First, Qurʾān 30:21 explains the purpose of marriage in unambiguous terms:

﴿وَمِنْ آيَاتِهِ أَنْ خَلَقَ لَكُمْ مِنْ أَنْفُسِكُمْ أَزْوَاجًا لِتَسْكُنُوا إِلَيْهَا وَجَعَلَ بَيْنَكُمْ مَوَدَّةً وَرَحْمَةً﴾

> And among His signs is that He created mates for you from among yourselves, so that you may find peace and comfort with them, and He created love and affection between you.

Judging the matter solely on the basis of the Qurʾānic wisdom for marriage in a situation in which the religious reports are so contradictory and unreliable, and in which the early Muslim authorities disagreed so sharply, a nonpartisan jurist may legitimately argue that when permanent marriage is out of the question for one reason or another,[110] such as, according to some opinions, a difference in religious affiliation between the partners,[111]

110 Such situations may include instances in which the wife does not want to move to the residence of the husband and prefers to stay in her own, a scenario that Islamic family law allows in a *mutʿa* marriage but not in a permanent marriage. A somewhat similar form of marriage that tried to address this dilemma, though on a permanent basis, has been known in Islamic law since the late first century as *nahāriyya* (see *al-Mawsūʿa al-fiqhiyya* [Kuwait], 41:376–77; also Ibn Abī Shayba, *Muṣannaf*, 6:121 and other sources named in the editor's footnote therein) and in more recent times as *ziwāj misyār* (for the position of Jaʿfar al-Ṣādiq and his father on this category of marriage, see ʿAyyāshī, *Tafsīr*, 1:447; Kulaynī, *Kāfī*, 5:402–3; Ṭūsī, *Tahdhīb*, 7:372, 374). There are other dispensations from the general rules of a permanent marriage that are permissible in a *mutʿa*: No obedience is required of the wife to the husband in *mutʿa*, nor is there any financial obligation from the husband to the wife. Unlike in a permanent marriage, in a *mutʿa* marriage the two parties can agree on any condition and limitation that they wish, specifying no children, no intercourse, or the like. Any violation by the husband of the terms and limits that the two parties have agreed upon for sexual relations is deemed tantamount to rape, unless consistent with terms newly agreed upon by both parties.

111 This has been a common cause for *mutʿa* marriages in the Shīʿī community in the past and the present. Most reports in Shīʿī *ḥadīth* collections, and the majority opinion in Shīʿī law, restrict the possibility of marriage between Muslim men and non-Muslim women belonging to the People of the Book to temporary marriage for a specified period, often set at ninety-nine years, although some jurists have concerns about a term that exceeds the normal longevity of human beings, at least as of now. They argue that such a time frame renders the marriage

time-limited arrangements to secure mutual peace and comfort as well as love and affection fall under the original legality of *mutʿa*, provided that all other essential conditions of an Islamic marriage[112] are met and that the evils warned against in Qurʾān 4:25 and 5:5 are avoided.[113]

This, however, can in no way justify reports that *encourage* the practice of *mutʿa*,[114] except insofar as those reports reflect an irritated reaction to the demonization of *mutʿa* by members of the opposing camp.[115] Moreover, as warned in works on *ḥadīth* forgery in the sections on foods, sweets, and fruits, one must be very suspicious of reports in cases that deal with human desires and temptations as well as those that involve social, local, and tribal bias, such as reports that praise or blame specific towns and regions.

With the school of Mecca being in favor of the lawfulness of *mutʿa* until the mid-second century and its chief jurist, ʿAbd al-Malik b. ʿAbd al-ʿAzīz b. Jurayj (d. 150), having married sixty,[116] seventy,[117] or ninety[118] *mutʿa* wives in the course of his life, it is evident that Muslims could still freely practice *mutʿa* without significant problems, at least in Mecca.[119] The fact that Jaʿfar al-Ṣādiq and his father openly argued for the continued lawfulness of *mutʿa* clearly indicates that there was no need to observe precautionary secrecy

---

in effect permanent. It should also be noted that according to several reports from Jaʿfar al-Ṣādiq and his father (Aḥmad b. Muḥammad b. ʿĪsā, *Nawādir*, 119; Kulaynī, *Kāfī*, 5:356, 358, 360), an interfaith marriage is an option for a Muslim man only when marriage with a free or enslaved Muslim wife is not possible:

> لا ينبغي للمسلم الموسر أن يتزوّج الأمة إلّا أن لا يجد حرّة، وكذلك لا ينبغي له أن يتزوّج امرأةً من أهل الكتاب إلّا في حال ضرورة لا يجد مسلمة حرّةً ولا أمةً.
>
> A financially able Muslim should not marry a slave woman unless he is not able to find a free woman [to marry]. Likewise, he should not marry a woman from the People of the Book except in a case of necessity, when he finds neither a free nor an enslaved Muslim woman (Kulaynī, *Kāfī*, 5:360).

112 As is well known to students of Islamic family law, Abū Ḥanīfa and his followers allow an unchaperoned marriage for a mature, sane woman (*al-Mawsūʿa al-fiqhiyya* [Kuwait], 41: 248–49), and many early jurists do not require witnesses for marriage (Ibn Qudāma, *Mughnī*, 9:347–48).

113 The same can be said about cases in which, in the absence of a permanent wife, there is an exchange of care and protection for a woman for any other legal and ethical purpose, as in the pre-Islamic Meccan practice of providing moral, tribal, and financial support, and the formula endorsed by the Prophet as mentioned above. Reasonable purposes, such as having a child for someone whose permanent wife is infertile, or a male issue when one is missing in the family, can legitimately fall within the same framework in the situations previously described.

114 E.g., Ḥimyarī, *Qurb al-isnād*, 44; Kulaynī, *Kāfī*, 5:465; Ibn Bābawayh, *Faqīh*, 3:294–97.

115 See Ibn Bābawayh, *Faqīh*, 3:295: خلافًا على من أنكرها.

116 Dhahabī, *Taʾrīkh al-Islām*, 3:920.

117 Dhahabī, *Mīzān al-iʿtidāl*, 2:659.

118 Dhahabī, *Siyar aʿlām al-nubalāʾ*, 6:333; Dhahabī, *Tadhkirat al-ḥuffāẓ*, 1:171. These three figures can corrupt to one another in the Arabic script.

119 The situation was different in Medina. See Kulaynī, *Kāfī*, 5:467.

on the subject in their lifetimes. Yet there is not a single report to suggest that either of the two Imams ever entered a *mutʿa* marriage, although if they seriously wanted to encourage their followers to do so, the best and most effective way would have been to do it personally and make it known to the community of their followers.[120]

Second, *mutʿa* as a category of marriage[121] has the same essential conditions as permanent marriage,[122] most importantly the required waiting period after the termination of the union.[123] However, the way in which it was practiced in the first half of the second century, when supporters of its legality were still present among the majority, did not at times fully accord with the terms and conditions of an Islamic marriage. It was a misinformed, misunderstood, and corrupt practice that Jaʿfar al-Ṣādiq constantly complained about, as demonstrated by some of the statements quoted above.[124]

The reports from Jaʿfar al-Ṣādiq and his father emphasized that the Prophet never abrogated the legality of the category of marriage called *mutʿa* and that ʿUmar, as the leader of the Muslim community, had no authority to abrograte it, and in fact never intended nor tried to do this. What he did was ban a practice that had given rise to a pattern of widespread abuse of the law in his time. *Mutʿa* as a legal category was, therefore, still lawful in principle. The focus of the debate was thus on the theoretical and theological aspects of the question of *mutʿa*. That never meant that every member of society, those with permanent wives in particular,[125] should or would in fact engage in the practice.

120 For a parallel situation in a non-Shīʿī school, see the Ibāḍī Shiqṣī, *Manhaj al-ṭālibīn*, 15:386 (see also Kindī, *Muṣannaf*, 19:445), where the author comments, after giving a list of Ibāḍī jurists and *imāms* who considered *mutʿa* lawful:

ولم نعلم أنّ أحدًا من أصحابنا فَعَل تزويج المتعة. ونحن بهم نقتدى وبنورهم نهتدى.

But we do not know if any of our companions ever practiced the marriage of *mutʿa*. We take them as our role models and find guidance by their light.

121 Mufīd, *al-Masāʾil al-Ṣāghāniyya*, 41–42.

122 Figure 1 shows how this worked in practice.

123 See Aḥmad b. Muḥammad b. ʿĪsā, *Nawādir*, 83; Kulaynī, *Kāfī*, 5:458; Ibn Bābawayh, *Faqīh*, 3:296; Ṭūsī, *Tahdhīb*, 7:265.

124 In a report from Muḥammad al-Bāqir in Kulaynī, *Kāfī*, 5:453, he, too, advised caution:

أبو مريم قال: سُئل أبو جعفر عن المتعة فقال: إنّ المتعة اليوم ليست كما كانت قبل اليوم. إنهّن كنّ يُؤمَنّ يومئذ واليوم لا يُؤمَنّ.

[Abū Maryam:] Abū Jaʿfar [al-Bāqir] was asked about *mutʿa*, and he replied, "*Mutʿa* today is not like it used to be. Women used to be trustworthy [in their claim to be chaste], but today they are no longer trustworthy."

125 That *mutʿa* was not meant for those with permanent wives is clearly understood from the frequently cited statement from ʿAlī and Ibn ʿAbbās (as noted before), لولا أنّ عمر نهى عن المتعة ما زنى إلّا شقيّ, as it assumes that the person would not have an alternative recourse to satisfy his

Figure 1

This is an example of a document illustrating the terms of a *mutʿa* marriage, from early thirteenth-century Yazd (in the central region of Iran), published in Jafarian, *Nuskha-khwānī*, 24:166–67.

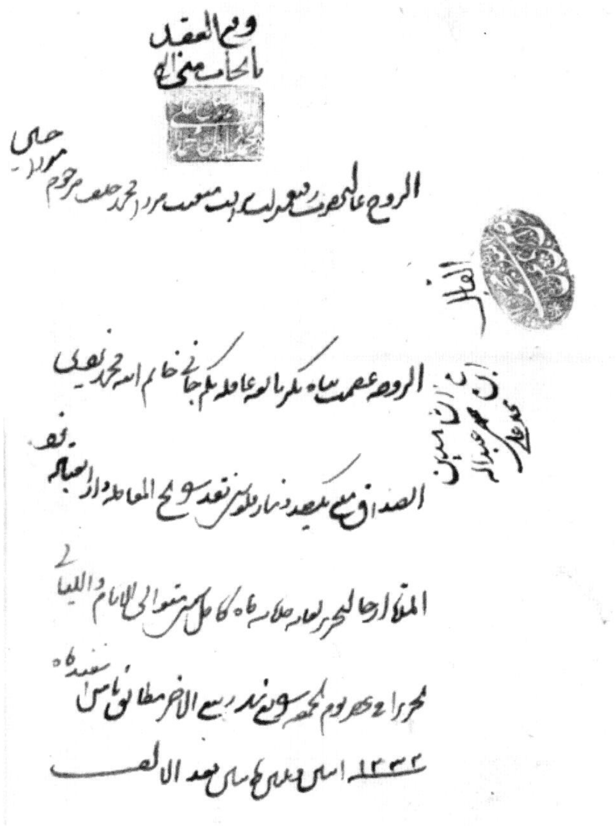

Document text:

- Husband: Mīrzā Muḥammad, son of the late Mīrzā Ḥusayn.
- Wife: Jānī Khānum, daughter of Muḥammad Yazdī.
- *Ṣadāq* [the nuptial gift]: The amount of one hundred dinars of *fulūs*, of common usage in the Dār al-ʿIbāda of Yazd [commonly known as *ṣannār*, this was the lowest valued Iranian coin at the time].
- Duration: From the date of this document for three successive, full solar months [the duration of time required for a pilgrimage from Yazd to Mashhad and back].
- Date: In the afternoon of Friday, 4 Rabīʿ al-Thānī = 8 of [the Persian solar month of] Isfand of the year 1232.

Top of document: The [marriage] formula of *ījāb* [that is, the offer of marriage on behalf of the woman] was recited by me [the seal of the marriage officiant with the name of Muḥammad].

Right margin of the document: The acceptor [of the marriage on behalf of the man] [the seal of the person who represented the husband in accepting the marriage, also with the name of Muḥammad].

Right margin of the document, below the testimony of the husband's representative: [We are] from among the witnesses: [I] ʿAbd Allāh, son of Muḥammad [II] Muḥammad ʿAlī.

The third and final point is that when it came to marital relations, many ethnic, tribal, and regional cultures among the Muslims frowned upon the concept of temporary marriage, in the same way that many contemporary Muslims frown upon bigamy, and when they hear about a case of it, their spontaneous reaction is to ask, "What was wrong?"[126] Many families would never sanction anything short of a permanent relationship for either their sons or their daughters. It was never a choice for men and women from noble, upper-class families, either.[127] To a great extent, this was because of the mentality created by the misconceptions of the ignorant and the misconduct of unethical, licentious people as condemned by Jaʿfar al-Ṣādiq, but also because of a class and family culture that had nothing to do with lawfulness and unlawfulness, as explained above.

In sum, the fact that *mutʿa* was lawful did not mean that it was advisable, in good taste, or desirable to all. There were—and are—numerous other "lawful" things that many people would nonetheless never approach.[128]

To those who might insist that anyone who considers a practice legal should be ready to do it themselves, the following brief examples should provide clarification. A number of *ḥadīth*-oriented jurists in the early and later periods considered the urine of a camel to be lawful to drink,[129] even

lust other than fornication. See also the following reports in Kulaynī, *Kāfī*, 5:452–53 (the first report also in Aḥmad b. Muḥammad b. ʿĪsā, *Nawādir*, 87):

علي بن يقطين قال: سألت أبا الحسن عن المتعة فقال: ما أنت وذاك وقد أغناك الله عنها؟

[ʿAlī b. Yaqṭīn:] I asked Abū al-Ḥasan [Mūsā al-Kāẓim] about *mutʿa*. He said, "What do you have to do with that? God has made you free of this need."

الفتح بن يزيد قال: سألت أبا الحسن عن المتعة فقال: هي حلال مباح مطلق لمن لم يغنه الله بالتزويج.

[Fatḥ b. Yazīd:] I asked Abū al-Ḥasan about *mutʿa*. He said, "It is lawful for the one whom God has not made free of need by marriage."

كتب أبو الحسن إلى بعض مواليه: لا تشتغلوا بها عن فُرُشكم وحرائركم.

Abū al-Ḥasan wrote to some of his clients: "Do not let it [*mutʿa*] divert your attention from your families and free wives."

126 Similarly, many families and groups also frown on their sons or daughters marrying a widow or a widower as their first marital experience. Likewise, the overemphasis on the hymen in many Muslim communities, even though the Imams (e.g., Kulaynī, *Kāfī*, 5:413) and other early authorities of Islam (e.g., ʿAbd al-Razzāq, *Muṣannaf*, 7:106) emphasized that it was a bodily feature that could easily be damaged by simple physical acts, is another example of a cultural behavior that has nothing to do with Islamic tradition and norms.

127 See the advice of Jaʿfar al-Ṣādiq in Ṭūsī, *Tahdhīb*, 7:253 against entering into temporary relationships with "believing women." There is at least one monograph against the practice of *mutʿa* with female descendants of the Prophet. See *Risāla fī ḥurmat al-tamattuʿ bi'l-ʿAlawiyyāt*, mentioned in Āghā Buzurg al-Ṭihrānī, *Dharīʿa*, 6:395.

128 In several statements quoted earlier, the Imam said that something was not unlawful, but "people feel disgust and desist from it, and so we [too] feel disgust and desist from it." See, for instance, ʿAyyāshī, *Tafsīr*, 2:126, 3:4; Ṭūsī, *Tahdhīb*, 9:6, 18.

129 See *al-Mawsūʿa al-fiqhiyya* (Kuwait), 40:91–92. The case of *mutʿa* was certainly different, as it was not an idea of "some jurists" but was unanimously agreed to have been endorsed by

if not as a remedy for certain illnesses, as some people in ancient times had advocated. But did this mean that a certain ʿAbd Allāh b. ʿUmayr al-Laythī,[130] who in a conversation about *mutʿa* with Muḥammad al-Bāqir confused lawfulness with desirability,[131] drank a glass of "camel cola" with his daily breakfast? Perhaps he did, but the overwhelming majority of human beings never shared his enthusiasm. Similarly, some early jurists and later schools considered lizards, jerboas, and whole frogs to be lawful for consumption,[132] but did ʿAbd Allāh b. ʿUmayr al-Laythī enjoy these items for his daily lunch and dinner? Perhaps he did, but not everybody would find these items as appetizing as he did. The oft-repeated question of some opponents of the concept of *mutʿa* as to whether those who believed in its lawfulness would allow their female relatives to practice it[133] is thus irrelevant.

IV. Triple Divorce

The question of whether a man may divorce his wife by uttering a single statement of divorce pronounced as three divorces all at once or three statements of divorce on a single occasion has been well covered. Some prominent jurists from other schools,[134] as well as the personal status codes of some Muslim countries, adopted Jaʿfar al-Ṣādiq's position that requires divorce pronouncements to be issued one by one, in three different sessions. There is no need to delve into this issue deeply, as it is covered in each and every work on Islamic family law.[135] It should suffice to note that Qurʾān 2:229–30 set the standard for legal divorce, and it does not permit a triple divorce to be uttered in a single pronouncement. However, in response to specific circumstances in his time, ʿUmar declared that, as a matter of discipline, he would hold people responsible for reckless utterances

---

the Prophet, at least once upon a time, and was attested to have been practiced by a good number of distinguished Companions during his lifetime. However, the question of whether those who consider something lawful should be happy to apply it to themselves and their families applies to both cases alike.

130 Possibly the same as ʿAbd Allāh b. ʿUbayd b. ʿUmayr al-Laythī al-Makkī (d. 113). See Mizzī, *Tahdhīb al-Kamāl*, 15:259–61, and the sources cited in the editor's footnotes.

131 Aḥmad b. Muḥammad b. ʿĪsā, *Nawādir*, 86; Kulaynī, *Kāfī*, 5:449.

132 See Cook, "Early Islamic Dietary Law," especially 220–32, 252–53.

133 For another early example of that genre, see Kulaynī, *Kāfī*, 5:450 (also Marzubānī, *Akhbār shuʿarāʾ al-Shīʿa*, 88; Ibn al-Nadīm, *Fihrist*, 224 [in the footnote, from a manuscript of the work]). This was an alleged conversation between Abū Ḥanīfa and the Shīʿī theologian Ṣāḥib al-Ṭāq. However, a variant of the story is attributed to a conversation between Abū Ḥanīfa and Ibn Abī Laylā in Muwaffaq b. Aḥmad al-Makkī, *Manāqib Abī Ḥanīfa*, 1:145.

134 For what happened to two Mālikī jurists who supported this opinion, one in Seville in the third century and the other in Córdoba in the fourth century, see respectively Qāḍī ʿIyāḍ, *Madhāhib al-ḥukkām*, 284–85 and Wansharīsī, *Miʿyār*, 4:436–40.

135 For a very basic explanation of the topic, see the entry on *ṭalāḳ* in *Encyclopaedia of Islam* II, 10:151–56 [J. Schacht].

of a triple divorce. His ruling remained the norm in the Sunnī schools of law, which considered triple divorce in a single pronouncement wrong, but nevertheless granted it full legal effect. Jaʿfar al-Ṣādiq and his father disagreed with this ruling, arguing that only a legal divorce should have legal effect. The following reports explain their viewpoints and arguments:

> رُوي عن الأئمّة – عليهم السلام – أنّ طلاق السنّة هو أنّه إذا أراد الرجل أن يطلّق امرأته تربّص بها حتّى تحيض وتطهر ثمّ يطلّقها بشاهدين عدلين في موقف واحد بلفظة واحدة، فإن أشهد على الطلاق رجلاً وأشهد بعد ذلك الثاني لم يَجز ذلك الطلاق إلّا أن يشهدهما جميعًا في مجلس واحد. فإذا مضت بها ثلاثةُ أطهار فقد بانت منه. فإن تزوّجها بعد ذلك تزوّجها بمهر جديد. فإن أراد طلاقها طلّقها للسنّة على ما وصفت. ومتى طلّقها طلاق السنّة فجائز له أن يتزوّجها بعد ذلك. وكلّ طلاق خالف السنّة فهو باطل. ومن طلّق امرأته للسنّة فله أن يراجعها ما لم تنقضِ عدّتها. فإذا انقضت عدّتها بانت منه. وعلى المطلِّق للسنّة نفقة المرأة والسكنى ما دامت في عدّتها، وهما يتوارثان حتّى تنقضي العدّة.[136]
>
> It was reported from the Imams that a [valid] divorce according to the Sunna is that the man who wants to divorce his wife waits until she commences and then concludes a menstrual cycle, and then he may divorce her in the presence of two upright witnesses, in one setting, and in one pronouncement. If one man witnesses the divorce and another man bears witness to it at a later time, the divorce is not effective until they bear witness together in a single setting. Once three periods of purity have elapsed, then the wife is separated from the husband. If he remarries her after that, he does so with a new dower. If he decides to divorce her [again], he should do so according to the Sunna, as described. When he divorces her according to the Sunna, he is permitted to marry her again. Any divorce contrary to the Sunna is invalid. Whoever divorces his wife according to the Sunna may take her back so long as her waiting period has not concluded; if her waiting period concludes, she is separated from him. Whoever divorces according to the Sunna owes his wife maintenance and lodging as long as she is in her waiting period, and they inherit from one another until the waiting period is concluded.

136 Ibn Bābawayh, *Faqīh*, 3:320.

أبو بصير عن أبي عبد الله قال: سألته عن طلاق السُنّة؟ فقال: طلاق السُنّة إذا أراد الرجل أن يطلّق امرأته يدعها إن كان قد دخل بها حتّى تحيض ثم تطهر، فإذا طهرت طلّقها واحدة بشهادة شاهدين، ثمّ يتركها حتى تعتدّ ثلاثة قروء، فإذا مضت ثلاثة قروء فقد بانت منه بواحدة، وكان زوجها خاطبًا من الخطّاب، إن شاءت تزوّجته وإن شاءت لم تفعل. فإن تزوّجها بمهر جديد كانت عنده على اثنتين باقيتين وقد مضت الواحدة. فإن هو طلّقها واحدة أخرى على طهر من غير جماع بشهادة شاهدين ثمّ تركها حتّى تمضي اقراؤها، فإذا مضت اقراؤها من قبل أن يراجعها فقد بانت منه باثنتين، وملكت أمرها، وحلّت للازواج، وكان زوجها خاطبًا من الخطّاب، إن شاءت تزوّجته وإن شاءت لم تفعل. فإن هو تزوّجها تزويجًا جديدًا بمهر جديد كانت معه بواحدة باقية وقد مضت اثنتان، فإن أراد أن يطلّقها طلاقًا لا تحلّ له حتّى تنكح زوجًا غيره، تركها حتّى إذا حاضت وطهرت وأشهد على طلاقها تطليقة واحدة، ثمّ لا تحلّ له حتى تنكح زوجًا غيره.

وأمّا طلاق الرَّجعة فأن يدعها حتّى تحيض وتطهر ثمّ يطلّقها بشهادة شاهدين ثمّ يراجعها ويواقعها ثمّ ينتظر بها الطُّهر. فإذا حاضت وطهرت أشهد شاهدين على تطليقة أخرى ثمّ يراجعها ويواقعها ثمّ ينتظر بها الطُّهر، فإذا حاضت وطهرت أشهد شاهدين على التطليقة الثالثة. ثمّ لا تحلّ له أبدًا حتّى تنكح زوجًا غيره. وعليها أن تعتدّ ثلاثة قروء من يوم طلّقها التطليقة الثالثة. فإن طلّقها واحدة على طهر بشهود ثمّ انتظر بها حتّى تحيض وتطهر ثمّ طلّقها قبل أن يراجعها [لم] يكن طلاقه الثاني طلاقًا لأنّه طلّق طالقًا، لأنّه إذا كانت المرأة مطلّقة من زوجها كانت خارجة من ملكه حتّى يراجعها، فإذا راجعها صارت في ملكه ما لم يطلّق التطليقة الثالثة. فإذا طلّقها التطليقة الثالثة فقد خرج مِلك الرَّجعة من يده، فإن طلّقها على طهر بشهود ثمّ راجعها وانتظر بها الطهر من غير مواقعة فحاضت وطهرت ثمّ طلّقها قبل أن يدنّسها بمواقعة بعد الرجعة لم يكن طلاقه لها طلاقًا، لأنه طلّقها التطليقة الثانية في طهر الأولى ولا ينقض الطهر إلّا بمواقعة بعد الرجعة، وكذلك لا تكون التطليقة الثالثة إلّا بمراجعة ومواقعة بعد المراجعة ثمّ حيض وطهر بعد الحيض ثمّ طلاق بشهود حتّى يكون لكلّ تطليقة طهر من تدنيس المواقعة بشهود.[137]

137 Kulaynī, *Kāfī*, 6:66–67.

[Abū Baṣīr:] I asked Abū ʿAbd Allāh about divorce according to the Sunna. He said, "Divorce according to the Sunna is when a man who wants to divorce his wife avoids her [that is, does not have intercourse with her], if he has already had intercourse with her [after her last menstrual period], until she starts menstruating and then stops. When the menstrual period ends, he divorces her once with two witnesses present. He then leaves her for a waiting period of three menstrual cycles. Once three menstrual cycles pass, she is separated from him by one statement of divorce. [Should she want to remarry], her former husband can be one of her suitors, and she is free to marry him or not. If he marries her with a new dower, she is with him with two [divorces] remaining, one having been used. If he divorces her once again when she is in a state of purity during which they have not had intercourse, in the presence of two witnesses, and then leaves her until her [three] menstrual cycles pass, then once her menstrual cycles elapse and he has not assumed her back, she has separated from him twice. Once again, she has authority over her own affairs and is permitted to marry others. Her [former] husband can again be one of the suitors, and she is free to marry him or not. If he marries her anew with a new dower, she is with him with one remaining [divorce], two having been used. If he wishes to divorce her—[such that] she would no longer be lawful for him until she has married someone else—he must leave her until she commences and concludes a menstrual cycle and a single divorce is issued and witnessed. Then she is not lawful for him until she has married someone else.

"The recurrent divorce is when he avoids her until she commences and concludes her menstrual cycle, then he divorces her in the presence of two witnesses, then he takes her back [that is, they recommence the union] and has intercourse with her, and then he waits until she concludes a menstrual cycle. Once she has commenced and concluded a menstrual cycle, he secures two witnesses to another divorce; then he returns to her, has intercourse with her, and awaits the conclusion of another menstrual cycle. Once she has commenced and concluded a menstrual cycle, and he has secured two witnesses to a third divorce, she is no longer lawful to him until she has married someone else. She must wait three menstrual cycles from the day he divorces her for the third time.

"If he divorced her once in the presence of witnesses, waited for the commencement and conclusion of a menstrual cycle, and then divorced her before taking her back, that does not count as a second divorce because he only divorced her once. That is because if a woman is divorced by her husband, she is no longer under his authority until he takes her back. If he takes her back, she is under his authority so long as he does not proclaim a third divorce. If he divorces her a third time, he no longer has the authority to take her back. If he divorced her while she was in a state of ritual purity and in the presence of witnesses, then assumed her back and waited until she concluded her period of purity without having intercourse with her, then she commenced and concluded a menstrual cycle, and then he divorced her without having soiled her with intercourse after taking her back, that does not count as a divorce. This is because he issued the second divorce while she was still in a state of purity following the first [divorce], and the requisite period of ritual purity does not elapse until there is intercourse after he has taken her back. Likewise, the third divorce does not occur unless he has taken her back, they have had intercourse after she has come back, and her menstruation commences and concludes; [only] then can the divorce occur in the presence of witnesses. Each divorce must be done with witnesses [after] assuming a state of purity following the soiling of intercourse."

V. Other Matters Pertaining to Private Life

The school of Medina was known in the early periods as espousing peculiar opinions that were criticized by the jurists of the school of Iraq and others.[138] A case in point was an unusual opinion on sexual behavior that affirmed the availability of the wife's entire body for the husband's pleasure,[139] allowing abnormal sexual relations between husband and wife.[140] Such relations were strictly forbidden by other schools and jurists.

Nāfiʿ attributed a view in favor of this position to ʿAbd Allāh b. ʿUmar, a claim that was denied by ʿAbd Allāh's son Sālim and others.[141] There were others, too, who were quoted as endorsing it.[142] Early Mālikīs in the western part of the Muslim world attributed the same opinion to Mālik,[143] although

---

138 See Ibn Ḥajar, *Talkhīṣ al-ḥabīr*, 3 380. (See also Ḥākim al-Naysābūrī, *Maʿrifat ʿulūm al-ḥadīth*, 251.)

139 E.g., Wansharīsī, *al-Miʿyār al-muʿrib*, 3:259.

140 E.g., Ḍirār b. ʿAmr, *Taḥrīsh*, 131; Jāḥiẓ, *al-Shārib wa'l-mashrūb*, 277; ʿAyyāshī, *Tafsīr*, 1:224 (also Ṭūsī, *Tahdhīb*, 7:415); Ibn Taymiyya, *Musawwada*, 519.

141 Ṭabarī, *Jāmiʿ al-bayān*, 2:405–6.

142 Ṭabarī, *Jāmiʿ al-bayān*, 2:407; Qurṭubī, *Jāmiʿ*, 4:8.

143 See especially Ibn Rushd, *al-Bayān wa'l-taḥṣīl*, 18:460–61, quoting the third-century Mālikī law text *ʿUtbiyya* (by Muḥammad b. Aḥmad b. ʿAbd al-ʿAzīz al-Qurṭubī [d. 254–55]) on which *al-Bayān wa'l-taḥṣīl* is a commentary. It is interesting that the original work used cryptography here so that the rank and file could not understand what the jurists were talking about. Ibn Rushd explained how to decipher the codes (18:462) and the editor of the work has transliterated the text into normal Arabic in the footnotes. See also Ibn Ḥajar, *Talkhīṣ al-ḥabīr*, 3:374–76.

other Mālikīs denied the attribution.[144] There are some fairly detailed discussions of the topic in the law books of the Mālikīs[145] and others.[146]

Numerous reports from Jaʿfar al-Ṣādiq strongly condemn such sexual practices.[147] As is usual in this genre, there are also reports that ascribe to him the opposite position, known to have been supported by other jurists of Medina at the time. But this is a clear misattribution.[148] Besides, a statement from the Imam,[149] quoted earlier in this chapter, addressed situations involving contradictory reports and advised his followers to follow the report that contradicted the dominant opinion of the community—in this case, the Medinan view that such behavior was permissible.

In the time of Muḥammad al-Bāqir, this type of sexual behavior even led to a death, and the case was brought to his attention.[150] It is difficult to imagine that jurists who came to know of such fatalities could have deemed the acts that caused them legally and ethically acceptable.[151]

There was also a peculiar opinion among the jurists of Mecca at the time that allowed a master to offer his or her female slave to someone else for the purpose of sexual relations between the latter and the slave, such as a mother offering her female slave to her son when he reached puberty, a phenomenon that seems to have been not uncommon. This opinion was

---

144 See especially Qurṭubī, *Jāmiʿ*, 4:8–10.

145 E.g., Ibn Rushd, *al-Bayān wa'l-taḥṣīl*, 18:460–63; Ibn Ḥajar, *Talkhīṣ al-ḥabīr*, 3:379; Wansharīsī, *al-Miʿyār al-muʿrib*, 3:258–59. See also Ṭarsūsī, *Tuḥfat al-Turk*, 90.

146 There was a similar disagreement among the Shāfiʿīs in the early centuries. See Māwardī, *al-Ḥāwī al-kabīr*, 11:433–39, where the author says:

ذهب بعض أصحابنا إلى إحلاله وآخرون إلى تحريمه.

> Some of our colleagues supported its lawfulness, others its prohibition.

(See also Ibn Ḥajar, *Talkhīṣ al-ḥabīr*, 3:372–73; cf. Shāfiʿī, *Umm* [Manṣūra, 2001], 7:511.)

147 ʿAyyāshī, *Tafsīr*, 1:225; ʿAlī b. Ibrāhīm, *Tafsīr*, 1:73. Zaydī Shīʿa, too, reject the practice. See Yaḥyā al-Hādī, *Aḥkām*, 1:409–10; ʿAlawī, *al-Jāmiʿ al-kāfī*, 4:190–91.

148 One of the most prominent Shīʿī jurists of all time, who investigated the chains of transmission of various reports on this topic in the Shīʿī sources, concluded that not a single report had a reliable *isnād* (Shahīd al-Thānī, *Masālik al-afhām*, 7:58–59).

149 Ṭūsī, *Tahdhīb*, 8:98.

150 Ibn Bābawayh, *Faqīh*, 4:111; Ṭūsī, *Tahdhīb*, 10:233.

151 The editor of Mizzī, *Tahdhīb al-Kamāl* [Beirut, 1983], 26:150, line 15, and the accompanying note (no. 1) attributed this behavior to a group of Ghulāt whom this editor identified as *Kharibiyya*, to which the poet Kuthayyir ʿAzza (d. 107) belonged. This is a clear misreading of the name *Khashabiyya* (the supporters of Mukhtār al-Thaqafī, the governor of Kūfa in 66–67, whose name the editor read and recorded correctly in line 15 of the same page, again as the group with which the same poet was affiliated). However, no historical or heresiographical source seems to have attributed that practice to this group, nor even named a group as *Kharibiyya* (except occasionally as a corruption of the name *ḥarbiyya* [or *ḥarthiyya*], the supporters of a certain ʿAbd Allāh b. ʿAmr b. Ḥarb [or Ḥārith], who joined ʿAbd Allāh b. Muʿāwiya al-Ṭālibī [d. 129] in his revolt against the Umayyads). Ṭabarī, *Jāmiʿ al-bayān*, 4:403–13, on the other hand, named other groups and individuals who continued to advocate this unethical behavior in the early Muslim community.

supported by a number of eminent students of Ibn ʿAbbās such as ʿAṭāʾ, Ṭāwūs, Jābir b. Zayd, and their students.[152] Once again, some transmitters attributed statements in favor of the practice to Jaʿfar al-Ṣādiq, whose legal positions in numerous other cases were similar to those of Ibn ʿAbbās.[153] In this specific case, however, there is no evidence to suggest that Ibn ʿAbbās in fact supported the opinion as such.[154] Even if he did so, Jaʿfarī law does not systematically follow his views; numerous opinions quoted from him in early sources do not agree with the positions of Jaʿfarī law.[155] Zaydī[156] and Ismāʿīlī[157] Shīʿa, too, were against the practice, unless the master gave the slave as a gift (*hiba*), and thus transferred the ownership of the slave to the recipient. This also might have been how Ḥasan al-Baṣrī (d. 110) understood the concept of offering one's female slave to someone else, as he held that the recipient would then have the option of manumitting the slave if he so wished.[158]

This is not the right place to discuss the question of slavery and how it was introduced into Islam. However, since it is related to the matter at hand, I briefly mention that early in Islamic history, there were scholars and groups who considered slavery unlawful and, even more emphatically, deemed a master's sexual relations with his female slave to be unlawful. The present author has discussed these viewpoints in more detail elsewhere.[159]

VI. Wiping over Boots in Ritual Ablution (*al-Masḥ ʿalā al-Khuffayn*)[160]

Qurʾān 5:6 instructs Muslims to wash their faces and hands to the elbows and to wipe over their heads and feet up to the ankles before starting prayer. This is the meaning of the passage at face value, and it is the meaning that the House of the Prophet followed. The majority of the Muslims since the early times, however, wash their feet instead of wiping over them. They

---

152 ʿAbd al-Razzāq, *Muṣannaf*, 7:215–17; Mufīd, *al-Masāʾil al-Ṣāghāniyya*, 71. See further Ibn Ḥazm's discussion in *Muḥallā*, 9:207–9.

153 See Madelung, "ʿAbd Allāh b. ʿAbbās and Shīʿite Law," 14–21.

154 There is only an ambiguous report from him concerning this behavior in ʿAbd al-Razzāq, *Muṣannaf*, 7:216. That, however, does not fully accord with what his students maintained in this case.

155 See Madelung, "ʿAbd Allāh b. ʿAbbās and Shīʿite Law," 23–24.

156 ʿAlawī, *al-Jāmiʿ al-kāfī*, 4:209.

157 Qāḍī Nuʿmān, *Daʿāʾim al-Islām*, 2:245–46.

158 See the reports from Ḥasan in ʿAbd al-Razzāq, *Muṣannaf*, 7:215–17.

159 Modarressi, "Nawādir-i fiqhī-yi Khawārij wa Muʿtazila," 208, 215–18. See further Motzki, "Wa'l-muḥṣanātu mina n-nisāʾ"; Rabb, *Doubt in Islamic Law*, 50–51 and note 6 (with references).

160 Most of the discussions and references in this section are adapted from the text of a paper delivered by the author at a conference in 2013 and published in the proceedings of the conference: Michalak-Pikulska et al. (eds.), *Ibadi Jurisprudence: Origins, Developments, and Cases*, 111–19.

have their own way of explaining the text of the Qurʾān in this case. There are numerous reports from the Companions and others in the Sunnī *ḥadīth* collections that confirm this latter understanding.

Arguing for the Sunnī practice of washing the feet rather than wiping over them as suggested by the Qurʾān, Ibn Ḥazm, who was a great scholar of Arabic in addition to being an eminent jurist, and who supported the majority opinion in this case, commented:

> وممّا نسخ فيه السنّةُ القرآنَ قوله تعالى: ﴿وَامْسَحُوا بِرُءُوسِكُمْ وَأَرْجُلَكُمْ إِلَى الْكَعْبَيْنِ﴾ فإنّ القراءة بخفض أرجلكم وبفتحها كلاهما لا يجوز إلّا أن يكون معطوفًا على الرؤوس في المسح ولا بدّ، لأنّه لا يجوز البتّة أن يحال بين المعطوف والمعطوف عليه بخبرٍ غير الخبر عن المعطوف عليه، لأنّه اشكال وتلبيس وإضلال لا بيان. فلمّا جاءت السنّة بغسل الرجلين صحّ أنّ المسح منسوخٌ عنهما، وهكذا عمل الصحابة فإنّهم كانوا يمسحون على أرجلهم. وكذلك قال ابن عبّاس: نزل القرآن بالمسح.[161]

> An instance in which the Sunna abrogated the Qurʾān is where He, the Exalted, said, "Wipe your heads and feet up to the ankles [Qurʾān 5:6]." *Feet* is recited in both the genitive and accusative cases, but it must be read in conjunction with *heads* with respect to wiping. Interference between two words in a [*conjunctive*] *construction* can absolutely not occur with a predicate that differs from the one predicated on the first term in the conjunctive phrase, because instead of clarity, that would yield confusion, obscurity, and error. When the Sunna established that the feet should be washed, it proved that wiping had been abrogated for both. This was the practice of the Companions; they used to wipe over their feet. And so Ibn ʿAbbās said, "The Qurʾān prescribed wiping."[162]

Accepting this explanation requires assuming that the Prophet amended the instructions conveyed in the passage almost immediately after their revelation in the brief period of three months or so that elapsed between the revelation of the passage and his death, replacing the divine order to wipe over the feet with washing. If abrogations occurred when changing circumstances required new rules, as suggested by many authorities of the Muslim tradition, one might wonder why God, the All Knowing, should have bothered to send down a revelation that He knew He would have to

161 Ibn Ḥazm, *Muḥallā*, 4:112–13.

162 See further Sharaf al-Dīn, *Masāʾil fiqhiyya*, 80–83, where similar statements are quoted from several other major authorities in *tafsīr* and *ḥadīth*, all confirming the same points.

abrogate almost immediately through the voice of His Prophet. In addition, a report from ʿĀʾisha about the *sūra* of the Qurʾān in which the passage in question appears (*sūrat al-Māʾida*) asserts that no passage in this *sūra* was abrogated:

أما انّها آخر سورة نزلت فما وجدتم فيها من حلال فاستحلّوه وما وجدتم فيها من حرام فحرّموه.[163]

> Know that it was the last *sūra* that was revealed. So whatever you find in it as lawful, deem it lawful, and whatever you find in it as unlawful, deem it unlawful.[164]

The Qurʾānic passage in question was concerned only with washing and wiping over parts of the body, with no reference to footwear. However, a report suggests that during the Battle of Tabūk (a military expedition directed against Byzantium in the year 9 of the *hijra*), the Prophet allowed the Muslim warriors to keep their boots on and wipe over them as the last item of the minor ritual ablution before performing their prayers. As suggested by a large number of reports,[165] the majority of the first-generation Muslims followed this practice even when they were not in the midst of a battle or on the road.[166] A relatively smaller number of Companions of the Prophet, ʿAlī and Ibn ʿAbbās in particular, disagreed. They argued that the practice predated, and hence had been abrogated by, the Qurʾānic passage.[167]

Ever since the early centuries of Islam, Sunnī schools and scholars have unanimously supported the first opinion and maintained that wiping over boots in ablution was a valid and legitimate practice.[168] This opinion and the

163 Ḥākim al-Naysābūrī, *Mustadrak*, 2:370.

164 Cf. Ibn al-ʿArabī, *Masālik*, 2:146, where the author insists that this *sūra* was revealed before the Battle of Tabūk in the year 9.

165 See, for instance, Bayhaqī, *Sunan*, 1:405–13.

166 This may indicate that the practice had long been established as a general rule and was not just an exception made for the battlefield in the year 9 of the *hijra* as suggested by the above-mentioned report. Muslims were performing prayers, presumably with the required ritual ablution, long before the last year of the Prophet's life, the assumed date of revelation of the fifth *sūra* of the Qurʾān, in which the passage in question appears, and consequently the date of that passage, too. (This is certainly the case if one accepts the commonly supported proposition that all passages of a *sūra* were revealed in succession and that no passages were inserted into various *sūra*s either at random or on some other basis at the time of the Qurʾān's compilation, and if, in turn, one accepts the accuracy of the extremely doubtful story of the collection of the Qurʾān. See Modarressi, "Early Debates.") It might thus be suggested that Muslims originally wiped over their boots all along until the new rules were set by the Qurʾānic passage in question.

167 Ibn Abī Shayba, *Muṣannaf*, 1:338; Ṭūsī, *Tahdhīb*, 1:361–62.

168 Ibn al-Mundhir, *Ijmāʿ*, 20; Ibn Qudāma, *Mughnī*, 1:358.

practice it sanctioned were commonly rejected by the Shīʿa and the Ibāḍīs[169] on the basis of the explicit designation in the aforementioned Qurʾānic passage, which mentions only face, hands, head, and feet and which, in their view, abrogated the previous practice.[170] The dispute thus turned into a sectarian issue, with prominent Sunnī authorities declaring the practice inherent to the Sunna,[171] more meritorious than washing the feet[172] and even obligatory,[173] and proclaiming belief in its legality to be part of the Sunnī creed.[174] Certain scholars among the majority who had no inclination to compromise and who preferred to raise the fences as high as possible called any opponent of the practice a heretic;[175] some even feared that such

169 Marwazī, *Sunna*, 257; Ashʿarī, *Maqālāt al-Islāmiyyīn*, 2:161; Nawawī, *Majmūʿ*, 1:513; Fakhr al-Dīn al-Rāzī, *Tafsīr*, 11:163; ʿAynī, *ʿUmdat al-qārī*, 2:97; Ibn Ḥajar, *Fatḥ al-Bārī*, 1:404. The two groups share parts of their legal heritage thanks to the time that they spent together in ʿAlī's camp in Kūfa before the Arbitration (*taḥkīm*).

170 Rabīʿ b. Ḥabīb, *Musnad*, no. 123; Sharīf al-Murtaḍā, *Rasāʾil*, 3:183–84. See also Marwazī, *Sunna*, 257, and Fakhr al-Dīn al-Rāzī, *Tafsīr*, 11:163, quoting the opponents' argument.

171 Ashʿarī, *Ibāna*: 26; Ashʿarī, *Maqālāt al-Islāmiyyīn*, 1:295; Ibn Baṭṭa, *Ibāna*, 312; Barbahārī, *Sharḥ al-sunna*, 79.

172 Lālakāʾī, *Sharḥ*, 1:171 (quoting Sufyān al-Thawrī):

> يا شعيب بن حرب! لا ينفعك ما كتبت لك حتى ترى المسح على الخفّين دون خلعهما أعدل عندك من غسل قدميك.
>
> O Shuʿayb b. Ḥarb! What I have written for you will not benefit you until you see that wiping over boots without removing them is better than washing your feet.

See also Ibn Qudāma, *Mughnī*, 1:361; Ibn Taymiyya, *Majmūʿat fatāwā*, 22:423; Ibn Ḥajar, *Fatḥ al-Bārī*, 1:404 (quoting Ibn al-Mundhir).

173 Abū Ḥanīfa (attr.), *Waṣiyya*, 50: المسح على الخفّين واجب. The statement is, however, problematic, as neither Abū Ḥanīfa nor any other Muslim authority ever considered the practice obligatory; cf. Abū Ḥanīfa (attr.), *al-Fiqh al-akbar*, 186: المسح على الخفّين سُنّة.

174 Taftāzānī, *Sharḥ al-Maqāṣid*, 104 (quoting the Companion Anas b. Mālik); ʿAynī, *ʿUmdat al-qārī*, 2:97 (quoting Abū Ḥanīfa); Aḥmad, *Ṣifat al-muʾmin*, 294; Lālakāʾī, *Sharḥ*, 1:205 (quoting Sahl b. ʿAbd Allāh al-Tustarī); Ṭaḥāwī, *ʿAqīda*, 49; Ashʿarī, *Ibāna*, 26; Ashʿarī, *Maqālāt al-Islāmiyyīn*, 1:295; Nasafī, *ʿAqāʾid*, 1:80.

175 Abū Nuʿaym, *Ḥilyat al-awliyāʾ*, 7:32 (quoting Sufyān al-Thawrī: "Accuse whoever who does not wipe over boots of deviation from religion"); Ibn Baṭṭa, *Ibāna*, 312 ("No one rejects wiping over boots except a heretic"); Taftāzānī, *Sharḥ al-Maqāṣid*, 104 ("Whoever does not regard wiping over boots as valid is a heretic"). See also Ibn Daqīq al-ʿĪd, *Iḥkām al-aḥkām*, 1:111:

> وقد اشتهر جواز المسح على الخفّين عند علماء الشريعة حتّى عدّ شعارًا لاهل السنّة وعدّ انكاره شعارًا لاهل البدع.
>
> The permissibility of wiping over boots has become so widespread among the scholars of the *sharīʿa* that it counts as a symbol of the *ahl al-sunna* and its rejection constitutes a symbol of the heretics.

The point is put even more forcefully by Ibn al-ʿArabī, *Masālik*, 2:145:

> الحكم الجليل الّذى به فُرّق بين أهل السنّة وأهل البدع وهو المسح على الخفّين، لا يُنكره إلاّ مخذول مبتدع خارج عن جماعة المسلمين أهل السنّة والأثر، لا خلاف بينهم فيه، إلاّ قوم ابتدعوا وأنكروا

opponents might qualify as infidels.[176] As in all cases of sectarian dispute in which the minority opinion sounded more in line with the Qurʾān, an extensive and impressive body of *ḥadīth*s was contributed by *ḥadīth* transmitters to fill the gap in support of the majority opinion.[177]

وقالوا: إنّه خلاف القرآن وغير القرآن قد نسخه، ومعاذ الله أن يخالف رسول الله – صلّى الله عليه وسلّم – كتاب الله.

The noble ruling that divides followers of the Sunna from heretics is the one about [the legality of] wiping over boots. No one rejects this ruling except a wretched heretic who has left the community of Muslims, that is, the followers of the Sunna and established practices, who all agree on this point, except for some heretics who deny [the legality of] the practice and say, "The ruling is against the Qurʾān, and what [is claimed to have] abrogated the Qurʾānic rule was non-Qurʾānic." [The author comments:] Far be it from the Prophet to have ever acted against the Book of God. [Needless to say, the jurists who are against the practice do not believe in the truth of the reports that ascribed it to the Prophet].

176 Abū Ḥanīfa, *Waṣiyya*, 50: ومن أنكر يُخشى عليه الكفر; Taftāzānī, *Sharḥ al-Maqāṣid*, 104, quoting Abū al-Ḥasan al-Karkhī: أخاف الكفر على من لا يرى المسح على الخفّين. The argument was that those who denied the validity of the practice rejected a widely transmitted (*mutawātir*) *ḥadīth* (as explained below), an act that some considered tantamount to denying an essential component of Islam (see Modarressi, "Essential Islam," 206–7). The prominent Ḥanafī jurist Abū Bakr al-Sarakhsī was more conciliatory in his discussion of different categories of widespread transmission (Sarakhsī, *Uṣūl*, 1:293):

وقسمٌ لا يُضَلَّل جاحده ولكن يُخَطّأ ويُخشى عليه الاثم وذلك نحو خبر المسح بالخفّ.

There is a kind [of widespread transmission] that one would not be called a heretic for rejecting but one will be condemned as misled, and the concern will be that one is sinful. An example [of that kind of transmission] is [denying] the report regarding wiping over boots.

177 As noted earlier, the number of transmissions produced by the supporters of the legality of wiping over boots was so impressive that the issue was thought to constitute an example of *tawātur*, belonging to the collective memory of the community of the faithful. In the words of Ibn Abī al-ʿIzz al-Dimashqī, *Sharḥ*, 2:551:

تواترت السنّة عن رسول الله بالمسح على الخفّين والرافضة تخالف هذه السنّة المتواترة.

Reports from the Messenger of God about the *sunna* of wiping over boots are widely transmitted (*mutawātir*), but the Rāfiḍa oppose this mass-transmitted *sunna*.

However, in Abū Ḥanīfa, *Waṣiyya*, 50, the relevant reports are described as being "close to *tawātur*." The Shāfiʿī scholar Badr al-Dīn al-Zarkashī (d. 794) suggested that citations on the two issues of wiping over boots and stoning as a punishment for adultery became widespread only in the second to fourth generations of Muslims. He argued that the reports in both cases nevertheless qualify as *mutawātir* and are as such valid beyond discussion (Zarkashī, *al-Baḥr al-muḥīṭ*, 3:307, also 313). They have to be so for important reasons: in the first case (wiping over boots), to prove abrogation of a Qurʾānic passage (5:6), which can be established only through *tawātur*, and in the second (stoning), to close the door against any suggestion that Qurʾān 24:2, which advised lashing, might have abrogated the long-established, pre-Islamic custom of the Arabs and others to stone adulterers. In the latter case, however, some scholars found a shortcut around the *tawātur* requirement by suggesting that Qurʾān 24:2 had been qualified by another Qurʾānic revelation that had sadly been lost; they maintained that the sheet of paper on which it had been written was gobbled up by a domestic animal shortly after the death of the Prophet while his household was preoccupied with his funeral arrangements (see Modarressi, "Early Debates," 10–11, and the sources cited therein).

In line with the tradition of the House of the Prophet, which always aligned with ʿAlī's opinion, Jaʿfar al-Ṣādiq, too, considered the Qurʾānic passage to apply in perpetuity:

الحلبي قال: سألت أبا عبد الله عن المسح على الخفّين فقال: لا تمسح. إنّ جدّي قال: سبق الكتاب الخفّين.[178]

[Muḥammad al-Ḥalabī:] I asked Abū ʿAbd Allāh about wiping over boots. He said, "Do not wipe. My grandfather [ʿAlī] said, 'The Book outlawed the [practice of wiping over] boots.'"

حسّان المدائنى قال: سألت جعفر بن محمّد عن المسح على الخفّين فقال: لا تمسح، ولا تصلّ خلف من يمسح.[179]

[Ḥassān al-Madāʾinī:] I asked Jaʿfar b. Muḥammad about wiping over boots. He said, "Do not wipe [over boots], and do not pray behind anyone who wipes [over boots]."

الكلبي النسّابة عن جعفر بن محمّد قال: قلت له: ما تقول في المسح على الخفّين؟ فتبسّم ثمّ قال: إذا كان يوم القيامة وردّ الله كلّ شيء إلى سببه،[180] وردّ الجلد إلى الغنم، سترَى أصحاب المسح أين يذهب وضوؤهم![181]

[Kalbī al-Nassāba:] I said to Jaʿfar b. Muḥammad, "What is your opinion on [the permissibility of] wiping over boots?" He smiled and said, "When the Day of Resurrection arrives and God returns everything to its origin and returns the hide to the sheep,[182] the people who wipe [over boots] will see where their ablution will go!"

عن جعفر بن محمّد قال: إنّ مِن أشدّ الناس حسرةً يوم القيامة من رأى وضوءه على جلد غيره.[183]

178 Ṭūsī, *Tahdhīb*, 1:361.
179 Ḥimyarī, *Qurb al-isnād*, 162.
180 The word is corrupted in the edition of the source used here to شيئه.
181 Kulaynī, *Kāfī*, 1:350.
182 As commonly known, shoes in premodern times were normally made of leather. The Mālikīs, whose opinions usually represented the customs of Medina in the second century, specified that only boots made of leather could be wiped over in ritual ablution. See *al-Mawsūʿa al-fiqhiyya* (Kuwait), 37:265.
183 Ibn al-Rāzī, *Kitāb al-Ghāyāt*, 232. Cf. Ibn Bābawayh, *Faqīh*, 1:30 where the statement is quoted by ʿĀʾisha from the Prophet.

Jaʿfar b. Muḥammad said, "Some of those who will have the most regrets on the Day of Resurrection are those who see their ablution on another's skin."

موسى بن جعفر عن أبيه جعفر بن محمّد قال: أخبرني جدّي القاسم بن محمّد بن أبي بكر قال: سمعت عائشة تقول: لئن شلّت يدي أحبّ إليّ من أن أمسح على الخفّين.[184]

[Mūsā b. Jaʿfar:] Jaʿfar b. Muḥammad said, "My [maternal] grandfather, Qāsim b. Muḥammad b. Abī Bakr, informed me that he heard ʿĀʾisha say, 'I would prefer my arm to be paralyzed to wiping over boots.'"

موسى بن جعفر عن أبيه جعفر بن محمّد قال: نشد عمر بن الخطّاب الناس من رأى رسول الله – صلّى الله عليه وآله وسلّم – مسح على الخفّين؟ فقام ناس من أصحاب رسول الله – صلّى الله عليه وآله وسلّم – فشهدوا أنّهم رأوا رسول الله – صلّى الله عليه وآله وسلّم – مسح على الخفّين. فقال علي: سَلهم أقبل نزول المائدة أم بعدها؟ فقالوا: لا ندري! فقال علي: لكنّي أدري. إنّه لمّا نزلت سورة المائدة رُفع المسح [على الخفّين].[185]

[Mūsā b. Jaʿfar:] Jaʿfar b. Muḥammad reported, "ʿUmar b. al-Khaṭṭāb asked those who saw the Messenger of God (may God's prayer and peace be upon him and his Family) wipe over his boots to come forth to testify. Some of the Companions of the Messenger of God (may God's prayer and peace be upon him and his Family) came forth and testified that they saw the Messenger of God (may God's prayer and peace be upon him and his Family) wipe over his boots. ʿAlī said, 'Ask them whether it was before or after the revelation of [the *sūra* of] *Māʾida*.' They said, 'We do not know!' ʿAlī said, 'But I know. When the *sūra* of *Māʾida* was revealed, it abrogated wiping [over boots].'"[186]

---

184 Ibn al-Ashʿath, *Ashʿathiyyāt*, 24. See also ʿAbd al-Razzāq, *Muṣannaf*, 1:221, where ʿĀʾisha is quoted as saying:

لَئن يُقطع قدمى أحبّ إليّ من أن أمسح على الخفّين.

> I would prefer having my foot cut off to wiping over boots.

And Ibn Bābawayh, *Amālī*, 744 where she is quoted as saying:

لَئن أمسح على ظهر عَيرٍ بالفلاة أحبّ إليّ من أن أمسح على خُفّي.

> I would prefer wiping over the back of a wild donkey in the desert to wiping over boots.

185 Ibn al-Ashʿath, *Ashʿathiyyāt*, 24.

186 See further on this dispute Sharaf al-Dīn, *Masāʾil fiqhiyya*, 93–101.

VII. Reciting the Opening Formula Aloud (*al-Jahr bi'l-Basmala*)

With a single exception,[187] all *sūras* of the Qurʾān open with the phrase "In the name of God, the Beneficent, the Merciful." There was a dispute among Muslims about whether this opening formula was an integral part of the *sūras*. The Shāfiʿīs concluded that the opening formula was a part of the first *sūra* of the Qurʾān, *Fātiḥat al-Kitāb*, but they disagreed among themselves on the other *sūras*.[188] The other three Sunnī schools maintained that the formula was not a part of any *sūra*, and—with the exception of the Ḥanafīs, who read it silently[189]—they omitted it altogether when reciting the Qurʾān in prayers, reasoning that it constituted a non-Qurʾānic element.[190]

The dispute can be traced back to the early days of Islam. ʿAlī is known to have considered the opening formula an integral part of each and every *sūra* in which it appeared and recited it aloud in his prayers.[191] By contrast, the Umayyads, who habitually disparaged and discouraged anything closely associated with ʿAlī's name,[192] banned the practice.[193] The Shīʿa[194] and the Ibāḍīs[195] subsequently disagreed with the Sunnīs on this point. They continued to regard the opening formula as part and parcel of each *sūra* in which it appears and to recite it in their prayers. The members of both schools recite the phrase aloud in those prayers that are required to be performed audibly, but the Imāmī Shīʿa recite it aloud even when the rest of the prayer is to be performed quietly,[196] a practice interpreted as a symbol of defiance

187 The ninth *sūra*, the *sūra* of Repentance.

188 See, for instance, Nawawī, *Majmūʿ*, 3:290.

189 Ibn Qudāma, *Mughnī*, 2:148–50.

190 Ibn Qudāma, *Mughnī*, 2:151–53.

191 Bayhaqī, *Sunan*, 2:70; Fakhr al-Dīn al-Rāzī, *Tafsīr*, 1:205:

أمّا أنّ علي بن أبي طالب كان يجهر بالتسمية فقد ثبت بالتواتر.

That ʿAlī b. Abī Ṭālib used to recite "In the name of God, the Beneficent, the Merciful" aloud is established through mass transmission.

192 See references to this in section I on p. 237 of the present chapter.

193 Fakhr al-Dīn al-Rāzī, *Tafsīr*, 1:206 (quoted previously):

إنّ عليًا كان يبالغ في الجهر بالبسملة فلمّا وصلت الدولة إلى بني أميّة سعوا إلى إبطال آثار علي.

ʿAlī used to recite "In the name of God, the Beneficent, the Merciful" out loud. When the Umayyads came to power, they worked hard to erase his influence.

194 They included both the Imāmīs (see, for instance, Jawād al-ʿĀmilī, *Miftāḥ al-karāma*, 7:65–66 and the many sources and authorities cited therein) and the Zaydīs (e.g., Aḥmad b. ʿĪsā, *Amālī*, 1:114–23; ʿAlawī, *al-Jāmiʿ al-kāfī*, 2:100–102, both with long lists of the legal authorities of the House of the Prophet who agreed on this point; see also the decree by the Dāʿī Ḥasan b. Zayd, ruler of Ṭabaristān [r. 250–70], in Ibn Isfandiyār, *Tārīkh-i Ṭabaristān*, 1:240). See further Shahristānī, *Mafatīḥ al-asrār*, 1:74.

195 Sālimī, *Maʿārij al-āmāl*, 4:84, 93–95. See also Shammākhī, *Īḍāḥ*, 1:478.

196 Jawād al-ʿĀmilī, *Miftāḥ al-karāma*, 7:201–5, and other sources cited therein. The Zaydīs disagree on this point, reciting the formula quietly in those prayers (ʿAlawī, *al-Jāmiʿ al-kāfī*, 2:103).

and a mark of their opposition to the Umayyads.[197] The anti-Umayyad significance of the practice persuaded the Shīʿa to identify it as one of the five indicators of the faith—the five symbolic actions that draw a line between a Shīʿī and a non-Shīʿī in the Muslim community.[198] This in turn prompted some Sunnī scholars to react by advising against the practice as a matter of creed, because of its symbolic significance.[199]

Here are a few reports on the matter from Jaʿfar al-Ṣādiq that demonstrate his position on the opening formula and his uniform adherence to the practice of reciting it aloud:

محمّد بن مسلم قال: سألت أبا عبد الله عن «السبع المثاني والقرآن العظيم»، أهي الفاتحة؟ قال: نعم! قلت: بسم الله الرحمن الرحيم من السبع؟ قال: نعم! هي أفضلهنّ.[200]

[Muḥammad b. Muslim:] I asked Abū ʿAbd Allāh whether the "seven oft-repeated [passages] and the Mighty Qur'ān"[201] refer to the *Fātiḥat* [*al-Kitāb*]. He said, "Yes!" I said, "Is 'In the name of God, the Beneficent, the Merciful' part of the seven?" He said, "Yes! It is the best of them."

مسمع البصري قال: صلّيت مع أبي عبد الله فقرأ «بسم الله الرحمن الرحيم الحمد لله ربّ العالمين».[202]

[Mismaʿ al-Baṣrī:] I prayed with Abū ʿAbd Allāh, and he recited "In the name of God, the Beneficent, the Merciful. Praise be to God, Lord of the Universe" [the opening of the first *sūra*].

صفوان الجمّال قال: صلّيت خلف أبي عبد الله أيّامًا، فكان إذا كانت صلاة لا يجهر فيها جهر ببسم الله الرحمن الرحيم [وأخفى ما سوى ذلك]. وكان يجهر في السورتين جميعًا.[203]

197 Sālimī, *Maʿārij al-āmāl*, 4:95.

198 Ṭūsī, *Tahdhīb*, 6:52.

199 Lālakā'ī, *Sharḥ*, 1:171 (quoting Sufyān al-Thawrī):

> يا شعيب بن حرب! لا ينفعك ما كتبت حتّى يكون إخفاء بسم الله الرحمن الرحيم في الصلاة أفضل عندك من أن تجهر بها.
>
> O Shuʿayb b. Ḥarb! What I have written for you will not benefit you until you consider reciting "In the name of God, the Beneficent, the Merciful" quietly during prayer more praiseworthy than reciting it aloud.

Ibn Baṭṭa, *Ibāna*, 315 ("It is *sunna* to not recite the *basmala* aloud"); Ibn Taymiyya, *Majmūʿat fatāwā*, 22:423; Ibn Taymiyya, *Minhāj al-sunna*, 4:151. See also Rāfiʿī, *Fatḥ al-ʿAzīz*, 2:453.

200 Ṭūsī, *Tahdhīb*, 2:289. Also in Sayyārī, *Qirā'āt*, 13, through a different transmitter.

201 From Qur'ān 15:87.

202 Ṭūsī, *Tahdhīb*, 2:288.

203 Sayyārī, *Qirā'āt*, 11; Kulaynī, *Kāfī*, 3:315; Ṭūsī, *Tahdhīb*, 2:68 (all with variations).

[Ṣafwān al-Jammāl:] I prayed behind Abū ʿAbd Allāh for several days. When the prayer was one in which recitation was done quietly, he would recite "In the name of God, the Beneficent, the Merciful" aloud [and recited everything else quietly]. He would recite it aloud in both *sūras*.[204]

حنان بن سدير قال: صلّيت خلف أبي عبد الله فتعوّذ بإخفاء[205] ثم جهر ببسم الله الرحمن الرحيم.[206]

[Ḥanān b. Sadīr:] I prayed behind Abū ʿAbd Allāh. He recited the *taʿawwudh/istiʿādha* [that is, the declaration seeking refuge in God from the accursed devil, which precedes recitations of the Qurʾān] quietly, and then he recited "In the name of God, the Beneficent, the Merciful" aloud.

أبو حفص الصائغ قال: صلّيت خلف جعفر بن محمّد فجهر ببسم الله الرحمن الرحيم.[207]

[Abū Ḥafṣ al-Ṣāʾigh:] I prayed behind Jaʿfar b. Muḥammad and he recited "In the name of God, the Beneficent, the Merciful" aloud.

عبد الله بن يحيى الكاهلي قال: صلّى بنا أبو عبد الله في مسجد بني كاهل، فجهر مرّتين ببسم الله الرحمن الرحيم.[208]

[ʿAbd Allāh b. Yaḥyā al-Kāhilī:] Abū ʿAbd Allāh led us in prayer in the mosque of the Banū Kāhil[209] and he twice recited "In the name of God, the Beneficent, the Merciful" aloud.

---

204 That is, in the first *sūra*, *Fātiḥat al-Kitāb*, and in whichever *sūra* he happened to recite after it in the second of a prayer's two Qurʾānic recitations.

205 The source reads باجهار, which is most likely a corruption of بإخفاء or بإخفات, as is suggested by the words ثمّ جهر immediately after it. The author who quoted this report in his *Tahdhīb* (Ṭūsī) tells us in his *Kitāb al-Khilāf* (1:326–27) of a unanimous opinion among the Shīʿa to recite the *istiʿādha* quietly. This is the majority opinion in Sunnī law, too. See Ibn Qudāma, *Mughnī*, 2:146; *al-Mawsūʿa al-fiqhiyya* (Kuwait), 4:12–13.

206 Ṭūsī, *Tahdhīb*, 2:289, with a variant in Ḥimyarī, *Qurb al-isnād*, 124 (but the text in the manuscript of this latter work used by Ḥurr al-ʿĀmilī in *Wasāʾil al-Shīʿa*, 6:135 is closer to the version quoted in Ṭūsī).

207 Ṭūsī, *Amālī*, 273.

208 Ṭūsī, *Tahdhīb*, 2:288.

209 A mosque in Kūfa. See Modarressi, *Tradition and Survival*, 1:163.

عبد الرحمن بن محمّد قال: صلّيت خلف جعفر بن محمّد المغرب فجهر ببسم الله الرحمن الرحيم.[210]

[ʿAbd al-Raḥmān b. Muḥammad:] I prayed *the maghrib* prayer behind Jaʿfar b. Muḥammad and he recited "In the name of God, the Beneficent, the Merciful" aloud.

VIII. Other Issues Concerning Prayer

*A. The Call to Prayer (***Adhān***)*

The story of the introduction of the call to prayer (*adhān*) has been recounted in different ways by the two main traditions in Islam. Whereas the Sunnī tradition ascribed the origin of the call to prayer to a dream[211] had by a certain Companion, ʿAbd Allāh b. Zayd,[212] the tradition of the House of the Prophet insisted that the *adhān* was not human in origin but rather was taught to the Prophet by the angel Jibrīl (Gabriel).[213] Statements attributed to Jaʿfar al-Ṣādiq censure those who trace the *adhān* to a dream:

إنّ دين الله أعزّ من أن يُرى في النوم.[214]

The religion of God is too honorable to be dreamed of in one's sleep.

يتنزّل الوحي على نبيّكم وتزعمون أنّه أخذ الأذان من عبد الله بن زيد؟[215]

Your Prophet receives revelation, and you say that he adopted the call to prayer from ʿAbd Allāh b. Zayd?

According to reports quoted from Jaʿfar al-Ṣādiq,[216] the original *adhān* included a call to the "best of acts" (حيّ على خير العمل), understood in the context to refer to the prayer. The phrase was reportedly taken out during the caliphate of ʿUmar because of a shift of the caliphate's current priorities

210 Aḥmad b. ʿĪsā, *Amālī*, 1:123.

211 On the value of dreams as a possible source of Islamic laws, see the discussion in Zarkashī, *al-Baḥr al-muḥīt*, 1:62–63 and 6:106, where he assigns no value to dreams (see further Sharīf al-Murtaḍā, *Masʾala fī al-manāmāt* in his *Amālī*, 2:392–85 and *Rasāʾil*, 2:7–14). However, some Muslim jurists at times mentioned dreams to support an argument. See, for instance, Sarakhsī, *Mabsūṭ*, 1:28, 75. See also Ibn Ṭāwūs, "Risāla fī ʿadam muḍāyaqat al-fawāʾit," 345–48; Modarressi, "Dukhāniyyāt-i fiqh," 188–89.

212 ʿAbd al-Razzāq, *Muṣannaf*, 1:455–56, 461–62; Ibn Abī Shayba, *Muṣannaf*, 1:215, 2:5–8; Ibn Mājah, *Sunan*, nos. 706–7; Abū Dūwūd, *Sunan*, nos. 498–99; Tirmidhī, *Sunan*, no. 189.

213 Kulaynī, *Kāfī*, 3:302.

214 Kulaynī, *Kāfī*, 3:482.

215 Qāḍī Nuʿmān, *Daʿāʾim al-Islām*, 1:172. See also Shahīd al-Awwal, *Dhikrā al-Shīʿa*, 3:195.

216 Ṭūsī, *Istibṣār*, 1:306; Ṭūsī, *Tahdhīb*, 2:59–61.

from prayer to *jihād*.[217] ʿAlī b. al-Ḥusayn Zayn al-ʿĀbidīn called the version that included the extra sentence "the original *adhān*" (*al-adhān al-awwal*).[218] Sunnī sources tell us that ʿAbd Allāh b. ʿUmar and ʿAlī b. al-Ḥusayn Zayn al-ʿĀbidīn included it in their *adhān*.[219] Other members of the House of the Prophet,[220] including Muḥammad al-Bāqir,[221] Jaʿfar al-Ṣādiq,[222] and Zayd b. ʿAlī,[223] as well as some other early Muslims,[224] did the same, as did the Khārijī Najda al-Ḥarūrī, and presumably other Khawārij, too.[225]

*B. Combining Prayers (*al-Jamʿ bayn al-Ṣalātayn*)*

The four major schools of Sunnī law agree that every daily prayer has a specific time when it should be performed and that performing the noon and afternoon or the dusk and evening prayers together is unlawful, except in specific cases and circumstances. Some early jurists of the Ḥijāz[226] and a few later jurists, mainly among the Mālikīs, disagreed[227] on the basis of a statement from Ibn ʿAbbās, who reported that the Prophet used to perform those prayers together even when there were no specific circumstances:

217 Aḥmad b. ʿĪsā, *Amālī*, 1:92; Ibn Bābawayh, *ʿIlal al-sharāʾiʿ*, 2:56 (from Ibn ʿAbbās); ʿAlawī, *Adhān*, 21–25, 30, 63, 70, 72–73, 76–77, 79.

218 Bayhaqī, *Sunan*, 1:625; ʿAlawī, *Adhān*, 22–23, 63–73, 7679.

219 ʿAbd al-Razzāq, *Muṣannaf*, 1:460, 464; Ibn Abī Shayba, *Muṣannaf*, 2:27–28; Bayhaqī, *Sunan*, 1:624–25. See also ʿAlawī, *Adhān*, 21–23, 55–77.

220 See Aḥmad b. ʿĪsā, *Amālī*, 1:92; Yaḥyā al-Hādī, *Aḥkām*, 1:84; Qāḍī Nuʿmān, *Daʿāʾim al-Islām*, 1:172–75; Iṣbahānī, *Maqātil al-Ṭālibiyyīn*, 446; ʿAlawī, *Adhān*, 54, 80, 84, 86–91; Ibn al-Murtaḍā, *al-Baḥr al-zakhkhār*, 2:189. See also the aforementioned decree by the Dāʿī Ḥasan b. Zayd in Ibn Isfandiyār, *Tārīkh-i Ṭabaristān*, 1:240.

221 Aḥmad b. ʿĪsā, *Amālī*, 1:92; ʿAlawī, *Adhān*, 75, 78–80.

222 Ṭūsī, *Istibṣār*, 1:306; ʿAlawī, *Adhān*, 85.

223 ʿAlawī, *Adhān*, 82–83.

224 Bayhaqī, *Sunan*, 1:625; ʿAlawī, *Adhān*, 54–75. There is a monograph on the topic by a contemporary scholar, ʿAlī al-Shahristānī, titled *al-Adhān bayna al-aṣāla wa'l-taḥrīf: Ḥayyi ʿalā khayr al-ʿamal, al-sharʿiyya wa'l-shiʿāriyya*, with useful references and historical information.

225 Ibn Abī al-Zamanayn, *Uṣūl al-sunna*, 283.

226 Ḥākim al-Naysābūrī, *Maʿrifat ʿulūm al-ḥadīth*, 251, quoting Awzāʿī (also Ibn Ḥajar, *Talkhīṣ al-ḥabīr*, 3:379).

227 See the monograph on the topic by a Moroccan scholar, Aḥmad b. Muḥammad b. al-Ṣiddīq al-Ghumārī: *Izālat al-khaṭar ʿamman jamaʿa bayn al-ṣalātayn fī al-ḥaḍar*, 44–45; see also Āl al-Mujaddid al-Shīrāzī, "Ḥukm al-jamʿ bayn al-ṣalātayn," for a useful review of some of the main discussions on the topic.

ابن عبّاس قال: جمع النبي – صلّى الله عليه وسلّم – بين الظهر والعصر [والمغرب والعشاء] بالمدينة في غير سفر ولا مطر.[228] قلت: يا أبا العبّاس![229] ولِمَ فعل ذلك؟ قال: أراد أن لا يُحرج أمّته.[230]

Ibn ʿAbbās said, "The Prophet (may God's prayer and peace be upon him) combined the *ẓuhr* and *ʿaṣr* prayers [as well as the *maghrib* and *ʿishāʾ* prayers] in Medina without being in a situation of travel or rain." I said, "O Abū al-ʿAbbās! Why did he do that?" He said, "He did not want to impose hardship on his community."

Jaʿfar al-Ṣādiq and his father endorsed the report and told their followers that combining prayers was permissible, despite their strong emphasis on performing each prayer in its respective *best time*:[231]

زرارة عن أبي عبد الله قال: صلّى رسول الله – صلّى الله عليه وآله وسلّم – بالناس الظهر والعصر حين زالت الشمس في جماعة من غير علّة وصلّى بهم المغرب والعشاء الآخرة قبل سقوط الشفق في جماعة من غير علّة. وإنّما فعل رسول الله – صلّى الله عليه وآله وسلّم – [ذلك] ليتّسع الوقت على أمّته.[232]

[Zurāra:] Abū ʿAbd Allāh said, "The Messenger of God (may God's prayer and peace be upon him and his Family) led the people in the *ẓuhr* and *ʿaṣr* prayers in congregation when the sun had passed its

---

228 The last word, مطر, is also given as سفر / خطر / خوف, which suggests that later transmitters were quoting a written text, with different transmitters reading it differently. There are many similar examples in the Sunnī *ḥadīth* collections. A similar case in a Shīʿī *ḥadīth* work is a report from ʿAlī:

من جدّد قبرًا أو مثّل مثالاً فقد خرج عن الإسلام.

> Whoever rebuilds a grave or sets up an image [as a representation of a deity] abandons Islam.

The first verb in this sentence is read by respected Shīʿī *ḥadīth* authorities as جدّد / حدّد / خدّد / جدّث, with the first variant (جدّد) interpreted in two different ways. See Ibn Bābawayh, *Faqīh*, 1:120–21; Ṭūsī, *Tahdhīb*, 1:459–60. For a partial parallel, see Bukhārī, *Ṣaḥīḥ*, no. 3949.

229 This was the teknonym of Ibn ʿAbbās after the name of his first son, ʿAbbās. See Balādhurī, *Ansāb al-ashrāf*, 4:93.

230 ʿAbd al-Razzāq, *Muṣannaf*, 2:555; Muslim, *Ṣaḥīḥ*, no. 705; Aḥmad b. Ḥanbal, *Musnad*, 3:421–22, 4:338, 5:289, 345 (and other sources cited in the editors' footnotes therein). Also transmitted by Jābir b. Zayd in Rabīʿ b. Ḥabīb, *Musnad*, no. 253. As usual, there is also a report that quotes Ibn ʿAbbās as saying that combining two prayers is a major sin for a non-traveler (Ibn al-Jawzī, *Nāsikh al-ḥadīth wa-mansūkhuh*, 246 and the many sources cited in the editor's footnote, n. 5).

231 E.g., Kulaynī, *Kāfī*, 3:136, 267.

232 Ṭūsī, *Tahdhīb*, 2:263. Also Ibn Bābawayh, *ʿIlal al-sharāʾiʿ*, 2:11.

zenith without there being a reason, and he led them in the *maghrib* and *ʿishāʾ* prayers in congregation before twilight had disappeared without there being a reason. The Messenger of God (may God's prayer and peace be upon him and his Family) did that so that his community would have more flexibility in the timing [of prayers]."

عبد الله بن سنان عن أبي عبد الله أنّ رسول الله – صلّى الله عليه وآله وسلّم – جمع بين الظهر والعصر بأذانٍ وإقامتين، وجمع بين المغرب والعشاء من غير علّة باذانٍ واحد وإقامتين.[233]

[ʿAbd Allāh b. Sinān:] Abū ʿAbd Allāh said, "The Messenger of God (may God's prayer and peace be upon him and his Family) combined the *ẓuhr* and *ʿaṣr* prayers with one *adhān* and two *iqāmas*, and he combined the *maghrib* and *ʿishāʾ* prayers, without cause, with one *adhān* and two *iqāmas*."

عبد الملك القمّي عن أبي عبد الله قال: قلت له: أَجمَعُ بين الصلاتين من غير علّة؟ قال: قد فعل ذلك رسول الله – صلّى الله عليه وآله وسلّم. أراد التخفيف عن أمّته.[234]

[ʿAbd al-Malik al-Qummī:] I asked Abū ʿAbd Allāh, "Shall I combine the two prayers without cause?" He said, "The Messenger of God (may God's prayer and peace be upon him and his Family) did that. He wanted to ease matters for his community."

إسحاق بن عمّار قال: سألت أبا عبد الله: نجمع بين المغرب والعشاء في الحضر قبل أن تغيب الشفق[235] من غير علّة؟ قال: لا بأس.[236]

[Isḥāq b. ʿAmmār:] I asked Abū ʿAbd Allāh, "May we combine the *maghrib* and *ʿishāʾ* prayers while in residence, before the disappearance of the twilight, without cause?" He said, "There is nothing wrong with that."

---

233 Ibn Bābawayh, *Faqīh*, 1:186.
234 Ibn Bābawayh, *ʿIlal al-sharāʾiʿ*, 2:10.
235 The word is corrupted to الشمس in the edition of the source used here; cf. Ṭūsī, *Istibṣār*, 1:272.
236 Ṭūsī, *Tahdhīb*, 2:263.

IX. Shares Exceeding the Estate (the Question of *ʿAwl*)

The Qurʾān, at 4:11–12, 176, assigns fixed shares of inheritance to certain categories of heirs. At times, the sum total of these shares exceeds the estate. Consider this example: A husband and two full sisters survive a woman. The fixed share assigned to the husband is half and the share assigned to the two sisters is two thirds. The sum total of the two numerical quantities is one sixth more than the estate. The earliest recorded case of this kind of conflict occurred during the caliphate of ʿUmar, who decided to reduce the shares proportionately. Ibn ʿAbbās disagreed. The dispute is well covered in all books on the Islamic law of inheritance.[237]

Jaʿfar al-Ṣādiq and his father agreed with Ibn ʿAbbās. There are two categories of heirs in the Qurʾān. The first consists of parents and spouses, whose possibly conflicting shares were already considered by the Qurʾān, and two different rates, one higher, the other lower, were assigned to address the potential conflict. These two types of heirs always receive their shares of the inheritance in full, according to rates specified for them in the Qurʾān for different situations. The second category contains relatives who were assigned a single rate of inheritance, such as sisters and daughters. Their share can fluctuate as a result of conflicting claims.[238] The following reports attributed to Jaʿfar al-Ṣādiq spell out his position:

أبو بكر الحضرمي عن أبي عبد الله قال: كان ابن عبّاس يقول : إنّ الّذي أحصى رمل عالج ليعلم أنّ السهام لا تعول من ستّة.[239]

[Abū Bakr al-Ḥaḍramī:] Abū ʿAbd Allāh said, "Ibn Abbas used to say, 'He Who counted the sand grains of the desert surely knows that the denominator of [inheritance] shares never increases beyond six.'"

بكير بن أعين عن أبي عبد الله قال: أصل الفرائض من ستّة أسهم، لا تزيد على ذلك ولا تعول عليها.[240]

[Bukayr b. Aʿyan:] Abū ʿAbd Allāh said, "The basis of inheritance is the denominator six. That figure never increases and the division by six never changes."

237 Also, in general, works such as *al-Mawsūʿa al-fiqhiyya* (Kuwait), 3:47–49; *Encyclopaedia of Islam* II, 1:764–65.

238 See further Ibn Ḥazm, *Muḥallā*, 9:264.

239 Ibn Bābawayh, *Faqīh*, 4:187.

240 Kulaynī, *Kāfī*, 7:81.

أبو بصير عن أبي عبد الله قال: أربعة لا يدخل عليهم ضرر في الميراث: الوالدان والزوج والمرأة.[241]

[Abū Baṣīr:] Abū ʿAbd Allāh said, "There are four categories of heirs who always get their shares in full: father, mother, husband, and wife."

بكير بن أعين عن أبي عبد الله قال: الوُلد والإخوة هم الّذين يزادون وينقصون.[242]

[Bukayr b. Aʿyan:] Abū ʿAbd Allāh said, "Children and siblings—these are the ones who get the increases and decreases [in their shares of inheritance]."

X. Three is Greater than Four: A Mathematical Paradox

In the discussion on restitution for mayhem (willful bodily injury) in his *Mughnī*, Ibn Qudāma says:

تُساوي جراح المرأة جراح الرجل إلى ثلث الدية، فان جاوز الثلث فعلى النصف. رُوي هذا عن عمر وابن عمر وزيد بن ثابت. وبه قال سعيد بن المسيّب وعمر بن عبد العزيز وعروة بن الزبير والزهري وقتادة والأعرج وربيعة ومالك. قال ابن عبد البرّ: وهوقول فقهاء المدينة السبعة وجمهور أهل المدينة. وحُكي عن الشافعي في القديم. ورُوي عن علي – رضى الله عنه – أنّها على النصف في ما قلّ أو كثر. ورُوي ذلك عن ابن سيرين. وبه قال الثوري والليث وابن أبي ليلى وابن شبرمة وأبو حنيفة وأصحابه وأبو ثور والشافعي في ظاهر مذهبه، واختاره ابن المنذر. قال ربيعة: قلت لسعيد بن المسيّب: كم في إصبع المرأة؟ قال: عشر. قلت: ففي إصبعين؟ قال: عشرون. قلت: ففي ثلاث أصابع؟ قال: ثلاثون. قلت: ففي أربع؟ قال: عشرون. قلت: لمّا عظمت مصيبتها قلّ عقلها؟! قال: هكذا السنّة يا ابن أخي![243]

The [restitution for] injury to a woman is equivalent to [the amount payable for] injury to a man, up to one-third of the blood-money [for a homicide]. If the [injury calculation] exceeds one-third, it will be half [of the blood-money]. This was reported from ʿUmar, Ibn ʿUmar, and Zayd b. Thābit, as well as Saʿīd b. al-Musayyib, ʿUmar b. ʿAbd al-Azīz, ʿUrwa b. al-Zubayr, Zuhrī, Qatāda, [ʿAbd al-Raḥmān] al-Aʿraj, Rabīʿa,

241 Kulaynī, *Kāfī*, 7:82.

242 ʿAyyāshī, *Tafsīr*, 1:375.

243 Ibn Qudāma, *Mughnī*, 12:57–58.

and Mālik. Ibn ʿAbd al-Barr said that this was the opinion of the Seven Jurists of Medina as well as other jurists of the town. It was also reportedly Shāfiʿī's old opinion. ʿAlī [on the other hand] is reported to have held that the [restitution for the injury of a woman] is half [of that of a man for every injury], whether small or large [and many other jurists agreed with this opinion]. Rabīʿa said, "I said to Saʿīd b. al-Musayyib, 'What is the restitution for a woman's finger?' He said, 'Ten [camels].' I said, 'What about two fingers?' He said, 'Twenty.' I said, 'What about three fingers?' He said, 'Thirty.' I said, 'What about four fingers?' He said, 'Twenty.' I said, 'When her injury worsens, her restitution decreases?' He said, 'That is the Sunna, O son of my brother!'"

The opinion attributed to ʿAlī in Ibn Qudāma's text, specifying a uniform standard of restitution for women's injuries, is recorded in both Sunnī[244] and Shīʿī[245] *ḥadīth* collections.[246] It clearly applies to cases of mayhem that lead to the loss of fingers, as in the scenario raised by Rabīʿa. The opposite opinion risks the paradox that Saʿīd b. al-Musayyib, the well-known late first-century jurist of Medina (d. 94), faced—namely, that the restitution for the loss of four fingers ended up being less than that for the loss of three.[247] Saʿīd b. al-Musayyib's answer is both mathematically paradoxical and legally incomprehensible.

A redaction of Saʿīd b. al-Musayyib's conversation with his student is attributed to an alleged conversation between Jaʿfar al-Ṣādiq and a learned disciple of his, Abān b. Taghlib.[248] Jaʿfar al-Ṣādiq advised his followers that when facing a case such as this one, in which a position that the common

244 Ibn Abī Shayba, *Muṣannaf*, 9:149; Bayhaqī, *Sunan*, 8:167.

245 Ṭūsī, *Tahdhīb*, 10:185.

246 There is, however, a discrepancy between two reports from ʿAlī in Sunnī *ḥadīth* collections: whereas one report quotes him as saying that the restitution for damages inflicted on a woman is half of that for damages to a man (Ibn Abī Shayba, *Muṣannaf*, 9:149), another quotes him as saying that it is the same for men and women (Ibn Abī Shayba, *Muṣannaf*, 9:150):

الشعبي عن علي: تستوي جراحات النساء والرجال في كلّ شيء.

The injuries of women and men are regarded equally in all matters.

To remove the discrepancy, one may suggest that the latter statement refers to equality between different parts of the body, not between the two genders. In other words, any finger of a man or of a woman should receive the same rate of restitution as another finger within the general Islamic law pattern of restitution for each gender, which assigns half of the restitution for a man's injury to a similarly injured woman.

247 Mālik, *Muwaṭṭaʾ* (recension of Yaḥyā b. Yaḥyā al-Laythī), 2:430 (no. 2507), and *Muwaṭṭaʾ* (recension of Abū Muṣʿab al-Zuhrī), 2:236 (no. 2278); Ibn Abī Shayba, *Muṣannaf*, 9:150; Bayhaqī, *Sunan*, 8:168.

248 Kulaynī, *Kāfī*, 7:299–300.

sense[249] could not understand was ascribed to the Imams, they should suspend judgment and refer the case to the Imams.[250] The standards of *ʿilm rijāl al-ḥadīth* concerning the reliability or lack thereof of transmitters were not applicable in such situations. The point made in the statements quoted from ʿAlī, Ibn ʿAbbās, and Muḥammad al-Bāqir about potentially conflicting inheritance shares—that there are no mathematical paradoxes in the religion of God[251]—also applies here:

إنّ الّذي أحصى رَمل عالج لَيعلم أنّ الفرائضَ لا تعول على أكثر من ستّة.

> He who counted the sand grains of the desert surely knows that the number of shares does not exceed six.

249 Various passages in the Qurʾān (e.g., 4:82, 6:50) recognize the common sense as valid. In the specific case of restitution, there seems to have been an early suggestion that the rules of restitution were administrative ordinances issued by the Prophet himself with no need for divine revelation (see, for instance, Ṣaffār al-Qummī [attr.], *Baṣāʾir al-darajāt*, 381 [see also 379–80], where a report ascribes the idea to Muḥammad al-Bāqir; see also a partially similar idea, regarding the administration of the penal code in general, attributed to the Muʿtazilī theologian Abū Hāshim al-Jubbāʾī in Ṭūsī, *Ghayba*, 94). Should such ordinances, and not direct divine revelation, have been the origin of the Islamic law of restitution, one would expect even more strongly a pattern of restitution understandable to the common sense of the time.

250 Kulaynī, *Kāfī*, 2:222.

251 Kulaynī, *Kāfī*, 7:79.

CHAPTER 4

A Selection of Legal Responses

As noted in the preceding chapters, there is an extremely large number of statements quoted from Jaʿfar al-Ṣādiq in Muslim works of diverse provenance. Multivolume collections have been assembled and published out of this material. According to one report,[1] the people who transmitted from him compiled four hundred books, including monographs on specific chapters of the law as well as notebooks: *uṣūl* or *ajzāʾ* of *ḥadīth*. They also supplied the original material for later Shīʿī *ḥadīth* collections such as *Kitāb al-Kāfī* and *Tahdhīb al-aḥkām*. A few of the original books and notebooks have survived and been published; others have been reconstructed from later collections and published in recent years, with more to come.

In the following pages, I present a small selection of this material, together with English translations. The emphasis is on texts that illustrate Jaʿfar al-Ṣādiq's style of legal interpretation and argumentation, which was a continuation of that of his father, Muḥammad al-Bāqir. To retain historical order and provide context, therefore, a few samples from Muḥammad al-Bāqir precede the selections from Jaʿfar, again with emphasis on reports that highlight the style of Muḥammad al-Bāqir's interpretation and argumentation.[2]

1 Jaʿfar b. al-Ḥasan al-Ḥillī, *Muʿtabar*, 1:26; Shahīd al-Awwal, *Dhikrā al-Shīʿa*, 1:59; Ḥusayn b. ʿAbd al-Ṣamad al-ʿĀmilī, *Wuṣūl al-akhyār*, 60; cf. Ibn Shahrāshūb, *Maʿālim al-ʿulamāʾ*, 13, where the figure of four hundred is mentioned as the number of the notebooks produced by transmitters from all the Imams, the majority understandably by the disciples of Jaʿfar al-Ṣādiq.

2 In both sections, the texts are arranged in the order in which their subject matters are addressed in traditional Islamic law books.

I. Samples of Imam Muḥammad al-Bāqir's Responses to Legal Questions

1

زرارة قال: قلت لأبي جعفر: رجلٌ كانت عنده دراهم أشهرًا فحوّلها دنانير فحال عليها منذ يوم ملكها دراهم حولٌ، أيزكّيها؟ قال: لا! ثمّ قال: أرأيت لو أنّ رجلاً دفع إليك مائة بعير وأخذ منك مائتي بقرة فلبثت عنده أشهرًا ولبثت عندك أشهرًا فموتت عندك إبله وموتت عنده بقرك، أكنتما تزكّيانها؟ فقلت: لا! قال: كذلك الذهب والفضّة. ثمّ قال: وإن حوّلت برًّا أو شعيرًا ثمّ قلبته ذهبًا أو فضّة فليس عليك فيه شيء، إلّا أن يرجع ذلك الذهب أو تلك الفضّة بعينها أو بعينه. فإن رجع ذلك عليك فإنّ عليك الزكاة، لأنّك قد ملكتها حولاً.[3]

[Zurāra:] I said to Abū Jaʿfar, "A man had some dirhams for some months and then converted them to dinars, and then a year passed from the day he had them as dirhams—does he pay *zakāt* on them?" He said, "No." Then he said, "What if a man were to give you one hundred camels and take two hundred cattle from you? [The cattle] remained with him for some months and [the camels] remained with you for some months, but then his camels died in your possession and your cattle died in his possession. Would you both have to pay *zakāt* on them?" I said, "No!" He said, "The same applies to gold and silver." Then he said, "If you convert wheat or barley and turn it into gold or silver, then you owe nothing on it unless that same gold or silver returns to you. If it returns to you, you owe *zakāt* because then you were in possession of it for one year."

2

سدير الصيرفيّ قال: قلت لأبي جعفر: ما تقول في رجل كان له مالٌ فانطلق به فدفنه في موضع، فلمّا حال عليه الحول ذهب ليخرجه من موضعه فاحتفر الموضع الّذي ظنّ أنّ المال فيه مدفونٌ فلم يصبه، فمكث بعد ذلك ثلاث سنين، ثمّ إنّه احتفر الموضع الّذي من جوانبه كلّه فوقع على المال بعينه، كيف يزكّيه؟ قال: يزكّيه لسنة واحدة، لأنّه كان غائبًا عنه وإن كان احتبسه.[4]

3 Ibn Bābawayh, *ʿIlal al-sharāʾiʿ*, 2:62.
4 Kulaynī, *Kāfī*, 3:519.

[Sadīr al-Ṣayrafī:] I said to Abū Jaʿfar, "What is your position on a man who had some money that he took and buried somewhere, and when a year had passed, he went to retrieve it and dug in the location in which he thought the money was buried but could not find it. Then three years passed. Then he dug up all the nearby locations and found it. How does he pay *zakāt* on it?" He said, "He pays *zakāt* on it in the amount due for one year, because it was inaccessible to him [for the intervening two years], even if he was the one who locked it away."

3

زرارة قال: قلت لأبي جعفر: رجلٌ كان عنده مائتا درهمٍ غير درهم أحد عشر شهرًا، ثمّ أصاب درهمًا بعد ذلك في الشهر الثاني عشر، فكملت عنده مائتا درهم. أعليه زكاتها؟ قال: لا! حتّى يحول عليه الحول وهي مائتا درهم. فإن كانت مائة وخمسين درهمًا فأصاب خمسين بعد أن يمضي شهر فلا زكاة عليه حتّى يحول على المائتين الحول. قلت: فإن كانت عنده مائتا درهمٍ غير درهم، فمضى عليها أيّامٌ قبل أن ينقضي الشهر ثم أصاب درهمًا فأتى على الدّراهم مع الدِّرهم حولٌ، أعليه زكاة؟ فقال: نعم! وإن لم يمض عليها جميعًا الحولُ فلا شيء عليه فيها.[5]

[Zurāra:] I said to Abū Jaʿfar, "A man had 200 dirhams minus one [that is, 199 dirhams] for eleven months. He then earned one dirham in the twelfth month and so had a full 200 dirhams. Does he have to pay *zakāt* on it?" He said, "No! Not until a year elapses while he has 200 dirhams. If he has 150 dirhams and then earns 50 dirhams one month later, he owes no *zakāt* until a year elapses on the 200." I said, "What if he had 200 dirhams minus one, and after some days but before the month ends, he earns one dirham, then a year elapses on the [199] dirhams in addition to the one dirham—does he owe *zakāt*?" He said, "Yes! But if a year does not elapse on the sum total of them, he owes nothing on it."

4

يزيد[6] الكناسيّ قال: قلت لأبي جعفر: متى يجوز للأب أن يزوّج ابنته ولا يستأمرها؟ قال: إذا جازت تسع سنين. فإن زوّجها قبل بلوغ التسع سنين كان الخيار لها إذا بلغت

5 Kulaynī, *Kāfī*, 3:525.

6 This is how the name appears in the printed version of the source (Ṭūsī, *Tahdhīb*, 7:382), but it is "Burayd" in Ḥurr al-ʿĀmilī, *Wasāʾil al-Shīʿa*, 20:278, on the basis of a manuscript of *Tahdhīb*. Corruption of one of these two names into the other in Arabic script is very easy and common. The Imam, however, addressed the transmitter in the conversation as "Abū Khālid."

تسع سنين. قلت: فإن زوّجها أبوها ولم تبلغ تسع سنين فبلغها ذلك فسكتت ولم تأب ذلك، أيجوز عليها؟ قال: ليس يجوز عليها رضى في نفسها ولا يجوز لها تأبّ ولا سخط في نفسها حتّى تستكمل تسع سنين، وإذا بلغت تسع سنين جاز لها القول في نفسها بالرضا والتأبّي وجاز عليها بعد ذلك وإن لم تكن أدركت مدرك النساء. قلت: أفتقام عليها الحدود وتؤخذ بها وهي في تلك الحال وإنّما لها تسع سنين ولم تدرك مدرك النساء في الحيض؟ قال: نعم! إذا دخلت على زوجها ولها تسع سنين ذهب عنها اليُتم ودُفع إليها مالها، وأقيمت الحدود التامّة عليها ولها. قلت: فالغلام يجري في ذلك مجرى الجارية؟ فقال: يا أبا خالد! إنّ الغلام إذا زوّجه أبوه ولم يُدرك كان بالخيار إذا أدرك وبلغ خمس عشرة سنة أو يُشعِر في وجهه أو ينبت في عانته قبل ذلك. قلت: فإن أدخلت عليه امرأته قبل أن يدرك فمكث معها ما شاء الله، ثمّ أدرك بعد فكرهها وتأبّاها؟ قال: إذا كان أبوه الّذي زوّجه ودخل بها ولذّ منها وأقام معها سنة فلا خيار له إذا أدرك، ولا ينبغي له أن يردّ على أبيه ما صنع، ولا يحلّ له ذلك. قلت: فإن زوّجه أبوه ودخل بها وهو غير مدرك، أتقام عليه الحدود وهو في تلك الحال؟ قال: أمّا الحدود الكاملة التي يؤخذ بها الرجل فلا، ولكن يجلد في الحدود كلّها على قدر مبلغ سنّه، يؤخذ بذلك ما بينه وبين خمس عشرة سنة. ولا تبطل حدود الله في خلقه، ولا تبطل حقوق المسلمين فيما بينهم. قلت له: جعلت فداك! فإن طلّقها في تلك الحال ولم يكن قد أدرك، أيجوز طلاقه؟ فقال: إن كان قد مسّها في الفرج فإنّ طلاقها جائز عليها وعليه. وإن لم يمسّها في الفرج ولم يلذّ منها ولم تلذّ منه، فإنّها تعزل عنه وتصير إلى أهلها فلا يراها ولا تقربه حتّى يدرك فيُسأل ويقال له: إنّك كنت قد طلّقت امرأتك فلانة. فإن هو أقرّ بذلك وأجاز الطلاق كانت تطليقة بائنة.[7]

[Yazīd al-Kunāsī:] I said to Abū Jaʿfar, "When is it permissible for a father to betroth his daughter to another without consulting her?" He said, "When she reaches the age of nine. If he betroths her before she reaches the age of nine, she has the option of annulling the marriage when she turns nine." I said, "What if her father betroths her before she reaches nine years of age and she learns of this, remains silent, and does not object; is it [that is, the betrothal] effective for her?" He said, "Her consent on behalf of herself, her refusal, and her discontent

That was, as said earlier, the default *kunya* for individuals whose name was Yazīd, indicating that the name here is in fact Yazīd, not Burayd.

7 Ṭūsī, *Tahdhīb*, 7:383.

on behalf of herself are not effective until she completes her ninth year. Once she reaches the age of nine, she may speak on her own behalf with respect to her consent or refusal, and it [that is, her decision] is then effective for her even if she has not reached womanhood." I said, "Can *ḥadd* punishments be applied to her and can she be liable for committing [*ḥadd* crimes] when she is at that stage [of minority], that is, when she is [at least] nine years old but has not reached womanhood by menstruating?" He said, "Yes! If she begins her marital life with her husband at nine, she can no longer be considered an orphan; she is given possession of her wealth, and the full *ḥadd* punishments can be imposed against her and on her behalf." I said, "Is the boy treated the same as a girl in that respect?" He said, "O Abū Khālid! If a boy is married off by his father and he has not attained [manhood], he has a choice once he attains manhood or reaches the age of fifteen or if he starts growing hair on his face or pubic region before then." I said, "What if his wife cohabits with him before he attains [manhood], and he remains with her for as long as God wills, but when he attains [manhood] he comes to hate her and refuses her?" He said, "If his father is the one who betrothed him and he [the boy] cohabits with his wife, takes pleasure in her, and resides with her for a year, then he has no option to annul [what has become a marriage] when he attains [manhood]. He should not renounce what his father did, and it is not lawful for him to do so." I said, "What if his father betroths him and he [the boy] cohabits with her before attaining [manhood]; are *ḥadd* punishments to be imposed on him at that stage?" He said, "Not the full *ḥadd* punishments that apply to men. Instead, he is to be flogged for all prescribed offenses according to his age. This is to be imposed on him on a proportional basis at the age of fifteen. God's punishments for His creation cannot be canceled and the rights of Muslims against one another are not annulled." I said to him, "May I be made your ransom! If he divorces her at that stage, before attaining [manhood], is his divorce effective?" He said, "If he has touched her in the vagina, divorcing her is effective for both of them. If he has not touched her in the vagina, and he has not taken pleasure in her nor has she taken pleasure in him, she is separated from him and returned to her family. He cannot see her nor can she go near him until he attains [manhood]. He is then told: 'You have divorced your wife so-and-so.' If he acknowledges this and approves of the divorce, the divorce is effective."

5

زرارة عن أبي جعفر، قال: سألته عن مملوك تزوّج بغير اذن سيّده. فقال: ذاك إلى سيّده، إن شاء أجازه وإن شاء فرّق بينهما. قلت: أصلحك الله! إنّ الحكم بن عتيبة وإبراهيم النخعي وأصحابهما يقولون: إنّ أصل النكاح فاسد، ولا تحلّ إجازة السيّد له. فقال أبو جعفر: إنّه لم يعص الله وإنّما عصى سيّده، فإذا أجازه فهو له جائز.[8]

[Zurāra:] I asked Abū Jaʿfar about a slave who marries without the permission of his master. He said, "The matter is for his master to decide. If he wishes he can approve it, and if he wishes he can separate them." I said, "May God put you on the right path! Ḥakam b. ʿUtayba,[9] Ibrāhīm al-Nakhaʿī,[10] and their companions say that the marriage is invalid from the start[11] and the approval of the master does not make it permissible for him." Abū Jaʿfar said, "He did not disobey God but rather disobeyed his master. So if he [the master] approves it, it is permissible for him."

6

محمّد بن مسلم عن أبي جعفر قال: إنّ أهل الكتاب وجميع من له ذمّة إذا أسلم أحد الزوجين فهما على نكاحهما، وليس له أن يخرجها من دار الإسلام إلى غيرها، ولا يبيت معها ولكنّه يأتيها بالنهار.[12]

[Muḥammad b. Muslim:] Abū Jaʿfar said, "For the People of the Book and all those who are protected, if one of the spouses becomes Muslim, their marriage stands. [Should the wife be the one who becomes Muslim,] he may not remove her from the land of Islam to someplace else. Nor may he spend the night with her, but he may visit her during the day."[13]

---

8 Kulaynī, *Kāfī*, 5:478.

9 Ḥakam b. ʿUtayba al-Kindī (d. 115), a Kūfan jurist and *ḥadīth* transmitter. He was a student of Ibrāhīm al-Nakhaʿī and Muḥammad al-Bāqir.

10 Ibrāhīm b. Yazīd al-Nakhaʿī, an eminent jurist of Kūfa (d. 96), as mentioned earlier.

11 This may refer to an earlier opinion from the two, as the opinion quoted from them in Ibn Abī Shayba, *Muṣannaf*, 6:31, agrees with Muḥammad al-Bāqir's position as stated here.

12 Kulaynī, *Kāfī*, 5:358.

13 The view is quoted in two reports from ʿAlī in Ibn Abī Shayba, *Muṣannaf*, 6:464. It is also attributed to him in Jāḥiẓ, *ʿUthmāniyya*, 90; Mufīd, *al-Masāʾil al-Ṣāghāniyya*, 65–66; Mufīd, *al-Fuṣūl al-mukhtāra*, 1:162–68. See also the following report in Ṭūsī, *Tahdhīb*, 2:199:

جميل بن دراج عن بعض أصحابنا عن أحدهما في اليهودي والنصراني والمجوسي إذا أسلمت امرأته ولم يُسلم [هو]. قال: هما على نكاحهما ولا يُفرّق بينهما، ولا يُترك أن يخرج بها من دار الإسلام.

7

أبو بصير قال: سألت أبا جعفر عن رجل تزوّج أربع نسوة في عقدة واحدة – أو قال: في مجلس واحد – ومهورهنّ مختلفة. قال: جائز له ولهنّ. قلت: أرأيت إن هو خرج إلى بعض البلدان فطلّق واحدة من الأربع، وأشهد على طلاقها قومًا من أهل تلك البلاد وهم لا يعرفون المرأة، ثمَّ تزوّج امرأة من أهل تلك البلاد بعد انقضاء عدَّة تلك المطلّقة، ثمَّ مات بعدما دخل بها، كيف يقسّم ميراثه؟ فقال: إن كان له ولدٌ فإنَّ للمرأة التي تزوّجها أخيرًا من أهل تلك البلاد رُبع ثُمن ما ترك. وإن عرفت الّتي طلقت من الأربع بعينها ونسبها فلا شيء لها من الميراث وليس عليها العدَّة. قال: ويقتسمن الثلاثة النسوة ثلاثة أرباع ثُمن ما ترك، وعليهنّ العدَّة. وإن لم تعرف الّتي طلّقت من الأربع اقتسمن الأربع نسوة ثلاثة أرباع ثُمن ما ترك بينهنَّ جميعًا، وعليهنّ جميعًا العدَّة.[14]

[Abū Baṣīr:] I asked Abū Jaʿfar about a man who marries four women with one contract (or [the narrator] said in one setting), each with a different dower. He said, "That is permissible for him and for them." I said, "What is your position on [a case in which] he [the man] goes to another land and divorces one of the four, and a group of people from that land witness the divorce but do not know the woman. He then marries a woman from the people of that land after the waiting period of the divorced one has concluded. He then dies after cohabiting with her [the new wife]. How is his inheritance divided?" He said, "If he has a child, the last woman he married from the people of that land receives one fourth of one eighth of what he leaves behind. If the identity and lineage of the woman who was divorced is known, she does not get any inheritance and she does not have a waiting period [for the death of her former husband]. The three other wives share three fourths of one eighth of what he left behind, and they have [to observe] a waiting period. If the identity of the woman who was divorced is unknown, the four women share between themselves three fourths of one eight of what he left behind, and they all have [to observe] a waiting period."

Regarding a Jew, Christian, or Magian whose wife becomes Muslim but he does not, he said, "Their marriage stands and they are not separated, and he is not allowed to take her out of the abode of Islam."

14 Kulaynī, *Kāfī*, 7:131.

8

زرارة عن أبي جعفر أنّه قال: كلُّ طلاق لا يكون على السنّة أو طلاق على العدَّة فليس بشيء. قال زرارة: فقلت لأبي جعفر: فَسِّر لي طلاق السنّة وطلاق العدَّة، فقال: أمّا طلاق السنّة فإذا أراد الرَّجل أن يطلّق امرأته فلينتظر بها حتّى تطمث وتطهر، فإذا خرجت من طمثها طلّقها تطليقة من غير جماع ويُشهد شاهدين على ذلك، ثمَّ يدعها حتّى تطمث طمثتين فتنقضي عدَّتها بثلاث حيض وقد بانت منه، ويكون خاطبًا من الخطّاب – إن شاءت تزوّجته وأن شاءت لم تتزوّجه. وعليه نفقتها والسكنى ما دامت في عدّتها، وهما يتوارثان حتّى تنقضي العدَّة. قال: وأمّا طلاق العدَّة الّذي قال الله عزَّ وجلَّ: ﴿فَطَلِّقُوهُنَّ لِعِدَّتِهِنَّ وَأَحْصُوا الْعِدَّةَ﴾ فإذا أراد الرَّجل منكم أن يطلّق امرأته طلاق العدَّة فلينتظر بها حتّى تحيض وتخرج من حيضها ثمَّ يطلّقها تطليقة من غير جماع، ويُشهد شاهدين عدلين، ويراجعها من يومه ذلك إن أحبَّ أو بعد ذلك بأيّام قبل أن تحيض، ويُشهد على رجعتها ويواقعها ويكون معها حتّى تحيض. فإذا حاضت وخرجت من حيضها طلّقها تطليقة أُخرى من غير جماع، ويُشهد على ذلك، ثمَّ يراجعها أيضًا متى شاء قبل أن تحيض، ويُشهد على رجعتها ويواقعها وتكون معه إلى أن تحيض الحيضة الثالثة. فإذا خرجت من حيضتها الثالثة طلّقها التطليقة الثّالثة بغير جماع. ويُشهد على ذلك، فإذا فعل ذلك فقد بانت منه ولا تحلُّ له حتّى تنكح زوجًا غيره. قيل له: فإن كانت ممّن لا تحيض؟ فقال: مثل هذه. تطلّق طلاق السنّة.[15]

[Zurāra:] Abū Jaʿfar said, "Any divorce not performed according to the Sunna or an *ʿidda* divorce is invalid." I said to Abū Jaʿfar, "Explain to me the proper divorce according to the Sunna and the *ʿidda* divorce." He said, "As for the divorce according to the Sunna, if a man wishes to divorce his wife he must wait until she starts and finishes a menstrual period. Once she concludes her period, he divorces her once without having intercourse with her, and two individuals bear witness to it. He then leaves her until she has undergone two menstrual cycles, so her waiting period is fulfilled by three cycles of menstruation while she is separated from him. He then becomes like a suitor among others; if she wishes she can marry him, and if she wishes not to, she need not. He is responsible for her maintenance and housing for the duration of her waiting period, and they inherit from one another until the waiting period has concluded." He said, "As for the *ʿidda* divorce, God, the

15 Kulaynī, *Kāfī*, 6:65.

Mighty and Majestic, said, 'Divorce them for [the term of] their waiting period and keep count of the waiting period.'[16] If a man among you wishes to divorce his wife with an *ʿidda* divorce, he should wait until she menstruates and concludes her menstruation, and then divorce her without having intercourse with her, with two upright individuals bearing witness. He may take her back on that same day if he wishes, or a few days later before she menstruates [again], and he has witnesses for taking her back. He has intercourse with her and remains with her until she menstruates. When she menstruates and concludes her menses, he then divorces her another time without having intercourse, and that is borne witness to. He then takes her back when he wishes before she menstruates, with witnesses, has intercourse with her, and remains with her until she menstruates for a third time. Once she concludes her third menstrual cycle he divorces her for the third time, without intercourse, and that is borne witness to. If he does so, she is separated from him and she is not lawful for him until she has married another man." It was said to him, "What if she is one of those who do not menstruate?" He said, "She is like this one [that is, the woman in the first type of divorce]. She will be divorced according to the Sunna."

9

بُريد العجلي قال: سألت أبا جعفر عن رجل كان عليه عتق رقبة فمات قبل أن يُعتِق، فانطلق ابنه فابتاع رجلاً من كيسه فاعتقه عن أبيه، وإنّ المعتَق أصاب بعد ذلك مالاً ثمّ مات وتركه، لمن يكون ميراثه؟ قال فقال: إن كانت الرقبة الّتي كانت على أبيه في نذر أو شكر أو واجبة عليه فانّ المعتَق سائبة لا سبيل لأحد عليه. قال: وإن كان توالى قبل أن يموت إلى أحد من المسلمين فضمن جنايته وجريرته، كان مولاه ووارثه، إن لم يكن له قريب يرثه. قال: وإن لم يكن توالى إلى أحد حتّى مات فإنّ ميراثه لإمام المسلمين، إن لم يكن له قريب يرثه من المسلمين. قال: وإن كانت الرقبة التي على أبيه تطوّعًا وقد كان أبوه أمره أن يعتق عنه نسمة فإنّ ولاء المعتَق هو ميراث لجميع وُلد الميّت من الرجال. قال: ويكون الذي اشتراه فاعتقه بأمر أبيه كواحد من الورثة، إذا لم يكن للمعتق قرابة من المسلمين أحرار يرثونه. قال: وإن كان ابنه الذي اشترى الرقبة أعتقها عن أبيه من ماله بعد موت أبيه تطوّعًا منه، من غير أن يكون

16 Qurʾān 65:1.

أبوه أمره بذلك، فإنّ ولاءه وميراثه للّذي اشتراه من ماله فأعتقه عن أبيه، إذا لم يكن للمعتق وارث من قرابته.[17]

[Burayd al-ʿIjlī:] I asked Abū Jaʿfar about a man who was obligated to manumit a slave but died before [doing so], so his son went and purchased a man out of his own wealth and manumitted him on his father's behalf. The manumitted individual then attained some wealth and died, leaving it behind. Who receives his inheritance? He said, "If the slave that the father was to manumit was [to be manumitted] because of a vow, as an act of gratitude [to God], or because of something obligatory for him [the owner], the manumitted individual is a *sāʾiba* [that is, a freed slave who no longer has any bond with the former master], and no one [from the former owner's family] has a right to [his inheritance]." He said, "If, before dying, he [the manumitted individual] became a client of a Muslim who assumed liability for his offenses and [other financial] liabilities, he [the latter] became his patron and his heir if he [the former] has no relative who inherits from him." He said, "If he [the manumitted individual] did not become the client of anyone before dying, then his inheritance goes to the leader of the Muslims if he has no relative among the Muslims to inherit him." He said, "If his father was going to free a slave voluntarily and ordered him [his son] to manumit an individual on his behalf, the right of succession to the inheritance of the manumitted individual becomes the inheritance of all male children of the deceased [father]." He said, "The one who purchased him and manumitted him according to his father's orders is treated as one of the heirs if the manumitted individual lacks free Muslim relatives to inherit him." He said, "If his son who purchased the slave out of his own wealth and manumitted him on behalf of his father after his father died did so voluntarily without an order from his father, the [manumitted slave's] inheritance goes to the one who purchased him with his wealth and manumitted him on his father's behalf if the manumitted individual does not have an heir among his relatives."

10

حُمران بن أعيَن قال: سألت أبا جعفر عن جارية لم تدرك، بنت سبع سنين، مع رجل وامرأة ادّعى الرجل أنّها مملوكة له وادّعت المرأة أنّها ابنتها. فقال: قد قضى في هذا علي. قلت: وما قضى في هذا؟ قال: كان يقول: الناس كلّهم أحرار إلّا من أقرّ على نفسه

17 Kulaynī, *Kāfī*, 7:171.

بالرقّ وهو مُدرك، ومن أقام بيّنة على من ادّعى من عبد أو أمة، فإنّه يُدفع إليه ويكون له رقًّا. قلت: فما ترى أنت؟ قال: أرى أن يُسئل الّذي ادّعى أنّها مملوكة له بيّنةً على ما ادّعى، فإن أحضر شهودًا يشهدون أنّها مملوكةٌ [له] لا يعلمونه باع ولا وهب، دفعت الجارية إليه، حتّى تُقيم المرأة من يشهد لها أنّ الجارية ابنتها حرّة مثلها، فلتُدفع إليها وتُخرج من يد الرجل. قلت: فإن لم يقم الرجل شهودًا أنّها مملوكة له؟ قال: تُخرج من يده. فإن أقامت المرأة البيّنة على أنّها ابنتها دفعت إليها. فإن لم يقم الرجل البيّنة على ما ادّعى ولم تقم المرأة البيّنة على ما ادّعت، خلّي سبيلُ الجارية، تذهب حيث شاءت.[18]

[Ḥumrān b. Aʿyan:] I asked Abū Jaʿfar about a girl who has not reached maturity, [a girl] of seven years [who is found] with a man and a woman. The man claims that she is his slave, and the woman claims that she is her daughter. He said, "ʿAlī rendered a judgment on this matter." I said, "What was his judgment on it?" He said, "He used to say, 'All people are free except for one who admits to being a slave and is mature and one who, whether male or female, [is claimed by] someone who produces evidence attesting to the person's being a slave; the person will be given to him and will be his slave." I said, "What is your position?" He said, "I believe that the one who claims she is his slave should be asked to produce evidence in support of his claim. If he produces witnesses who testify that she is a slave of his and they do not know him to have sold or gifted her, the girl is given to him, unless the woman brings forth someone to witness that the girl is her daughter and is free like her; then she is given to her and removed from the possession of the man." I said, "What if the man does not produce witnesses that she is his slave?" He said, "She is removed from his possession. If the woman produces evidence that she is her daughter, she is given to her. If the man does not produce evidence in support of his claim, and the woman does not produce evidence in support of her claim, the girl will be free to go wherever she pleases."

11

طربال عن أبي جعفر قال: سُئل عن رجل كانت له جارية فأغار عليه المشركون فأخذوها منه، ثمّ إنّ المسلمين بعدُ غزوهم أخذوها فيما غنموا منهم. فقال: إن كانت في الغنائم وأقام البيّنة أنّ المشركين أغاروا عليهم فأخذوها منه رُدّت عليه، وإن كانت اُشتريت وخرجت من المغنم فأصابها بعدُ رُدّت عليه برمّتها وأعطى الّذي اشتراها

18 Kulaynī, *Kāfī*, 7:420.

الثمن من المغنم من جميعه. قيل له: فإن لم يصبها حتّى تفرّق الناس وقسّموا جميع الغنائم فأصابها بعد؟ قال: يأخذها مِن الّذي هي في يده إذا أقام البيّنة، ويرجع الّذي هي في يده إذا أقام البيّنة على أمير الجيش بالثمن.[19]

[Ṭirbāl b. Rajāʾ al-Kūfī:] Abū Jaʿfar was asked about a man who had a slave girl. The polytheists attacked him and took her from him. When the Muslims attacked them, they took her from them as part of the booty. He said, "If she was part of the booty and evidence is produced that the polytheists attacked and took her from him, she will be returned to him. If she was purchased and taken from the booty and afterwards he finds her, she will be returned to him entirely[20] and the person who purchased her is given her value from the entirety of the booty." It was said to him, "What if he does not find her until after the people have parted ways and distributed all the booty?" He said, "If he produces evidence, he will take her from the person who has her in his possession, and if that person has evidence [of purchase], he is to appeal to the commander of the army for [compensation of] her value."

12

زرارة، عن أبي جعفر قال: سألته عن رجل قَتل فحُمل إلى الوالي وجاءه قوم فشهدوا عليه الشهود أنّه قتله عمدًا، فدفع الوالي القاتل إلى أولياء المقتول ليُقاد به، فلم يرتموا حتّى أتاهم رجل فأقرّ عند الوالي أنّه قتل صاحبهم عمدًا وأنّ هذا الرجل الّذي شهد عليه الشهود بريءٌ من قتل صاحبكم فلان، فلا تقتلوه به وخذوني بدمه. فقال أبو جعفر: إن أراد أولياء المقتول أن يقتلوا الّذي أقرّ على نفسه فليقتلوه ولا سبيل لهم على الآخر، ثمّ لا سبيل لورثة الّذي أقرّ على نفسه على ورثة الّذي شُهد عليه. وإن أرادوا أن يقتلوا الّذي شُهد عليه فليقتلوه ولا سبيل لهم على الّذي أقرّ، ثمّ ليؤدّى الّذي أقرّ على نفسه إلى أولياء الّذي شُهد عليه نصف الدية. قلت: أرأيت إن أرادوا أن يقتلوهما جميعا؟ قال: ذاك لهم، وعليهم أن يدفعوا إلى أولياء الّذي شُهد عليه نصفَ الدية خاصّةً دون صاحبه ثمّ يقتلوهما به. قلت: فإن أرادوا أن يأخذوا الدية؟ قال: الدية بينهما نصفان، لأنّ أحدهما أقرّ والآخر شُهد عليه. قلت: كيف جعلتَ لأولياء الّذي شُهد عليه على الّذي أقرّ على نفسه نصف الدية حين قُتل ولم تجعل لأولياء الّذي أقرّ

19 Ṭūsī, *Tahdhīb*, 6:160–61.

20 That is, the tax of one-fifth that is usually deducted from the booty of war will not be applied in this case. See *al-Mawsūʿa al-fiqhiyya* (Kuwait), 4:160, 31:305–6.

على أولياء الّذي شُهد عليه ولم يقتل؟ قال: لأنّ الّذي شُهد عليه ليس مثل الّذي أقرّ. الّذي شُهد عليه لم يقرّ ولم يُبرئ صاحبَه، والآخر أقرّ وأبرء صاحبَه، فلزم الّذي أقرّ وأبرء صاحبَه ما لم يلزم الّذي شُهد عليه ولم يقرّ ولم يُبرئ صاحبَه.[21]

[Zurāra:] I asked Abū Jaʿfar about a man who committed homicide and was taken to the governor. A group of people came and testified against him that he had killed [the victim] intentionally. The governor turned the killer over to the kin of the victim so that they could retaliate. But before they left, a man came to them and confessed in front of the governor that he had killed their companion intentionally and that the man against whom the witnesses testified was innocent of killing your companion, such-and-such. [The second man told them,] "Do not kill him [the first suspect] and take me instead on account of his [the victim's] blood." Abū Jaʿfar said, "If the kin of the victim wish to put to death the person who confessed his guilt, they may have him put to death and have no recourse against the other man [the first suspect]. The heirs of the person who confessed have no recourse against the heirs of the person who was testified against. If they [the victim's kin instead] wish to have the person who was testified against put to death, they may do so and have no recourse against the person who confessed, and the person who confessed must give the kin of the person who was testified against half of the blood-money." I said, "What is your position on [a case in which] they [the victim's kin] wish to have both of them put to death?" He said, "They may do so. They must pay half of the blood-money only to the kin of the person who was testified against and not the other, and then they may have both put to death." I said, "What if they want to accept the blood-money?" He said, "The [obligation to pay the] blood-money is split in half between the two, because one confessed and the other was testified against." I said, "How is it that you grant the kin of the person who was testified against half of the blood-money from the person who confessed when the former is killed, but you do not grant the kin of the person who confessed anything from the kin of the person who was testified against but was not killed?" He said, "This is because the person who was testified against is not like the one who confessed. The person who was testified against did not confess and he did not exonerate the other, whereas the second man confessed and exonerated the first. Thus, the person who confessed and exonerated the other has a duty

21 Kulaynī, *Kāfī*, 7:092, with minor corrections on the basis of a slightly different version of the text as recorded in Ṭūsī, *Tahdhīb*, 10:172–73.

that does not apply to the one who was testified against and who did not confess and thereby exonerate the other."

13

حبيب السجستاني قال: سألت أبا جعفر عن رجل قطع يدين لرجلين اليمينين. فقال: تُقطع يمينه للّذي قَطَع يمينه أوّلاً، وتُقطع يساره للرجل الذي قَطَع يمينه أخيرًا، لأنّه إنّما قطع يد الرجل الأخير ويمينه قصاص للرجل الأوّل. قال: فقلت: إنّ عليًا – عليه السلام – إنّما كان يقطع اليد اليمنى والرِجل اليسرى. فقال: إنّما كان يفعل ذلك فيما يجب من حقوق الله، فأمّا حقوق المسلمين فإنّه تؤخذ لهم حقوقهم في القصاص: اليد باليد إذا كانت للقاطع يد، والرِجل باليد إذا لم يكن للقاطع يد. فقلت له: أو ما تجب عليه الدية وتترك له رِجله؟ فقال: إنّما تجب عليه الدية إذا قطع يد رَجلٍ وليس للقاطع يدان ولا رجلان، فثمّ تجب عليه الدية لأنّه ليس له جارحة يقاصّ منها.[22]

[Ḥabīb al-Sijistānī:] I asked Abū Jaʿfar about a man who amputates the right hands of two men. He said, "His right hand is to be amputated for the right hand of the first person whose hand he amputated, and his left hand is to be amputated for the man whose right hand he cut last. This is because he cut the hand of the last man while his [own] right hand was due for amputation as retaliation for the first man." I said, "ʿAlī used to cut the right hand and the left foot." He said, "He used to do so where the rights of God were concerned. As for the rights of Muslims, their right of retaliation is applied as a hand for a hand if the amputator has a hand, and as a foot for a hand if the amputator does not have a hand." I said to him, "Can he be required to pay the blood-money and his foot be left alone?" He said, "The blood-money is owed if the person who amputates the hand of a man has no hands or feet. Then the blood-money is owed because he does not have a limb that can be retaliated against."

14

الحكم بن عتيبة قال: قلت لأبي جعفر: أصلحك الله! إنّ بعض الناس في فيه اثنان وثلاثون سنًّا وبعضهم لهم ثمانية وعشرون سنًّا، فعلى كم تُقسّم دية الأسنان؟ فقال: الخلقة إنّما هي ثمانية وعشرون سنًّا: اثنتا عشر في مقاديم الفم وستّة عشر سنًّا في مؤاخيره. فعلى هذا قسّمت دية الأسنان. فدية كلّ سنٍّ من المقاديم إذا كسرت حتّى

22 Kulaynī, *Kāfī*, 7:319.

يذهب خمسمائة درهم، فديتها كلّها ستّة آلاف درهم، وفي كل سنّ من المؤاخير إذا كسرت حتّى يذهب فإنّ ديتها مائتان وخمسون درهمًا. وهي ستة عشر سنًّا. فديتها كلّها أربعة آلاف درهم. فجميع دية المقاديم والمؤاخير من الأسنان عشرة آلاف درهم. وإنّما وضعت الدية على هذا، فما زاد على ثمانية وعشرين سنًّا فلا دية له، وما نقص فلا دية له. هكذا وجدناه في كتاب علي. قلت: إنّ الديات إنّما كانت تؤخذ قبل اليوم من الإبل والبقر والغنم؟ فقال: إنّما كان ذلك في البوادي قبل الإسلام، فلمّا ظهر الإسلام وكثرت الورق في الناس قسّمها أمير المؤمنين – عليه السلام – على الورق. قلت له: أرأيت من كان اليوم من أهل البوادي ما الّذي يؤخذ منهم في الدية اليوم، إبل أو ورق؟ فقال: الإبل اليوم مثل الورق، بل هي أفضل من الورق في الدية. إنّهم كانوا يأخذون منهم في دية الخطأ مائة من الإبل، يحسب بكلّ بعير مائة درهم، فذلك عشرة آلاف درهم. قلت له: فما أسنان المائة بعير؟ فقال: ما حال عليه الحول. ذُكران كلّها.

وسألت أبا جعفر عن أصابع اليدين وأصابع الرجلين: أرأيت ما زاد فيها على عشر أصابع أو نقص من عشرة فيها دية؟ فقال لي: يا حكم! الخلقة الّتي قسمت عليها الدية عشرة أصابع في اليدين، فما زاد أو نقص فلا دية له، وعشرة أصابع في الرجلين، فما زاد أو نقص فلا دية له. وفي كلّ أصبع من أصابع اليدين ألف درهم، وفي كلّ أصبع من أصابع الرجلين ألف درهم. وكلّ ما كان من شلل فهو على الثلث من دية الصحاح.[23]

[Ḥakam b. ʿUtayba:] I said to Abū Jaʿfar, “May God put you on the right path! Some people have thirty-two teeth in their mouths, and some have twenty-eight teeth. How is the restitution for teeth divided?” He said, “By nature, it is twenty-eight teeth: twelve teeth in the front, and sixteen teeth in the back. The restitution is divided according to this. The restitution for each tooth in the front, if it is knocked out, is 500 dirhams, so the total restitution is 6,000 dirhams. For each tooth in the back, if it is knocked out, the restitution is 250 dirhams; they are sixteen teeth in all, so the total restitution is 4,000 dirhams. The total restitution for all of the front and back teeth is 10,000 dirhams. The restitution is established on this basis, so there is no restitution for what is in excess of twenty-eight teeth and no restitution for anything less.[24] This is what we find in the book of ʿAlī.” I said, “Before, restitution

23 Kulaynī, *Kāfī*, 7:329–30.

24 This means that one has to pay, for instance, 9,750 dirhams in restitution for knocking out all the teeth in someone’s mouth, if one tooth at the back was missing from the beginning. So 250 dirhams will be deducted from the sum total of 10,000 dirhams, the value of restitution for all teeth, as there is no restitution payable for the missing tooth.

was paid with camels, cattle, and sheep." He said, "That was the case in the deserts before Islam. When Islam appeared and coined money became widespread among the people, the Commander of the Faithful [ʿAlī] divided the blood-money on the basis of coined money." I said to him, "What is your position on what desert-dwellers today have to pay for restitution, camels or coined money?" He said, "Camels today are like coined money, and even preferred over coined money for purposes of restitution. They used to pay 100 camels as the blood-money for an accidental death, and each camel was valued at 100 dirhams, so it was 10,000 dirhams." I said to him, "What age should the 100 camels be?" He said, "Camels that have lived one year, all of them male."

I questioned him [about restitution] with respect to fingers and toes: "Is restitution due when there are more or fewer than ten fingers?" He said to me, "O Ḥakam! The natural form according to which the restitution was divided was based on ten fingers between both hands, and there is no restitution if there are more or fewer; and ten toes between the two feet, and there is no restitution if there are more or fewer.[25] 1,000 dirhams [are due] for each finger, and one thousand dirhams [are due] for each toe. One-third of the restitution of anything healthy [is due] for what is paralyzed."

15

محمّد بن مسلم عن أبي جعفر قال: قلت له: ما تقول في امرأة ماتت وتركت زوجها وأخوتها لأُمّها وإخوة وأخوات لأبيها؟ قال: للزوج النصف: ثلاثة أسهم، ولإخوتها لأُمّها الثلث: سهمان – الذكر والأنثى فيه سواء، وبقي سهم فهو للإخوة والأخوات من الأب – للذكر مثل حظّ الأنثيين. لأنّ السهام لا تعول، وإنّ الزوج لا ينقص من النصف ولا الإخوة من الأُمّ من ثلثهم. لأنّ الله عزّ وجلّ يقول: ﴿فَإِنْ كَانُوا أَكْثَرَ مِنْ ذَلِكَ فَهُمْ شُرَكَاءُ فِي الثُّلُثِ﴾، وإن كان واحدًا فله السدس. إنّما عنى الله في قوله: ﴿إِنْ كَانَ رَجُلٌ يُورَثُ كَلَالَةً أَوِ امْرَأَةٌ وَلَهُ أَخٌ أَوْ أُخْتٌ فَلِكُلِّ وَاحِدٍ مِنْهُمَا السُّدُسُ﴾، إنّما عنى الله بذلك الإخوة والأخوات من الأُمّ خاصّة، وقال في آخر سورة النساء: ﴿يَسْتَفْتُونَكَ قُلِ اللَّهُ يُفْتِيكُمْ فِي الْكَلَالَةِ إِنِ امْرُؤٌ هَلَكَ لَيْسَ لَهُ وَلَدٌ وَلَهُ أُخْتٌ﴾ – يعني بذلك أختًا لأب وأُم وأختًا لأب – ﴿فَلَهَا نِصْفُ مَا تَرَكَ وَهُوَ يَرِثُهَا إِنْ لَمْ يَكُنْ لَهَا وَلَدٌ فَإِنْ كَانَتَا اثْنَتَيْنِ فَلَهُمَا الثُّلُثَانِ مِمَّا تَرَكَ وَإِنْ كَانُوا إِخْوَةً رِجَالًا وَنِسَاءً فَلِلذَّكَرِ مِثْلُ حَظِّ الْأُنْثَيَيْنِ﴾، وهم الّذين يزادون وينقصون. قال: ولو أنّ امرأة تركت زوجها وأُختيها لأُمّها وأُختيها

25 As explained in the previous footnote about a missing tooth.

لأبيها كان للزّوج النصف: ثلاثة أسهم، ولأُختيها لأُمّها الثلث: سهمان، ولأُختيها لأبيها السدس: سهم. وإن كانت واحدة فهو لها، لأنّ الأُختين من الأب لا يزادون على ما بقي، ولو كان أخٌ لأب لم يزد على ما بقي.[26]

[Muḥammad b. Muslim:] I said to Abū Jaʿfar, "What is your position regarding a woman who dies and leaves behind her husband, half siblings through her mother, and half brothers and sisters through her father?" He said, "The husband receives one-half, as three shares; the half siblings through her mother receive one-third, as two shares, with equal amounts to males and females; and a share remains for the half brothers and sisters through the father, with males getting the share of two females. That is because the shares do not change, the husband does not receive less than half, and the half siblings through the mother do not receive less than their third. Because God, the Mighty and Majestic, says, 'If they are more than that, they share a third,'[27] and if there is one, he gets one sixth. God's saying, 'If a man or a woman who is inherited has left neither ascendants nor descendants but has left a brother or a sister, to each of them goes one sixth,'[28] refers to brothers and sisters through the mother only. At the end of the *sūra* of Women, He says: 'They seek your legal verdict. Say, "God gives a ruling regarding those who leave no ascendants or descendants. If a man dies with no children and has a sister [meaning a full sister through both the mother and the father or a half-sister through the father], she receives half of what is left behind. And he inherits her [estate, that is, all her wealth] if she has no children. And if there are [both] brothers and sisters, males receive the share of two females."'[29] They are the ones whose [inheritance] can increase and decrease." He said, "If a woman leaves behind her husband, two half-sisters through her mother, and two half-sisters through her father, one-half goes to the husband, as three shares; one-third goes to the two half-sisters through the mother, as two shares; and one-sixth remains for the two half-sisters through the father, as one share. If there is only one sister, then [the remainder] goes to her because the two sisters through the father do not get more than what remains; and if it was a half-brother through the father, he would not get more than what remains."

26 Kulaynī, *Kāfī*, 7:103 (see also 7:101–2, where a variant of this report is attributed to Jaʿfar al-Ṣādiq).

27 Qurʾān 4:12.

28 Qurʾān 4:12.

29 Qurʾān 4:176.

16

بُكير بن أعيَن قال: جاء رجل إلى أبي جعفر فسأله عن امرأة تركت زوجها وإخوتها لأُمّها وأختًا لأبيها، فقال: للزوج النصف: ثلاثة أسهم، وللإخوة للأم الثلث: سهمان، وللأخت من الأب السدس: سهم. فقال له الرجل: فإنّ فرائض زيد وفرائض العامّة والقضاة على غير ذلك يا أبا جعفر! يقولون: للأخت من الأب ثلاثة أسهم، تصير من ستّة [و]تعول إلى ثمانية. فقال أبو جعفر: وَلِمَ قالوا ذلك؟ قال: لأنّ الله تبارك وتعالى يقول: ﴿وَلَهُ أُخْتٌ فَلَهَا نِصْفُ مَا تَرَكَ﴾. فقال أبو جعفر: فإن كانت الأخت أخًا؟ قال: فليس له إلّا السدس. فقال أبو جعفر: فما لكم نقصتم الأخ إن كنتم تحتجّون للأخت النصف بأنّ الله سمّى لها النصف، فإنّ الله قد سمّى للأخ الكلّ، والكلّ أكثر من النصف، لأنّه قال: ﴿فَلَهَا نِصْفُ﴾ وقال للأخ: ﴿وَهُوَ يَرِثُهَا﴾ – يعني جميع مالها – ﴿إِنْ لَمْ يَكُنْ لَهَا وَلَدٌ﴾. فلا تعطون الّذي جعل الله له الجميع في بعض فرائضكم شيئًا وتعطون الّذي جعل الله له النصف تامًّا؟ فقال له الرجل: وكيف تعطى الأخت النصف، ولا يعطى الذكر – لو كانت هي ذكرًا – شيئًا؟ قال: يقولون في أمّ وزوج وإخوة لأمّ وأخت لأب، فيعطون الزوج النصف، والأمّ السدس، والإخوة من الأمّ الثلث، والأخت من الأب النصف، فيجعلونها من تسعة، وهي من ستّة فترتفع إلى تسعة. قال: كذلك يقولون. قال: فإن كانت الأخت ذكرًا أخًا لأب قالوا ليس له شيء. فقال الرجل لأبي جعفر: فما تقول أنت جعلت فداك؟ فقال: ليس للإخوة من الأب والأمّ ولا الإخوة من الأمّ ولا الإخوة من الأب شيءٌ مع الأمّ.[30]

[Bukayr b. Aʿyan:] A man came to Abū Jaʿfar and asked him about a woman who left behind a husband, half-brothers through her mother, and a half-sister through her father. He said, "Half goes to the husband as three shares, a third goes to the half-brothers through the mother as two shares, and a sixth goes to the half-sister through the father as one share." The man said to him, "But the system of inheritance of Zayd [b. Thābit] and that of the majority [proto-Sunnīs] and the judges is different from that, O Abū Jaʿfar! They say, 'The half-sister through the father receives three shares; it [that is, the total number of inheritance shares] moves from six and goes up to eight.'" Abū Jaʿfar said, "Why do they say that?" He said, "Because God, the Praised and Exalted, says: 'And if he has a sister, she receives half of what he leaves behind.'"[31] Abū Jaʿfar said,

30 Kulaynī, *Kāfī*, 7:102–3.
31 Qurʾān 4:176.

"What if the sister is a brother?" He said, "He gets only one-sixth." Abū Jaʿfar said, "Why did you reduce [the share of] the brother if you claim one-half for the sister on the basis that God designated one-half for her, since God designated the full amount for the brother, and the full amount is greater than half? Because He said [about the sister], 'She receives half,' and about the brother He said, 'He inherits her [meaning all of her wealth] if she does not have a child.' So according to some of your inheritance rules you give nothing to the one for whom God designated the full amount, and you give everything to the one for whom God designated half?" The man said to him, "Why is the sister given half when the male would not be given anything if she were male?" He [the Imam] said, "Regarding [a decedent's] mother, husband, half-brothers through the mother, and half-sister through the father, they [the other jurists] give the husband half, the mother one-sixth, the half-brothers through the mother one-third, and the half-sister through the father half. They thus make it nine shares when it is six, so it is raised to nine." [The man] said, "That is [indeed] what they say." [The Imam] said, "And if the sister were a male [that is,] a half-brother through the father, they say, 'He gets nothing.'" The man said to Abū Jaʿfar, "And what is your position, may I be made your ransom?" He said, "Full brothers through the mother and the father, half-brothers through the mother, and half-brothers through the father get nothing when the mother is there."

17

بُكير بن أعيَن عن أبي جعفر قال: سأله رجلٌ عن أختين وزوج فقال: النصف والنصف. فقال الرجل: أصلحك الله! قد سمّى الله لهما أكثر من هذا! لهما الثلثان. فقال: ما تقول في أخ وزوج؟ فقال: النصف والنصف. فقال: أليس قد سمّى الله له المال فقال: ﴿وَهُوَ يَرِثُهَا إِنْ لَمْ يَكُنْ لَهَا وَلَدٌ﴾؟[32]

[Bukayr b. Aʿyan:] A man asked Abū Jaʿfar about [the inheritance shares of] two sisters and a husband. He said, "Half and half." The man said, "May God put you on the right path! God designated more than that for the two sisters! They get two thirds." He [Abū Jaʿfar] said, "What is your position about a brother and a husband?" He said, "Half and half." He [Abū Jaʿfar] said, "Did God not designate the entire wealth for him [the brother] by saying: 'He inherits her [estate] if she does not have a child'?"[33]

32 Kulaynī, *Kāfī*, 7:103.
33 Qurʾān 4:176.

18

أبو عبيدة قال: سألت أبا جعفر عن غلام وجارية زوَّجهُما وليّان لهما وهما غير مُدركين. قال: النكاح جائز. أيّهما أدرك كان له الخيار. فإن ماتا قبل أن يدركا فلا ميراث بينهما ولا مهر، إلّا أن يكونا قد أدركا ورضيا. قلت: فإن أدرك أحدهما قبل الآخر؟ يجوز ذلك عليه إن هو رضى. قلت: فإن كان الرجل هو الّذي أدرك قبل الجارية ورضى بالنكاح، ثمّ مات قبل أن تُدرك الجارية. أترثه؟ قال: نعم! يعزل ميراثها منهُ حتّى تُدرك وتحلف بالله ما دعاها إلى أخذ الميراث إلّا رضاها بالتزويج، ثمَّ يُدفع إليها الميراث ونصف المهر. قلت: فإن ماتت الجارية ولم تكن أدركت، أيرثها الزوج المدرك؟ قال: لا! لأنَّ لها الخيار إذا أدركت. قلت: فإن كان أبوها هو الّذي زوَّجها قبل أن تُدرك. قال: يجوز عليها تزويج الأب، ويجوز على الغلام، والمهر على الأب للجارية.[34]

[Bukayr b. Aʿyan:] I asked Abū Jaʿfar about a boy and a girl whose guardians betrothed them to each other before they had reached maturity. He said, "The marriage is permissible, and when each matures, each has the option [of annulling it]. If they die before attaining maturity, there is no inheritance between them nor a dower, unless they mature and consent [to the marriage]." I said, "What if one of them reaches maturity before the other?" He said, "It [the marriage] is permissible for him if he consents." I said, "What if the man becomes mature before the girl and consents to the marriage, but then dies before the girl matures, does she inherit from him?" He said, "Yes! Her inheritance from him is set aside until she matures, at which point she swears by God that she sought the inheritance only because of her consent to the marriage. The inheritance is then given to her along with half of the dower." I said, "What if the girl dies and she has not reached maturity; does her mature husband inherit from her?" He said, "No! Because she would have had the option [of annulling the marriage] had she reached maturity." I said, "What if it was her father who married her off before she reached maturity?" He said, "Her father's marriage for her has legal effect and the boy's father's marriage for the boy has legal effect for the boy, and the dower to the girl is owed by the father."

34 Kulaynī, *Kāfī*, 7:113.

19

مالك بن أعيَن عن أبي جعفر قال: سألته عن نصرانيّ مات وله ابن أخ مسلم وابن أخت مسلم وللنصراني أولاد وزوجة نصارى. فقال: أرى أن يعطى ابن أخيه المسلم ثلثي ما ترك، ويعطى ابن أخته ثلث ما ترك إن لم يكن له ولد صغار، فإن كان له ولد صغار فإنّ على الوارثين أن ينفقا على الصغار ممّا ورثا من أبيهم حتّى يدركوا. قيل له: كيف ينفقان؟ فقال: يُخرج وارث الثلثين ثلثي النفقة ويُخرج وارث الثلث ثلث النفقة، فإن أدركوا قَطَعا النفقة عنهم. قيل له: فإن أسلم الأولاد وهم صغار؟ فقال: يُدفع ما ترك أبوهم إلى الإمام حتّى يدركوا. فإن بقوا على الإسلام دفع الإمام ميراثهم إليهم، وإن لم يبقوا على الإسلام إذا أدركوا دفع الإمام ميراثه إلى ابن أخيه وابن أخته المسلمين. يُدفع إلى ابن أخيه ثلثي ما ترك ويُدفع إلى ابن أخته ثلث ما ترك.[35]

[Mālik b. Aʿyan:] I asked Abū Jaʿfar about a Christian man who died leaving a Muslim nephew through his brother, a Muslim nephew through his sister, and a Christian wife and children. He said, "My position is that the Muslim nephew through the brother is given two-thirds of what he left behind and the nephew through the sister gets one-third of what he left behind, if he did not have young children. If he had young children, the heirs should use the inheritance they receive from the children's father to pay for the maintenance of the young children until they reach maturity." It was said to him, "How are they paid the maintenance?" He said, "The heir of the two-thirds pays for two-thirds of the maintenance, and the heir of the one-third pays for one-third of the maintenance. Once they mature, the maintenance ceases." It was said to him, "What if the children convert to Islam when they have not yet reached the age of maturity?" He said, "What their father left behind is given to the *imām* until they mature. If they remain Muslim, the *imām* gives them their inheritance. If they do not remain Muslim when they reach maturity, the *imām* pays the inheritance to the Muslim nephew through his [the decedent's] brother and the Muslim nephew through his sister. The nephew through his brother receives two-thirds of what he [the decedent] left behind and the nephew through the sister receives one-third of what he left behind."

35 Kulyanī, *Kāfī*, 7:143–44.

20

أبو بصير عن أبي جعفر قال: سألته عن رجل مسلم مات وله أمّ نصرانيّة وله زوجة وولد مسلمون، قال: إن أسلمت أمّه قبل أن يقسّم ميراثه أعطيت السدس. قلت: فإن لم يكن له امرأة ولا ولد ولا وارث له سهم في الكتاب من المسلمين، وأمّه نصرانيّة، وله قرابة نصارى ممّن له سهم في الكتاب لو كانوا مسلمين، لمن يكون ميراثه؟ قال: إن أسلمت أمّه فإنّ جميع ميراثه لها، وإن لم تسلم أمّه وأسلم بعض قرابته ممّن له سهم في الكتاب فإنّ ميراثه له، وإن لم يسلم من قرابته أحدٌ فإنّ ميراثه للإمام.[36]

[Abū Baṣīr:] I asked Abū Jaʿfar about a Muslim man who died leaving a Christian mother and a Muslim wife and children. He said, "If his mother becomes Muslim before his estate is divided, she will be given one-sixth." I said, "If he does not have a wife or children, nor a Muslim heir from those [categories] that have been assigned a share of the inheritance in the Qurʾān, and his mother is Christian and he has Christian relatives who would have a share of the inheritance assigned to them in the Qurʾān if they were Muslim, to whom does his inheritance go?" He said, "If his mother becomes Muslim, she gets the entire inheritance. If his mother does not become Muslim, but some of the relatives to whom a share has been assigned in the Qurʾān become Muslim, they receive the inheritance. If none of his relatives becomes Muslim, his inheritance goes to the *imām*."

II. Samples of Imam Jaʿfar al-Ṣādiq's Responses to Legal Questions

On Ritual Purity

1

عبد الأعلى مولى آل سام قال: قلت لأبي عبد الله: عثرت فانقطع ظفري فجعلت على اصبعي مرارة فكيف أصنع بالوضوء؟ قال: يُعرَف هذا وأشباهه من كتاب الله: ﴿مَا جَعَلَ عَلَيْكُمْ فِي الدِّينِ مِنْ حَرَجٍ﴾. إمسح عليه.[37]

[ʿAbd al-Aʿlā, client of Āl Sām:] I said to Abū ʿAbd Allāh, "I tripped and my nail became detached, so I put balm on my toe. How should I perform ablution?" He said, "This and similar cases are known by the

36 Kulaynī, *Kāfī*, 7:144.

37 Kulaynī, *Kāfī*, 1:33. This report was also cited in Chapter 2 as an example of the Imam's argumentation using a Qurʾānic text.

Book of God: 'He did not place any difficulty upon you in religion.'[38] Wipe over it."

2

سألوا أبا عبد الله عن الحائض والسنّة في وقته، فقال: إنّ رسول الله – صلّى الله عليه وآله وسلّم – سنّ في الحائض ثلاث سنن بيّن فيها كلّ مشكل لمن سمعها وفهمها حتّى لا يدع لأحد مقالاً فيه بالرّأي. أمّا إحدى السّنن فالحائض الّتي لها أيّام معلومة قد أحصتها بلا اختلاط عليها ثمّ استحاضت واستمرّ بها الدّم وهي في ذلك تعرف أيّامها ومبلغ عددها، فإنّ امرأة[39] استحاضت فاستمرّ بها الدّم فأتت أمّ سلمة فسألت رسول الله – صلّى الله عليه وآله وسلّم – عن ذلك، فقال: تدع الصّلاة قدر إقرائها – أو قدر حيضها، وقال: إنّما هو عِرق، وأمرها أن تغتسل وتستثفر بثوب وتصلّي.

قال أبو عبد الله: هذه سنّة النبي – صلّى الله عليه وآله وسلّم – في الّتي تعرف أيّام إقرائها لم تختلط عليها. ألا ترى أنّه لم يسألها كم يوم هي، ولم يقل: إذا زادت على كذا يومًا فأنت مستحاضة، وإنّما سنّ لها أيّامًا معلومة ما كانت من قليل أو كثير بعد أن تعرفها. وكذلك أفتى أبي – وسئل عن المستحاضة – فقال: إنّما ذلك عِرق غابر أو ركضة من الشيطان، فلتدع الصّلاة أيّام إقرائها ثمّ تغتسل وتتوضّأ لكلّ صلاة. قيل: وإن سال؟ قال: وإن سال مثل المَثعب. قال أبو عبد الله: هذا تفسير حديث رسول الله – صلّى الله عليه وآله وسلّم – وهو موافق له. فهذه سنّة الّتي تعرف أيّام إقرائها، لا وقت لها إلّا أيّامها، قلّت أو كثرت.

---

38 Qur'ān 22:78.

39 In the edition of the source (Kulaynī's *Kāfī*) used in this study, the name of Fāṭima bt. Abī Ḥubaysh, the subject of the next story, appears here, clearly taken from a few lines later in the text. This is an obvious error, as the text explicitly makes a distinction between the two cases a few lines below:

أما تسمع رسول الله أمَرَ هذه بغير ما أمر به تلك؟

> Did you not hear the Messenger of God order this woman to do something differently from what he ordered the other woman to do?

Some Sunnī transmitters, too, confused the two stories (see the reports in Bayhaqī, *Sunan*, 1:507–18, 521). The *ḥadīth* of Umm Salama mentioned in this text does not name the woman (Abū Dāwūd, *Sunan*, nos. 274, 275, 278 and other sources cited in the editor's footnote there at 1:196–97 [of Beirut, 1996 edition]), except in a report by Ḥakam b. ʿUtayba from Muḥammad al-Bāqir, where she is named as Sawda [bt. Zamʿa, the second wife of the Prophet] (Abū Dāwūd, no. 281; Bayhaqī, 1:496; cf. 1:519–20, where she is said to have been Sahla bt. Suhayl [b. ʿAmr al-ʿĀmiriyya], and 1:523, where she is identified as Fāṭima bt. Qays [al-Fihriyya]).

وأمّا سنّة الّتي قد كانت لها أيّام متقدّمة ثمّ اختلط عليها من طول الدمّ فزادت ونقصت حتّى أغفلت عددها وموضعها من الشهر، فإنّ سنّتها غير ذلك. وذلك أنّ فاطمة بنت أبي حبيش أتت النبي – صلّى الله عليه وآله وسلّم – فقالت: إنّي أستحاض فلا أَطهر، فقال النبي – صلّى الله عليه وآله وسلّم: ليس ذلك بحيض. إنّما هو عِرق. فإذا أقبلت الحيضة فدعي الصّلاة وإذا أدبرت فاغسلي عنك الدَّم وصلّي.[40] وكانت تغتسل في كلّ صلاة وكانت تجلس في مركن لأختها وكانت صفرة الدَّم تعلو الماء.[41] فقال أبو عبد الله: أما تسمع رسول الله – صلّى الله عليه وآله وسلّم – أمر هذه بغير ما أمر به تلك؟ ألا تراه لم يقل لها: دعي الصلاة أيّام إقرائك، ولكن قال لها: «إذا أقبلت الحيضة فدعي الصلاة وإذا أدبرت فاغتسلي وصلّي»؟ فهذا يبيّن أنَّ هذه امرأة قد اختلط عليها أيامها، لم تعرف عددها ولا وقتها. ألا تسمعها تقول: إنّي أستحاض فلا أطهر؟ وكان أبي يقول إنّها استحيضت سبع سنين.[42] ففي أقلّ من هذا تكون الرَّيبة والاختلاط، فلهذا احتاجت إلى أن تعرف إقبال الدَّم من إدباره، وتغيّر لونه من السواد إلى غيره. وذلك أنَّ دم الحيض أسود يعرف، ولو كانت تعرف أيّامها ما احتاجت إلى معرفة لون الدَّم، لأنَّ السنة في الحيض أن تكون الصفرة والكدرة فما فوقها في أيّام الحيض إذا عرفت حيضاً كلّه إن كان الدَّم أسودًا و غير ذلك. فهذا يبيّن لك أنَّ قليل الدَّم وكثيره أيّام الحيض حيض كلّه إذا كانت الأيّام معلومة. فإذا جهلت الأيّام وعددها احتاجت إلى النظر حينئذ إلى إقبال الدَّم وإدباره وتغيّر لونه، ثمّ تدع الصلاة على قدر ذلك. ولا أرى النبي – صلّى الله عليه وآله وسلّم – قال: اجلسي كذا وكذا يومًا فما زادت فأنت مستحاضة، كما أمر الأُولى بذلك.[43] وكذلك أبي أفتى في مثل هذا، وذلك أنَّ امرأة من أهلنا استحاضت فسألت أبي عن ذلك، فقال: «إذا رأيت الدَّم البحراني فدعي الصلاة، وإذا رأيت الطّهر ولو ساعة من نهار فاغتسلي وصلّي». قال أبو عبد الله: وأرى جواب أبي ههنا غير جوابه في المستحاضة الأُولى. ألا ترى أنّه قال: «تدع الصلاة أيّام إقرائها»؟ لأنّه نظر إلى عدد الأيّام، وقال ههنا: إذا رأيت الدَّم البحراني فلتدع

40 Bukhārī, *Ṣaḥīḥ*, nos. 228, 320, 335; Muslim, *Ṣaḥīḥ*, no. 333; Abū Dāwūd, *Sunan*, nos. 286, 299–300; and many other sources listed in the editors' footnote in Aḥmad b. Ḥanbal, *Musnad*, 42:400–404.

41 Sunnī reports attribute this to the third case, that of Bint Jaḥsh. See Bayhaqī, *Sunan*, 1:486–87.

42 This specification, too, is attributed in some Sunnī works to the third case. See Bayhaqī, *Sunan*, 1:486.

43 In the edition of the source used in this study, this sentence appears as كما لم تؤمر الأُولى بذلك, which sounds like a correction by a later transmitter, copyist, or editor who did not follow the flow of the argument.

الصلاة. فأمر ههنا أن تنظر إلى الدَّم إذا أقبل وأدبر وتغيّر. وقوله: «البحراني» شبه معنى قول النبي – صلّى الله عليه وآله وسلّم: «أنَّ دم الحيض أسود يعرف». وإنّما سمّاه أبي بحرانيًّا لكثرته ولونه. فهذا سنّة النبيِّ – صلّى الله عليه وآله وسلّم – في الّتي اختلط عليها أيامها حتّى لا تعرفها، وإنّما تعرفها بالدَّم ما كان من قليل الأيّام وكثيره.

قال: وأمّا السنة الثّالثة فهي الّتي ليس لها أيّام متقدّمة ولم تر الدَّم قطُّ ورأت أوّل ما أدركت واستمرَّ بها، فإنَّ سنّة هذه غير سنّة الأُولى والثانية. وذلك أنَّ امرأة يقال لها: حَمنة بنت جحش[44] أتت رسول الله – صلّى الله عليه وآله وسلّم – فقالت: إنّي استحضت حيضة شديدة، فقال لها: «احتشي كرسفًا»، فقالت: إنّه أشدُّ من ذلك، إنّي أثجّه ثجًّا. فقال: تلجّمي وتحيّضي في كلّ شهر في علم الله ستّة أيّام – أو سبعة – ثمّ اغتسلي غسلاً وصومي ثلاثة وعشرين يومًا – أو أربعة وعشرين – واغتسلي للفجر غسلاً وأخّري الظّهر وعجّلي العصر واغتسلي غسلاً، وأخّري المغرب وعجّلي العشاء واغتسلي غسلا. قال أبو عبد الله: فأراه قد سنَّ في هذه غير ما سنَّ في الأُولى والثانية. وذلك لأنَّ أمرها مخالف لأمر هاتيك. ألا ترى أنَّ أيّامها لو كانت أقلّ من سبع، وكانت خمسًا أو أقلَّ من ذلك، ما قال لها: «تحيّضي سبعًا»، فيكون قد أمرها بترك الصلاة أيّامًا وهي مستحاضة غير حائض. وكذلك لو كان حيضها أكثر من سبع وكانت أيّامها عشرًا أو أكثر لم يأمرها بالصلاة وهي حائض. ثمَّ ممّا يزيد هذا بيانًا قوله لها: «تحيَّضي» وليس يكون التحيّض إلّا للمرأة الّتي تريد أن تكلّف ما تعمل الحائض. ألا تراه لم يقل [لِمن] لها أيّامًا معلومة: تحيّضي أيّام حيضك؟ وممّا يبيّن هذا قوله لها: «في علم الله»، لأنّه قد كان لها [ذلك] وإن كانت الأشياء كلّها في علم الله تعالى. وهذا بيّن واضح لأنّ هذه لم تكن لها أيّام قبل ذلك قطُّ. وهذه سنّة الّتي استمرَّ بها الدَّم أوّل ما تراه، أقصى وقتها سبع وأقصى طهرها ثلاث وعشرون، حتّى يصير لها أيّامًا معلومة فتنتقل إليها.

فجميع حالات المستحاضة تدور على هذه السنن الثلاثة، لا تكاد أبدًا تخلو من واحدة منهنّ: إن كانت لها أيامٌ معلومة من قليل أو كثير فهي على أيّامها وخلقها الّذي جرت عليه، ليس فيه عدد معلوم موقّت غير أيّامها. فإن اختلطت الأيّام عليها وتقدَّمت وتأخّرت وتغيّر عليها الدَّم ألوانًا فسنّتها إقبال الدم وإدباره وتغيّر حالته. وإن لم تكن

44 A sister of Umm Ḥabība bt. Jaḥsh, wife of the Prophet. Ḥamna's name appears in this story in Bayhaqī, *Sunan*, 1:488, 520, 523. However, most other reports attribute the story to her sister, Umm Ḥabība (Bayhaqī, 1:489, 490, 513–18, 521). The similarity in written Arabic between Jaḥsh, Ḥubaysh, and Qays, and between Ḥamna and Ḥabība, is striking.

لها أيّام قبل ذلك واستحاضت أوّل ما رأت فوقتها سبع وطهرها ثلاث وعشرون، فإن استمرّ بها الدّم أشهرًا فعلت في كلّ شهر كما قال لها، فإن انقطع الدّم في أقلّ من سبع أو أكثر من سبع فإنّها تغتسل ساعة ترى الطهر وتصلّي. فلا تزال كذلك حتّى تنظر ما يكون في الشهر الثاني، فإن انقطع الدم لوقته في الشهر الأوّل سواء حتّى توالي عليها حيضتان أو ثلاث فقد علم الآن أنّ ذلك قد صار لها وقتًا وخلقًا معروفًا تعمل عليه وتدع ما سواه وتكون سنّتها فيما تستقبل إن استحاضت، فقد صارت سنّة إلى أن تحبس إقراؤها. وإنّما جعل الوقت إن توالي عليها حيضتان أو ثلاث لقول رسول الله – صلّى الله عليه وآله وسلّم – للّتي تعرف أيّامها: «دعي الصلاة أيّام إقرائك»، فعلمنا أنّه لم يجعل القرء الواحد سنّة لها فيقول: «دعي الصلاة أيّام قرئك»، ولكن سنّ لها الأقراء، وأدناه حيضتان فصاعدًا. وإذا اختلط عليها أيّامها وزادت ونقصت حتّى لا تقف منها على حدّ ولا من الدم على لون، عملت بإقبال الدم وإدباره. وليس لها سنّة غير هذا، لقول رسول الله – صلّى الله عليه وآله وسلّم – : «إذا أقبلت الحيضة فدعي الصلاة وإذا أدبرت فاغتسلي»، ولقوله: «إنّ دم الحيض أسود يعرف»، كقول أبي: «إذا رأيت الدم البحرانيّ». فإن لم يكن الأمر كذلك ولكن الدم أطبق عليها فلم تزل الاستحاضة دارّة وكان الدم على لون واحد وحالة واحدة فسنّتها السبع والثلاث والعشرون، لأنّ قصّتها كقصّة حَمنة حين قالت: إنّي أثجّه ثجًّا.[45]

Abū ʿAbd Allāh was asked about a woman in a state of intermenstrual bleeding [that is, abnormal vaginal bleeding between periods][46] and the legal practice with respect to its duration. He said, "The Messenger of God (may God's prayer and peace be upon him and his Family) established three legal practices for a woman who continues to menstruate [beyond the normal course of her period]. Through them he clarified every issue for whoever hears and understands it, such that he did not leave room for anyone to give a personal opinion regarding the matter. In one of the legal practices established by him, the menstruating woman has a set number of days [of menstruation] that she has calculated without confusion, but now she continues to menstruate afterward and the blood persists, but she knows the normal days [of her period] and what they amount to. A woman [once] continued

45 Kulaynī, *Kāfī*, 3:83 88.

46 As indicated by the length and elaborateness of the present report, this was a significant question for Islamic ritual laws at the time, at least in Arabia. Detailed discussions are still devoted to this topic, and many of them can be found online under the Arabic term استحاضة.

to menstruate and her blood persisted, so she went to Umm Salama, who asked the Messenger of God (may God's prayer and peace be upon him and his Family) about it. He said, 'She should abstain from praying [only] for the duration of her [normal] days of menstruation.' And he said, 'This [additional blood] comes from a vein, and she must perform the full-body ablution and wear cloth pads [to prevent leakage] and pray.'"

Abū ʿAbd Allāh said, "This is the legal practice established by the Prophet (may God's prayer and peace be upon him and his Family) with respect to the woman who knows the duration of her menstrual period and it does not change for her. Is it not the case that he did not ask her about her [normal] duration, nor did he say that when she goes beyond that duration she is in a state of pseudomenstruation? He set for her [as her period of legal menstruation] the number of days, whether few or many, determined by what she knew. My father gave the same advice when he was asked about a woman in a state of pseudomenstruation. He said, 'That is an afflicted vein or an intended harm from the devil. She should abstain from prayer for the duration of her [normal] menstrual period and then perform the full-body ablution as well as the minor ablution for each prayer.' He was asked, 'Even if it flows?' He said, 'Even if it flows like a gutter!'" Abū ʿAbd Allāh said, "This is the explanation for the report from the Messenger of God (may God's prayer and peace be upon him and his Family), and it is consistent with it. This is the legal practice for the woman [in a state of pseudomenstruation] who knows the duration of her [normal menstrual] period, whether short or long.

"As for a woman who used to menstruate for a certain number of days but then the period became confused because its duration kept changing, to the point that she forgot the exact duration and time of the month [of her menstrual period], her legal practice is different. Regarding such cases, Fāṭima, daughter of Abū Ḥubaysh, went to the Prophet (may God's prayer and peace be upon him and his Family) and said, 'I continue to menstruate and never enter a state of purity.' The Prophet (may God's prayer and peace be upon him and his Family) said, 'That is not menstruation. It is a vein. When the menstruation commences, abstain from prayer, and when it concludes, wash away the blood and pray.' [Afterward], she would perform a full-body ablution for every prayer. She used to sit in her sister's washtub, and the yellow from the blood would surface on the top of the water." Abū ʿAbd Allāh said, "Did you not hear the Messenger of God (may God's prayer and peace be upon him and his Family) order this woman to do something different from what he ordered the other woman to do? Do you not see that he did not say to her, 'Abstain from prayer for the duration of your menstruation,' but instead said to her, 'When the menstruation commences, abstain from prayer, and when it concludes, wash your body and pray'? This clarifies that this woman was confused as to the duration [of her menstrual period]; she did not know the number [of days] or the timing. Did you not hear that she said, 'I menstruate but never enter a state of purity'? My father used to say, 'She menstruated for seven years.' It takes far less time to be in a status of doubt and confusion. For this reason, she needed to [look for signs such as] high and low flows and a change of color from black to something else. Menstrual blood is black and recognizable, and if she knew the duration [of her menstrual period] she would not need to watch out for the color of the blood, because it is normally yellow and cloudy, and it is all counted as part of menstruation [even] if she knew her menstrual blood to be black or otherwise. This clarifies that either a small or a large amount of blood during the days of menstruation is all considered menstrual if the duration [of the period] is known. But if she does not know the duration and number of days, she needs to watch out for high and low flows and the color change and then to abstain from prayer accordingly. I do not see the Prophet (may God's prayer and peace be upon him and his Family) say, 'Remain [in a state of presumed menstruation] for such-and-such a number of days, and for anything beyond that you are in a state of pseudomenstruation,' as he told the first woman. My father gave the same legal opinion in a similar case in which a female relative of ours continued to menstruate and asked my father about it. He said, 'If you see pouring red blood, abstain from prayer, and if you are clean of blood, even for just an hour in the day, perform a full-body ablution and pray.'" Abū ʿAbd Allāh said, "I see that my father's answer in this case is different from his answer to the first woman who was pseudomenstruating. Do you not see that he said [in the first case] that the woman should abstain from prayer for the duration of her menstrual period? This is because [in that case], he based his answer on the number of days, but in this case, he said that if she sees intensely red blood she should abstain from prayer. In this case he ordered her to look for high and low flows of blood and the change [in its color]. His phrase 'pouring red' bears a meaning similar to that of the saying of the Prophet (may God's prayer and peace be upon him and his Family), 'Menstrual blood is black and recognizable.' My father called it *baḥrānī* because of its large quantity and its color. This is the legal practice set by the Prophet (may God's prayer and peace be upon him and his Family) for a woman who is confused about the duration [of her menstrual period] to the point that she does not know it. She knows it only by blood, whether it lasts for a short or a long period."

He said, "As for the third legal practice, it applies to a woman who does not have a previously established duration [of her menstrual period] and has never seen blood before, but who then sees the first blood, which persists. The legal practice for this person is different from those for the first or the second. Regarding this issue, a woman named Ḥamna, daughter of Jaḥsh, went to the Messenger of God (may God's prayer and peace be upon him and his Family) and said, 'I have an intense menstrual flow.' He said to her, 'Stuff yourself with cotton.' She said, 'It is more intense than that. It is flowing profusely.' He said, 'Wear cloth pads [to prevent leakage], and for each month, by God's knowledge, count six or seven days as the period of your menstruation. Afterward, perform a full-body ablution once, fast [in the month of fasting] for the remaining twenty-three or twenty-four days, perform a full-body ablution for the *fajr* (pre-dawn) prayer once, delay the noon prayer and perform the afternoon prayer earlier with another full-body ablution for the two prayers, and delay the sunset prayer and pray the evening prayer earlier with another full-body ablution to cover both prayers.'" Abū ʿAbd Allāh said, "I see that he set for this woman a different practice from those that he set for the first and the second, and that is because the situation of this woman differs from those of the other two. Is it not the case that if the duration [of her menstrual period] was less than seven [days], being five or fewer, he would not say to her, '[Count] seven days.' Had he said that, he would have instructed her to miss her prayers for a number of days while she was in a state of pseudomenstruation and not one of menstruation. Likewise, if her menstrual period were longer than seven days with a duration of ten days or more, he would not instruct her to pray while menstruating. What clarifies this further is his saying, 'Count as the period of your menstruation,' and this order can apply only to a woman who wants to bear the responsibility of what a woman who is menstruating does. Do you not see that he did not say to the woman who had a certain, known [number of] days [of menstruation], 'Count as the period of your menstruation'? What also clarifies this is his saying, 'by God's knowledge,' because she actually had a certain span of time [for her menstruation]—even though all things fall under the knowledge of God, the Exalted. It is clear that she never had a [menstrual] period before this. This is the legal practice for a woman whose bleeding persists from the time she first sees it;

the maximum duration of her [legal] menstrual period is seven days and the maximum period of her state of purity is twenty-three days, until [her menstruation] becomes regular and she moves to that [category of regularity].

"All cases of pseudomenstruation fall within these three legal practices, and no case will not be covered by one of them. If a woman has a known duration, whether short or long, she bases her practice on the duration and her natural course; there is no set time period other than the days [of her normal menstrual period]. If a woman's period becomes confused, starting early or being delayed and the color of the blood changing, her legal practice is based on the high and low flows and the change [in the blood]. If a woman does not have a previously determined duration [for her menstrual period] and she menstruates for the first time, her [legal] menstrual period is set at seven days and [the duration of] her state of purity is set at twenty-three days. If the blood persists for months, she acts each month according to how she was instructed. If the bleeding ceases in less or more than seven days, she performs a full-body ablution the moment she sees purity and she prays. She continues in this way until she sees what occurs in the second month. If the blood ceases at the same time as it did in the first month, and this same [pattern] continues for two or three periods, it becomes known that she has a set duration and a known natural course that she can base herself on and ignore anything else. From then on, that legal practice continues until her menstruation stops. The duration is set when two or three of her successive menstrual cycles have passed, on the basis of the saying of the Messenger of God (may God's prayer and peace be upon him and his Family) to the one who knew her duration: 'Abstain from prayer for the duration of your menstrual cycles.' We thus know that he did not consider one menstrual cycle to establish a practice for her, in which case he would have said, 'Abstain from prayer for the duration of your menstrual cycle.' Rather, he named a plurality of menstruations, which means a minimum of two menstrual cycles. If the duration of a woman's period becomes confused, and it increases or decreases such that there is no limit or blood color she can rely on, then she bases herself on the high and low flows, and she has no set practice other than this because of the saying of the Messenger of God (may God's prayer and peace be upon him and his Family) 'When the menstruation flows high, abstain from praying, and when it flows low, perform a full-body ablution,' as well as his saying 'Menstrual blood is black and recognizable.' This is like my father's saying 'When you see the pouring red blood.' If the situation is not like this, and [the bleeding] is continuous and the pseudomenstruation does not cease and the blood remains the same color and consistent, her legal practice is based on seven and twenty-three [days], because her situation is like that of Ḥamna [daughter of Jaḥsh] when she said, 'it is flowing profusely.'"

On Prayer

3

قال هشام بن الحكم لأبي عبد الله: أخبرني عمّا يجوز السجود عليه وعمّا لا يجوز؟ قال: السجود لا يجوز إلّا على الأرض أو على ما أنبتت الأرض - إلّا ما أُكل أو لُبس. فقال له: جعلت فداك! ما العلّة في ذلك؟ قال: لأنّ السجود خضوع لله عزّ وجلّ، فلا ينبغي أن يكون على ما يُؤكل أو يُلبس لأنّ أبناء الدنيا عبيد ما يأكلون ويلبسون، والساجد في سجوده في عبادة الله عزّ وجلّ، فلا ينبغي أن يضع جبهته في سجوده على معبود أبناء الدنيا الّذين اغترّوا بغرورها. والسجود على الأرض أفضل لأنّه أبلغ في التواضع والخضوع لله عزّ وجلّ.[47]

Hishām b. al-Ḥakam asked Abū ʿAbd Allāh, "Tell me on what one may perform *sujūd* (prostration) and on what one may not?" He replied, "*Sujūd* is permitted only on the earth or what grows from it—except what is eaten or worn." [Hishām] said to him, "May I be made your ransom! What is the reason for this?" [Jaʿfar al-Ṣādiq] said, "Because *sujūd* is submission to God, the Mighty and Majestic, so it ought not to be done on what is eaten or worn, because the people of this world are slaves to what they eat and wear, and the prostrator worships God, the Mighty and Majestic, through his *sujūd*. During *sujūd* he should not place his brow on what the people of this world are slaves to, those who are seduced by its temptations. *Sujūd* on the earth is more meritorious because it is more emphatically humble and submissive toward God, the Mighty and Majestic."

4

أبو ولّاد قال: قلت لأبي عبد الله: إنّي كنت خرجت من الكوفة في سفينة إلى قصر ابن هبيرة - وهو من الكوفة على نحو عشرين فرسخًا في الماء - فسِرت يومي ذلك أقصّر الصلاة، ثمّ بدا لي في الليل الرجوع إلى الكوفة فلم أدر أصلّي في رجوعي بتقصير أم

47 Ibn Bābawayh, *Faqīh*, 1:177.

بتمام؟ وكيف كان ينبغي أن أصنع؟ فقال: إن كنت سِرت في يومك الّذي خرجت فيه بريدًا فكان عليك حين رجعت أن تصلّي بالتقصير، لأنّك كنت مسافرًا إلى أن تصير إلى منزلك. قال: وإن كنت لم تسر في يومك الّذي خرجت فيه بريدًا فانّ عليك أن تقضي كلّ صلاة صلّيتها في يومك ذلك بالتقصير بتمام، من قبل أن تريم من مكانك ذلك، لأنّك لم تبلغ الموضع الّذي يجوز فيه التقصير حتّى رجعت. فوجب عليك قضاء ما قصرت. وعليك إذا رجعت أن تتمّ الصلاة حتّى تصير إلى منزلك.[48]

[Abū Wallād:] I said to Abū ʿAbd Allāh, "I left Kūfā on a ship for the Palace of Ibn Hubayra,[49] which is at a distance of twenty *farsakhs* [each *farsakh* being about three and a half miles] from Kūfa by water. So I traveled that day, shortening my prayers by half, but at night I realized I had to return to Kūfa and did not know whether to pray half or in full on my return journey. What should I have done?" He said, "If on the day you left [Kūfa] you traveled a *barīd* [roughly, twelve miles], then you would have had to pray half during your return because you remained a traveler until you reached your residence. But if you did not travel a *barīd*, then you must make up in full each prayer you prayed half of that day before you leave that place, because you did not reach the distance at which praying half is permitted before coming back. So you must redo the prayers you prayed half. During your return journey you must perform prayers in full until you reach your residence."

5

سماعة قال: سألت أبا عبد الله عن الرجل يأتي المسجد وقد صلّى أهله، أيبتديء بالمكتوبة أو يتطوّع؟ فقال: إن كان في وقت حسن فلا بأس بالتطوّع قبل الفريضة، وإن كان خاف الفوت من أجل ما مضى من الوقت فليبدأ بالفريضة، وهو حقّ الله، ثمّ ليتطوّع ما شاء. الامر موسّع أن يصلّي الانسان في أول وقت الفريضة. والفضل إذا صلّى الانسان وحده أن يبدأ بالفريضة إذا دخل وقتها ليكون فضل الوقت للفريضة، وليس بمحظور عليه أن يصلّي النوافل من أوّل الوقت إلى قريب من آخر الوقت.[50]

[Samāʿa:] I asked Abū ʿAbd Allāh about a person who comes to the mosque and the people have [already] prayed [in congregation]; should he begin with the obligatory prayer or the supererogatory one [that usually precedes it]?" He said, "If a good amount of time is still left

48 Ṭūsī, *Tahdhīb*, 3:298–99.

49 A town that lay near Hāshimiyya, some eighty miles south of Baghdad.

50 Ṭūsī, *Tahdhīb*, 2:264.

[before the end of the prayer's allotted time], there is nothing wrong with performing the supererogatory prayer before the obligatory one. But if he fears the [time of the prayer] will pass because of the time that has [already] elapsed, he should begin with the obligatory prayer, which is the right of God, and then he may perform whatever supererogatory prayers he wishes. It is permitted for a person to pray [the supererogatory prayer] in the beginning of the time for the obligatory prayer. The preference for someone praying alone is to begin with the obligatory prayer when its time commences so that the preferred part of the [prayer's] time is devoted to the obligatory prayer. But it is not impermissible for him to pray the supererogatory prayer [at any point] from the start of the time until the time is nearly over."

6

عمّار بن موسى الساباطى عن أبي عبد الله قال: أجمع لك السهو كلّه في كلمتين: متى شككت فخذ بالأكثر، فإذا سلّمت فأتمّ ما ظننت أنّك قد نقصت. فإن كنت قد أتممت لم يكن عليك شيء، وإن ذكرت أنّك كنت نقصت كان ما صلّيت تمام ما نقصت.[51]

[ʿAmmār b. Mūsā:] Abū ʿAbd Allāh said, "I will sum up for you the entire issue of inattentiveness [in prayer, leading to uncertainty as to whether one has performed it in full] in two words: When in doubt, go with the more likely possibility. When you conclude the prayer, do [the prayer *rakʿa*s] that you think you probably missed. If you had completed the prayer in full, [redoing a *rakʿa* that you were doubtful about] does no harm. If you remembered that you had omitted something, what you prayed is the completion of what you omitted."

On Fasting

7

ابن سنان قال: سألت أبا عبد الله عن الرجل يسافر في شهر رمضان ومعه جارية له، أله أن يُصيب منها بالنهار؟ فقال: سبحان الله! أما يعرف حرمة شهر رمضان؟ إنَّ له في الليل سبحًا طويلاً! قلت: أليس له أن يأكل ويشرب ويقصّر؟ فقال: إنَّ الله – تبارك وتعالى – قد رخّص للمسافر في الإفطار والتقصير رحمةً وتخفيفًا لموضع التعب والنصب ووعث السفر، ولم يرخّص له في مجامعة النساء في السفر بالنهار في شهر

51 Ṭūsī, *Tahdhīb*, 2:943 (see also 2:193; Ibn Bābawayh, *Faqīh*, 1:225).

رمضان. وأوجب عليه قضاء الصيام ولم يوجب عليه قضاء تمام الصلاة إذا آب من سفره. ثمّ قال: والسنّة لا تقاس. وإنّي إذا سافرت في شهر رمضان ما آكل إلّا القوت وما أشرب كلّ الرّيّ.[52]

[Ibn Sinān:] I asked Abū ʿAbd Allāh about a man who travels in the month of Ramaḍān with a handmaiden of his: can he engage her during the day? He said, "Praise be to God! Does he not know about the sanctity of the month of Ramaḍān? He has so much time during the night!" I said, "Is it not the case that he eats, drinks, and prays half [while traveling]?" He said, "God, the Sublime and Exalted, has indeed provided a dispensation for the traveler with respect to breaking his fast and shortening his prayer out of mercy, to ease hardship, illness, and the difficulties of travel. He did not provide a dispensation for intercourse with women while traveling during the day in the month of Ramaḍān. He obligated him to make up the fast but not to make up the prayers in full once he completes his trip." He then said, "Analogies cannot be drawn from the Sunna. When I travel during the month of Ramaḍān, I eat only what helps me survive and I drink just enough to quench my thirst."

8

الحسن بن بسّام الجمّال عن رجل قال: كنت مع أبي عبد الله فيما بين مكّة والمدينة في شعبان وهو صائم، ثمّ رأينا هلال شهر رمضان فأفطر. فقلت له: جعلت فداك! أمس كان من شعبان وانت صائم، واليوم من شهر رمضان وانت مفطر؟! فقال: إنّ ذاك تطوّع ولنا أن نفعل ما شئنا، وهذا فرض فليس لنا أن نفعل إلا ما أُمرنا.[53]

[Ḥasan b. Bassām al-Jammāl:] I was with Abū ʿAbd Allāh between Mecca and Medina in the month of Shaʿbān, and he was fasting. We saw the crescent moon of Ramaḍān, and he broke his fast. I said, "May I be made your ransom! Yesterday was part of Shaʿbān and you were fasting, and today is part of Ramaḍān and you are breaking your fast?" He said, "That was a voluntary deed, so we could do what we wished, but this is an obligation, so we can do only what we have been commanded."

52 Kulaynī, *Kāfī*, 4:134.
53 Kulaynī, *Kāfī*, 4:131.

On Alms

9

زيد الصائغ قال: قلت لأبي عبد الله: إنّي كنت في قرية من قرى خراسان يقال لها بخارا فرأيت فيها دراهم تعمل ثُلث فضّة وثُلث مسّ وثُلث رصاص وكانت تجوز عندهم وكنت أعملها وأنفقها. فقال أبو عبد الله: لا بأس بذلك إذا كانت تجوز عندهم. فقلت: أرأيت إن حال عليها الحول وهي عندي وفيها ما يجب عليّ فيه الزكاة، أُزكّيها؟ قال: نعم! إنّما هو مالُك. قلت: فإن أخرجتها إلى بلدة لا يُنفق فيها مثلها فبقيت عندي حتّى يحول عليها الحول، أُزكّيها؟ قال: إن كنت تعرف أنّ فيها من الفضّة الخالصة ما يجب عليك فيها الزكاة فزكّ ما كان لك فيها من الفضّة الخالصة ودَع ما سوى ذلك من الخبيث. قلت: وإن كنت لا أعلم ما فيها من الفضّة الخالصة، إلّا أنّي أعلم أنّ فيها ما يجب فيه الزكاة؟ قال: فاسبكها حتّى تخلص الفضّة ويحترق الخبيث، ثمّ زكّ ما خلص من الفضّة لسنة واحدة.[54]

[Zayd al-Ṣāʾigh:] I said to Abū ʿAbd Allāh, "I was in one of the towns of Khurāsān, called Bukhārā, where I saw coins composed of one-third silver, one-third copper, and one-third lead. They were in circulation there, and I made them and used them." Abū ʿAbd Allāh said, "There is nothing wrong with that if they were in circulation there." I said, "What is your position if a year passes and the coins remain in my possession, and there is in them [the minimum requisite amount of silver] that requires me to pay *zakāt* on it; do I pay *zakāt* on it?" He said, "Yes! It is your wealth." I said, "What if I take them to a town where they are not used, and they remain in my possession until a year has passed; do I pay *zakāt* on it?" He said, "If you know that you have the amount of pure silver in the coins that meets the required minimum for *zakāt*, then pay *zakāt* on the portion of pure silver in them and leave alone the worthless part." I said, "What if I do not know how much pure silver is in them, but I generally know that it reaches the minimum required for *zakāt* to be owed?" He said, "Then smelt it until the silver becomes pure and the worthless part burns off, and then pay *zakāt* for one year on the pure silver that remains."

54 Kulaynī, *Kāfī*, 3:517.

10

هارون بن خارجة عن أبي عبد الله قال: قلت له: إنَّ أخي يوسف ولّى لهؤلاء القوم أعمالاً أصاب فيها أموالاً كثيرة، وإنّه جعل تلك الأموال حليًّا أراد أن يفرّ بها من الزكاة. أعليه الزكاة؟ قال: ليس على الحليِّ زكاة. وما أدخل على نفسه من النقصان في وضعه ومنعه نفسه فضلَه، أكثر ممّا يخاف من الزكاة.[55]

[Hārūn b. Khārija:] I said to Abū ʿAbd Allāh, "My brother Yūsuf worked for these people [that is, the caliphal administration], which earned him a lot of wealth, and he turned that wealth into jewels so he could avoid paying *zakāt* on it. Does he owe *zakāt*?" He said, "*Zakāt* is not owed on jewels. What he caused himself to lose out on by depriving himself of its benefit outweighs what he feared from [paying] *zakāt*."

11

سماعة عن أبي عبد الله قال: إذا أخذ الرجل الزكاة فهي كمالِه يصنع بها ما يشاء. إنَّ الله عزَّ وجلَّ فرض للفقراء في أموال الأغنياء فريضة لا يُحمَدون إلّا بأدائها وهي الزكاة، فإذا هي وصلت إلى الفقير فهي بمنزلة مالِهِ يصنع بها ما يشاء. فقلت: يتزوَّج بها ويحجّ منها؟ قال: نعم! هي مالُه. قلت: فهل يؤجَر الفقير إذا حجَّ من الزكاة كما يؤجَر الغنيّ صاحب المال؟ قال: نعم![56]

[Samāʿa:] Abū ʿAbd Allāh said, "If a person receives *zakāt*, it is like his own wealth and he can do with it what he pleases. God, the Mighty and Majestic, assigned an allocation to the poor from the wealth of the rich, who will not be commended without paying it, and that is *zakāt*. If it reaches a poor person, it is considered his wealth and he can do with it whatever he pleases." I said, "Can he use it to marry and to perform the *ḥajj*?" He said, "Yes! It is his wealth." I said, "Does the poor person get rewarded for performing the *ḥajj* with the money he received as *zakāt*, like the rich person who [originally] owned it?" He said, "Yes!"

12

سماعة قال: سألت أبا عبد الله عن الزكاة هل تصلح لصاحب الدار والخادم؟ فقال: نعم! إلّا أن تكون داره دار غلّة فيخرج له من غلّتها دراهم ما يكفيه لنفسه وعياله. فإن

55 Kulaynī, *Kāfī*, 3:518.
56 Kulaynī, *Kāfī*, 3:556.

لم تكن الغلّة تكفيه لنفسه وعياله في طعامهم وكسوتهم وحاجتهم من غير إسراف فقد حلّت له الزكاة، وإن كانت غلّتها تكفيهم فلا.[57]

[Samāʿa:] I asked Abū ʿAbd Allāh whether *zakāt* can be given to someone who owns a home and a servant. He said, "Yes! Unless his home is used for revenue and he receives from its revenue enough money to suffice him and his family. If the revenue is not enough for his and his family's food, clothing, and other basic needs in moderation, it is lawful for him to receive *zakāt*. But if the revenue suffices them, then no."

13

سماعة قال: سألته عن الرجل يكون عنده المتاع موضوعًا فيمكث عنده السنة والسنتين أو أكثر من ذلك؟ قال: ليس عليه زكاة حتّى يبيعه. إلّا أن يكون أعطى به رأس ماله فيمنعه من ذلك التماس الفضل، فإذا هو فعل ذلك وجبت فيه الزكاة. وإن لم يكن أعطى به رأس ماله فليس عليه زكاة حتّى يبيعه، وإن حبسه بما حبسه، فإذا هو باعه فإنّما عليه زكاة سنة واحدة.[58]

[Samāʿa:] I asked him about a man who has a commodity that remains with him for a year or two or more than that. He said, "He does not owe *zakāt* on it until he sells it, unless he received an offer [of purchase] at the price for which he obtained it but he rejected the offer in the hope of making a profit on it; if he did that, then *zakāt* is owed on it. But if he did not receive such an offer at the original price paid, he owes no *zakāt* until he sells it, however long he holds it. But when he sells it, he owes *zakāt* for one year."

14

سماعة قال: سألته عن الرجل يكون له الدَين على الناس أيجب فيه الزكاة؟ قال: ليس عليه فيه زكاة حتّى يقبضه، فإذا قبضه فعليه الزكاة. وإن هو طال حبسه على الناس حتّى يتم لذلك سنون فليس عليه زكاة حتّى يخرج، فإذا هو خرج زكّاه لعامه ذلك. وإن كان هو يأخذ منه قليلاً قليلاً فليزكّ ما خرج منه أوّلاً فأوّلاً. فإن كان متاعه ودينه وماله في تجارته الّتي يتقلّب فيها يومًا بيوم، يأخذ ويعطي ويبيع ويشتري، فهو يشبه العين في

57 Kulaynī, *Kāfī*, 3:561.
58 Kulaynī, *Kāfī*, 3:528.

يده فعليه الزكاة. ولا ينبغي له أن يغيّر ذلك إذا كان حال متاعه وماله على ما وصفت لك فيؤخّر الزكاة.[59]

[Samāʿa:] I asked him about a man who is owed money by people; does he owe *zakāt* on it? He said, "He does not owe *zakāt* on it until he receives it. Once he receives it, he owes *zakāt*. If it remains with the people for a long time such that years pass by, he still owes no *zakāt* until he receives it. If he receives it [all at once], he pays *zakāt* on it for that year. If he receives it little by little, he pays *zakāt* on what he receives in the order he receives it. If his goods, credit, and wealth are in his trade, which changes day by day—he takes, gives, sells, and buys—then it is like an object in his possession, so he owes *zakāt*. He should not change the situation, if the state of his goods and wealth is as I described to you, in order to delay the payment of *zakāt*."

15

سماعة قال: سألته عن الرجل يكون معه المال مضاربة، هل عليه في ذلك المال زكاة إذا كان يتّجر به؟ فقال: ينبغي له أن يقول لأصحاب المال: زكّوه. فإن قالوا: إنّا نزكّيه، فليس عليه غير ذلك. وإن هم أمروه أن يزكّيه فليفعل. قلت: أرأيت لو قالوا إنّا نزكّيه والرجل يعلم أنّهم لا يزكّونه؟ فقال: إذا هم أقرّوا بأنّهم يزكّونه فليس عليه غير ذلك، وإن هم قالوا إنّا لا نزكّيه فلا ينبغي له أن يقبل ذلك المال ولا يعمل به حتّى يزكّوه.[60]

[Samāʿa:] I asked him about a man managing someone else's wealth in a sleeping partnership—does he owe *zakāt* if he puts it to use? He said, "He must instruct the owners of the wealth to pay *zakāt* on it. If they say, 'We do pay *zakāt* on it,' then he does not have to do anything else, and if they order him to pay it, he should do so." I said, "What is your position if they say, 'We do pay *zakāt* on it,' but the man knows that they do not?" He said, "If they say they pay *zakāt* on it, then he does not have to do anything else. If they say, 'We do not pay *zakāt* on it,' then he should not accept the wealth or work with it until they pay *zakāt* on it."

16

عن زرارة قال: قلت لأبي عبد الله: رجل حلّت عليه الزكاة ومات أبوه وعليه دَين، أيؤدّي زكاته في دَين أبيه وللابن مال كثير؟ فقال: إن كان أبوه أورثه مالاً ثمّ ظهر عليه

59 Kulaynī, *Kāfī*, 3:519.
60 Kulaynī, *Kāfī*, 3:519.

دين لم يعلم به يومئذ فيقضيه عنه، قضاه من جميع الميراث ولم يقضه من زكاته. وإن لم يكن أورثه مالاً لم يكن أحدٌ أحقُّ بزكاته من دَين أبيه، فإذا أدّاها في دَين أبيه على هذه الحال أجزأت عنه.[61]

[Zurāra:] I said to Abū ʿAbd Allāh, "A man owes *zakāt* [after holding property for a year], and his father dies owing a debt. Can the son fulfill his *zakāt* obligation by paying off his father's debt, if the son has a lot of wealth?" He said, "If his father left wealth to him and he then came to know that his father owed a debt that he had not known of, the son pays it on his father's behalf from the entire inheritance, not from his own *zakāt* [obligations]. But if the father did not leave any wealth to him, nothing is more entitled to his *zakāt* than his father's debt. If he pays [his *zakāt*] by paying his father's debt in this situation, that suffices to cover his obligation."

17

عن زرارة قال: قلت لأبي عبد الله: هل في البغال شيء؟ فقال: لا! قلت: فكيف صار على الخيل ولم يصر على البغال؟ قال: لأنَّ البغال لا تلقح والخيل الإناث ينتجن، وليس على الخيل الذُّكور شيء. قلت: فما في الحمير؟ فقال: ليس فيها شيء. قلت: هل على الفرس أو البعير يكون للرجل يركبهما شيء؟ فقال: لا! ليس على ما يُعلف شيء. إنّما الصدقة على السائمة المرسلة في مرجها عامها الّذي يقتنيها فيه الرجل، فأمّا ما سوى ذلك فليس فيه شيء.[62]

[Zurāra:] I said to Abū ʿAbd Allāh, "Is anything owed on mules?" He said, "No!" I said, "Why is it that there is [a tax] on horses but not on mules?" He said, "Because mules cannot be impregnated whereas female horses reproduce, and nothing is owed on male horses." I said, "What about donkeys?" He said, "Nothing is owed on them." I said, "Is anything owed on a horse or a camel that a man uses for riding?" He said, "No! Nothing is owed on what is foddered. *Zakāt* is owed on livestock that are sent out to graze on common pasture, for the year in which one acquired them. Nothing is owed for anything else."

---

61 Kulaynī, *Kāfī*, 3:553.
62 Kulaynī, *Kāfī*, 3:530.

18

محمّد بن مسلم قال: قلت لأبي عبد الله: رجلٌ بعث بزكاة ماله لتقسّم فضاعت. هل عليه ضمانها حتّى تقسّم؟ فقال: إذا وجد لها موضعًا فلم يدفعها فهو لها ضامنٌ حتّى يدفعها، وإن لم يجد لها من يدفعها إليه فبعث بها إلى أهلها فليس عليه ضمان، لأنّها قد خرجت من يده. وكذلك الوصيُّ الّذي يوصى إليه يكون ضامنًا لِما دُفع إليه إذا وجد الّذي أمر ربّه بدفعه إليه، فإن لم يجد فليس عليه ضمان.[63]

[Muḥammad b. Muslim:] I said to Abū ʿAbd Allāh, "A man sent the *zakāt* on his wealth to be distributed, but it got lost. Is he liable for it until it has been distributed?" He said, "If he found someone [in need] to pay it to and did not do so, he is liable for it until he pays it. If he did not find anyone to pay it to and so sent it to those entitled to it, he is not liable because it is no longer in his possession. Likewise, a trustee who is entrusted [with distributing something] is liable for what is given to him if he finds a person to whom the owner has ordered him to pay it. But if he has not found [such person and the *zakāt* monies are lost], he is not liable."

19

محمّد بن مسلم قال: سألت أبا عبد الله عن رجل اشترى متاعًا وكسد عليه وقد كان زكّى ماله قبل أن يشتري المتاع، متى يزكّيه؟ فقال: إن كان أمسك متاعه يبتغي به رأس ماله فليس عليه زكاة، وإن كان حبسه بعد ما يجد رأس ماله فعليه الزكاة بعد ما أمسكه بعد رأس المال. قال: وسألته عن الرجل يوضع عنده الأموال يعمل بها، فقال: إذا حال الحول فليزكّها.[64]

[Muḥammad b. Muslim:] I asked Abū ʿAbd Allāh about a man who purchased a commodity and was unable to sell it, and he had paid *zakāt* on his property before purchasing the commodity. When should he pay *zakāt* [on the commodity]? He said, "If he abstained from selling it, hoping to sell it at the price that he paid for it, no *zakāt* is owed on it. But if he held on to it even after receiving an offer to sell it at that price, he must pay *zakāt* on it for declining to sell it at the original price that he paid for it." I [also] asked him about a man who is given wealth with which to conduct business. He said, "If a year passes, he pays *zakāt* on it."

63 Kulaynī, *Kāfī*, 3:530.
64 Kulaynī, *Kāfī*, 3:528.

20

عبيد بن زرارة قال: قلت لأبي عبد الله: رجل عارف أدّى زكاته إلى غير أهلها زمانًا، هل عليه أن يؤدّيها ثانيًا إلى أهلها إذا علمهم؟ قال: نعم! قلت: فإن لم يعرف لها أهلاً فلم يؤدّها أو لم يعلم أنّها عليه فعلم بعد ذلك؟ قال: يؤدّيها إلى أهلها لِما مضى. قلت له: فإنّه لم يعلم أهلها فدفعها إلى من ليس هو لها بأهل وقد كان طلب واجتهد ثمّ علم بعد ذلك سوء ما صنع؟ قال: ليس عليه أن يؤدّيها مرّة أُخرى.[65]

['Ubayd b. Zurāra:] I said to Abū ʿAbd Allāh, "A Shīʿī man distributed his *zakāt* to people not entitled to it for a long time—does he have to redistribute it to people entitled to it if he comes to know them?" He said, "Yes!" I said, "What if he did not know of people entitled to it, so he did not distribute it, or did not know that he had to pay it but later learned of the fact?" He said, "He distributes it to those entitled to it [to make up] for the time that has passed." I said to him, "What if he did not know people entitled to it, even though he searched and exerted himself [to find such people], and distributed it to people not entitled to it, but then later learns of his mistake?" He said, "He does not have to redistribute it."

21

عبيد بن زرارة قال: سألت أبا عبد الله عن رجل أخرج زكاة ماله ألف درهم فلم يجد موضعًا يدفع ذلك إليه فنظر إلى مملوك يباع فيمن يريده فاشتراه بتلك الألف الدِرهم الّتي أخرجها من زكاته فأعتقه. هل يجوز له ذلك؟ قال: نعم! لا بأس بذلك. قلت: فإنّه لمّا أن أُعتَق وصار حرًّا اتّجر واحترف وأصاب مالاً ثمّ مات وليس له وارث، فمن يرثه إذا لم يكن له وارث؟ قال: يرثه الفقراء المؤمنون الّذين يستحقّون الزكاة، لإنّه إنّما اشتُرى بمالِهم.[66]

['Ubayd b. Zurāra:] I asked Abū ʿAbd Allāh about a man who set aside one thousand dirhams as *zakāt* on his wealth but found nobody to distribute it to. He then saw a slave on sale to potential buyers, so he purchased him with those one thousand dirhams that he had set aside as his *zakāt* and manumitted him. Could he do that?" He said, "Yes! There is nothing wrong with that." I said, "When [the slave] was manumitted and became free, he then traded, worked, and amassed wealth,

65 Kulaynī, *Kāfī*, 3:546.
66 Kulaynī, *Kāfī*, 3:557.

and then died without any heirs. Who inherits him if he has no heir?" He said, "He will be inherited by the poor among the believers who are entitled to *zakāt*, because he was purchased with their wealth."

22

أبو بصير قال: قلت لأبي عبد الله: إنّ شيخًا من أصحابنا يقال له عمر، سأل عيسى بن أعيَن وهو محتاج. فقال له عيسى بن أعيَن: أما إنَّ عندي من الزكاة ولكن لا أُعطيك منها. فقال له: ولِمَ؟ فقال: لأنّي رأيتك اشتريت لحمًا وتمرًا. فقال: إنّما ربحت درهمًا فاشتريت بدانقين لحمًا وبدانقين تمرًا ورجعت بدانقين لحاجة. قال: فوضع أبو عبد الله يده على جبهته ساعةً، ثمّ رفع رأسه ثمّ قال: إنّ الله تبارك وتعالى نظر في أموال الأغنياء، ثمّ نظر في الفقراء فجعل في أموال الأغنياء ما يكتفون به. ولو لم يكفهم لزادهم. بل يعطيه ما يأكل ويشرب ويكتسي ويتزوّج ويتصدّق ويحجّ.[67]

[Abū Baṣīr:] I said to Abū ʿAbd Allāh, "An elderly person among our companions, called ʿUmar, asked [for help] from ʿĪsā b. Aʿyan when he was in need. ʿĪsā b. Aʿyan said to him, 'I have some *zakāt* with me, but I will not give you any of it.' ʿUmar said, 'Why not?' ʿĪsā said, 'Because I saw you buy meat and dates.' ʿUmar said, 'I earned a dirham, so I bought meat with two *dāniqs*[68] and dates with two *dāniqs*, and I saved two *dāniqs* for [later] need.'" Abū ʿAbd Allāh put his hand on his forehead for a while, then lifted his head and said, "God, the Sublime and Exalted, considered the wealth of the rich and then considered the poor. He then made the wealth of the rich enough for the poor [too]. If it had not been enough for the poor, He would have increased their wealth. One has to give the poor [not only] what they eat, drink, and wear [but also what they] marry, pay charity, and perform the *ḥajj* with."

23

أبو بصير قال: سمعت أبا عبد الله يقول: يأخذ الزكاة صاحب السبعمائة إذا لم يجد غيره. قلت: فإنّ صاحب السبعمائة تجب عليه الزكاة؟ قال: زكاته صدقة على عياله ولا يأخذها إلّا أن يكون إذا اعتمد على السبعمائة أنفدها في أقلّ من سنة فهذا يأخذها. ولا تحلّ الزكاة لمن كان محترفًا وعنده ما يجب فيه الزكاة.[69]

67 Kulaynī, *Kāfī*, 3:556.

68 A *dāniq* was a coin valued at one-sixth of a dirham, as in Maqrīzī's *Shudhūr al-ʿuqūd*.

69 Kulaynī, *Kāfī*, 3:560.

[Abū Baṣīr:] I heard Abū ʿAbd Allāh say, "The owner of seven hundred [dirhams] can receive *zakāt* if he has nothing else." I said, "But doesn't the owner of seven hundred [dirhams] owe *zakāt*?" He said, "His *zakāt* is charity for his family. He cannot receive *zakāt* unless [he is in a situation in which] he depends on the seven hundred [dirhams] and he will exhaust them in less than a year. Such a person can receive *zakāt*. But *zakāt* is not lawful for someone who works and has enough [wealth] to owe *zakāt* on."

24

أبو بصير قال: سألت أبا عبد الله عن رجل من أصحابنا له ثمانمائة درهم وهو رجلٌ خفّاف وله عيال كثيرة، أله أن يأخذ من الزكاة؟ فقال: يا أبا محمّد! أيربح في دراهمه ما يقوت به عياله ويفضل؟ قال: قلت: نعم! قال: كم يفضل؟ قلت: لا أدري. قال: إن كان يفضل عن القوت مقدار نصف القوت فلا يأخذ الزكاة، وإن كان أقلّ من نصف القوت أخذ الزكاة. قلت: فعليه في ماله زكاة تلزمه؟ قال: بلى! قلت: كيف يصنع؟ قال: يوسّع بها على عياله في طعامهم وشرابهم وكسوتهم، وإن بقي منها شيء يناوله غيرهم. وما أخذ من الزكاة فضّه على عياله حتّى يلحقهم بالناس.[70]

[Abū Baṣīr:] I asked Abū ʿAbd Allāh about a man among our colleagues who has eight hundred dirhams, works as a shoemaker, and has a large family; can he receive *zakāt*? He said, "Does he earn enough money to feed his family and have some left over?" I said, "Yes!" He said, "How much is left over?" I said, "I do not know." He said, "If the remaining surplus exceeds half the value of what he spends on food [for his family], he cannot receive *zakāt*. But if [the surplus] is [worth] less than half of his food expenses, he can receive *zakāt*." I said, "But then he owes *zakāt* on his wealth?" He said, "Indeed!" I said, "What does he do?" He said, "He uses it to improve the life of his family in matters of food, drink, and clothing. If any of it remains, he gives it to someone besides them. Whatever he receives as *zakāt*, he spends on his family until they reach [the normal standard of living of] other people."

25

إسماعيل بن عبد الخالق قال: سأله سعيد الأعرج وأنا أسمع فقال: إنّا نكبس الزيت والسمن نطلب به التجارة فربّما مكث عندنا السنة والسنتين، هل عليه زكاة؟ فقال:

70 Kulaynī, *Kāfī*, 3:560.

إن كنت تربح فيه شيئًا أو تجد رأس مالك فعليك زكاته، وإن كنت إنّما تربّص به لأنّك لا تجد إلّا وضيعة فليس عليك زكاته حتّى يصير ذهبًا أو فضّة، فإذا صار ذهبًا أو فضّة فزكّه للسنة الّتي اتّجرت فيها.[71]

[Ismāʿīl b. ʿAbd al-Khāliq:] Saʿīd al-Aʿraj asked him while I was listening, "We store oil and butterfat in order to trade them, and sometimes it remains with us for one or two years. Do we owe *zakāt* on it?" He said, "If you profit at all from it or are offered for it the equivalent of what you paid for it, you owe *zakāt* on it. If you hold it back because you could only sell it at a loss, you do not owe *zakāt* on it until it is turned into gold or silver. If it is exchanged for gold or silver, pay *zakāt* on it for the year in which you traded [with it]."

On Ḥajj

26

بريد بن معاوية العجلي قال: سألت أبا عبد الله عن رجل خرج حاجًّا ومعه جمل ونفقة وزاد فمات في الطريق. فقال: إن كان صرورة فمات في الحرم فقد أجزأت عنه حجّة الإسلام، وإن مات قبل أن يُحرم وهو صرورة جُعل جمله وزاده ونفقته في حجّة الإسلام، فإن فضل من ذلك شيء فهو لورثته. قلت: أرأيت إن كانت الحجّة تطوّعًا فمات في الطريق قبل أن يُحرم لمن يكون جمله ونفقته وما ترك؟ قال: لورثته. إلّا أن يكون عليه دَين فيُقضى عنه، أو يكون أوصى بوصيّة فيُنفذ ذلك لمن أوصى ويُجعل ذلك من الثُلث.[72]

[Burayd b. Muʿāwiya al-ʿIjlī:] I asked Abū ʿAbd Allāh about a man who left to perform the *ḥajj*, bringing with him a camel, cash, and provisions, but who died during the journey. He said, "If he had not performed the *ḥajj* before this and he died within the sacred precinct (*ḥaram*), he is considered to have performed the Islamic obligation of the *ḥajj*. If he died before entering the state of pilgrim sanctity (*iḥrām*) and had never performed the *ḥajj* before this, his camel, provisions, and cash should be spent on the Islamic obligation of the *ḥajj*, and whatever is left over goes to his heirs." I said, "What is your position if his *ḥajj* was voluntary and he died during the journey before entering the state of pilgrim sanctity; to whom belong his camel, cash, and

71 Kulaynī, *Kāfī*, 3:529.
72 Ṭūsī, *Tahdhīb*, 5:407.

what he left behind?" He said, "To his heirs, unless he owes a debt, in which case that is paid off [first], or he made a bequest, in which case they must be given to the recipient, and it will be counted toward the one-third [of his estate that he is entitled to allocate as he wishes]."

27

أبو الربيع الشامي قال: سُئل أبو عبد الله عن قول الله عزّ وجلّ: ﴿وَلِلَّهِ عَلَى النَّاسِ حِجُّ الْبَيْتِ مَنِ اسْتَطَاعَ إِلَيْهِ سَبِيلاً﴾، فقال: ما يقول الناس؟ فقلت له: الزاد والراحلة. فقال أبو عبد الله: قد سُئل أبو جعفر عن هذا فقال: هلك الناس إذَن! لَئِن كان من كان له زاد وراحلة قدرَ ما يقوت عياله ويستغني به عن الناس، ينطلق إليه فيسلبهم إيّاه لقد هلكوا إذَن. فقيل له: فما السبيل؟ فقال: السعة في المال، إذا كان يحجّ ببعض ويبقي بعضًا لقوت عياله. أليس قد فرض الله الزكاة فلم يجعلها إلّا على من يملك مائتي درهم؟[73]

[Abū al-Rabīʿ al-Shāmī:] Abū ʿAbd Allāh was asked about the statement of God, the Mighty and Majestic, "Pilgrimage to the House [of God] is a duty upon humankind before God for anyone who can afford a way to do so."[74] He said, "What do the people [that is, the jurists among the majority] say [about the concept of ability to afford it]?" I said, "[Having] provisions and a riding camel." Abū ʿAbd Allāh said, "Abū Jaʿfar [Muḥammad al-Bāqir] was asked about this. He said, 'People will perish then! If someone who has a riding camel and provisions as well as [the minimum] required to feed his family without needing people's help departs for the *ḥajj* and deprives his family of that [minimum], they [the family] will perish.' It was said to him, 'What does "a way" mean, then?' He said, 'A good amount of wealth such that he can perform the *ḥajj* with some of it and leave some to feed his family. Did God not make *zakāt* obligatory only for those who own two hundred dirhams?'"

28

حمّاد بن عيسى عن أبي عبد الله قال: من دخل مكّة متمتّعًا في أشهر الحجّ لم يكن له أن يخرج حتّى يقضي الحجّ، فإن عرضت له حاجة إلى عسفان أو إلى الطائف أو إلى ذات عرق، خرج محرمًا ودخل ملبّيًا بالحجّ فلا يزال على إحرامه، فإن رجع إلى مكّة رجع محرمًا ولم يقرب البيت حتّى يخرج مع الناس إلى مِنى على إحرامه، وإن شاء وجّهه

73 Kulaynī, *Kāfī*, 4:267.
74 Qurʾān 3:97.

ذلك إلى مِنى. قلت: فإن جهل فخرج إلى المدينة أو إلى نحوها بغير إحرام، ثمّ رجع في ابّان الحجّ في أشهر الحجّ يريد الحجّ، فيدخلها محرمًا أو بغير إحرام؟ قال: إن رجع في شهره دخل بغير إحرام، وإن دخل في غير الشهر دخل محرمًا. قلت: فأيّ الإحرامين والمتعتين، متعته الأولى أو الأخيرة؟ قال: الأخيرة هي عمرته، وهي المحتبس بها الّتي وصلت بحجّته. قلت: فما الفرق بين المفردة وبين عمرة المتعة إذا دخل في أشهر الحجّ؟ قال: أحرم بالعمرة وهو ينوي العمرة، ثمّ أحلّ منها ولم يكن عليه دم، ولم يكن محتبسًا بها، لأنّه لا يكون ينوي الحجّ.[75]

[Ḥammād b. ʿĪsā:] Abū ʿAbd Allāh said, "Whoever enters Mecca for the *ḥajj* of *tamattuʿ* during the months of the *ḥajj* cannot leave until he has performed the *ḥajj*. If he has a need to go to ʿAsafān, Ṭāʾif, or Dhāt ʿIrq,[76] he must leave in a state of pilgrim sanctity and enter Mecca while performing the *talbiya*. He thus continues to be in the state of pilgrim sanctity. So when he returns to Mecca, he returns in a state of pilgrim sanctity and does not go to the House [of God, the Kaʿba] until he goes out with the people to Minā in his state of pilgrim sanctity. If he wishes, he can go directly to Minā [on his way back from his trip]." I said, "What if he is ignorant and leaves for Medina or its like without being in a state of pilgrim sanctity, and returns during the time of the *ḥajj*, in the *ḥajj* months, seeking to perform the *ḥajj*—should he enter in a state of pilgrim sanctity or not?" He said, "If he comes back within a month [of leaving Mecca], he does not enter in a [new] state of pilgrim sanctity. But if he enters after the month has passed, he should enter in a [new] state of pilgrim sanctity." I said, "Which of the two states of pilgrim sanctity and the two lapses in between [count toward his *tamattuʿ*], the first or the second?" He said, "The second one, which is the *ʿumra* that he is bound to and the one that will be connected to his *ḥajj*." I said, "What is the difference between the *ʿumra mufrada* and the *ʿumra* performed with the *tamattuʿ* when he enters during the months of the *ḥajj*?" He said, "[*ʿUmra mufrada* is when] he enters a state of pilgrim sanctity for the *ʿumra* intending [only] the *ʿumra*, then exits that state and does not have to offer a sacrifice, and he is not confined to it because he did not intend [to perform] the *ḥajj*."

75 Kulaynī, *Kāfī*, 4:441–42.

76 These are regions around Mecca, within an approximate distance of 55 to 60 miles from it.

29

سعيد السمّان قال: كنت أحجُّ في كلِّ سنة. فلمّا كان في سنة شديدة أصاب الناس فيها جهد، فقال لي أصحابي: لو نظرت إلى ما تريد أن تحجَّ العام به فتصدّقتَ به كان أفضل. فقلت لهم: وترون ذلك؟ قالوا: نعم! قال: فتصدَّقت تلك السنة بما أُريد أن أحجَّ به وأقمت. قال: فرأيت رؤيا ليلة عرفة وقلت: والله لا أعود ولا أدع الحجَّ. قال: فلمّا كان من قابل حججت، فلمّا أتيت مِنى رأيت أبا عبد الله وعنده النّاس مجتمعون، فأتيته فقلت له: أخبرني عن الرجل – وقصصت عليه قصّتي – وقلت: أيّهما أفضل: الحجُّ أو الصدقة؟ فقال: ما أحسن الصدقة – ثلاث مرّات. قال: قلت: أجل! فأيّهما أفضل؟ قال: ما يمنع أحدكم من أن يحجَّ ويتصدَّق؟ قال: قلت: ما يبلغ مالُه ذلك ولا يتّسع. قال: إذا أراد أن يُنفق عشرة دراهم في شيء من سبب الحجّ أنفق خمسة وتصدَّق بخمسة، أو قصّر في شيء من نفقته في الحجِّ فيجعل ما يحبس في الصدقة فإنَّ له في ذلك أجرًا. قلت: هذا لو فعلناه استقام. قال: ثمَّ قال: وأنّى له مثل الحجِّ؟ – قالها ثلاث مرّات – إنَّ العبد ليخرج من بيته فيعطى قسمًا حتّى إذا أتى المسجد الحرام طاف طواف الفريضة، ثمَّ عدل إلى مقام إبراهيم فصلّى ركعتين، فيأتيه ملك فيقوم عن يساره فإذا انصرف ضرب بيده على كتفيه فيقول: يا هذا! أمّا ما مضى فقد غُفر لك وأمّا ما يستقبل فجَدِّ.[77]

[Saʿīd al-Sammān:] I used to perform the *ḥajj* each year. Then when the people were afflicted with hardship during a difficult year, my associates said to me, "If you calculated how much you would spend on performing the *ḥajj* this year and gave it in charity instead, that would be better." I said to them, "That is your opinion?" They said, "Yes!" So I gave charity that year with what I would have spent on the *ḥajj* and stayed home. On the night of ʿArafa, I had a dream, and I said, "By God, I will never do that again and will not abandon the *ḥajj*." When I performed the *ḥajj* the next year and went to Minā, I saw Abū ʿAbd Allāh with the people congregated around him. I went to him and said, "Tell me about a man"—and I told him my story and said, "Which is better, to perform the *ḥajj* or to give charity?" He said, "How good it is to give charity!" three times. I said, "Indeed! So which one of them is better?" He said, "What prevents one of you from doing both, performing the *ḥajj* and giving charity?" I said, "His money is not enough

77 Kulaynī, *Kāfī*, 4:257.

for that and does not reach that goal." He said, "If he wishes to spend ten dirhams on something that goes toward the *ḥajj*, he can spend five and give five in charity, or else he can save some of what he spends on the *ḥajj* and spend that in charity; he will be rewarded for that." I said, "If we do this, that will be possible." He said, "And can he have anything like the *ḥajj*?"—he said this three times. "A worshipper leaves his house, reaches the Sacred Mosque, and performs the obligatory circumambulation. He then goes to the Station of Ibrāhīm and prays two *rakʿas* of prayer. He is then approached by an angel, who stands to his left, and when he finishes, [the angel] pats his shoulder with his hand and says, 'O you! You have been forgiven for all that has occurred in the past, so try to do [your best] from now on.'"

30

معاوية بن عمّار عن أبي عبد الله قال: سمعته يقول: المحصور غير المصدود. المحصور المريض، والمصدود الّذي يصدُّه المشركون – كما ردُّوا رسولَ الله – صلّى الله عليه وآله وسلّم – وأصحابَه – ليس من مرض. والمصدود تحلُّ له النساء، والمحصور لا تحلُّ له النساء. قال: وسألته عن رجل أُحصر فبعث بالهدي، قال: يواعد أصحابه ميعادًا. إن كان في الحجِّ فمحلُّ الهدي يوم النحر، فإذا كان يوم النحر فليقصّ من رأسه، ولا يجب عليه الحلق حتّى يقضي المناسك. وإن كان في عمرة فلينظر مقدار دخول أصحابه مكّة والساعة الّتي يعدهم فيها، فإذا كان تلك الساعة قصّر وأحلَّ. وإن كان مرض في الطريق بعد ما أحرم فأراد الرجوع، رجع إلى أهله ونحر بدنة أو أقام مكانه حتّى يبرأ إذا كان في عمرة. وإذا برء فعليه العمرة واجبة. وإن كان عليه الحجُّ فرجع أو أقام ففاته الحجُّ، فإنَّ عليه الحجُّ من قابل. فإنّ الحسين بن علي خرج معتمرًا فمرض في الطريق، فبلغ عليًا ذلك وهو في المدينة، فخرج في طلبه فأدركه بالسقيا وهو مريض بها. فقال: يا بنيِّ! ما تشتكي؟ فقال: أشتكي رأسي. فدعا عليٌّ – عليه السلام – ببدنة فنحرها وحلق رأسه وردَّه إلى المدينة، فلمّا برء من وجعه اعتمر. قلت: أرأيت حين برء من وجعه قبل أن يخرج إلى العمرة حلّت له النساء؟ قال: لا تحلّ له النساء حتّى يطوف بالبيت وبالصفا والمروة. قلت: فما بال رسول الله – صلّى الله عليه وآله وسلّم – حين رجع من الحديبيّة حلّت له النساء ولم يطف بالبيت. قال: ليسا سواء. كان النبيُّ – صلّى الله عليه وآله وسلّم – مصدودًا والحسين محصورًا.[78]

78 Kulaynī, *Kāfī*, 4:369–70.

[Muʿāwiya b. ʿAmmār:] I heard Abū ʿAbd Allāh say, "A person who is restricted is different from a person who is prevented. The one restricted is [like one who is] ill, and the one prevented is [like one who is] prevented by the polytheists, just as they turned away the Prophet (may God's prayer and peace be upon him and his Family) and his Companions; it was not because of illness. The prevented person is permitted women, but the restricted person is not permitted women." I asked him about a man who is restricted but sends a sacrificial animal. He said, "He should arrange to meet up with his companions. If it is during the *ḥajj*, [he should meet them] at the place of sacrifice on the day of the sacrifice. When the day of the sacrifice arrives, he should cut his hair but does not have to shave until he performs the rites. If it is during the *ʿumra*, he should consider when his companions will enter Mecca and what time he will meet them. When that hour arrives, he should cut his hair and nails and exit the state of pilgrim sanctity. If he falls ill on the road after entering the state of pilgrim sanctity and wishes to return, he should return to his family and offer a sacrifice or else remain in that place until he recovers if it is during the *ʿumra*. If he recovers, performing the *ʿumra* becomes obligatory for him. If he was performing the *ḥajj* and returned, or remained but missed the *ḥajj*, he must redo it in the future. Ḥusayn b. ʿAlī left [Medina] to perform the *ʿumra* and fell ill on the road. ʿAlī heard of this while he was in Medina, so he left to seek him and found him ill at Suqyā [on the road from Medina to Mecca]. He said, 'O my son! What is your pain?' He said, 'My head hurts.' ʿAlī (peace be upon him) called for a sacrificial animal, slaughtered it, shaved [Ḥusayn's] head, and sent him back to Medina. When he recovered from his pain, he performed the *ʿumra*." I said, "Do you think that when he recovered from his pain, but before he embarked on the *ʿumra*, women were permissible for him?" He said, "Women would not have been permissible for him until he had circumambulated the House [of God] and [walked the distance between] Ṣafā and Marwa." I said, "So why were women permitted for the Prophet (may God's prayer and peace be upon him and his Family) when he returned from Ḥudaybiyya, although he had not circumambulated the House?" He said, "The two cases are not the same. The Prophet (may God's prayer and peace be upon him and his Family) was prevented, whereas Ḥusayn was restricted."

On Jihād *and Public Administration*

31

حفص بن غياث قال: كتب إليّ بعض إخواني أن أسأل أبا عبد الله عن مسائل من السير، فسألته وكتبت بها إليه. وكان فيما سألت:

أخبرني عن الجيش إذا غزوا أرض الحرب فغنموا غنيمة، ثمّ لحقهم جيش آخر قبل أن يخرجوا إلى دار الإسلام ولم يلقوا عدوًّا حتّى يخرجوا إلى دار الإسلام، هل يشاركونهم فيها؟ قال: نعم!

وعن سريّة كانوا في سفينة فقاتلوا وغنموا وفيهم من معه الفرس وإنّما قاتلوهم في السفينة ولم يركب صاحب الفرس فرسه، كيف تقسّم الغنيمة بينهم؟ فقال: للفارس سهمان وللراجل سهم. قلت: وإن لم يركبوا ولم يقاتلوا على أفراسهم؟ فقال: أرأيت لو كانوا في عسكر فتقدم الرجّالة فقاتلوا وغنموا، كيف تقسّم بينهم؟ ألم تجعل للفارس سهمين وللراجل سهمًا وهم الّذين غنموا دون الفرسان؟

قلت: فهل يجوز للإمام أن ينفل؟ فقال: له أن ينفل قبل القتال، فأمّا بعد القتال والغنيمة فلا يجوز ذلك لأنّ الغنيمة قد أحرزت.[79]

[Ḥafṣ b. Ghiyāth:] One of my brothers wrote to me asking me to question Abū ʿAbd Allāh about some issues related to *jihād*, so I did so and wrote [the answers] to him. Among the questions that I asked were [the following]:

"Tell me about an army that attacked enemy territory and obtained some booty, but before leaving to go back to the abode of Islam was joined by another army that had not encountered the enemy until they all left for the abode of Islam; do they [the newly joined army] share with the former in the booty?" He said, "Yes!"

[I asked] about a brigade on a ship that fought and acquired some booty, and there were cavalrymen among them; they fought onboard the ship, so the cavalrymen did not ride their horses. How is the booty divided among them? He said, "A cavalryman gets two shares and an infantryman gets one." I said, "Even if they did not ride and fight on their horses?" He said, "What would you say if they were in an army and the infantrymen went forth to fight and acquire some booty; how would it be divided among them? Would not the cavalrymen get two

79 Kulaynī, *Kāfī*, 5:44.

shares and the infantrymen one, even though the latter were the ones who acquired the booty without the cavalrymen?"

I asked, "Can the ruler give extra [booty]?" He said, "He can give extra before the battle, but after the battle, once the booty has been acquired, he cannot, because the booty has been won."

32

قال حفص: كتب إليّ بعض إخواني أن أسأل أبا عبد الله عن مسائل من السير فسألته وكتبت بها إليه. فكان فيما سألته:

أخبرني عن النساء كيف سَقَطت الجزية عنهنّ ورُفِعَت عنهنّ؟ فقال: لأنّ رسول الله – صلّى الله عليه وآله وسلّم – نهى عن قتل النساء والولدان في دار الحرب إلّا أن يقاتِلن، وإن قاتلت أيضًا فامسِك عنها ما أمكنك ولم تخف خللًا، فلمّا نهى عن قتلهنّ في دار الحرب كان ذلك في دار الإسلام أولى. ولو امتنعت أن تؤدّي الجزية لم يمكنك قتلها، فلمّا لم يمكن قتلها رفعت الجزية عنها. فلو امتنع الرجال وأبوا أن يؤدّوا الجزية كانوا ناقضين للعهد وحلّت دماؤهم وقتلهم، لأنّ قتل الرجال مباح في دار الشرك. وكذلك المُقعَد من أهل الذمّة والأعمى والشيخ الفاني والمرأة والولدان ليس عليهم جزية لأنّه لا يمكن قتلهم، لما نهى رسول الله – صلّى الله عليه وآله وسلّم – عن قتل المُقعد والأعمى والشيخ الفاني والمرأة والولدان في دار الحرب. فمن أجل ذلك رفعت عنهم الجزية.[80]

[Ḥafṣ:] One of my brothers wrote to me, asking me to ask Abū ʿAbd Allāh about some issues related to *jihād*, so I asked him and wrote [the answers] to the person. Among the questions that I asked was [the following]:

"Tell me how the *jizya* [poll tax on non-Muslims] was dropped and removed from women." He said, "[It was] because the Messenger of God (may God's prayer and peace be upon him and his Family) forbade killing women and children in the abode of war, unless they fight. Even if a woman fights, avoid her as much as you can and do not fear major harm. Since it is forbidden to fight them in the abode of war, that applies a fortiori in the abode of Islam. You cannot kill women if they refuse to pay *jizya*, and since you cannot kill them, *jizya* does not apply to them. If the men refuse to pay *jizya*, they are repudiating

80 Barqī, *Maḥāsin*, 327–28, and with a missing line in Kulaynī, *Kāfī*, 5:28–29.

their covenant [of safety with the Muslims], and [taking] their lives and fighting them become lawful. That is because it is permissible to fight men in the territory of polytheism. Likewise, the crippled among the people of *dhimma* [that is, protected status by covenant] and the blind, the elderly, women, and children are not subject to *jizya* because they cannot be killed, as the Messenger of God (may God's prayer and peace be upon him and his Family) forbade killing the crippled, the blind, the elderly, women, and children in the abode of war. For this reason, they are relieved of the *jizya*."

33

حفص بن غياث قال: سمعت أبا عبد الله يقول – وسئل عن قسم بيت المال – فقال: أهل الإسلام هم أبناء الإسلام، أسوّي بينهم في العطاء، وفضائلهم بينهم وبين الله، فأجعلهم كبني رجل واحد، لا يفضّل أحدٌ منهم لفضله وصلاحه في الميراث على آخر ضعيف منقوص. قال: وهذا هو فعل رسول الله – صلّى الله عليه وآله وسلّم – من بدو أمره. وقد قال غيرنا: أقدّمهم في العطاء بما قد فضّلهم الله بسوابقهم في الإسلام، إذ كانوا بالإسلام قد أصابوا ذلك. فأنزلهم على مواريث ذوي الأرحام، بعضهم أقرب من بعض وأوفر نصيبًا لقربه من الميت وإنّما ورثوا برحمهم. وكذلك كان عمر يفعله.[81]

[Ḥafṣ b. Ghiyāth:] I heard Abū ʿAbd Allāh say, when he was asked about distributing the treasury, "The people of Islam are the children of Islam; I consider them equal with respect to their receipts [from the Muslim treasury], and their merits are between them and God. I treat them as the children of the same man, none of whom is favored in the area of inheritance for his preeminence and righteousness over another who is weak and lacking." He said, "This was the practice of the Prophet (may God's prayer and peace be upon him and his Family) from the beginning. Others said, 'I prioritize [individuals'] payments [from the Muslim treasury] according to how God has favored them in their past records in Islam, since it was by Islam that they obtained these [financial resources].' He treated everyone according to the standards of inheritance among relatives: some are closer [to the deceased] than others and receive a bigger share because of their closeness to the deceased, because they inherit according to their relationship. This was how ʿUmar dealt with this matter."

81 Ṭūsī, *Tahdhīb*, 6:146, with corrections on the basis of a manuscript of the work used by Ḥurr al-ʿĀmilī, *Wasāʾil al-Shīʿa*, 15:106.

34

حفص بن غياث عن أبي عبد الله قال: سأل رجل أبي عن حروب أمير المؤمنين – عليه السلام. فقال له أبو جعفر: بعث الله محمّدًا – صلّى الله عليه وآله وسلّم – بخمسة أسياف. ثلاثة منها شاهرة لا تُغمد إلى أن تضع الحرب أوزارها، ولن تضع الحرب أوزارها حتّى تطلع الشمس من مغربها، فيومئذٍ ﴿لَا يَنْفَعُ نَفْسًا إِيمَانُهَا لَمْ تَكُنْ آمَنَتْ مِنْ قَبْلُ أَوْ كَسَبَتْ فِي إِيمَانِهَا خَيْرًا﴾، وسيف منها مكفوف، وسيف منها مغمود، سلّه إلى غيرنا وحكمه إلينا. فأمّا السيوف الثلاثة الشاهرة فسيف على مشركي العرب. قال الله تعالى: ﴿فَاقْتُلُوا الْمُشْرِكِينَ حَيْثُ وَجَدْتُمُوهُمْ﴾. فهؤلاء لا يُقبل منهم إلّا القتل أو الدخول في الإسلام. والسيف الثاني على أهل الذمّة. قال الله تعالى: ﴿قَاتِلُوا الَّذِينَ لَا يُؤْمِنُونَ بِاللَّهِ وَلَا بِالْيَوْمِ الْآخِرِ﴾ – الآية. فهؤلاء لا يقبل منهم إلّا الجزية أو القتل. والسيف الثالث سيف على مشركي العجم، يعني الترك والخزر والديلم. قال الله تعالى: ﴿فَضَرْبَ الرِّقَابِ حَتَّىٰ إِذَا أَثْخَنْتُمُوهُمْ﴾. فهؤلاء لا يُقبل منهم إلّا القتل أو الدخول في الإسلام، ولا يحلّ لنا نكاحهم ما داموا في [دار] الحرب. وأمّا السيف المكفوف فهو على أهل البغي والتأويل. قال الله تعالى: ﴿وَإِنْ طَائِفَتَانِ مِنَ الْمُؤْمِنِينَ اقْتَتَلُوا فَأَصْلِحُوا بَيْنَهُمَا فَإِنْ بَغَتْ إِحْدَاهُمَا عَلَى الْأُخْرَىٰ فَقَاتِلُوا الَّتِي تَبْغِي حَتَّىٰ تَفِيءَ إِلَىٰ أَمْرِ اللَّهِ﴾. وكانت السيرة فيهم من أمير المؤمنين – عليه السلام – ما كان من رسول الله – صلّى الله عليه وآله وسلّم – في أهل مكّة يوم فتح مكّة، فإنّه لم يسب لهم ذريّةً وقال: «من أغلق بابه وألقى سلاحه أو دخل دار أبي سفيان فهو آمن»، وكذلك قال أمير المؤمنين – عليه السلام – يوم البصرة فيهم: «لا تسبوا لهم ذريّةً ولا تجهزوا على جريح ولا تتبعوا مدبرًا، ومن أغلق بابه وألقى سلاحه فهو آمن». وأمّا السيف المغمود فالسيف الّذي يقام به القصاص. قال الله تعالى: ﴿النَّفْسَ بِالنَّفْسِ﴾ – الآية. فسلّه إلى أولياء المقتول وحكمه إلينا. فهذه السيوف التي بعث الله تعالى نبيّه – صلّى الله عليه وآله وسلّم – بها، فمن جحدها أو جحد واحدًا منها أو شيئًا من سيرها وأحكامها فقد كفر بما أنزل الله على محمّد – صلّى الله عليه وآله وسلّم.[82]

[Ḥafṣ b. Ghiyāth:] Abū ʿAbd Allāh said, "A man asked my father about the wars of the Commander of the Faithful [ʿAlī] (peace be upon him).

82 Ṭūsī, *Tahdhīb*, 6:136–37. A longer version of this report is recorded in ʿAlī b. Ibrāhīm, *Tafsīr*, 2:320; Kulaynī, *Kāfī*, 5:10–12. I have used this longer version to correct a few errors in the version quoted in *Tahdhīb*.

Abū Jaʿfar said to him, 'God sent Muḥammad (may God's prayer and peace be upon him and his Family) with five swords. Three of them are unsheathed and will never be sheathed until the burdens of war are lifted, and the burdens of war are not lifted until the sun rises from the west. On that day, "believing will do no good to a person who did not believe beforehand";[83] one of the swords is held back, and one of the swords is sheathed: it is up to others to unsheath it, but the judgment about it is up to us. As for the three unsheathed swords, the first of them is for the Arab polytheists. God, the Exalted, said, "Fight the polytheists wherever you find them."[84] Nothing can be accepted from them except being killed or entering Islam. The second sword is for the non-Muslim people of scripture. God, the Exalted, said, "Fight those who do not believe in God or the Last Day [among those who were given the Book, till they pay the *jizya*]"—to the end of the passage.[85] Nothing is accepted from these people beyond payment of *jizya* or being killed. The third sword is for the non-Arab polytheists: Turks, Khazars, and Daylamites. God, the Exalted, said, "Then strike at their necks until you have subdued them."[86] Nothing can be accepted from them except being killed or entering Islam, and we cannot marry them as long as they are in enemy territory. As for the sword that is held back, it is for the rebels and those who have their own interpretation [of the teachings of Islam]. God, the Exalted, said, "If two groups among the believers fight, reconcile them, but if one of them aggresses against the other, fight those who aggress until they return to God's command."[87] The practice of the Commander of the Faithful [ʿAlī] toward them was like the practice of the Messenger of God (may God's prayer and peace be upon him and his Family) toward the people of Mecca on the day of the conquest of Mecca. He did not enslave their progeny, and he said, "Whoever closes his door and drops his weapon or joins the house of Abū Sufyān—he is safe." The Commander of the Faithful said the same thing on the Day of Baṣra: "Do not enslave their progeny, do not kill a wounded person, and do not pursue anyone who runs away. Whoever closes his door and drops his weapon is safe." As for the sheathed sword, it is the sword used for retaliation. God, the Exalted, said, "A life for a life"—to the end of the passage.[88] Unsheathing [this sword] is the right of the family of the slain, and its judgment is up to us. These are

83 Qur'ān 6:158.

84 Qur'ān 9:5.

85 Qur'ān 9:29.

86 Qur'ān 47:4.

87 Qur'ān 49:9.

88 Qur'ān 5:45.

the swords with which God, the Exalted, sent his Prophet (may God's prayer and peace be upon him and his Family). Whoever repudiates them, or repudiates one of them or an aspect of their practice and rulings, has disbelieved what God revealed to Muḥammad (may God's prayer and peace be upon him and his Family).'"

35

حفص بن غياث قال: سألت أبا عبد الله عن الأسير هل يتزوّج في دار الحرب؟ فقال: أكره ذلك له، فإن فعل في بلاد الروم فليس بحرام وهو نكاح، وأمّا الترك والخزر والديلم فلا يحلّ له ذلك.[89]

[Ḥafṣ b. Ghiyāth:] I asked Abū ʿAbd Allāh whether a prisoner of war can marry in the abode of war. He said, "I dislike that for him. If he does it in the land of the Rūm [Byzantium], it is not impermissible and it is a marriage. But in the [lands of the] Turks, the Khazars, and the Daylamites, it is not permissible for him [to marry]."

36

حفص بن غياث قال: سألت أبا عبد الله عن الطّائفتين من المؤمنين، إحداهما باغية والأُخرى عادلة فهزمت العادلة الباغية؟ فقال: ليس لأهل العدل أن يتبعوا مدبرًا ولا يقتلوا أسيرًا ولا يجهزوا على جريح. وهذا إذا لم يبق من أهل البغي أحدٌ ولم يكن لهم فئة يرجعون إليها. فإذا كان لهم فئة يرجعون إليها فإنّ أسيرهم يقتل ومدبرهم يتبع وجريحهم يجهز [عليه].[90]

[Ḥafṣ b. Ghiyāth:] I asked Abū ʿAbd Allāh about two parties among the believers, one rebellious and the other upright, and the upright party defeats the rebels. He said, "The upright party should not pursue anyone who runs away, kill prisoners of war, or finish off their wounded. This is the case so long as none of the rebels remains and they do not have a group they can return to [and regroup]. If they have a group they can return to, then the prisoners can be killed, those who run away can be pursued, and their wounded can be finished off."

89 Ṭūsī, *Tahdhīb*, 6:152.
90 Kulaynī, *Kāfī*, 5:32–33.

37

محمّد الحلبي قال: سُئل أبو عبد الله عن السواد ما منزلته؟ فقال: هو لجميع المسلمين، لمن هو اليوم ولمن يدخل في الإسلام بعد اليوم ولمن لم يخلق بعد. قلنا: الشراء من الدهاقين؟ قال: لا يصلح، إلّا أن يشتري منهم على أن يصيّرها للمسلمين، فإن شاء وليّ الأمر أن يأخذها أخذها. قلنا: فإن أخذها منه؟ قال: يردّ إليه رأس ماله وله ما أكل من غلّتها بما عمل.[91]

[Muḥammad al-Ḥalabī:] Abū ʿAbd Allāh was asked about the status of the land of the Sawād [Mesopotamia]. He said, "It belongs to all Muslims—those existing today, those who will enter Islam after today, and those who do not yet exist." We said, "[What about] buying it from [its original, non-Muslim] farmers?" He said, "[Such a purchase] is not valid, unless a person purchases it from them in order to turn it over to the Muslims. Then if the government wants to take it, it may take it." We said, "And [what happens] if it takes it from him?" He said, "His principal is to be returned to him, and whatever he consumed of the produce from the land to the extent that he worked [on it] belongs to him."

38

محمّد بن مسلم: قلت لأبي عبد الله: أرأيت ما يأخذ هؤلاء من هذا الخمس من أرض الجزية ويأخذ من الدهاقين جزية رؤوسهم، أما عليهم في ذلك شيء موظّف؟ فقال: كان عليهم ما أجازوا على أنفسهم. وليس للإمام أكثر من الجزية، إن شاء الإمام وضع ذلك على رؤوسهم وليس على أموالهم شيء، وإن شاء فعلى أموالهم وليس على رؤوسهم شيء. فقلت: فهذا الخمس؟ فقال: إنّما هذا شيء كان صالحهم عليه رسول الله – صلّى الله عليه وآله وسلّم.[92]

[Muḥammad b. Muslim:] I said to Abū ʿAbd Allāh, "What is your position on what these people [that is, the caliphal administration] take—the one-fifth from the land of the non-Muslims and the *jizya* taken from the non-Muslim farmers; do they not have a specific legal obligation in this regard?" He said, "They became responsible for what they agreed to pay, but the *imām* cannot take more than the *jizya*. If he wishes, the *imām* can apply it to each individual and take nothing from

91 Ṭūsī, *Tahdhīb*, 7:147.
92 Kulaynī, *Kāfī*, 3:567.

their wealth, and if he wishes, he can apply it to their wealth and nothing is owed for each individual." I said, "What about the one-fifth?" He said, "That is something they agreed on with the Messenger of God (may God's prayer and peace be upon him and his Family)."[93]

39

إسماعيل بن الفضل الهاشميّ قال: سألت أبا عبد الله عن رجل اكترى أرضًا من أرض أهل الذمّة من الخراج وأهلها كارهون، وإنّما تقبّلها من السلطان لعجز أهلها عنها أو غير عجز. فقال: إذا عجز أربابها عنها فلك أن تأخذها إلّا أن يضارّوا، وإن أعطيتهم شيئًا فسخت أنفس أهلها لكم بها فخذوها. قال: وسألته عن رجل اشترى منهم أرضًا من أراضي الخراج فبنى فيها أو لم يَبنِ، غير أنَّ أُناسًا من أهل الذمّة نزلوها. أله أن يأخذ منهم أجور البيوت إذا أدّوا جزية رؤوسهم؟ قال: يشارطهم فما أخذ بعد الشّرط فهو حلال.[94]

[Ismāʿīl b. al-Faḍl al-Hāshimī:] I asked Abū ʿAbd Allāh about a man who leased a piece of *kharāj* land belonging to the people of *dhimma*, but its people were not in agreement. He accepted it from the government either because the people failed [to maintain and pay *kharāj* on] it or for another reason. He said, "If its owners failed, you can take it unless it would be harmful to them. If you give them something and the people of [the land] become happy with you, take it." I [also] asked about a man who purchased from them a tract of *kharāj* land and then either built [houses] on it or did not do so, but the people of the *dhimma* took up residence in it; can he collect rent for the houses if they paid the *jizya* they owe? He said, "He is to reach an agreement with them, and whatever he takes after he reaches an agreement with them is permissible."

40

إسماعيل ابن الفضل الهاشميّ عن أبي عبد الله قال: سألته عن رجل استأجر من السلطان من أرض الخراج بدراهم مسمّاة أو بطعام مسمّى، ثمَّ آجرها و شرط لمن يزرعها أن يقاسمه النصف أو أقلّ من ذلك أو أكثر، وله في الأرض بعد ذلك فضل، أيصلح له ذلك؟ قال: نعم! إذا حفر نهرًا أو عمل لهم شيئًا يُعينهم بذلك فله ذلك. قال: وسألته عن الرجل استأجر أرضًا من أرض الخراج بدراهم مسمّاة أو بطعام معلوم، فيؤاجرها

93 For details, see Modarressi, *Kharāj in Islamic Law*, 147–50.
94 Kulaynī, *Kāfī*, 5:282.

قطعة قطعة أو جريبًا جريبًا بشيء معلوم، فيكون له فضل فيما استأجره من السلطان ولا ينفق شيئًا، أو يؤاجر تلك الأرض قِطَعًا على أن يعطيهم البذر والنفقة فيكون له في ذلك فضل على إجارته وله تربة الأرض أو ليست له. فقال: إذا استأجرت أرضًا فأنفقت فيها شيئًا أو رممت فيها فلا بأس بما ذكرت.[95]

[Ismāʿīl b. al-Faḍl al-Hāshimī:] I asked Abū ʿAbd Allāh about a man who leases a tract of *kharāj* land from the government for a specific amount of money or produce and then leases it out and stipulates on whoever sows it to divide [the crops with him] fifty-fifty, or receives less than half or more than half, and he [the original lessee] will make profit from the land; is that valid for him to do? He said, "Yes! If he digs a water canal or performs any labor that would help [the sub-lessee], he can do that." I also asked him about a man who leases a tract of *kharāj* land for a specified payment or a known amount of produce and then leases it out plot by plot, or patch by patch, for a specified amount, and he makes money from what he has leased from the government without having responsibility to pay for anything. Or he leases out the land by plots on the condition of giving the sublessee the seeds and covering the expenses [of cultivation], so that he will make extra money off his lease on the land, whether he owns the soil of the land or not. He said, "If you lease land and spend something on it or renovate something in it, there is nothing wrong with what you have described."

41

مولى لعلي بن الحسين قال: كنت بالكوفة فقدم أبو عبد الله الحيرة، فأتيته فقلت له: جعلت فداك! لو كلّمت داود بن علي أو بعض هؤلاء فأدخل في بعض هذه الولايات. فقال: ما كنت لأفعل! قال: فانصرفت إلى منزلي فتفكّرت فقلت: ما أحسبه منعني إلّا مخافة أن أظلم أو أجور. والله لآتينّه ولأعطينّه الطلاق والعتاق والأيمان المغلّظة ألّا أظلم أحدًا ولا أجور ولأعدلنّ. قال: فأتيته فقلت: جعلت فداك! إنّي فكّرت في إبائك عليّ فظننت أنّك إنّما منعتني وكرهت ذلك مخافة أن أجور أو أظلم، وإنّ كلّ امرأة لي طالق وكلّ مملوك لي حرٌّ، وعليّ وعليّ إن ظلمت أحدًا أو جُرت عليه وإن لم أعدل!

95 Kulaynī, *Kāfī*, 5:272.

قال: كيف قلت؟ قال: فأعدت عليه الأيمان. فرفع رأسه إلى السماء فقال: تناول السماء أيسر عليك من ذلك.[96]

[A client of ʿAlī b. al-Ḥusayn:] I was in Kūfa when Abū ʿAbd Allāh arrived in Ḥīra, so I went to him and said, "May I be made your ransom! What if you spoke to Dāwūd b. ʿAlī [governor of Kūfa at the time] or some of these people so that I could enter into a government position?" He said, "I would not do that!" I went home, thought about it, and said [to myself] that he would not have refused my request except out of fear that I would commit injustice or oppression. [I said to myself,] "By God, I will go to him and make vows to him of divorce and manumission, and give binding oaths that I will not be unjust toward or oppress anyone and that I will be just." So I went to him and said, "May I be made your ransom! I thought about your refusal [of my request], and I concluded that you forbade me and disliked it out of fear that I would commit injustice or oppression. May all my wives be divorced, and all my slaves be free, and . . . and . . . if I do injustice toward or oppress anyone, and if I do not act justly!" He said, "What did you say?" I repeated the oaths to him. He raised his head to the sky and said, "Grabbing the sky is easier for you than that is."[97]

96 Kulaynī, *Kāfī*, 5:108.

97 See also the following two reports from the Imam about unjust rulers (Kulaynī, *Kāfī*, 5:108):

جهم بن حميد قال: قال لي أبو عبد الله: أما تغشى سلطان هؤلاء؟ قلت: لا! قال: ولِمَ؟ قلت: فرارًا بديني. قال: فعزمت على ذلك؟ قلت: نعم. فقال لي: الآن سلم لك دينُك.

[Jahm b. Ḥumayd:] Abū ʿAbd Allāh said to me, "Do you get involved with these authorities?" I said, "No!" He said, "Why not?" I said, "[I am] escaping with my religion!" He said, "And you are resolute on that?" I said, "Yes!" He said, "Now your religion is safe."

فُضيل بن عياض قال: سألت أبا عبد الله عن أشياء من المكاسب فنهاني عنها وقال: يا فضيل! والله لضرر هؤلاء على هذه الأُمّة أشدُّ من ضرر الترك والدَيلم. قال: وسألته عن الورع من الناس فقال: الّذي يتورَّع عن محارم الله عزَّ وجلَّ ويجتنب هؤلاء، وإذا لم يتّق الشبهات وقع في الحرام وهو لا يعرفه، وإذا رأى المنكر فلم ينكره وهو يقدر عليه فقد أحبّ أن يعصى الله عزَّ وجلّ، ومن أحبَّ أن يعصى الله فقد بارز الله عزَّ وجلَّ بالعداوة، ومن أحبَّ بقاء الظالمين فقد أحبَّ أن يعصى الله. إنَّ الله تعالى حمد نفسه على هلاك الظالمين فقال: ﴿فَقُطِعَ دَابِرُ الْقَوْمِ الَّذِينَ ظَلَمُوا وَالْحَمْدُ لِلَّهِ رَبِّ الْعَالَمِينَ﴾.

[Fuḍayl b. ʿIyāḍ:] I asked Abū ʿAbd Allāh about some business matters, and he forbade me from engaging in them. He said, "O Fuḍayl! By God, the harm these people [the rulers] exact on this community (*umma*) is greater than the harm caused by the Turks and the Daylamites." I asked him, "Who among the people exhibit piety?" He said, "[Piety is found in] the one who heeds the prohibitions of God, the Mighty and Majestic, and avoids those people. If he does not shield himself from doubtful matters, he will fall into sin without knowing it. If he sees a wrong but does not forbid it even though he is capable of doing so, then he likes to see God, the Mighty and Majestic, disobeyed. Whoever likes to see God disobeyed has come out against

On Contracts

42

أبو الرَبيع الشامي قال: سألت أبا عبد الله عن رجل أربا بجهالة ثمّ أراد أن يتركه. فقال: أمّا ما مضى فله، وليتركه فيما يستقبل. ثمّ قال: إنّ رجلاً أتى أبا جعفر فقال إنّي قد ورثت مالاً وقد علمت أنّ صاحبه كان يربو، وقد سألت فقهاء أهل العراق وفقهاء أهل الحجاز فذكروا أنّه لا يحلّ أكله. فقال أبو جعفر: إن كنت تعرف منه شيئًا معزولاً تعرف أهله وتعرف أنّه ربًا فخذ رأس مالك ودع ما سواه، وإن كان المال مختلطًا فكُله. فإنّ المال مالك. واجتنب ما كان يصنع صاحبك، فإنّ رسول الله – صلّى الله عليه وآله وسلّم – قد وضع ما مضى من الربا، فمن جهله وسعه أكله فإذا عرفه حرم عليه أكله، فإن أكله بعد المعرفة وجب عليه ما وجب على آكل الربا.[98]

[Abū al-Rabīʿ al-Shāmī:] I asked Abū ʿAbd Allāh about a man who issued usurious loans out of ignorance and then wanted to give up this practice. He said, "What he earned in the past belongs to him, and he should put an end to it going forward." Then he said, "A man once came to Abū Jaʿfar [Muḥammad al-Bāqir] and said, 'I have inherited wealth that I know came from an owner who used to engage in usury. I asked the jurists of Iraq and the jurists of the Ḥijāz, and they said that consuming it is impermissible.' Abū Jaʿfar said, 'If you know that a distinct portion of it came from certain owners and was derived from usury, take your principal and leave the rest. But if the wealth is all mixed together, consume it, as the wealth is yours. Avoid what the man was doing, because the Prophet (may God's prayer and peace be upon him and his Family) forgave what was previously earned usuriously. Whoever is ignorant about [the origin of] money may consume it, but when he comes to know [of ill-gotten gains], consuming it becomes impermissible for him. If he consumes it after acquiring knowledge, he will face the same consequences that the consumer of usury will face.'"

Him as an enemy. Whoever likes for oppressors to remain, he likes that God be disobeyed. God praises Himself for destroying the oppressors. He says, 'The people who committed injustice were eliminated. Praise be to God, Lord of the Universe' [Qurʾān 6:45]."

98 Kulaynī, *Kāfī*, 5:146.

43

الحلبي عن أبي عبد الله قال: الحكرة أن يشتري طعامًا ليس في المصر غيره فيحتكره، فإن كان في المصر طعام أو يباع غيره فلا بأس بأن يلتمس بسلعته الفضل. قال: وسألته عن الزيت، فقال: إن كان عند غيرك فلا بأس بإمساكه.[99]

['Ubayd Allāh al-Ḥalabī:] Abū ʿAbd Allāh said, "Hoarding means purchasing all of the food in a city and having exclusive possession of it. If there is [still] food in the city or other food is being sold, there is nothing wrong with profiting from one's commodity." I also asked him about cooking oil. He said, "If other people besides you have it, there is nothing wrong with retaining it."

44

سالم الحنّاط قال: قال لي أبو عبد الله: ما عملك؟ قلت: حنّاط، وربّما قدمت على نفاق وربّما قدمت على كساد فحبست. فقال: فما يقول من قِبلَك فيه؟ قلت: يقولون: محتكر. فقال: يبيعه أحد غيرك؟ قلت: ما أبيع أنا من ألف جزء جزءًا. قال: لا بأس! إنّما كان ذلك رجل من قريش يقال له حكيم بن حزام، كان إذا دخل الطعام المدينة اشتراه كلّه. فمرَّ عليه النبيُّ – صلّى الله عليه وآله وسلّم – فقال: يا حكيم بن حزام! إيّاك أن تحتكر.[100]

[Sālim al-Ḥannāṭ:] Abū ʿAbd Allāh said to me, "What is your occupation?" I said, "I am a wheat-seller. Sometimes the market is thriving and sometimes it is depressed, so I retain [the supply]." He said, "What do people around you say about this?" I said, "[They call me] a hoarder." He said, "Does anyone besides you sell it?" I said, "What I sell is not even one-thousandth of the market." He said, "There is nothing wrong with that! There was a man from the Quraysh called Ḥakīm b. Ḥizām,[101] who bought the entire food stock when it arrived Medina. The Prophet (may God's prayer and peace be upon him and his Family) passed by him and said, 'O Ḥakīm b. Ḥizām! Do not hoard!'"

---

99 Kulaynī, *Kāfī*, 5:164–65.

100 Kulaynī, *Kāfī*, 5:165.

101 A nephew of Khadīja, the first wife of the Prophet. He converted to Islam on the day of the conquest of Mecca in the year 8 and moved to Medina, where he lived and eventually died in the year 54.

45

سعيد بن محمّد الطاهريّ، عن أبيه، عن أبي عبد الله قال: سأله رجلٌ عن بيع الجواري المغنّيات فقال: شراؤهنّ وبيعهنّ حرام، وتعليمهنّ كفر، واستماعهنّ نفاق.[102]

[Saʿīd b. Muḥammad al-Ṭāhirī:] A man asked Abū ʿAbd Allāh about the sale of singing slave girls. He said, "Buying and selling them is impermissible, training them is unbelief, and listening to them shows lack of faith."[103]

46

الحلبيّ عن أبي عبد الله في رجل ابتاع من رجل طعامًا بدراهم فأخذ نصفه وترك نصفه، ثمّ جاء بعد ذلك وقد ارتفع الطعام أو نقص. قال: إن كان يوم ابتاعه ساعره أنّ له كذا وكذا فإنّما له سعره، وإن كان إنّما أخذ بعضًا وترك بعضًا ولم يسمّ سعرًا فإنّما له سعر يومه الّذي يأخذ فيه ما كان.[104]

[ʿUbayd Allāh al-Ḥalabī:] Regarding a man who purchased food from another man but took only half of it and left the other half, then came later and found the food price increased or decreased, Abū ʿAbd Allāh said, "If on the day he purchased it they agreed on the price, he gets it at that price. But if he took some and left some without setting a price, he gets it [the second half] at the price of the day on which he takes what is left."

102 Kulaynī, *Kāfī*, 5:120.

103 See also the following reaction from his son, Mūsā al-Kāẓim (Kulaynī, *Kāfī*, 5:120):

إبراهيم بن أبي البلاد قال: أوصى إسحاق بن عمر عند وفاته بجوارٍ له مغنيّات أن نبيعهنّ ونحمل ثمنهنَّ إلى أبي الحسن. قال إبراهيم: فبعت الجواري بثلاثمائة ألف درهم وحملت الثمن إليه، فقلت له: إنَّ مولىً لك يقال له إسحاق بن عمر قد أوصى عند موته ببيع جوارٍ له مغنيّات وحمل الثمن إليك، وقد بعتهنَّ وهذا الثمن ثلاثمائة ألف درهم. فقال: لا حاجة لي فيه. إنَّ هذا سحت، وتعليمهنَّ كفر، والاستماع منهنَّ نفاق، وثمنهنَّ سحت.

[Ibrāhīm b. Abī al-Bilād:] Isḥāq b. ʿUmar entrusted [me] on his deathbed to sell his singing girls and take the money to Abū al-Ḥasan [Mūsā al-Kāẓim]. [Ibrāhīm said:] I sold the slave girls for 300,000 dirhams and took the money to him. I said to him, "A client of yours named Isḥāq b. ʿUmar entrusted [me] on his deathbed [with ensuring] that his singing slave girls are sold and the money is brought to you. I sold them, and this is the money, 300,000 dirhams." He said, "I have no need for it. This is ill-gotten [wealth]. Teaching them is unbelief, listening to them shows lack of faith, and the money [earned from their sale] is ill-gotten."

104 Kulaynī, *Kāfī*, 5:181.

47

الحلبي قال: سُئل أبو عبد الله عن رجل أسلم دراهمه في خمسة مخاتيم من حنطة أو شعير إلى أجل مسمّى، وكان الّذي عليه الحنطة والشعير لا يقدر على أن يقضيه جميع الّذي له إذا حلَّ، فسأل صاحب الحقّ أن يأخذ نصف الطعام أو ثلثه أو أقلّ من ذلك أو أكثر، ويأخذ رأس مال ما بقي من الطعام دراهم؟ قال: لا بأس. [وعن] الزعفران يسلم فيه الرجل دراهم في عشرين مثقالاً أو أقلَّ من ذلك أو أكثر؟ قال: لا بأس إن لم يقدر الّذي عليه الزعفران أن يعطيه جميع ما لَه، أن يأخذ نصف حقّه أو ثلثه أو ثلثيه، ويأخذ رأس مال ما بقي من حقّه.[105]

['Ubayd Allāh al-Ḥalabī:] Abū ʿAbd Allāh was asked about a man who paid in advance for five barrels of wheat or barley to be delivered later on a specified date. The person who owed the wheat and barley was unable to deliver it all when the time came, so he asked the person with the right [to the food] to take half, a third, or more or less of the food and to take the principal for the rest in the form of cash. He said, "There is nothing wrong [with that]." And he was asked about a man who pays in advance for twenty *mithqāl*s, or more or less, of saffron. He said, "If the person who owes the saffron is unable to deliver it all, there is nothing wrong with [the buyer's] taking half, a third, or two-thirds of what he is owed in kind and the remainder of what he is owed as principal [in cash]."

48

عن رزيق قال: كنت عند أبي عبد الله يومًا إذ دخل عليه رجلان. فقال أحدهما إنّه كان عليّ مال لرجل من بني عمّار، وله بذلك ذكر حقّ وشهود، فأخذ المال ولم أسترجع منه الذكر بالحق، ولا كتبت عليه كتابًا، ولا أخذت منه براءة، وذلك لأنّي وثقت به وقلت له: مزّق الذكر بالحق الّذي عندك. فمات وتهاون بذلك ولم يمزّقها. وعقب هذا أن طالبني بالمال ورّاثه وحاكموني وأخرجوا بذلك الذكر بالحقّ، وأقاموا العدول فشهدوا عند الحاكم فأُخذت بالمال، وكان المال كثيرًا فتواريت من الحاكم فباع عليّ قاضي الكوفة معيشة لي وقبض القوم المال، وهذا رجل من إخواننا إبتلى بشراء معيشتي من القاضي. ثمّ أنّ ورثة الميّت أقرّوا أنّ المال كان أبوهم قد قبضه وقد سألوه أن يردّ عليّ معيشتي ويعطونه في أنجم معلومة، فقال: إنّي أُحبّ أن نسأل أبا عبد الله

105 Kulaynī, *Kāfī*, 5:186.

عن هذا. فقال الرجل – يعني المشتري – جعلني الله فداك! كيف أصنع؟ فقال: تصنع أن ترجع بمالك على الورثة وتردّ المعيشة إلى صاحبها، وتخرج يدك عنها. قال: فإذا أنا فعلت ذلك له أن يطالبني بغير هذا؟ قال: نعم! له أن يأخذ منك ما أخذتَ من الغلّة ثمن الثمار، وكلّ ما كان مرسومًا في المعيشة يوم اشتريتها يجب أن تردّ ذلك، إلّا ما كان من زرع زرعته أنت، فإنّ للزارع إمّا قيمة الزرع وإمّا أن يصبر عليك إلى وقت حصاد الزرع، فإن لم يفعل كان ذلك له وردّ عليك القيمة وكان الزرع له. قلت: جعلت فداك! فإن كان هذا قد أحدث فيها بناء وغرس؟ قال: له قيمة ذلك أو يكون ذلك المحدِث بعينه يقلعه ويأخذه. قلت: أرأيت إن كان فيها غرس أو بناء فقلع الغرس وهدم البناء؟ فقال: يردّ ذلك إلى ما كان أو يغرم القيمة لصاحب الأرض، فإذا ردّ جميع ما أخذ من غلّاتها إلى صاحبها وردّ البناء والغرس وكلّ محدَث إلى ما كان أو ردّ القيمة كذلك يجب على صاحب الأرض أن يردّ عليه كل ما خرج عنه في إصلاح المعيشة من قيمة غرس أو بناء أو نفقة في مصلحة المعيشة، ودفع النوائب عنها. كلّ ذلك فهو مردود إليه.[106]

[Ruzayq b. al-Zubayr:] I was with Abū ʿAbd Allāh one day when two men came to him. One of them said, "I owed money to a man from Banū ʿAmmār.[107] He had a written document of the debt and witnesses. He received the borrowed money back, but I did not take back the written document from him, nor did I prepare a document to that effect, nor did I receive a document from him to certify that I have been released of my legal duty. This was because I trusted him, and I said to him, 'Tear up the document that you have of the debt.' He then died, but had been negligent in this matter and not torn up the document. As a result, his heirs requested the money from me and sued me, producing the written document. The [two] upright witnesses testified to the judge, and I was held liable for the money. The money was a large sum, so I hid from the judge. Then the judge of Kūfa sold my land, from which I earned my livelihood, and the heirs took possession of the money. This man is one of our brothers who fell into trouble by buying my land from the judge. Then the heirs acknowledged that their

106 Ṭūsī, *Amālī*, 697–99.

107 Generally speaking, this can mean either a family, such as the one to which Isḥāq b. ʿAmmar, the moneychanger, and his four brothers belonged (a prominent and wealthy Shīʿī family in Kūfa at the time, as Najāshī, *Rijāl*, 71 reports; see also Kashshī, *Rijāl*, 402, 408), a tribe, or a district in the town where the members of the tribe predominantly lived. In the case at hand, however, the first option is most likely.

father had received the money, so they asked the man to return my land to me and they would pay him in a set number of installments. The man said, 'I would like us to ask Abū ʿAbd Allāh about this matter.'" So the man—the purchaser—said, "May God make me your ransom! What should I do?" Abū ʿAbd Allāh said, "You should get your money from the heirs and give the land to its owner and give up possession of it." He said, "If I do that, can he demand anything else of me?" Abū ʿAbd Allāh said, "Yes! He can take whatever money you earned from the crops, and anything that was recorded to have been on the land on the day you purchased it must be returned, except for what you tilled yourself. As the tiller you either receive the value of [your work] or wait until the harvest; if he [the owner] does not [give you part of the harvest], the owner keeps it and the value [of the harvest] is paid to you, and the harvest belongs to him." I said, "May I be made your ransom! What about if he built on the land and planted [trees]?" Abū ʿAbd Allāh said, "He gets their value, or he can remove and take away that newly added thing." I said, "What is your position if it [the land] had plants or buildings on it [when it came into the possession of the purchaser], and he uprooted the plants and demolished the building?" Abū ʿAbd Allāh said, "It will be returned to its original condition, or the value [of what has been removed] is paid to the owner of the land. When he [the purchaser] returns all of the produce to the owner and the plants and buildings and everything newly added to its original status, the owner has to give him in return the value of whatever the man did to improve the land, be it the value of what he planted or built or of the improvements he made and the disasters he prevented. All that is to be paid back to him."

49

سماعة قال: سألته عن بيع الثمرة هل يصلح شراؤها قبل أن يخرج طلعها؟ فقال: لا! إلّا أن يشتري معها شيئًا غيرها، رطبة أو بقلاً، فيقول: أشتري منك هذه الرطبة وهذا النخل وهذا الشجر بكذا وكذا، فإن لم تخرج الثمرة كان رأس مال المشتري في الرطبة والبقل. وسألته عن ورق الشجر هل يصلح شراؤه ثلاث خرطات أو أربع خرطات؟ فقال: إذا رأيت الورق في شجرة فاشتر منه ما شئت من خرطة.[108]

[Samāʿa:] I asked him whether it is valid to buy fruit before its inflorescence. He said, "No! Not unless one buys something else along with fresh produce or herbs and says, 'I buy this fresh produce from you,

108 Kulaynī, *Kāfī*, 5:176.

this date palm, and this tree for such-and-such.' If no fruit is borne, the buyer's principal is in the fresh produce and herbs." I also asked him whether it is valid to buy three or four stripped-off bunches of tree leaves. He said, "If you see the leaves on the tree, buy however many stripped-off bunches you wish."

50

علي بن أبي حمزة قال: سألت أبا عبد الله عن رجل اشترى بستانًا فيه نخل وشجر، منه ما قد أُطعم ومنه ما لم يُطعم. قال: لا بأس به إذا كان فيه ما قد أُطعم. قال: وسألته عن رجل اشترى بستانًا فيه نخل ليس فيه غير بُسر أخضر. فقال: لا! حتّى يزهو. قلت: وما الزَّهو؟ قال: حتّى يتلوَّن.[109]

['Alī b. Abī Ḥamza:] I asked Abū 'Abd Allāh about a man who purchased an orchard containing date palms and trees, some of which had ripe fruit and some of which did not. He said, "There is nothing wrong with that if some of it was already ripe." I also asked him about a man who purchased an orchard with date palms that only had green, unripe dates. He said, "No! Not until they flourish." I said, "What is flourishment?" He said, "When they get color."

51

ابن سنان قال: سألت أبا عبد الله عن الرجل يشتري الدابّة. ويشترط إلى يوم أو يومين فيموت الدابّة أو يحدث فيه الحدث. على من ضمان ذلك؟ فقال: على البائع حتّى ينقضي الشرط ثلاثة أيّام ويصير المبيع للمشتري، شرط له البائع أو لم يشترط. قال: وإن كان بينهما شرط أيّامًا معدودة فهلك في يد المشتري قبل أن يمضي الشرط فهو من مال البائع.[110]

[Ibn Sinān:] I asked Abū 'Abd Allāh about a man who purchases a riding animal, with an option [to cancel the sale] for one or two days, but the beast then dies or a misfortune befalls it. Who is liable? He said, "The seller, until three days have elapsed on the option and ownership of the sold merchandise has passed to the buyer, whether or not the seller accepted the option. If they agreed to an option for a specified number of days, and the merchandise perishes in the possession of the buyer before the option has lapsed, the loss falls on the seller."

---

109 Kulaynī, *Kāfī*, 5:176.
110 Kulaynī, *Kāfī*, 5:169–70.

52

معاوية بن عمّار قال: قلت لأبي عبد الله: يجيئني الرجل يطلب متاع الحرير وليس عندي شيء منه فيقاولني عليه وأقاوله في الربح والأجل حتّى نجتمع على شيء، ثمّ أذهب فاشتري له الحرير فأدعوه إليه. فقال: أرأيت إن وجد بيعًا هو أحبّ إليه ممّا عندك أيستطيع أن ينصرف إليه ويدعك؟ أو إن وجدت أنت ذلك أتستطيع أن تنصرف عنه وتدعه؟ قلت: نعم! قال: لا بأس.[111]

[Muʿāwiya b. ʿAmmār:] I said to Abū ʿAbd Allāh, "A man comes to me seeking to buy silk, but I do not have any, so he negotiates with me for it and I negotiate with him over the profit and time limit until we come to an agreement. Then I go, buy the silk for him, and call him [to pick it up]." He said, "If he finds an option that he likes more than what you have, can he opt for it and turn you down? Or if you find a better option, can you then renounce [the sale] and turn him down?" I said, "Yes!" He said, "There is nothing wrong with that."

53

هذيل بن حيّان أخي جعفر بن حيّان الصيرفي قال: قلت لأبي عبد الله: إنّي دفعت إلى أخي جعفر مالاً فهو يعطيني ما أنفقه وأحجُّ منه وأتصدَّق، وقد سألت مَن قِبَلنا فذكروا أنّ ذلك فاسد لا يحلّ، وأنا أُحبّ أن أنتهي إلى قولك. فقال لي: أكان يصلك قبل أن تدفع إليه مالك؟ قلت: نعم. قال: فخذ منه ما يعطيك فكُل منه واشرب وحجّ وتصدّق، فإذا قدمت العراق فقل: جعفر بن محمّد أفتاني بهذا.[112]

[Hudhayl b. Ḥayyān:] I said to Abū ʿAbd Allāh, "I gave money to my brother Jaʿfar, and [now] he gives me what I spend on living and on performing the *ḥajj* and on donating. I asked [the Sunnī jurists] in our district and they told me this is invalid and unlawful, and I want to follow your opinion." He said to me, "Was he giving you support before you gave him your money?" I said, "Yes." He said, "Take what he gives you and use it to eat, drink, perform the *ḥajj*, and donate. And when you arrive in Iraq, say: 'Jaʿfar b. Muḥammad gave me this legal edict.'"

111 Kulaynī, *Kāfī*, 5:200.
112 Kulaynī, *Kāfī*, 5:103.

54

إبراهيم الكرخيّ قال: قلت لأبي عبد الله: أُشارك العِلج فيكون من عندي الأرض والبذر والبقر ويكون على العِلج القيام والسقي والعمل في الزرع حتّى يصير حنطة وشعيرًا ويكون القسمة فيأخذ السلطان حقّه ويبقى ما بقي، على أنّ للعِلج منه الثلث ولي الباقي؟ قال: لا بأس بذلك. قلت: فلي عليه أن يردّ عليَّ ممّا أخرجت الأرض البذر ويقسّم الباقي؟ قال: إنّما شاركتَه على أنّ البذر من عندك وعليه السقي والقيام.[113]

[Ibrāhīm al-Karkhī:] I said to Abū ʿAbd Allāh, "I enter into a partnership with a non-Muslim [farmer] in which I contribute my land, seeds, and cattle and the non-Muslim [farmer] does the work, watering and cultivating the crops until they become wheat and barley. Upon distribution, the government takes its share, and of what remains, the non-Muslim [farmer] takes one-third and I take the rest." He said, "There is nothing wrong with that." I said, "From what grows from the earth, does he [first] owe me seeds [in an amount equivalent to what I provided] before the rest is divided?" He said, "You partnered with him on the basis that you provide the seeds and he waters and maintains."

55

يعقوب بن شعيب عن أبي عبد الله قال: سألته عن الرجل يكون له الأرض من أرض الخراج فيدفعها إلى الرجل على أن يعمرها ويصلحها ويؤدّي خراجها وما كان من فضل فهو بينهما. قال: لا بأس. وسألته عن الرَّجل يعطي الرجل أرضه وفيها رمّان أو نخل أو فاكهة، فيقول: إسق هذا من الماء واعمره ولك نصف ما أخرج. قال: لا بأس. قال: وسألته عن الرجل يعطي الرجل الأرض فيقول: اعمرها وهي لك ثلاث سنين أو خمس سنين أو ما شاء الله. قال: لا بأس. قال: وسألته عن المزارعة. فقال: النفقة منك والأرض لصاحبها، فما أخرج الله منها من شيء قُسّم على الشطر. وكذلك أعطى رسول الله – صلّى الله علي وآله وسلّم – أهل خيبر حين أتوه فأعطاهم إيّاها على أن يعمروها ولهم النصف ممّا أخرجت.[114]

[Yaʿqūb b. Shuʿayb:] I asked Abū ʿAbd Allāh about a man who owns a piece of *kharāj* land and gives it to another man on the condition that the latter cultivate it, improve it, and pay the tax on it, and that they

113 Kulaynī, *Kāfī*, 5:268.
114 Kulaynī, *Kāfī*, 5:268.

share whatever surplus remains. He said, "There is nothing wrong with that." I asked him about a man who gives his land, containing pomegranate trees, date palms, or fruit trees, to another man and says, "Water it and keep it cultivated, and you get half of the produce." He said, "There is nothing wrong with that." I asked him about a man who gives land to another man and says, "Cultivate it and it is yours for three years, or five years, or whatever God wills." He said, "There is nothing wrong with that." I asked him about sharecropping. He said, "The cost is on you and the land belongs to its owner. Whatever God causes it to produce is divided in half. That is how the Prophet (may God's prayer and peace be upon him and his Family) gave [the land] to the people of Khaybar when they came to him. He gave it to them on the condition that they cultivate it, and their share would be half of what it produced."

56

سماعة قال: سألته عن مزارعة المسلم المشرك فيكون من عند المسلم البذر والبقر وتكون الأرض والماء والخراج والعمل على العلج. قال: لا بأس به. قال: وسألته عن المزارعة فقلت: الرجل يبذر في الأرض مائة جريب أو أقلّ أو أكثر طعامًا أو غيره فيأتيه رجل فيقول: خذ منّي نصف ثمن هذا البذر الّذي زرعته في الأرض ونصف نفقتك عليَّ وأشركني فيه. قال: لا بأس. قلت: وإن كان الّذي يبذر فيه لم يشتره بثمن وإنّما هو شيء كان عنده؟ قال: فليقوّمه قيمةً كما يباع يومئذ فليأخذ نصف الثمن ونصف النفقة ويشاركه.[115]

[Samāʿa:] I asked him about sharecropping between a Muslim and a polytheist, when the Muslim provides the seeds and cattle, and the land, water, tax, and labor are provided by the non-Muslim [farmer]. He said, "There is nothing wrong with that." I asked him about [a specific case of] sharecropping and said, "A man sows one hundred acres, or more or less, of wheat or otherwise. Another man then comes to him and says, 'Take from me half the value of the seeds you planted in the earth, and I will owe you half of the cost [of your labor], and you take me as a partner in this.'" He said, "There is nothing wrong with that." I said, "What if the person who sowed the earth did not buy [the seeds] for money but had them from before?" He said, "Then he will assess them according to their sale price that day [that is, the day of planting] and take half the value and half the cost [of his labor], and they form a partnership."

115 Kulaynī, *Kāfī*, 5:268.

57

سماعة قال: سألته عن رجل اشترى مرعى يرعى فيه بخمسين درهمًا أو أقلّ أو أكثر فأراد أن يُدخل معه من يرعى فيه ويأخذ منهم الثمن. قال: فليُدخل معه من شاء ببعض ما أعطى، وإن أدخل معه بتسعة وأربعين وكانت غنمه بدرهم فلا بأس، وإن هو رعى فيه قبل أن يُدخله بشهر أو شهرين أو أكثر من ذلك بعد أن يبيّن لهم فلا بأس، وليس له أن يبيعه بخمسين درهمًا ويرعى معهم ولا بأكثر من خمسين ولا يرعى معهم. إلّا أن يكون قد عمل في المرعى عملاً: حفر بئرًا أو شقّ نهرًا أو تعنّى فيه برضا أصحاب المرعى فلا بأس ببيعه بأكثر ممّا اشتراه به، لأنّه قد عمل فيه عملاً فبذلك يصلح له.[116]

[Samāʿa:] I asked him about a man who buys [the grass in] a pasture to use for grazing for fifty dirhams, or more or less. He then wants to bring in other people to use it with him and pay him the value. He said, "He can bring in whomever he wants for payment of part of the price he paid [for the pasture]. If he takes them in for [payment of] forty-nine dirhams and his own sheep [use it for the cost of the remaining] one dirham, that is fine. If he has already used the pasture for grazing for one or two months, or more, before granting access to the others but after making [the situation] known to them, that is fine. He cannot sell [the grass in] it for fifty dirhams and still graze on it himself with them, nor for more than fifty dirhams [on the condition that] he does not graze on it with them, unless he worked on the pasture by digging a well or a water canal or labored on it with the permission of the pasture's owners. Then there is nothing wrong with selling [the usufruct of] it for more than he bought it for, because he labored to improve it, and thus [making profit] is permissible for him."

58

أبو ولّاد الحنّاط قال: اكتريت بغلاً إلى قصر ابن هبيرة ذاهبًا وجائيًا بكذا وكذا وخرجت في طلب غريم لي، فلمّا صرت قرب قنطرة الكوفة خُبّرت أنّ صاحبي توجّه إلى النيل، فتوجّهت نحو النيل، فلمّا أتيت النيل خُبّرت أنّه توجّه إلى بغداد فأتبعته وظفرت به وفرغت ممّا بيني وبينه ورجعت إلى الكوفة. وكان ذهابي ومجيئي خمسة عشر يومًا. فأخبرت صاحب البغل بعذري وأردت أن أتحلّل منه ممّا صنعت وأُرضيه فبذلت له خمسة عشر درهمًا فأبى أن يقبل، فتراضينا بأبي حنيفة فأخبرته بالقصّة وأخبره الرَّجل. فقال لي: وما صنعت بالبغل؟ فقلت: قد دفعته إليه سليمًا. قال: نعم! بعد خمسة

116 Kulaynī, *Kāfī*, 5:273.

عشر يومًا! فقال: فما تريد من الرجل؟ قال: أُريد كرى بغلي فقد حبسه عليَّ خمسة عشر يومًا. فقال: ما أرى لك حقًّا، لأنّه اكتراه إلى قصر ابن هبيرة فخالف وركبه إلى النيل وإلى بغداد فضمن قيمة البغل وسقط الكرى، فلمّا ردّ البغل سليمًا وقبضتَه لم يلزمه الكرى. قال: فخرجنا من عنده وجعل صاحب البغل يسترجع، فرحمتُه ممّا أفتى به أبو حنيفة فأعطيته شيئًا وتحلّلت منه. فحججت تلك السنّة فأخبرت أبا عبد الله بما أفتى به أبو حنيفة، فقال: في مثل هذا القضاء وشبهه تحبس السماء ماءها وتمنع الأرض بركتها. قال: فقلت لأبي عبد الله: فما ترى أنت؟ قال: أرى له عليك مثل كرى البغل ذاهبًا من الكوفة إلى النيل ومثل كرى البغل راكبًا من النيل إلى بغداد ومثل كرى البغل من بغداد إلى الكوفة، توفيه إيّاه. قال: فقلت: جعلت فداك! إنّي قد علّفته بدراهم فلي عليه علفه؟ فقال: لا! لأنّك غاصب. فقلت: أرأيت لو عطب البغل ونفق أليس كان يلزمني؟ قال: نعم! قيمة بغل يوم خالفته. قلت: فإن أصاب البغل كسر أو دبر أو غمز؟ فقال: عليك قيمة ما بين الصحّة والعيب يوم تردُّه عليه. قلت: فمن يعرف ذلك؟ قال: أنت وهو. إمّا أن يحلف هو على القيمة فتلزمك، فإن ردَّ اليمين عليك فحلفت على القيمة لزمه ذلك، أو يأتي صاحب البغل بشهود يشهدون أنَّ قيمة البغل حين أكرى كذا وكذا فيلزمك. قلت: إنّي كنت أعطيته دراهم ورضي بها وحلّلني. فقال: إنّما رضي بها وحلّلك حين قضى عليه أبو حنيفة بالجور والظلم، ولكن ارجع إليه فأخبره بما أفتيتك به، فإن جعلك في حلّ بعد معرفته فلا شيء عليك بعد ذلك. قال أبو ولّاد: فلمّا انصرفت من وجهي ذلك لقيت المكاري فأخبرته بما أفتاني به أبو عبد الله وقلت له: قل ما شئت حتّى أُعطيكه. فقال: قد حبّبت إليَّ جعفر بن محمّد ووقع في قلبي له التفضيل وأنت في حلّ، وإن أحببتَ أن أردَّ عليك الّذي أخذت منك فعلت.[117]

[Abū Wallād al-Ḥannāṭ:] I hired a mule to go to the Palace of Ibn Hubayra,[118] going there and coming back, for such-and-such a price. I went to attend to a debtor of mine. When I was near the aqueduct of Kūfa, I was told the man had gone to the Nīl,[119] so I went to the Nīl. When I arrived at the Nīl, I was told that he had gone to Baghdad,[120] so

117 Kulaynī, *Kāfī*, 5:290–91.

118 A town that lay near Hāshimiyya, some eighty miles south of Baghdad, as mentioned earlier.

119 This is the Nīl of Euphrates, in the region of Bābil, south of Baghdad.

120 This should mean the region of small villages with this name where the modern city was subsequently built by Manṣūr in 145–50. Jaʿfar al-Ṣādiq died in 148 when the construction of the city was in progress.

I followed him and caught up to him. Then I settled what was between us and returned to Kūfa. My trip lasted fifteen days. I informed the owner of the mule of my excuse and wanted to be absolved of liability for what I had done and conciliate him. So I gave him fifteen dirhams, but he refused to accept it. We agreed to have the matter settled by Abū Ḥanīfa, so I told Abū Ḥanīfa what had happened and the man told him [his side]. Abū Ḥanīfa said to me, "What did you do with the mule?" I said, "I returned it to him in good condition." The owner of the mule said, "Yes! After fifteen days!" Then Abū Ḥanīfa asked the man, "What do you want?" He said, "I want the price for the hire of my mule; he kept it from me for fifteen days." Abū Ḥanīfa said, "I do not think you have a claim, because he hired it to take it to the Palace of Ibn Hubayra but breached [the agreement] and rode it to the Nīl and Baghdad, so he was liable for the value of the mule and the hire price was voided. Because he has returned the mule in good condition and you took possession of it, he is not liable for the hire price." We then left him, and the owner of the mule began to sigh.[121] I felt pity for him for the verdict that Abū Ḥanīfa gave, so I gave him something and absolved myself of him.

I went to the *ḥajj* that year and told Abū ʿAbd Allāh about Abū Ḥanīfa's verdict. He said, "It is because of such judgments and their like that the sky withholds its water and the earth withholds its blessings." I said to Abū ʿAbd Allāh, "So what, then, is your position?" He said, "I believe you owe him the price for hiring the mule to ride from Kūfa to the Nīl, and the price for hiring the mule to ride from the Nīl to Baghdad, and the price for hiring the mule to ride from Baghdad to Kūfa; you should deliver all of that to him." I said, "May I be made your ransom! I spent some money to feed [the mule]. Can I claim the money I paid back?" He said, "No! Because you were a usurper." I said, "Do you think that if the mule died, I would not be liable?" He said, "Yes! [You would be liable for] the price of the mule on the day you took it." I said, "What if the mule suffers a fracture or injuries on its back, or develops a limp?" He said, "You owe the difference between its price when it was healthy and its price when it had acquired the defect with which you returned it to him." I said, "Who determines that?" He said, "You and he. He either swears to its price and it becomes binding on you, or he makes you swear an oath and you swear to its price, and that then becomes binding on him. Or the owner of the mule may produce

121 The expression used in the text is *jaʿala yastarjiʿ*, that is, he began to repeat the sentence mentioned in Qurʾān 2:156 as what the faithful say when struck by misfortune: "Those who say, when afflicted with a misfortune: 'To God We belong, and to Him we return.'"

witnesses who testify that the price of the mule when it was hired was such-and-such, and it becomes binding on you." I said, "I gave him some money, which he agreed to, and he absolved me." He said, "He agreed to it and absolved you when Abū Ḥanīfa issued an unjust and oppressive judgment against him. Go back to him and inform him of the verdict I gave to you. If he absolves you after knowing this, you owe nothing after that."

When I went back, I found the person who had rented the mule and informed him of the verdict Abū ʿAbd Allāh issued to me. I said, "Tell me what you want so I can give it to you." He said, "You made Jaʿfar b. Muḥammad beloved to me and my heart developed a preference for him. You are absolved. If you would like me to return what I took from you, I will do so."

On Obligations

59

الحلبي عن أبي عبد الله في رجل حلف بيمين أن لا يتكلّم ذا قرابة له، قال: ليس بشيء، فليكلّم الّذي حلف عليه. وقال: كلُّ يمين لا يراد بها وجه الله عزّ وجلّ فليس بشيء، في طلاق أو عتق. قال: وسألته عن امرأة جعلت ما لها هديًا لبيت الله إن أعارت متاعها لفلانة وفلانة، فأعار بعض أهلها بغير أمرها. قال: ليس عليها هدي. إنّما الهدي ما جُعل لله هديًا للكعبة فذلك الّذي يوفَى به إذا جُعل لله، وما كان من أشباه هذا فليس بشيء، ولا هدي لا يُذكر فيه اسم الله عزّ وجلّ. وسُئل عن الرجل يقول عليّ ألف بدنة وهو محرم بألف حجّة. قال: ذلك من خطوات الشيطان.[122]

[ʿUbayd Allāh al-Ḥalabī:] Regarding a man who vowed to not speak to a relative of his, Abū ʿAbd Allāh said, "It [the vow] is not effective. He may speak to the person he made the vow against." And he said, "Any vow that is not made for the sake of the countenance of God, the Mighty and Majestic, is ineffective, whether the vow is for divorce or for manumission." I asked him about a woman who vowed to give her provisions as a sacrifice to the House of God if she ever loaned her provisions to certain persons. [It happened that] some of her family members loaned her things [to one of those persons] without her permission. He said, "She does not owe a sacrifice. The sacrifice is only what God has designated as a sacrifice to the Kaʿba, and that is to be fulfilled when is made for the sake of God. Things of this sort are

122 Kulaynī, *Kāfī*, 7:441.

ineffective. There is no [legal] sacrifice over which the name of God, the Mighty and Majestic, has not been invoked." He was asked about a man who vowed to make one thousand sacrifices in a state of pilgrim sanctity for one thousand *ḥajj* pilgrimages. He said, "This is an illusion of the devil."

60

محمّد بن يحيى الخثعميّ قال: كنّا عند أبي عبد الله جماعة إذ دخل عليه رجلٌ من موالي أبي جعفر فسلّم عليه ثمّ جلس وبكى، ثمّ قال له: جعلت فداك! إنّي كنت أعطيت الله عهدًا إن عافاني الله من شيء كنت أخافه على نفسي أن أتصدّق بجميع ما أملك، وإنّ الله عزّ وجلّ عافاني منه، وقد حوّلت عيالي من منزلي إلى قبّة من خراب الأنصار وقد حملت كلّ ما أملك فأنا بايع داري وجميع ما أملك فأتصدّق به. فقال أبو عبد الله: انطلق وقوّم منزلك وجميع متاعك وما تملك بقيمة عادلة وأعرف ذلك، ثمّ أعمد إلى صحيفة بيضاء فاكتب فيها جملة ما قوّمت، ثمّ انظر إلى أوثق الناس في نفسك فادفع إليه الصحيفة وأوصيه ومُره إن حدث بك حدث الموت أن يبيع منزلك وجميع ما تملك فيتصدّق به عنك، ثمّ ارجع إلى منزلك وقُم في مالك على ما كنت فيه فكُل أنت وعيالك مثل ما كنت تأكل، ثمّ انظر بكلّ شيء تُصدّق به فيما تستقبل من صدقة أو صلة قرابة أو في وجوه البرّ فاكتب ذلك كلّه وأحصه، فإذا كان رأس السنة فانطلق إلى الرجل الّذي أوصيت إليه فمُره أن يخرج إليك الصحيفة، ثمّ اكتب فيها جملة ما تصدّقت وأخرجت من صلة قرابة أو برّ في تلك السنة، ثمّ افعل ذلك في كلّ سنة حتّى تفي لله بجميع ما نذرت فيه ويبقى لك منزلُك ومالُك إن شاء الله. قال: فقال الرّجل فرّجت عنّي يابنَ رسول الله! جعلني الله فداك![123]

[Muḥammad b. Yaḥyā al-Khathʿamī:] A group of us were with Abū ʿAbd Allāh when a man came to him from the clients of Abū Jaʿfar.[124] He greeted Abū ʿAbd Allāh and then sat down and wept. Then he said to Abū ʿAbd Allāh, "May I be made your ransom! I made a covenant with God that if he cured me of something that I feared for myself, I would give everything I owned in charity. God, the Mighty and Majestic, cured me of it. So I moved my family from my home to a dome in the slums of the Anṣār. I took everything I owned to sell my house and all that I possessed in order to give it away in charity." Abū ʿAbd Allāh

123 Kulaynī, *Kāfī*, 7:458–59.

124 This refers to Muḥammad al-Bāqir, not Manṣūr, the Abbasid caliph.

said, "Go and assess your house and all your provisions and belongings at a fair price, and clarify their worth. Then take a white piece of paper and write on it the total value. Go to the most reliable person you know, give him the paper, and entrust him and tell him to sell your house and all your belongings if death befalls you and to donate it on your behalf.[125] Then go back to your house and live on your wealth as you used to, and carry on with your lives, you and your family, as you did before. Then keep track of everything you donate in the future as charity or gift to your kin or provide in other charitable donations and write it all down and calculate [its value]. At the beginning of the year, go to the man you entrusted and ask him to give you the paper and write on it everything you donated and spent as gifts to your kin or as charitable donations in that year. Do that every year until you fulfill your entire vow to God. You will keep your home and belongings, God willing." The man said, "You have relieved me, O son of the Messenger of God! May God make me your ransom!"

61

قال الصادق [وقد سُئل عن اللقطة]: أفضل ما يستعمله الإنسان في اللقطة إذا وجدها ألّا يأخذها ولا يتعرّض لها، فلو أنّ الناس تركوا ما يجدونه لجاء صاحبه فأخذه. وإن كانت اللقطة دون درهم فهي لك لا تعرّفها، وأن وجدت في الحرم دينارًا مطلّسًا فهو لك لا تعرّفه، وإن وجدت طعامًا في مفازة فقوّمه على نفسك لصاحبه ثمّ كُله فإن جاء صاحبه فردّ عليه القيمة، وإن وجدت لقطة في دار وكانت عامرة فهي لأهلها، وإن كانت خرابًا فهي لمن وجدها.[126]

[Jaʿfar al-Ṣādiq:] The best thing a man can do with lost property that he finds is to refrain from taking it and avoid it. If everyone left it alone, its owner would [eventually] come and take it. If the lost property is worth less than a dirham, you can keep it and you do not have to make it known. If you find an unengraved dinar in the sacred precinct, you can keep it and you do not have to make it known. If you find food in a desert, make note of its value for its owner and consume it. If its owner comes, give him its value. If you find lost property in an inhabited home, it belongs to the residents. If the home is in ruins, it belongs to whoever finds it.

---

125 The text is silent on what will happen to the man's family if the house and all his belongings are donated on his behalf, an indication that something is missing from the text (see also texts 24 on p. 345 and 27 on p. 347 above).

126 Ibn Bābawayh, *Faqīh*, 3:190.

62

ابن أخي الفضيل بن يسار قال: كنت عند أبي عبد الله فدخلت امرأة وكنت أقرب القوم إليها، فقالت لي: إسأله، فقلت: عمّا ذا؟ فقالت: إنّ ابني مات وترك مالاً كان في يد أخي فأتلفه، ثمّ أفاد مالاً فأودعنيه، فلي أن آخذ منه بقدر ما أتلف من شيء؟ فأخبرته بذلك فقال: لا! قال رسول الله – صلّى الله عليه وآله وسلّم: أدّ الأمانة إلى من ائتمنك ولا تخن من خانك.[127]

[Ḥasan, the nephew of al-Fuḍayl b. Yasār:] I was with Abū ʿAbd Allāh when a woman came in, and I was the nearest to her. She said to me, "Ask him." I said, "About what?" She said, "My son died and left behind some wealth that was in the possession of my brother, but he squandered it. He then earned some wealth and entrusted me with it. Can I take from it the amount that he squandered?" I informed him [Jaʿfar al-Ṣādiq] of this and he said, "No! The Messenger of God (may God's prayer and peace be upon him and his Family) said, 'Pay the deposit [back] to whoever deposited it with you, and do not betray the person who betrayed you.'"

On Gifts

63

إبراهيم الكرخي قال: سألت أبا عبد الله عن الرجل يكون له الضيعة الكبيرة فإذا كان يوم المهرجان والنيروز أهدوا إليه الشيءَ ليس هو عليهم، يتقرّبون بذلك الشيء إليه. فقال: أليس هم مصلّين؟ قلت: بلى! قال: فليقبل هديتهم وليكافهم.[128]

[Ibrāhīm al-Karkhī:] I asked Abū ʿAbd Allāh about a man who owns a large estate. On the [Persian feast] days of Mihrgān and Nawrūz, they [the celebrators] give him gifts. They do not have to do it, but they want to make friends with him by that gift. He said, "Do they not pray?" [that is: Are they not Muslims?] I said, "Yes!" He said, "He should accept their gift and reciprocate it."

64

إسحاق بن عمار قال: قلت لأبي عبد الله: ما تقول في رجل يهب لعبده ألف درهم أو أقلّ أو أكثر فيقول: حلّلني من ضربي إيّاك أو من كلّ ما كان منّي إليك وممّا أخفتك

127 Ṭūsī, *Tahdhīb*, 6:348.

128 Kulaynī, *Kāfī*, 5:141; Ibn Bābawayh, *Faqīh*, 3:191.

وأرهبتك، فيحلّله ويجعله في حلّ رغبةً فيما أعطاه، ثمّ إن المولى بعدُ أصاب الدراهم التّي أعطاه في موضع قد وضعها فيه العبد فأخذها المولى، أحلال هي له؟ فقال: لا! فقلت له: أليس العبد وماله لمولاه؟ قال: ليس هذا ذاك. ثمّ قال: قل له فليردّها عليه فإنّه لا يحلّ له، فإنه افتدى بها نفسه من العبد مخافة العقوبة والقصاص يوم القيامة.[129]

[Isḥāq b. ʿAmmār:] I said to Abū ʿAbd Allāh, "What is your position regarding a man who gifts his slave one thousand dirhams, or more or less, and says, 'Absolve me for beating you or for everything I have done to you and for frightening and intimidating you.' He absolves him because of what he gave him. Later, the master finds the money he gave to his slave in the place where the slave put it, and the master takes it. Is it lawful for him?" He said, "No!" I said to him, "Do the slave and his wealth not belong to his master?" He said, "This is not such a case." Then he said, "Tell him to return the money to him [the slave], because it is not lawful for him [the master]. He sacrificed it on behalf of himself for the slave out of fear of punishment and retaliation on the Day of Resurrection."

65

عمر الحلبي عن أبي عبد الله قال: سألته عن دار لم تقسّم فتصدّق بعض أهل الدار بنصيبه من الدار؟ قال: يجوز. قلت: أرأيت إن كانت هبة؟ قال: يجوز. قال: وسألته عن رجل أسكن رجلاً داره حياته. قال: يجوز له، وليس له أن يُخرجه. قلت: فله ولعقبه؟ قال: يجوز. وسألته عن رجل أسكن رجلاً ولم يوقّت له شيئًا. قال: يخرجه صاحب الدّار إذا شاء.[130]

[ʿUmar al-Ḥalabī:] I asked Abū ʿAbd Allāh about a home that is not divided, and one of the owners of the house donates his share of it as charity. He said, "That is permissible [and effective]." I said, "What is your position if he gave it as a gift?" He said, "That is permissible." I asked him about a man who houses another man in his home for the duration of that man's life.[131] He said, "That is permissible, and he cannot evict him." I said, "[What if it is] for him and his successors?" He said, "That is permissible." I asked him about a man who houses another man for an indefinite amount of time. He said, "The owner of the house can evict him if he wants."

129 Ibn Bābawayh, *Faqīh*, 3:146.

130 Kulaynī, *Kāfī*, 7:34.

131 This is the concept of a gift of residence for life (*ʿumrā*), as allowed in a number of reports from the Prophet and endorsed by the jurists. For details, see Ibn Qudāma, *Mughnī*, 8:281–89; *al-Mawsūʿa al-fiqhiyya* (Kuwait), 30:311–12.

66

جعفر بن حيّان قال: سألت أبا عبد الله عن رجل وقف غلّة له على قرابة من أبيه وقرابة من أُمّه، وأوصى لرجل ولعقبه من تلك الغلّة، ليس بينه وبينه قرابة، بثلاثمائة درهم في كلّ سنة، ويقسّم الباقي على قرابته من أبيه وقرابته من أُمّه. قال: جائز للّذي أوصى له بذلك. قلت: أرأيت إن لم يخرج من غلّة الأرض الّتي وقفها إلّا خمسمائة درهم؟ قال: أليس في وصيّته أن يعطى الّذي أوصى له من الغلّة ثلاثمائة درهم ويقسّم الباقي على قرابته من أُمّه وقرابته من أبيه؟ قلت: نعم! قال: ليس لقرابته أن يأخذوا من الغلّة شيئًا حتّى يوفي الموصى له بثلثمائة درهم، ثمّ لهم ما يبقي بعد ذلك. قلت: أرأيت إن مات الّذي أوصى له؟ قال: إن مات كانت الثلاثمائة درهم لورثته يتوارثونها ما بقي أحد، فإذا انقطع ورثته ولم يبق منهم أحدٌ كانت الثلاثمائة درهم لقرابة الميّت تردُّ إلى ما يخرج من الوقف، ثمّ يقسّم بينهم يتوارثون ذلك ما بقوا وبقيت الغلّة. قلت: فللورثة من قرابة الميّت أن يبيعوا الأرض إذا احتاجوا ولم يكفهم ما يخرج من الغلّة؟ قال: نعم! إذا رضوا كلّهم وكان البيع خيرًا لهم باعوا.[132]

[Jaʿfar b. Ḥayyān:] I asked Abū ʿAbd Allāh about a man who established a pious endowment for his paternal and maternal relatives with his revenues [from a piece of land]. He also bequeathed some of this revenue to a man and his successors who were not related to him, at an amount of three hundred dirhams per year. The rest was to be divided between his paternal and maternal relatives. He said, "The bequest is legally valid for those for whom it was made." I said, "What is your position if the revenue from the land he donated yields only five hundred dirhams?" He said, "Does his will not mention a bequest of three hundred dirhams from the revenue for a specific person and the rest to be divided between his paternal and maternal relatives?" I said, "Yes!" He said, "His relatives cannot take anything from the revenue until the person bequeathed three hundred dirhams has received it in full. Then they receive the remainder." I said, "What is your position if the beneficiary of the bequest passes away?" He said, "If he dies, the three hundred dirhams go to his heirs, who inherit it as long as one of them remains. If he no longer has heirs and nobody remains, the three hundred dirhams go to the relatives of the deceased [that is, the original owner]; they revert to the proceeds from the pious endowment, and that is then divided and those who remain inherit it as long

132 Kulaynī, *Kāfī*, 7:35.

as the revenue [from the land] persists." I said, "Can the heirs who are related to the deceased sell the land if they need to and the revenue from it is not enough for them?" He said, "Yes! If they all agree and the sale is good for them, they may sell it."

On Manumission

67

بعض آل أعين عن أبي عبد الله قال: من كان مؤمنًا فقد عتق بعد سبع سنين، أعتقه صاحبه أم لم يعتقه. ولا تحلّ خدمة من كان مؤمنًا بعد سبع سنين.[133]

[A member of Āl Aʿyan:] Abū ʿAbd Allāh said, "Any believer is manumitted after seven years, whether or not his master manumits him. It is not lawful to receive the services of a believer after seven years."[134]

68

يعقوب بن شعيب عن أبي عبد الله قال: سألته عن الرجل يكون له الخادم تخدمه فيقول هي لفلانٍ تخدمه ما عاش، فإذا مات فهي حرّة. فتأبّق الأمة قبل أن يموت الرجل بخمس سنين أو ستّة، ثمّ يجدها ورثته. ألهم أن يستخدموها قدر ما أبقت؟ قال: إذا مات الرجل فقد عُتقت.[135]

[Yaʿqūb b. Shuʿayb:] I asked Abū ʿAbd Allāh about a man with a handmaiden who serves him. Then he says that she belongs to so-and-so, that she must serve him for the rest of his life and that she will be free after his death. The slave runs away five or six years before the man dies, and then the heirs of the man find her somewhere. Can they make use of her for the length of time she was on the run? He said, "When the man died, she was manumitted."

69

عبد الله بن طلحة عن أبي عبد الله قال: سألته عن رجل مات وترك مالاً كثيرًا وترك أُمًّا مملوكة وأُختًا مملوكة، فقال: تُشتريان من مال الميّت ثمّ تُعتقان وتورثان. قلت: أرأيت إن أبى أهل الجارية كيف يصنع؟ قال: ليس لهم ذلك وتُقوّمان قيمةَ عدل ثمّ

133 Kulaynī, *Kāfī*, 6:196–97.

134 A reminder of Deuteronomy 15:12–15.

135 Kulaynī, *Kāfī*, 7:34.

يُعطى مالهم على قدر القيمة. قلت: أرأيت لو أنّهما اشتريا ثمّ أُعتقا ثمّ وُرّثا من بعد من كان يرثهما؟ قال: يرثهما موالي ابنهما لأنّهما اشتريا من مال الابن.[136]

[ʿAbd Allāh b. Ṭalḥa:] I asked Abū ʿAbd Allāh about a man who died and left behind a great amount of wealth. He was survived by an enslaved mother and an enslaved sister. He said, "They will be bought using the wealth of the deceased and are manumitted and will inherit from him." I said, "What is your position if the owners of the slave woman refuse?" He said, "They do not have that right. They [the two slave women] will be evaluated fairly and paid for according to their value." I said, "If they are both purchased and manumitted and then leave an inheritance in the future, who do you think inherits them?" He said, "They will be inherited by the patrons of their [deceased] son, because they were bought using his wealth."

70

محمّد بن مسلم قال: قلت لأبي عبد الله: رجل ورث غلامًا وله فيه شركاء فأعتق لوجه الله نصيبه؟ فقال: إذا أعتق نصيبه مضارًّا وهو موسرٌ ضمن للورثة، وإذا أعتق نصيبه لوجه الله كان الغلام قد أعتق منه حصّةَ من أعتق ويستعملونه على قدر ما لهم فيه، فإن كان نصفه عمل لهم يومًا وله يومٌ. وإن أعتق الشريك مضارًّا وهو معسر فلا عتق له لأنّه أراد أن يفسد على القوم، ويرجع القوم على حصصهم.[137]

[Muḥammad b. Muslim:] I said to Abū ʿAbd Allāh, "A man inherits a male slave and has partners with a stake in his ownership, and then he manumits his share in him for the sake of God." He said, "If he manumits his share to harm the partners, and he is well off, he is liable to the other heirs [for whatever harm has he inflicted on them]. If he manumits him for the sake of God, the slave is manumitted with respect to the share of the manumitter; they [that is, the partners] can make use of him according to how much of him is still owned by them. If half of him is still owned, he is to work for them for one day and then have one day for himself. If he manumits his share to harm the partners and he is poor, his manumission is ineffective because he wished to harm the partners, so the owners will continue to own him according to their original shares."

136 Kulaynī, *Kāfī*, 7:147.
137 Ibn Bābawayh, *Faqīh*, 3:68.

71

الفضيل بن يسار قال: عبد مسلم عارف أعتقه رجل فدخل به على أبي عبد الله. قال: يا هذا من هذا السندي؟ قال الرجل: عارف وأعتقه فلان. فقال أبو عبد الله: ليت إني كنت أعتقته. فقال السندي لأبي عبد الله: إنّي قلت لمولاي: بعني بسبعمائة درهم وأنا أعطيك ثلاثمائة درهم. فقال أبو عبد الله: إن كان يوم شرطتَ لك مال فعليك أن تعطيه، وإن لم يكن لك مال يومئذ فليس عليك شيء.[138]

[Al-Fuḍayl b. Yasār:] A Shīʿī Muslim slave was manumitted by someone and was then brought to Abū ʿAbd Allāh. He said, "O you! Who is this Sindī [that is, a man from the Indian subcontinent]?" The man said, "He is a Shīʿī Muslim manumitted by so-and-so." Abū ʿAbd Allāh said, "I wish I were the one who manumitted him." The Sindī said to Abū ʿAbd Allāh, "I said to my master, 'Sell me for seven hundred dirhams and I will give you three hundred dirhams.'" Abū ʿAbd Allāh said, "If on the day you made that commitment you had money, you must pay him, but if you did not have money at the time, you owe nothing."

On Agency

72

هشام بن سالم عن أبي عبد الله في رجل وكّل آخر على وكالة في أمر من الأمور وأشهد له بذلك شاهدين، فقام الوكيل فخرج لامضاء الأمر، فقال: اشهدوا أنّي قد عزلت فلانًا عن الوكالة. فقال: إن كان الوكيل أمضى الأمر الذي وكّل عليه قبل أن يعزل عن الوكالة فإنّ الأمر واقعٌ ماض على ما أمضاه الوكيل، كره الموكّل أم رضي. قلت: فإنّ الوكيل أمضى الأمر قبل أن يعلم بالعزل أو يبلغه أنّه قد عُزل عن الوكالة فالأمر على ما أمضاه؟ قال: نعم! قلت: فإن بلغه العزل قبل أن يمضي الأمر ثمّ ذهب حتّى أمضاه لم يكن ذلك بشيء؟ قال: نعم! إنّ الوكيل إذا وكّل ثمّ قام عن المجلس فأمره ماض أبدًا، والوكالة ثابتة حتّى يبلغه العزل عن الوكاله بثقة يبلغه أو مشافهة بالعزل عن الوكالة.[139]

[Hishām b. Sālim:] Regarding a man who delegated another as an agent in a matter and had two witnesses attest to it on his behalf, and the agent then went to fulfill the task and then the principal said, "Bear witness that I have dismissed so-and-so of his agency," Abū ʿAbd Allāh

138 Kulaynī, *Kāfī*, 6:193.

139 Ibn Bābawayh, *Faqīh*, 3:49–50.

said, "If the agent fulfilled the task for which he was delegated before he was dismissed from his agency, the task has been fulfilled on the basis of the agent's actions, whether the principal likes it or not." I said, "So if the agent fulfilled the task before he learned of his dismissal or received the news that he has been dismissed from his agency, his fulfillment of the task is effective?" He said, "Yes!" I said, "So if he learns of his dismissal before fulfilling the task but then fulfills it anyway, is his action ineffective?" He said, "Yes! If the agent was delegated and then departed from the setting in which he was appointed, his actions are perpetually effective and his agency affirmed until he receives notice of his dismissal by being informed by a reliable person or receiving a verbal communication of dismissal from his agency."

On Marriage

73

علاء بن سيابة قال: سألت أبا عبد الله عن امرأة وكّلت رجلاً بأن يزوّجها من رجل فقبل الوكالة وأشهدت له بذلك فذهب الوكيل فزوّجها، ثمّ إنّها أنكرت ذلك عن الوكيل وزعمت أنها عزلته عن الوكالة وأقامت شاهدين أنّها عزلته، فقال: ما يقول من قِبَلكم في ذلك؟ قلت: يقولون يُنظَر في ذلك، فإن كانت عزلته قبل أن يزوّج فالوكالة باطلة والتزويج باطل، وإن عزلته وقد زوّجها فالتزويج ثابت على ما زوّج الوكيل وعلى ما اتّفق معها من الوكالة إذا لم يتعدّ شيئاً مما أمرت به واشترطت عليه في الوكالة. قال: يعزلون الوكيل عن وكالتها ولم تُعلمه بالعزل؟! فقلت: نعم! يزعمون أنها لو وكّلت رجلاً وأشهدت في الملأ وقالت في الملأ اشهدوا أنّي قد عزلته، بطلت وكالته وإن لم يُعلم بالعزل وينقضون جميع ما فعل الوكيل في النكاح خاصّة، وفي غيره لا يبطلون الوكالة إلّا أن يعلم الوكيل بالعزل، ويقولون: المال منه عوض لصاحبه والفرج ليس منه عوض إذ وقع منه الولد. فقال: سبحان الله ما أجور هذا الحكم وأفسده! إنّ النكاح أحرى وأحرى أن يحتاط فيه وهو فرج ومنه يكون الولد. إنّ علياً – عليه السلام – أتته امرأة مستعدية على أخيها فقالت: يا أمير المؤمنين! وكّلت أخي هذا بأن يزوّجني رجلاً وأشهدت له ثمّ عزلته من ساعته تلك، فذهب فزوّجني ولي بيّنةٌ أنّي قد عزلته قبل أن يزوّجني وأقامت البينة. فقال الأخ: يا أمير المؤمنين! إنّها وكّلتني ولم تُعلمني أنّها عزلتني عن الوكالة حتّى زوّجتها كما أمرتني به. فقال لها: ما تقولين؟ قالت: قد أعلمته يا أمير المؤمنين! فقال لها: ألك بيّنة بذلك؟ فقالت: هؤلاء

شهودي يشهدون. فقال لهم: ما تقولون؟ قالوا: نشهد إنّها قالت اشهدوا أنّي قد عزلتُ أخي فلانًا عن الوكالة بتزويجي فلانًا وأنّي مالكة لأمري قبل أن يزوّجني فلانًا. فقال: أشهَدَتكم على ذلك بعلم منه ومحضر؟ قالوا: لا! قال: أفتشهدون أنّها أعلمته العزل كما أعلمته الوكالة؟ قالوا: لا! قال: أرى الوكالة ثابتة والنكاح واقعًا! أين الزوج؟ فجاء. فقال: خذ بيدها. بارك الله لك فيها. قالت: يا أمير المؤمنين! أحلفه أنّي لم أُعلمه العزل وأنّه لم يعلم بعزلي إيّاه قبل النكاح. فقال: وتحلف؟ قال: نعم يا أمير المؤمنين! فحلف، فأثبت وكالته وأجاز النكاح.[140]

[ʿAlāʾ b. Sayāba:] I asked Abū ʿAbd Allāh about a woman who appointed a man as an agent to wed her to a man. He accepted the agency and she had witnesses attest to it, so the man went and contracted the marriage [for her]. Then she denied the agent's actions and claimed that she had dismissed him from his agency, and she produced two witnesses to that effect. He said, "What do the [jurists] in your town say about this?" I said, "They say it depends. If she dismissed him before he contracted the marriage, the agency is void and the marriage invalid. If she dismissed him after he contracted the marriage, the marriage is valid on the basis of the agent's actions and within the terms of the agency agreement, so long as he did not exceed his authority with respect to what she ordered him to do and what she stipulated for his agency." He said, "They dismiss the agent from her assignment without her informing him of his dismissal?" I said, "Yes! They maintain that if she appointed a man and had a crowd witness it, and then said to the crowd, 'Witness that I have dismissed him,' his agency is voided even if he does not know about the dismissal. They void all of the agent's actions with respect to marriage exclusively; for other things they do not void the agency unless the agent learns of his dismissal. They say, 'Money can be replaced for the one who loses it, but [sexual access] cannot be replaced because it may result in a child.'" He said, "Praise be to God! How unjust and wicked this ruling is! It is much more appropriate to safeguard marriage [that is to say, a contract of marriage should be deemed irrevocable as far as possible]; it bestows sexual access and may result in a child. ʿAlī was approached by a woman making a claim against her brother. She said, 'O Commander of the Faithful! I appointed my brother as an agent to marry me to a man, and I had witnesses for this. Then I dismissed him shortly thereafter, but he went and married me [to the man anyway].

140 Ibn Bābawayh, *Faqīh*, 48–49.

I have evidence that I dismissed him before he married me off.' And she produced the evidence. The brother said, 'O Commander of the Faithful! She appointed me as an agent but did not inform me that she had dismissed me from the agency until I had married her off as she had ordered me to.' ʿAlī said to her, 'What do you say?' She said, 'I informed him, O Commander of the Faithful!' ʿAlī said to her, 'Do you have evidence for that?' She said, 'These are my witnesses who will testify.' ʿAlī said to them, 'What do you say?' They said, 'We testify that she said, "Witness that I have dismissed my brother so-and-so from his agency to marry me to so-and-so, and that I am in charge of my affairs, before he marries me to so-and-so."' ʿAlī said, 'She had you witness to this with his knowledge and in his presence?' They said, 'No!' ʿAlī said, 'Do you testify that she informed him of his dismissal just as she informed him of his appointment?' They said, 'No!' ʿAlī said, 'I hold that the agency is valid and the marriage is effected. Where is the husband?' The husband came and ʿAlī said, 'Take her hand. May God bless you with her.' She said, 'O Commander of the Faithful! Make him swear that I did not inform him of his dismissal and that he did not know that I had dismissed him before the marriage.' ʿAlī said [to the brother], 'Do you swear?' He said, 'Yes, O Commander of the Faithful!' He swore and ʿAlī affirmed his agency and approved the marriage."

74

عمر بن حنظلة عن أبي عبد الله قال: سألته عن رجل قال لآخر: إخطب لي فلانة فما فعلتَ شيئًا مما قاولتَ من صداق أو ضمنتَ من شيء أو شرطتَ فذلك لي رضًى وهو لازم لي، ولم يُشهد على ذلك. فذهب فخطب له وبذل عنه الصداق وغير ذلك ممّا طالبوه وسألوه، فلمّا رجع إليه أنكر ذلك كلّه. قال: يغرم لها نصف الصداق عنه، وذلك أنّه هو الذي ضيّع حقّها. فلمّا لم يُشهد لها عليه بذلك الّذي قال له حلّ لها أن تتزوّج، ولا يحلّ للأول فيما بينه وبين الله عز وجل إلّا أن يطلّقها، لأنّ الله تعالى يقول: ﴿فَإِمْسَاكٌ بِمَعْرُوفٍ أَوْ تَسْرِيحٌ بِإِحْسَانٍ﴾. فإن لم يفعل فإنّه مأثوم فيما بينه وبين الله عزّ وجلّ، وكان الحكم الظاهر حكم الإسلام، وقد أباح الله عزّ وجلّ لها أن تتزوّج.[141]

[ʿUmar b. Ḥanẓala:] I asked Abū ʿAbd Allāh about a man who said to another man, "Marry so-and-so for me. Whatever you negotiate as the dower, and whatever liabilities you assume or conditions you make, I agree to and will be bound by." However, he did not ask anyone to

141 Ibn Bābawayh, *Faqīh*, 3:49.

witness this. He [the agent] went and contracted the marriage and paid the dower on his [the groom's] behalf in addition to other things they [the bride's family] requested. When he [the agent] returned, [the groom] repudiated everything. He said, "He [the agent] will be charged for half of her dower on behalf of the man, because he [the agent] is the one who caused her to lose her right. Because he [the agent] did not get any witnesses for the bride's benefit to testify to what the man had said to him, it is permissible for her to marry [someone else], and it is obligatory for the man [who supposedly ordered the agent], between him and God, the Mighty and Majestic, to divorce her, because God, the Exalted, says: 'Retain in honor or release in kindness.'[142] If he does not do so, he has sinned with respect to what is between him and God, the Mighty and Majestic, but the legal presumption is what the law of Islam requires: God, the Mighty and Majestic, made it permissible for her to marry [whomever she wishes]."

75

أبو عبيدة عن أبي عبد الله في رجل أمر رجلاً أن يزوّجه امرأة من أهل البصرة من بني تميم فزوّجه امرأة من أهل الكوفة من بني تميم، قال: خالف أمره، وعلى المأمور نصف الصداق لأهل المرأة، ولا عدّة عليها ولا ميراث بينهما. فقال بعض من حضره: فإن أمره أن يزوّجه امرأة ولم يسمّ أرضًا ولا قبيلة، ثمّ جحد الآمر أن يكون أمره بذلك بعد ما زوّجه؟ فقال: إن كان للمأمور بيّنة أنّه كان أمره أن يزوّجه كان الصداق على الآمر، وإن لم يكن له بيّنة كان الصداق على المأمور لأهل المرأة، ولا ميراث بينهما ولا عدّة عليها، ولها نصف الصداق إن كان فرض لها صداقًا.[143]

[Abū 'Ubayda:] Regarding a man who ordered another man to wed him to a Baṣran woman from the Banū Tamīm, but he wed him to a Kūfan woman from the Banū Tamīm, Abū 'Abd Allāh said, "He contravened his order. The ordered person owes half of the dower to the family of the woman, and she does not have to observe a waiting period, and they [the woman and the person who gave the order] do not inherit from one another." One of those in attendance said, "What if he ordered him to wed him to a woman without specifying her place of origin or tribe, and then the person who gave the order denied that he had given such an order after the marriage had already been contracted." Abū 'Abd Allāh said, "If the agent has proof [that is, witnesses] that he ordered

142 Qur'ān 2:229.

143 Ibn Bābawayh, *Faqīh*, 3:264–65; Ṭūsī, *Tahdhīb*, 7:490.

him to marry him [to an unspecified woman], the dower is owed by the person who gave the order. If he does not have proof, the dower is owed to the woman's family by the agent. The two [the woman and the person who gave the order] will not inherit from one another and the woman does not have to observe a waiting period. She gets half the dower if a [specific amount of] dower was assigned to her."

76

أبو ولّاد الحنّاط قال: سُئل أبا عبد الله عن رجل أمر رجلاً أن يزوّجه امرأةً بالمدينة وسمّاها له، والّذي أمره بالعراق، فخرج المأمور فزوّجها إيّاه ثمّ قدم إلى العراق فوجد الّذي أمره قد مات. قال: ينظر في ذلك. فإن كان المأمور زوّجها إيّاه قبل أن يموت الآمر ثمّ مات الآمر بعده فإنّ المهر في جميع ذلك الميراث، بمنزلة الدَين. وإن كان زوّجها إيّاه بعد ما مات الآمر فلا شيءَ على الآمر ولا على المأمور، والنكاح باطل.[144]

[Abū Wallād al-Ḥannāṭ:] Abū ʿAbd Allāh was asked about a man who ordered another man to wed him to a woman in Medina, and he provided him with her name. The person who gave the order was in Iraq. The ordered person departed and wed her to him, then returned to Iraq and found that the person who ordered him had died. He [Jaʿfar al-Ṣādiq] said, "It depends [on the dates of the two events]. If the ordered person wed her to him before he died, and the person who gave the order died afterward, her dower is deducted from the entire estate. It is like a debt. If he wed her to him after he had died, the person who gave the order owes nothing, nor does the ordered person, and the marriage is invalid."

77

عن أبي عبد الله في رجل قبض صداق ابنته من زوجها ثمّ مات، هل لها أن تطالب زوجها بصداقها أو قبضُ أبيها قبضُها؟ فقال: إن كانت وكّلته بقبض صداقها من زوجها فليس لها أن تطالبه، وإن لم تكن وكّلته فلها ذلك ويرجع الزوج على ورثة أبيها بذلك. إلّا أن تكون حينئذٍ صبيّة في حجره فيجوز لأبيها أن يقبض صداقها عنها. ومتى طلّقها قبل الدخول بها فلأبيها أن يعفو عن بعض الصداق ويأخذ بعضًا، وليس له أن

144 Ibn Bābawayh, *Faqīh*, 3:271.

يدع كلّه. وذلك قول الله عز وجل: ﴿إِلَّا أَنْ يَعْفُونَ أَوْ يَعْفُوَ الَّذِي بِيَدِهِ عُقْدَةُ النِّكَاحِ﴾ – يعني الأب والّذي توكّله المرأة وتولّيه أمرها من أخ أو قرابة أو غيرها.[145]

Regarding a man who received his daughter's dower from her husband and then died; can she demand her dower from her husband, or does her father's receipt [of it] amount to her receipt? Abū ʿAbd Allāh said, "If she appointed him to receive her dower from her husband, she cannot demand it. If she did not appoint him, she has that right, and the husband can turn to her father's heirs for it. However, if she was a minor under his legal guardianship, her father is permitted to receive her dower on her behalf. If her husband divorces her before consummating [the marriage] with her, her father can forgo part of the dower and accept [the other] part, but he cannot forgo it entirely. This is what God, the Mighty and Majestic, says: 'Unless they forgo or the person who has authority over the marriage contract forgoes.'[146] This refers to the father and whomever the woman appoints and entrusts her affairs to, such as a brother, a relative, or someone else."

On Divorce

78

أبو ولّاد الحنّاط عن أبي عبد الله قال: سألته عن امرأة ادّعت على زوجها أنّه طلّقها تطليقة طلاق العدّة طلاقًا صحيحًا – يعني على طهر من غير جماع – وأشهد لها شهودًا على ذلك، ثمّ أنكر الزوج بعد ذلك؟ فقال: ان كان إنكاره الطلاق قبل انقضاء العدّة فانّ إنكاره للطلاق رجعة لها، وإن كان أنكر الطلاق بعد انقضاء العدّة فإنّ على الإمام أن يفرّق بينهما بعد شهادة الشهود، بعد أن تُستحلف[147] أنّ إنكاره للطلاق بعد انقضاء العدّة.[148]

[Abū Wallād al-Ḥannāṭ:] I asked Abū ʿAbd Allāh about a woman who claimed that her husband divorced her with a single, revocable divorce in a valid divorce—that is, it took place when she was in a state of purity without intercourse—and witnesses testified to the divorce on her behalf, but the husband later denied it. He said, "If he denied the divorce before the waiting period had concluded, his denial counts as

145 Ibn Bābawayh, *Faqīh*, 3:50–51.

146 Qurʾān 2:237.

147 In the edition of the source used in this work: يُستحلف, which was corrected by Ḥurr al-ʿĀmilī, *Wasāʾil al-Shīʿa*, 22:136, as is also required by the context.

148 Kulaynī, *Kāfī*, 6:74.

taking her back [that is, recommencing the union]. If he denied the divorce after the conclusion of the waiting period, the *imām* [represented by the court] must separate them from one another following the testimony of the [two] witnesses [to the divorce] and after the woman takes an oath that her husband's denial of the divorce took place after the conclusion of the waiting period."

79

الحسن بن صالح قال: سألت جعفر بن محمّد عن رجل طلّق امرأته وهو غائب في بلدة أخرى وأشهد على طلاقها رجلين، ثمّ إنّه راجعها قبل انقضاء العدّة ولم يُشهد على الرجعة، ثمّ إنّه قَدِم عليها بعد انقضاء العدّة وقد تزوّجت رجلاً، فأرسل إليها إنّي كنت قد راجعتكِ قبل انقضاء العدّة ولم أُشهد؟ فقال: لا سبيل له عليها لأنّه قد أقرّ بالطلاق وادّعى الرجعة بغير بيّنة فلا سبيل له عليها، ولذلك ينبغي لمن طلّق أن يُشهِد ولمن راجع أن يُشهِد على الرجعة كما أشهد على الطلاق. وإن كان قد أدركها قبل أن تزوّج كان خاطبًا من الخطّاب.[149]

[Ḥasan b. Ṣāliḥ:] I asked Jaʿfar b. Muḥammad about a man who divorced his wife while he was in another town and had two men witness the divorce. Then he [verbally] took her back before the conclusion of the waiting period but did not have witnesses to his taking her back. Then he went to her after the conclusion of the waiting period and found that she had already married somebody else. He then sent a message to her, "I took you back before the conclusion of the waiting period but did not have witnesses to that." He [Jaʿfar al-Ṣādiq] said, "He has no legal access to her, because he admitted to the divorce but claimed to have taken her back without proof. So he has no legal access to her. For this reason, a man who divorces [his wife] should call forth witnesses, and a man who takes his wife back should call forth witnesses, just as he called forth witnesses for the divorce. Had he reached her before she remarried, he could have been one of her suitors."

80

سماعة قال: سألت أبا عبد الله عن قول الله عزّ وجلّ: ﴿فَابْعَثُوا حَكَمًا مِنْ أَهْلِهِ وَحَكَمًا مِنْ أَهْلِهَا﴾، أرأيت إن استأذن الحكمان فقالا للرجل والمرأة: أليس قد جعلتما أمركما إلينا في الإصلاح والتفريق؟ فقال الرجل والمرأة: نعم! فأشهدا بذلك شهودًا

149 Kulaynī, *Kāfī*, 6:80.

عليهما، أيجوز تفريقهما عليهما؟ قال: نعم! ولكن لا يكون إلّا على طهر من المرأة من غير جماع من الزَّوج. قيل له: أرأيت إن قال أحد الحكمين قد فرَّقت بينهما وقال الآخر لم أُفرّق بينهما؟ فقال: لا يكون تفريق حتّى يجتمعا جميعًا على التفريق، فإذا اجتمعا على التفريق جاز تفريقهما.[150]

[Samāʿa:] I asked Abū ʿAbd Allāh about the saying of God, the Mighty and Majestic, "Appoint an arbitrator from his family and an arbitrator from her family":[151] "What is your position on [a case in which] the arbitrators ask permission and say to the man and the woman, 'Did you not put your situation in our hands to restore or to separate?' The man and the woman say yes and two witnesses witness it. Will the decision of the arbitrators to separate them have legal effect?" He said, "Yes! But only if she is in a state of purity, during which time she has had no intercourse with the husband." It was said to Abū ʿAbd Allāh, "What is your position if one of the arbitrators says he separated them and the other says he did not separate them?" He said, "There will be no separation until they both agree to separate them. If they agree on the separation, the separation will have legal effect."[152]

81

بريد بن معاوية قال: سألت أبا عبد الله عن المفقود كيف تصنع امرأته؟ قال: ما سكتت عنه وصبرت يُخلّى عنها، فإن هي رفعت أمرها إلى الوالي أجّلها أربع سنين، ثمّ يكتب إلى الصقع الّذي فُقد فيه فيُسأل عنه، فإن خُبر عنه بحياة صبرتْ وإن لم يُخبر عنه بشيء حتّى تمضي الأربع سنين دُعي وليّ الزوج المفقود فقيل له: هل للمفقود مال؟ فإن كان له مال أنفق عليها حتّى يعلم حياته من موته، وإن لم يكن له مال قيل للوليّ: أنفق عليها، فإن فعل فلا سبيل لها إلى أن تتزوّج، وإن لم يُنفق عليها أجبره الوالي على

150 Kulaynī, *Kāfī*, 6:147.

151 Qurʾān 4:35.

152 See also the following report in Kulaynī, *Kāfī*, 6:146:

الحلبي عن أبي عبد الله قال: سألته عن قول الله عزّ وجلّ: ﴿فَابْعَثُوا حَكَمًا مِنْ أَهْلِهِ وَحَكَمًا مِنْ أَهْلِهَا﴾. قال: ليس للحكمين أن يُفرّقا حتّى يستأمرا الرجل والمرأة ويشترطا عليهما إن شئنا جمعنا وإن شئنا فرّقنا، فإن جمعا فجائز وإن فرّقا فجائز.

['Ubayd Allāh al-Ḥalabī:] I asked Abū ʿAbd Allāh about the saying of God, the Mighty and Majestic, "Appoint an arbitrator from his family and an arbitrator from her family." He said, "The two arbitrators cannot separate them until they consult the man and the woman and stipulate to them, 'If we want, we can unite you, and if we want, we can separate you.' Then, if they unite them, it is valid, and if they separate them, it is valid."

أن يطلّق تطليقة في استقبال العدّة وهي طاهر، فيصير طلاق الوليّ طلاق الزوج، فإن جاء زوجها من قبل أن تنقضي عدّتها من يوم طلّقها الوليّ فبدا له أن يراجعها فهي امرأته وهي عنده على تطليقتين، فإن انقضت العدّة قبل أن يجيىء أو يراجع فقد حلّت للأزواج ولا سبيل للأوّل عليها.[153]

[Burayd b. Muʿāwiya:] I asked Abū ʿAbd Allāh what the wife of a missing person should do. He said, "As long as she is quiet and patient, she is left alone. If she raises her case to the governor, he asks her to wait for four years, [during which time] he sends a letter to the region where [the husband] disappeared, asking about him. If he is informed that he is alive, she remains patient. If there is no news of him after four years, the husband's patron is called and asked, 'Does the missing person have wealth?' If he has wealth, she will be paid her maintenance until it is known whether he is alive or dead. If he does not have wealth, the patron will be ordered to maintain her financially. If he does so, she cannot get married. If he does not, the governor forces him to divorce her [on the missing husband's behalf] while she is in a state of purity in order to commence the waiting period. So the divorce of the patron counts as the divorce of the husband. If her husband returns before the conclusion of the waiting period that began on the day she was divorced by the patron, he may take her back and she is his wife. She is with him with two divorces [remaining before they are fully separated]. If the waiting period concludes before his arrival or before he takes her back, she is lawful for other grooms and the first [husband] has no legal access to her."[154]

On the Administration of Justice

82

يونس بن عبد الرحمن، عن بعض رجاله، عن أبي عبد الله قال: سألته عن البيّنة إذا أُقيمت على الحقّ، أيحلّ للقاضي أن يقضي بقول البيّنة من غير مسألة إذا لم يعرفهم؟ فقال: خمسة أشياء يجب على الناس الأخذ فيها بظاهر الحكم: الولايات، والمناكح،

153 Kulaynī, *Kāfī*, 6:147–48.

154 This was a judgment issued by ʿUmar, reportedly supported by ʿAlī and Ibn ʿAbbās. See ʿAbd al-Razzāq, *Muṣannaf*, 7:86–88; Ibn Abī Shayba, *Muṣannaf*, 6:151–52; Saʿīd b. Manṣūr, *Sunan*, 3:400–402; Dāraquṭnī, *Sunan*, 4:482. The Mālikīs and most Ḥanbalīs offer the same solution. See Ibn Qudāma, *Mughnī*, 11:247–49; *al-Mawsūʿa al-fiqhiyya* (Kuwait), 38:268–69.

والمواريث،[155] والذبائح، والشهادات. فإذا كان ظاهر الرجل ظاهرًا مأمونًا جازت شهادته ولا يسأل عن باطنه.[156]

[Yūnus b. ʿAbd al-Raḥmān:] I asked Abū ʿAbd Allāh about testimony given in support of a claim: Can the judge decide on the basis of oral testimony without further questioning when he does not know the witnesses? He said, "People must take five matters at face value: guardianship, marriage, inheritance [that is, lineage], ritual slaughter, and testimony. If a man appears to be trustworthy, his testimony is accepted, and he will not be asked about his internal state."

83

علقمة قال: قال الصادق وقد قلت له: يا ابن رسول الله! أخبرني عمّن تقبل شهادته ومن لا تقبل؟ فقال: يا علقمة! كلّ من كان على فطرة الإسلام جازت شهادته. قال: فقلت له: تقبل شهادة مقترف بالذنوب؟ فقال: يا علقمة! لو لم تقبل شهادة المقترفين للذنوب لما قبلت إلّا شهادة الأنبياء والأوصياء، لأنّهم المعصومون دون سائر الخلق. فمن لم تره بعينك يرتكب ذنبًا أو لم يشهد عليه بذلك شاهدان، فهو من أهل العدالة والستر، وشهادته مقبولة وإن كان في نفسه مذنبًا.[157]

[ʿAlqama:] I said to [Jaʿfar] al-Ṣādiq, "O son of the Messenger of God! Inform me whose testimony is accepted and whose is not." He said, "O ʿAlqama! The testimony of anyone who has the innate disposition of Islam is accepted." I said to him, "Is the testimony of someone who has committed sins accepted?" He said, "O ʿAlqama! If the testimony of sinners is not accepted, only the testimony of prophets and their successors could be accepted, because they are the only infallible beings in all creation. Anyone whom you have not seen committing a sin with your eye, or who has not been seen doing so by two witnesses, is one of the upright and concealed people. His testimony is accepted even if he is internally sinful."

84

عبد الله بن أبي يعفور قال: قلت لأبي عبد الله: بِمَ تعرف عدالة الرجل بين المسلمين حتّى تقبل شهادته لهم وعليهم؟ فقال: أن تعرفوه بالستر والعفاف وكفّ البطن

155 This is والأنساب in Ibn Bābawayh, *Faqīh*, 3:9.
156 Kulaynī, *Kāfī*, 7:431; Ibn Bābawayh, *Faqīh*, 3:9 with minor variations.
157 Ibn Bābawayh, *Amālī*, 163–64.

والفرج واليد واللسان، ويعرف باجتناب الكبائر التي أوعد الله عز وجل عليها النار من شرب الخمور والزنا والربا وعقوق الوالدين والفرار من الزحف وغير ذلك. والدلالة على ذلك كلّه أن يكون ساترًا لجميع عيوبه حتّى يحرم على المسلمين ما وراء ذلك من عثراته وعيوبه وتفتيش ما وراء ذلك، ويجب عليهم تزكيته وإظهار عدالته في الناس، ويكون منه التعاهد للصلوات الخمس إذا واظب عليهن وحفظ مواقيتهن بحضور جماعة من المسلمين وأن لا يتخلّف عن جماعتهم في مصلّاهم إلّا من علة، وإذا كان كذلك لازمًا لمصلاّه عند حضور الصلوات الخمس فإذا سئل عنه في قبيلته ومحلّته قالوا: ما رأينا منه إلّا خيرًا، مواظبًا على الصلوات، متعاهدًا لأوقاتها في مصلّاه، فإنّ ذلك يجيز شهادته وعدالته بين المسلمين. وذلك أنّ الصلاة ستر وكفّارة للذنوب، وليس يمكن الشهادة على الرجل بأنّه يصلّي إذا كان لا يحضر مصلّاه ويتعاهد جماعة المسلمين. وإنّما جعل الجماعة والاجتماع إلى الصلاة لكي يُعرف من يصلّي ممّن لا يصلّي، ومن يحفظ مواقيت الصلوات ممّن يُضيع، ولولا ذلك لم يمكن لأحد أن يشهد على آخر بصلاح لأن من لا يصلّي لا صلاح له بين المسلمين، فإنّ رسول الله – صلّى الله عليه وآله وسلّم – همّ بأن يُحرق قومًا في منازلهم لتركهم الحضور لجماعة المسلمين، وقد كان منهم من يصلّي في بيته فلم يقبل منه ذلك، وكيف تقبل شهادة أو عدالة بين المسلمين ممّن جرى الحكم من الله عزّ وجلّ ومن رسوله – صلّى الله عليه وآله وسلّم – فيه الحرق في جوف بيته بالنار، وقد كان يقول رسول الله – صلّى الله عليه وآله وسلّم: لا صلاة لمن لا يصلّي في المسجد مع المسلمين إلّا من علّة.[158]

[ʿAbd Allāh b. Abī Yaʿfūr]: I said to Abū ʿAbd Allāh, "How is the uprightness of a Muslim man known so that his testimony can be accepted for and against other Muslims?" He said, "They will know him by his concealment [that is, no one has ever seen him commit a sin], his chastity, and his restraint of his stomach, genitals, hands, and tongue. And he will be known by his avoidance of the major sins for which God, the Mighty and Majestic, promised hellfire, including drinking wine, fornication, usury, disrespect to one's parents, and fleeing war, among other things. This is all indicated by his concealment of all his faults, such that delving into anything beyond that of his [possible] mistakes and faults, and investigating beyond that, becomes unacceptable for Muslims. They should vindicate him and establish his uprightness among the people. [For his part,] he should demonstrate his commitment to

158 Ibn Bābawayh, *Faqīh*, 3:24–25.

the five prayers by being careful to perform them and maintain their timeliness by joining the congregation of Muslims, and by trying not to miss joining their congregation in their place of prayer, except for a [valid] reason. If he is committed to his place of prayer when the times for the five prayers arrive, his tribe and neighborhood, if asked about him, would say, 'We have seen only good from him, diligence in performing the prayers, and a commitment to performing them on time in his place of prayer.' All this makes his testimony acceptable and establishes his uprightness among the Muslims. That is because the prayer is a concealer and an expiator of sins. It is not possible to testify that a man prays if he does not attend his place of prayer or commit to the Muslim congregation. The congregation and gathering for prayer were established so that it would be known who prays and who does not, and who prays on time and who does not. Otherwise, nobody would be able to testify about the righteousness of another, because whoever does not pray is not righteous among the Muslims. The Messenger of God (may God's prayer and peace be upon him and his Family) attempted to burn the houses of those who abandoned the Muslims' congregation. Some of them would pray in their homes, but that would not be accepted from them. How can Muslims accept the testimony or uprightness of someone whom God, the Mighty and Majestic, and His Messenger (may God's prayer and peace be upon him and his Family) decreed be burned inside their homes with fire? The Messenger of God (may God's prayer and peace be upon him and his Family) used to say, 'There is no prayer for someone who does not pray in the mosque with the Muslims, except for a [valid] reason.'"

85

أبو بصير قال: سألت أبا عبد الله عن الرجل يأتي القوم فيدّعي دارًا في أيديهم ويُقيم الّذي في يده الدار البيّنة أنّه ورثها عن أبيه ولا يدري كيف كان أمرها؟ فقال: أكثرهم بيّنة يستحلف وتدفع إليه. وذكر أنّ عليًا – عليه السلام – أتاه قوم يختصمون في بغلة فقامت البيّنة لهؤلاء أنّهم انتجوها على مذودهم ولم يبيعوا ولم يهبوا، وأقام هؤلاء البيّنة أنّهم انتجوها على مذودهم لم يبيعوا ولم يهبوا، فقضى بها لأكثرهم بيّنة واستحلفهم. قال: فسألته حينئذ فقلت: أرأيت إن كان الّذي ادَّعى الدار قال إن أبا هذا الّذي هو فيها أخذها بغير ثمن، ولم يقم الّذي هو فيها بيّنةً إلّا أنّه ورثها عن أبيه. قال: إذا كان أمرها هكذا فهي للّذي ادّعاها وأقام البيّنة عليها.[159]

159 Kulaynī, *Kāfī*, 7:418.

[Abū Baṣīr:] I asked Abū ʿAbd Allāh about a man who comes to a people and makes a claim to a house in their possession, and the person who possesses the house produces evidence that he inherited it from his father and was unaware of the circumstances surrounding it. He said, "Whoever has more evidence will be made to swear an oath, and it is then given to him." He mentioned that ʿAlī was approached by a people disputing about a mule. Evidence was brought in support of one side [to the conflict], claiming that they had bred it in their stable and never sold or gifted it; the other side brought evidence in support of their claim that they bred it in their stable and never sold or gifted it. ʿAlī judged in favor of those who brought more evidence and made them swear an oath. I then asked Abū ʿAbd Allāh, "What is your position on [a case in which] the person who claims the house says, 'The father of this person who lives in it took it without paying for it,' and the person living in it does not produce evidence beyond [the statement] that he inherited it from his father?" He said, "If that is the case, it belongs to the person who claims it and produces evidence in support of his claim."

On Crimes

86

حمزة بن حُمران قال: سألت أبا عبد الله عن سارق عدا على رجل من المسلمين فعقره وغصب ماله. ثمّ إنّ السارق بعد تاب، فنظر إلى مثل المال الّذي كان غصبه من الرجل فحمله إليه وهو يريد أن يدفعه إليه ويتحلّل منه ممّا صنع به. فوجد الرجل قد مات. فسأل معارفه هل ترك وارثا؟ وقد سألني أن أسألك عن ذلك حتّى ينتهي إلى قولك. فقال أبو عبد الله: إن كان الرجل الميّت توالى إلى رجل من المسلمين فضمن جريرته وحدثه وأشهد بذلك على نفسه فإنّ ميراث الميّت له، وإن كان الميّت لم يتوال إلى أحد حتّى مات فإنّ ميراثه لإمام المسلمين. فقلت له: فما حال الغاصب فيما بينه وبين الله تعالى؟ فقال: إذا هو أوصل المال إلى إمام المسلمين فقد سلم، وأمّا الجارحة فإنّ الجروح تُقتصّ منه يوم القيامة.[160]

[Ḥamza b. Ḥumrān:] I asked Abū ʿAbd Allāh about a thief who transgressed against a Muslim man by wounding him and seizing his wealth. Afterward the thief repented, so he took the same amount of wealth that he had stolen from the man and brought it to him with the

160 Ṭūsī, *Tahdhīb*, 10:130–31.

intention of paying it back and being relieved of liability toward him for what he had done, but he found that the man had died. He asked the man's acquaintances whether he had left behind any heirs, and he asked me to ask you about the matter so he could follow your opinion. Abū ʿAbd Allāh said, "If the deceased is a client of a Muslim man who assumed liability for his offenses and actions, and he has witnesses to this effect, the inheritance of the deceased goes to him.[161] If the deceased was not a client of anyone when he died, his inheritance goes to the leader of the Muslims." I said to him, "What is the situation of the usurper regarding what is between him and God, the Exalted?" He said, "If he delivers the wealth to the leader of the Muslims, he is safe [as far as his financial liability is concerned]. As for the wounds, they will be retaliated against on the Day of Resurrection."

87

[حفص بن غياث النخعي][162] قال: سألت أبا عبد الله عن رجل من المسلمين أودعه رجل من اللصوص دراهم أو متاعًا واللص مسلم فهل يردّه عليه؟ قال: لا يردّه عليه، فإن أمكنه أن يردّه على صاحبه فعل، وإلّا كان في يده بمنزلة اللقطة يصيبها فيعرّفها حولًا، فإن أصاب صاحبها وإلّا تصدّق بها، فإن جاء صاحبها بعد ذلك خُيّر بين الأجر والغرم، فإن اختار الأجر فله الأجر، وإن اختار الغرم غرم له وكان الأجر له.[163]

[Ḥafṣ b. Ghiyāth al-Nakhaʿī:] I asked Abū ʿAbd Allāh about a Muslim man who was entrusted with some money or provisions by a thief, the thief being Muslim. Should the man return it to the thief? He said, "He should not return it to him. If he can return it to its owner, he should do so. Otherwise, it will be in his possession like lost property that he found. So he is to advertise it to the public for one year. If he finds its owner [he will give it to him]; otherwise he can donate it. If the owner comes after [a year], the owner has a choice between accepting the divine reward [for the donation] or requesting compensation. If he chooses the reward, he gets the reward. If he chooses the compensation, [the donor] should compensate him for it and the reward goes to him [the donor]."

161 The assumption is that the man died leaving no family member behind to inherit his estate.

162 From Ibn Bābawayh, *Faqīh*, 3:190.

163 Kulaynī, *Kāfī*, 5:803.

88

عبد الله بن سنان عن أبي عبد الله قال: سُئل عن المؤمن يقتل المؤمن متعمّدًا أله توبة؟ فقال: إن كان قتله لإيمانه فلا توبة له، وإن كان قتله لغضب أو لسبب شيء من أمر الدنيا فإنّ توبته أن يُقاد منه، فإن لم يكن علم به أحد انطلق إلى أولياء المقتول فأقرّ عندهم بقتل صاحبهم، فإن عفوا عنه فلم يقتلوه أعطاهم الدية وأعتق نسمة وصام شهرين متتابعين وأطعم ستّين مسكينًا توبةً إلى الله عزّ وجلّ.[164]

[ʿAbd Allāh b. Sinān:] Abū ʿAbd Allāh was asked about a believer who kills another believer intentionally: Can he repent? He said, "If he killed him because of his belief, there is no repentance. If he killed him out of anger or because of some worldly matter, his repentance is that the rule of retaliation is applied to him. If nobody knows [of his offense], he must go to the successors of the victim and admit to having killed their man. If they pardon him and do not kill him, he is to pay the blood-money to them, manumit a slave, fast for two consecutive months, and feed sixty poor individuals in repentance to God, the Mighty and Majestic."

89

أبو الصباح الكناني قال: قلت لأبي عبد الله: إنّ لنا جارًا من همدان يقال له الجعد بن عبد الله وهو يجلس إلينا فنذكر عليًا أمير المؤمنين – عليه السلام – وفضله فيقع فيه، أفتأذن لي فيه؟ فقال لي: يا أبا الصباح! أفكنت فاعلاً؟ فقلت: إي والله! لَئن أذنت لي فيه لأرصدنّه فإذا صار فيها اقتحمت عليه بسيفي فخبطته حتّى أقتله. فقال: يا أبا الصباح! هذا الفتك، وقد نهى رسول الله – صلّى الله عليه وآله وسلّم – عن الفتك. يا أبا الصباح! إنّ الإسلام قيّد الفتك.[165]

[Abū al-Ṣabbāḥ al-Kinānī:] I said to Abū ʿAbd Allāh, "We have a neighbor from [the tribe of] Hamdān named Jaʿd b. ʿAbd Allāh who sits with us, and when we mention ʿAlī, the Commander of the Faithful, and his virtues, he slanders him. Do you give me permission [to punish him]?" He said to me, "O Abū al-Ṣabbāḥ! Would you do it?" I said, "Yes, by God! If you give me permission, I will look out for him, and when he is there, I will rush at him with my sword and strike him to death." He said, "O Abū al-Ṣabbāḥ! This is assassination, and the Messenger of God

164 Kulaynī, *Kāfī*, 7:276.
165 Kulaynī, *Kāfī*, 7:375.

(may God's prayer and peace be upon him and his Family) forbade assassination.[166] O Abū al-Ṣabbāḥ! Islam did away with assassination."

90

سماعة قال: سألت أبا عبد الله عن الرجل يقذف الرجل بالزنى فيعفو عنه ويجعله من ذلك في حلّ، ثمّ إنّه بعد يبدو له في أن يقدّمه حتّى يجلده. فقال: ليس له حدٌّ بعد العفو. فقلت له: أرأيت إن هو قال: «يا ابن الزانية» فعفا عنه وترك ذلك لله؟ فقال: إن كانت أُمّه حيّةً فليس له أن يعفو. العفو إلى أُمّه. متى شاءت أخذت بحقّها. وإن كانت أُمّه قد ماتت فإنّه وليُّ أمرها يجوز عفوه.[167]

[Samāʿa:] I asked Abū ʿAbd Allāh about a man who slanders another man for fornicating, but the victim pardons him and relieves him of liability. Afterward, he [changes his mind and] decides to bring the offender forth to be flogged in punishment. He said, "There is no prescribed (*ḥadd*) punishment after a pardon." I said to him, "What is your position on [a case in which] the offender says, 'O son of a harlot!' but the victim pardons him and leaves the matter to God?" He said, "If his mother is alive, he does not have the right to pardon. The right to pardon belongs to his mother, and she can enforce her right whenever she wishes. If his mother is dead, he is the executor of her affairs and his pardon takes effect."

91

عمّار الساباطي عن أبي عبد الله قال: سمعته يقول: إنّ الحدّ لا يورث كما تورث الدية والمال والعقار، ولكنّ من قام به من الورثة فطلبه فهو وليّه، ومن تركه فلم يطلبه فلا حقّ له. وذلك مثل رجلٍ قذف رجلاً [في أمّه] وللمقذوف أخ، فإن عفا عنه أحدهما كان للآخر أن يطلبه بحقّه،لأنّها أمّهما جميعًا والعفو لهما جميعًا.[168]

166 ʿAbd al-Razzāq, *Muṣannaf*, 5:299; Aḥmad b. Ḥanbal, *Musnad*, 3:45; Abū Dāwūd, *Sunan*, no. 2769; Ṭabarānī, *Musnad al-Shāmiyyīn*, 3:350 (all as الإيمان قيد الفتك).

167 Kulaynī, *Kāfī*, 7:252.

168 Kulaynī, *Kāfī*, 7:552.

[ʿAmmār al-Sābāṭī:] I heard Abū ʿAbd Allāh say, "A *ḥadd* punishment is not inherited the way blood-money, wealth, and real estate are. However, whoever among [a victim's] heirs chooses to pursue it will have the right to it, and whoever abandons it has no right. It is like when a man slanders another man's mother, and the slandered man has a brother; even if one of them forgives him, the other can pursue his right because she is the mother of both of them and the right to forgive belongs to both of them together."

92

عبد الرحمن عن أبي عبد الله قال: سألته عن رجل قتل رجلين عمدًا ولهما أولياء فعفا أولياء أحدهما وأبى الآخرون؟ فقال: يَقتل الّذين لم يعفوا، وإن أحبّوا أن يأخذوا الدية أخذوا. قال عبد الرحمن: فقلت لأبي عبد الله: فرجلان قتلا رجلاً عمدًا وله وليّان فعفا أحد الوليّين؟ فقال: إذا عفا بعض الأولياء دُرِئ عنهما القتل وطرح عنهما من الدية بقدر حصّة من عفا، وأدّيا الباقي من أموالهما إلى الّذين لم يعفوا.[169]

[ʿAbd al-Raḥmān:] I asked Abū ʿAbd Allāh about a man who intentionally killed two men. They both had successors; the successors of one of them pardoned [him] and the others refused. He said, "Those who did not pardon may kill [the killer] or take the blood-money if they wish to do so." I said to Abū ʿAbd Allāh, "Two men together intentionally killed a man who had two successors, and one of the successors pardoned [him]." He said, "If some of the successors pardon, neither [of the two killers] can be killed. The share of the blood-money of the one who pardoned is subtracted and the rest is paid to those who did not pardon."

93

أبو ولّاد الحنّاط قال: سألت أبا عبد الله عن رجل مسلم قتل رجلاً مسلمًا عمدًا، فلم يكن للمقتول أولياء من المسلمين إلّا أولياء من أهل الذمّة من قرابته. فقال: على الإمام أن يعرض على قرابته من أهل بيته الإسلام، فمن أسلم منهم فهو وليّه، يُدفَع القاتل إليه، فإن شاء قتل وإن شاء عفا وإن شاء أخذ الدية. فإن لم يُسلم أحدٌ كان الإمام وليّ أمره، فإن شاء قتل وإن شاء أخذ الدية، يجعلها في بيت مال المسلمين. لأنّ جناية المقتول كانت على الإمام فكذلك يكون ديته لإمام المسلمين. قلت: فإن عفا عنه

169 Kulaynī, *Kāfī*, 7:358.

الإمام؟ فقال: إنّما هو حقّ جميع المسلمين، وإنّما على الإمام أن يقتل أو يأخذ الدية، وليس له أن يعفو.[170]

[Abū Wallād al-Ḥannāṭ:] I asked Abū ʿAbd Allāh about a Muslim man who intentionally kills another Muslim man, but the slain man has no Muslim successors and only *dhimmī* successors among his relatives. He said, "The *imām* should invite his relatives from his household to convert to Islam. Whoever converts to Islam becomes his successor. The killer will be delivered to him, and if he wishes he can have him killed, pardon him, or accept the blood-money. If nobody converts to Islam, the *imām* has authority over his affairs. If he wishes, he can kill [the killer] or he can accept the blood-money and place it in the Muslim public treasury. Had the slain man ever committed a crime, it would be for the *imām* [to compensate], and likewise his blood-money goes to the *imām* of the Muslims." I said, "What if the *imām* pardons him?" He said, "It is the right of all the Muslims, so the *imām* must either kill [him] or accept the blood-money; he cannot pardon."

94

الحلبيّ عن أبي عبد الله أنّه سُئل عن الرجل يمرُّ على طريق من طرق المسلمين فتصيب دابّته إنسانًا برجلها؟ فقال: ليس عليه ما أصابت برجلها ولكن عليه ما أصابت بيدها، لأنَّ رجلها خلفه إن ركب، وإن كان قادها فإنّه يملك بإذن الله يدها يضعها حيث يشاء. قال: وسئل عن بُختيّ اغتلم فخرج من الدار فقتل رجلاً فجاء أخو الرجل فضرب الفحل بالسيف فعقره؟ فقال: صاحب البُختيّ ضامن للديّة ويقبض ثمن بُختيّه. وعن الرجل ينفّر بالرجل فيعقره وتعقر دابّته رجلاً آخر؟ فقال: هو ضامن لما كان من شيء.[171]

[ʿUbayd Allāh al-Ḥalabī:] Abū ʿAbd Allāh was asked about [a case in which] a man travels along one of the roads of the Muslims and his riding animal hits a person with its hind leg. He said, "He is not liable for what it hits with its hind legs but is liable for what it hits with its forelegs.[172] That is because its hind legs are behind him when he rides, but if he leads the animal, then he controls, by God's permission, its forelegs to be put where he wishes." He was asked about a

170 Kulaynī, *Kāfī*, 7:359.

171 Kulaynī, *Kāfī*, 7:351; Ṭūsī, *Tahdhīb*, 10:224.

172 For the disagreements between early jurists and various schools on this question, see Ibn ʿAbd al-Barr, *Istidhkār*, 25:212–14, where it is reported that Mālik, Awzāʿī, and Layth b. Saʿd agreed with the opinion given by Jaʿfar here.

Bactrian camel that becomes excited, leaves the building, and then kills a man. The brother of the man strikes the animal with a sword and cripples it. He said, "The owner of the Bactrian camel is liable for the blood-money [of the man] and is owed the price for the camel." As for a man who scares another man and injures him, and his riding animal injures another man, he said, "He [the first man] is liable for it all."

On Inheritance

95

زرارة قال: هذا مما ليس فيه اختلاف عند أصحابنا عن أبي عبد الله وعن أبي جعفر أنّهما سُئلا عن امرأة تركت زوجها وأُمّها وابنتيها؟ فقالا: للزوج الرُّبع وللامِّ السُدُس وللابنتين ما بقي، لأنّهما لو كانا رجلين لم يكن لهما [شيء] إلّا ما بقي، ولا تزاد المرأة أبدًا على نصيب الرجل لو كان مكانها.

وإن ترك الميّت أُمًّا أو أبًا وامرأة وابنة فإنّ الفريضة من أربعة وعشرين سهمًا: للمرأة الثمن ثلاثة أسهم من أربعة وعشرين، ولأحد الأبوين السُدس أربعة أسهم، وللابنة النصف اثنى عشر سهمًا، وبقي خمسة أسهم [هي] مردودة على سهام الابنة وأحد الأبوين على قدر سهامهما، ولا يردّ على المرأة شيء.

وإن ترك أبوين وامرأة وبنتًا فهي أيضًا من أربعة وعشرين سهمًا: للأبوين السُدسان ثمانية أسهم – لكلّ واحد [منهما] أربعة أسهم – وللمرأة الثمن ثلاثة أسهم، وللابنة النصف اثنى عشر سهمًا، وبقي سهم واحد مردود على الابنة والأبوين على قدر سهامهم، ولا يردّ على المرأة شيء.

وإن ترك أبًا وزوجًا وابنةً فللأب سهمان من اثني عشر [سهمًا] وهو السدس، وللزوج الربع ثلاثة أسهم من اثني عشر [سهمًا]، وللابنة النصف ستّة أسهم من اثني عشر [سهمًا]، وبقي سهم واحد مردود على الابنة والأب على قدر سهامهما، ولا يردّ على الزوج شيء.

ولا يرث أحد من خلق الله مع الولد إلّا الأبوان والزوج والزوجة. فإن لم يكن [له] ولد وكان ولد الولد، ذكورًا كانوا أو اناثًا، فإنّهم بمنزلة الولد، [و]ولد البنين بمنزلة البنين يرثون ميراث البنين، وولد البنات بمنزلة البنات يرثون ميراث البنات، ويحجبون

الأبوين والزوج والزوجة عن سهامهم الأكثر، وإن سفلوا ببطنين وثلاثة وأكثر، يرثون ما يرث ولد الصلب ويحجبون ما يحجب ولد الصلب.[173]

[Zurāra:] There is no disagreement among our companions, on the authority of Abū ʿAbd Allāh and Abū Jaʿfar, that they were asked about a woman who [died and] left behind her husband, mother, and two daughters. They both said, "The husband gets one-quarter, the mother gets one-sixth, and the two daughters get the remainder, because if they were men they would get the remainder, and a woman does not get more than what a man would get if he were in her position.

"If the deceased leaves behind either a mother or a father, as well as a wife and a daughter, the inheritance comprises twenty shares: one-eighth to the wife (three shares out of the twenty), one-sixth to the parent (four shares), and one-half to the daughter (twelve shares); five shares remain, and these are added to the shares of the daughter and the parent according to their shares. Nothing is added to the shares of the wife.

"If the deceased leaves behind two parents, a wife, and a daughter, then it also comprises twenty shares: one-sixth to the two parents (eight shares, so each of them gets four shares), one-eighth to the wife (three shares), and one-half to the daughter (twelve shares). One share remains, which goes to the daughter and the parents according to their shares. Nothing additional goes to the wife.

"If the deceased leaves behind a father, a husband, and a daughter, the father gets two shares out of twelve, which is one-sixth; one-fourth, or three shares out of twelve, goes to the husband; and one-half, or six shares out of twelve, goes to the daughter. One share remains, which goes to the daughter and the father according to their shares, and nothing additional goes to the husband.

"No one among God's creation inherits along with a child except for the parents, the husband, and the wife. If the deceased does not leave a child but only a grandchild, male or female, the grandchild is counted as a child. The children of sons count as sons and inherit as sons; the children of daughters count as daughters and inherit as daughters; and they [both] preclude the parents, the wife, and the husband from inheriting at their higher rate. Even if the grandchildren are separated by two, three, or more generations, they inherit just like direct offspring do, and they preclude others from inheriting [at their higher rate] just like direct offspring do."

173 Kulaynī, *Kāfī*, 7:79.

96

بكير بن أعيَن قال: قلت لأبي عبد الله: امرأة تركت زوجها وإخوتها لأُمّها وإخوتها وأخواتها لأبيها؟ فقال: للزوج النصف ثلاثة أسهم، وللأخوة من الأُمّ الثلث – الذكر والانثى فيه سواء – وبقي سهم فهو للأخوة والأخوات من الأب – للذكر مثل حظّ الأُنثيين – ، لأنّ السهام لا تعول، ولا ينقص الزّوج من النصف ولا الأخوة من الأمّ من ثلثهم. لأنّ الله عزّ وجلّ يقول: ﴿فَإِنْ كَانُوا أَكْثَرَ مِنْ ذَلِكَ فَهُمْ شُرَكَاءُ فِي الثُّلُثِ﴾، وإن كانت واحدة فلها السدس. والّذي عنى الله تبارك وتعالى في قوله: ﴿وَإِنْ كَانَ رَجُلٌ يُورَثُ كَلَالَةً أَوِ امْرَأَةٌ وَلَهُ أَخٌ أَوْ أُخْتٌ فَلِكُلِّ وَاحِدٍ مِنْهُمَا السُّدُسُ فَإِنْ كَانُوا أَكْثَرَ مِنْ ذَلِكَ فَهُمْ شُرَكَاءُ فِي الثُّلُثِ﴾ إنّما عنى بذلك الإخوة والأخوات من الأُمّ خاصّة. وقال في آخر سورة النساء: ﴿قُلِ اللَّهُ يُفْتِيكُمْ فِي الْكَلَالَةِ إِنِ امْرُؤٌ هَلَكَ لَيْسَ لَهُ وَلَدٌ وَلَهُ أُخْتٌ فَلَهَا نِصْفُ مَا تَرَكَ﴾ يعني أُختًا لأُمّ وأب أو أُختًا لأب ﴿وَإِنْ كَانُوا إِخْوَةً رِجَالًا وَنِسَاءً فَلِلذَّكَرِ مِثْلُ حَظِّ الْأُنْثَيَيْنِ﴾ فهم الّذين يزادون وينقصون، وكذلك أولادهم الّذين يزادون وينقصون. ولو أنّ امرأة تركت زوجها وإخوتها لأمّها وأُختيها لأبيها كان للزوج النصف ثلاثة أسهم، وللإخوة من الأُمّ سهمان، وبقي سهم فهو للأختين للأب. وإن كانت واحدة فهو لها لأنّ الأُختين لأب لو كانتا أخوين لأب لم يزادا على ما بقي، ولو كانت واحدة أو كان مكان الواحدة أخ لم يزد على ما بقي، ولا يزاد أُنثى من الأخوات ولا من الولد على ما لو كان ذكرًا لم يزد عليه.[174]

[Bukayr b. Aʿyan:] I said to Abū ʿAbd Allāh, "A woman [died and] left behind her husband, [half-]siblings through her mother, and [half-] brothers and sisters through her father." He said, "One-half goes to the husband (three shares); one-third [two shares] goes to siblings through the mother, the male and the female being equal; and one share remains and goes to the siblings through the father, with the male receiving the share of two females. That is because the shares do not change. The husband does not suffer a loss to his half nor do the siblings through the mother to their third, because God, the Mighty and Majestic, says, 'If they are more than that, they share in a third.'[175] If there is only one [sibling through the father, and she is female], she gets one-sixth. With the saying of God, the Praised and Exalted, 'If a

174 Kulaynī, *Kāfī*, 7:101–2 (see also 7:103, where a variant of this report is attributed to Muḥammad al-Bāqir, as quoted earlier).

175 Qurʾān 4:12.

man or a woman who is to be inherited has left no parent or child, but has left a brother or a sister, each of them receives one-sixth, and if they are more than that, they share in a third,'[176] He meant siblings through the mother only. At the end of the *sūra* of Women, He says, 'They seek your legal verdict. Say, "God gives a ruling regarding those who leave no parent or child. If a man dies with no child and has a sister, she receives half of what is left behind." This means a full sister or a paternal sister. "And if there are brothers and sisters, the male receives the share of two females."'[177] They and their children are the ones whose inheritance can increase and decrease. If a woman leaves behind her husband, sisters through her mother, and two sisters through her father, one-half goes to the husband, as three shares; two shares go to the sisters through the mother; and one share remains for the two sisters through the father. If there is only one sister [through the father], it [the share] goes to her, because if the two sisters through the father were two brothers through the father, they would not get anything above what remained. If there was one sister, or in the place of the one there was a brother, nothing would be added to the remainder. Nothing is added for either female siblings or children because if they were male, there would be nothing additional."

97

عن زرارة قال: سألت أبا عبد الله عن رجل ترك أخاه لأبيه وأمّه وجدّه. قال: المال بينهما نصفان. ولو كانا أخوين أو مائة كان الجدّ معهم كواحد منهم، للجدّ ما يصيب واحدًا من الأخوة. قال: وإن ترك أُخته فللجدّ سهمان وللأخت سهم. وإن كانتا أختين فللجدّ النصف وللأُختين النصف. قال: وإن ترك إخوة وأخوات من أبٍ وأُمٍّ كان الجدّ كواحد من الإخوة، للذكر مثل حظّ الأُنثيين.[178]

[Zurāra:] I asked Abū ʿAbd Allāh about a man who [died and] left behind a [full] brother through his father and mother, as well as a grandfather. He said, "The wealth is split evenly between them. If there are two or one hundred brothers, the grandfather is counted as one of them. The grandfather receives whatever one brother receives." He said, "If he left a sister, the grandfather gets two shares and the sister gets one share. If there are two sisters, the grandfather receives half and the two sisters receive half." He said, "If he left behind [full] brothers and

176 Qur'ān 4:12.
177 Qur'ān 4:176.
178 Kulaynī, *Kāfī*, 7:110.

sisters through his mother and father, the grandfather is counted as one of the brothers—a male receives the share of two females."

98

عبّاد بن صهيب عن أبي عبد الله في رجل فرّط في إخراج زكاته في حياته، فلمّا حضرته الوفاة حسب جميع ما كان فرّط فيه ممّا لزمه من الزكاة ثمّ أوصى به أن يُخرج ذلك فيدفع إلى من يجب له؟ قال: جائز، يُخرج ذلك من جميع المال. إنّما هو بمنزلة دَينٍ لو كان عليه ليس للورثة شيء حتّى يؤدُّوا ما أوصى به من الزّكاة.[179]

[ʿAbbād b. Ṣuhayb:] On the question of a man who neglected paying *zakāt* during his lifetime but, when he was about to die, calculated all that he had neglected to pay of the *zakāt* he owed and then entrusted someone with taking it [from his wealth] and paying it to those to whom it was owed, Abū ʿAbd Allāh said, "That is permitted. It will be taken from the entirety of his wealth. It is like a debt; if he owes it, his heirs receive nothing until they pay the *zakāt* that he willed [to be paid]."

99

عبد الرحمن بن الحجّاج قال: سألت أبا عبد الله عن الزّوج والمرأة يهلكان جميعًا فيأتي ورثة المرأة فيدّعون على ورثة الرجل الصداق. قال: وقد هلكا وقُسّم الميراث؟ فقلت: نعم! قال: ليس لهم شيء. قلت: فإن كانت المرأة حيّة فجاءت بعد موت زوجها تدّعي صداقها؟ قال: لا شيء لها وقد أقامت معه مقرّة حتّى هلك زوجها. فقلت: فإن ماتت وهو حيٌّ فجاءت ورثتها يطالبونه بصداقها. قال: وقد أقامت معه حتّى ماتت لا تطلبه؟ فقلت: نعم! فقال: لا شيء لهم. قلت: فإن طلّقها فجائت تطلب صداقها؟ قال: وقد أقامت لا تطلبه حتّى طلّقها؟ لا شيء لها. قلت: فمتى حدُّ ذلك الّذي إذا طلبته لم يكن لها؟ قال: إذا أُهديت إليه ودخلت بيته ثمّ طلبت بعد ذلك فلا شيء لها.[180]

[ʿAbd al-Raḥmān b. al-Ḥajjāj:] I asked Abū ʿAbd Allāh about a husband and a wife who both die, and then the wife's heirs demand the wife's dower from the husband's heirs. He said, "Has the inheritance already been divided after their death?" I said, "Yes!" He said, "They are not entitled to anything." I said, "What if the wife is alive and after her

179 Kulaynī, *Kāfī*, 3:547; Ṭūsī, *Tahdhīb*, 9:170.
180 Kulaynī, *Kāfī*, 5:385–86.

husband's death she demands her dower?" He said, "She is not entitled to anything if she lived with her husband until he died." I said, "What if she died and he is alive, and her heirs demand the dower from him?" He said, "Did she live with him until her death without demanding it?" I said, "Yes!" He said, "They are not entitled to anything." I said, "What if he divorced her and then she demanded her dower?" He said, "And she lived with him without demanding her dower until he divorced her? She is not entitled to anything." I said, "What is the point at which she is no longer entitled to request her dower?" He said, "If she was delivered to him and entered his house [to live with him] and thereafter made the demand, she is not entitled to anything."[181]

100

عبد الرحمن بن الحجّاج قال: سألت أبا عبد الله عن الحميل. فقال: وأيُّ شيء الحميل؟ قلت: المرأة تسبى من أهلها معها الولد الصغير فتقول هذا ابني، والرجل يسبى فيلقي أخاه فيقول هو أخي، وليس لهم بيّنة إلّا قولهم. قال: ما يقول فيهم الناس عندكم؟ قلت: لا يورّثونهم، لأنّه لم يكن لهم على ولادتهم بيّنة وإنّما هي ولادة الشرك. فقال: سبحان الله! إذا جاءت بابنها أو ابنتها ولم تزل مقرّة به، وإذا عرف أخاه وكان ذلك في صحّة منهما ولم يزالا مقرّين بذلك، ورث بعضهم من بعض.[182]

[ʿAbd al-Raḥmān b. al-Ḥajjāj:] I asked Abū ʿAbd Allāh about *ḥamīl*. He said, "What is *ḥamīl*?" I said, "A woman who is enslaved [and taken] from her family together with a small child and who says, 'This is my son,' or a man who is enslaved, finds his brother, and says, 'This is my brother,' but neither has any evidence other than their word." He said, "What do the people [that is, the jurists among the majority] in your region say about them?" I said, "They do not allow them to inherit from one another, because there is no evidence of [a legally valid] birth [that can prove shared lineage]; rather, it is the birth [system followed] by the polytheists." He said, "Praise be to God! If she comes with her son or daughter and continues to acknowledge them, and if he recognizes his brother, and they both confirm it while they are of sound mind and continue to acknowledge that, they inherit from one another."

181 The answer was based on a long-established practice in Medina of women asking for their dowers before moving to the matrimonial home. See Ḥurr al-ʿĀmilī, *Wasāʾil al-Shīʿa*, 21:254, and, for reports about this Medinan tradition, 21:254–60.

182 Kulaynī, *Kāfī*, 7:165–66.

Concluding Remarks

I hope this book was successful in serving its purpose: to define the nature and main characteristics of the legal thought of Imam Jaʿfar al-Ṣādiq, a highly esteemed jurist of Medina in the first half of Islam's second century whose mastery of Islamic religious law was a matter of unanimous agreement in Muslim society in his time and after.

The school of Jaʿfar al-Ṣādiq, as the most learned and esteemed member of the House of the Prophet in his time, represented the legal tradition of the House. This tradition was characterized by a focus on the text of the Qurʾān and the Sunna of the Prophet as the sources of the law, and on the transmission, interpretation, and practice of ʿAlī, as known to and transmitted by the learned among his descendants, as the interpretive model for everything Islamic. It lay very much within the general legal discourse of late Umayyad and early Abbasid times, but was known to differ in certain approaches from the other main legal schools of these same early Muslim periods.

Examples of Jaʿfar al-Ṣādiq's legal opinions that are quoted in the Sunnī and Shīʿī works of Islamic law reflect the main characteristics of his school as well as occasional disagreements between him and other jurists of the time. It was common for the judges and jurists of the period to maintain sharp differences of opinion and to disagree on just about every point. The community had accepted this diversity of opinion alongside a core that all Muslim jurists agreed upon and that formed the essential elements of Islamic religious thought and culture.

With the advancement of legal "orthodoxy" and the growing popularity of a small number of legal schools, many early opinions, including much that was supported by or attributed to the school of Jaʿfar al-Ṣādiq, gradually disappeared from the legal discourse of the majority Sunnī tradition. His school, however, continued unabated according to the roadmap drawn by him for the future generations whom he expected to be able to derive rulings for specific cases from the legal norms that they had learned. This is how the Imam explained the division of labor between himself and future generations:

إنّما علينا أن نُلقي إليكم الأصول وعليكم أن تُفرِّعوا.

It is our duty to teach you the principles, and it is your duty to derive legal rules for specific cases.

والحمد لله الّذي بِنعمته تَتمّ الصالحات

Praise to God by Whose grace good deeds are completed

Bibliography

ʿAbd Allāh b. Yazīd al-Fazārī (late 2nd century). *Kitāb al-Tawḥīd*. In *Early Ibāḍī Theology*, edited by Wilferd Madelung and Abd al-Rahman al-Salimi, 198–227. Leiden, 2014.

ʿAbd al-Jalīl al-Qazwīnī (mid-6th century). *Kitāb al-Naqḍ*. Tehran, [1980].

ʿAbd al-Quddūs al-Anṣārī. *Āthār al-Madīna al-munawwara*. Medina, 1985.

ʿAbd al-Razzāq b. Hammām al-Ṣanʿānī (d. 211). *al-Muṣannaf*. Beirut, 1970.

Abou El Fadl, Khaled. "Law of Duress in Islamic Law and Common Law: A Comparative Study." *Islamic Studies* 30, no. 3 (Autumn 1991): 305–50.

Abū al-Aṣbagh ʿĪsā b. Sahl al-Asadī al-Jiyānī (d. 486). *Dīwān al-aḥkām al-kubrā*. Riyadh, 1997.

Abū ʿAwwāna Yaʿqūb b. Isḥāq al-Isfarāʾīnī (d. 316). *Musnad Abī ʿAwwāna*. Beirut, 1998.

Abū Dāwūd al-Sijistānī (d. 275). *Kitāb al-Marāsīl*. Riyadh, 2001.

———. *Sunan Abī Dāwūd*. Beirut, 1996.

Abū Ḥanīfa (d. 150) (attr.). *al-Fiqh al-akbar*. [Cairo, 1909].

———(attr.). *Waṣiyyat al-imām Abī Ḥanīfa al-Nuʿmān*. Beirut, 1997.

Abū Hilāl al-ʿAskarī (d. 395). *Kitāb al-Awāʾil*. Riyadh, 1980.

Abū Khirāsh al-Hudhalī (d. 15). *Dīwān*. Aleppo, 1996.

Abū Manṣūr al-Ṭabarsī (early 6th century). *al-Iḥtijāj ʿalā ahl al-lijāj*. Qum, [1992].

Abū al-Muʾayyad al-Khwārazmī (d. 655). *Jāmiʿ masānīd Abī Ḥanīfa*. Hyderabad, [1914].

Abū Muḥammad al-Ḥārithī (d. 340). *Musnad Abī Ḥanīfa*. Beirut, 2008.

Abū Nuʿaym al-Iṣbahānī (d. 430). *Dhikr akhbār Iṣbahān*. Leiden, 1931.

———. *Ḥilyat al-awliyāʾ*. Cairo, 1932.

Abū al-Qāsim al-Jawharī (d. 381). *Musnad al-Muwaṭṭaʾ*. Beirut, 1997.

Abū al-Shaykh al-Iṣbahānī (d. 369). *Akhlāq al-Nabī*. Riyadh, 1998.

———. *Ṭabaqāt al-muḥaddithīn bi-Iṣbahān wa'l-wāridīn ʿalayhā*. Beirut, 1992.

Abū Ṭāhir al-Silafī (d. 576). *Muʿjam al-safar*. Damascus, 1993.

Abū Ṭālib al-Hārūnī, Yaḥyā b. al-Ḥusayn (d. 424). *Amālī = Taysīr al-maṭālib min Amālī al-imām Abī Ṭālib*. Amman, 2002.

Abū Tammām al-Ṭāʾī (d. 231). *Dīwān Abī Tammām bi-sharḥ al-Khaṭīb al-Tabrīzī*. Cairo, 1964.

Abū al-Ṭufayl ʿĀmir b. Wāthila al-Kinānī (d. around 102). *Dīwān*. In *Silsilat dawāwīn al-shuʿarāʾ min aṣḥāb ʿAlī Amīr al-Muʾminīn*, edited by Qays al-ʿAṭṭār, vol. 9. Qum, [2000].

Abū Yūsuf (d. 182). *al-Radd ʿalā siyar al-Awzāʿī*. Hyderabad, 1938.

Āghā Buzurg al-Ṭihrānī (d. 1389). *al-Dharīʿa ilā taṣānīf al-Shīʿa*. Najaf, 1934.

Aḥmad b. Ḥanbal (d. 241). *al-ʿIlal wa-maʿrifat al-rijāl: riwāyat al-Marrūdhī wa-Ṣāliḥ b. Aḥmad wa'l-Maymūnī*. Bombay, 1988.

———. *Masāʾil al-imām Aḥmad b. Ḥanbal: Riwāyat ibnih ʿAbd Allāh b. Aḥmad*. Beirut and Damascus, 1981.

———. *Musnad al-imām Aḥmad b. Ḥanbal*. Beirut, 1993–2001.

———. *Ṣifat al-muʾmin min Ahl al-Sunna wa'l-Jamāʿa*. In Abū Yaʿlā al-Farrāʾ, *Ṭabaqāt al-Ḥanābila*, 2:293–94. Riyadh, 1999.

Aḥmad b. ʿĪsā b. Zayd b. ʿAlī b. al-Ḥusayn (d. 247). *Amālī = Kitāb al-ʿUlūm*. Compiled by Muḥammad b. Manṣūr al-Murādī al-Kūfī (alive 290). [Ṣanʿāʾ], n.d.

Aḥmad b. Muḥammad b. ʿĪsā al-Ashʿarī (mid-3rd century) (attr.). *Kitāb al-Nawādir*. Qum, [1987].

ʿAjlūnī (d. 1162). *Kashf al-khifāʾ wa-muzīl al-ilbās*. Beirut, n.d.

Akhṭal (d. 90). *Dīwān al-Akhṭal*. Beirut, 1994.

Āl Kāshif al-Ghiṭāʾ, Muḥammad Ḥusayn (d. 1373). *Aṣl al-Shīʿa wa-uṣūluhā*. Beirut, 1990.

———. *Taḥrīr al-Majalla*. Qum, 2001.

Āl al-Mujaddid al-Shīrāzī, Ḥasan. "Ḥukm al-jamʿ bayn al-ṣalātayn ʿalā ḍawʾ al-madhāhib al-fiqhiyya." *Turāthunā* 35–36 [1994]: 75–127.

ʿAlāʾ b. Razīn al-Qallāʾ al-Kūfī (2nd century). *Kitāb ʿAlāʾ b. Razīn al-Qallāʾ*. In *al-Uṣūl al-sittat-ʿashar*, 357–68. Qum, [2002].

ʿAlawī, Abū ʿAbd Allāh (d. 445). *al-Adhān bi-ḥayya ʿalā khayr al-ʿamal*. N.p., [1979].

———. *al-Jāmiʿ al-kāfī*. Ṣaʿda, 2014.

ʿAlī b. Abī Ṭālib (d. 40). *Dīwān Imām ʿAlī*. Tehran, [1994].

ʿAlī b. Asbāṭ al-Kūfī al-Muqriʾ (3rd century). *Nawādir ʿAlī b. Asbāṭ*. In *al-Uṣūl al-sittat-ʿashar*, 337–52. Qum, [2002].

ʿAlī b. Ibrāhīm al-Qummī (alive 307). *Tafsīr*. Najaf, [1966].

ʿAlī b. Jaʿfar al-ʿUrayḍī (d. ca. 220). *Masāʾil ʿAlī b. Jaʿfar*. Mashhad, 1989.

ʿAlī b. al-Ḥusayn Zayn al-ʿĀbidīn (d. 95). *al-Ṣaḥifa al-kāmila al-Sajjādiyya*. With *The Psalms of Islam*, translated by William C. Chittick. London, 1988.

ʿAlī b. al-Muṭahhar al-Ḥillī (late 7th century). *al-ʿUdad al-qawiyya*. Qum, [1988].

ʿAlī al-Qārī (d. 1014(. *Sharḥ al-Fiqh al-akbar*. Cairo, [1909].

ʿAlī al-Ṭabrisī (early 7th century). *Mishkāt al-anwār*. Qum, [2002].

Ālūsī, Maḥmūd (d. 1270). *Rūḥ al-maʿānī*. Cairo, 1960s.

Āmidī, ʿAbd al-Wāḥid (mid-6th century). *Ghurar al-ḥikam*. Beirut, 1987.

Ashʿarī, Abū al-Ḥasan ʿAlī b. Ismāʿīl (d. 324). *Maqālāt al-Islāmiyyīn*. Cairo, 1950.

Ashtor, Eliyaha. *Histoire des prix et des salaires dans l'orient medieval*. Paris, 1969.

ʿĀṣim b. Ḥumayd al-Ḥannāṭ (mid-2nd century). *Kitāb ʿĀṣim b. Ḥumayd al-Ḥannāṭ*. In *al-Uṣūl al-sittat-ʿashar*, 147–85. Qum, [2002].

Averroes = Ibn Rushd the Grandson (d. 595). *Bidāyat al-mujtahid*. Beirut, 1996.

ʿAynī, Badr al-Dīn (d. 855). *al-Bināya: Sharḥ al-Hidāya*. Beirut, 2000.

———. *ʿIqd al-jumān fī taʾrīkh ahl al-zamān*. Cairo, 2010.

———. *ʿUmdat al-qārī: Sharḥ Ṣaḥīḥ al-Bukhārī*. Beirut, 1970.

ʿAyyāshī, Muḥammad b. Masʿūd (late 3rd century). *Kitāb al-Tafsīr*. Qum, [2000].

Azharī, Abū Manṣūr (d. 370). *Tahdhīb al-lugha*. Cairo, 1966.
Azraqī, Abū al-Walīd (mid-3rd century). *Ta'rīkh Makka = Akhbār Makka wa-mā jā'a fīhā min al-āthār*. Cairo, 2004.
Balādhurī (d. 279). *Ansāb al-ashrāf*. Beirut, 1996.
Balawī, Yūsuf b. Muḥammad al-Māliqī al-Mālikī (d. 604). *Alif-bā'*. Cairo, 1870.
Bāqillānī (d. 402). *al-Tamhīd*. Beirut, 1957.
Barbahārī (d. 329). *Sharḥ al-Sunna*. Medina, 1993.
Barqī, Aḥmad b. Muḥammad b. Khālid (d. 274/280). *Kitāb al-Maḥāsin*. Tehran, [1951].
Basyawī, Abū al-Ḥasan (late 4th century?). *Jāmiʿ Abī al-Ḥasan al-Basyawī*. Muscat, 1984.
Bayhaqī (d. 458). *Dalā'il al-nubuwwa*. Beirut, 1985.
———. *Maʿrifat al-sunan wa'l-āthār*. Cairo, 1991.
———. *Shuʿab al-īmān*. Beirut, 1990.
———. *al-Sunan al-kubrā*. Beirut, 1994.
Bazanṭī, Aḥmad b. Muḥammad b. Abī Naṣr (d. 221). *Jāmiʿ*. In Ibn Idrīs al-Ḥillī (d. 598), *Mustaṭrafāt al-Sarā'ir*, 97–117. Qum, [2008].
———. *Nawādir*. In Ibn Idrīs al-Ḥillī, *Mustaṭrafāt al-Sarā'ir*, 41–61. Qum, [2008].
Bukhārī (d. 256). *Ṣaḥīḥ*. Riyadh, 1998.
———. *al-Ta'rīkh al-kabīr*. Hyderabad, [1941].
Calder, Norman. *Studies in Early Muslim Jurisprudence*. Oxford, 1993.
Chittick, William C. *The Psalms of Islam*. London, 1988.
Conrad, Lawrence I. "The Plague in the Early Medieval Near East." PhD dissertation. Princeton, 1981.
Cook, Michael. *Commanding Right and Forbidding Wrong in Islamic Thought*. Cambridge, 2000.
———. "Early Islamic Dietary Law." *Jerusalem Studies in Arabic and Islam* 7 (1986): 217–77.
———. "Early Medieval Christian and Muslim Attitudes to Pagan Law: A Comparison." In *Islam and Its Past: Jahiliyya, Late Antiquity, and the Qur'an*, edited by C. Bakhos and M. Cook, 213–46. Oxford, 2017.
———. "Magian Cheese: An Archaic Problem in Islamic Law." *Bulletin of the School of Oriental and African Studies* 47, no. 3 (Oct. 1984): 449–67.
———. "The Opponents of the Writing of Tradition in Early Islam." *Arabica* 44, no. 4 (Oct. 1997): 437–530.
Coulson, Noel. *Succession in the Muslim Family*. Cambridge, 1971.
Dāraquṭnī (d. 385). *Sunan*. Beirut, 2004.
Dārimī, ʿAbd Allāh b. ʿAbd al-Raḥmān (d. 255). *Sunan*. Riyadh, 2000.
Dhahabī (d. 748). *al-ʿIbar fī khabar man ghabar*. Kuwait, 1966.
———. *Mīzān al-iʿtidāl*. Cairo, [1964].
———. *Siyar aʿlām al-nubalā'*. Beirut, 1981.
———. *Tadhkirat al-ḥuffāẓ*. Hyderabad, 1955.
———. *Ta'rīkh al-Islām*. Beirut, 1988.
Ḍirār b. ʿAmr al-Ghaṭfānī (late 2nd century). *Kitāb al-Taḥrīsh*. Istanbul, 2014.
Durust b. Abī Manṣūr al-Wāsiṭī (2nd century). *Kitāb Durust b. Abī Manṣūr*. In *al-Uṣūl al-sittat-ʿashar*, 281–98. Qum, [2002].

Elad, Amikam. *The Rebellion of Muḥammad al-Nafs al-Zakiyya in 145/762: Ṭālibids and Early ʿAbbāsids in Conflict.* Leiden, 2015.

Encyclopaedia Iranica. Edited by Ehsan Yarshater. London, 1982.

Encyclopaedia of Islam II = *The Encyclopaedia of Islam*, 2nd ed. Edited by H. A. R. Gibb et al. Leiden, 1960.

Encyclopaedia of Islam III = *The Encyclopaedia of Islam, Three.* Edited by Kate Fleet et al. Leiden, 2007–.

Ess, Josef van. *Theologie und Gesellschaft im 2. und 3. Jahrhundert Hidschra: Eine Geschichte des religiösen Denkens im frühen Islam.* Berlin, 1991.

Faḍl b. Ḥasan al-Ṭabrisī (d. 548). *Iʿlām al-warā.* Najaf, 1970.

———. *Tāj al-mawālīd.* In *Majmūʿa nafīsa fī taʾrīkh al-Aʾimma*, 78–155. Qum, [1986].

Fakhr al-Dīn al-Rāzī (d. 606). *al-Maḥṣūl fī ʿilm al-uṣūl.* Beirut, 1997.

———. *al-Tafsīr al-kabīr.* Cairo, 1934.

Fasawī, Yaʿqūb b. Isḥāq (d. 277). *al-Maʿrifa wa'l-taʾrīkh.* Baghdad, 1974.

al-Fatāwā al-Hindiyya = *Fatāwā ʿĀlamgīriyya.* Calcutta, 1831.

Fattanī, Muḥammad Ṭāhir (d. 986). *Tadhkirat al-mawḍūʿāt.* Beirut, [1960].

Fayyāḍ, Muḥammad Isḥāq. *Muḥāḍarāt fī uṣūl al-fiqh.* Qum, [1998].

Furāt b. Ibrāhīm al-Kūfī (early 4th century). *Tafsīr.* Tehran, 1990.

Ghaffārī, Qāḍī Aḥmad (d. 975). *Tārīkh-i nigāristān.* Tehran, [1960].

Ghumārī, Aḥmad b. Muḥammad b. al-Ṣiddīq (d. 1380). *Izālat al-khaṭar ʿamman jamaʿa bayn al-ṣalātayn fī al-haḍar.* Irbid (Jordan), 2006.

Goitein, S. D. *A Mediterranean Society.* Los Angeles, 1967.

Habash, Hasan Qasim. *Riḥlat al-Muṣḥaf al-sharīf min al-jarīd ilā al-tajlīd.* Beirut, 1993.

Ḥaḍramī, Muḥammad b. ʿAqīl al-ʿAlawī (d. 1350). *al-ʿAtb al-jamīl ʿalā ahl al-jarḥ wa'l-taʿdīl.* Beirut, 1971.

———. *al-Naṣāʾiḥ al-kāfiya li-man yatawallā Muʿāwiya.* Qum, 2006.

Haider, Najam. *The Origins of the Shīʿa.* Cambridge, 2011.

Ḥākim al-Naysābūrī (d. 405). *Maʿrifat ʿulūm al-ḥadīth.* Beirut, 2003.

———. *al-Mustadrak ʿalā al-Ṣaḥīḥayn.* Cairo, 1997.

Harawī, Abū ʿUbayd (d. 401). *al-Gharībayn: Gharībay al-Qurʾān wa'l-Ḥadīth.* Hyderabad, 1985.

Ḥārithī, Sālim b. Ḥamad. *al-ʿUqūd al-fiḍḍiyya fī uṣūl al-Ibāḍiyya.* Muscat, 1983.

Ḥasan, Sulāf Faḍl Allāh. *Dawr al-jawārī wa'l-qahramānāt fī dār al-khilāfa al-ʿAbbāsiyya.* Damascus, 2013.

Ḥasan b. Faḍl al-Ṭabrisī (mid-6th century). *Makārim al-akhlāq.* Qum, [1993].

Ḥasan b. Maḥbūb al-Sarrād (d. 224). *al-Mashyakha.* In Ibn Idrīs al-Ḥillī, *Mustaṭrafāt al-Sarāʾir*, 135–63. Qum, [2008].

Ḥasan b. Zayn al-Dīn al-ʿĀmilī (d. 1011). *Muntaqā al-jumān.* Qum, [1983].

Haythamī (d. 807). *Majmaʿ al-zawāʾid.* Beirut, 2015.

Ḥimyarī, ʿAbd Allāh b. Jaʿfar (late 3rd century). *Qurb al-isnād.* Qum, 1993.

Hishām al-Kalbī = Ibn al-Kalbī (d. 204). *Mathālib al-ʿArab.* Beirut, 1998.

Ḥurr al-ʿĀmilī (d. 1104). *Wasāʾil al-Shīʿa.* Qum, [1988].

Ḥusayn b. ʿAbd al-Ṣamad al-ʿĀmilī (d. 984). *Wuṣūl al-akhyār ilā maʿrifat al-akhbār.* Qum, [1981].

Ḥusayn b. Saʿīd al-Ahwāzī (early 3rd century). *Kitāb al-Zuhd.* Qum, [1982].

Ibn ʿAbd al-Barr (d. 463). *al-Istīʿāb fī maʿrifat al-Aṣḥāb*. Cairo, 1960.
———. *al-Istidhkār al-jāmiʿ li-madhāhib fuqahāʾ al-amṣār*. Damascus, 1993.
———. *Jāmiʿ bayān al-ʿilm wa-faḍlih*. Dammām, 1994.
———. *al-Tamhīd*. Rabat, 1981.
Ibn ʿAbd al-Ḥakam (d. 257). *Futūḥ Miṣr wa'l-Maghrib*. Cairo, 1995.
Ibn ʿAbd Rabbih (d. 328). *al-ʿIqd al-farīd*. Cairo, 1940.
Ibn Abī al-Dunyā (d. 281). *al-Ishrāf ʿalā manāqib al-ashrāf*. Beirut, 1992.
———. *Kitāb al-Maṭar wa'l-raʿd wa'l-barq wa'l-rīḥ*. Riyadh, 1997.
Ibn Abī al-Ḥadīd (d. 655). *Sharḥ Nahj al-balāgha*. Cairo, 1959.
Ibn Abī Ḥātim (d. 327). *al-Jarḥ wa'l-taʿdīl*. Hyderabad, 1952.
Ibn Abī al-ʿIzz al-Dimashqī (d. 792). *Sharḥ al-ʿAqīda al-Ṭaḥāwiyya*. Beirut, 1987.
Ibn Abī al-Khayr, Yaḥyā b. Sālim al-ʿImrānī (d. 558). *al-Bayān fī madhhab al-imām al-Shāfiʿī*. Jeddah, 2000.
Ibn Abī Shayba (d. 235). *al-Muṣannaf*. Riyadh, 2004.
Ibn Abī al-Thalj (d. 325). *Taʾrīkh al-Aʾimma*. In *Majmūʿa nafīsa fī taʾrīkh al-Aʾimma*, 2–63. Qum, [1986].
Ibn Abī al-Zamanayn (d. 399). *Uṣūl al-sunna*. Medina, 1995.
Ibn ʿĀbidīn (d. 1252). *Radd al-muḥtār*. Cairo, 1966.
Ibn ʿAdī (d. 365). *al-Kāmil fī ḍuʿafāʾ al-rijāl*. Beirut, 1984.
Ibn al-ʿArabī, Abū Bakr (d. 543). *Aḥkām al-Qurʾān*. Cairo, 1957.
———. *al-Masālik fī sharḥ Muwaṭṭaʾ Mālik*. Beirut, 2007.
———. *al-Qabas fī sharḥ Muwaṭṭaʾ Mālik b. Anas*. Beirut, 1998.
Ibn ʿAsākir (d. 573). *Taʾrīkh madīnat Dimashq*. Beirut, 1995.
Ibn al-Ashʿath, Muḥammad b. Muḥammad al-Kūfī (mid-4th century). *al-Ashʿathiyyāt = al-Jaʿfariyyāt*. With the first edition of ʿAbd Allāh b. Jaʿfar al-Ḥimyarī's *Qurb al-isnād*. Tehran, n.d.
Ibn al-Athīr (d. 630). *al-Kāmil fī al-taʾrīkh*. Beirut, 1965.
Ibn ʿAyyāsh al-Jawharī, Aḥmad b. Muḥammad b. ʿUbayd Allāh al-Baghdādī (d. 401). *Muqtaḍab al-athar fī al-naṣṣ ʿalā al-Aʾimma al-ithnāʿashar*. Qum, [1960].
Ibn Bābawayh (d. 381). *al-Amālī*. Qum, [1996].
———. *Faḍāʾil al-Shīʿa*. With the author's *Kitāb al-Mawāʿiẓ*, 269–335. Qum, [2000].
———. *ʿIlal al-sharāʾiʿ*. Qum, [1957].
———. *al-Iʿtiqādāt*. Qum, [1992].
———. *Kamāl al-dīn*. Tehran, [1970].
———. *Kitāb al-Khiṣāl*. Tehran, [1969].
———. *Maʿānī al-akhbār*. Tehran, [1969].
———. *Man lā yaḥḍuruh al-faqīh*. Najaf, 1957.
———. *Ṣifāt al-Shīʿa*. With the author's *Kitāb al-Mawāʿiẓ*, 185–266. Qum, [2000]
———. *Kitāb al-Tawḥīd*. Tehran, [1967].
———. *Thawāb al-aʿmāl*. Tehran, [1971].
———. *ʿUyūn akhbār al-Riḍā*. Qum, [1958].
Ibn Baṭṭa (d. 387). *al-Ibāna al-ṣughrā = al-Sharḥ wa'l-ibāna ʿalā uṣūl al-sunna wa'l-diyāna*. Medina, 2002.
Ibn Bisṭām al-Zayyāt, ʿAbd Allāh and Ḥusayn (4th century). *Ṭibb al-Aʾimma*. Najaf, 1965.

Ibn Daqīq al-ʿĪd (d. 702). *Iḥkām al-aḥkām*. Cairo, 1955.
Ibn Dāwūd al-Ḥillī (early 8th century). *Kitāb al-Rijāl*. Najaf, 1972.
Ibn Farḥūn al-Mālikī (d. 799). *Irshād al-sālik ilā afʿāl al-manāsik*. Carthage, 1989.
Ibn Ḥabīb al-Hāshimī al-Baghdādī (d. 245). *al-Muḥabbar*. Hyderabad, 1942.
Ibn Ḥajar al-ʿAsqalānī (d. 852). *Fatḥ al-Bārī bi-sharḥ Ṣaḥīḥ al-Bukhārī*. Cairo, 1978.
———. *Inbāʾ al-ghumr*. Cairo, 1969.
———. *al-Iṣāba*. Cairo, 1970.
———. *Lisān al-Mīzān*. Beirut, 2002.
———. *Tabṣīr al-muntabih*. Cairo, 1964.
———. *Tahdhīb al-Tahdhīb*. Hyderabad, [1933].
———. *Talkhīṣ al-ḥabīr*. [Cairo], 1995.
Ibn Ḥamdūn, Bahāʾ al-Dīn Muḥammad b. al-Ḥasan al-Baghdādī (d. 562). *al-Tadhkira al-Ḥamdūniyya*. Beirut, 1996.
Ibn Ḥawqal (mid-4th century). *Ṣūrat al-arḍ*. Leiden, 1939.
Ibn Ḥazm (d. 456). *al-Fiṣal fī al-milal wa'l-ahwāʾ wa'l-niḥal*. Beirut, 1995.
———. *al-Iḥkām fī uṣūl al-aḥkām*. Cairo, [1926].
———. *al-Muḥallā*. Damascus, [1928].
Ibn Ḥibbān (d. 354). *Kitāb al-Majrūḥīn min al-muḥaddithīn*. Aleppo, 1976.
———. *Mashāhīr ʿulamāʾ al-amṣār*. Beirut, 1995.
———. *Ṣaḥīḥ = al-Iḥsān fī taqrīb Ṣaḥīḥ Ibn Ḥibbān*. Beirut, 1991.
———. *Kitāb al-Thiqāt*. Hyderabad, 1973.
Ibn al-Humām = Kamāl b. al-Humām (d. 861). *Fatḥ al-Qadīr*. Cairo, 1970.
Ibn Isfandiyār (early 7th century). *Tārīkh-i Ṭabaristān*. Tehran, [1941].
Ibn Iyās (d. ca. 930). *Badāʾiʿ al-ẓuhūr fī waqāʾiʿ al-duhūr*. Cairo, 1984.
Ibn al-Jawzī (d. 597). *Akhbār al-ẓurrāf wa'l-mutamājinīn*. Beirut, 1977.
———. *Gharīb al-ḥadīth*. Beirut, 1985.
———. *Manāqib Amīr al-Muʾminīn ʿUmar b. al-Khaṭṭāb*. Bahrain [Manama], 2013.
———. *Kitāb al-Mawḍuʿāt*. Riyadh, 1997.
———. *Nāsikh al-ḥadīth wa-mansūkhuh*. Beirut, 2002.
Ibn al-Junayd, Ibrāhīm b. ʿAbd Allāh (mid-3rd century). *Suʾālāt Ibn al-Junayd li-Yaḥyā b. Maʿīn*. Beirut, 1990.
Ibn Kathīr (d. 774). *al-Bidāya wa'l-nihāya*. Beirut, 1994.
———. *Tafsīr al-Qurʾān al-ʿaẓīm*. Riyadh, 1997.
Ibn Khalfūn al-Awnabī (d. 636). *Asmāʾ shuyūkh Mālik b. Anas al-Aṣbaḥī*. Riyadh, 2004.
Ibn Khallikān (d. 681). *Wafayāt al-aʿyān*. Beirut, 1978.
Ibn al-Khashshāb (d. 567). *Taʾrīkh mawālīd al-Aʾimma wa-wafayātihim*. In *Majmūʿa nafīsa fī taʾrīkh al-Aʾimma*, 158–202. Qum, [1986].
Ibn Khurdādhbih (late 3rd century). *Kitāb al-Masālik wa'l-mamālik*. Leiden, 1928.
Ibn Khuzayma (d. 311). *Ṣaḥīḥ*. Beirut, 1979.
Ibn Mājah (d. 273). *Sunan*. Beirut, 1998.
Ibn Manẓūr (d. 711). *Lisān al-ʿArab*. Beirut, 1955.
Ibn al-Mashhadī (6th century). *al-Mazār al-kabīr*. Qum, [1999].
Ibn Mufliḥ (d. 763). *al-Ādāb al-sharʿiyya*. Beirut, 1997.
Ibn al-Mundhir (d. 318). *al-Ijmāʿ*. Beirut, 1986.

Ibn al-Murtaḍā (d. 840). *al-Baḥr al-zakhkhār*. Beirut, 1989.

Ibn al-Muṭahhar al-Ḥillī, al-ʿAllāma (d. 726). *Khulāṣat al-aqwāl* (published as *Rijāl al-ʿAllāma al-Ḥillī*). Najaf, 1961.

———. *al-Mustajād min Kitāb al-Irshād*. In *Majmūʿa nafīsa fī taʾrīkh al-Aʾimma*, 291–558. Qum, [1986].

———. *Tadhkirat al-fuqahāʾ*. Qum, 1993.

Ibn al-Muzayyin, Abū al-ʿAbbās al-Qurṭubī (d. 656). *al-Mufhim li-mā ashkala min kitāb Talkhīṣ Muslim*. Damascus, 1996.

Ibn al-Nadīm (late 4th century). *Kitāb al-Fihrist*. Tehran, [1071].

Ibn Namā al-Ḥillī (d. 645). *Sharḥ al-thār*. In Muḥammad Bāqir al-Majlisī, *Biḥār al-Anwār*, 45:346–87. Beirut, 1983.

Ibn Nāṣir al-Dīn al-Dimashqī (d. 842). *Jāmiʿ al-āthār fī mawlid al-Nabī al-mukhtār*. Beirut, 2009.

Ibn Nujaym (d. 970). *al-Ashbāh waʾl-naẓāʾir ʿalā madhhab Abī Ḥanīfa al-Nuʿmān*. Beirut, 1999.

Ibn al-Qayyim (d. 751). *Jalāʾ al-afhām*. Mecca, [2004].

———. *al-Ṭuruq al-ḥukmiyya*. N.p. (Maktabat Dār al-Bayān), n.d.

Ibn Qiba al-Rāzī (early 4th century). *Naqḍ Kitāb al-Ishhād*. In Hossein Modarressi, *Crisis and Consolidation in the Formative Period of Shīʿite Islam*, 171–201. Princeton, 1993.

Ibn Qudāma (d. 620). *al-Mughnī*. Cairo, 1986.

Ibn Qūlawayh al-Qummī (d. 369). *Kāmil al-ziyārāt*. Najaf, [1937].

Ibn Qutayba al-Dīnawarī (d. 276). *al-Maʿārif*. Cairo, 1960.

Ibn Rajab (d. 795). *Fatḥ al-Bārī: Sharḥ Ṣaḥīḥ al-Bukhārī*. Riyadh, 1996.

Ibn al-Rāzī, Jaʿfar b. Aḥmad al-Qummī (late 4th century). *Kitāb al-Ghāyāt*. With the author's *Jāmiʿ al-aḥādīth*, 169–235. Mashhad, [1993].

Ibn Rushd, the Grandfather (d. 520). *al-Bayān waʾl-taḥṣīl*. Beirut,1984.

Ibn Saʿd (d. 230). *Kitāb al-Ṭabaqāt al-kabīr*. Cairo, 2001.

Ibn al-Sāʿī, ʿAlī b. Anjab al-Khāzin al-Baghdādī (d. 674). *Nisāʾ al-khulafāʾ*. Cairo, [1968].

Ibn al-Ṣalāḥ (d. 643). *Adab al-muftī waʾl-mustaftī*. N.p., 1986.

Ibn Samka, Abū ʿAlī Aḥmad b. Ismāʿīl al-Bajalī al-Qummī (early 4th century). *al-ʿAbbāsī*. (Published as *Akhbār al-dawla al-ʿAbbāsiyya*). Beirut, 1971.

Ibn Sayyid al-Nās (d. 734). *ʿUyūn al-āthār*. Beirut, [1993].

Ibn Shabba (d. 262). *Taʾrīkh al-Madīna al-munawwara = Akhbār al-Madīna al-Nabawiyya*. Beirut, 1990.

Ibn Shahrāshūb (d. 588). *Maʿālim al-ʿulamāʾ*. Tehran, [1934].

———. *Manāqib Āl Abī Ṭālib*. Qum, 1958.

———. *Mathālib al-Nawāṣib*. Baghdad, 2015.

Ibn al-Shalabī, Shihāb al-Dīn (d. 947). *Ḥāshiyat al-Shaykh al-Shalabī ʿalā Tabyīn al-ḥaqāʾiq*. With Zaylaʿī's *Tabyīn al-ḥaqāʾiq*. Beirut, 2000.

Ibn Shuʿba al-Ḥarrānī (possibly 5th or 6th century). *Tuḥaf al-ʿuqūl*. Beirut, 2002.

Ibn Sīda (d. 458). *al-Muḥkam waʾl-muḥīṭ al-aʿẓam*. Beirut, 2000.

Ibn Taghrībirdī (d. 874). *al-Manhal al-ṣāfī waʾl-mustawfī baʿda al-wāfī*. Cairo, 1984.

———. *al-Nujūm al-zāhira*. Cairo, 1963.

Ibn Ṭāwūs, Raḍī al-Dīn ʿAlī (d. 664). *al-Amān min akhṭār al-asfār wa'l-azmān*. Qum, [1988].

———. *al-Iqbāl al-aʿmāl*. Qum, [1993].

———. *al-Luhūf*. Qum, n.d.

———. *Muhaj al-daʿawāt*. Tehran, [1995].

———. "Risāla fī ʿadam muḍāyaqat al-fawā'it." *Turāthunā* 6–7 ([1987]): 331–59.

Ibn Taymiyya (d. 728). *Majmūʿat fatāwā Shaykh al-Islām Aḥmad b. Taymiyya*. Beirut, 1997.

———. *Minhāj al-sunna*. Cairo, 1986.

Ibn al-Wazīr (d. 840). *Tarjīḥ asālīb al-Qur'ān*. Cairo, 1931.

Idlibi, Salah al-Din. "Asbāb ʿudūl al-imām al-Bukhārī ʿan al-takhrīj li'l-Imām Jaʿfar al-Ṣādiq fī Ṣaḥīḥih." *Hadis Tetkikleri Dergisi* 9 (2011): 55–74.

Imāmī Khātūnābādī, Muḥammad Riḍā b. Muḥammad Mu'min (early 12th century). *Jannāt al-khulūd*. Tehran, [1958].

Irbilī, Bahā' al-Dīn ʿAlī b. ʿĪsā (d. 692). *Kashf al-ghumma fī maʿrifat al-A'imma*. Qum, [2005].

Iṣbahānī, Abū al-Faraj (d. 356). *Kitāb al-Aghānī*. Cairo, 1927.

———. *Maqātil al-Ṭālibiyyīn*. Cairo, 1949.

Isnawī (d. 772). *al-Tamhīd fī takhrīj al-furūʿ ʿala al-uṣūl*. Beirut, 1980.

Jaʿfar al-Ḥaḍramī (mid-2nd century). *Kitāb Jaʿfar b. Muḥammad b. Shurayḥ al-Ḥaḍramī*. In *al-Uṣūl al-sittat-ʿashar*, 213–52. Qum, [2002].

Jaʿfar b. al-Ḥasan al-Ḥillī, al-Muḥaqqiq (d. 676). *al-Muʿtabar*. Qum, 1985.

Jafarian. *Nuskha-khwānī. Āyina-i pizhūhish* (Qum), 187 (2021): 159–70.

Jāḥiẓ (d. 255). *al-Shārib wa'l-mashrūb*. In *Rasā'il al-Jāḥiẓ*, edited by ʿAbd al-Salām Muḥammad Hārūn, 4:261–84. Cairo, 1979.

———. *al-Tabaṣṣur bi'l-tijāra*. Cairo, 1994.

———. *al-ʿUthmāniyya*. Cairo, 1955.

Jaṣṣāṣ, Abū Bakr Aḥmad b. ʿAlī al-Rāzī (d. 370). *Aḥkām al-Qur'ān*. Beirut, n.d. [ca. 1978].

———. *al-Fuṣūl fī al-uṣūl*. Kuwait, 1994.

Jawād al-ʿĀmilī (1226). *Miftāḥ al-karāma*. Qum, [1999].

Juwaynī, Imām al-Ḥaramayn (d. 478). *al-Burhān fī uṣūl al-fiqh*. Doha, 1979.

Juynboll, G. H. A. "Nāfiʿ, the *Mawlā* of Ibn ʿUmar and His Position in Muslim *Ḥadīth* Literature." *Der Islam* 70 (1993): 207–44. Reprinted in *Studies in the Origins and Uses of Islamic Hadith*, edited by G. H. A. Juynboll, ch. 9. Aldershot, 1996.

Kardarī, Muḥammad al-Bazzāzī al-Khwārazmī (d. 827). *al-Manāqib al-Kardariyya fī sīrat al-imām Abī Ḥanīfa*. With Muwaffaq al-Dīn Aḥmad al-Makkī al-Khwārazmī (d. 568), *Manāqib Abī Ḥanīfa*. Beirut, 1981.

Kāsānī (d. 587). *Badā'iʿ al-ṣanā'iʿ*. Cairo, 1968.

Kashshī, Abū ʿAmr Muḥammad b. ʿUmar (early 4th century). *Kitāb al-Rijāl*. Mashhad, 1970.

Khaṭīb al-Baghdādī (d. 463). *al-Faqīh wa'l-mutafaqqih*. Beirut, 1996.

———. *Ta'rīkh Baghdād = Ta'rīkh Madīnat al-salām*. Beirut, 2001.

Khazzāz al-Qummī (mid-5th century). *Kifāyat al-athar*. Qum, [1981].

Khu'ī, Abū al-Qāsim (d. 1413). *Muʿjam rijāl al-ḥadīth*. Beirut, 1983.

Khumaynī, Rūḥ Allāh (d. 1409). *Risāla fī al-taqiyya*. In the author's *al-Rasāʾil*, 2:173–210. Qum, [1965].
Kindī al-Nazwī (d. 557). *al-Muṣannaf*. Muscat, 1979.
Kitāb Sulaym b. Qays al-Hilālī (early 2nd century). Qum, [1994].
Kohlberg, Etan. *A Medieval Muslim Scholar at Work*. Leiden, 1992.
———. "The Position of the *Walad Zinā* in Imāmī Shīʿism." *Bulletin of the School of Oriental and African Studies* 48 (1985): 237–66. Reprinted in Kohlberg, *Belief and Law in Imāmi Shīʿism*, ch. 11. Aldershot, 1990.
———. "Al-Uṣūl al-arbaʿumiʾa." *Jerusalem Studies in Arabic and Islam* 10 (1987): 128–66. Reprinted in Kohlberg, *Belief and Law in Imāmi Shīʿism*, ch. 7. Aldershot, 1990.
Kulaynī, Muḥammad b. Yaʿqūb (d. 329). *Kitāb al-Kāfī*. Tehran, [1957].
Kushājim (d. 360). *al-Maṣāyid wa'l-matārid*. Baghdad, 1954.
Kutbī, Muḥammad b. Shākir al-Dimashqī (d. 764). *Fawāt al-wafayāt*. Beirut, 1973.
Kuthayyir ʿAzza (d. 107). *Dīwān*. Beirut, 1993.
Lālakāʾī (d. 418). *Sharḥ uṣūl iʿtiqād Ahl al-Sunna wa'l-Jamāʿa*. Riyadh, 1994.
Madelung, Wilferd. "ʿAbd Allāh b. ʿAbbās and Shīʿite Law." In *Law, Christianity, and Modernism in Islamic Society*, edited by U. Vermeulen et al., 13–25. Leuven, 1998.
Majd al-Dīn Ibn al-Athīr (d. 606). *al-Nihāya*. Cairo, 1963.
Majlisī, Muḥammad Bāqir (d. 1110). *Biḥār al-anwār*. Beirut, 1983.
Mālik b. Anas (d. 179). *al-Mudawwana al-kubrā: Riwāyat Saḥnūn*. Cairo, [1906].
———. *al-Muwaṭṭaʾ*. Recension of Abū Muṣʿab al-Zuhrī. Algiers, 2015.
———. *al-Muwaṭṭaʾ*. Recension of Yaḥyā b. Yaḥyā al-Laythī. Beirut, 2015.
Maqrīzī (d. 845). *Ighāthat al-umma bi-kashf al-ghumma*. al-Haram (Giza), 2007.
———. *Imtāʿ al-asmāʿ*. Beirut, 1999.
———. *Khiṭaṭ = al-Mawāʿiẓ wa'l-iʿtibār bi-dhikr al-khiṭaṭ wa'l-āthār*. Cairo, 1911.
———. *Shudhūr al-ʿuqūd fī dhikr al-nuqūd = al-Nuqūd al-Islāmiyya*. Najaf, 1967.
———. *Shudhūr al-ʿuqūd = al-Nuqūd al-Islāmiyya*. Constantinople, [1881]. (Also in the collection *Thalāth rasāʾil*, 2–19.)
———. *al-Sulūk li-maʿrifat duwal al-mulūk*. Beirut, 2015.
Marghīnānī (d. 593). *al-Hidāya*. Cairo, 1975.
Marwazī, Muḥammad b. Naṣr (d. 294). *Kitāb al-Sunna*. Riyadh, 2001.
Marzubānī (d. 384). *Akhbār shuʿarāʾ al-Shīʿa*. Najaf, 1968.
———. *Muʿjam al-shuʿarāʾ*. Beirut, 1991.
Masʿūdī (d. 346). *Murūj al-dhahab*. Beirut, 1965.
Māwardī (d. 452). *al-Ḥāwī al-kabīr*. Beirut, 1994.
al-Mawsūʿa al-fiqhiyya. Kuwait, 1983.
Mawsūʿat al-fiqh al-Islāmī, ṭibqan li-madhhab Ahl al-Bayt. Qum, 2002.
Māzarī (d. 536). *al-Muʿlim bi-fawāʾid Muslim*. Beirut, 1992.
Miskawayh (d. 421). *Tajārib al-umam*. Beirut, 2003.
Mizzī (d. 742). *Tahdhīb al-Kamāl*. Beirut, 1985.
Modarressi, Hossein. "Common Ibāḍī-Shīʿite Legacy: Examples from the Ritual Law." In *Ibadi Jurisprudence: Origins, Developments, and Cases*, edited by Barbara Michalak-Pikulska et al., 111–19. Hildesheim, 2015.
———. *Crisis and Consolidation in the Formative Period of Shīʿite Islam*. Princeton, 1993.

———. "Dukhāniyyāt-i fiqh." In Hossein Modarressi, *Tārīkhiyyāt*, 179–204. New Jersey, 2009.

———. "Early Debates on the Integrity of the Qur'ān." *Studia Islamica* 77 (1993): 5–39.

———. "Essential Islam: The Minimum That a Muslim is Required to Acknowledge." In *Accusations of Unbelief in Islam*, edited by Camilla Adang et al., 395–412. Leiden, 2015.

———. "Facts or Fables? Muslims' Evaluation of Historical Memory." *Studia Islamica* 114 (2019): 205–18.

———. *An Introduction to Shīʿī Law*. London, 1984.

———. *Kharāj in Islamic Law*. London, 1983.

———. *Maktab dar farāyand-i takāmul.* Persian translation of the author's *Crisis and Consolidation in the Formative Period of Shīʿite Islam*, with added footnotes from the author. Tehran, 2007.

———. "Mutual Understanding and Harmonious Relations between Ibāḍī and Shīʿite Communities in 2nd/8th-Century Iraq." In *Local and Global Ibadi Identities*, edited by Y. Kondo and A. Ziaka, 33–40. Hildesheim, 2019.

———. "Nawādir-i fiqhī-yi Khawārij wa Muʿtazila." In Modarressi, *Tārīkhiyyāt*: 205–26. New Jersey, 2009.

———. *Tradition and Survival: A Bibliographical Survey of Early Shīʿite Literature.* Vol. 1. Oxford, 2003.

Motzki, Harald. "*Quo vadis Ḥadīṯ*-Forschung? Eine kritische Untersuchung von G. H. A. Juynboll: 'Nāfiʿ, the *Mawlā* of Ibn ʿUmar and His Position in Muslim *Ḥadīth* Literature.'" *Der Islam* 73 (1997): 40–80.

———. "Wa'l-muḥṣanātu mina n-nisā'i illā mā malakat aimānukum (Koran 4:24) und die Koranische Sexualethik." *Der Islam* 63 (1986): 192–218.

Muʿāwiya b. ʿAmmār al-Duhnī (d. 175). *Kitāb Muʿāwiya b. ʿAmmār*. In Ibn Idrīs al-Ḥillī, *Mustaṭrafāt al-Sarā'ir*, 35–39. Qum, [2008].

Mubārak, ʿAlī Pāshā (d. 1311). *al-Khiṭaṭ al-Tawfīqiyya*. Cairo, 1969.

Mubarrad (d. 286). *al-Kāmil*. Cairo, 1956.

Mufīd (d. 413). *Aḥkām al-nisā'*. In *Muṣannafāt al-Shaykh al-Mufīd*, vol. 9. Qum, [1992].

———. *al-Amālī*. Qum, [1983].

———. *al-Fuṣūl al-mukhtāra.* Najaf, ca. 1950.

———(attr.). *al-Ikhtiṣāṣ*. Tehran, [1959].

———. *al-Irshād*. Najaf, 1962.

———. *Khulāṣat al-Ījāz fī al-mutʿa*. In *Muṣannafāt al-Shaykh al-Mufīd*, vol. 6. Qum, [1992].

———. *al-Masā'il al-Ṣāghāniyya*. In *Muṣannafāt al-Shaykh al-Mufīd*, vol. 3. Qum, [1992].

Muḥammad b. ʿAbd al-Hādī al-Sindī (d. 1138). *al-Hāshiya ʿalā al-Bukhārī*. In the margins of Bukhārī, *al-Jāmiʿ al-ṣaḥīḥ*. Cairo, [1883].

Muḥammad b. ʿAlī b. Maḥbūb al-Ashʿarī (mid-3rd century). *Nawādir al-Muṣannaf.* In Ibn Idrīs al-Ḥillī, *Mustaṭrafāt al-Sarā'ir*, 165–207. Qum, [2008].

Muḥammad b. al-Muthannā al-Ḥaḍramī (2nd century). *Kitāb Muḥammad b. al-Muthannā al-Ḥaḍramī*. In *al-Uṣūl al-sittat-ʿashar*, 253–75. Qum, [2002].

Muslim b. al-Ḥajjāj al-Naysābūrī (d. 261). *Ṣaḥīḥ*. Beirut, 1995.

Muṭahharī, Murtaḍā (d. 1399). *Niẓām-i ḥuquq-i zan dar Islām*. Qum, [1980].

Muttaqī al-Hindī (d. 975). *Kanz al-ʿummāl*. Aleppo, 1969.

Muwaffaq b. Aḥmad al-Makkī (d. 568). *Manāqib Abī Ḥanīfa*. Beirut, 1981.

Nafrāwī (d. 1126). *al-Fawākih al-dawānī*. Cairo, [1913].

Nahj al-balāgha. A selection of ʿAlī's sayings by Sharīf al-Raḍī (d. 406). Beirut, 1967.

Nāʾīnī, Muḥammad Ḥusayn (d. 1355). *Fawāʾid al-uṣūl*. Qum, [1989].

Najāshī (d. 450). *Rijāl = Fihrist asmāʾ muṣannifī al-Shīʿa*. Qum, [1987].

Nasafī, Abū Ḥafṣ (d. 537). *al-ʿAqāʾid al-Nasafiyya*. In *Shurūḥ wa-ḥawāshī al-ʿAqāʾid al-Nasafiyya*. Beirut, 2013.

Nasāʾī (d. 303). *Sunan*. Beirut, 2001.

Naṣr b. Muzāḥim (d. 212). *Waqʿat Ṣiffīn*. Cairo, 1982.

Nawawī (d. 606). *al-Majmūʿ: Sharḥ al-Muhadhdhab*. Cairo, 1966.

———. *Sharḥ Ṣaḥīḥ Muslim*. Beirut, 1987.

Nuʿaym b. Ḥammād al-Marwazī (d. 228). *Kitāb al-Fitan*. Mecca, 1991.

Nuʿmānī, Muḥammad b. Ibrāhīm (mid-4th century). *Kitāb al-Ghayba*. Tehran, [1977].

Qāḍī ʿIyāḍ (d. 544). *Ikmāl al-muʿlim bi-fawāʾid Muslim*. Beirut, 1998.

———. *al-Shifā bi-taʿrīf ḥuqūq al-Muṣṭafā*. Damascus, 1972.

——— and his son, Qāḍī Muḥammad b. ʿIyāḍ (d. 575). *Madhāhib al-ḥukkām fī nawāzil al-aḥkām*. Beirut, 1990.

Qāḍī Nuʿmān (d. 363). *Daʿāʾim al-Islām*. Cairo, 1951.

———. *Sharḥ al-akhbār*. Qum, [1989].

Qāḍī Ṣafad, Muḥammad b. ʿAbd al-Raḥmān al-Dimashqī (late 8th cantury). *Raḥmat al-umma fī ikhtilāf al-Aʾimma*. Beirut, 1994.

Qalqashandī (d. 821). *Ṣubḥ al-aʿshā*. Cairo, 1913.

Qazwīnī, Muḥammad Kāẓim (d. 1415). *Mawsūʿat al-Imām Jaʿfar al-Ṣādiq*. Qum, 1993.

Quḍāʿī, Muḥammad b. Salāma (d. 454). *Dustūr maʿālim al-ḥikam*. Beirut, 1981.

Qurṭubī, Abū ʿAbd Allāh (d. 671). *al-Jāmiʿ li-aḥkām al-Qurʾān*. Beirut, 2006.

Rabb, Intisar A. "The Curious Case of Bughaybigha, 661–883: Land and Leadership in Early Islamic Societies." In *Justice and Leadership in Early Islamic Courts*, edited by Intisar A. Rabb and Abigail Krasner Balbale, 23–46. Cambridge, MA, 2017.

———. *Doubt in Islamic Law: A History of Legal Maxims, Interpretation, and Islamic Criminal Law*. Cambridge, 2015.

———. "Islamic Legal Minimalism." In *Law and Tradition in Classical Islamic Thought*, edited by Michael Cook et al., 145–66. New York, 2016.

Rabīʿ b. Ḥabīb al-Farāhīdī (late 2nd century). *Musnad = al-Jāmiʿ al-ṣaḥīḥ*. Oman, 2003.

Rāfiʿī (d. 623). *Fatḥ al-Azīz fī sharḥ al-Wajīz*. Beirut, 1997.

Rāghib al-Iṣfahānī (early 5th century). *Muḥāḍarāt al-udabāʾ*. Beirut, 1961.

Rakīnī, Ḥaydar Riḍā (d. 1198). *Jabal ʿĀmil fī qarn*. Beirut, 1997.

Raqqām, Muḥammad b. ʿImrān al-ʿAbdī al-Baṣrī (early to mid-4th century). *Kitāb al-ʿAfw waʾl-iʿtidhār*. Riyadh, 1981.

Rāwandī, Quṭb al-Dīn (d. 573). *al-Kharāʾij waʾl-jarāʾiḥ*. Qum, [1989].

Rifāʿī, ʿAbd al-Jabbār. *Muʿjam mā kutib ʿan al-Rasūl waʾl-Aʾimma*. Tehran, [1992].

Saʿd b. ʿAbd Allāh al-Ashʿarī (d. 299–301). *Kitāb al-Maqālāt wa'l-firaq*. Tehran, 1963.
Ṣafadī (d. 764). *al-Wāfī bi'l-wafayāt*. Istanbul, 1931.
Ṣaffār, Fāḍil. *Fiqh al-maṣāliḥ wa'l-mafāsid: Tazāḥum al-ahamm wa'l-muhimm fī al-aḥkām wa'l-awlawiyyāt al-sharʿiyya*. Beirut, 2008.
Ṣaffār al-Qummī (d. 290) (attr.). *Baṣāʾir al-darajāt*. Tabriz, [1961].
Saʿīd b. Manṣūr (d. 227). *Sunan*. Bombay, 1982.
Sakhāwī (d. 902). *al-Ḍawʾ al-lāmiʿ*. Cairo, 1934.
Sālimī, Nūr al-Dīn (d. 1332). *Maʿārij al-āmāl*. Oman, 2010.
Samʿānī (d. 562). *al-Ansāb*. Hyderabad, 1962.
Sarakhsī, Abū Bakr (d. 483). *Kitāb al-Mabsūṭ*. Cairo, [1906].
———. *Uṣūl al-Sarakhsī*. Beirut, 1973.
Sayyārī, Aḥmad b. Muḥammad (late 3rd century). *Kitāb al-Qirāʾāt*. Leiden, 2009.
Sayyid al-Ḥimyarī (d. 173). *Dīwān*. Beirut, 1966.
Shāfiʿī (d. 204). *al-Risāla*. Cairo, 1938.
———. *Kitāb al-Umm*. Beirut, 1993.
Shahīd al-Awwal, Muḥammad b. Makkī al-ʿĀmilī (d. 786). *Dhikrā al-Shīʿa*. Qum, [1998].
Shahīd al-Thānī, Zayn al-Dīn b.ʿAlī al-ʿĀmilī (d. 965). *Masālik al-afhām*. Qum, 1997.
Shahristānī, ʿAlī. *al-Adhān bayn al-aṣāla wa'l-taḥrīf: Ḥayyi ʿalā khayr al-ʿamal, al-sharʿiyya wa'l-shiʿāriyya*. Qum, [2003].
Shahristānī, Muḥammad b. ʿAbd al-Karīm (d. 548). *Mafatīḥ al-asrār wa-maṣābīḥ al-abrār*. Tehran, 2008.
———. *al-Milal wa'l-niḥal*. Beirut, 1990.
Shammākhī, ʿĀmir b. ʿAlī (d. 792). *Kitāb al-Īḍāḥ*. Beirut, 1970.
Sharaf al-Dīn, ʿAbd al-Ḥusayn (d. 1377). *Masāʾil fiqhiyya*. Tehran, 1997.
Sharīf al-Murtaḍā (d. 436). *Amālī al-Murtaḍā = Ghurar al-fawāʾid*. Cairo, 1954.
———. *Rasāʾil al-Sharīf al-Murtaḍā*, Qum, 1984.
Shaybānī (d. 189). *al-Iktisāb fī al-rizq al-mustaṭāb*. Cairo, 1938.
Shiqṣī al-Rustāqī. *Manhaj al-ṭālibīn wa-balāgh al-rāghibīn*. Muscat, 1979.
Shīrāzī, Abū Isḥāq (d. 476). *Kitāb al-Lumaʿ*. Bahrain, 2013.
———. *al-Tabṣira fī uṣūl al-fiqh*. Damascus, 1980.
Ṣūrī, Sadīd al-Dīn (6th century). *Qaḍāʾ ḥuqūq al-muʾminīn*. Qum, [1988].
Suyūṭī (d. 911). *al-Ashbāh wa'l-naẓāʾir fī qawāʿid wa-furūʿ fiqh al-Shāfiʿiyya*. Beirut, 1983.
———. *al-Itqān fī ʿulūm al-Qurʾān*. Cairo, 1984.
———. *Jāmiʿ al-uṣūl*. Beirut, 1994.
———. *al-Laʾālī al-maṣnuʿa fī al-aḥādīth al-mawḍūʿa*. Cairo, 1934.
———. *Rafʿ al-khidr ʿan qaṭʿ al-sidr*. In the author's *al-Ḥāwī li'l-fatāwī*, 2:51–55. Beirut, 2000.
Syed, Mairaj. *Coercion and Responsibility in Islam*. Oxford, 2017.
Ṭabarānī (d. 360). *al-Muʿjam al-awsaṭ*. Cairo, 1995.
———. *al-Muʿjam al-kabīr*. Beirut, 1990s.
———. *Musnad al-Shāmiyyīn*. Beirut, 1989.
Ṭabarī (d. 310). *Jāmiʿ al-bayān = Tafsīr al-Ṭabarī*, edited by Aḥmad Shākir and Maḥmūd Shākir. Cairo, 1954.

———. *Taʾrīkh al-rusul waʾl-mulūk*. Cairo, 1960.

Taftāzānī, Saʿd al-Dīn (d. 792). *Sharḥ al-ʿAqāʾid al-Nasafiyya*. Cairo, 1987.

———. *Sharḥ al-Maqāṣid*. Beirut, 1989.

Ṭaḥāwī, Abū Jaʿfar (d. 321). *al-ʿAqīda al-Ṭaḥāwiyya*. Beirut, 1978.

———. *Sharḥ Mushkil al-āthār*. Reorganized by Khālid Maḥmūd al-Rabāṭ as *Tuḥfat al-akhyār bi-tartīb Sharḥ Mushkil al-āthār*. Riyadh, 1999.

Tanūkhī (d. 384). *al-Faraj baʿd al-shidda*. Beirut, 1978.

Ṭarsūsī, Najm al-Dīn Ibrāhīm b. ʿAlī (d. 758). *Tuḥfat al-Turk fī mā yajib ʿan yuʿmal fī al-mulk*. Beirut, 1992.

Tawḥīdī, Abū Ḥayyān (late 4th–early 5th centuries). *al-Imtāʿ waʾl-muʾānasa*. Cairo, 1953.

Thaʿālibī (d. 429/430). *al-Tamthīl waʾl-muhāḍara*. Cairo, [1961].

———. *Thimār al-qulūb*. Cairo, [1964].

Thaʿlabī, Abū Isḥāq Aḥmad b. Muḥammad al-Naysābūrī (d. 427). *al-Kashf waʾl-bayān fī tafsīr al-Qurʾān*. Beirut, 2002.

Tirmidhī (d. 279). *al-Jāmiʿ al-kabīr = Sunan*. Beirut, 1996.

Ṭurayḥī, Fakhr al-Dīn (d. 1085). *Majmaʿ al-baḥrayn*. Najaf, 1961.

Ṭūsī, Abū Jaʿfar Muḥammad b. al-Ḥasan (d. 460). *al-Amālī*. Qum, [1993].

———. *Kitāb al-Fihrist*. Najaf, [1937].

———. *Kitāb al-Ghayba*. Qum, 1991.

———. *al-Istibṣār*. Najaf, 1956.

———. *Kitāb al-Khilāf*. Qum, [1987].

———. *Kitāb al-Rijāl*. Qum, [1994].

———. *Tahdhīb al-aḥkām*. Najaf, 1958.

———. *al-Tibyān fī tafsīr al-Qurʾān*. Qum, [2011].

———. *ʿUddat al-uṣūl*. Qum, 1983.

Tustarī, Muḥammad Taqī (d. 1415). *Qāmūs al-rijāl*. Qum, [1990].

ʿUqaylī (d. 322). *Kitāb al-Ḍuʿafāʾ*. Beirut, 1984.

Wakīʿ, Muḥammad b. Khalaf (d. 306). *Akhbār al-quḍāt*. Cairo, 1947.

Wansharīsī (d. 914). *al-Miʿyār al-muʿrib*. Rabat, 1981.

al-Wazīr al-Maghribī, Ḥusayn b. ʿAlī (d. 418). *al-Maṣābīḥ fī tafsīr al-Qurʾān al-ʿaẓīm*. Edited as a doctoral thesis by ʿAbd al-Karīm al-Zahrānī. Umm al-Qurā University, 2000. https://dorar.uqu.edu.sa/uquui/handle/20.500.12248/95483?locale=en.

Weiss, Bernard. *The Spirit of Islamic Law*. Athens, GA, ca. 1998.

Yāfiʿī, ʿAbd Allāh b. Asʿad (d. 768). *Mirʾāt al-jinān*. Beirut, 1997.

Yaḥyā b. Ādam (d. 203). *Kitāb al-Kharāj*. Cairo, 1964.

Yaḥyā al-Hādī (d. 298). *Kitāb al-Ahkām*. N.p. (Yemen), 1990.

Yaḥyā b. Maʿīn (d. 233). *Taʾrīkh*. Mecca, 1979.

Yaʿqūbī (alive 292). *Taʾrīkh*. Beirut, 1960.

Zabīdī (d. 1205). *Tāj al-ʿarūs*. Kuwait, 1965.

Zamakhsharī (d. 538). *al-Fāʾiq fī gharīb al-ḥadīth*. Cairo, 1969.

———. *Rabīʿ al-abrār*. Baghdad, 1976.

Zarkashī (d. 794). *al-Baḥr al-muḥīt*. Kuwait, 1992.

Zarqā, Aḥmad (d. 1357). *Sharḥ al-qawāʿid al-fiqhiyya*. Damascus, 1989.

Zayd b. ʿAlī b. al-Ḥusayn (d. 122) (attr.). *Musnad al-imām Zayd*. Beirut, 1966.

Zaylaʿī, Fakhr al-Dīn (d. 743). *Tabyīn al-ḥaqāʾiq*. Beirut, 2000.
Ziriklī (d. 1396). *al-Aʿlām*. Beirut, 1989.
Zubayr b. Bakkār (d. 256). *al-Akhbār al-Muwaffaqiyyāt*. Baghdad, [1972].
Zurqānī (d. 1122). *Sharḥ al-Mawāhib al-ladunniyya*. Cairo, [1911].

Index of Names

Index of Terms and Topics